THE
EXCEPTIONAL
CHILD

McGRAW-HILL SERIES IN SPECIAL EDUCATION

ROBERT M. SMITH, *Consulting Editor*

ROBERT M. SMITH

Virginia Polytechnic Institute and State University

JOHN T. NEISWORTH

The Pennsylvania State University

FRANCES M. HUNT

The Pennsylvania State University

McGRAW-HILL BOOK COMPANY

New York | St. Louis | San Francisco
Auckland | Bogotá | Hamburg
Johannesburg | London | Madrid
Mexico | Montreal | New Delhi
Panama | Paris | São Paulo | Singapore
Sydney | Tokyo | Toronto

SECOND EDITION

The Exceptional Child

A FUNCTIONAL APPROACH

TO
ANITA DAUB

THE
EXCEPTIONAL
CHILD
A FUNCTIONAL APPROACH

1234567890   DOCDOC   89876543

ISBN 0-07-058976-3

This book was set in Zenith by Rocappi, Inc.
The editors were Christina Mediate and Barry Benjamin;
the designer was Nicholas Krenitsky;
the production supervisor was Phil Galea.
The cover photograph was taken by Annette Shaw Breukelman;
other photographs were taken by Elizabeth A. Llewellyn,
Jim Lukens, Paul J. Quinn, and Chuck Zovko.
New drawings were done by J & R Services, Inc.
R. R. Donnelley & Sons Company was printer and binder.

Library of Congress Cataloging in Publication Data
Main entry under title:

The Exceptional child.

    (McGraw-Hill series in special education)
    Rev. ed. of: The exceptional child / Robert M.
Smith, John T. Neisworth. 1975.
    Bibliography: p.
    Includes indexes.
    1. Exceptional children—Education—Addresses,
essays, lectures.   I. Smith, Robert McNeil.
II. Neisworth, John T.   III. Hunt, Frances M.
IV. Smith, Robert McNeil.   Exceptional child.
V. Series.
LC3965.E86   1983   371.9   82-14016
ISBN 0-07-058976-3

CONTENTS

LIST OF
CONTRIBUTORS

STEPHEN J. BAGNATO
Department of Psychiatry
Hershey Medical Center
The Pennsylvania State University

CHESTON M. BERLIN, Jr.
Departments of Pediatrics and
  Pharmacology
Milton S. Hershey Medical Center
The Pennsylvania State University

JOSEPH P. FRENCH
School Psychology Program
The Pennsylvania State University

JANELL I. HANEY
Department of Clinical Psychology
University of Pittsburgh

FRANCES M. HUNT
Division of Special Education and
  Communication Disorders
The Pennsylvania State University

RUSSELL T. JONES
Department of Clinical Psychology
University of Pittsburgh

EDWARD KLEIN
Speech and Hearing Clinic
Whittier College

P. DAVID KURTZ
Departments of Social Work and
  Counselor Education
University of Georgia

ELIZABETH A. LLEWELLYN
Division of Special Education and
  Communication Disorders
The Pennsylvania State University

RONALD A. MADLE
Center for Program Development
  and Evaluation
Laurelton Center, PA

DONALD F. MOORES
Center for Studies in Education and
  Human Development
Gallaudet College

JOHN T. NEISWORTH
Division of Special Education and
  Communication Disorders
The Pennsylvania State University

RALPH L. PEABODY
Department of Special Education
University of Pittsburgh

L. ALLEN PHELPS
Office of Career Development for
  Special Populations
University of Illinois at Urbana-
  Champaign

GREG REID
Department of Physical Education
McGill University, Montreal

JOHN SALVIA
Division of Special Education and
  Communication Disorders
The Pennsylvania State University

PATRICIA SEIBEL
Carbon-Lehigh Intermediate Unit
Jim Thorpe, PA

PAUL SINDELAR
Division of Special Education and
  Communication Disorders
The Pennsylvania State University

ROBERT M. SMITH
Dean, College of Education
Virginia Polytechnic Institute and
    State University

JAMES W. TAWNEY
Division of Special Education and
    Communication Disorders
The Pennsylvania State University

LINDA L. VARNER
Department of Special Education
California State University at
    Hayward

x

To a large extent, the success of *The Exceptional Child,* first Edition, has been due to the continuing movement toward a noncategorical approach for dealing with the educational needs of exceptional students. Though much debated, a distinct and separate training for each conventional category of exceptionality can no longer be academically defended. Further, the economics of the 1980s will probably not permit separate methods and materials courses to be offered in teacher-education programs. Finally, the massive integration of handicapped with nonhandicapped students has accentuated the need for more generic training in working with special-needs students.

For the second edition of *The Exceptional Child* we have enlarged the generic, noncategorical content of the book to include chapters on early special education and vocational/career education. Although non- and cross-categorical information is extensive, we have also greatly enlarged the coverage of conventional specific categories. The information summaries on traditional categories of the first edition have been developed into full chapters which discuss curriculum content, materials, applications of teaching strategies, and research *within* categories of exceptionality. Many of these chapters were contributed by recognized specialists within the diverse field of special education in order to reflect the unique concerns and the most recent development within each specialty area. This text is, then, really *two books in one:* both noncategorical (common) concerns *and* category-specific chapters provide the most comprehensive coverage available at the undergraduate level.

Since the first edition, the field of special education has undergone some major changes, both political and substantive. Undoubtedly, the single most dramatic event has been the passage in 1975 of Public Law 94-142, which guarantees free appropriate public education to all handicapped children. Plans for providing special education services were immediately formulated in every state to comply with this federal mandate. Regular and special educators, parents, nurses, therapists, and other ancillary personnel participated in extensive in-service training programs. Colleges and universities scrambled to meet the sudden demand for educators specially trained to design and implement programs for exceptional children. Millions of dollars were made available for research and evaluation of special education techniques. And though practitioners may only now be adjusting to requirements of P.L. 94–142, the trend to reduce federal aid to education and other social programs is likely to threaten the availability of resources for meeting the most basic needs of the handicapped.

Despite this nearly continuous state of flux, special educators have maintained constancy in their intervention philosophy and its underlying tenets. As with the first edition, the following tenets form the foundation for the content of this text: (a) every child must have a quality, appropriate education; (b) both regular and special educators need specialized training to work with exceptional children; (c) teachers need to develop a point of view or approach that they believe will provide a consistent learning environment; (d) intervention should be based on progress through steps of the diagnostic prescriptive model (to locate, screen, diagnose, treat, and evaluate); (e) intervention should be planned and implemented using a multidisciplinary approach, with education the focal point of that intervention; and (f) treatment must not be based on categorical requirements, but on the individual needs of the child. This text highlights these continuing, basic themes.

The second edition of *The Exceptional Child,* is appropriate not only for use in preservice training of both regular and special educators but also for preservice and in-service training of ancillary personnel including nurses, physical therapists, speech therapists, and school psychologists.

The comprehensive coverage of this text would have been impossible without the dedicated efforts of many of our colleagues. Special thanks go to the many contributing authors for their time and thoughtful suggestions, and for their patience throughout the long preparation period. Linda Regan, Jo Ann Gorman, Judy Lynch, and Denise Calhoun provided assistance in preparing the glossary and reference sections. We are also grateful to the many photographers who contributed their works, particularly Chuck Zovko and Paul J. Quinn. For his thorough and unquestioning servitude, our gratitude is extended to Howard Gallop. Secretarial help throughout the revision process was most supportive, thanks to the dedication and professionalism of Jo Ann Dreibelbis and Anita Daub. Finally, we extend our sincere thanks to the many colleagues who used the first edition and made suggestions for changes in content and format. We believe this edition will now provide the most comprehensive and practical coverage of the dynamic field of special education.

Robert M. Smith
John T. Neisworth
Frances M. Hunt

PART ONE COMMON CONCERNS WITHIN SPECIAL EDUCATION

Robert M. Smith
John T. Neisworth
Frances M. Hunt

CHAPTER 1
SPECIAL EDUCATION: A CHALLENGING AND CHANGING PROFESSION

(Courtesy of Chuck Zovko.)

This book is about children with problems. It is a book for regular educators as well as for prospective teachers who have a special interest in disabled and handicapped children. The U.S. Congress and the courts have mandated that all children, whatever their individual levels or types of disability, are to be provided a free public school education within the least restrictive environment possible. As a result, scores of disabled youngsters have moved in and out of regular classrooms. The need for regular-class teachers to know more about exceptional children and conditions has never been more pronounced. Such teachers are now responsible for providing appropriate and facilitating educational environments and experiences for *all* youngsters. Those who intend to become teachers, therefore, must be prepared to deal with exceptional children, because more is expected of today's teachers than ever before. These changes promise the individual preparing for a career in this field a challenging and dynamic profession.

CHANGES IN SOCIAL PHILOSOPHY, TECHNOLOGY, AND LEARNING THEORY

American society has historically interpreted education as a privilege to be extended only to those who were thought to benefit from it. The belief that human development and competence were not malleable but, rather, were controlled by heredity was behind much of of the logic to exclude children from school. Individual development was thought to be predestined and inevitable—the result of a biological master plan. A philosophy of fatalism particularly permeated the intervention efforts toward the disabled and abnormal. As a result, it was "logical" that education, therapy, and other such services for exceptional children, could at most ameliorate or contain the many unfortunate conditions that frustrate development.

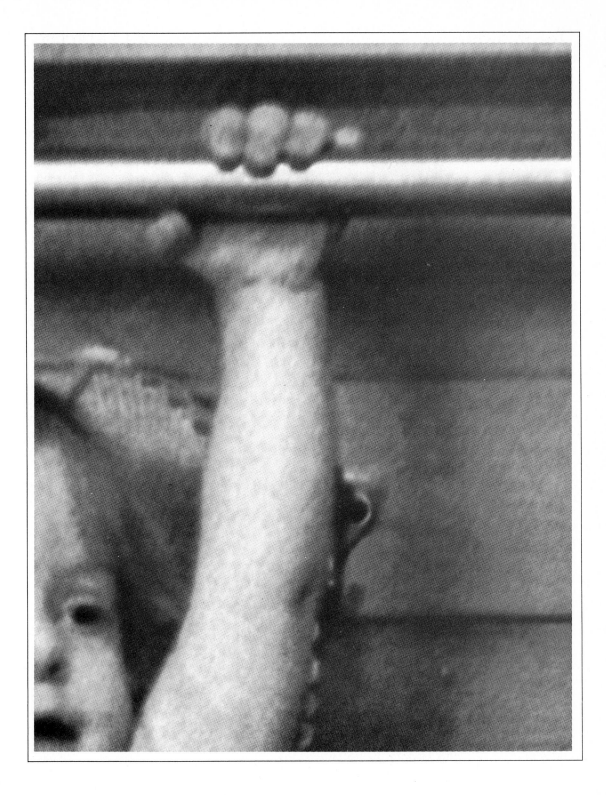

At one time handicapped children were prohibited from attending American public schools. (*President's Committee on Mental Retardation.*)

As methods for studying and understanding behavior and human development have become more refined and reliable, it has become clear that the environment interacts in a continuous way with the individual's biological makeup. Society's attitudes toward the handicapped and those who are "socially defective" have changed as evidence has emerged that individual development results from a complex interplay of "nature and nurture."

Finally, a revolution in learning theory has provided the push necessary to transform education from an art to a systematic manipulation of environmental variables. Initially, learning research was of little relevance to education, practical psychology, or other human-service fields. But the application of newly discovered learning principles to humans was inevitable. Initial success with experiments centered around the most severe problems of institutionalized persons rapidly led to the application of modern learning theory to a wide range of problems, persons, and situations. These profound and exciting changes have had a significant impact on special education. It is now recognized that intellectual, social, sensory, and physical deficiencies are not exclusively the result of a defective constitution. Rather, such deficiencies are the product of personal characteristics interacting with environmental variables. Constitution and environment affect each other, and neither is the exclusive cause or basis for handicap.

New assessment procedures make it possible to more accurately evaluate the learning needs of children. Educational practices are more efficient,

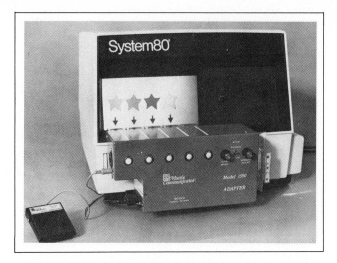

Teaching machines like this System 80 model help educators provide appropriate and individualized learning experiences. (*Borg-Warner Corp.*)

more effective, and better documented than ever before. Educators with a particular interest in exceptional children now make more use of behavioral objectives, programmed instruction, motivational management procedures, and competency-based curricula. Complementary instructional materials are also being developed. Hardware (teaching machines and other electrical and mechanical gadgets) and software (such as programmed texts) are changing the role of the educator.

TEN NEW DIRECTIONS IN SPECIAL EDUCATION
The following ten statements give focus to the latest views and directions for the education of exceptional children:

1. Categories based on causes and medical conditions are considered *less* important than groupings based on educational functioning (for example, problems related to learning, communication dysfunction, motoric capabilities, and social interaction).

2. Exceptional children must be integrated with nonhandicapped students when possible (least restrictive environment).

3. Programs for preschoolers and those who have left school are available in many communities to extend the scope of professional help available to exceptional persons and their families.

4. A key goal of society is the normalization of exceptional children (that is, children are to be placed in, or returned to, settings that require more normal levels of functioning on their part).

5. Robotlike psychological testing has been deemphasized as a requirement for receiving special education services.

6. The teacher's role has become more prominent in the diagnosis and

education of exceptional children. (Physicians and psychologists have assumed a more consultative role.)

7. Educational services are to be provided to all children whatever their degree or type of disability.

8. As a preventative measure, more emphasis is being given to early attention to problems.

9. Formal and continuous training is now available to professionals and paraprofessionals who have some responsibility for exceptional children.

10. Parent involvement in designing and carrying out a child's program is being emphasized, with the special educator playing a key role in educating and working with parents.

SPECIAL EDUCATION AND THE LAW

"Students may be expelled if they display continuous disorderly conduct or have a depressing or nauseating effect on the teachers and school children. The rights of a child of school age to attend school cannot be insisted upon when his presence is harmful to the best interest of the school." (*Beattie v. the State Board of Education,* 1919)

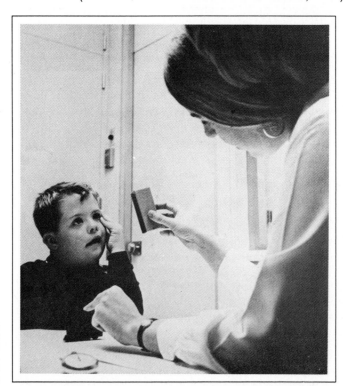

Because exceptional children are educated in the least restrictive environment, all educators must be *special* educators. (*President's Committee on Mental Retardation.*)

This statement, taken from a 1919 court decision, accurately reflected the belief held by most people that education in the United States was a privilege, *not a right*. In fact, only in the last twenty-five years has education been viewed differently. Coupled with the simultaneous changes in social philosophy, technology, and understanding of learning theory, basic changes in the interpretation of the constitutional rights of all individuals have produced a continuing revolution in education.

These changes have significantly altered the quantity, quality, and consistency of education in the United States. The events which led to the establishment of the Education For All Handicapped Children Act of 1975 spanned a period of twenty years. Pressure from parent and child-advocacy groups increased as numerous court decisions indicated that education, and equal access to it, were *constitutionally guaranteed.* P.L. 94-142 spells out the right of handicapped children to appropriate education and describes a framework for changes in the education system to ensure this right.

The most important features of P.L. 94-142 are outlined in Table 1-1. In the 1980s it is essential for the educator to be familiar with the elements of this law because part of your job will be to act as a responsible member of a team to implement it.

TABLE 1-1
Important Facts about P.L. 94–142

Public Law 94–142, the Education for All Handicapped Children Act, was passed by the U.S. Congress in 1975.

P.L. 94–142 has four major purposes:

1. to guarantee free and public special education programming to handicapped children who need it

2. to assure fairness and appropriateness in decision making about providing special education to handicapped children and youth

3. to establish management and auditing requirements and procedures regarding special education at all levels of government

4. to help state and local governments implement the law by providing federal funds

All states must serve children between the ages of 6 and 18; states that have independently provided services to children from 3 to 5 (kindergarten) or from 18 to 21 must also provide services for exceptional children between those ages.

Children must be educated in the least restrictive environment.

An individualized education program (IEP) must be developed, maintained, and evaluated for each child.

States must assure nondiscrimination testing, confidentiality, and due process procedures for all handicapped children and their parents.

States must actively attempt to identify children in need of special services.

States must provide a comprehensive system of personnel development.

Concern for the handicapped as expressed in P.L. 94-142 remains undiminished in spite of dramatic changes in other economic, social, and political policy. Whether the prevailing government is liberal or conservative, Democrat or Republican, there continues to be strong support for the rights and education of exceptional children. Economic constraints, however, may create some restrictions in implementing aspects of the law.

CAREERS IN SPECIAL EDUCATION

In years past, special education classes have been segregated from the mainstream of regular education. The children enrolled in them were grouped according to the traditional, more medically related disability categories. The special educator was responsible for conducting a program of education that was to be tailored to certain types of exceptional children, such as emotionally disturbed, blind, deaf, and so on. This concept of the special educator's role has changed dramatically. Special educators are now called upon to design and implement educational programs for disabled preschoolers, schoolchildren, and people who are no longer in school. Prevention of handicap is of equal importance as remediation and care.

In addition to working within self-contained classrooms, special educators serve routinely as consultants to teachers of regular classes, parent-training programs, and administrators. Because educational opportunities are mandated for all children in all possible settings within the school environment, special education teachers and consultants now have wider responsibilities than before. Eligibility for special education services is not restricted to children who exhibit only extreme deviations. Youngsters with special learning problems (such as addition problems, difficulties in motivation, or conduct problems) are now referred to a specialist.

As you probably suspect, a wide range of careers is possible in special education: teacher's aide, resource-room specialist, consultant to regular-class teachers, diagnostic and remedial specialist in certain subjects or skills, counselor to parents, recreation specialist, supervisor and program administrator, researcher, and teacher trainer, among others.

EXCEPTIONAL CHILDREN AND SPECIAL EDUCATION

Authors in the field of special education have chosen to define exceptional children in different ways. Here are three.

1. An exceptional child is one who deviates from the average or normal child in mental characteristics, sensory abilities, neuromuscular or physical characteristics, social behavior, or communication abilities. Such deviation must be of such an extent that the child requires a modification of school practices, or special education services, to develop to maximum capacity (Kirk & Gallagher, 1979, p. 3).

2. An exceptional pupil is so labeled only for that segment of his or her school career (1) when the deviating physical or behavioral charac-

teristics are of such a nature as to manifest a significant learning asset or disability for special education purposes; and, therefore, (2) when it has been determined through trial provisions that the child can make greater all-around adjustment and scholastic progress with direct or indirect special education services than with a typical regular school program (Dunn, 1973, p. 7).

3. The exceptional child is one whose educational requirements are so different from the average or normal child, that he or she cannot be effectively educated without the provision of special educational programs, services, facilities, or materials (Gearheart, 1972, p. 2).

Most definitions have focused on the attributes, deficiencies, or defects of the child. There is a danger that this may lead to (1) inappropriate labeling of the child, thereby making the child a scapegoat (that is, blaming the child for his or her problems); (2) imprecision in defining the prominent learning needs of each individual child (for example, calling a child "mentally retarded" does not lead to a specification of instructional needs); and (3) emphasizing the management of problems without directing concern to the prevention of future disorders or the elimination of circumstances that promote handicaps.

A slightly different perspective is to focus on what is to be done to the child educationally. We feel that such a definition minimizes the weaknesses inherent in focusing on the characteristics of the child. Therefore, we have chosen to define special education rather than exceptional children. *Special education is that profession concerned with the arrangement of educational variables leading to the prevention, reduction, or elimination of those conditions that produce significant deficits in the intellectual, communicative, motoric, social, and emotional functioning of children.*

Here, emphasis is on the major goal of special education, that is, arranging and structuring educational variables. The definition is educational. It does not focus on medical, constitutional, or hidden reasons for deficiencies in the child's performance. It embraces functional areas of performance, all of which can be observed directly and measured objectively. It implies that special education should be concerned with the prevention of disabilities as it has traditionally been about the reduction of the impact of the disabilities. It suggests that a child can be "exceptional" at one time and not at another, or in one situation but not in another. And finally, criteria can be established for a "significant deficiency" in one or more of the functional areas.

BASIC THEMES OF THIS BOOK

There are several basic themes in this book. These messages have common elements. Being alert to them will help you to identify and develop a consistent philosophy regarding your role as a teacher, the nature of exceptional conditions, and the meaning of special education. Your future performance as a teacher will be influenced by your philosophy. It is for that reason that we want you to know some of the tenets underlying the point of view emphasized in this text.

This book has five main themes:

1. *Interaction:* The behavior of a child, the differences expressed among children, and their individual strengths and weaknesses are the product of the interaction of a child with his or her environment. Behavioral defects or limitations are the result of interaction between the child and the environment and do not reside with the child exclusively.

2. *Behavior:* This book emphasizes behavior. Descriptions of children are descriptions of functioning or behavior. We have tried to avoid speaking about such things as a youngster's internal state or psychic strength. The design and delivery of educational programs will emphasize manipulation of the external environment as well as the collection of data that can be observed directly as a way of assessing instructional effectiveness.

3. *Development:* The attributes evidenced by children do not suddenly appear; they have a history of development to which all teachers must be alert.

4. *Prevention:* Most things which have not been learned can be; many problems of children can be reversed or certainly lessened, many can be prevented by early detection and special education.

5. *Normalization:* Children should be educated in as normal an environment as possible. If some form of atypical, more restricted instructional environment is required, the decision as to what form that environment should take must be based on where the child can function best.

SUMMARY

Education is a profession undergoing many rapid changes. Advances in social philosophy, learning theory, and technology have produced a continuing revolution which makes it exciting but sometimes difficult to be a special educator. In the past, it was believed that special education, therapy, and other services could serve only to ameliorate, contain, or provide care for the many unfortunate conditions that frustrate an individual's development.

A contemporary philosophy is emerging that emphasizes not only remediation, but prevention and normalization. Intellectual, emotional, sensory, and physical deficiencies are no longer seen as residing exclusively with the child and as the result of a defective constitution. Rather, such deficiencies are the product of personal characteristics interacting with environmental variables. Constitution and environment affect each other, and neither is static. This new position means that special education may be viewed as planned intervention designed to reduce, eliminate, or preclude deficiencies. A contemporary philosophy of special education, then, rejects the idea of merely caring for or maintaining persons with deficiencies or helping them to adjust. Instead, it emphasizes prevention and correction. Thus, retarded or distorted development and physical handicaps represent problems to be reversed, drastically reduced, or compensated for, with the goal of successive steps toward normalization. The goal must, in all cases, be progressive improvement in the direction of normal functioning. P.L. 94-142, which guarantees the right of every child to a "free appropriate public education," is based on this philosophy.

Exceptional children have been defined in a variety of ways by leaders in the field of special education. An alternative approach is to focus on the definition of special education. Special education is that profession concerned with the arrangement of educational variables leading to the prevention, reduction, or elimination of those conditions that produce significant deficits in the functioning of children. The major purpose of this book is to describe the skills and information educators will need to begin effectively to orchestrate environmental variables to the benefit of the child.

John T. Neisworth
Robert M. Smith

CHAPTER 2
EDUCATIONAL
SIMILARITIES
AND DIFFERENCES

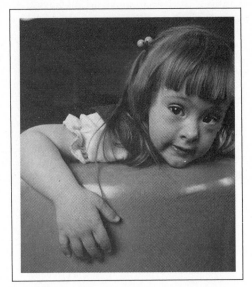

(Courtesy of Chuck Zovko.)

In this book we shall look at both the general and specific aspects of educational practice with exceptional children and adults. To be effective the regular teacher and the special educator or therapist must be knowledgeable about and competent in these two areas. The depth of knowledge will, of course, vary for the special and the regular educator.

At this point we will take an overview of the common denominators or generic considerations important to special educators. These general dimensions will be examined in greater detail in the next twelve chapters.

EDUCATIONAL SIMILARITIES

Whether the teacher is working with preschoolers or adults, with problems of retardation, emotional disturbance, or physical disability, the building blocks that form the foundation for effective education consist of the information and skills that have general application to the education and treatment of people with exceptional conditions. Like physicians in various medical specialties or different kinds of engineers, educators share a common base of information and skill. Fortunately, there is a growing professional core of information and techniques. Three areas of common concern are knowledge of the common causes of exceptionality, assessment, and educational intervention (Figure 2-1). Parts II and III of this book present details on each of these professional core areas.

CAUSES OF EXCEPTIONALITY

"Exceptionality" refers to the educational and developmental deviations shown by children who require educational adjustments or special consideration. Both biological and environmental variables are involved in causing

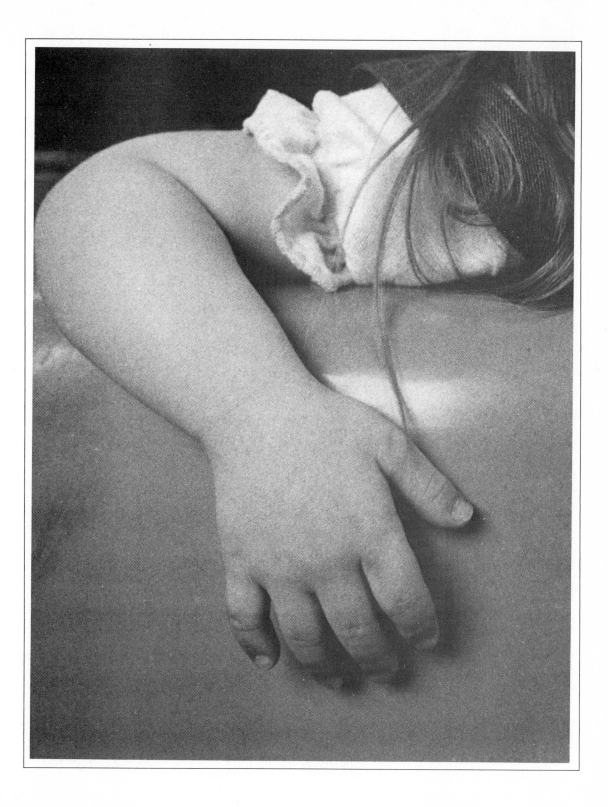

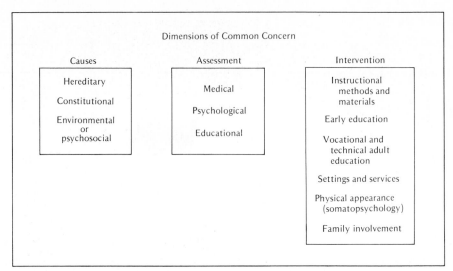

FIGURE 2-1
Three basic dimensions
that are of common
concern to educators who
work with exceptional
children.

exceptionalities. Regardless of their area of disability specialization, educators must be aware of the common or typical constitutional and environmental factors that frequently form the basis for disorder. Maternal nutrition, for example, can affect the health of the fetus and be a basis for a number of disabilities. Also, environmental variables, such as parenting practices, stimulation at home, and opportunities for responding can all influence the rate and direction of development. Chapters on these topics provide a general foundation of knowledge for the educator.

ASSESSMENT
Regardless of the disability area involved, assessment is crucial for educational planning. While teachers are not expected to be school psychologists or psychometricians, they should be familiar with the materials and techniques associated with medical, psychological, and educational assessment of exceptional children.

INTERVENTION
Of greatest concern to the educator are the common basic issues related to educational intervention.

Instructional Methods and Materials
Methods and materials can be specific to a disability area: braille and sign language are examples. Nevertheless, most good instructional practice rests on a general foundation of sound principles of learning and teaching. These include an understanding of and ability to use: specific appropriate objectives, precision teaching and other instructional strategies, varied room arrangements, and appropriate materials. To work with exceptional children effectively, the contemporary educator *must* be an instructional expert and must *apply* this knowledge *deliberately*.

Teachers of exceptional children must acquire expertise in the use of precision-teaching methods. (*President's Committee on Mental Retardation.*)

Appropriate Goals

In addition to the traditional goals of education, such as those related to academic and vocational skills, the contemporary special educator must be concerned with establishing objectives that will eventuate in the normalization of the child. These objectives may include elimination of or compensation for certain telltale characteristics which may serve as signals to others of a more pervasive handicap. Posture, facial expression, gait, and aspects of social interaction are some of the characteristics studied by those in the area of *somatopsychology*. Educators must be concerned with the problems of looking and acting differently, which can result in an additional social problem for the handicapped child.

Directly related to somatopsychological concerns is the use of *prostheses*—such devices as hearing aids, glasses, wheelchairs, braces, and a variety of gadgets that are used to compensate for or reduce the effect of handicaps. Additionally, there are prosthetic arrangements, such as ramps and braille signs, that can be built into the child's environment. Special educators are frequently inadequately trained to help children learn how to use and care for these prosthetic devices. All these matters are of educational importance and should be within the competence of the educator who works with significant exceptionality.

Family problems are prevalent with almost any area of disability. Not only parental reactions to the child but sibling adjustment and family dynamics generally can be an asset or liability to the child. Increasingly, educators are being called on to provide parent and family conferences, parent-child programming, and actual parental education.

The special educator has traditionally been confined to a special class or school. It is only recently that this conception of the *education setting of exceptional students* has been broadened. Most of the contemporary positions on placement involve a series of teaching environments that move progressively from highly contrived to more natural, normal arrangements. Exceptional children, then, can progress from one setting to another by design, according to their individual level of performance and instructional requirements. The ultimate goal is to move children as far into the mainstream of regular education as possible. The regular class setting is the goal for many (but not all) exceptional children.

Increasingly, not only does special education programming take place in more varied settings but resources for intervention come from a wider context. The most basic and ultimately influential resource is community support. Local, regional, and national commitment to research and services for people with handicaps is directly related to the financial support, cooperation, and prestige afforded to special education. Our country has lagged behind several other less affluent nations in this respect. Fortunately, however, special education and rehabilitation are now receiving greater attention and concern, and special educators can expect a broader base of support and respect for their efforts. Right-to-education laws, child advocacy, career ladders in special education, increased articulation among agencies, better public relations, and the growing proportion of handicapped people all bring special education into a more visible and prominent place. Contemporary educators see not only the school but the community as a ready resource. They may enlist the help of volunteers, paraprofessionals, civic and religious organizations, and university personnel to work directly with children and to assist in the continuing education of each other.

Early education is an area that cuts across all disability categories. Regardless of the handicap or potential problem, early intervention can prevent many secondary problems. Certainly, special educators should be apprised of the availability and promise of early special education. In turn, they can encourage parents to enroll children who risk additional problems in appropriate preschools. Recent legislation is bringing us closer to free and appropriate early education for handicapped children.

Parallel to the concern for early education is the trend toward *vocational and technical adult education.* Simply dumping exceptional persons into the population after traditional schooling is obviously misguided. We must attempt to engineer a smooth transition into adult life. Certainly, preparation for work, whenever possible, is a critical mission for professionals in education and rehabilitation.

All the foregoing topics and issues are relevant to a comprehensive educator. These are the core issues that form the foundations on which the effective contemporary educator must build. In addition to these generic

Parents are encouraged to take active roles in early intervention with their child. (*National Down Syndrome Society.*)

areas, the special educator must be well versed in the details of specific exceptionalities, as was mentioned at the beginning of this section.

CATEGORIES OF EXCEPTIONALITY

Conventional categories of exceptionality have evolved over the past thirty years. These categories have been useful in defining, describing, and organizing information on exceptional conditions and their etiologies. Table 2-1 shows two estimates of the prevalence of various types of exceptionality. A comparison of the 1979 and 1980 estimates illustrate how estimates can vary depending on the definitions and procedures used in the estimation process. Figure 2-2 shows the number of handicapped children receiving special education.

We have organized the various categories of exceptionality under four broad areas of development or behavioral functioning (Figure 2-3). Ask yourself, for example, what the relevance is to the educator of a child being categorized as crippled. What area of *functioning* might be expected to be deficient and therefore of prime interest? If motor functioning is impaired, this usually has direct implications for the provision of education. If a child is mentally retarded, what *functional area* is typically implicated? Intellectual or cognitive functioning is usually the major area of concern. Likewise, the phrase "emotional disturbance" might have legal, medical, or psychological implications for other professionals, but for the educator, the training of social and emotional skills is the major area of concern. The hearing impaired and visually handicapped obviously have sensory deficits that demand unique and special provisions. We have grouped these sensory difficulties under the functional area of "communication."

TABLE 2-1

Estimated number of handicapped children, using two different sets of identification criteria

PERCENT	ESTIMATED NUMBER	CATEGORY	PERCENT	ESTIMATED NUMBER
3.50	2,660,000	Speech impaired	2.42	1,170,538
3.00	2,280,000	Learning-disabled	3.03	1,468,047
2.30	1,748,000	Mentally retarded	1.74	844,321
2.00	1,520,000	Emotionally disturbed	0.72	348,965
0.58	437,000	Hearing-impaired	.16	81,376
0.58	380,000	Motorically impaired	0.12	59.664
0.10	76,000	Visually impaired	0.06	33,005
0.06	45,600	Deaf, blind, other multihandicapped	.34	172,029
12.10	9,146,600	Total	8.65	4,177,945

SOURCE: These figures are 1979 estimates of the number children ages 0–19 with various handicapping conditions. These data may be inflated because children with more than one handicapping condition may be included in more than one category (Bureau for the Education of the Handicapped, 1979).

SOURCE: These figures are 1980 estimates of the number of school-age children participating in special education programs, classified by primary disability. Children who receive services from private schools are not included (Special Education Programs, Department of Education, Personal Communication, 1982).

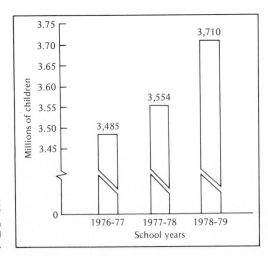

FIGURE 2-2
The number of handicapped children receiving special education.

Handicapped populations are not homogeneous. Each of these children have different social, emotional, and educational needs; different likes and dislikes. Each person is an individual!

Remember that children can bear one or several labels based on their medical, psychological, or even legal condition. The educator must ask, "So what?" and then determine what *functional* difficulties the child may present in the educational setting. You may be told, for instance, that Mary Lou is cerebral palsied. So what? What can she *do* and not do? In addition to problems with motor functioning, she may have learning, communication, social, and emotional problems. Or she may not. Always be alert to identifying *areas of functional deficit;* the medical or psychological "condition" is, at best, of secondary concern to the educator.

Functional Areas			
Learning	Socioemotional	Communication	Neuromotor
Gifted	Emotionally disturbed	Speech and language impaired	Crippled
Mentally retarded	Socially maladjusted	Hard of hearing	Other health impaired (seizure-prone children, progressive and chronic disease)
Learning-disabled		Deaf	
		Visually handicapped	
Severely handicapped	Severely handicapped	Severely handicapped	Severely handicapped

FIGURE 2-3
The conventional exceptionality categories organized under the four major areas of functioning.

While each child is unique, there are ways in which a child's specific dysfunctions or disabilities can be classified with respect to problems in school-related activities. Basically, there are four major areas of functional concern: learning (cognitive); social-emotional (affective); communication (language); and neuromotor.

There are other professions allied to education that are interested in the origin of disorder, details of biological differences, assumed conditions, and other features often common to a category of disorder. Regular and special educators must communicate with these allied professionals. In order to facilitate communication and familiarize educators with the problems common to a category, Part II of this book includes details on each conventional category of exceptionality. For now, we have provided an overview of these various exceptionality categories. This will help to acquaint you with the major distinctions among the categories. Begin to see the specific *and* general concerns addressed in this book.

DIFFERENCES IN LEARNING

It is clear that children differ greatly in their receptivity to and rate of learning, memory capability, skill in relating previous information to new knowledge, sensitivity to the environment, and ability to generate adequate responses to problems. Exceptionality ranges from superior functioning to significant general and specific dysfunction.

GIFTEDNESS

It was not until about fifty years ago that major efforts were begun in public schools to identify, study, and promote giftedness. Special programs were launched during the 1950s—the Sputnik era—when there was national concern that the Russians and others were getting ahead of the United States in technological development.

For purposes of this book, giftedness is included under *intellectual* functioning. Recent definitions, however, include superiority in other areas of competence, such as leadership and motor ability. Nevertheless, a measured IQ of about 130 or above has been and continues to be the major criterion for inclusion in the gifted category. At times, other criteria, such as achievement, teacher appraisal, and unusual talent are also used to qualify a child for special programming.

Teachers of gifted children must be ready to deal with problems associated with quick learners. It is a real challenge to keep ahead of a group of bright youngsters. Lesson plans and resources are soon exhausted. The special educator dedicated to promoting a sound instructional environment for these students must be energetic, open, and tolerant. Here, there is little room for compulsive adherence to the lesson; flexibility in instruction as well as concern with preplanned objectives is important. As with any notion of diversity, giftedness is not without its problems. Frequently, rapid learners do not experience the full social acceptance given to intellectually normal peers. Sometimes, then, there are adjustment problems to which the teacher must be alert. The teacher of gifted children is responsible for facilitating full development of these children—not just in their sometimes narrow area of superiority.

MENTAL RETARDATION

Certain children exhibit a generalized deficit in learning ability in contrast to other youngsters of the same age. Traditionally, such children have been labeled "mentally retarded" if their performance is significantly below that of their peers. The criterion for what constitutes a meaningful deviation from the norm is a point of debate among professionals. Usually, however, a score significantly lower than the norm on a standardized intelligence test is the primary criterion for the label "retarded."

The causes for a general learning deficit (mental or learning retardation) are varied and complex. It has been estimated that between 75 and 94 percent of individuals who are identified as mentally retarded exhibit that condition for reasons which cannot be adequately documented (Dunn, 1973). As is true with other areas of exceptionality, mental retardation is disproportionately expressed among various segments of the population. More children from lower rather than higher socioeconomic levels are defective in functioning. The relative influence of poor prenatal care, genetics, and the environment at various stages of development and functioning is an area of intense study. It seems clear that identification of the various causes of intellectual retardation will eventually lead to sophisticated preventive procedures.

General learning problems seem more resistant to change than deficiencies in single skills. Persons with retarded development typically show low-frequency behaviors in those areas in which they have previously failed, such as in many of the academic subject areas. So often these people lack opportunity in their early years for gaining those skills necessary to be successful in school and society. As a result, "the retarded" often exhibit socially inappropriate and developmentally obstructive behaviors. Self-stimulation, self-abuse, communication problems, stereotypic behaviors, and withdrawal are examples of behaviors that have been learned in the absence of a helpful environment. Institutions for the retarded are notorious settings for the development and maintenance of such unfortunate behaviors.

Compounding the problems of these children is the high incidence of other disorders. Motor problems, speech and language weaknesses, and psychosocial disorders head the list. These become more serious and frequent in children who are considered to be moderately or severely retarded. For youngsters with physical deformities or cosmetic defects, psychological complications inevitably arise because of the complex social consequences of the handicap. In addition, along with these primary problems, the mentally retarded and their families often suffer severe distress. These complications magnify basic learning difficulties and in a real sense enlarge management and instructional problems. For example, retarded children who experience constant failure in school and embarrassment before their peers may well develop significant behavior and adjustment problems. For such children, then, the layer upon layer of problems that result serve to blur the assignment of the child to a category.

There is unanimity of feeling among professionals that persons labeled mentally retarded are heterogenous as a group and therefore need an instructional program that is suited to their individual needs. The range of their educational needs is broad. Although there is diversity of opinion regarding which of the many psychological theories is most easily translatable for use in educational programs, most educators agree that principles of learning such as reinforcement of success, proper sequencing, programming in small steps, teaching direct applications, and practice have special pertinence in dealing effectively with the educational difficulties of the retarded.

The concept of *normalization* has emerged as a central theme throughout education, especially in the field of mental retardation. *Normalization* generally refers to the process of helping exceptional persons achieve more typical functioning through progressively more normal educational and treatment methods. *Mainstreaming* is one aspect of normalization and refers to the placement of exceptional persons in the same environment as the nonhandicapped.

The attempt to integrate exceptional youngsters into the mainstream of society has several points of origin. First, dramatic changes were reported in the performance of severely retarded persons through the use of systematic instructional programming, commonly referred to as behavior modification. Second, certain segments of society became concerned and vocal about the poor treatment many institutions for the mentally retarded were providing. Third, research confirmed the suspicion held by many people that certain commonly accepted practices in the education and management of the mentally retarded were in fact making the functional condition worse. Finally, behavioral scientists became convinced, upon the urging of parent groups, that one cannot expect normal functioning from a retarded person who lives or is educated in an abnormal environment. These events have led to a renewed interest in how best to deal with the problems of mental retardation.

LEARNING DISABILITY

The field of learning disabilities is a relatively recent addition to the exceptionality categories. Although historically there have been pockets of serious interest in the causes and characteristics of wide performance discrepancies in certain children, educators did not evidence an intense and all-abiding interest in such children until the early 1960s. It was only after the publication of several classic texts on this general subject and pressure by parent groups that organized professional interest developed. The publication of several promising diagnostic tests that were designed to pinpoint specific areas of performance disability (mainly in the academic subjects) gave impetus to the movement. Before that time the subject of specific learning disabilities had been focused within the context of the medical specialties.

As has been true in many relatively new fields of inquiry, professionals have not agreed on some basic concepts of learning disabilities. For example, the literature shows differences in definitions: some believe that brain damage is a necessary condition for a child to be classified as learning-disabled, others choose not to include social or personal deviations within the category, and still others hold the belief that education embraces all learning disabilities. Obviously, the definition of a phenomenon is the key to other considerations, including incidence, characteristics, identification, prevention, and therapeutic approaches. Without agreement on whom we are talking about, it is virtually impossible to agree on how many there are and what characteristics they exhibit. This inconclusiveness, of course, is typical of most fields of inquiry during early stages of formulation and development.

In spite of the problems related to such new areas, there is general agreement that children with learning disabilities exhibit a performance discrepancy of significant magnitude in one or more academically related areas. In contrast, their level of functioning in other fields is usually approximately normal. Mentally retarded children, in contrast, function poorly in most academic and psychosocial areas.

The diagnostic approaches that are used to evaluate the various nuances of learning disability are quite close to those used in the field of mental retardation. An interdisciplinary approach has been recommended. The fundamental principles of assessment of mental retardation and of learning disabilities are very similar, as are the problems of evaluation: test validity and reliability, test bias, comparative data, and the effectiveness of the tester.

The basic causes of learning disabilities are unclear, although there is general agreement that poor early school experiences, emotional problems, inept child-rearing practices, diseases, and accidents are major contributors to the problem. Prenatal and perinatal complications, to be discussed in a later chapter, are probably related in certain instances, but the exact relationships are unclear.

Finally, the best methods and procedures for dealing with children with learning disabilities are not agreed upon. Numerous points of view and philosophical propositions have been advanced in favor of one approach or another. Most of these strategies have not been tested enough to be proved valid.

SOCIAL AND EMOTIONAL DIFFERENCES

EMOTIONAL DISTURBANCE
This and other general terms such as "mental illness," "psychosis," and "neurosis" include numerous conditions such as schizophrenia, phobias,

obsessions, compulsions, autism, and so on. Each of these categories of disturbance has characteristics that separate it from the others. Typically, children who exhibit emotionally disturbed behavior are excessively aggressive, withdrawn, or both. Their central problem is not always reflected in violation of social rules or the mores and folkways of the culture; they are, however, usually very unhappy people.

As was mentioned in the preceding section, imprecision in the definition of a problem makes clear assessment impossible in other important areas, such as frequency of the exceptionality, its characteristics, its diagnosis, and its treatment. The broad area covered by the term "emotional disturbance" or "behavior disorders" suffers from the same definitional ambiguity as learning disabilities, with all of the related consequences. The statement that 12 percent or more of children in school have significant behavior disorders really has little meaning without an agreed-upon functional definition of the term.

There are a multitude of behaviors associated with social and emotional problems. Checklists have been developed to aid in alerting teachers to conduct and personality problems. For most teachers, extreme behaviors of a child stand out to such an extent that such lists are not necessary. Teachers and diagnosticians are frequently guilty of "playing psychiatrist" and speculating about strange behaviors as if they were facts. This procedure only leads to labeling, an intensification of existing problems, achievement disorders, and other types of complications. There is no question that social and emotional problems have multiple causes, but the presumed origin of any child's emotional or social disorder is clearly outside the expertise of most school personnel.

The treatment and management of behavior disorders by teachers and psychologists within the public school have taken many directions. Individual and group therapy, behavioral and drug intervention, educational or psychoanalytical procedures, and contrived or natural procedures have been implemented. Each method has its advocates, and all have histories of success and failure.

The field of behavior disorders is fraught with great imprecision, perhaps more than most other areas of exceptionality. This imprecision is not surprising, since the whole area of personal affect and social interaction has historically been explained by theories that themselves were vague. Educators have become increasingly concerned about these areas since the late 1950s, mainly as a result of having recognized that adjustment problems seem more prevalent among children with other types of disabling conditions than in nonhandicapped youngsters. There appears to be a double disability, with emotional disturbance being especially prominent. Some label this "emotional overlay." These observations by teachers, then, have contributed to a real interest among educators in more precise definition, more accurate observation and diagnosis, and more effective ways to prevent or treat the various adjustment problems that schoolchildren exhibit.

In contrast to emotional disturbance, social maladjustment refers basically to behavior which violates social or cultural rules. The behavior may be acceptable within the context of the child's subculture, but not in society at large. In fact, within the child's immediate social milieu rule-violating behavior (such as throwing stones at school windows) may be rewarded.

The incidence of social maladjustment is higher among low socioeconomic groups, but this picture is changing. More and more, middle-class children are engaging in shoplifting, drug abuse, and gang involvement. These children exhibit conduct disorders; they are caught up in activities that provide excitement, that declare independence, and that rebel against authority.

Frequent behaviors that result in a child being labeled socially maladjusted are shoplifting, school truancy, running away from home, drug involvement, rape, theft, and violence. These children show little realization for the long-range consequences of their behavior. Immediate gratification through antisocial acts is frequent. Showing off, partying, and disregard for the feelings and property of others typify the activities of socially maladjusted children.

In general, when these actions are committed by children under 16 years old, they do not fall under adult criminal provisions. Instead, juvenile delinquency and predelinquent provisions are available to help manage the problems. Of course, the legal system is not the appropriate one to prevent or really remedy social maladjustment. Community, home, and school environments are in the best position to detect and turn around children who cope poorly with social codes.

Children involved in antisocial activities do not usually do well in school. Since they resent authority, socially maladjusted children often avoid school or engage in countercontrol. Cheating, of course, is rampant. Children with a nasty reputation do not have a positive image among teachers, so if academic progress is attempted, it may go unnoticed.

As with emotional disturbance, there is enormous imprecision in the definition and treatment of social maladjustment within the field of education. Complications become even greater because the law is involved. Irate business people, aggravated citizens, worried and frustrated parents frequently urge simply "teaching him a lesson" or "getting rid of her." Retarded or disturbed children may violate norms but frequently have a pathology to explain their behavior. With no relatively clear pathology present, the child is blamed for misconduct.

Social maladjustment must be treated as a significant problem by educators, since it *does* intrude on school achievement and leads to further problems for the child and society. Programs are emerging that emphasize high-interest curricula, community participation, and career and vocational preparation. Parent involvement becomes crucial in working with socially maladjusted or sociopathic children. Home and school can work together to provide positive avenues for development. Positive motivation, realistic and interesting tasks, alignment with desirable models (especially peers) and a few real teacher friends can go a long way to avoiding or getting off the road to delinquency and academic tailspin.

COMMUNICATION DIFFERENCES

SPEECH AND LANGUAGE DYSFUNCTION

Speech is human verbal expression. Language, which may involve speech, gestures, or written symbols, is the way humans convey messages and ideas. Both fall under the broad rubric "communication" and together make up the area of disability that involves the highest percentage of children. Estimates of the incidence range from 5 percent to over 10 percent of school-age children.

The way speech and language develop normally is fairly well documented. The very earliest stages in communication are reflexive vocalization, babbling, vocal play, lallation, and echolalic utterances, all of which play important roles in the character and strength of subsequent communication capabilities. At around 1 year of age, the child's first words appear—usually single-syllable, consonant-vowel combinations, as in "ma-ma" or "da-da." Each month thereafter new, more complex words appear in the child's repertoire. At age 2, under facilitating circumstances, nearly 300 words can be expressed in combinations and in appropriate ways. As youngsters grow older, their skills in making complex speech sounds and their vocabularies increase dramatically. Under normal circumstances, a 6-year-old child has a comprehension vocabulary of more than 2,000 words.

Especially during the early stages of development, speech and language develop simultaneously. If something occurs to impede the development of one of these areas of functioning during this crucial early period, the other area will be negatively influenced. Perhaps the greatest source of difficulty in this respect is a child's being around poor or inadequate models. When adults either do not speak to their youngsters or err in their patterns of speech and language, children will not learn to communicate properly. Other functional causes for communication disorders are poor teaching methods, emotional problems, fatigue, and low energy levels. Problems with the organs involved in verbal communication, as well as those of the central nervous system, can interfere with the establishment and enhancement of speech and language. Hearing loss, brain or nerve damage, seizure, pathology of the vocal cords, problems with the soft or hard palate, swollen adenoids, paralyzed oral structures, growths, and glandular dysfunction are associated with organic weaknesses or malfunctions.

Speech defects are typically classified in terms of (1) articulation problems (sound omissions, substitutions, distortions, or additions); (2) disorders in rhythm or speech flow (stuttering or cluttering); (3) voice deviations (quality, pitch, or volume); (4) cleft palate; (5) cerebral-palsied speech; and (6) those speech defects directly related to hearing problems. Professional speech personnel have over the years developed special types of evaluative procedures to screen for and comprehensively assess elements of the various speech disorders. Evaluative procedures and treatment approaches are intimately related to the particular theory that the therapist subscribes to. Chapter 5 provides a review of the prominent diagnoses and treatment perspectives related to speech disorders. The diversity of opinion in these areas among eminent speech pathologists should be studied carefully in order to gain a full appreciation of the state of this very large and important area of special education.

Children with language problems have difficulty dealing with linguistic symbols. This can be manifested in numerous ways, including failure to understand the meaning of what is said or written, difficulty in relating the meanings of words to the information the child has previously acquired, weakness in expressing meaning to others through the written or spoken word, problems in focusing on specifics or in formulating generalizations, disorders of auditory or visual recall, or combinations of any of these.

This area gained increasing attention during the 1960s as a result of great advances in the field of psycholinguistic testing. The Illinois Test of Psycholinguistic Abilities has been instrumental in fostering research, development, and experimentation in the broad area of language. Specialists in the field of learning disabilities have chosen to include language disorders as part of their general area of expertise. The field is still in a relatively embryonic stage and is in serious need of rigorous and extended research and experimentation. This state affords numerous opportunities to students who are interested in an area of special education that is presently undergoing great change.

AUDITORY DYSFUNCTION

Several dimensions and criteria have been used to classify auditory disorders. The location of the problem (outer ear, middle ear, or inner ear), the degree of hearing impairment (as measured by an audiometric evaluation), the age at onset (before or after birth), and types of auditory disorders (conductive, sensory-neural, central, or psychogenic) illustrate the range of possibilities for establishing categories. By far the most helpful and frequently used classification system for education purposes is degree of hearing loss. This has most functional relevance and is tied directly to hearing behavior, which, in turn, provides specific information on the nature of a child's special educational needs.

Hearing disorders can be traced to the same basic sources as other disabilities. Prenatal, perinatal (at the time of birth) and postnatal difficulties can affect the functioning of components of the auditory system to varying degrees. Some dysfunctions are effectively managed by medical intervention, either short-term or long-term, while other auditory probems cannot be prevented, reversed, or medically ameliorated. Psychological and social difficulties are frequently related to hearing disorders and often serve to worsen the consequences of the hearing problem itself. Deaf people, for example, often hesitate to speak. When they do speak, they exhibit a characteristically unique pattern of speech and language that signals abnormality to the listener. The reactions of listeners to deaf speech can be extreme enough to influence the hearing-impaired person in very negative ways. Some have trouble in personal and social areas; others are influenced in their academic functioning.

Relatively sophisticated approaches have been developed by audiologists (hearing specialists) and otologists (ear doctors) to observe and measure the characteristics of the auditory system. Technical advances in this field are impressive and have led to major changes in past practices and philosophies. For example, because of progress in physiological audiometry, infant hearing tests are much more valid and reliable than in the past. Advances in microsurgery of the ear have also proved extremely effective in reversing significant auditory disorders.

Instructional programs for children with hearing defects require highly skilled professionals. The most immediate issue of concern, quite logically, is to help the hearing-impaired child develop acceptable skills in expressing and understanding ideas. There is controversy among special educators and therapists on the proper focus for this instruction. Some emphasize training in oral expression, others emphasize sign language, while still others opt for a combination of these approaches. Debate also appears in the literature and at professional meetings on the most appropriate location for educating hearing-impaired children and youth. Some believe that residential schools provide the best environment. An equally vocal group of professionals holds that these children should be educated within the public schools.

VISUAL DYSFUNCTION

In 1979, the Bureau for the Education of the Handicapped (BEH) estimated that between 0.1 percent and 0.4 percent of children of school age have significant visual disorders. This is the smallest group of exceptional children. A standard classification system has been adopted by almost all professional groups who have an interest in visual defects. The legal definition of blindness is used to dictate the types of social services for which the blind can qualify. It has little meaning educationally, so special educators have chosen to classify as blind those who cannot read print. The *partially sighted* are youngsters who can read print with special low-vision aids.

The causes of visual disorders parallel the causes of the other disabilities that involve clear organ dysfunction. Accidents, poisoning, infections, tumors, hereditary difficulties, and nutritional deficiencies stand out as major contributors to visual problems. There are a multitude of types of visual defects. Problems with the area surrounding the eye, refractive errors, muscle imbalance and failure, defects in the receptive mechanisms, cataracts, glaucoma, and albinism are among the most prominent forms of ocular difficulties. Each has different causes and demands unique intervention.

Teachers have an important place in the early diagnosis of visual problems in young children. As problems are suspected, more elaborate screening devices can be used to assess the validity of the teacher's hunch. These tests measure visual acuity, depth perception, possible muscular problems, and the range of the child's visual field.

NEUROMOTOR DIFFERENCES

At birth a physician looks for certain motor behaviors in the infant that together indicate that the child is reasonably healthy. Sucking, swallowing, grasping, the contraction of pupils in reaction to bright lights, and several forms of reflexive behavior are signs that suggest a normal pattern of motor behavior in a newborn. As children approach their first birthday, they make tremendous advances in motor performance. Certain basic reflexive behaviors become less obvious: children reach in response to objects, move from side to side, and exhibit control over the head and upper body; fine motor coordination between fingers and thumbs develops rapidly, and the rudiments of locomotion skills become obvious. Ages 2, 3, and 4 constitute significant landmark periods, during which children gain ever-increasing control over their bodies and become skilled in executing complex motor behaviors.

As they grow older, most children begin to run, skip, hop, jump, and climb steps with facility. By ages 6 and 7 youngsters demonstrate relatively mature patterns in fine motor skills, as in writing, throwing, and a wide spectrum of physical activities of substantial complexity.

Many motor disorders occur during the prenatal period or during the process of birth. Relatively few are the result of postnatal difficulties, such as some unusually traumatic experience like amputation, brain tumor, poisoning, or a serious blow to the head.

CEREBRAL PALSY

Of all the types of motor disorders, cerebral palsy is the most common, affecting approximately 1 to 3 per 1,000 school-age youngsters. The original problem is not with the child's muscles; the motor disorder is caused by brain damage that has affected the motor areas of the brain in either a specific or a generalized fashion. The inability of these children to use their extremities and control other neuromuscular behavior (such as positioning and balance) results in further complications, weaknesses, and disabilities through disuse. Muscles contract, fibers become excessively tense, and additional deformities result.

There are various forms of cerebral palsy, each of which is theoretically characterized by unique symptomatology. Most astute clinicians are able to diagnose a cerebral-palsied child as spastic, athetoid, ataxic, with tremor, or rigid, even though the presumably unique characteristics of each type overlaps in reality. As in the other disability areas, there is enormous variability among children in the degree of handicap, the presumed time of onset, the number and location of the extremities influenced, and the extent to which other systems are involved. Cerebral palsy illustrates in an obvious and dramatic way the great difficulty in logically or pragmatically classifying chil-

CHAPTER 2
EDUCATIONAL
SIMILARITIES AND
DIFFERENCES

dren according to the traditional disability groups and the lack of meaning that such categories have for education. What is the point in debating whether a child with hearing, speech, motor, and learning problems is mentally retarded, cerebral palsied, or deaf? Most complex patterns of disability simply cannot be separated into such neat categories. In fact, the cerebral-palsied are so heterogeneous that the category itself has almost no meaning for education and rehabilitation.

These propositions notwithstanding, over the years several of the professions have given varied, thoughtful, and consistent attention to the issue of the cerebral-palsied child. Speech and hearing specialists and physical and occupational therapists have led the way in designing treatment and management programs for the cerebral-palsied. The theories advocated are as numerous as they are diverse in point of view. For the most part their collective, common focus seems to be on helping the youngster with the problem gain more strength and independence in muscle functioning. Some attack the problem by dealing with the muscles themselves, while other more extreme perspectives suggest working on the child's higher neurological centers. Medical and surgical procedures are used in varying degrees to provide support, remedy deformities, and facilitate the increased usage of the child's motor capabilities.

There is no standard special education program for cerebral-palsied children. Their learning needs are individual, dependent on their characteristics, background, and ambitions. Of course, the types of special education options available in a community will dictate to a very great extent how well the youngster's educational requirements can be met.

EPILEPSY

Neurological disturbance can result in seizures of varying intensity and frequency. This is referred to as epilepsy. Motor dysfunction accompanies the seizures in most cases. Muscles become stiff and contract, and violent muscular jerking may occur. In some instances only certain sections of the body may be influenced. The condition occurs rather infrequently (1 per 1,000 school-age children); it usually results from brain damage during the prenatal or perinatal period, and the major treatment is drug therapy. The condition is a perplexing one for many teachers, especially when the teacher is unaware of how best to deal with a child's seizure.

OTHER DISORDERS

Spina bifida occurs with the same frequency as epilepsy. The defect is congenital (present at birth) and is characterized by an opening in the child's spine. Neural tissue frequently protrudes, and this results in varying degrees of paralysis of the legs. Bladder and sphincter control are often lost. The condition varies in intensity, and treatment may involve early surgery, corrective braces and hygienic practices.

Muscular dystrophy is a progressive disease in which the muscle tissues degenerate and waste away. There are several types of muscular dystrophy.

The disease is hereditary, and because no successful treatment is available the patient usually dies at an early age.

Motor disorders are also the consequence of such infrequent conditions as polio, clubfeet, congenital amputation, rheumatoid arthritis, and curvature of the spine. The patterns of deviation range from complete to very mild involvement, and remediation in most of the cases can significantly improve the child's level of functioning.

Several evaluative devices have been developed to assess motor development in children. Some of these instruments are for very young children and can be used to detect significant delays in development. These data are then used to decide what kind of procedures can be taken to prevent a worsening of the condition and, if possible, to reverse its outcome.

The whole area of motor disorders exemplifies the general character of exceptionalities. The psychosocial complications, the multiplicity of deviations that are frequently present, the time of onset and the reasons for the disabilities, the process involved in assessment and diagnosis, and the varieties of therapies used are broadly similar to the other forms of exceptionalities we have briefly described. Most exceptional youngsters have functional problems that are complex and that interact with each other and with the environment in unique ways. It is most important that the special educator recognize these core issues and focus attention on the establishment of instructional programs.

SEVERE, PROFOUND, AND MULTIPLE HANDICAPS

We have been able to place each of the conventional categories of exceptionality into the four functional areas: learning, social-emotional, communication, and neuromotor functioning. Severe handicap, however, cuts across these areas. "Severe handicap" can refer to extreme difficulty in one or more areas of functioning. Indeed, it is frequently the case that severe handicap in one area is associated with problems in other areas. Also, *severe* and *profound* difficulties tend to require measurement and treatment tactics that differ considerably from those required for milder disorders.

The special educator who elects to work with the severely handicapped is bound to encounter many frustrations. Often, bizarre behavior patterns are practiced by severely handicapped children and adults. When institutionalized, these persons often develop unproductive behaviors in response to the low-stimulus, routine environment typical of most institutions.

Fortunately, there is movement away from institutionalization and toward alternative classes within regular schools, and even regular classes within regular schools are being used to serve the educational needs of the severely handicapped. Group homes and real-home placement are being used increasingly. Instruction of the severely handicapped is making more and more use of behavioral techniques and prosthetic arrangements. Special technology to facilitate stimulus reception and permit acceptable responding is available. The special educator who works with severely handicapped children must be technician, therapist, educator, and friend! Data from several projects with the severely handicapped show promising results: good programming can lead to remarkable improvement in functioning.

SUMMARY

Special education is both *education* and *special*. That means that we must first consider exceptional children as children who deserve an education—like any other children. Secondly, we must consider exceptional children as students who need specialized materials, methods, and environments in order to help them progress. As educators, we must be expert in both the educational provisions common to all children and to the special considerations required for categories of exceptionality. The common concerns include acquaintance with the basic *causes* of exceptionality so that we can better understand and work with children in need. Basic knowledge of developmental factors, nutrition, parenting practices, and the effect of various environmental qualities can help the educator see the broader context of normality and exceptionality. Likewise, there are a number of common considerations in the assessment of children and educational problems. There are, fortunately, a number of factors related to educational intervention that deal with all children. Certain learning principles and practices, curricula, grouping arrangements, and well-established teaching procedures have applicability not only across categories of exceptionality but to all children. These generic considerations, relevant to educational intervention, are basic to good teaching and form the foundation for all educators.

On the other hand, special educators are faced with the challenge of working with children who are different in educationally significant ways. We have grouped these differences according to areas of behavioral or developmental functioning. Thus, special and regular educators must work at promoting child progress in the *functional* areas of learning, social and emotional capabilities, communication, and motor abilities. Exceptional children have numerous and significant *differences* that produce *problems* within the standard educational setting. These problems must be accommodated through specialized arrangements so that they no longer present obstacles to educational progress. Knowledge and skill in *special* child characteristics, materials, and teaching tactics built on a foundation of understanding of *common* factors will result in a top-notch regular or special educator.

John Salvia
Patricia Seibel

CHAPTER 3
LABELING
AND CLASSIFICATION
IN SPECIAL EDUCATION

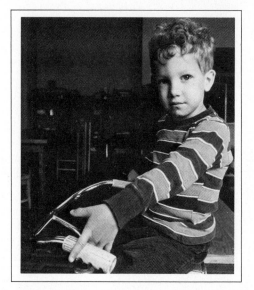

(Courtesy of Chuck Zovko.)

Classification and labeling serve useful social and scientific ends. Sciences use classification systems to order information, to provide a framework for understanding new information, and to shape the directions of future inquiries. The merits and limitations of classifications of handicaps depend on their social utility and impact. Labeling for what purpose? What outcomes result from labeling? Our emphasis will be on the social and educational consequences of labeling.

Social systems rely heavily on classifications to maintain order and to promote the welfare of the citizenry. There are many socially useful and valid categories and labels; a few of the more common labels are based on categories of:

Age (for example, infant, adolescent, minor, adult)

Enfranchisement (for example, citizen, registered voter)

Occupation (for example, teacher, senator, unemployed)

Physical characteristics (for example, male, paraplegic, slim, blind)

Educational attainment (for example, preschooler, second-grader, high school dropout, college graduate)

COMPLICATIONS OF LABELING AND CLASSIFICATION

The overriding question is, Do the benefits of labeling outweigh the liabilities? This seemingly simple question has three complications: the benefits to the individual and to society may be contradictory; categorized groups are heterogeneous; and there is overlap within and among various systems of classification. Let us examine each of these problems separately.

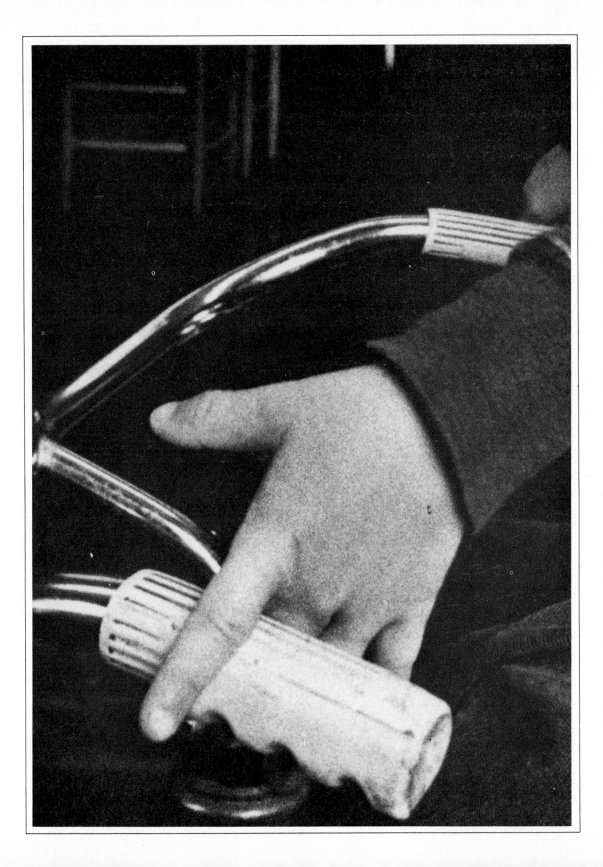

CONTRADICTORY BENEFITS

Farber (1968) draws a careful distinction between "incompetence" and "deviance." Incompetent people present little threat to the social order, while deviant individuals do. To the extent that handicapped persons are viewed as incompetent (that is, wishing to conform to society's values but unable to do so), they are likely to be given special or extra consideration to overcome their incompetence—or at least benignly neglected. On the other hand, if handicapped persons are viewed as deviant (that is, posing a threat to society), they are likely to be dealt with more harshly. These opposing views are always present in society and at any one time produce social ambivalence toward the handicapped (Lewis, 1973). Because of this ambivalence, social policy tends to be contradictory: at any one time the effects of categorization and labeling may be both beneficial and harmful.

Benefits to Society

Several practices illustrate society's attempts to protect itself from the handicapped. Handicapped persons have been prohibited from serving on juries, voting, attending public schools, or marrying (Wald, 1976). Perhaps nowhere is society's fear of handicapped people as clear as in the eugenics movement which began in the nineteenth century. The basic tenet was that humanity is weakened genetically if unfit persons are allowed to reproduce. Charles Darwin, writing in 1874, stated the position succinctly:

> With savages, the weak in body or mind are soon eliminated; and those that survive commonly exhibit a vigorous state of health. We civilized men, on the other hand, do our utmost to check the process of elimination; we build asylums for the imbecile, the maimed, and the sick; we institute poor-laws; and our medical men exert their utmost skill to save the life of every one to the last moment. . . . Thus the weak members of civilized societies propagate their kind. No one who has attended to the breeding of domestic animals will doubt that this must be highly injurious to the race of man. It is surprising how soon a want of care, or care wrongly directed, leads to the degeneration of a domestic race; but, excepting in the case of man himself, hardly any one is so ignorant as to allow his worst animals to breed.

Shirer (1961) notes that Nazi Germany's sterilization laws and national policy of elimination of mental defectives was carried out under the guise of mercy killings. The eugenic motive behind the laws and killings was quite clear: those people were not useful to that society. In 1974, twenty-six states in the United States had eugenics statutes which permitted the sterilization of minors or mental incompetents, and these statutes were being used. In the state of North Carolina, for example, 1,620 such individuals were sterilized between 1960 and 1968 (Coburn, 1974).

Will the label of mental retardation limit expectations of what this child's capabilities are? (*President's Committee on Mental Retardation.*)

Benefits to Individuals

At the same time that society seeks to protect itself from the handicapped, it also provides them with kind and humane treatment. Various organizations have been created to serve particular categories of handicapped individuals: state associations for the retarded or for children with learning disabilities, the Society for Crippled Children, the Easter Seal Society for Crippled Children and Adults, the National Foundation (March of Dimes), the Epilepsy Foundation of America, United Cerebral Palsy, and the Muscular Dystrophy Association, to name a few. Moreover, service clubs and charities—for example, Shriners' hospitals for crippled children and various United Way agencies—often support activities or facilities that benefit the handicapped. It would be virtually impossible to list the particular services that these organizations provide to handicapped individuals and their families. In general terms, they provide diagnostic, treatment, counseling, and medical services as well as prosthetic devices (for example, glasses, artificial limbs), and community education and awareness programs. Finally, one should not overlook the actions of individual employers who make it a policy to hire the handicapped.

Government agencies have increasingly provided for various identified and labeled categories of handicapped persons. At the state level, departments of public welfare may provide or support such services as emergency care, inpatient, outpatient, and rehabilitation services, sheltered workshops, halfway houses or group homes, foster care, short-term and long-term residential care, and so on. State departments of vocational rehabilitation may provide a variety of services to handicapped persons, including assessment, rehabilitation, training, counseling, and securing employment.

At the federal level, handicapped persons are often identified for special benefits. For example, Supplemental Security Income is a federal program to help blind or disabled persons of any age in financial need. Public support for increased benefits for groups of handicapped persons has become evident during the 1960s and 1970s, including the creation in 1966 of the Bureau for the Education of the Handicapped within the United States Office of Education. However, three events in the early 1970s are especially noteworthy as indicators of support for the handicapped. In 1972, a class action suit was brought in the District of Columbia by parents and guardians of handicapped children not being served by the public schools. In *Mills v. Board of Education of the District of Columbia,* the court ruled that all school-age children were entitled to a free and appropriate public education regardless of the severity of their handicaps. In 1973, Section 504 of the Vocational Rehabilitation Amendments of P.L. 93-112 became a civil rights act for the handicapped. It stated in part:

> No otherwise qualified handicapped individual in the United States shall, solely by reason of his handicap, be excluded from the participation in, be denied the benefits of, or be subjected to discrimination under any program or activity receiving federal financial assistance.

In 1975, the Education for All Handicapped Children Act (P.L. 94-142) was passed. Section 3(c) states:

Do the benefits outweigh the disadvantages of labeling? The research is not conclusive. (*National Down Syndrome Society.*)

It is the purpose of this Act to assure that all handicapped children have available to them a free appropriate public education which emphasizes special education and related services designed to meet their unique needs, to assure that the right of handicapped children and their parents or guardians are protected, to assist State and localities to provide for the education of all handicapped children, and to assess and assure the effectiveness of efforts to educate handicapped children.

While there are many reasons to be hopeful about the potential benefits that classification and labeling can bring to handicapped persons, the benefits that are actually delivered are still unclear. Labels can become social signals for both positive and negative consequences.

HETEROGENEOUS GROUPS

Severity of the Handicap

Although persons within a category share a common characteristic (that is, a particular handicap), and although one commonly finds stereotypic references to the handicapped, various groups of handicapped persons are not homogeneous. At the simplest level, disability varies along a continuum of severity (from profound to mild retardation, from the absence of light perception to myopic vision, and so forth).

Visibility of the Handicap

Another important but often overlooked consideration is the conspicuousness of the handicap. Handicapping conditions range from the obvious to the subtle. Some, such as paraplegia, prelingual deafness, mutism, severe speech impediments, profound mental retardation, and some forms of psychosis, are immediately apparent to untrained observers after casual contact with the person. Often, but not always, the more severe the handicap, the more conspicuous it is. The highly visible handicap probably acts as an anchor or reference point for stereotypes of handicapping behavior. For example, when a child has been labeled "emotionally disturbed," there may be a tendency to think of severe acting-out behavior rather than mild withdrawal.

Other conditions are apparent only to skilled or trained observers during diagnostic assessment. Examples of more subtle handicaps include mild mental retardation, minor errors in articulation, mild hearing loss, partial vision, some forms of neurosis, and mild forms of cerebral palsy. Untrained persons may recognize that the person is "different," while not being aware that the person is handicapped. Finally, there comes the point where handicapped and nonhandicapped (normal) merge. Here, experts often disagree over the classification of individuals, and "handicapped" and "normal" become indistinguishable categories.

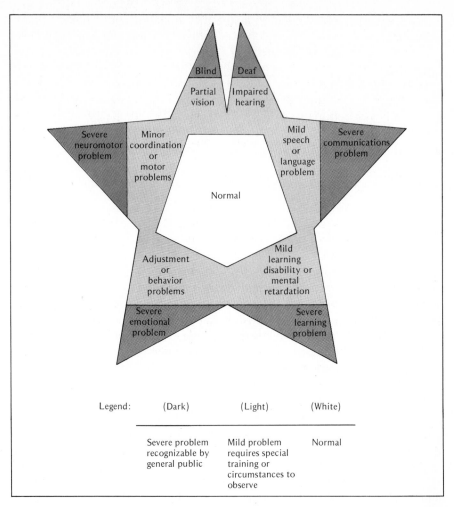

FIGURE 3-1
The salience of extreme
forms of handicap and the
gradual loss of distinction
as the category
approaches normality.

The benefits and liabilities of categorization probably differ as a function of the visibility of the handicapping condition. Labels emphasize *differences* from the norm rather than similarities to it. Many handicapped persons may try to pass for normal, although they know that they are handicapped. As Wright notes:

A person may fully accept a particular fact about himself and yet conceal it because of the belief that awareness on the part of others would contribute to disturbed social relations. This is one basis on which the cosmetic hand instead of the hook or no prosthesis is recommended in casual relationships (Dembo & Tane-Baskin, 1955). Realistically recognizing that the knowledge that one is . . . an amputee, or hard-of-hearing may create social barriers to full acceptance by others.

Other handicapped persons may deny outright that they are handicapped. Edgerton (1967) reports the statement of a former resident of a state hospital for the retarded:

You know, I was worried did they really think I was like them others. The ones that couldn't do nothing or learn nothing. I used to think that I'd rather be dead than be like them. I found out OK that nobody thought I was really like them others. I wasn't no mental problem or nothing like them others. If I was like them others, God, I would have really killed myself. (Wright, 1960, p. 20–21)

For these people, the intended benefits of labeling are outweighed by the stigma of public identification. Moreover, the history of mental retardation is filled with examples of once-identified "retardates" fading into the general population (Baller, 1936; Charles, 1953; Ginzberg & Bray, 1953; President's Committee on Mental Retardation, 1969). Being handicapped is certainly not a status that people usually seek to acquire or maintain.

At the other extreme, persons with highly visible handicaps will likely suffer no more because they are officially labeled, since their handicaps are obvious already, and they are usually unable to pass for normal. For example, a person in a wheelchair is perceived as handicapped because the condition is obvious to the observer. The salience of the handicapping condition, rather than the label itself, will more likely influence the conclusions the observer will reach. The consequences for the handicapped person would be about the same, with or without the label.

OVERLAP WITHIN AND AMONG CLASSIFICATION SYSTEMS
The third complication of labeling is that there is considerable overlap in the classification of handicaps. This problem is twofold. First, there are multiple systems of classification used in social contexts. A number of different professions are interested in various exceptionalities. Each discipline brings with it its own theoretical orientations and often somewhat different classification systems. Thus, a child with a *specific learning disability* (educational label) may be *organically brain-damaged* (medical label) and may be a *ward of the court* living with foster parents (legal labels). Actually, the situation is more complicated because within various professional disciplines there may be several schools of thought, each with its own set of definitions and classification systems. As an example, Gallagher, Forsythe, Ringelheim, and Weintraub (1975) reviewed the labels used by four federal programs that dealt with persons who could be considered handicapped. They found that the Rehabilitation Services Administration used twenty labels and categories, the Law Enforcement Assistance Administration used thirty-five labels, and the National Institute of Mental Health used forty-one labels. The U.S. Office of Special Education uses eight categories: mentally retarded, hearing impaired, visually handicapped, speech handicapped, emotionally disturbed, specific learning disabilities, crippled and other health impaired,

CHAPTER 3
LABELING AND
CLASSIFICATION IN
SPECIAL EDUCATION

and multiply handicapped. Garrett and Brazil (1979) surveyed state departments of education to ascertain what categories were used. Their results are reprinted in Table 3-1. It can be seen that categories used by the Bureau for the Education of the Handicapped have had a pronounced effect on the categories used by the state departments; the two notable exceptions are the provision of services for the gifted and the classification, "children in need of special services."

TABLE 3-1
Categories Used for Identification and Education of Exceptional Children

STATE	BLIND	DEAF-BLIND	EARLY CHILDHOOD SPECIAL EDUCATION	GIFTED, TALENTED	HARD OF HEARING	MENTALLY RETARDED	MULTIPLE HANDICAPPED	ORTHOPEDICALLY IMPAIRED	OTHER HEALTH PROBLEMS	SERIOUSLY EMOTIONALLY DISTURBED	SPECIAL LEARNING DISABILITIES	SPEECH IMPAIRED	VISUALLY IMPAIRED
Alabama	X	X	X	X	X	X	X		X	X	X	X	X
Alaska	X				X	X	X	X	X	X	X		X
Arizona	X				X	X	X		X	X	X	X	X
Arkansas	X	X			X	X		X	X	X	X	X	X
California	X				X	X	X	X	X	X	X	X	X
Colorado	X				X	X	X	X		X	X	X	X
Connecticut	X			X	X	X	X	X		X		X	X
Delaware	X				X	X		X	X	X	X	X	X
D.C., Wash.	X	X			X	X		X	X	X	X	X	X
Florida	X					X		X		X	X	X	X
Georgia	X	X	X	X	X	X	X			X	X	X	X
Hawaii	X				X	X	X			X	X	X	X
Idaho	X	X		X	X	X	X	X	X	X	X	X	X
Illinois	X				X	X	X	X	X	X	X	X	X
Indiana	X				X	X	X	X		X	X	X	X
Iowa	X				X	X		X		X	X	X	X
Kansas	X	X			X		X	X		X	X	X	X
Kentucky	X				X	X	X		X	X	X	X	X
Louisiana	X	X		X	X	X	X			X	X	X	X
Maine	X				X	X	X	X		X	X	X	X
Maryland	X				X	X	X	X		X	X	X	X
Massachusetts	Children in need of special services												
Michigan	X				X	X	X	X	X	X	X	X	X
Minnesota	X				X	X		X		X	X	X	X
Mississippi	X	X		X	X	X	X		X	X	X	X	X
Missouri	X			X	X	X	X	X	X	X	X	X	X
Montana	X				X	X		X		X	X	X	X

The second problem is overlap within a classification system. Within special education, children with two or more severe handicaps are likely to be diagnosed as multiply handicapped (for example, deaf-blind). For children with one mild and one severe handicap, the severely handicapping condition is of such salience that, for purposes of classification and labeling, it overshadows the other less prominent and milder handicap. For example, a severely retarded person with an emotional problem would be classified as

TABLE 3-1 (cont.)
Categories Used for Identification and Education of Exceptional Children

STATE	BLIND	DEAF-BLIND	EARLY CHILDHOOD SPECIAL EDUCATION	GIFTED, TALENTED	HARD OF HEARING	MENTALLY RETARDED	MULTIPLE HANDICAPPED	ORTHOPEDICALLY IMPAIRED	OTHER HEALTH PROBLEMS	SERIOUSLY EMOTIONALLY DISTURBED	SPECIAL LEARNING DISABILITIES	SPEECH IMPAIRED	VISUALLY IMPAIRED
Nebraska	X				X	X		X	X	X	X	X	X
Nevada	X			X	X	X	X	X		X	X	X	X
New Hampshire	X				X	X		X	X	X			X
New Jersey	X				X	X	X	X	X	X	X	X	X
New Mexico	X			X	X	X	X	X		X	X	X	X
New York	X				X	X	X	X		X	X	X	X
North Carolina	X			X	X	X	X			X	X	X	X
North Dakota	X	X	X		X	X	X		X	X	X	X	X
Ohio	X	X	X	X	X	X	X	X	X	X	X	X	X
Oklahoma	X				X	X		X		X			X
Oregon	X				X	X		X			X	X	X
Pennsylvania	X	X		X	X	X			X	X	X	X	X
Rhode Island	X				X	X	X		X	X	X	X	X
South Carolina	X	X			X	X		X		X	X	X	X
South Dakota	Children in need of special services												
Tennessee	X	X	X	X	X	X	X	X	X	X	X	X	X
Texas	X	X	X		X	X	X		X	X	X	X	X
Utah	X	X			X	X	X		X	X	X	X	X
Vermont	X				X	X	X	X	X	X	X	X	X
Virginia	X		X		X	X	X	X		X	X	X	X
Washington	X				X	X	X	X	X	X	X	X	X
West Virginia	X	X		X	X	X		X		X	X	X	X
Wisconsin	X	X	X		X	X	X	X	X	X	X	X	X
Wyoming	X	X			X	X			X	X	X	X	X

SOURCE: Garrett & Brazil, 1979, pp. 291–292.

retarded and receive services for the mentally retarded. The emotional problem is usually presumed to be secondary. The difficulty arises with mild handicaps because the clarity and salience of the handicaps are lost. It becomes difficult to discriminate among categories of learning disabled, mentally retarded, and emotionally disturbed. As shown in Table 3-1, there is a great deal of overlap among these categories. Moreover, the distinctions between each of these three categories of handicap and normality are difficult to perceive.

UNDERLYING ASSUMPTIONS ABOUT LABELING AND CLASSIFICATION

HANDICAPS EXIST WITHOUT LABELING

The first assumption underlying classification of the handicapped is that disabilities are absolute and are not just a vicious result of the labeling and categorization process: disabled people are different and in need of special consideration. The labeling and categorization process allows policy makers to target special programs to these groups of people. This assumption is probably valid for the severely and obviously handicapped. For example, Murphy (1976) reports that even among very primitive peoples, clear-cut psychosis exists and is recognized as abnormal behavior. Kanner (1948) described long ago the condition of absolute feeblemindedness, retardation so severe that it would be recognized in any society. Biblical accounts of physical handicaps—blindness, deafness, orthopedic handicaps—are numerous and frequently cited.

The validity of this assumption is questionable for the mildly handicapped. Many children are identified as handicapped only while attending public schools. They are not considered handicapped before school entry or after they complete their schooling. Furthermore, if they move to a school that does not provide special educational services (for example, a parochial school), they may no longer be considered handicapped. Finally, some children are handicapped only for the time they are in school (for example, the 6-hour retarded child). Thus, some handicaps are handicaps only under special circumstances—when someone (usually the school) is looking for them.

CLASSIFICATION AFFECTS OUTCOME

The second assumption is that the intended social consequences of the classification, "handicapped"—the protection of society and the provision of benefits to the individual—are inherent in the classification process. In other words, to be eligible for services for the handicapped one must first be certified as handicapped. To ascertain if the desired effect of labeling is being achieved, it is necessary to examine the impact of such labels on individuals.

When policy makers plan services for the handicapped, they anticipate that the services will work. However, good intentions and demonstrated efficacy are not synonymous. The first question to be asked is always, "Do children who are labeled and given special services do better than similar children who are not labeled and not given special services?"

A detailed analysis of the efficacy of special education programs is beyond the scope of this chapter. However, several excellent reviews are available. The majority of empirical studies involve evaluations of special education programs for the mentally retarded. Kirk (1964) and Guskin and Spicker (1968) have provided detailed analyses of this research. The general conclusions to be drawn from these reviews are as follows: (1) the achievement of educable mentally retarded children in self-contained classes is poorer than the achievement of mentally retarded children left in regular classes; (2) the benefits of schooling for trainable mentally retarded students are unclear; (3) the social and emotional benefits of special self-contained classes are also unclear. In a more recent review of resource-room programs, Sindelar and Deno (1978) reached similar conclusions: there are no clear-cut benefits—either social or academic—from placing educable mentally retarded pupils in resource-room programs.

The evidence bearing on the efficacy of other special education programs is far less abundant. Hirshoren, Schultz, Manton, and Henderson (1970) reviewed the literature comparing regular educational services and self-contained classes for emotionally disturbed children. Most of the studies they reviewed showed that special education produced gains in achievement, improved behavior, and better adjustment. Sindelar and Deno reviewed several studies which examined the benefits of resource-room programs for emotionally disturbed and learning disabled students. In summarizing their analyses of academic gain, they reported that:

> The findings from efficacy studies of nonretarded populations served in resource programs are more conclusive. Several studies . . . were well-designed and methodologically sound, providing a firm basis for interpretation. . . . These studies compared regular-class placement with resource support to regular-class placement with no resource support. All obtained results favored resource programming. (1978, p. 24)

In summarizing their analyses of studies dealing with social and personal development, they concluded, "Neither static assessment nor experimentation has established the efficacy of resource programming in improving the personal and social adjustment of children so placed" (Sindelar & Deno, 1978, p. 24).

It appears that while there may indeed be benefits for the handicapped from special education programs, these benefits are far fewer than the policy makers had hoped for.

BENEFITS OUTWEIGH LIABILITIES
The third assumption is that the presumed benefits of categorization and labeling outweigh the liabilities—calling attention to a person's handicap

brings little harm but considerable good. As we have seen, in comparing the identified and the unidentified handicapped child, the benefits derived from various special services are unclear. The liabilities, however, are clearer. From the preceding discussion of salience of handicap, it is clear that labeling probably does not create additional burdens for the obviously or the severely handicapped. However, the liabilities for the mildly handicapped have been documented.

Labels do tend to lower teachers' expectations for handicapped pupils (Foster & Keech, 1977; Foster, Ysseldyke, & Reese, 1975; Gillung & Rucker, 1977; Salvia, Clark, & Ysseldyke, 1973). Labels also affect teacher judgments of pupil performance by focusing attention on behaviors associated with the label and distort teachers' observation. Pupil performance tends to be interpreted in accordance with stereotypes. Thus, when normal children are labeled gifted, they may be seen as using better verbalizations and having better attitudes toward their own performance than when they are labeled normal (Salvia et al., 1973). When children are labeled emotionally disturbed, they may be seen as exhibiting disordered behavior, whereas when they are labeled normal their behavior is seen as appropriate (Foster et al., 1975). Similarly, the label of learning disabled affects perceptions of school-related behavior (Foster & Salvia, 1977; Ysseldyke & Foster, 1978). The label of hyperkinesis causes observers to see more instances of hyperactivity (Neisworth, Kurtz, Jones, & Madle, 1974). Perhaps the most frightening effect of labels is that observers may actually see things that are not there (Foster & Salvia, 1977). It is unclear whether or not the label of normal affects observations of deviant behavior.

Labels also affect a teacher's interactions with students. Teachers may treat pupils on the basis of stereotypes and expectations rather than actual characteristics and behavior (Beez, 1968; Meichenbaum, Bowers, & Ross, 1969; Palardy, 1969; Rubovitz & Maehr, 1973; Sutherland, 1976). And altered teacher behavior affects pupil behavior—a self-fulfilling prophecy. While much of the research dealing with self-fulfilling prophecy has been appropriately criticized, there is a small body of research that supports it. In a careful review of the literature, Sutherland (1976) noted that self-fulfilling prophecies do operate when the experimenter reinforces expectations already held by the teachers and when those teachers work with either individuals or small groups of students.

The effect on those who are labeled is less clear. Handicapped persons often deny or try to hide the fact that they are handicapped or enrolled in special education. Studies investigating the self-concepts of handicapped individuals have been reviewed by Wright (1960) and by Guskin, Bartel, and MacMillan (1975). There does not appear to be a consistent relationship between self-concept and handicap. One study is worth special mention, however. Meyerowitz (1962) studied the self-concepts of 120 educable mentally retarded (EMR) students randomly assigned to either special education or regular education programs. He found that the self-concepts of EMRs who were labeled and given special services were lower than those of EMRs who were unlabeled and received regular education. Although the effects of label and treatment are confounded, nevertheless the *two,* either singly or in combination, appear to produce lower self-esteem in a mildly handicapped population.

The effect of labeling and classification on the social acceptance of handicapped persons is a complex area of study. The effects of the handicapped person's behavior and characteristics must be separated from the effects of labeling. Handicapped children, although unlabeled, are often rejected by their peers (Johnson, 1950; Johnson & Kirk, 1950). Integrated EMRs may be rejected more often than segregated EMRs (Goodman, Gottlieb, & Harrison, 1972). Similarly, normal children may be more accepted than undiagnosed students receiving services in a resource-room program, who may in turn be more accepted than EMRs in an integrated program (Iano, Ayers, Heller, McGettigan, & Walker, 1974).

Gottlieb (1974) and Foley (1978) used videotapes to evaluate behavior and label separately. Gottlieb found that the label did not affect acceptance adversely. Foley (1979) found that the label actually increased acceptance; the label may justify to peers otherwise unacceptable behavior.

SUMMARY

Labeling and classification represent different problems for mildly handicapped and severely handicapped persons. For the conspicuously handicapped, labels probably do little to call additional attention to handicaps. Consequently, the effects of labeling on peer acceptance, self-concept, reactions of teachers, and so forth are probably inconsequential. In instances where the social policy is beneficial to the handicapped, labeling and categorization entitle handicapped persons to desirable services.

For the mildly handicapped, labels call attention to handicaps that might otherwise go unrecognized. Consequently, the label may disrupt teacher-pupil relations and affect peer relationships. Although the consequences of labeling and categorization are supposed to be beneficial, this may not be the case; the liabilities may outweigh the limited benefits for the mildly handicapped.

Labeling and classification have consequences for the nonhandicapped as well. Generally, these consequences are discussed in terms of a cost-benefit analysis to society of enabling the handicapped to become productive workers who pay taxes. There is another benefit which is seldom discussed: there is a special education industry—university professors, teachers, therapists, school psychologists, state and federal bureaucrats, textbook writers, publishers, and so on—that benefit financially from having the handicapped identified and served. There is also a potential benefit that is seldom discussed. Normal children may benefit from the removal of handicapped children from their classrooms. We know of no definitive data on the achievement and adjustment of normal children before and after handicapped children are either removed or mainstreamed.

Special education is indeed a challenging and changing profession, with its clientele—exceptional children—being constantly reconceptualized, reconsidered, and renamed.

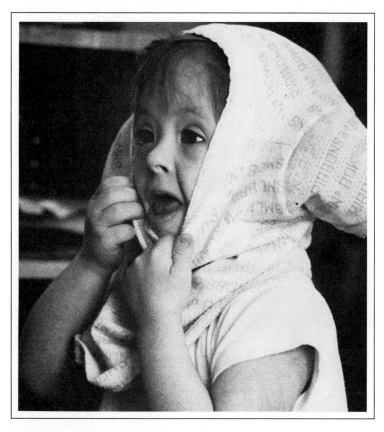

PART TWO
CAUSES
AND
ASSESSMENT
OF EXCEPTIONALITY

Cheston M. Berlin, Jr.

CHAPTER 4
BIOLOGICAL CAUSES
OF EXCEPTIONALITY

(*Courtesy of the National Down Syndrome Society.*)

Our society is now facing two large medical problems: chronic disease and the prevention of conditions which may lead to lifelong medical and social handicaps.

About 3 percent of all newborn infants (about 120,000 per year) will have a handicap that will place them in the category of developmental delay or developmental disability. An equal number of infants are born each year with significant medical conditions capable of causing other types of medical or social handicaps or both. A great deal has been learned concerning the *causes* of these conditions, but more must be learned about their precise mechanisms. Much more must be learned about their *prevention.*

For purposes of discussion, it is useful to group the biological causes of handicap into four major periods: *prenatal* (prior to birth), *perinatal* (the time period immediately surrounding actual delivery of the child), *postnatal* (after delivery) and *neonatal* (newborn period, considered by some to last up to two weeks). We will briefly discuss the four periods and the major problems within each that give rise to handicapping conditions.

HEREDITARY DEFECTS
We must look further into the past, beyond immediate prenatal conditions to *preconception,* the period before the egg is fertilized by the sperm. This is particularly important for the female, who is born with her lifetime complement of eggs or ova. About 2 million primary (first stage) ova are present in the ovaries of the newborn female. No additional ova will be formed during the woman's life. Only about 25,000 of these are usable at the time of puberty. Since only one ovum is expelled each month during the menstrual cycle, only about 350 to 400 ova will be available for fertilization during the entire reproductive cycle of the woman. During the years that the ova are dormant, ample opportunities exist for these germ cells to be damaged.

The formation of sperm cells in males is entirely different. Not until

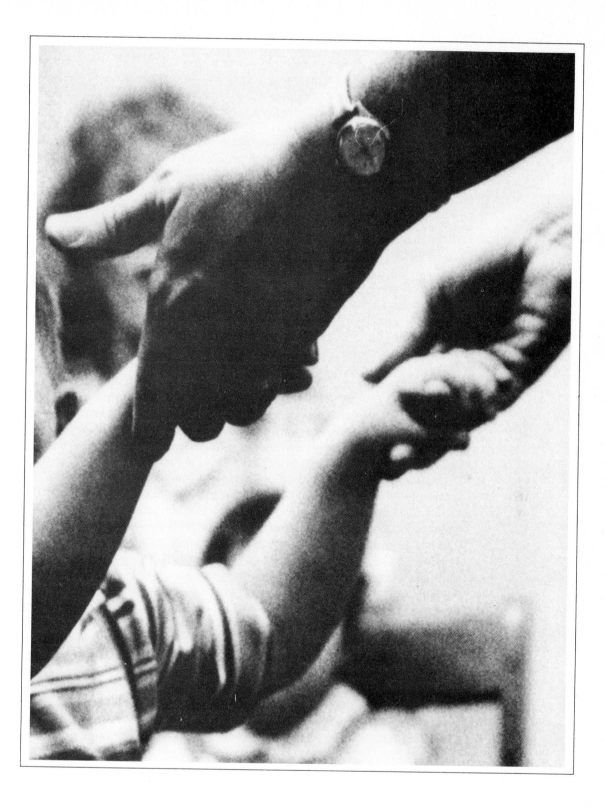

puberty does an active process begin which results in mature sperm capable of fertilizing ova. These sperm are made continually in the pubescent and adult male. Potentially damaging events will affect only a small number of the total output of a male. Nonetheless, dangers do exist for the male as well as for the female.

Heredity obviously determines a significant part of the nature of the developing fetus. The genetic material is contained within the nucleus of the germ cells in structures called chromosomes. Human beings have forty-six of these chromosomes arranged in twenty-three pairs. Twenty-two pairs have identical partners and are termed the autosomes; one pair determines the sex of the offspring and are called the sex chromosomes. Errors in both groups exist and may result in profound handicaps.

DNA (deoxyribonucleic acid) is the chemical material in chromosomes. It determines not only what information is passed on to daughter cells during cell division but also directs the chemical processes within the cells. The human embryo begins with the fusion of ovum and sperm. When they divide, each daughter cell receives an equivalent amount of genetic material. This is made possible by the doubling of the chromosomes just prior to cell division, with equal numbers going to each daughter cell.

EXPOSURE TO TOXIC MATERIALS

Protection of the germ cells (ova and sperm) is critical. All young people, even infants, should avoid any unnecessary exposure to radiation, such as x-rays and radioactive isotopes, and to certain industrial chemicals, such as heavy metals (lead, cadmium) and the plasticizing agent, vinyl chloride. Such exposure may result in damage to or change in the individual's reproductive material (DNA). These changes may not show up until the individual attempts to reproduce.

If the DNA is changed, one of four consequences may occur. (1) The individual may be sterile. (2) There may be difficulty in maintaining the pregnancy because of spontaneous abortion. (3) The damage may be repaired. Information is now available that human cells, like bacterial cells, possess the ability to repair some or possibly all of this damage. Perhaps humans cells do this constantly throughout the life of the individual.

Fourth, if the fertilized ovum survives, it may express one or more abnormalities at birth. These are referred to as hereditary anomalies, that is problems introduced *at* the point of reproduction. If the body cells of the fetus are affected, the changes *could* lead, for example, to the development of malignancy or the reproduction of a specific hereditary anomaly. Although it has not yet been demonstrated in humans, in animals significant genetic damage causes premature aging of cells.

All of these changes may be passed on to subsequent generations. Because the human generation time is so long (twenty to twenty-five years), the long-term effects of genetic damage are not yet well defined. For example, data are being collected on the survivors (and their offspring) of the

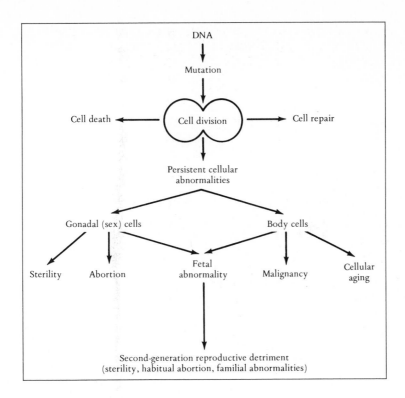

atomic bomb blasts at Hiroshima and Nagasaki in 1945. It now appears that in the survivors the risk of developing solid tumors (discovered in the decade 1960–1970) is increased, as well as the risk for developing leukemia (discovered in the decade 1950–1960).

Currently the information connecting preconception exposure to drugs, chemicals, or radiation and the occurrence of birth defects is scanty and based largely on animal models, which do not always provide an accurate indication of human biology.

METABOLIC ERRORS

Hereditary characteristics are dependent on the genetic information on these chromosomes. Characteristics such as physical stature, skin color, and possibly intelligence are dependent on information from many genes and are termed *polygenic* characteristics. Other characteristics are determined by single pairs of genes. Very small deviations from normal, perhaps only a single small chemical alteration, may cause a severe disease, such as sickle-cell anemia. The group of diseases caused by abnormal genetic material are known as "metabolic errors" (inborn errors of metabolism). This name is used because the normal chemistry (metabolism) of the cell is altered by the inability to provide or dispose of a critical chemical or protein.

These inherited metabolic errors now form a large group—perhaps nearly

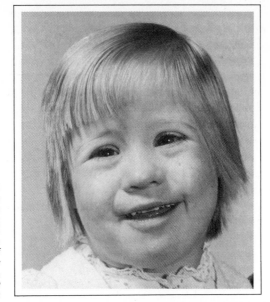

This child's physical features are characteristic of Down's syndrome: slanted eyes with epicanthic folds, round face, depressed nose bridge. (*Department of Pediatrics, Hershey Medical Center, Pennsylvania State University.*)

2,000. They involve errors in every aspect of the body's chemistry: proteins, amino acids, fats, sugars, vitamins, bile salts, and hormones. Table 4-1 lists a few of the more common inherited metabolic errors.

Many of these metabolic errors can be treated: insulin for diabetes, special diet for PKU and galactosemia, and blood transfusions for the large

TABLE 4-1
Common Inherited Metabolic Errors

DISEASE	COMPOUND INVOLVED	CONSEQUENCE
Phenylketonuria (PKU)	Phenylalanine (too much)	Mental retardation, seizures, eczema
Sickle-cell anemia	Hemoglobin (wrong one made)	Poor delivery of oxygen to tissues; abnormal red blood cells are easily destroyed by body and clog blood vessels
Tay-Sachs disease	Ganglioside (excess fatty substance stored in brain)	Deterioration of all brain function leading to death in first or second year
Diabetes	Insulin (not produced)	High blood sugar; possible early development of degenerative changes in nearly all body tissues
Galactosemia	Galactose (increased sugar in blood)	Mental retardation, cataracts, liver disease

group of hemoglobin disorders. Early diagnosis and treatment is mandatory to prevent permanent changes. PKU is an excellent example. A simple blood test (Guthrie) is available for diagnosis in the newborn period. (Previously, a less reliable urine test was done). If the disease is confirmed, prompt institution of a diet low in phenylalanine (the compound which is not properly handled and which accumulates) will, in most cases, prevent mental retardation. With other diseases, such as Tay-Sachs disease, treatment does not exist, and attention is currently being focused on prevention.

For a small number of metabolic diseases, currently about forty, it is possible to detect whether a woman is carrying an affected fetus by means of *amniocentesis.* Amniocentesis is a procedure whereby a small amount of amniotic fluid is withdrawn from the uterus through a needle in the mother's abdominal wall. Chemical analysis of this fluid and the cells suspended in this fluid can determine if the fetus is affected. If it is, therapeutic abortion may be elected to terminate the pregnancy. The ethical issues plus the rather small number of diseases which can be so identified argue very strongly for another approach to prevention, treatment, or both.

CONGENITAL DEFECTS
The two major areas of concern after conception are providing the best possible fetal environment and protecting the fetus from direct exposure to potentially damaging influences. Table 4-2 summarizes these influences.

MATERNAL DISEASE CONDITIONS

Chronic Renal Disease
Renal refers to the kidney and its function. In mothers with chronic renal disease the placenta fails to provide nutrients to the baby effectively. The precise mechanism is unknown. The placenta is smaller than normal and frequently has areas of degeneration and calcium deposits. The baby does not grow properly and is smaller and scrawnier than expected for gestational age. The pregnancy may be stormy, with hypertension (high blood

TABLE 4-2
Postconception Influences on the Fetus

MATERNAL DISEASE CONDITIONS	DIRECT DANGER TO FETUS
Anemia	Drugs and chemicals
Chronic renal disease	Infection
Diabetes	Rubella (German measles)
Hyperemesis (severe vomiting)	Syphilis
Infection	Toxoplasmosis
Nutrition	Cytomegalic inclusion disease
Rh problems	Herpes
Toxemia	Tuberculosis
	Radiation

CHAPTER 4
BIOLOGICAL CAUSES OF
EXCEPTIONALITY

pressure), edema (retention of water), and presence of protein in the mother's urine. Premature birth with attendant problems is common. The danger to the mother may be great around the time of delivery: hypertension and edema may cause a condition known as toxemia, which may lead to convulsions and threaten the lives of both mother and fetus. The successful conclusion of such a pregnancy demands meticulous medical supervision and the full cooperation of the patient.

Diabetes

A similar problem exists with the diabetic mother. First, sterility may be a major problem. If the mother is not sterile and pregnancy occurs, spontaneous abortion during the first three months (trimester) is common. Later in pregnancy strict regulation of the mother's diabetic state is mandatory. In spite of the best possible management the infant may face a considerable array of problems. Premature birth occurs commonly, not only naturally but as a result of early deliberate induction of birth, which may be medically necessary to prevent fetal death. The pregnancy may have to be terminated as early as the beginning of the eighth fetal month (eight weeks early) and almost always by the ninth fetal month. These infants run an increased risk of developing hyaline membrane disease, a serious respiratory difficulty. The baby may have problems with blood sugar just after birth because of overactivity of the pancreas (increased output of insulin). This occurs in response to wide fluctuations in the mother's blood sugar. These babies run an increased risk of the occurrence of congenital abnormalities. Many of the pregnancies must be terminated by cesarean section, which offers additional hazards (operation and anesthesia) to both mother and infant.

Nutrition

Perhaps the most important and controversial issue in producing a healthy baby is the nutrition of the mother. There is now abundant experimental evidence in animals that failure to provide adequate *caloric* intake and adequate *protein* to the mother has profound effects on the offspring. These effects are in two areas: body size and brain development. It is now known that the growth of a fetus is of two types: first, an increase in the *number* of cells of the body; second, an increase in cell *size.* Later in pregnancy and during postnatal life, growth occurs chiefly by an increase in the *size* of cells—that is, very few new cells are made, while the existing cells simply get bigger. If the mother is deprived of calories, protein, or both, the offspring is small. If the deprivation is severe enough, the infant remains small. This is critical where the brain is concerned.

The sensitive phase appears to involve the increase in number of cells. Poor maternal nutrition results in a fetal brain (as well as other organs) with a markedly reduced number of cells. This number *cannot* be increased by postnatal feeding. There appears to be a point during the development of the fetus after which attempts to reverse the effects of malnutrition are fruitless. This fact has been demonstrated in experiments with animals but is less well documented in humans. The chief reason for this is that populations likely to be undernourished are also likely to live in socioeconomic conditions detrimental to the growing infant. Most human studies have focused on areas in Central and South America. Mothers in these studies are deprived of adequate protein and calories and do give birth to infants with significantly reduced birth weights compared to well-nourished populations.

Autopsy studies are few but do show that the brains of infants whose mothers were undernourished are smaller and have fewer cells than the brains of infants whose mothers were not undernourished. However, follow-up studies of infants born to malnourished mothers are partly inconclusive because such children live in an environment in which infectious disease, poverty, malnutrition, and psychological neglect are common and important factors in the child's intellectual development. Current studies are providing increased calories and proteins (by food supplements) to these mothers. The rate of low-birth-weight babies is dramatically decreased.

The literature on the problem of malnutrition during pregnancy and its outcome is becoming more abundant all the time. Much of the work has been done on animals, but some tentative conclusions with regard to humans can be made.

1. The better the mother's state of nutrition *before* conception, the less the effect of malnutrition during pregnancy. A supporting illustration comes from the events of World War II. There was a severe famine (individual intake less than 750 calories per day) in parts of Holland during seven months of 1944–1945. A study of males (age 19 at time of study) whose mothers were pregnant in 1944–1945 showed no difference in mental performance between the group whose mothers were in the famine zone during pregnancy and the group whose mothers were in a part of Holland that did not suffer so severely. The mothers who were malnourished during pregnancy had had adequate nutrition before conception.

2. Birth weight is related to weight gain by mothers during pregnancy.

3. Birth weight is related to placental weight. Small placentas may be caused by poor nutrition, smoking, infections, and chronic maternal disease.

4. In humans, the spurt in brain growth probably extends from midpregnancy to the postnatal age of two years. Interference with this spurt of growth at *any* time within this range *may* cause a permanent decrease in brain size which *may* lead to suboptimal mental performance. It is also widely believed that, within limits, adequate nutrition may compensate for deprivation if instituted before the end of the spurt in brain growth. There is an optimal time to guarantee adequate brain growth; this opportunity may occur only during a short period of time.

CHAPTER 4
BIOLOGICAL CAUSES OF
EXCEPTIONALITY

5. Postnatal influences, especially socioeconomic conditions, may be the major factor determining whether and to what extent malnutrition affects intellectual function. Good nutrition is not a guarantee that all will be well, but it is a start; and logistically and financially it is comparatively easy to achieve. Table 4-3 for example, illustrates how prudent buying may purchase the most protein at least cost. It is often necessary to educate parents in this regard.

Rh Disease

One of the most exciting and satisfying advances in pediatrics and obstetrics has been the discovery (1932) and definition (1940) of the Rh blood factor, and the treatment (1946) and prevention (1964) of Rh disease. All this was accomplished within a period of thirty-two years.

Humans have four basic blood groups: A, B, O, and AB. But there are over twenty other blood factors involved in typing blood. The Rh factor (named after the rhesus monkey in which it was discovered) is the most important. About 85 percent of Caucasians and almost 100 percent of blacks are Rh positive (they have the factor); 15 percent of Caucasians are Rh negative (they do not have the factor). If an Rh-negative woman becomes pregnant by an Rh-positive man, there is a good chance that the baby will be Rh-positive. During the first part of any pregnancy a small number of the fetus's

TABLE 4-3
Costs of Protein in Food*

FOOD	PROTEIN CONTENT (%)	COST PER ⅓ RDA (CENTS)†
Peanut butter	26.1	15.2
Dried lima beans	20.7	15.9
Milk, powdered	3.5	16.0
Cottage cheese	19.5	18.3
Chicken	20.3	18.4
Eggs	12.8	25.3
Milk, skimmed	3.5	27.9
Tuna, canned	29.0	27.9
Milk, whole	3.5	28.8
Hamburger	22.0	34.5
American processed cheese	23.0	40.1
Natural cereal, dry	12.0	41.2
Rib roast	24.0	53.5
Pork chops	23.0	53.7
Fish	18.7	58.3
Steak, porterhouse	23.0	76.3
Frankfurter	11.7	76.9

*Plant proteins are equal to animal proteins when combined—for example, rice and beans. They are also cheaper, contain no cholesterol, less fat, and fewer additives.
†RDA (Recommended Dietary Allowances) per day is calculated as 65 grams for a pregnant woman. With three items from this list, total day cost for an adequate intake can be less than $1.00 (costs based on prices in January 1979). Not all proteins are equal in food value; egg and milk protein are superior. Plant protein usually needs supplementation with egg or milk for full effectiveness.

red blood cells invariably leak across the placenta into the mother's bloodstream. This may be enough to stimulate the production of antibodies in the Rh-negative mother. These antibodies cross the placenta to the fetus, attach to its red blood cells, and render them very unstable and subject to easy destruction. The baby may then die from severe anemia and attendant heart failure.

The second effect is that free hemoglobin, which is normally carried to the bloodstream in the red blood cells, is released into the circulation and promptly broken down. A product of this breakdown is a compound called "bilirubin." All red blood cells have a definite life span of 120 days. Destruction of these cells and the disposition of the freed bilirubin presents no problem to normal children and adults. It is handled easily in the liver and is excreted mostly through the bile and hence evacuated with stools (a minor amount is excreted through the urine). The presence of bilirubin in the fetus is not serious, as it crosses the placenta and is well handled by the mother's liver. However, because of the large amount of bilirubin freed in the sensitized newborn and the immaturity of liver function in newborns, large amounts build up in the blood. This bilirubin is very soluble in fats, and since the fat content of brain tissue is very high, significant amounts may be deposited in the brain. This bilirubin is toxic and causes a condition called "kernicterus" ("yellow kernel," so named because the areas of the brain will be stained yellow). Kernicterus causes a clinical condition very similar to some forms of cerebral palsy, with spasticity of certain muscle groups and mental retardation.

Kernicterus may be treated by early removal of the bilirubin by changing the infant's blood (exchange transfusion). This procedure has now been developed to the point where risks are very small. Multiple transfusions may be required with as many as ten to fifteen in extreme cases, but usually fewer than three to five. It is now possible—but riskier—to provide the fetus with new blood while it is still in the uterus. This must be done when evidence of severe sensitization exists at a time when the fetus is too young to be delivered (before thirty-two weeks' gestation). A small amount of adult red blood cells are given to the baby by the insertion of a needle through the mother's abdomen, through the uterus, and into the baby's abdominal cavity. Blood is well absorbed by the abdominal cavity and this added blood will prevent the fetus from dying of severe anemia and heart failure. This procedure is technically difficult, and the hazards to both mother and baby are high.

Prevention of any disease is always safer and easier than treatment. Mothers who have been sensitized by having an Rh-positive baby have in their serum a detectable antibody against Rh-positive red cells. This antibody, which belongs to the gamma globulin class, can be highly purified by laboratory methods. It has now been conclusively demonstrated that giving this antibody (vaccine) to Rh-negative mothers immediately after they have their first Rh-positive baby or a miscarriage of an Rh-positive fetus will prevent Rh disease in the next pregnancy. (First pregnancies rarely cause Rh disease even if the fetus is Rh-positive. If the disease does occur in a first term pregnancy, then prior sensitization very likely has occurred, either by a miscarriage or the administration of mismatched blood.) This vaccine was first introduced in the mid-1960s and has resulted in a virtual disappearance of the disease. However, there are still cases occurring in mothers who were sensitized before the vaccine was available, who failed to receive it after a pregnancy or miscarriage, or who have unknowningly received Rh-positive blood.

Rh disease is not the only cause of increased bilirubin in newborn infants. The list of causes is very long and includes infection, incompatibility with other blood groups, drugs, and prematurity. These cases can usually be handled by the judicious use of exchange transfusions and exposure of the infant to high-intensity light, which hastens the destruction of bilirubin in the skin circulation before it is absorbed by brain tissue. It is important to emphasize that normal infants *may* have transient elevation of bilirubin to dangerous levels. Doctors who work with newborns must be vigilant to detect and treat the bilirubin level *before* it gets too high.

It has been estimated that there are at least 200,000 infants per year in the United States who risk developing Rh disease. That we are now in a position to prevent *all* cases of Rh incompatibility between mother and infant must rank with the development of the polio vaccine as one of the great achievements in pediatrics in the last twenty years.

Toxemia

Edema, hypertension, and protein in the urine during the last trimester of pregnancy are evidence of a syndrome called toxemia. If the condition is severe enough, the blood pressure becomes extreme and convulsions may occur. This condition is known as eclampsia. Although some of these mothers may have identifiable kidney disease, many do not, and the condition may occur without warning, especially in first pregnancies. This is only one of many reasons for careful prenatal care. The danger to the fetus is twofold: normal growth may be impaired (because of insufficient placental nourishment), and treatment of the mother—especially at or near the time of birth—may affect the baby. For example, one of the drugs given to mothers with toxemia or eclampsia is magnesium sulfate. The magnesium ion crosses the placenta easily and quickly. In high enough concentrations, it may seriously depress the newborn's breathing and heart action.

DIRECT DANGERS TO THE FETUS

Drugs and Chemicals

To date, the drugs that are definitely known to cause structural fetal damage are few in number (see Table 4-4). Most of these compounds are known to interfere chemically with fetal DNA. The first four drugs are used in the treatment of various malignancies. It was established very early in the development of these drugs that they could cause fetal damage. Case reports are not common because most women with cancer do not become pregnant, and if they do, they frequently are unable to complete their pregnancy. However, the drug *methotrexate* is now being used to treat a skin condition called psoriasis. This condition does not interfere with pregnancy, and the patient may forget she is taking a drug that can cause serious damage to the baby she is carrying.

The *thalidomide* story is an unparalleled catastrophe of human pharmacology. This drug was developed as an effective and safe sedative (which it is). It was distributed widely in Western Europe in the late 1950s and early 1960s. A very small amount was distributed in this country for clinical trials. In 1960 and 1961 many disturbing reports were published of children born with a heretofore rare abnormality called "phocomelia"—absence of part of a limb. The remaining limb (or limbs) may be disfigured. The limbs resembled flippers. Other defects are known: deafness, abnormal ears and eyes, congenital heart disease, abnormal kidneys, and narrowed portions of the

TABLE 4-4
Drugs and Chemicals Known to Cause Fetal Damage

DRUG OR CHEMICAL	USE	DAMAGE
Methotrexate	Treatment of cancers	Multiple bony anomalies
Busulfan	Treatment of cancers	Multiple anomalies
Aminopterin	Treatment of cancers	Miscarriage; any major congenital anomalies may occur
Cyclophosphamide	Treatment of cancers	Abnormal digits and palate
Thalidomide	Sedative	Anomalies of heart, eye, ear, limbs, kidney, intestinal tract
Diphenylhydantoin	Treatment of epilepsy	Cleft palate (risk twice normal)
Progestational compounds	Prevention of miscarriage	Masculinization of female baby
Diethylstilbesterol (DES)	Prevention of miscarriage (no longer used for this)	Risk of female baby's developing vaginal cancer in young adulthood
Ethyl alcohol	Prevent premature labor; a social drug	Profound growth and brain damage
Methyl mercury	Industrial use in making plastics	All organs, especially brain; cerebral palsy-like damage
Tetracycline	Antibiotic	Stains teeth; affects bone growth

intestinal tract. Connection was rapidly made with maternal ingestion of thalidomide during early pregnancy. In fact, the critical period of ingestion is extremely narrow: between the thirty-fifth and fiftieth days from the beginning of the last menstrual cycle. Only two animal species are known to be similarly affected by this drug: the rabbit and the monkey. It is difficult or impossible to produce congenital abnormalities in any other animal tested. This tragedy may result in the requirement that any drug which may be given during pregnancy must first be tested on monkeys. Thousands of thalidomide babies were born in Europe before the connection was determined. The drug was never officially on the market in the United States. Thus, there are less than twenty affected American babies and many of these were born in families who acquired the drug while in Europe. It appears that this drug is virtually guaranteed to cause fetal damage if ingested during the critical period.

Diphenylhydantoin (phenytoin) is a valuable anticonvulsant drug. The realization that its ingestion by a pregnant woman might be dangerous to the fetus required the collection of a large group of such mothers—literally thousands—because the risk is not the same as with thalidomide. In this country the general risk of having a child with a significant birth defect is about 1 in 15. It takes a large number of such children to create suspicion and then to statistically connect a drug with a defect. It may well be shown that this subtle but real increase in risk is present for many more drugs and chemicals.

In 1973 appeared the first report of the effect of maternal *alcohol* consumption on offspring. The effect is extremely serious. Infants of women who are truly alcoholic during pregnancy have *severe* mental and growth retardation as well as skeletal (especially facial) anomalies. Why did we not know about this prior to 1973? Alcoholic women usually do not become pregnant (they do not ovulate), so there was no large prenatal population of alcoholics to alert us. Secondly, the physical characteristics of the affected infants are frequently subtle. Obvious facial features, such as those evidenced by the child with Down's syndrome, are lacking. Now that the fetal alcohol syndrome has been identified, physicians are finding cases not only in alcoholic women but also in women who would not fit that definition. There is concern that as few as two drinks (60 cubic centimeters) of liquor per day is deleterious. Many physicians now advocate no alcohol intake whatsoever during pregnancy.

Besides the chemical compounds listed in Table 4-4, there are many other drugs for which suspicion is high but definite proof is lacking. Everyone does agree that the safest course is to avoid exposure to chemicals and, whenever possible, the ingestion of *all* drugs, whether prescribed or purchased over the counter.

Infection
Research since 1960 has made it clear that of all the infections that threaten the fetus, five are responsible for the most damage. These five are rubella (German measles), syphilis, toxoplasmosis, cytomegalic inclusion disease

(CID), and herpes. Four of these infections are intrauterine, that is, they occur within the mother's uterus during pregnancy; herpetic infections of the newborn are acquired during passage through the birth canal (see "Perinatal Causes of Handicap").

Rubella, or German measles, is a virus infection which causes very mild disease in children or adults. The rubella virus may damage the fetus at *any* time during pregnancy, but the first trimester is the period of greatest risk. Consequences of rubella infection may range from fetal death to mild hearing loss. The outcome is more likely to be somewhere between these extremes. Virtually every organ system can be involved, singly or in combination. The most common defects are mental retardation, cataracts, hearing loss, congenital heart disease, and small stature (height and weight). Once the mother becomes infected with the virus, spread to the fetus cannot be prevented. The chance of having an affected offspring is so high if infection occurs early in the first trimester (at least 60 percent in the first month) that many parents will choose to have a therapeutic abortion. Rehabilitative procedures are certainly possible and may be quite effective: eye surgery, glasses, hearing aids (not very effective as the deafness is due to nerve damage, not conductive damage), and surgery for the congenital heart disease.

Fortunately, we can prevent this tragedy completely: the rubella vaccine is effective and safe. Every woman of childbearing age should know whether she has had rubella. She can find out through a simple blood test (rubella titer). A history of having had rubella is unreliable: many viruses unrelated to rubella may produce similar symptoms. If the blood test shows that the woman has *not* had rubella, *she should receive the vaccine.* This vaccine must not be given to pregnant women, and pregnancy should be avoided for three months after administration of the vaccine. The determination of the rubella status should be part of the health supervision of all adolescent girls or should be included in the premarital examination. Rubella babies should become as rare as acute poliomyelitis.

Syphilis is an infection caused by a bacterium called a spirochete (because of its corkscrew shape under the microscope). When infection is present in the mother, the spirochetes cross the placenta and invade all fetal tissue. Fetal infections probably occur after the fifth month of development. Syphilis is a particularly treacherous disease because initially all organ systems may be involved (including the brain) and this involvement may not be apparent until months or years have elapsed. The time of the appearance of some symptoms may be judged from the size of the infecting bacteria transferred across the placenta from mother to fetus. With a heavy infection, during the first two months the infant may exhibit persistent watery nasal discharge, enlarged liver and spleen, skin rash, eye changes, and bone changes (seen by x-ray only). Frequently these symptoms are ignored or are entirely missed, and the child appears at a later age with well-established destructive lesions which may involve *any* organ system, especially the brain.

Like congenital rubella, this disease is entirely preventable. Unlike rubella, it is also treatable. Blood tests for the presence of syphilis must be done on all pregnant women. They should be done on *each* pregnancy and are best performed twice during pregnancy. A woman with a negative blood test in her first trimester of pregnancy may be infected during her seventh month with disastrous consequences to the fetus.

Newborn infants should have their cord blood tested and if the test is positive, they should receive treatment. Penicillin is still effective and the drug of choice for both mother and infant. Early treatment will usually prevent permanent damage.

Toxoplasmosis may be a relatively mild illness in adults: slight fever, malaise, occasional skin rash. The illness is similar to a mild case of infectious mononucleosis. Affected infants are born with significant involvement of the brain and eye. Serious mental retardation may result. The only prevention possible is for the pregnant woman to avoid anyone with an infectious disease, especially children. There is a drug treatment currently under investigation at several medical centers; it is too early to predict whether such treatment will prevent permanent damage.

Cytomegalic inclusion disease is similar to rubella, although maternal illness may not be apparent. The infant may have severe involvement of the brain and eye but other organ systems are usually not involved. No prevention (except avoidance of infection) and no treatments are known.

Research work is being done which may lead to the development of vaccines for both toxoplasmosis and cytomegalic inclusion disease. If they become available, all four of the common prenatal infections will be preventable, treatable, or both. A large proportion of cases of significant mental retardation will disappear. The incidence of these prenatal infections may be as high as 1 in 700 to 1 in 1,000 in some populations.

Two infections of the fetus occur not during pregnancy but during the actual process of birth. These are herpes and tuberculosis. *Herpes* is best known as the virus responsible for cold sores or fever blisters (at the corners of the mouth and around the nostrils). Another type of herpes causes ulcers on the genitalia and is liable to affect the infant as it comes down the birth canal. The brain is severely affected. This disease in newborns is usually rapidly fatal; should recovery occur, the damage is profound. Treatment with an antiviral drug, Vidarabine, is now available. Survivors still have a considerable risk of permanent damage. Herpes in the newborn may be prevented by recognition of the disease in the mother (good prenatal care) and delivery of the child by cesarean section.

If a mother has active *tuberculosis,* the infant must be separated from the mother after birth and closely observed for signs of tuberculosis. The mother must be treated and the infant repeatedly tested. If tuberculosis occurs, prompt treatment with drugs is effective. Should the infant acquire tuberculosis and not be treated, the illness may be severe and terminate in tuberculosis meningitis (infection of the membrane lining the brain and spinal cord).

Intrauterine and perinatal infections are also known by the acronym

*TORCH: T*oxoplasmosis, *O*ther, *R*ubella, *C*ytomegalic inclusion disease, *Herpes*. This grouping refers to those diseases caused by viral or protozoal agents and excludes bacterial diseases such as syphilis and tuberculosis. The category "other" will assume greater importance as further research identifies new viral agents implicated in fetal and newborn damage. At present it is only conjecture what other viruses may be implicated. It should be appreciated that all of these infectious agents multiply rapidly in fetal and newborn tissues. The diseases are more severe than in adults, and if the infant recovers permanent damage may be profound.

Radiation

Exposure of pregnant animals to large amounts of radiation in the form of x-rays predictably causes severe congenital anomalies in the offspring. The evidence for humans is less sharp, particularly with regard to what amounts are hazardous. Exposure to large amounts in the human has caused bone defects and microcephaly (small head and, invariably, mental retardation). There is vigorous debate over how much exposure is dangerous. For example, some investigators claim the exposure of the pregnant mother to a single abdominal x-ray significantly increases the chances of the infant's acquiring a malignancy. These arguments are based on the statistics in thousands of cases. Everyone agrees that the pregnant woman should avoid *all* x-ray exposure unless *absolutely* necessary. This would include routine chest and dental x-rays.

Because of the tragic experience of Hiroshima and Nagasaki we know that exposure to large amounts of radiation is hazardous to the fetus. Pregnant women close to the center of the explosion had a very high rate of

Feeding time provides a good opportunity to observe the child's motor movements, alertness and responsiveness. (*Courtesy of Elizabeth A. Llewellyn.*)

spontaneous abortion. A high percentage of the babies subsequently born alive had microcephaly. Because a human generation is about twenty-five years, it is still too early to determine what long-term effects this exposure might have. It may well take 100 years of careful observation to determine how damaging a chemical or an x-ray exposure may be. You will recall the concern over radiation hazards released by the 1979 Three Mile Island nuclear power plant disaster. Studies of the possible effects on pregnancies are currently underway. It will be at least several years before any definite results can be reported.

The effects of other types of radiation—cosmic rays, microwaves, low-frequency radio waves—are completely unknown. They appear not to have a significant effect at doses recently studied in both humans and animals.

CHROMOSOMAL ERRORS

As stated earlier each human cell possesses forty-six chromosomes—twenty-two autosomal (identical) pairs and a twenty-third pair that determines the sex of the individual. The ova contain only the X chromosomes. Sperm contain either X or Y chromosomes. If the ovum is fertilized by an X-bearing sperm, the result is a female (XX), if it is fertilized by a Y-bearing sperm, the result is a male (XY). For identification, the chromosomes are placed in groups according to their configuration (see Figure 4-2).

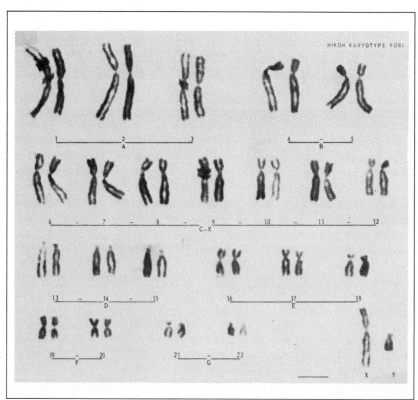

When cell division results in an unequal distribution of chromosomes, one cell will contain, for example, forty-seven chromosomes, the other forty-five. If this occurs early during maturation of the ovum before fertilization (meiosis), then all further cells will have the same abnormal number of chromosomes. As an example, an ovum just before fertilization should have twenty-three chromosomes (one from each pair) to match with the twenty-three from the sperm. Suppose the ovum has twenty-four: one complete pair plus twenty-two single chromosomes. Fertilization occurs with a normal sperm (twenty-three single chromosomes). The fertilized egg, which now begins to produce daughter cells, has twenty-four plus twenty-three, or forty-seven, chromosomes: one "pair" has three instead of two chromosomes. This is called "trisomy." If this occurs in Group G, a Down's syndrome child results. There are now many examples of patients with chromosome numbers in excess of the normal forty-six.

The major components of Down's syndrome are: folds of skin over the upper inside part of the eyes, a round face, a flattened head, and a depressed nose bridge. These children have poor muscle tone (they are "floppy" during infancy) and are small for their age. Mental retardation is virtually always present although its severity varies widely. A large proportion have congenital heart disease. Numerous other structural problems may be present. These children always need special medical and educational care. It is not possible to predict in infancy the degree of permanent retardation: requirements for schooling may change in the course of an individual's life span.

A child may have fewer than forty-six chromosomes. If one of the female sex chromosomes is missing, only one X chromosome remains. Although these children appear to be female, their ovaries are not developed; they are infertile and puberty does not occur. The latter fact is frequently what brings them to the physician. The administration of sex hormones will allow sexual maturation to occur, but infertility is permanent. The therapeutic induction of sexual maturation is critical for psychological well-being in these patients and allows gender identification. Mental retardation does occur in a number of cases.

The sex chromosomes may contain numerous other errors resulting in three or more chromosomes. A Y chromosome must be present to confer maleness. Most individuals with three or more sex chromosomes are sterile and have some degree of mental retardation.

Although the number of chromosomes may be normal, there may be changes in their structures—that is, breaks, rings, and pieces missing. The consequences may not be obvious, but these changes are a source of great concern because of animal and bacterial experiments that do show changes in subsequent generations. This explains the concern over exposure to ionizing radiation (for example, the Three Mile Island accident) and some chemicals, which in certain doses are known to disrupt the normal chromosome pattern. The incidence of chromosomal abnormalities especially increases with maternal age. The current recommendation is that all pregnant women over 35 or with a previous family history of an affected infant be offered amniocentesis, which is carried out between fourteen to eighteen weeks after conception.

PERINATAL CAUSES OF HANDICAP

The birth process is the single major challenge to the newborn. In a matter of minutes it must surrender the fetal protection of the uterus for the hostile outside environment. The period of labor and delivery and of adaptation to self-support are times of maximal danger. Damage that occurs during this period is frequently severe and irreversible. All of the conditions that have been discussed previously are dependent on prenatal events, but the following problems occur *during* or immediately after the birth process.

GESTATIONAL AGE

Premature birth* is an unfortunately common event occurring between 10 and 12 times per 100 births. Many factors are known to be highly correlated with prematurity. These include maternal illness (diabetes, kidney disease), the presence of more than one fetus, history of premature delivery, Rh sensitization, incompetent cervix, and premature rupture of the membranes. Trauma is rarely a cause. Very often the cause is not apparent. Premature infants born at between thirty-five and thirty-seven weeks' development have an excellent outlook. As prematurity increases, the immediate complications become more of a problem, especially the most common cause of mortality and morbidity in all newborns: hyaline membrane disease. This disease affects the lungs and is caused by the formation of a membrane between the lung capillaries and the tiny air sacs (alveoli), which markedly interferes with the passage of oxygen *into* the blood and carbon dioxide *out of* the body. The amount of oxygen in the baby's blood may fall to low levels, causing irreversible brain damage or death. Before the late 1960s, the results of treatment of severe hyaline membrane disease were discouraging. However, in one of the most exciting advances in pediatrics in the last thirty years, a breathing method has been developed which has not only markedly increased the survival rate of these infants but also produced very encouraging follow-up results in their neurological status. In spite of this procedure, prevention is obviously preferable.

A recent advance in prevention involves the administration to the mother of a cortisone drug by injection during premature labor. If twenty-four hours elapses before the infant's birth, the chance of acquiring hyaline membrane disease is considerably reduced.

Techniques are available to predict fetal maturity before delivery. These include x-ray for fetal bone maturation and analysis of certain chemical constituents in the amniotic fluid. The latter is technically easier, more precise, and does not involve radiation. Very recently ultrasound has been used

*A premature infant is usually defined as a baby born at less than thirty-seven weeks' gestation (normal gestation is forty weeks). Mothers may be uncertain or incorrect about their last menstrual period; the determination is then done on physical examination of the infant. Any infant of less than twenty-six weeks' gestation is considered "immature."

to assess fetal growth. The determination of fetal age helps to determine the best time for delivery.

One very simple prevention measure is prenatal care. In a recent Pennsylvania study adequate prenatal care was shown to cut the prematurity rate by a factor of 6—from 35 to 6 cases per 1,000 births.

Postmature infants, that is, infants born later than their due date, are also at risk, but for a different reason. They rarely have lung problems but may have marked difficulty with their blood-sugar levels. Blood sugar is a very necessary source of energy for the brain. Low blood sugar can be as devastating as low oxygen content in the blood. However, even postmature infants without detectable decreases in blood sugar may have neurological problems in later life—especially learning disabilities. Adequate monitoring of blood sugar is mandatory for such infants.

BIRTH WEIGHT

Infants whose birth weights are much lower than expected for their gestational age (small for date) are also at risk. Cigarette smoking by the mother may result in a low-birth-weight infant. Like the postmature babies, they may also have blood-sugar problems. For example, an infant born at term normally weighs about 3,000 grams (6½ pounds). A small-for-date infant (term baby) may weigh 2,000 grams (4½ pounds). This implies marked difficulty with placental nutrition; it may occur with or without maternal disease. These infants also must be closely monitored, especially for decreases in blood sugar. Early feedings may help prevent problems.

A fourth group of infants is very large for their gestational age. A term baby of a mother who is a diabetic may weigh 4,500 grams (10 pounds) or more. They are also at increased risk for low blood sugar. This may be due to an increase in the baby's circulating insulin in response to the diabetic mother's high blood sugar. Often the mother does not have diabetes or even prediabetes, and the cause is obscure. These infants can be well managed with early feeding and careful monitoring of blood sugar. If they have a smooth neonatal course, they appear not to be at increased risk for later problems.

MECHANICS OF LABOR

Uterine contraction should be a smooth process. The fetus must continue to receive its blood supply from the mother during labor. Prolonged or severely irregular contractions will compromise this blood flow. A number of problems can arise during the labor and delivery period.

Presentation of the Fetus

This refers to the position of the fetus within the birth canal. Head first is the most common and safest presentation, but the head should be so positioned that the top (vertex) comes first. Face or brow presentation may result in very high pressure being applied to the head, with resultant skin and (occasionally) intracranial bleeding. Breech presentations (buttocks or feet first) need special handling. Transverse presentations (long axis of baby is at right angles to the outlet), if not corrected to a head or breech, requires cesarean section.

Location of Placenta
If the placenta lies over the cervix (the mouth of the uterus), immediate cesarean section is necessary to avoid massive bleeding—potentially fatal to mother and infant alike. A partial placental praevia may also cause significant bleeding if the margins are torn before the baby is safely delivered.

Rupture of Membranes
The membranes surrounding the fetus must, of course, be ruptured before delivery can occur. In fact, this rupturing frequently stimulates the onset of labor. Rupture usually occurs near the time of delivery or within the previous 24 hours. The amniotic fluid thus released is normally a clear, amber-colored fluid. It is also an excellent culture medium for bacteria: if the membranes are ruptured more than twenty-four hours before delivery, both mother and infant are at high risk for infection. This infection may cause very serious and irreversible damage to the baby. Also, if a fetus is subjected to unusual stress within the uterus, it may respond by defecating. The content of the bowel at this time of development is a black substance called "meconium." Meconium-stained amniotic fluid is green-black in color and signals intrauterine distress and hence a high-risk delivery.

Analgesia and Anesthesia
Drugs given to women in labor and delivery for relief of pain are nearly all depressants of brain function. Because they all cross the placenta with ease, the fetus also receives and is influenced by them. Should the dose be sufficiently high, or the period from administration to birth sufficiently long (to permit drug accumulation in the infant), the infant's central nervous system will be depressed. It may not be able to breathe independently and will then require an antidote, prompt respiratory support, or both.

Multiple Births
Multiple pregnancies do carry increased risk to the offspring, primarily in the area of prematurity. Twins are more likely to be born prematurely than single fetuses and thus be subject to all the risks of prematurity. In addition, one twin may "steal" most of the placental nutrition and be significantly larger than the other. The smaller twin is at increased risk for a number of problems. Blood supply may be affected during labor, and one twin will be anemic, the other plethoric. Both are hazardous conditions: anemia may be severe enough to cause circulatory failure, while plethora (excess blood) may be severe enough to cause clotting within blood vessels, especially in the brain.

Fetal Monitoring
Technology now exists to monitor the status of the infant during labor. With relatively simple means both the fetus's heart rate and the intrauterine pres-

sure can be continually monitored. When disturbing patterns occur, certain maneuvers can be used to diminish the threat or speed up the delivery, or if necessary prompt cesarean section can be performed. This technique has been invaluable in the prevention of neonatal problems.

The application of forceps may be necessary. Forceps are used commonly and usually skillfully. However, it must be recognized that since they are applied to the head, very hard pressure or twists may cause physical damage to the face, the nerves outside the cranium, and the brain and upper spinal cord. Likewise, the use of anesthesia during this final part of the birth process may cause significant depression of the central nervous system, since the infant alone will be responsible for handling the anesthetic agent. Cesarean section represents a distinct hazard when general anesthesia is used; most sections are performed in less than ten minutes of general anesthesia time.

APGAR SCORE

In an attempt to evaluate the newborn's adaption to extrauterine life, Dr. Virginia Apgar (1953) developed a scoring technique based on clinical observation of five areas of functioning, which together indicate the well-being of a newborn infant. They are:

1. Heart rate

2. Respiratory effort

3. Muscle tone

4. Reflex irritability

5. Skin color

Each response is graded 0 ("absent"), 1, or 2 ("normal") for a total score of 10. The evaluation is done at 1, 3, and 5 minutes after delivery. A score of 7 or under is cause for concern; low scores at one and three minutes might indicate problems in the immediate newborn period. A low five-minute score, especially if below 5, has now been shown to be associated with a significant increase in abnormal neurological findings at 1 year of age. A large study is ongoing, and further data will indicate how well the Apgar score may indicate increased risk for possible handicap.

POSTNATAL CAUSES OF HANDICAP

Late detection of handicapping conditions does not always mean that the biologic result occurred *after* birth. Usually it means late recognition of a condition present before or since birth. However, certain conditions do occur after birth and may have severe consequences, even death. By far the most common is physical trauma. Accidents have always been the leading cause of death in children of all ages (about 60,000 per year under the age of 18); they are also the commonest cause of permanent disabilities. The resulting handicap is every bit as real as that of the child brain-damaged at birth—and usually more preventable. These accidents usually cause damage to limbs, head, or spinal cord. The rehabilitation of the children thus damaged requires an intensive multidisciplinary team approach.

Simple measures like traffic education, use of automobile seat belts (or infant restraints), and poison prevention would eliminate many of these tragic and preventable accidents. One trauma that is of serious concern is that of the battered child—a child who is deliberately beaten physically *or* emotionally. It is estimated that 1,600,000 children per year fall into this group with perhaps as many as 2,000 deaths. This enormous and complicated problem will require a multidisciplinary team—physician, nurse, psychiatrist, lawyer, social worker, public officials—for a successful resolution.

A smaller number of children suffer permanent disability from diseases, for example, infection, degenerative nerve diseases, and late onset of genetic disease. Proper child health supervision has eliminated many of the scourges. There is now no excuse for a child's contracting acute poliomyelitis. We are thankful that there are now fewer than twenty cases of polio per year in this country. Measles is a severe disease, seldom fatal but frequently crippling; the vaccine should, if widely used, eliminate this disease also. Prompt, judicious use of antibiotics should control most of the bacterial illness that may lead to permanent disability if untreated—for example, meningitis and rheumatic fever. The degenerative diseases, such as rheumatoid arthritis, have no known means of prevention as yet. Certain genetic diseases, such as muscular dystrophy, are still puzzles. Much more research will be needed to put the pieces into place.

Two especially common handicapping conditions should be mentioned to illustrate many of the points considered in this chapter:

Cerebral palsy is a term used to describe brain damage resulting in spasticity of muscles and (sometimes) coexisting mental retardation. The cause is usually direct physical damage or deprivation of oxygen to the brain. The cause may be set early in pregnancy with poor nutrition or at the time of delivery with a very hard labor and forceps damage. The range of damage may be great—from severe disability requiring total care to slight spasticity in one limb. Degree of muscle involvement does not determine mental damage: some children are so severely crippled as to be unable to walk or even push a wheelchair; yet they may not be truly retarded. The term has fallen into disuse among some pediatricians, because it is vague and because better understanding of the causes has resulted in more precise diagnostic labels.

"Hyperactivity" is a term which should be reserved for the child with extreme motor activity, poor or absent attention span, marked learning difficulties, and a great degree of responsiveness to the use of stimulant drugs (such as methylphenidate). Its cause is unknown. Organic brain damage in these children is not usually detectable. Many nervous, fidgety children do not have this problem and the widespread use of drugs for this type of "hyperactivity" (as well as in the exuberant normal child) is to be deplored. The diagnosis should be made by a pediatrician conversant with this problem, not by the parent, teacher, or school nurse.

SUMMARY

While biomedical research has made spectacular achievements in the past twenty years, professionals are clearly beginning to emphasize *prevention* of handicaps through better pre- and postnatal care of the mother and infant. Good postnatal care of the infant includes comprehensive early intervention to ameliorate or prevent the development of handicaps. Prenatal care begins before conception. Protection of reproductive cells from radiation and industrial chemicals is essential, as overexposure can cause genetic mutations in these cells, which can have a variety of consequences, including death to the cell or mutations in the offspring.

Postconception influences on the fetus include both maternal conditions which interfere with the fetal environment, and direct dangers to the fetus. Conditions in the mother which may interfere with the fetal environment include high alcohol intake, anemia, chronic renal disease, diabetes, cancer, hyperemesis, nutrition, infection, Rh problems, toxemia, and cigarette smoking. Infection radiation exposure, and drugs or chemicals may directly influence the development of the fetus.

Perinatal causes of handicapping conditions are related to the maturity of the infant at birth, conditions of birth and conditions in the infant. Infants who are premature may risk developing a variety of complications such as hyaline membrane disease. Postmature infants are also at risk of developing complications, specifically difficulty with blood-sugar levels. Complications may also be present in infants with very high or very low birth weights.

Conditions of birth which can negatively effect the infant include abnormal labor, or presentation of the fetus, placenta location, and membrane rupture. Other factors which may affect the infant at birth are the use of drugs to relieve pain in the mother during labor and delivery, and multiple births. Prevention of neonatal problems has been greatly enhanced by technology developed to monitor the fetus's heart rate and intrauterine pressure.

Postnatal causes of handicapping conditions in children include trauma—physical and emotional—resulting from accidents, poisoning, and battering of the child. Infectious disease is less frequently disabling, thanks to the development of preventive vaccine, but causes of the puzzling genetic and degenerative diseases are, unfortunately, not yet well understood.

The explosion of medical knowledge within the last thirty years has equipped us with very powerful tools to prevent most of the handicapping conditions of childhood. Great strides have already been made in the elimination of certain diseases. Expertise is available to the pediatrician and the obstetrician to identify and treat potentially damaging illness. We need only three conditions to assure each developing child of the most fertile social, intellectual, and physical environment: continued research into the unsolved problems, provision of known medical solutions to all parts of the population, and love.

Cheston M. Berlin, Jr.

CHAPTER 5
MEDICAL ASSESSMENT
OF EXCEPTIONALITY

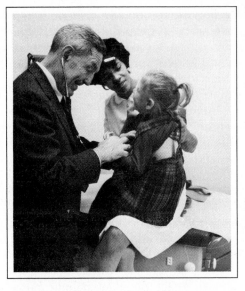

This chapter presents an overview of the crucial steps involved in the medical assessment of exceptional conditions. It is important for the special educator to be familiar with these steps because much of the educator's successful intervention depends on the careful and deliberate integration of the perspectives provided by several disciplines. The medical assessment can give the professional educator information that helps in designing programs for children. Often certain activities or foods will be limited, duration of activities may be restricted, and various constructive experiences may be recommended. Also, the educator and physician can frequently work together to monitor the effects of drugs and other interventions.

Usually, the family physician or the pediatrician is the first professional consulted in the medical investigation of a handicap. The assessment begins with a careful history. The patient is then examined. Finally, tests—both laboratory and achievement tests—are ordered, depending upon the findings of the history and the physical examination.

THE HISTORY
The medical history of an individual has always been very crucial to medical care. It directs the physician both to possible diagnoses and to avenues of further investigation. In some instances a careful history can directly result in the diagnosis.

FAMILY HISTORY
A handicap may have had its beginnings before the conception of the patient. Questions must be asked concerning the family history of any diseases. Although they occasionally appear for the first time in the patient being investigated, genetic disorders may be discovered in near or distant ancestors. Is family inbreeding present? Frequently a distant common relative may be discovered, or a mother and father may discover that their

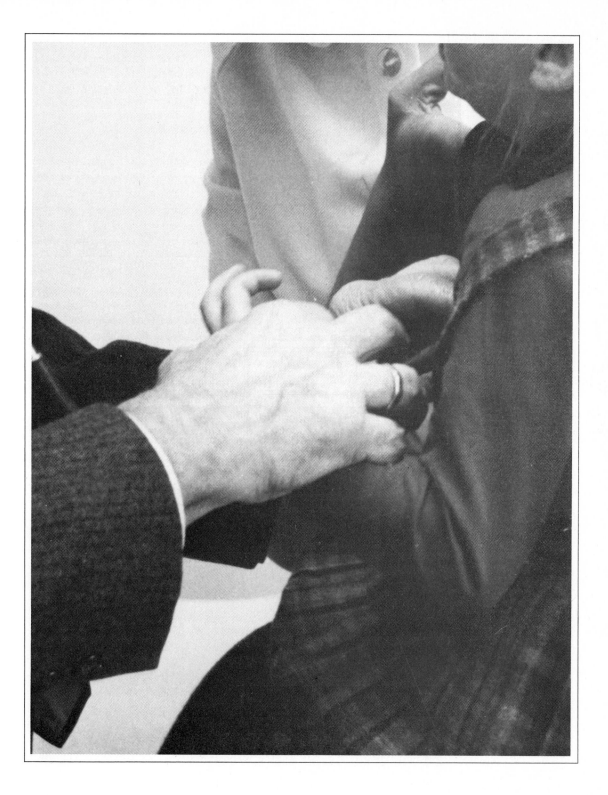

families originally came to America from the same small town in Europe. A family tree is an excellent way to take a history; when possible, it should be extended back at least three generations. Specific questions must be asked about miscarriages, early infant deaths, odd-looking individuals, and the occurrence of mental retardation. In many families these are considered skeletons in the closet, and often information must be obtained by very detailed and specific questioning.

PREGNANCY
Often events occurring during the pregnancy can provide clues for the focus of medical assessment. Was the pregnancy unusual? Was there bleeding or infection? Was birth weight low? Were any drugs taken during pregnancy? Was there exposure to potentially toxic drugs? Did the mother use alcohol or tobacco? A positive response to any of these questions helps the physician in conducting and ordering tests for conditions that may have their origin in circumstances surrounding the pregnancy.

LABOR AND DELIVERY
Because so many handicaps result from perinatal difficulties it is particularly important to ascertain the details of birth and the newborn period. Was labor prolonged (over twelve hours) or unusually difficult? Were the membranes ruptured more than twenty-four hours before onset of labor—thus predisposing mother and fetus to infections? Was there any significant bleeding before or during delivery? How much analgesia and anesthesia were necessary? Was there difficulty getting the baby to breathe? How long did the baby have to stay in the hospital? Was jaundice (yellow skin) present? Was the baby blue? Was there any Rh incompatibility? Was oxygen needed? Are Apgar scores available? A low five-minute Apgar places the infant at increased risk for neurological problems at 1 year of age.

Use of drugs, alcohol, tobacco, and other such substances must be avoided during pregnancy. When used, the physician should be told, since this will influence the next steps in the examination. (*Courtesy of Paul J Quinn.*)

One of the best estimates of the well-being of a child is growth, both height and weight. Children will grow at *rates* which are surprisingly constant for each child. Growth charts are available on which height and weight may be plotted against age. The resulting curve follows a percentile, the latter derived from long-term follow-ups of normal children. Most such children will grow in the boundaries between 25 percent and 75 percent of the normal population. The percentile is not by itself important. Normal children may be between the third and ninety-seventh percentile; they are obviously small or large for their age. It is only a decrease or increase in the *rate* of growth that alerts the physician to a possible change in nutrition, hormonal balance, or metabolic processes. Any type of illness may cause depression in growth: chronic infection (tuberculosis), thyroid disease, intestinal malabsorption of foodstuffs, and an inadequate emotional environment. A few illnesses may even cause sudden abnormal spurts of growth. Failure of a child to maintain a consistent rate of growth may be the first clue to the physician that the child has a problem.

The acquisition of skills at definite ages (developmental landmarks) is perhaps the most sensitive measurement the physician possesses. Within certain age ranges infants learn these skills in a predictable sequence. Table 5-1 lists the landmarks and the ages at which some of these are accomplished. More extensive lists are available: lists of gross motor skills, fine motor skills, and socialization skills. In early infancy, the normal range is very wide. Even at 1 and 2 years of age, considerable variation is permissible. This explains the reluctance of physicians to label a child at an early age as "slow" or "retarded" unless there is obvious, significant delay in many of these landmarks. The Denver Developmental Screening Test has become a widely used device for detecting early developmental problems.

SCHOOLING

The first indication that a child may not be developing normally may be in school performance. Even in kindergarten the child's adaptation to and performance of routine tasks such as coloring, identification of left and right, and simple drawing may alert the teacher to a potential or actual handicap. Early identification is crucial to prompt evaluation and meaningful suggestions for appropriate special educational intervention. It is also astonishing to see how many children with an obvious learning problem are not identified until starting school. This is often the case, since many handicaps have no direct or obvious associated physical abnormalities.

SOCIAL HISTORY

Many children with a relatively normal medical history do poorly in competitive situations such as school. The reason may be a very unstable social environment. The physician dealing with children is very much oriented to the critical role played by emotional factors in the child's development. Indeed, there is a syndrome, now well described but not well explained,

TABLE 5-1
Major Developmental Landmarks

AGE	GROSS MOTOR RESPONSE	FINE MOTOR RESPONSE	SOCIALIZATION AND COMMUNICATION
Birth	Startle response; Moro		Eyes fix briefly on bright red object
1 month	Lifts head off table while prone		Watches face
2-3 months	Lifts head to 90° angle from table		Smiles, laughs
4-5 months	Rolls back to stomach	Grabs object	
8-9 months	Sits with support and briefly without support; stands briefly with support	Transfers object from one hand to other	Fear of strangers
10 months	Pulls self to standing position; attempts to get toy placed out of reach	Pincer grasp	Says "Da-da," "Ma-ma"; plays "peekaboo"
12 months	Cruises—walks holding on to furniture	Plays pat-a-cake	May have several words in vocabulary
18 months	Walks well	Rolls ball	Indicates wants; mimics parents' work (household chores)
2 years	Walks backward and up stairs	Kicks ball; takes off clothes; scribbles with pencil	Start of play with peers; toilet training may start
2½ years	Runs well	Throws ball overhand	Sentences
3 years	Jumps in place	Rides tricycle	Able to attend nursery school; partial to complete toilet training is achieved

called "failure to thrive." The failure usually has a nonorganic background (that is, no identifiable physical or medical problem). This clinical syndrome, sometimes referred to as "maternal deprivation," seems to stem from an absence of love from the infant's caretakers. The infant's environment is so deficient in love, stimulus and response opportunities, and interpersonal reinforcement that the child fails to develop in all areas: mental, physical, and social. The problems presented by such a background are considerable and are frequently insurmountable. Broken home, divorce, death of a parent, neglect or abuse of a child may require a team approach involving the physician, the parent or parents, teachers, social workers, and others, such as a psychologist, relatives, the family pastor, and lawyer.

In the absence of obvious medical conditions, difficulties in social adjustment may be traced (even in the well-balanced family) to a single traumatic event—for example, the death of a close family member or multiple geographic moves. Given a secure home situation this problem can be dealt with through a good counseling program.

Of particular importance is the identification of traumatic episodes occurring during crucial periods in the child's development. The period from birth to about age 2 (infant to toddler) is a time for identification of self as opposed to the rest of the world. The preschool period from age 2 to age 6 is a time during which children differentiate between male and female and take on appropriate sex roles. Also of importance in this period is the increasing growth toward independence—such as brief separations from parents, independent play, and formation of personal friendships. The period from age 6 to age 12 is typically characterized by rapid physical growth, good health, expansion of social contacts, increasing concern for personal appearance—but all the while the maintenance of strong parental attachments. Any major disruptions in the family, such as the death of a parent, may have a more traumatic impact during this age period than during an earlier period. It now appears to many pediatricians and psychologists that this is a most critical time. Clinical observations of emotionally disturbed young adults indicate that many of them have suffered significant losses during this period.

The teenage years have their own well-known problems to be faced: sexual development, decisions about vocation, self-image, and independence from parents. The physician is alert to this time and appreciates the significance that major social events might have in the individual's development.

THE PHYSICAL EXAMINATION
The physical examination must be complete. The physician surveys the following order.

GENERAL APPEARANCE
The physician is attentive to how appropriate a response the child gives for its age—for example, an 18-month-old is *not* always cooperative. Is the child well cared for? Is there evidence of unusual bruising, cuts, old scars? Height and weight are absolutely critical, as discussed previously.

VITAL SIGNS
The vital signs include temperature, pulse, respiration, and blood pressure. Of these, the latter is the most important for alerting the physician to possible chronic disease. Children with elevated blood pressure must be thor-

oughly investigated for significant medical problems, kidney disease being the most common.

SKIN
Because the skin and the nervous system (brain and spinal cord) develop from the same embryonic tissue (ectoderm), lesions of the skin may be the first clue to abnormalities of the brain. Areas of change in pigmentation are particularly important. The presence of unusual numbers of bruises in unaccustomed areas (face, back) may raise suspicion that the child has been abused or may indicate diseases of the blood and bone marrow.

HEAD
The physician measures head circumference to determine if it falls within the normal range for the child's age. In general the head grows because the brain grows. The actual circumference is not as important as is the maintenance of a *rate* of growth. A very small head (less than the third percentile) is not always an indication of mental retardation, but in a child whose development is not normal, it certainly greatly increases suspicion that the brain is not growing normally.

Unusual facial appearance can indicate the presence of a serious medical condition. A few examples are Down's syndrome (mongolism), Hurler's syndrome (gargoylism), Sturge-Weber's syndrome (large birthmark over the face and also over the underlying surface of the brain), and hypothyroidism (cretinism). With most of these syndromes (a term meaning a constellation of findings similar from patient to patient) mental retardation of varying degrees is present.

EYES
The following ocular abnormalities may indicate the presence of systemic medical disorders: wide-set eyes, cataracts, dislocated lenses, or changes in the pigmentation of the retina. Vision must be screened in children capable of cooperation (usually age 4 and older). Many learning problems are due to poor vision, and improvement is dramatic with appropriate lenses. Muscle balance is important: the eyes should move together (conjugate gaze). With severe muscle imbalance (strabismus), vision may be markedly impaired.

EARS
Repeated episodes of middle-ear infections may result in the chronic accumulation of fluid within the middle-ear chamber. When hearing is impaired in the young infant, speech and language development will be delayed. There are also congenital causes of mild to profound deafness. Since children with hearing loss do not learn to speak, a screening audiogram is important in all children with delayed or abnormal speech. Special techniques have been developed to assess hearing in very young infants (age 1 year).

The presence of malformed or low-set ears, or both, suggests structural abnormalities in other organ systems, especially the kidney. Many patients with chromosomal problems have ear abnormalities.

MOUTH, THROAT, AND NECK

Abnormalities to be looked for here are mostly concerned with infection. Carious teeth, chronically infected tonsils, and continuous enlargement of the lymph nodes (glands) may indicate infection which needs further investigation and appropriate correction. The neck must be palpated for abnormalities of the thyroid gland. Ordinarily this gland cannot be felt in children. If enlarged, it may suggest either overactivity or underactivity.

HEART AND LUNGS

Attention here is focused on determining those conditions that may indicate chronic lung disease, such as asthma, or congenital or rheumatic heart disease. Children with involvement in either of these areas risk significant handicap. They are rarely retarded, but their physical activity may be so restricted that serious emotional consequences may result, affecting development, school progress, or both.

ABDOMEN

Enlargement of the liver or the spleen may indicate the presence of a "storage disease." These diseases are characterized by abnormal accumulation of certain biochemicals which interfere with the functioning of the organ. Several of these diseases may also involve the brain.

GENITALIA

Many chromosomal disorders have as part of their clinical syndrome ambiguous genitalia (assignment of sex is difficult). Abnormal genitalia indicate a serious medical situation in two respects: (1) other abnormalities must be sought, and (2) the social and emotional consequences to the patient and the family may by themselves cause considerable emotional handicap unless a definite assignment of sex can be made immediately.

EXTREMITIES

Extra digits or deformities of the extremities may be associated with severe handicap. The abnormal limbs of the children whose mothers took thalidomide are examples. Very frequently abnormal extremities indicate defects in other organ systems (especially heart and kidney). Abnormal size or proportion of limbs in relation to body and head size are present in many syndromes. Frequently retardation is also present.

NERVOUS SYSTEM

Examination of this part of the body is perhaps the most important in determining not only a diagnosis but also the degree of any existing developmental retardation. Because young children do not cooperate and follow directions, this examination is often best done by observation. Important points are (1) type and symmetry of locomotion (crawling, walking, running, hopping, skipping); (2) ease and coordination of movement of each side of face and body; (3) responses to sound, sights, and other stimuli; (4) pupil size and reaction to light; (5) reflex response on each side of the body; and (6) performance on tests of balance.

Perhaps the most valuable investigatory tool is observation. This is particularly valuable if the situation is not artificially contrived. Surprisingly accurate estimates as to the presence and degree of handicap can be made by watching the child play for thirty minutes. Frequently educators and parents can provide valuable observational findings to the physician that assists in diagnosis and treatment.

Many of the above points of assessment can be made only by using several observers in combination. The team approach to diagnosis is crucial. Parents, teachers, and family must be consulted for information on the child's actual performance level. The primary physician may wish to seek further consultation depending on his or her own findings. Consultants may include a psychologist, a pediatric neurologist, a speech therapist, specialists in the eye and ear, and, of course, the special educator.

LABORATORY TESTS

There are numerous laboratory tests available to the physician for support in determining the diagnosis in a child with a potential handicap. Only a few of the important ones will be mentioned. (These are in addition to the routine examinations used for normal health maintenance.)

CHROMOSOME ANALYSIS

This test includes a count and an examination of the structure of the genetic material. It should be performed only on children who have abnormalities in various body structures, such as cleft palate, abnormal fingers and toes, in addition to mental retardation. It is expensive, time-consuming, and requires highly trained technical personnel.

EXAMINATION OF BLOOD AND URINE

Blood and urine analysis for excesses of normal body chemicals or presence of abnormal compounds should include analyses of glucose (sugar), certain fats, and amino acids (the building blocks of proteins). Nearly all metabolic (body chemistry) disorders involve an error in one of these three groups.

HORMONES

Those related to the thyroid, pituitary, and gonads are especially critical to development and should be examined if appropriate.

X-RAYS

The maturation of the bones is an important indicator of general body development. Bone age can be determined by x-rays of the wrist and knee and may alert the physician to a discrepancy between skeletal and chronological age that will be an aid in the diagnosis of exceptional growth.

It remains for the physician to synthesize all of the areas of evaluation that have been discussed. The diagnosis is only the beginning: an estimate of the degree of handicap would then permit an adequate plan of education and rehabilitation. The complexity of these problems of special education demands the involvement of *all members* of the child's work to ensure the most successful program.

SUMMARY

Some of the information which the educator uses to develop a multidisciplinary intervention strategy for the child with special needs comes from the medical assessment. This assessment includes information about the family's history, the pregnancy, labor and delivery, the child's growth and development, school performance, and social history. The actual physical examination assesses factors such as the child's general appearance, vital signs, skin, head, eyes, ears, mouth, throat and neck, heart and lungs, abdomen, genitalia, extremities and nervous system. A number of laboratory tests may also provide detailed information about the child.

A basic understanding of the process of medical assessment is important to the educator for several reasons. Minor physical abnormalities may be overlooked by the parents or only begin to emerge when the child enters school. While the educational plan for the child is *not* centered around the medical assessment results, some restrictions on certain activities, special diets, and use of medications or prosthetic devices frequently affect the implementation of the educational plan. Finally, the educator can facilitate an understanding of this process in both the parent and child, who may be both curious and apprehensive about the medical assessment.

John T. Neisworth
Robert M. Smith

CHAPTER 6
PSYCHOSOCIAL CAUSES
OF EXCEPTIONALITY

(*National Down Syndrome Society.*)

We shall begin this chapter with a caution: The psychological, social, and educational factors related to disability surveyed in this chapter are not distinct and isolated from the biomedical causes previously discussed. Development is a process continuously influenced by the total complex of factors experienced throughout an individual's history. Throughout one's lifetime, individual characteristics interact with the environment to produce new traits that change constantly. Genetic and environmental factors work together to form a "package" that is the person. No two persons are alike because no two persons have exactly the same package. Even identical twins can often be quite different in their development and behaviors because their experiences differ.

In the film *The Boys from Brazil,* a Nazi scientist collaborating with Adolf Hitler laid plans to clone several duplicates of Hitler. (Cloning is a process of using a living cell from an organism as the basis for the development of an identical genetic duplicate. It has not been demonstrated with humans yet.) Several women in Brazil were used as "hosts" for Hitler's cells, and a number of boys were born who were, indeed, identical to Hitler. The scientist then proceeded to contact the boys, hoping to nurture at least one of them as a resurrection of *der Führer.* When contact was made, about twelve years had passed and the scientist anxiously met and talked with one of the boys. He assumed the "little Hitler" would have the same tendencies, traits, ambitions, and bigotry of Adolf Hitler. Bewildered and frustrated, the scientist discovered that the boy, genetically identical to Hitler, was quite different in personality. The boy's experiences had made him a very different person from Hitler, regardless of heredity.

What determines the development of disabilities? Are they genetically or environmentally produced? Can disabilities be remediated or "cured?" Are mental retardation, emotional disturbance, and learning disabilities discrete and independent? Are they reversible? Does the age at which a condition occurs determine whether or not it can be changed? Responses to these

questions depend heavily on how individuals feel behavior is determined. If they believe that development is determined at conception, then interest in the reversibility or modification of development will be minimal. If they believe that a disability is almost entirely environmentally produced, then they would be interested in figuring out how and when (not whether) developmental problems can be rectified. Even problems that seem biologically based may be reversed or compensated for through the right technology. At this time we simply can't draw the line between heredity and environment and between reversible and irreversible.

HISTORICAL POSITIONS ON DEVELOPMENT

In this section, we will review four different views of development, each of which has different implications for intervention. The first three views—preformationism, predeterminism, and environmentalism—have historical significance. The fourth view, interactionism, represents a more currently acceptable position for educators.

HEREDITARY DETERMINISM

A hereditary determinism approach to development denies any qualitative developmental process. The view proposes that everything about an individual is formed at conception. All bodily characteristics, talents, interests, and competencies are "signed, sealed, and delivered" at the moment the sperm fertilizes the egg. Development is nothing more than an increase in size; the environment has no role whatsoever. Progressively and inevitably, the individual unfolds on a preset schedule. New features and characteristics of the person are merely the result of predestined fate.

During past centuries, when the hereditary-determinism view was dominant, the child was seen as a miniature adult. All adult traits were believed to be present in the child but were simply less pronounced. Even the paintings of this era depicted children as little men and women. Formal education and training were reserved for children of upper-class families.

The hereditary-determinism view of developmental disability was straightforward. Developmental retardation, disturbed behavior, and other disabilities not clearly attributable to exogenous factors such as physical insult were simply the result of "defective stock." Little or nothing could be or was done, since the defect was believed to be inborn and not amenable to change.

As a result of writings by Jean-Jacques Rousseau (1712–1778), a modified hereditary-determinism position replaced former developmental theories and became the dominant view until the early 1900s. This hereditary view asserted that all characteristics and tendencies are locked up within the child from birth. This modified view differs from the older view, however, in two important ways. First, Rousseau recognized qualitative changes in development. Childhood was seen as important in its own right and qualitatively different from adulthood. Various qualitatively different stages in the progression of development were described and said to be somewhat universal for all children.

Second, Rousseau's view departed from the strict earlier hereditary view in recognizing some degree of environmental influence. The environment was seen as providing conditions for development. "Innate potential," "latent talent," and "natural goodness" would invariably unfold according to a natural (genetic) master plan. Rousseau emphasized the corrupting influence of the environment. If, he argued, we could provide the child with free and permissive surroundings, then capacities would emerge in undistorted and full expression. The unstructured child-centered models in education, counseling, and therapy prominent in the last several decades are rooted in a Rousseauian tradition.

While the Rousseau position considers the environment, it does not give to the environment any positive role in the developmental process. An appropriate environment is necessary to trigger or release genetic potential, but the environment does not actually contribute to qualitative changes in development. According to Rousseau, the environment can distort and corrupt development, but not positively influence it. The attainment of developmental landmarks by the child is still said to be caused by the person's heredity. Educators and developmentalists have revived the Rousseauian position in varying forms. Thus the essence of Rousseau—the concept that development is innate and that heredity is preeminent—seems evident in such propositions as child-centered early education (Froebel, 1826), "internal ripening" (Gesell, 1948), and the "spontaneous self-regulation" postulated by Piaget.

What implications does Rousseau's view of development have for the causes, prevention, and treatment of disability? Briefly, hereditary determinism (and Rousseau's theory) views disability as the outcome of either unfortunate genetic potential or the intrusion of extreme corrupting environmental influences. Drugs, disease, physical trauma, and severe deprivation may act to warp or destroy developmental potential. These factors do not contribute to the developmental process but are obstacles to or distortions of otherwise natural development. You can become less than, but no better than, your predetermined potential.

Until recently, views of normal intelligence, mental retardation, emotional disturbance, and other disabilities were predominantly hereditary. Definitions and suggested treatment techniques for mental retardation provide good illustrations of the influence of the predeterministic view. Widely accepted until recently, Tredgold's definition of mental retardation emphasized the endogenous, or internal, determination of defective intelligence: "A state of incomplete mental development of such a kind and degree that the individual is incapable of adapting himself to the normal environment of his fellows in such a way as to maintain existence independently of supervision, control or external support" (1937, p. 4).

Intelligence, from this view, is with the person at birth and can be hindered by negative environmental factors (Tredgold and Soddy, 1956). Documented cases of children originally diagnosed as mentally retarded who were placed in improved environments and subsequently showed sharp gains in intelligence (Goldfarb, 1945a, 1945b; Schmidt, 1946; Skeels & Dye, 1939; Skeels & Harms, 1948; Skodak & Skeels, 1949) were dismissed as instances of "pseudo mental retardation," since true mental retardation was not reversible. If reversal occurred, it simply meant that the original diagnosis was wrong because mental retardation was felt to be essentially incurable.

Similarly, definitions and concepts of emotional disturbance, slow learning, psychosis, and even "criminal personality" have had a hereditary ring to them. Developmental problems are seen as aberrations from a "natural" direction, pattern, and rate of development.

Since hereditary determinism regards biological factors as having the basic role in development, the focus of treatment and prevention is biological. Surgery, drug therapy, and hormone treatment are used in attempts to alter the constitution of the person and, thus, the assumed basis of the problems.

Perhaps the most extreme example of intervention related to a hereditary premise is the *eugenics* approach to improving humanity. Eugenics presumes that many defects are genetically based, predetermined, and irreversible. Selective mating among individuals with good qualities, and sterilization of defective persons are measures proposed to reduce the occurrence of defects. While these practices might cause some improvement in our species, several factors operate against the eugenics approach. First, modern genetics has established that if there is a hereditary basis for such complex characteristics as intelligence, temperament, and talent, it is *polygenic* rather than simple. That is, many genes operating in groups provide the base for complex traits. The effects of single genes are changed by other genes and most complex human characteristics are due to gene networks. (For a discussion of multiple-factor or quantitative genetics, see McClearn, 1970).

Such networks (not simple gene pairs) provide the hereditary portion for human defects that occur frequently. Selective mating and sterilization of the "unfit" might be feasible where characteristics have a relatively simple genetic basis. Selection is not feasible where heredity is complex. There are some extreme problems that indeed are due to relatively simple gene action. These problems are rare, however, and mating control or sterilization would not make much difference. Further, in many of these extreme cases, the individuals affected are naturally sterile or do not live to reproduce.

Second, since focus is on heredity, eugenics overlooks the possibilities for improvement through controlled changes in the environment, improvement that can be made within a generation as opposed to genetic improvement that takes hundreds of generations (Ausubel & Sullivan, 1970).

Finally, many problems among children labeled as "exceptional" do not have an hereditary basis, at least not in the way conceived of by those who advocate selective mating. As examples, most children diagnosed as mentally retarded show no organic defect and have no identifiable history of defective heredity (Reese & Lipsitt, 1970b; Sarason, 1953; Tredgold & Soddy, 1956). Likewise, other common problems observed by special educators (for example, disturbed behavior, many problems of motor control, sensory limitations) cannot be attributed to heredity.

In summary, hereditary determinism states that the environment provides a context in which biologically predestined development can take place. The environment does not cause development, but merely serves as a place for it to occur. Disability is believed to result from inborn defect or an extremely distressed environment. Since development is seen as biologically determined, intervention is almost exclusively directed toward biological or medical manipulation.

ENVIRONMENTALISM

Hereditary determinism represents an extreme point of view that gives almost exclusive emphasis to the biological basis of development. The concepts of environmentalism are equally extreme in emphasizing nonbiological (or situational) factors in development. John Locke is the philosophical father of what has come to be called the *tabula rasa* or "blank slate" theory. Locke suggested that children are born with no storehouse of memories, instinctive thoughts, or cognitive processes. The blank slate view, however, has also been associated with even more extreme positions in which no biological role in development is assumed. John Watson once said:

> Give me a dozen healthy infants, well formed, and my own specified world to bring them up in and I'll guarantee to take any one at random and train him to become any type of specialist I might select—doctor, lawyer, artist, merchant, chief, and yes, even beggarman and thief, regardless of his talents, peculiarities, tendencies, abilities, vocations, and race of his ancestors. (1925, p. 82)

Itard (1932), Montessori (1912), Seguin (1866), and others championed the position that even extreme developmental problems could be changed through "sensory training." Humanism in education, behaviorism in psychology, and cultural determinism in sociology and anthropology are more recent, but less extreme, examples of environmentalist approaches. Essentially, the environmentalist concepts of development deemphasize biological determinants and emphasize environmental variables. In the extreme, human beings are considered infinitely flexible with no limits on development. The environment, registered through the senses, is seen as responsible for the kind, the direction, and the rate of development.

Those who believe that personal development is almost exclusively the product of environmental forces will probably speak of intervention as being of absolute importance. Accordingly, intellectual retardation, disturbed behavior, and various learning problems will be seen as problems created by and treatable through the environment.

Rather than dwell on further details of environmentalism, especially its

CHAPTER 6
PSYCHOSOCIAL CAUSES
OF EXCEPTIONALITY

extreme versions, let's move to a discussion of the currently most accept-able position on the control of development, interactionism.

INTERACTIONISM

This position views development as the result of interaction between he-reditary and environmental factors. Personal development, whether positive or negative, is the result of the complex interplay of hereditary materials with the physical and social environment. *Interactionism* encompasses two ideas: no living thing develops in isolation, and heredity and environment are two broad classes of variables that are not independent. Heredity and environment are, however, usually separated only for purposes of discus-sion. Developmental problems are a product of heredity times environment. Neither heredity nor environment can be proclaimed the sole, real, or basic determinant of development. Each influences the role of the other. A per-son's attributes, intelligence, emotionality, interests, talents, and physique are the cumulative product of the continuous interchange between heredity and environment (Birch, 1968; Gordon, 1971).

The moment of conception, when parental genetic materials unite, is perhaps the only time when heredity operates alone. At that moment, the qualities of the zygote (the organism resulting from union of egg and sperm) are due to parental contributions. From this point on the environ-ment of the organism modifies the expression of the genetic material and actively contributes to developmental trends.

The notion of interaction is not a simple one. It involves the constant accumulation of heredity-times-environment *products,* which again interact with the environment. Although seeming overly simplistic, we have chosen the following expressions to summarize the concept of interactionism.

H = the hereditary influence on development, exclusively at conception.

$(H \times E)$ = the composite product of H (hereditary) variables interacting with E (environmental) variables. This product now constitutes the pack-age of determinants that will subsequently influence further interaction and, thus, development.

$(H \times E) \times E$ = the new product that is available for interaction.

$(H \times E) \times E \times E$, etc. = the continuously accumulating composite that interacts with E from moment to moment.

What is at one time an external, environmental influence registers on the individual and becomes part of the person. The now-changed personal characteristics interact with the environment to produce a new (perhaps only slightly changed) set of characteristics. From this point of view, it is clear that at any moment developmental characteristics are the result of environmental influences interacting with the product of previous interac-tions.

Even though heredity and environment interact to generate developmental characteristics, one might ask, What are the relative contributions of each for particular characteristics? Traits with a relatively simple genetic base are less variable and less subject to changing environments than are traits that have a complex or polygenic heredity pattern. Characteristics such as eye color, skin pigmentation, migraine headache, aniridia (a type of blindness), congenital deafness, kerotosis (a skin disorder), and color-blindness have a single, double, or sex-linked gene basis. The environment has little, if any, effect on these characteristics. Characteristics such as intelligence, temperament, aptitude, and talent have a complex gene base and are expressed widely over a range of environments.

What does all of this mean? With the exception of some, genetically identifiable defects result from an unfortunate interaction between heredity and environment and can be minimized, compensated for, or eliminated through appropriate environmental intervention.

ENVIRONMENTAL VARIABLES RELATED TO DISABILITIES

RESTRICTED RANGE OF SENSORY STIMULATION

Human development does not take place in a vacuum. Without question, the presence of sensory stimulation is a most crucial environmental contribution to one's development. Several important classic studies which involved the removal of retarded children from one environment to another with greater stimulation (Klineberg, 1935; Skeels, 1966; Skeels & Dye, 1939; Skodak & Skeels, 1949) were instrumental in shaking the then-dominant view that qualitative differences in early experience had little effect on later development.

Many early studies involved animals with relatively uncomplicated nervous systems. As similar studies were repeated with animals possessing more complex central nervous systems, it became clear that the higher the level of complexity, the more important the early experience in normal development. Today, the study of infancy is considered a crucial domain of developmental psychology (White, 1971). In fact, early experience is not only important for the general development of competence but also for the development of the organs and the nervous system (Beach & Jaynes, 1954; Harlow, 1961; Harlow & Zimmerman, 1959; Thompson, 1955).

The vagueness of phrases such as "adequate or optimal stimulation" and "poor environment" are beginning to be replaced with more precise definitions of stimulation. The volume of stimulation does not seem as crucial as the *range*. Stimulation from the standpoint of physics is not equivalent to stimulation from a developmental or psychological perspective. For example, the continuous background noise of traffic is a stimulus that will register on a meter, but its lack of variety reduces its stimulating properties. Therefore, it is not the presence of stimuli alone but their variety that is developmentally important (Friedlander, 1967; Kagan, 1970; Rheingold, 1963). During the first year or so of life, appropriate sensory stimulation

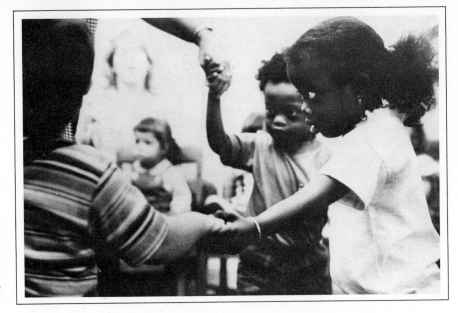

Early play experiences may be as important as academic ones in the promotion of physiological and psychosocial development. (*National Down Syndrome Society.*)

seems especially crucial. Infants must have a chance to do plenty of looking, listening, touching, tasting, and smelling.

Finally, stimulation is important not only for activation of the sense organs and the nervous system but also as cues for behavior. Reaching, grasping, pointing, asking—in general, *reacting*—require the presence of specific objects and events that evoke such behavior. *Reacting to* and *acting on the environment* build a file of responses that become increasingly more complex. This enables the child to interact with the physical and social environment in progressively more detailed and complex ways.

FACTORS CONTRIBUTING TO LOW STIMULATION

"Cultural deprivation," "cultural impoverishment," and more recent terms such as "disadvantaged' are all general descriptions of child-rearing environments that presumably are deficient.in stimulating development. These terms are usually applied to low socioeconomic circumstances. Low income, large families, and uneducated management of resources are usually associated with restricted developmental stimulation because objects are fewer and variety is limited. As a consequence, *there are fewer objects to label, differentiate among, react to, and behave toward.*

Auditory as well as visual stimulation may be less varied and less detailed. Music in the home, for example, is likely to be simple, repetitive, and lacking in range of style, content, and meaning. The language used in a lower socioeconomic environment typically involves fewer words with less elaboration, variability, and nuances of meaning (Bereiter & Engelmann, 1966; Bernstein, 1961, 1970; Deutsch & Brown, 1964). Verbal skills play an important part in development. Impoverished language usage, particularly by parental and important caregiver models, is of special concern. Limited language, like limited physical objects, provides fewer cues for behavior. Language development, auditory discrimination, and verbal reasoning must suffer retardation in an environment where words have little value beyond use in coping with the dreary daily routine. "Restricted" rather than "elaborate" (Bernstein, 1961; Robinson, 1965, 1968) and "low signal-to-noise ratio" (Deutsch, Katz, & Teusen, 1968) are terms that have been used to describe the language and other auditory stimulation associated with high risk environments for problematic development.

Let us now turn attention away from the context in which a child is reared in order to consider the child per se. Even if relatively adequate sensory stimulation is provided within the home, the child may come into the world with less than normal sensory capabilities. A blind or deaf child is an extreme example. But aside from such extremes, sensory perception may vary considerably among newborns. From the moment of birth, the child is enrolled in a learning program. Sensory receptors interact with the environment. Visual, auditory, tactile, and olfactory learning develops much earlier than we previously believed (Piaget, 1952; White, 1968). Some children have a head start. Not only are their environments rich in effective stimulation, but their sensory apparatus is fully functioning and develops rapidly. Other children may have defects and not be able to perceive and process environmental stimulation. In short, they are handicapped at the outset. Research to measure precisely an infant's sensory capabilities is not absolutely clear because it has received systematic and comprehensive attention only recently (Reese & Lipsitt, 1970a; White, 1971). It seems clear, though, that early detection of sensory deficits can lead to compensatory intervention to reduce the possibility of later problems. Prosthetic devices (like hearing aids and glasses) attached to the child or to the environment can be employed to boost stimulation and thereby offset sensory handicaps. Studies of infancy and early experience suggest the possibilities of assuring children a sensory head start in life (see Mussen, 1970, for a review).

LIMITATIONS ON OPPORTUNITIES FOR RESPONSE

The very same factors responsible for impoverished sensory stimulation also restrict the building and practice of responses by a child. Fewer objects to see and hear are also fewer objects to manipulate. Economic factors certainly play a direct role in this respect. Crowded conditions limit response opportunities because of the excessive need for sharing opportunities, the quick wearing out of objects, and the sheer frustration of living under crowded conditions.

Children experience response restrictions for several reasons. First, adults may not play with and otherwise interact with their children. Instead, children are often left on their own with little to do. In fact, they are frequently isolated. Second, handicapped children who undergo long periods of sickness and are confined to a crib, bed, or wheelchair must have response opportunities brought to them in order to develop in a reasonable way. Third, a great number of exceptional children have differences in their bodies that make some responses difficult. The usual ways to react to the environment are altered or missing because of a missing limb, paralyzed arms, defective speech mechanism, or poor locomotor control. Whether the response problem originates from defective heredity, prematurity, birth defect, or postnatal injury or illness, it is critical to help make the stimulus clearer and a response by the child possible. Greatly reduced opportunities to examine, use, and act on the environment will inevitably retard developmental progress.

Finally, a highly visible body defect can psychologically and socially repel adults and other children. This can dramatically reduce learning opportunities for exceptional children. Adults who force themselves to help children who are severely deviant in appearance often do so in an unreliable and artificial manner. Such adults will typically avoid physical closeness with the child and deny affection which the youngster might otherwise experience from a more suitable individual. It is this problem—inappropriate responses to the behavior of children—to which we now turn.

DEFECTIVE REACTIONS TO CHILDREN'S RESPONSES

Behavior is developed and maintained as a result of the qualities of one's environment. The literature on behavior modification demonstrates convincingly that changes in children's competencies can be brought about by simple rearrangements of behavior consequences (National Society for the Study of Education, 1972; O'Leary & O'Leary, 1972; Reese & Lipsitt, 1970b; Ross, 1981). When consequences are positive or reinforcing, a child's ac-

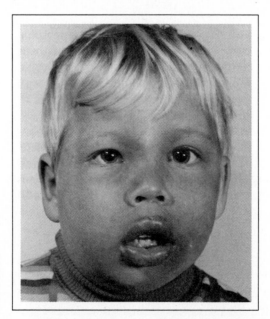

A "different" appearance in a child is apt to affect the attitudes, actions, and expectations of other people. (*Milton S. Hershey Medical Center.*)

Maladaptive behavior patterns may develop if more constructive social and academic behaviors are unrewarded. (*Courtesy of Paul J. Quinn.*)

tivity is strengthened and responses are built. Behavior must be physically or socially reinforcing if it is to survive. From what has been discovered about principles of behavior, developmental retardation or distortions can be produced through several unfortunate kinds of consequences to a child's behavior, namely, lean reinforcement, noncontingent reinforcement, and punishment.

LEAN REINFORCEMENT

First, *reinforcement for behavior can be stingy—too infrequent, too little, or both.* Institutional care is often characterized by a paucity of reinforcement. Investigations of retarded children have noted the devastating results of a prolonged stay in an institution (Braginsky & Braginsky, 1971; Kirk, 1958; Provence & Lipton, 1962; Skeels & Dye, 1939) and the positive shifts in development, especially intelligence, that arise when children are removed to more stimulating and reinforcing situations (Provence & Lipton, 1962; Skeels & Dye, 1939; Skodak & Skeels, 1949). Parents or caretakers may be too busy, may not know how to encourage constructive behavior, or may not be good at interacting with children. Whatever the reason, the net effect of nonreinforcement is the reduction of constructive behavior. A scarcity of reinforcement precludes the development of specific behaviors as well as producing a generalized retardation of intellectual, emotional, and motor functioning (Ullman & Krasner, 1969).

REINFORCEMENT DELAY

Delay in reinforcement is a defective procedure if one is interested in building a repertoire of behavior. Parents who are uninvolved with their children on a sustained basis will occasionally heap rewards upon them. Reinforcement is effective only if it immediately follows the desired behavior. A frustrated, busy, or unalert parent who is not there to provide the smile, the kind word, the hug (in short, a reinforcing reaction) when children behave appropriately will not see the behavior established. Delays in reinforcement result in strengthening whatever behavior has occurred at the time of reinforcement, and that behavior may be horribly inappropriate rather than desired. Many unwanted behaviors are, inappropriate, rather than desired. Many unwanted behaviors are, therefore, accidentally built.

NONCONTINGENT REINFORCEMENT

When reward or punishment is not dependent on specific behavior, many of the same problems arise as in instances of nonreinforcement. Developmental progress of children's behavior will not evolve rapidly in homes where reinforcement does not depend on appropriate behavior of the children. When children aren't required to ask for things, label objects, explain their wants, go to objects, or generally act on their surroundings, behavior will become stunted. Parents who consistently anticipate their children's needs or helpers who offer potent reinforcers (such as food and attention) independent of desired behavior responses by children are missing an important instructional strategy. Behavior will not progress or be maintained by noncontingent reinforcement.

Just as adults and siblings can fail to reinforce constructive behavior, they can also unwittingly reinforce *undesirable, maladaptive behavior.* Much antisocial, disturbed, and institutional behavior comes from inadvertent encouragement (Ullman & Krasner, 1969). This occurs because adults, like children, want to eliminate or reduce irritations. The child who does not attend to an important task may be offered other more personally attractive activities. This has the effect of reinforcing withdrawal from learning tasks. How many times have you seen fussing and tantrums by a child followed by the parent's or teacher's attention and diversion of the child to a pleasant activity so as to reduce the noise level? Reinforcing undesirable behaviors restricts opportunities for learning. Because "nasty children" are avoided by other children and adults, there is a lessening of the kinds of social, emotional, intellectual, and motor experiences that are guided and encouraged by others. Also, strong maladaptive behaviors can become a characteristic way for children to respond to even minor disappointments. This, in turn, further increases opportunities for the reinforcement of aversive behavior, escalates the problem, and furthers retarded development.

To close our discussion on defective reactions, let us examine *punishment.* As used in the behavioral literature, the term "punishment" refers to any reaction that acts to weaken or suppress behavior. Punishment is not necessarily intentional or exclusively physical. A frown may be as punishing to one child as a slap is to another. Failure to positively reinforce behavior which has been reinforced in times past may also function as punishment (Bijou & Baer, 1960; Marquis, 1943).

Repeated punishment, or even a single, severe punishment, usually eliminates behavior. Adults deliberately employ punishment to get rid of unwanted behavior. We do not advocate total abstinence from the use of punishment when it is in the long-range interests of children. There are, however, several outcomes associated with punishment that potentially contribute to developmental problems.

When punishment is repeatedly delivered by specific persons or within specific settings, the child associates those persons and places with the punishment. In other words, children learn not only to avoid those behaviors that produce negative consequences but also stay away from the people and places connected with punishment. Parents, teachers, and attendants begin to acquire negative properties the more frequently they rely on aversive means. This is especially unfortunate, for parents or other important models don't want to become aversive to their youngsters. It clearly diminishes occasions for important positive interaction. If a number of persons employ punishment, generalized avoidance will result. Children will not discriminate threatening from nonthreatening adults and begin to avoid most adult interaction (Bijou & Baer, 1967; Mearham & Wiesen, 1971; Neisworth & Smith, 1973). Fear of adults and unscheduled punishment for a variety of behaviors will cause emotional disturbance as well as retardation of a social character.

Children avoid behavior that produces punishment. Playing hooky or daydreaming in school can suggest that the child may be exposed to aversive stimulation too frequently or intensely. Severe punishment over time produces complete avoidance, such as refraining from any speech, and especially so if talking gets the child into trouble. Being forced to eat, under threat of punishment, may encourage vomiting or anorexia nervosa.

Severe or persistent punishment can also create numerous biological side effects. Loss of bladder and bowel control, gastrointestinal disorders, and other somatic (body) disorders may emerge under conditions of stress (Lachman, 1972). These disorders further limit the child's exchange with the learning environment.

We mentioned earlier that punishment may not be intentional. Indeed, the process of punishment can be hidden and even go unnoticed even by alert adults. This may especially occur among exceptional children who often must have painful treatment because of illness or other body dysfunctions. Chronic illness, with its pain and immobilization, can dampen and distort developmental progress.

But treatment itself may also act to suppress behavior. Repugnant medications, painful apparatus, and forced training procedures can punish behavior. Additionally, as with intentional punishment, generalization across persons and situations may occur. Whenever possible, parents, therapists, and nurses should not deliver aversive medication or treatment when the child is happy or otherwise engaged in developmentally constructive activity.

SUMMARY

Parents and teachers must pay attention to the content, timing, and sequence of events which children experience. Rearing and educating normal children is tough enough. The physical and behavioral deficiencies of exceptional children present special challenges and demands. Existing dysfunctions are easily amplified and one problem can set the stage for another. But intervention can make a difference and, if properly applied, may even undo long-standing disorders. Development is a modifiable process which is controlled by both biological and environmental variables. Special educators can be instrumental in providing unique environments that prevent, control, and even reverse handicaps.

Stephen J. Bagnato

CHAPTER 7
PSYCHOLOGICAL AND EDUCATIONAL ASSESSMENT OF EXCEPTIONALITY

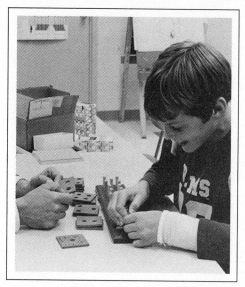

(Courtesy of Jim Lukens.)

Assessing the abilities of learners with special needs is a complex and continuous process which requires work by a team of specialists. With a team approach, the school psychologist, educational specialist, speech therapist, physician, school counselor, and parents combine their judgments about the child. These group decisions about the child's strengths, weaknesses, and needs serve as a foundation for the construction of an individualized plan of instruction.

The unifying theme of this chapter is that *assessment and educational programming are interdependent*. Assessment has little purpose or value unless it leads to individualized programming; programming without assessment is an imprecise and wasteful activity. Moreover, both assessment and educational programming must be tailored to the individual needs of the handicapped child.

ASSESSING SPECIAL NEEDS
Significant changes have occurred in the organization and provision of psychological and educational services to handicapped learners. The Education for All Handicapped Children Act of 1975 and the Developmental Disabilities Act of 1978 provide guidelines for educational planning for exceptional learners. At the center of these educational services is the individualized education program (IEP), a written document which serves to link individualized methods of assessment with individualized methods of instruction. "It is a management tool designed to assure that, when a child requires special education, the special education designed for that child is appropriate to his or her special learning needs, and that the special education designed is actually delivered and monitored" (Torres, 1977).

DEVELOPMENTAL LEARNING PERSPECTIVE
Behavior is the result not of a single influence but rather of multiple influences. All behavior can be viewed as the cumulative result of hereditary

factors interacting with environmental factors at specific moments in time. These unique interrelationships give rise to individual differences in a child's range of capabilities. In educational terms, children's strengths, weaknesses, and needs are determined by complex interactions between their increasing developmental skills, the type, amount, and quality of their learning experiences, and the timing of this stimulation at critical periods during life.

Children with special needs, whether mentally or physically handicapped, most often share disabilities in both learning and development across several different areas of behavior—physical, intellectual, linguistic, perceptual, social, emotional. Each disability area is not an exclusive category but rather overlaps with other areas. Effective changes in a youngster's development and learning depend upon the accuracy of pinpointing individual developmental needs and the planning of educational treatments matched with these needs.

FUNCTIONAL APPROACH

Accurate estimates of an individual's skills and deficits require precise descriptions of those behaviors that are present or absent. These descriptions of behavior provide examples of the child's *current levels of functioning,* that is what he or she *can and cannot do* at a certain time. This functional approach enables educational specialists to plan instructional activities. Analysis of the child's skills should include functioning in language, perceptual, cognitive, adaptive, self-help, emotional, social, gross and fine motor, and academic areas.

In contrast, a strictly categorical approach to assessment assumes that specialists can estimate children's abilities in general and then place them in a diagnostic category which presumes to tell specialists how to treat them—as mentally retarded, learning disabled, emotionally disturbed, and so forth. This latter approach has had little success. A functional approach to child treatment, then, emphasizes assessment of current performance and levels of functioning, which, in turn, leads to the development of an appropriate educational plan and program.

PURPOSEFUL GOALS AND PRACTICAL OUTCOMES

Accurate psychoeducational assessment is not a single operation which happens at a particular time. It is continuous and involves a general-to-specific evaluation process.

Robb, Bernardoni, and Johnson (1972) present five major purposes for conducting diagnostic assessment: (1) to screen and identify exceptional children; (2) to make decisions about appropriate educational placements; (3) to design individualized education plans; (4) to monitor individual child progress; and (5) to evaluate program effectiveness. When viewed as a *general-to-specific sequence,* each of these assessment purposes and activities is dependent upon the preceding one (see Figure 7-1).

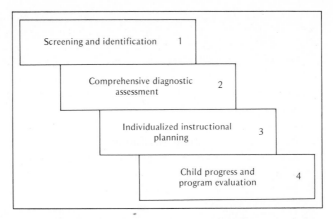

FIGURE 7-1
Interlinking purposes in psychoeducational assessment.

Children must be *screened,* that is, evaluated in a general way, so that potential problems can be tentatively identified and highlighted. It helps if parents and teachers are taught to observe and identify physical, emotional, and educational difficulties.

When suspected problems are identified, more *comprehensive assessment* methods can be used to focus on these presumed difficulties. Through continuous assessment of the child's functioning (in a variety of environments) teachers, school psychologists, and other specialists pool their judgments to increase accuracy in describing the children's strengths, weaknesses, and needs.

Based upon the assessment results, then, each child with special needs is provided with an *individualized plan* of educational goals that details the instructional modifications that will help the youngster meet specific objectives. Finally, ongoing assessment of skill development by teachers and periodic reevaluations by other specialists enable the school to document both *child progress* and the effectiveness of the instructional program.

SCREENING AND IDENTIFICATION

Screening is a sorting activity which seeks to distinguish those children who are suspected of being developmentally and learning disabled from those who are problem-free. The identification of significant differences between demonstrated and expected capabilities serves as a basis for more detailed assessment later.

Recent trends toward early identification and intervention for developmental and learning disabilities are based on a preventive service model (Meier, 1976). This model assumes that the early detection of problems in high-risk populations will lead to programs that will prevent the development of more complex learning problems later in life. The use of behavior-management strategies and parent-training procedures provides positive evidence that existing developmental and learning disorders can be reversed or at least ameliorated (Neisworth & Smith, 1973).

For example, kindergarten screening tests are used to identify children

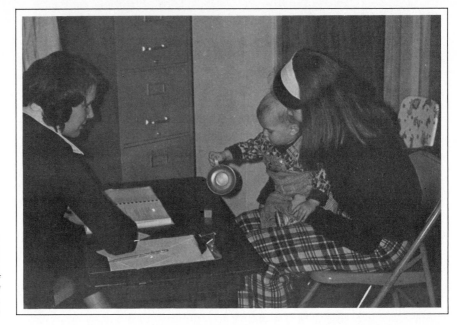

Early screening tests can help identify children in need of more detailed assessment and preventive measures. (*Courtesy of HICOMP Preschool Project, University Park, PA.*)

who do not have the required readiness skills to perform well in a structured school environment. Early identification efforts for infants and preschoolers employ developmental screenings on a mass community basis to identify children who have a high probability of having problems that can be alleviated through intervention (Kurtz, Neisworth, & Laub, 1977; Zehrbach, 1975). These efforts are most effective when many human-service agencies and professionals and paraprofessionals in a community coordinate their work.

SCREENING MEASURES

Early identification efforts frequently involve the use of developmental checklists, behavior-problem rating scales, readiness measures, and basic concept inventories. Detection of developmental and learning problems typically involves the use of such scales as the Denver Developmental Screening Test (Frankenburg, Dodds, & Fandal, 1975), the Developmental Activities Screening Inventory (Dubose & Langley, 1977), the Preschool Attainment Record (Doll, 1966), the Boehm Test of Basic Concepts (Boehm, 1971), and the Metropolitan Readiness Tests (Nurss & McGauvran, 1976).

The Denver Developmental Screening Test is one of the most frequently used developmental screening measures. Capable of being used with children aged 1 month to 6 years, the DDST surveys the child's functioning on landmark developmental tasks. It covers such areas as gross motor skills, fine motor adaptive skills, language behaviors, and psychosocial capabilities. Activities along this scale are placed within age ranges at which normal children can generally accomplish them. Passes and failures on these activities provide an estimate of how delayed a child's development appears to be.

Early screening and identification procedures highlight areas of suspected problems so that more focused, comprehensive assessments can provide an in-depth analysis of these problems. Screening at best *selects* children who are significantly different. It does not provide details for an analysis of the differences.

Since learners can experience difficulty in a variety of behavioral areas, screening must attempt to survey as many skills as possible in a short amount of time. Delays in the detection of problems result in delays in the remediation of problems. At an early age, when physical and neurological growth is rapid, unnecessary delays can be devastating for the child's future.

COMPREHENSIVE ASSESSMENT

Combinations of instruments and procedures are necessary to describe comprehensively the capabilities of the exceptional schoolchild. In fact, reliable diagnostic assessment depends upon the synthesis of both *qualitative* and *quantitative* information from a variety of sources, such as the direct observation of behaviors; classroom-climate scales; behavior ratings; actual child performance; interviews with parents, teachers, and the child; school achievement; and impressions from anecdotal records and diaries. This wide array of data makes us aware that a child's performance and learning are shaped by both personal characteristics and the context of the environment.

The following overview of the major types of general assessment methods shows what is available for conducting comprehensive evaluations of all learners.

BEHAVIORAL OBSERVATIONS AND RATINGS

Direct observation of a child's behavior as it occurs in the natural setting is one of the most useful and instructionally relevant diagnostic tools of the teacher. Structured observation involves looking carefully at and recording the child's behavior within the classroom. Emphasis is on determining what the child does in the presence of specific environmental conditions and his or her interaction with other children and adults. The central question to be answered is, What specific conditions (stimuli) affect the youngster's behavior (positive and negative responses)? For example, under what conditions and how often does the child have a tantrum, get out of the seat, hit others, fail to complete assignments, withdraw from activities, or talk out of turn in class? Behavioral observation can range from highly technical and precise systems of recording minute aspects of behavior to simple checklists or anecdotal records of behavior over periods of time.

Three observation techniques are frequently used with children experiencing developmental and learning problems: time-sampling methods, event-sampling methods, and rating scales and checklists.

Time-sampling techniques require the teacher or observer to record be-

CHILD _Larry H._   OBSERVER _R.L._

BEHAVIOR & SETTING _Inappropriate vocalizations during small group activities_

TIME PERIOD _60 min._   RECORDING INTERVAL _5 min._

DATE	1	2	3	4	5	6	7	8	9	10	11	12	%
5/10	+	+	+	−	+	+	−	−	+	+	+	+	75
5/11	−	−	−	+	−	+	+	+	+	+	+	+	66
5/12	+	−	−	−	+	+	−	−	+	+	−	+	50
5/13	+	+	+	+	+	+	−	−	+	+	+	+	83

FIGURE 7-2
Time-sampling method using intervals. (Adapted from Gardner, W.I., _Learning and behavior characteristics of exceptional children and youth._ Boston: Allyn & Bacon, 1977.)

havior only during a specific span of time. Data from this method reveals the frequency and duration of a certain behavior pattern, such as a child's screaming or fighting behavior when separated from his mother (Figure 7-2).

Event-sampling methods differ from the time techniques in that behavioral events are described in detail with this method. A chain or sequence of preceding and succeeding behaviors during such times as playground activities or small-group projects are narratively portrayed in event sampling. Anecdotal records are one form of event-sampling techniques (Figure 7-3). _Rating scales and checklists_ are probably the simplest and most frequently used observational methods to screen and diagnose developmental and learning difficulties. These informal techniques involve predetermined lists or sequences of behaviors, skills, and problems which are rated according to their frequency of occurrence, level of attainment, or severity. Essentially, rating scales and checklists are methods which attempt to structure to our _subjective impressions_ about children, which—as one might expect—tend to be relatively imprecise, since different perceptions color people's judgments. Cartwright and Cartwright (1974) and Iscoe and Payne (1972) stress that the rating approach helps to focus attention on important behaviors related to instruction and learning which are often overlooked in testing. In addition, precision can be added to this system by including behavioral definitions of each activity that is to be rated, thus facilitating more standardized judgments and better communication among parents, teachers, and other specialists (Bagnato, Neisworth, & Eaves, 1978). Examples of such rating methods include developmental checklists, lists of reading readiness skills, and behavior problem checklists (Figures 7-4 & 7-5).

Behavioral observation methods in assessing children with special needs and their environments are functional ones. They have certain advantages: they are embedded within the natural environment, relatively simple to construct and use, and instructionally and behaviorally specific.

```
ANTECDOTAL RECORD

                              Larry H.
                            (Child's name)

                               R.L.
                             (Observer)

                               6/14
                              (Date)
```

CHILD BEHAVIORS			TEACHER BEHAVIORS	
Words said	Words comprehended	Words attempted	Reinforcers used successfully	Events being paired with reinf.
up down toy cookie water soda	wheel cup come here	hello hot	raisins crackers	hugs kisses "good-boy"

General tasks enjoyed	Specific behaviors at those tasks	Vocabulary used	Situation in which used
playing piano	playing with 1 finger going up and down keys; humming		
water play	turning water on pouring from cup plugging sink	pour splash hot, cold	at the sink
riding toy giraffe	"nibbling" giraffe's ears	up down	with blocks in motor area

OTHER COMMENTS: He began to watch where the teacher kept the reinforcers.

FIGURE 7-3
Sample anecdotal record to guide programming.

NORM-REFERENCED ASSESSMENT

Norm-referenced scales are employed to compare a particular child's knowledge, performance, and skills with those of a representative group of peers. Norm-referenced testing often results in an age or grade score, which provides a standard for comparing a child's performance with that typical for the age or grade in school. It is *quantitative.* For example, if a fifth-grade child receives a grade score of 1.2 on a reading comprehension test, it means that compared to other fifth graders his comprehension level in reading is at the first-grade level. Intelligence tests and achievement tests are two familiar examples of norm-referenced scales.

Directions: Use the following symbols to indicate quality of performance on developmental objectives: (+) full skill   (−) absent skill   (±) emerging skill

OBJECTIVE NUMBER	GENERAL OBJECTIVE	PRETEST	POSTTEST	COMMENTS
M-3-1	Fundamental Movement (Gross Motor)			
M-3-1.1	Walks on tiptoe, demonstrated	+	+	
M-3-1.2	Begins a simple somersault	+	+	
M-3-1.3	Stands on balance beam with both feet	+	+	
M-3-1.4	Jumps from bottom step	−	±	
M-3-1.5	Walks up stairs, alternating feet	−	+	
M-3-1.6	Walks down stairs, alternating feet	−	−	
M-3-1.7	Walks on line on floor	±	+	
M-3-1.8	Rides a tricycle using pedals	−		
M-3-1.9	Stands on one foot, momentarily	±	+	
M-3-1.10	Catches large ball by holding it against body	−	+	
M-3-1.11	Jumps with both feet over low objects (1″-2″ high)	−		

FIGURE 7-4
Sample checklist of gross motor developmental skills.

Norm-referenced tests are important in the process of determining general levels of skill development and in placing children in special instructional classes. These scales must be used with caution in making educational decisions for two fundamental reasons. Some normative scales lack the technical sophistication needed to place confidence in their use (Salvia & Ysseldyke, 1978). Also, the skills sampled on such tests are often not the same as those taught in the classroom. When a strong relationship exists between behaviors tested and those taught, norm-referenced scales have much greater instructional application (Bagnato & Neisworth, 1979; Mac-Turk & Neisworth, 1978; Newland, 1971).

CRITERION-REFERENCED ASSESSMENT

Whereas norm-referenced assessment quantitatively compares a child to a representative group of peers, criterion-referenced assessment is essentially *qualitative*. In the latter case, emphasis is on the mastery of specific educational skills and content rather than on the relative standing of individuals (Ysseldyke, 1978).

Criterion-referenced measures sample each child's development of specific educational and prerequisite skills over time. These measures are instructionally relevant. For example, such tests enable the teacher to analyze skills that a child has and has not acquired along a given instructional sequence. This breakdown of skills is known as *task analysis*. Once this assessment is completed, the educator then focuses on the undeveloped skills. After a period of instruction, criterion-referenced tests are used again to evaluate mastery of these skills and overall educational progress. The scales

CHILD OBSERVATION AND EDUCATIONAL PLANNING FORM

BEHAVIOR DEFICITS AND NEEDS	0	1	2	3	INDIVIDUAL GOALS	INSTRUCTIONAL STRATEGIES
Impulsivity					List a series of prerequisite goals that you would work on with this child.	List the kinds of instructional techniques and educational settings you would use to work with this child.
Distractibility						
Persistence						
Frustration tolerance					1.	1.
Motivation						
Attention skills					2.	2.
Following directions						
Language skills					3.	3.
Readiness skills					4.	4.
Need for structure						
Need for limits					5.	5.
Need for cues and prompts					6.	6.
					7.	7.
					8.	8.

The following factors are important elements for defining individual differences in development and learning and for planning individual educational strategies:

1. Identify skills deficits and needs
2. Identify settings that control behavior
3. Select appropriate materials and activities
4. Create curriculum goals based on individual differences
5. Plan instructional techniques

help to pinpoint both deficient skills and the method to be used to help the child solve problems with a measure of independence.

FIGURE 7-5
Sample rating scale and program planning form.

ADAPTIVE ASSESSMENT

The assessment of a youngster's capabilities is most valuable when combined with diagnostic information obtained from a variety of evaluation methods. The limitations of each of these approaches are most evident when any one method is used to the exclusion of others. Problems are magnified when specialists assess children with multiple handicaps—youngsters who cannot demonstrate what they know on traditional instruments. Modifications must be made in assessment to accommodate their handicaps (Figure 7-6).

Nondiscriminatory Procedures

Evaluation methods need to be as free of bias as possible. Trends in special education have increased concerns about the effect of discriminatory

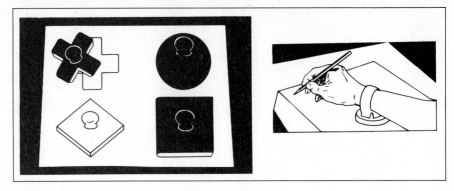

FIGURE 7-6
Adaptive materials for
assessing the learner with
special needs.

assessment practices on the education of culturally different populations (Cleary, Humphreys, Kendrick, & Wesman, 1975).

Diagnostic specialists face a particular challenge when asked to evaluate exceptional children. No matter what the handicap, an accurate estimate of the child's capabilities and limitations across several functional areas and situations must be obtained. But the child's impairments will often make a complete standardized assessment impossible. Departing dramatically from standardized procedures could invalidate norm-referenced comparisons. On the other hand, using strictly standardized procedures makes a comprehensive evaluation of current functioning difficult at best.

Children's social competence can be most appropriately assessed in actual social situations. (*President's Committee on Mental Retardation.*)

At the core of this dilemma, P.L. 94-142 makes explicit certain underlying assumptions regarding the assessment venture.

1. Assessments must be handicap-appropriate.

2. Assessments must be free of cultural and linguistic bias.

3. Assessment data must come from multiple sources and be directed toward programming.

4. Assessment results must provide comprehensive descriptions of *current* levels of functioning.

In order to effectively meet these goals guidelines are needed to facilitate the efforts of the specialist.

Adaptive Options
Several approaches have evolved over the years that are designed to alleviate the dilemma of assessing children with handicaps. These have centered on three possible options:

1. Developing specialized test materials standardized on the handicapped group in question (Hiskey, 1966; Newland, 1971)

2. Modifying traditional instruments to allow certain handicapped children to respond through other means (French, 1964; Maxfield & Buchholz, 1957; Sattler & Tozier, 1970)

3. Administering age-appropriate measures just as they were constructed for normal children to estimate the handicapped child's functioning under "realistic" social demands without regard to handicap (Anastasi, 1976; Louttit, 1957)

All of these options have certain limitations of reliability and validity, the possibility of nonrepresentative behavior samples, and an emphasis that serves to potentially exclude the exceptional child (Chase, 1975; Haeussermann, 1958; Wolf & Anderson, 1969).

DIAGNOSIS AND PRESCRIPTION

The comprehensive evaluation of handicapped children uses different methods from many sources and involves a team of specialists in order to analyze and profile the strengths, limitations, and needs of the child with learning difficulties (Hatch, Murphy, & Bagnato, 1979; Johnston & Magrab, 1976; Meier, 1976). As an outgrowth of the screening process, comprehensive assessment strives to probe more specifically into various functional areas that are viewed as problems by others, usually parents and teachers.

Most specialists use the *diagnostic-prescriptive* model (Cartwright & Cartwright, 1974). Diagnosis of educational strengths, weaknesses, and

CHILD _Paul E._   DATE _2/18/78_

SCHOOL _Head Start program_   AGE _5-0_

DEVELOPMENTAL SERVICES TEACHER INFORMATION SHEET

Paul is a very active, distractible, and impulsive five-year-old child who has been in my program for 4 weeks. In the classroom, Paul has trouble working on activities that require his attention and ability to listen. Often, he will rush into drawing, assembling puzzles, and picking out pictures in a book without thinking first or watching what he is doing. My other teachers and aides must be constantly with him to control his behavior.

In many respects, Paul seems to be like a somewhat younger child. He has difficulty controlling his own behavior especially in group play activities with other children his age. Because he disrupts games, Paul is ignored by other children, and he will often express his frustration in tantrums. On the playground, he moves about fairly well but appears to be awkward and clumsy and frequently falls.

At this time, I am mostly concerned about his speech and language difficulties and his general lack of readiness for first grade next year. Paul's speech is hard to understand but he does not speak very often in the classroom. He appears to have a limited vocabulary although he uses short three-word sentences.

Paul requires much work in coloring between lines, cutting with scissors, completing puzzles, and working with numbers, colors, shapes, and prereading tasks.

Right now, I feel that we need an estimate of what Paul is capable of doing so we can plan a variety of activities that will help him to get ready for first grade. Does he have any problem in his ability to learn? We are concerned that he may have a mild auditory problem also.

Rebecca Martina

Head Teacher
First Chance Classroom

FIGURE 7-7
Referral information on Paul, a 5-year old child with special needs.

needs defines a child's current levels of functioning and can lead to the construction of instructional objectives and activities. Using a team approach, various specialists focus their diagnostic work on the different areas of the child's functioning, including developmental, intellectual, linguistic, perceptual-motor, psychosocial, and educational. This assessment, coupled with conferences with the teacher and others, helps to *diagnose* and *pinpoint* problems and areas requiring special intervention. After the diagnostic work is completed, the specialists combine their judgments about the child's characteristics and suggest recommendations and strategies which match the student's characteristics and needs.

In the following sections the process of assessing learners with special needs is discussed and illustrated. We will look at specific tests and assessment methods for use with children who experience developmental learning problems. The case of Paul, a 5-year-old boy with special learning needs, illustrates the diagnostic sequence from screening to comprehensive assessment to individualized educational planning to evaluation (see Figures 7-7, 7-8, and 7-9).

Developmental Assessment

Developmental diagnosis involves the collection of information from various sources, such as parental reports of developmental progress, results of medical examinations, teacher observation, and actual child performance on structured tasks. Such information provides a clear picture of when and how a child stands, walks, runs, jumps, balances, and throws a ball. How a child manipulates objects manually, draws designs, uses speech and language, and plays with other children provides important information on readiness for working in a school environment. Data regarding the child's ability to wash, dress, feed, and use the toilet demonstrate the level of independence and social maturity.

Once suspected developmental problems have been screened and identified, more in-depth assessment can focus on areas of concern in order to define strengths and weaknesses. Measures such as the Bayley Scales of Infant Development (Bayley, 1969) and the Gesell Developmental Schedules (Knobloch & Pasamanick, 1974), which include a large number of items, provide precise analyses of wide-ranging language, motor, psychosocial, and problem-solving skills in young children from birth to 6 years of age. In addition, a curriculum-based instrument like the Learning Accomplishment Profile (Sanford, 1978) gives a rating of developmental age functioning, and also a breakdown of specific objectives that the child needs to accomplish before moving on to more complex activities. The child demonstrates ability to use developmental skills to manipulate the environment by completing such activities as formboards, puzzles, block towers, bead-stringing, picture-naming and identification, pegboards, paper cutting and folding, doll play, and drawing. The child's ability to complete items expected for his or her age gives evidence of the level of readiness, maturity, and developmental status.

Intellectual Assessment

Intelligence is a complex concept which attempts to explain a learner's ability to "think rationally, to act purposefully, and to deal effectively with his environment" (Sprinthall & Sprinthall, 1979, p. 479). We know that no individual test adequately samples the wide range of specific abilities thought to comprise the concept of intelligence (Guilford, 1967). However, instruments designed to assess reasoning and problem-solving abilities tend to sample mostly information that is highly verbal and culturally loaded. When a child experiences problems in any area, the capacity and opportunity to acquire information and to perform on traditional tests can be seriously impaired.

FIGURE 7-8
Paul's performance on the *Gesell Developmental Schedules.* (Reprinted with permission of Psychological Corporation).

42 months

MOTOR
- ± Stands: on 1 foot, 2 sec.
- + Walking bds: walks on both feet
- − Drawing: traces diamond

ADAPTIVE
- + M. Cubes: builds bridge from model
- + Geometric forms: points to 6
- ± Digits: repeats 3 (2 or 3 trials)
- − Weights: gives heavy block (2 of 3 trials)

LANGUAGE
- ± Picture cd: names all
- − Action: agent: 9 correct
- − Comprehen. Quest. A: answers 2

PERSONAL-SOCIAL
- + Dressing: washes, dries hands, face
- ± Play: assoc. play replaces parallel play

48 months

MOTOR
- + Stairs: walks down, foot to step
- − Skips: on 1 foot only (*60 m)
- ± Jumps: run, or stand, broad jump
- + Ball: throws overhand
- − Stands: on 1 foot, 4-8 sec.
- − Walking bds: 6 cm. bd., touches ground 1 (*60 m)
- ± Pellets: 10 into bo. in 25 sec.

ADAPTIVE
- − M. Cubes: imitates gage
- ± Pellets: 10 into bo. in 25 sec.
- + Drawing: man with 2 parts
- + Drawing: copies cross
- + Drawing: adds 3 parts incomplete man
- − Drawing: 1 bubble correct
- − Paper: (dem.) folds & creases 3 times
- − Geometric forms: points to 8
- − Sentences: repeats 1 of 3 (12-13 syll.)
- ± Missing parts: 1 correct
- − Counts: with correct point. 3 obj.
- − Weights: selects heavier invariably

LANGUAGE
- − Action agent: 18 correct
- − Color cd: names 1
- − Prepositions: obeys 4, ball & chair

PERSONAL-SOCIAL
- ± Dressing: washes & dries face & hands, brushes teeth
- ± Dressing: dresses & undresses, superv. (*60 m)
- − Dressing: laces shoes
- + Dressing: disting. front & back of clothes
- + Play: cooperates with children
- − Play: builds building with blocks
- − Develop. detach: goes on errands outside home

54 months

MOTOR
- ± Hops: on 1 foot
- − Articulation: not infantile
- − Drawing: traces cross
- D.A. = 42-48 mo.

ADAPTIVE
- − M. Cubes: makes gate from model
- + Drawing: copies square
- − Drawing: 3 bubbles correct
- − Geometric forms: points to 9
- − Counts: 5 obj. & ans. "how many?"
- + Aesthetic comparison: correct
- − Missing parts: 2 correct
- − Digits: repeats 4 (1 of 3 trials)
- D.A. = 42-48 mo.

LANGUAGE
- − Action agent: 14 correct
- − Defines: 4 in terms of use
- − Comprehen. Quest. 8: 1 correct
- D.A. = 36-42 mo.

PERSONAL-SOCIAL
- − Commun: calls attention to own perform.
- − Commun: relates fanciful tales (*60 m)
- − Commun: bosses & criticizes (*60 m)
- ± Play: shows off dramatically (*60 m)
- D.A. = 42-48 mo.

Adaptive and comprehensive assessment procedures require that the exceptional child's true abilities be sampled using methods which avoid any impairment. The adaptive options previously discussed offer practical alternatives to the diagnostic specialist. If a child is hindered from acquiring information because of a handicap, that child will be different from others of the same age. Because of this difference, members of a diagnostic team must strive to distinguish *process* abilities (underlying psychological strategies which develop naturally and are prerequisite to later learning) from *product* abilities (acquired, school-related, and cultural information) in order to describe the capabilities of the exceptional child.

Meaningful intellectual measurement must sample such skills as discrimination, generalization, perceptual-motor abilities, general information, vocabulary, induction, comprehension, sequencing, detail recognition, analogies, abstract reasoning, memory, and other related skills (Salvia & Ysseldyke, 1978). Tests like the Stanford-Binet Intelligence Scale (Terman & Merrill, 1973) and the Wechsler Intelligence Scale for Children-Revised (Wechsler, 1974) are widely used measures to describe levels of intellectual functioning and differences between children. Nevertheless, traditional intellectual measures are often inappropriate when used with children who evidence dysfunctions in the areas of motoric ability, affect, hearing and vision, and communication.

For this reason, diagnostic specialists must use instruments which avoid as much as possible the response-deficits of handicapped children (Langley, 1978). As well as having standardized alternative administration procedures, some instruments have separate norm groups for certain types and degrees of exceptionality. For example, the Pictorial Test of Intelligence (French, 1964) uses oversized picture cards and a simple gestural response to sample the learning capabilities of children with cerebral palsy and language disorder. The Leiter International Performance Scale (Arthur, 1950) uses pantomime directions and a unique format of matching designed blocks with a series of cards in a wooden frame to sample intellectual abilities of children with hearing and language problems. The Hiskey-Nebraska Test of Learning Aptitude (Hiskey, 1966) and the Blind Learning Aptitude Test (Newland, 1969) both contain separate norm groups and response formats for deaf and blind individuals, respectively.

Language Assessment
The quantity and quality of a child's receptive and expressive language skills are vital to later success in school. At an early age the developed and learned aspects of language interact with thought in ways that will transform dramatically the child's reasoning, memory, and problem-solving abilities. Language plays a vital role in the development and refinement of self-control behaviors in children as well (Meichenbaum, 1973). Schools employ speech and language specialists to aid in the detection and remediation of communication disorders. Disorders in communication may surface in several areas, such as speech sounds, word order, meaning, vocabulary, com-

prehension, and expression. It is important to distinguish, however, between language *competence* and language *performance* (Bloom & Lahey, 1978). A wide array of instruments designed to assess the various components of language are described in detail in other sources (Dale, 1972; Irwin & Marge, 1972).

Perceptual-motor Assessment

Psychologists and educators generally assume that well-developed perceptual-motor capabilities are important correlates to academic success. Assessment of these skills is usually accomplished by having a child draw increasingly more complex designs. Caution must be observed not to place children in programs designed to remediate perceptual-motor skills at the expense of ignoring academic needs. If used cautiously as part of a larger diagnostic battery, perceptual-motor tests have value in detecting disorders in normal development of neuromotor and visual-motor behavior and in generally indicating a child's level of readiness for school.

Several frequently used perceptual-motor measures sample such behaviors as eye-hand coordination, figure-ground perception, spatial relations, memory for design detail, balance and posture, form discrimination, ocular control, and body image. The most well known measures are the Bender Visual-Motor Gestalt Test (Koppitz, 1975), the Developmental Test of Visual-Motor Integration (Beery & Buktenica, 1967), the Memory for Designs Tests (Graham & Kendall, 1960), and the Non-Motoric Visual Gestalt Test (Foster & Sabatino, 1976).

Psychosocial Assessment

The assessment of emotional state, interpersonal relations, and adaptive behavior is complex and requires the gathering of information from various sources. The practical assessment of dysfunction in psychosocial adaptability must focus on the interaction between person variables and situation variables as they are expressed in different behavior patterns (Mischel, 1973). Measures exist to assess such aspects of behavior as self-concept, goal-setting, social maturity, adaptive behavior and independence, degree of anxiety, hyperactivity, aggressiveness, and classroom climate.

The assessment of adaptive behavior or social competence in children is important for many reasons, but especially so when retarded mental development is suspected. Adaptive behavior focuses mainly on the child's developing ability to function independently within a social context. The Vineland Social Maturity Scale (Doll, 1965), Adaptive Behavior Scale, (Nihira, Foster, Shellhaas, & Leland, 1969) and The Maxfield-Buchholz Scale of Social Maturity for Blind Preschool Children (Maxfield & Buchholz, 1957) are interview-informant measures that rate adaptive social functioning in various areas.

Assessment of personal characteristics of the child is a crucial concern. Diagnostic specialists have found such measures as the Piers-Harris Children's Self-Concept Scale (Piers & Harris, 1969), and the Human Figure

Drawing Test (Koppitz, 1968) particularly useful in assessing self and interpersonal perceptions as well as goal-directed behavior. With higher-functioning learners, measures such as incomplete sentence blanks and behavior-problem checklists are often used.

And finally in this area, specialists serve an important function by conducting systematic observations of child behavior in various school situations when the youngster is under the influence of different people. This type of analysis helps to identify conditions or people who tend to be associated with the child's problem behaviors. Home visits by social workers provide a valuable comparative source of data to pinpoint differences in a child's behavior at home and in school. Structured interviews with individual children and limited play therapy sessions also aid in problem identification. Psychologists find the use of classroom-climate scales important for analyzing pupil-pupil and teacher-pupil contacts and the types of verbal and nonverbal behaviors which maintain or discourage those contacts.

Educational Assessment

The primary purpose of evaluating children with developmental and learning disabilities is to collect data from multiple sources in order to plan an individualized instructional program (Hammill & Bartel, 1978; Wallace & Larsen, 1978). Educational assessment results provide data on a child's pattern of strengths and weaknesses—information that can be transformed directly into individualized curriculum plans.

The teacher, especially, must develop skills in observing and rating functioning in areas such as attention and listening, reading and comprehension, computation, oral and written expression, memory, and visual-motor capabilities. General achievement tests, informal educational-skill inventories, work samples, and criterion-referenced instructional batteries all help to screen, assess, and pinpoint specific educational needs requiring intervention. And in most instances, these evaluation devices can be administered, scored, and interpreted by teachers.

Such sources as Smith and Neisworth (1982), Salvia and Ysseldyke (1981), and Wallace and Larsen (1978) provide comprehensive and practical reviews of both formal and informal diagnostic methods used to assess educational disorders.

In educational diagnosis, norm-referenced (NRA) and criterion-referenced assessment (CRA) approaches must be effectively combined. Whereas NRA compares each child's level of performance to a norm group, CRA rates each child's level of performance against an absolute criterion of mastery within skill areas and, thus, tends to be more instructionally specific. The most frequently used NRA methods are such individually administered scales as the Peabody Individual Achievement Test (Dunn & Markwardt, 1970) and the Wide Range Achievement Test (Jastak & Jastak, 1965). In contrast, the Standford Achievement Test (Madden, Gardner, Rudman, Kavisen, & Merwin, 1973) has criterion-referenced qualities and separate norms for hearing- and visually impaired populations. Requiring individualized programs for exceptional children has increased the popularity of CRA instruments. The Woodcock Reading Mastery Tests (Woodcock, 1973) and the Brigance Diagnostic Inventory of Basic Skills (Brigance, 1977) are skill-specific diagnostic measures with CRA qualities. Most educational batteries assess prerequisite skills in the general categories of reading, mathematics, language arts, and readiness.

Environmental Assessment

Historically, educators and psychologists have concentrated on assessing individual characteristics, that is, intelligence, achievement, motivation, social maturity, to obtain information for appropriate educational placement and programming. However, it is also vital to stress the extraordinary importance of assessing the educational environment—the classroom climate, and the processes of instruction afforded to each child. Current thinking in education and psychology holds that a learner performs poorly in school because of a combination of problems related to the child's functional skills and the instructional environment. This perspective has encouraged specialists to identify *aptitude-treatment interactions* (ATI), that is, identify optimal matches between child characteristics and instructional variables (Smith, Neisworth, Greer, 1978; Ysseldyke, 1978). Although this trend has had mixed results, it provides us with some guidelines for assessing the quality of the instructional environment so that it can best meet his educational needs.

Teaching involves the "arrangement of conditions deliberately designed to effect relatively permanent demonstrable changes in behavior" (Smith, et al., 1978, p. 10). To help ensure effective teaching, teachers and psychoeducational specialists need to assess the following dimensions of educational environments through checklists, rating scales, and systematic observation methods.

1. Physical environment: instructional space, architectural design, seating arrangements

2. Instructional arrangements: content and characteristics of the curriculum, teaching methods, adaptive educational materials, and instructional media

3. Classroom climate: teacher-child and child-child interactions, group dynamics, and social relationships

Detailed and reliable evaluation of these educational dimensions allows teachers and cooperating specialists to plan individualized educational programs which will match each learner's needs and thus promote learning and growth.

INDIVIDUALIZED EDUCATIONAL PLANNING

Effective educational practice requires that assessment and intervention be linked in ways which are practical and meaningful for the teacher. The diagnostic-prescriptive model stresses assessment as a vehicle for describing patterns of strengths and weaknesses and for planning individual interventions designed to enhance deficit skills. *Observable* skills and *measurable* objectives are the keys to the reliability, validity, and practicality of such an approach.

The individualized education program is a direct outcome of the diagnostic process. The IEP is a statement of current levels of psychoeducational functioning within and across multiple areas of behavior (see Figure 7-9). It should describe in sequence appropriate annual and short-term goals. Essentially, the IEP highlights and describes each child's range of individual differences and then serves to identify objectives which can form the basis of an instructional or curriculum plan. In effect, then, the IEP systematizes the assessment and program planning process and helps to ensure that person-environment interactions influence our view in educational work with exceptional children. The relationship between testing and teaching has been called an "assessment/curriculum linkage" (Bagnato & Neisworth, 1979).

Several elements must merge to result in a well-developed and individualized prescriptive plan. Members of the program planning team must be specific about three major variables:

1. Behavior variables: The psychoeducational behaviors or goals that are desired outcomes of the proposed interventions.

2. Person variables: The child's range of individual differences—handicaps, educational strengths, weaknesses, and needs—which describe current levels of functioning.

3. Environmental variables: The types of instructional methods, strategies, and environmental arrangements which match and interact optimally with the child's range of individual differences to promote learning (Hunt & Sullivan, 1974).

Current levels of functioning in such skill areas as reading, math, written and oral expression, and perceptual-motor behaviors must be specified and strengths and weaknesses defined. Next, a sequence of desired performance levels or goals in each functional area must be established to guide teaching. These goals provide accountability, facilitate communication between parents, teachers, and specialists, ensure teaching precision by focusing learning activities, and motivate students if the goals are appropriate and the materials are attractive and manageable.

Finally, the team must attempt to specify the types of environmental arrangements which will match individual differences and thus promote learning for the handicapped child. Behavioral strategies which focus on differential methods of presenting materials and providing feedback need to be established. The pacing, sequencing, and breakdown of material lead-

DEVELOPMENTAL OBJECTIVE	INSTRUCTIONAL METHODS	CHILD PROGRESS EVALUATION			
		ASSESSMENT METHODS	PRE	POST	GAIN
1. Attends & listens during focused tasks	Physical-verbal prompts in low distraction, structured setting with simplified activities	Time-sampling anecdotal records			
2. Scans activities in an organized way before responding	self-instructional steps with teacher guidance & prompts in simple tasks	Duration measures Anecdotal records			
3. Copies & traces increasingly complex geometric forms	Large colorful form cards and templates	LAP Profile			
4. Names, identifies & matches a variety of shapes	one-one setting DLM materials	LAP Profile			
5. Names, identifies & matches primary & secondary colors	one-one setting DLM materials	LAP Profile			
6. Names & identifies & classifies pictured & concrete objects	one-one setting DLM materials	teacher developmental checklist			
7. Explains action & relationships in stories	one-one and small group (2-5) settings; Peabody Lang. Kit	Gesell Agent-actions Anecdotal records			
8. Demonstrates understanding of positional & comparative concepts	one-one and small group settings	CSAB Battery teacher checklist			
9. Counts objects 1-10	one-one setting; pair verbal and motor behaviors	CSAB Battery teacher checklist			
10. Identifies missing parts in pictured situations	one-one setting structure attention	Binet Missing Parts			
11. Defines objects in terms of use	one-one setting small group	CSAB; Peabody Lang. Kit			
12. Draws basic man form and places parts on incomplete man	one-one setting use models & prompts	Gesell & Binet tasks			

FIGURE 7-9
Example of an extended single domain IEP for Paul involving goals and methods in the cognitive/readiness area.

ing to the accomplishment of each goal will require precise teaching and systematic follow-up assessment.

EVALUATION OF CHILD PROGRESS AND PROGRAM EFFECTIVENESS

Programs claiming to help children with special needs are required to provide evidence of their effectiveness. Program evaluation procedures must account for both changes in children's learning of skills and the characteristics of their individual program which helped make those gains possible (Bagnato & Neisworth, 1980; Simeonsson & Weigerink, 1975). Evidence of progress is dependent upon the accuracy with which previous assessments identified needs and suggested related goals. Comprehensive evaluation procedures combine diagnostic information from achievement tests, child observation, teacher reports, and behavior ratings to measure child progress and program effectiveness.

FORMATIVE EVALUATION PROCEDURES

These have practical value for the teacher because they provide ongoing information about the learning of specific skills, the efficacy of certain instructional strategies, and the need to modify the existing methods or objectives for particular children. Criterion-referenced measures and behav-

PART II
CAUSES AND
ASSESSMENT OF
EXCEPTIONALITY

ioral-observation methods are appropriately used in formative evaluation. If necessary, modifications can be made in the child's program while the instructional plan is in effect (Ysseldyke, 1978).

SUMMATIVE EVALUATION

Such procedures provide the teacher with a method of measuring the overall effectiveness of the program by assessing comparative progress of individuals and groups *at the end* of participation in a program. Combinations of norm-referenced and criterion-referenced measures are most useful for summative evaluation purposes.

SUMMARY

The growing involvement of teams of diagnostic-prescriptive specialists in serving learners with special needs is an important trend in special education. Assessment and intervention must be linked in ways that are practical for the teacher and instructionally specific for the special child.

Thus, a team of specialists is needed to comprehensively assess the wide range of functional abilities. With P.L. 94-142 as a guide, systematic purposes and individualized methods of assessment allow for the planning of individualized treatment plans. The more defined the relationship between a child's pattern of capabilities and the plan of instruction, the more effective the total educational experience. The school psychologist's diagnostic skills are a vital link in this chain.

The end result of this screening, assessment, and goal-planning process is a tangible product—an initial individualized instructional contract forged through the cooperative efforts of a variety of individuals who are significant in the exceptional child's life. The individualized plan serves effectively to guide curriculum planning, is sensitive to the handicapped child's unique needs, and facilitates the monitoring of child progress and program effectiveness.

PART THREE
SPECIAL
EDUCATION
INTERVENTION

Robert M. Smith
John T. Neisworth

CHAPTER 8
FUNDAMENTAL
INSTRUCTIONAL PRACTICES

(Courtesy of Chuck Zovko.)

All children have a great deal in common, even youngsters with significant disabilities. This chapter will discuss a number of instructional considerations relevant to the special education of exceptional children. There are four aspects of instruction discussed in the following pages that are important for the educator to master.

The first component is the *curriculum, goals, or target behaviors.* Teachers need to decide what curricular goals are appropriate for each youngster. There are hierarchies of skills in which certain behaviors are dependent on more elementary skills. Special educators must be aware of this ordering of skills, for the consequences of placing a child in a program in which the tasks are too difficult can be devastating.

The second aspect of instruction is the *methodology, or procedures to be employed in the instructional setting.* This aspect is of secondary importance to the goals—one must have a firm decision on where to go before deciding how to get there. Methodology is a complex area and contains many components, some of which are: selecting the mode of presentation of a stimulus (for example, visual, auditory, or both); deciding on types of responses required of students; using positive or aversive consequences appropriately; knowing when and how to cue students; properly fading stimuli to maintain a correct response; using lecture, discussion, and demonstration correctly; and knowing how to group children for instruction. These techniques are more complex than most teachers realize and can be used successfully with certain instructional problems but not with others. This second aspect is a very important element in the education of exceptional children. As part of methods, we can include evaluation of learning progress. No program for a child can go very far unless there is deliberate and appropriate evaluation. Special educators need to have skills in detect-

Teaching methods include ways of focusing and maintaining attention, shaping performance, and motivating the student. (*Pennsylvania State University Child Development Laboratories.*)

ing changes in student behavior. These measures indicate child progress and provide feedback on the effectiveness of instruction.

A third component is the *choice of instructional materials.* Materials are facilitators; they enhance the methodologies so that the appropriate objectives can be more nearly achieved. A poor choice of materials can easily neutralize and perhaps even stifle the methodological procedures a teacher uses even if the methods are correctly selected and used. For example, a teacher would not select a primary visual device or instructional material for auditory instruction. Nor would a teacher use a game that punishes a child for a certain response when the method used rewards the very same or approximately the same behavior. Methods and materials should go hand-in-glove.

The fourth factor is the setting or place in which the unique combination of curriculum, methods, and materials can most efficiently and effectively be delivered. Since we will discuss in a subsequent chapter the major ramifications involved in selecting a setting, we will simply emphasize at this point how important this aspect of the child's environment is for increasing his or her performance. The place of delivery and the skills of the teacher in that place are directly related to how well each child acquires the desired skills.

This unique mix of curriculum, methods, materials, and setting is the essence of special education. If each is chosen appropriately, with frequent evaluation checks built into the system, it is very reasonable to expect continued progress from exceptional children.

The remainder of this chapter will center on general instructional guide-

lines and specific practical recommendations to make all educators more
effective.

127

TEACHER ATTITUDE

ACCEPT THE CHILD

Many children with whom special educators work come from lower socio-economic circumstances, may be neglected, and have learned a host of negative behaviors. They may look odd, smell bad, speak offensively, and have antisocial habits. This is the way it is, and it is your responsibility to assess your feelings about youngsters like these. Frequently such characteristics set the stage for the teacher either to avoid or even to punish the student. Guard against the formation of a negative halo or attitude that may cause your personal feelings about a student to interfere with your functioning as a real educator. Whether you intend to be a special or regular educator, you should be aware of these possibilities before you make a decision about your own career.

The potential consequences of being unable to overlook these negative attributes in children are (1) less progress by the children in schoolwork; (2) increased hostility and alienation between the teacher and the student; and (3) a relatively poor instructional experience throughout the students' schooling. An aide or assistant can be used to monitor a teacher's behavior toward individual children in order to detect possible instances of unfairness, favoritism, and unequal opportunity or even personal vendettas. It is important to be monitored by someone else because these problems in interpersonal relationships occur in very subtle ways and without recognition or awareness until the situation clearly gets out of hand.

REALIZE THAT EVERY CHILD CAN DO BETTER

Historically, special educators have tended to underestimate the progress exceptional children can make. Too often, psychometric information, medical reports, school records, diagnostic labels, and first impressions are translated into limited expectations for development. Lowered expectations will inevitably result in a decreased effort by that teacher and, thus, in lowered performance by the child.

Remember that children's progress is a function of their interaction with the environment. How far they succeed will depend not only upon their personal characteristics as they presently exist but upon the quality of the environment. When children are not improving, do not assume that they will never be able to do so. Instead, your responsibility is to adjust your instructional practices until you detect improvement. Developmental potential does not reside within the child but is a product of the complex interaction that occurs between the child and the environment. As a teacher, your attitude toward children and the instructional setting you provide are important components of their environment and will ultimately influence their progress and potential.

MAINTAIN YOUR OWN MOTIVATION
Being a teacher of exceptional children is not an easy job. It is an exacting profession and requires time and particular expertise. To be sure, it is rewarding to help exceptional children achieve competence and dignity. Do not depend on these altruistic motivations, however, to maintain your persistence during periods of frustration and discouragement. Consider using some of the learning principles we have mentioned to maintain your own professional activity. Many teachers, for example, find it useful to "premack" or otherwise reinforce getting their own class preparation done. That is, reward yourself by going shopping, eating out, or going on a coffee break only after having completed a certain facet of your preparation. You cannot be faulted for practicing what you preach.

OTHER TEACHING RESOURCES
Remember that the instructional situation is larger than either the teacher or the classroom. Children learn at home and in the broader community. Consider using facilities and personnel both in and out of school to achieve your objectives. Specifically, potential school resources include (1) audiovisual equipment, (2) instructional materials, (3) specialized consultants, and (4) other special educators or remedial specialists. One should not overlook the potential offered by programs in such fields as industrial arts, home economics, physical education, music, marketing education, agricultural education, and vocational-industrial education.

THE COMMUNITY
Recognize the wide range of help your community can provide. Professional clubs, social and civic organizations, local colleges, parent groups, local businesses, churches, regional centers that provide special education instructional materials, community recreation facilities, and local professionals who are interested in exceptional children should be contacted for purposes of assessing the contributions that they could make to the child's instructional environment. For example, the Lion's Club has a history of providing visual aids and braille apparatus, certain dentists specialize in providing dental care to handicapped children, and some corporations have chosen to employ handicapped persons wherever feasible. Possibilities for field trips, special events, and donations ought to be investigated as well.

Be sure to inquire of other teachers about the resources they have found useful. Mobilize the efforts of parents and other special educators to get a more coordinated effort in making efficient use of all community assets.

OTHER PROFESSIONALS
Special educators are usually overwhelmed with various points of view from coworkers on how best to deal with difficult instructional and deportment

problems. This is especially true when certain children are particularly resistant or when the teacher is fairly new on the job. Those teachers who have graduated recently or had some additional university training are likely to have acquired reasonably current skills and knowledge. Older colleagues, in contrast, may have somewhat outdated instructional practices, but they may have a broader, more practical perspective on educational strategies. New teachers will want to take advantage of the wisdom and maturity of more experienced staff members without compromising their own views of more contemporary philosophies and teaching approaches. So be alert for the recommendations and suggestions of others. You may wish to consider building them into your own philosophical framework.

The time will come when you will be confronted with a well-credentialed professional, like a school psychologist, whose pronouncements are contradictory to your beliefs and instructional approach. Now what do you do? We suggest that you give the person a full hearing, accept the information provided, and then request that the recommendations be translated into practical classroom procedures. You can then judge the utility of those suggestions and tell the consultant—in a courteous way, of course—your view of the relevance of the report's recommendations. By all means, avoid being so abrasive and dogmatic that you alienate those whose intentions are to help.

If you accept the perspective expressed in this book, as a teacher you will undoubtedly be concerned by a school psychologist's report in which a child has "an IQ of 54 with minimal cerebral dysfunction and can't be expected to do well in school," "dyslexia and a poor prognosis for achievement in reading," "undifferentiated perceptual integration problems that require patterning therapy," or "identification problems." When you receive these kinds of reports, your task will be to inquire about the educational implications for you—that is, what do these numbers and labels offer with respect to instructional strategy? If the response to your question is simply more labels and numbers, it would probably be wise to lay aside such reports in favor of more accurate and meaningful ones. It may be better for you to simply operate on your own by systematically collecting performance data on children in an informal way (Salvia and Ysseldyke, 1978; Smith, 1969). In sum, be gracious and open, respond in a professional manner, use whatever information passes the test of pragmatism, and maintain your own records on the achievement of each child.

Remember, too, that you no doubt have skills that can be of help to others, including those whose instructional responsibilities may not be with exceptional children. Don't be shy about sharing that information and the specific techniques that you have acquired during your training, but there is no need to hit them over the head with your newfound competencies. One of the best ways to be of assistance is by example. If you have a well-managed and effective classroom, the word soon gets around. Other teachers will eventually seek your advice—but play it cool and don't be a know-it-all.

TEACHER'S AIDES

Some teachers may be fortunate enough to have the services of a part-time or even full-time aide. Increasingly, teacher's aides and other paraprofessionals are receiving training that enables them to provide a valuable helping hand in the educational enterprise. While paraprofessional training programs vary considerably in their length and content, teacher's aides often become acquainted with many of the practical problems encountered in the classroom, such as establishing rapport with children, student deportment, assistance with schoolwork, operation of audiovisual equipment, and odds and ends like helping children with their coats and boots, seeing that they get on the correct bus, and even preparing snacks.

Regardless of the aide's preparation or previous experience with children, the teacher must provide an orientation and an explicit description of the division of labor between teacher and aide. In every instance the teacher must be the final authority. Some teachers prefer that the aide function in a subordinate role, whereas other teachers use the aide in a quasi-teaching role.

In situations in which the aide is used in a teacherlike role, absolute consistency must exist between the teacher and the aide with respect to the approach selected in working with the children. In all cases, the aide must support the teacher so that the children do not play one against the other. This often happens in families in which one parent is more lenient or more protective than the other. Inconsistency can lead to mismanagement of the students and conflict between the teacher and the aide.

Perhaps the best recommendation for the preparation of an effective teacher's aide and the establishment of a positive working relationship is to assign the aide relatively simple duties at first, ones that do not require extensive interaction with the children. This will provide the aide with a chance to observe the teacher, to understand the teacher's style, and to follow the model provided by the teacher. It is important at this point, even in the execution of routine activities with the children, that the aide's approach be consistent with that of the teacher's. For example, if the teacher has established a rule that crying, whining, and fussing will be ignored, it would be wrong for the aide to attend to that kind of behavior while removing boots, distributing materials, or cleaning up after lunch. If the aide does so, the goals of the instructional program will be subverted.

Gradually and progressively, as the aide becomes skilled in routine activities and understands the teacher's methodology, the aide's role can be expected to expand and include a variety of instructional activities. We recommend that the teacher develop behavioral objectives for the aide. For example, you may require that your aide be able to:

Thread a 16 mm projector

Demonstrate to children how to put on their coats

Conduct snack time

Tutor children in cursive writing

It is important to systematically evaluate and provide feedback on the aide's performance. Look for how well the objectives are being accomplished by using a checklist, rating scale, self-report, or weekly conference with the aide. While this may seem time-consuming, it is a vital part of your total program because it will eliminate a host of possible problems.

Like aides, volunteers can be very helpful, but only if adequate preparation and role descriptions have been developed by the teacher. If a teacher is unable or unwilling to consider these details prior to the involvement of classroom assistants, it would probably be best to do without such help.

PARENTS

Some parents of exceptional children have the knowledge, time, and patience to bring the school's program into the home—but most parents do not. A substantial number of parents of exceptional children are from lower socioeconomic circumstances. While they may value education, poor people have resource problems that restrict their opportunities to devote the time they might otherwise like to give to the youngster's school problems.

Since exceptional children come from all social classes, teachers must be prepared to relate to parents from middle and upper socioeconomic levels as well as from the lower levels. Sometimes parents are too eager to help. They unwittingly destroy the impact of the classroom program (1) by uncritically accepting "therapies" or "cures" that they have heard about that have little scientific credibility; (2) by being so eager to help their child that their haste leads to the inaccurate and detrimental application of suggestions made by the teacher; (3) by forcing the child to practice at home

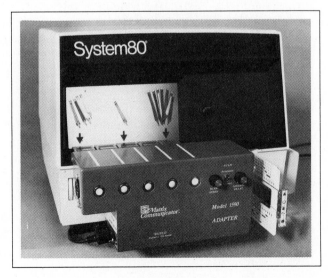

The right technology can greatly aid in teaching basic lessons and in reviewing and expanding on newly learned material. (*Borg-Warner Corp.*)

beyond a constructive point and thus tainting the teacher's efforts; (4) by entering their child into competition with others instead of looking at individual progress; and (5) by being unwilling to accept that their child is in need of special education.

In order to involve parents realistically and effectively, we recommend the following policy:

1. Schedule periodic conferences with parents. Conferences will be time-consuming; therefore, decide on a realistic commitment to these activities.

2. On the basis of the conference and any other available information, estimate the parents' competence in working with you. Are they naive, misinformed, pushy, prone to compare the child with siblings, apparently incapable of following a supplemental program of any complexity, or too demanding of the child?

3. Avoid discussion of possible causes of the child's problems, the history of the situation, and hunches as to prognosis. Reports should be meaningful, simply stated, and free of educational jargon.

4. Since many parents of exceptional children will read things into your statements and mannerisms in order to support their own biases and hunches, stick to the educational objectives for the child, progress toward achieving those objectives, the procedures you are using to help achieve them, and suggestions as to how the parents can help.

5. As the parents become cooperative and informed, progressively involve them in home-school programming for their child. Initially, you may request that the parents simply be with the child for a portion of the evening in any type of simple exchange. Later, the parents may assist the child in completing homework exercises. Eventually you might recommend that the parents tutor the youngster, develop behavioral objectives, and establish a management program for use at home. This will require careful preparation by the parents and monitoring by you.

6. Depending on the child's problems and the parents' capabilities you may wish to recommend a variety of sources to the parents, including manuals, seminars, and continuing education programs in child development and special education. You may also want to recommend that a parent become a teaching assistant if time permits.

7. Whenever possible you should encourage parents to keep records on their child's behavior at home so that their reports to you about how the child is doing will not be filled with unreliable impressions. Again, recommend a number of sources to the parents for keeping such records.

Instructional objectives can frequently be achieved through the use of games which provide automatic, imbedded reinforcement. (*Courtesy of Paul J. Quinn.*)

8. Be realistic about the extent to which parents can contribute to the education of their child. Most parents of exceptional children will have a tendency to overestimate the amount of time and energy they have available for working with their child. Don't blame them if the child is not progressing in your classroom. Their collaboration will facilitate the child's progress, but do not depend on their participation.

THE EDUCATIONAL SETTING

PLAN THE LAYOUT OF YOUR CLASSROOM

Classrooms are organized for different purposes. Some teachers arrange the physical environment with aesthetics in mind. Their major concern is how pleasing to the eye their classroom appears. Their focus is on public relations. For example, bulletin boards are lavish and not to be touched by the children—they are designed more for adult appeal than for the instruction of the children. Furniture is selected and arranged to suit the taste of the teacher and not primarily for utility.

Another rationale for the organization of the classroom is administrative convenience. In this case, the teacher is principally concerned with minimizing his or her own efforts—making life easier at the possible expense of instructional effectiveness. In this type of classroom, materials and supplies are stored so that children do not have access to them. Youngsters are seated alphabetically so that records are more easily maintained. Provision for individual learning areas is at a minimum, and the teacher's desk is usually isolated from the pupils' activities.

There are, of course, other personal and noninstructional criteria for organizing the classroom. Indeed, some teachers "organize" the classroom in a most haphazard way, changing the layout on the basis of whim or temporary expediency. What is lacking in all of the preceding bases for organizing the classroom is a *consistent instructional rationale*. The classroom is an environment for learning. All other considerations must be subordinate.

In arriving at an effective physical arrangement, it is important to see what modern learning theory has to offer. One clear conclusion is that learning efficiency and effectiveness are influenced by the characteristics of the physical context. That is, either because of accidental or intentional prior arrangements, activities come to be associated with, and thus influenced by, certain stimuli. For example, if you are accustomed to napping in your favorite easy chair, the chair becomes a cue for napping. Reading becomes difficult in that setting, since the napping competes with the reading. Or if you frequently eat while you watch television, the television becomes a cue for eating. As a result, you may search around for a snack when the television is on even though you may have just finished eating supper.

Within a school setting it is not surprising that schoolchildren are messy at their lunch table if this is the same table on which they are encouraged to smear paint during the art period. Such settings are technically called "discriminative stimuli"; they set the occasion for certain behaviors that occur

These children worked hard at a lesson they would have avoided in order to play Toss the Bean Bag. (*Pennsylvania State University Child Development Laboratories.*)

in a specific setting and that are reinforced in that environment. Successful teachers have found that children are more likely to be quiet, attentive, and persistent in activities such as reading or arithmetic in a corner or area that has been specifically set aside for that activity and in which behaviors incompatible with those activities do not occur. This principle, the control of behavior by cues, can be expanded to include not only location in the room but any other stimulus that can be used to set the occasion for desired behavior. To illustrate, the teacher may set a timer during which the children are expected and reinforced for being quiet in their seats. Color cues can also be used in various ways, for example, a blue card held up by the teacher signals that quiet talking is permissible. The characteristics of the physical setting, therefore, are important components of the instructional enterprise.

In planning of the classroom layout, the following factors are pertinent:

1. Decide what major student competencies you want to see exhibited and where they are to be demonstrated within the classroom. You might list certain activities such as reading, spelling, writing, arts and crafts, or group conversations and select specific areas where these activities are encouraged.

2. Determine which activities require the students to see or hear certain stimuli. The Distar Reading Program, for example, requires instruction in small groups because the children need to see small visual presentations and be within reaching distance of the teacher.

3. Assess where within the classroom the target activity can most easily be achieved by the children. It would be unwise, for example, to have an activity which requires concentration occurring side by side with one which involves group discussion.

4. Arrange the setting so that you can actively interact with the students. This means that your desk and resources should not be isolated from the learning environment. Your position should be part of, not apart from, the children's environment.

5. Consider whether group or individual materials are required and arrange the classroom accordingly.

6. Be sure to consider the importance of making traffic patterns in the classroom efficient and nondisruptive. During transitions between tasks children should move into the adjacent areas and not crisscross throughout the room.

7. It is important to identify the characteristics of the environment outside the classroom in which the skills you are teaching will be practiced. For example, if you wish the children to practice reading at home, a stimulated living room setting in the classroom where reading is taught may facilitate the transfer of this activity to the home.

BE PRACTICAL IN YOUR PLANS FOR GROUPING CHILDREN

While it is true that individualized instruction is desirable in many instances, such an arrangement is simply not possible within most classrooms. Instruction in small groups can possess many of the advantages of individualized instruction and, in fact, be more efficient. Do not be too fastidious about the similarity of children in a group. Obviously, we recommend that you group by achievement from your analysis of each child's performance. You may have to compromise—not all children will be at the same level. Some will be slightly behind and others will be slightly ahead. Some children will be placed in a less than optimum grouping situation just to be manageable. As a general rule, try not to have more than three groups operating at any one time in your classroom.

INSTRUCTIONAL MATERIALS

Teachers are often rushed to select instruction materials at either the beginning or the end of the school year. In haste, teachers will order materials on the basis of whatever catalog happens to be available, whether a salesperson is handy, or whether some other teacher has told them that a particular device is interesting. The combination of sales pitch and the sheer number of available materials leaves most teachers in a quandary over how to make the best selection.

We probably need not emphasize the importance of instructional materials. Along with instructional strategies, they are the essence of teaching. To help you select the most appropriate instructional devices and materials, we suggest the following guidelines, which have been derived from learning theory and research. We have attempted to provide a rather comprehensive group of suggestions because of the critical role materials play in the instructional program.

1. Materials should specify objectives for performance in explicit behavioral terms that allow for reliable measurement to assess student's achievement.

2. The material should be organized in such a way that one can teach and test for unit mastery, that is, achievement of groups of skills arrangement in a progressively more difficult sequence.

3. Success is probable at each step in the sequence. The steps should be small enough so that students can succeed and not be frustrated because of inordinately large gaps between skills objectives.

4. There are explicit criteria for success at each step, which the student will have to demonstrate to be considered competent at each step.

5. Pretests are available and evaluative checks for progress are built into the materials. These provide not only checks for the child but feedback for the teacher, who must be alert to the need for adjust-

ing instruction and establishing the child's proper location within the system.

6. Opportunities for positive reinforcement are integral to the materials. Reinforcement should follow the successful accomplishment of an objective and should be either provided by the teacher or intrinsic to the materials. For example, the use of humor or relatively easy materials should follow more difficult materials in the total sequence, providing built-in rewards for persistence.

7. No punishment, even of a subtle variety, should be involved in the materials. For example, poor sequencing may punish the student because of frustration in not being able to accomplish successful objectives.

8. Materials should allow for the use of standardized signals or cues for responses by students. This is especially important in materials that involve interaction between student and teacher where students are expected to answer or repeat during the lesson. In the Distar Reading Program, for example, the teacher must learn certain hand signals to cue the students concerning when and how to respond. This avoids confusion, situations in which the same child always is first to respond, and other forms of instructional inefficiency.

9. The materials should encompass a wide range of accomplishments and not be restricted to a range of skills. In the former instance, all students can use the materials at a level appropriate to their current status. Materials with a restricted range are usually more intensive and detailed in their steps and sequence and often more useful in remedial situations.

10. Students should be able to become actively involved with the materials. Active participation, which requires frequent responding in the selection of answers and in the production of correct behavior, is much preferred over materials in which the child is a passive agent. Programmed workbooks, which require student responses of various types throughout the material, are generally superior to materials that solicit answers at the end of a lesson.

11. Materials should provide for frequent and varied repetition of correct behavior. Repetition has been demonstrated to be one of the most critical factors in learning. It should not be boring formal drill but rather should require the review of previously achieved skills.

12. Materials should hold the interest of children at different ages and at various levels of socialization.

13. Materials should incorporate remedial provisions that will return a child who has failed at a certain level to a prescribed level for correction.

14. Students should be able to use the material or device independently or with a teacher's aide or another child, not just with a teacher.

15. Multisensory involvement should be possible. Generally speaking, learning is enhanced when several senses are involved, as in materials that present a concept visually, aurally, and tactilely. However, children who don't have use of certain senses should not be penalized by the materials.

16. The materials can be used with groups as well as with individuals. It is important to know how large a group is feasible.

17. Is cheating possible? Certain programmed texts, for example, include answers so that students can peek at the answers, fill in the blanks, and claim to have completed the assignment.

18. If you are considering purchasing a mechanical instructional device, the available materials for use with the machine should meet the aforementioned programming criteria. Some machines are marvelous, but the programs for software are instructionally inferior.

19. Teachers should be able to make up their own programs or extend existing ones for use with the teaching machine or material.

20. Is at-home involvement possible for the pupil? Some materials contain take-home exercises and projects in which students can practice skills alone or with their parents.

21. The material or device should fit in with other parts of the daily program. Such material should be of high priority for purchase as opposed to programs that have specialized and relatively little routine use.

22. Research data are available on the effectiveness of the materials. What is the source of these data—the publisher, the author, or relatively unbiased sources?

23. If the material requires extensive teacher training, this should be considered before purchase of the materials. For example, the Distar series assumes teacher's participation in an intensive workshop.

24. Teachers can and do become excited about using the materials. No matter how good the materials are with students, if the teacher does not enjoy them or is irritated when using them, the materials will inevitably end up in storage.

25. The materials are easily transportable. Can they be borrowed? Can students take them home? Do they have to be located in a special place?

26. The materials are cost-effective, including the initial cost and the cost of repairs or replacements. Are the materials durable and reusable?

Few materials will meet all of the above criteria. Nevertheless, materials should be selected that meet as many of these guidelines as possible.

PROGRAM PLANNING

There are many published curricula in special education that can be drawn upon as resources for content, sequence, and activities (Bereiter and Englemann, 1966; Goldstein, 1969; Meyen, 1972; Stephens, 1970; Tawney, 1980). Each has its own philosophical rationale, range of content, degree of specificity, and practical relevance. There are strengths and weaknesses in all of them, and you should not feel wedded to any single approach because of its current popularity. As you analyze these curricula and decide for yourself the kinds of instructional focus you believe to be appropriate, consider the following:

1. After you have determined the major subject areas to be included in the curriculum, progressively differentiate each curricular topic into subunits and sequence them according to their dependence on each other.

2. Make sure that your program of study stretches far enough to include the lower and upper boundaries of skills likely to be exhibited by the children. Use these boundaries to establish a list of skills to be acquired by the entire group. As each child demonstrates each skill, he or she can be checked off and proceed to the next skill in the sequence.

3. Keep in mind the range of learning objectives that will predictably be required of each child as the youngster moves toward independent living. Your curriculum should be relevant to the child's future. In addition to the usual tool subjects, the teacher's objectives should focus on social, vocational, personal, and family dimensions. Sex education, respect for authority, proper grooming and personal hygiene, and prevocational skills should be as important as skills in the tool subjects.

4. At the beginning of each school year, the teacher should focus immediately on social, personal, and attitudinal competencies that are fundamental to further instruction. For example, many children need to be taught how to pay attention, follow instruction, take turns, volunteer, and avoid being disruptive toward other children. The teacher should definitely decide on the ground rules for operation of the classroom before the students arrive. These are the dos and don'ts of the classroom, and they should be clearly posted and discussed with the children almost daily initially and as frequently thereafter as necessary. Start out with only a few rules. Academic

Objective Number	General Objective	Pretest	Date Begun	Date Ended	Strategy*	Evaluation Technique*	Comments: Activities: Materials:
0-3-1	Meeting social conventions and developing values						
0-3-1.1	States simple rule when asked e.g., "What do we do before snack?" "Pick up toys."				5	3	
0-3-1.2	Follows a simple rule concerning care of materials, e.g., picks up toys before snack				3, 5, 6	3	
0-3-1.3	Follows a simple rule concerning treatment of pets and/or other children, e.g., doesn't squeeze gerbil				3, 5, 6	3	
0-3-1.4	Follows a simple rule concerning eating behavior, e.g., saying please when asking for food				3, 5	3	
0-3-1.5	Follows a simple rule concerning courtesy, e.g., listens while children "share" news				3, 5, 6	3	
0-3-1.6	Enjoys performing simple tasks independently with minimal prompting by others, e.g., tries to zip own coat				1, 3, 5	3	
0-3-1.7	Enjoys demonstrating and practicing newly learned skills, e.g., will zip others' zippers				1, 5, 6	3	
0-3-1.8	Enjoys completing tasks, e.g., assembling a puzzle				9, 1, 5	3	

*See Comp-Curriculum Guide (Willoughby-Herb, Neisworth, & Laub, 1977)

FIGURE 8-1
Sample page of the
HICOMP Curriculum
(Willoughby-Herb &
Neisworth, 1982)

skills should be introduced gradually as social and personal skills are shaped.

5. Break down curricular goals into explicit and specific performance objectives. This breakdown will require the development of lists of behavioral objectives which permit measurement of their attainment. Such objectives become the content for your lesson plans. This process is called "task analysis."

Not all these suggestions can be accomplished before the children arrive in your classroom, but the overall curriculum plan, the determination of the subunits, and initial sets of behavioral objectives for the first few weeks of the school year should be developed. This degree of organization will minimize confusion and frustration during those first few weeks.

The individualized educational program usually requires the following information although the specifics may vary from state to state:

PART III
SPECIAL EDUCATION
INTERVENTION

1. Present educational level of the child

2. Annual goals with related short-term objectives

3. Methods and materials to be used in accomplishing the objectives

4. Evaluative procedures to be employed to detect progress on each objective

5. Specification of criteria of success for each objective

6. Any special services arranged for the child and the degree of involvement scheduled for the youngster

7. Date when special services are to begin and their expected duration

Every handicapped child must have an IEP *before* entry into special education: the IEP must indicate the need for special education. Once placed with the special arrangements, the child's placement status must be reviewed at least annually. Upon reevaluation, a new program may be devised that includes more or less special educational programming.

TEACHING METHODS

CONSIDER HOW CONSEQUENCES AFFECT BEHAVIOR

It is well established that the kinds of events that occur immediately after a behavior exert great influence on the future of that behavior. Behaviors that are ignored are likely to be weakened, whereas behaviors that are followed by rewarding outcomes will subsequently occur with greater frequency, intensity, and duration. Consequently, the teacher should study the advantages in controlling consequences as a means of accomplishing curricular objectives. The techniques involved in the effective management of consequences in the classroom include the following:

1. Built-in reinforcement: The teacher should select or design lessons that have built into them high interest and pleasant consequences for participation. Humor, improbable events, current activities, and the use of actual names of children within the group can be woven into a lesson to maintain their involvement.

2. The Premack Principle: Activities that children do not find exciting should be followed by high-interest activities if performance in the low-preference activities has been at a satisfactory level. Don't cluster music, art, recess, and snack time together at the beginning of the day, only to be followed by what are frequently low-preference activities, such as reading, arithmetic, spelling, and writing. Tasks should be appropriately alternated. What is a high-preference activity for one child may not be for another. Assess the situation carefully and sequence the activities somewhat individually, as is practical.

3. Social reinforcement: Attention, praise, and approval from an adult are powerful social reinforcers for children. While it is difficult, teachers must learn to refrain from paying attention to incorrect or inappropriate behavior during lessons and at other times. Be sure to demonstrate immediate approval of even small instances of progress on the part of children. Your approval can take the form of verbal praise, a pat on the back, a smile, or shaking the child's hand. Saying something positive about a youngster within his or her hearing may help to increase a particular behavior.

4. Charting progress: When the teacher or child keeps track of individual accomplishments, the mere charting of such progress often serves as a reinforcement. In a sense, it is like charting your own weight loss while on a diet.

5. Material rewards: Much has been written about the efficacy of using prizes to reward certain progressive behaviors. Trinkets, candy, games, and various other forms of material goods can serve as primary reinforcers. Token economies have been widely used in special education settings. Poker chips, stamps, check marks, or holes punched in a card can be accumulated by a student and exchanged for privileges and tangible rewards. A system of this sort enables a teacher to "credit" children quickly and thus reinforce their performance, without disrupting the classroom routine by having to immediately provide a material reward. Usually children cash in their tokens at a convenient time during the day.

All of these approaches to management of consequences can be employed to boost and maintain motivation and persistence in the classroom. Frequently parents can be trained in using these same approaches in the home in order to effect transfer from one setting to another. One of the important goals in using these rewards is to move children from dependence on material rewards to social rewards and, eventually, to the rewards associated with achievements of the task itself. This movement varies from child to child and situation to situation. A youngster may generally be motivated by achievement of a task but still require extrinsic motivation for attempting new and more difficult tasks.

STUDY CURRENT INSTRUCTIONAL TECHNIQUES

Instructional approaches have been presented in the literature of special education, and specific teaching strategies have been developed that are held to be effective with various categories of instructional problems. For example, there are numerous approaches for responding to perceptual-motor disorders—each of which has its own idiosyncrasies. The greatest diversity of approaches occurs in the treatment of behavior disorders. Many of the people espousing these approaches disagree among themselves. Many of the approaches are promoted with evangelistic fervor, and many have very little empirical validity. We do not mean to imply that these techniques are without merit. There are, however, at least two issues that must be clarified before one can have confidence in using them.

First, most of the approaches that have been developed are supposed to have specific and differential utility for children within a specific category of disability. Certain perceptual-motor approaches are presumed to be applicable to children with learning disabilities and not to youngsters with mental retardation. There are reading techniques for those who are emotionally disturbed, others for the retarded, and still others for slow learners. But this categorical specificity of instructional techniques is undocumented, unwarranted, and inefficient.

Second, portions of each instructional approach are undoubtedly effective; however, the segments contained in each have not been separately analyzed. One is usually faced with the choice of adopting a whole approach or selecting segments from various programs that have face validity.

There are some common characteristics in almost all of the prominent instructional approaches that have been developed for dealing with exceptional children. Many of these features come from learning theory, and the probable effectiveness of these various instructional approaches depends on the extent to which they incorporate the major principles of learning. In the following list we have identified a number of the most prominent of these principles which have applicability for effective instruction across traditional disability categories and instructional situations.

1. Identify teaching targets: In an earlier section we discussed the great importance of specifying clear instructional objectives. This is an important first step in whatever approach you select.

2. Provide motivation: A fundamental of any teaching-learning situation is that students be excited, interested, attentive, and eager to participate. A major component of the teaching task is to arrange for motivation rather than taking for granted that it will occur spontaneously. Management of consequences, especially the role of positive reinforcement and incentive programming, has been discussed as a primary means for motivational control. Do not lose sight of the fact that continued reinforcement can be accentuated or gradually withdrawn as appropriate behavior becomes established.

3. Arrange for repetition and practice: There is no question that repeated presentation of instructional stimuli is crucial to good teaching. Repetition can be multisensory; that is, stimuli can be presented visually, aurally, or tactilely. Generally speaking, multisensory repetition will enhance learning.

    Likewise, children should be given numerous opportunities to practice making responses. Multiresponse practice by students will help to consolidate learning. Children should practice correct responses by writing, speaking, or even demonstrating. A related consideration is to have the newly learned skill practiced in a variety of contexts. Keep in mind the need for the child to be able to generalize responses to different situations. Make sure to provide opportunities for youngsters to repeat and apply skills, once they are learned, in subsequent portions of your curriculum throughout the year. In summary, practice of correct responses should occur in three dimensions: in various response modes, in different situations, and intermittently throughout the school year. Since repetition is a vital part of instructional techniques, do not allow repetition of errors to occur.

4. Use shaping procedures: A common characteristic of most instructional approaches is the incorporation of a sequence from easy to hard. To assure the smooth progress of students, learning objectives and tasks should be ordered in terms of increasing difficulty. Students should be rewarded as they approximate achievement of each objective. Be patient but persistent; reinforce any sign of progress no matter how slight.

5. Be consistent: Perhaps one of the most devastating errors teachers and parents can make is to be inconsistent in their approach to children. Use consistent and standard stimulus cues for behavior you wish to establish and encourage. There are standard hand cues that can be used to signal the children to pay attention or to speak out. Certain activities can be scheduled for consistent times of the day, routine should be established at the outset of the second year, and verbal instructions must be the same from one time to the next in order to minimize confusion. Consider the possible ambiguity in the directions as perceived by a child in the following activity. Teachers may want a child to add $2 + 2$ and use the following inconsistent phrases at different times: "2 and 2 are 4," "2 plus 2 is 4," "2 added to 2 is 4," "the sum of 2 and 2 is 4." This is obviously perplexing to children who haven't learned the identity and meaning of the various terms. Therefore, choose one consistent phrasing at the outset until the skill is learned and then begin to introduce synonyms or variations.

A major dimension that demands consistency is the way the teacher reacts to behaviors. The same behavior should not at different times be rewarded, ignored, or punished depending on the mood of the teacher. Establishing new learning requires the consistent use of positive reinforcement. Only after the behavior is well established should you consider using reinforcement on a variable basis. Likewise, behaviors that you choose to punish should be punished in every instance. Do not let the youngsters get away with unwanted behavior without your reacting in an appropriate and consistent fashion. Finally, if the decision has been reached to ignore certain behaviors, technically termed "extinction," it would be a big mistake to attend to the behaviors from time to time.

6. Reduce the child's dependence on you: One of your primary goals as a special educator is to develop independence in the learner. At the beginning of an instructional sequence use consistent cues. For example, you may ask each child to "put your finger on the little hand; it tells you what time it is." "What time is it?" Gradually you may fade out the initial prompting so that eventually the youngster will state the correct time with the question, "What time is it?" In helping children put on their coats, help them through most of the sequence and then let them do the last step themselves. Gradually complete less of the task, letting the children do more and more of the activity. Similarly, children should become independent of you as the primary source for reinforcement. Associate tangible rewards with social incentives and gradually shift from contrived to more natural reinforcers. It is just as wrong to "crutch-trap" a child as to deny him the crutch in the first place. Finally, consider the advantages of having children work independently or with other children without your immediate presence. Your teacher's aide can be used in this regard as well. This will serve to increase the probability that the child will continue to progress with other adults and not just when you are available.

7. Continuously evaluate: We have already stressed the central role of evaluations of progress. It cannot be separated from proper instructional techniques.

For details on what to look for in a good instructional program, we refer you to *Evaluating Educational Environments* (Smith, Neisworth, and Greer, 1978). This paperback tells you what to look for and how to evaluate the instructional setting, methods, materials, social circumstances, and community resources.

AVOID DEAD TIME

Like a good play or television production, every minute of instructional time is important. Unplanned time will lead students to be restless and teachers to be haphazard. With exceptional children particularly, thorough organization is critical because greater focus must be given to intentional instruction. In short, you cannot leave skill acquisition to chance.

Often dead time results from teachers not having previously organized the classroom. For example, before school begins decisions should be reached on the location of materials, the things that will be in the students' desks, and the placement of routine school supplies.

PROGRAM EVALUATION

Reliable, valid, and systematic measurement is an essential activity of any science, basic or applied. Like the civil engineer, physician, or other technical professional, the educator must employ procedures and instruments of measurement that provide sufficiently precise information to accomplish professional goals. The educator's goals, of course, center around bringing about progressive and positive changes in students' competence. Teaching must be assessed by its intended result: learning. A teacher has not taught when children have not learned. Measurement, then, is crucial not only for gauging the student's status and progress but also for guiding the teacher's behavior.

Unfortunately, measurement in education has been predominately *normative* and *summative*. Children have most frequently been compared with other children in terms of performance rather than with their own past performance. Age norms and grade norms are examples of measures of average attainment with which children are compared. These normative measures are usually administered in the schools at the beginning or at the end of the school year. Summative evaluation is generally unsatisfactory for at least two reasons. First, end-of-year achievement tests, for example, do not provide enough detail to enable the teacher to pinpoint the specific learning problem or steps that may be responsible for lack of progress. Second, year-end testing is simply too late. Teachers discover after the school year is over that certain children show marked incompetence in areas where they could have been helped had the teacher been supplied that information in the earlier part of the school year.

The fundamental solution to the problems of normative and summative testing is not to do away with these types of evaluation, since they do have value, but to employ an ongoing program of *formative evaluation* based on competencies. Briefly, this involves the identification of specific objectives or competencies and frequent evaluation or checks on progress to provide the feedback that makes possible continual adjustments in methods and materials.

In addition to deciding on evaluative procedures (that is, formative or summative, based on competency or norms), the major content areas and priorities for measurement must be determined. Not everything can be measured in the same detail. Decisions will have to be made about what is important to evaluate, when certain skills should be assessed, and how or to what extent they must be measured. Making these decisions will certainly depend upon a number of factors, and no two teachers will pursue exactly the same program of evaluation. However, the following recommendations may assist in at least focusing attention on the issues or concerns involved before you become preoccupied with the day-to-day problems of the classroom.

1. Regard achievement, intelligence, and aptitude tests as global measures of the student's current status. Examine the results to provide suggestions for curriculum emphasis.

2. Supplement the formal achievement tests with your own informal assessments of each child's competence in each major subject area—

reading, language, writing, and arithmetic. Complete the initial formal and informal assessment before you begin regular systematic instruction toward specific objectives. Indeed, the objectives for your instructional programs are derived from the initial assessments.

3. Identify and measure social behavior critical to the smooth functioning of the educational program. Initial estimates of punctuality, honesty, cooperativeness, politeness, acceptance of disappointment, and other social and emotional behaviors may be difficult to obtain. It is difficult to define such terms clearly enough to permit reliable measurement. However, it is worth the effort because the social and emotional behavior of children often makes or breaks their careers in the classroom.

4. Decide how formative evaluation will be accomplished. Some teachers make daily checks of progress on what is presumably being taught. It is not possible, nor rquired, to check on every child in every learning area every day. Rather, many teachers reserve five minutes at the end of each instructional session to find out quickly what children can and cannot demonstrate in terms of the skills that are emphasized in each lesson. Some teachers systematically select, for example, five children each day for more comprehensive checks. In this fashion, not every child is checked daily, not too much time elapses between checks, and the burden on the teacher is not quite as great.

5. Consider the various options for collecting data. You may want to observe and record the behavior of just one or two children all day, especially if they are your major problems. Usually, however, it is most feasible to collect samples of performance. You may decide to record a particular behavior at a particular time for all or some of the children. For example, volunteering to answer or to accept tasks can be counted and recorded just during cleanup time. Similarly, you can set aside five minutes sometime during the morning and afternoon periods of seat work to scan the room to see which children are attending to their work.
Not only should the time and place for measurement be considered, but the type of data. You should consider the use of frequency and duration data, checklists, and rating scales. Sometimes simply counting the frequency of a behavior is the easiest and best measure. The number of times selected pupils get out of their seat during an hour, the number of words they read during a ten-minute session, and the frequency with which they say "please" and "thank you" during the day are instances of frequency data. Duration is sometimes the most practical measure of a behavior, especially when children seem to take too much time to do a particular assignment. Objective checklists, on which attainment of specified skills can be marked off and dated, are helpful in providing a record of a student's progress. Often

you will want to rate or judge a skill rather than count it, especially if the skill deals with social characteristics that are difficult to define as precisely as would be required to permit frequency counts. "Tolerance to criticisms," "initiative during free play," and "cooperativeness on the playground" are examples of behavior that can be rated. After this behavior has been somewhat objectified, measures of greater precision than ratings can be employed.

6. Finally, review the possibilities for helping in conducting evaluations of students. Sometimes students can test themselves, especially if you use self-instructional, programmed materials. A teacher's aide can be quite valuable as an assistant in this respect. Also, do not overlook the possibility of having one student check another's progress.

Evaluation can be comprehensive and frequent, and it need not be confusing or burdensome if the teacher takes advantage of possible shortcuts and assistance. Perhaps the best admonition is "a little at a time and a little every day"—systematic, routine checking of the progress of a few children in a few dimensions each day will supply the necessary information for a comprehensive assessment of each student's progress so that teaching strategies and materials can be monitored and modified.

SUMMARY
Exceptional children need a lot of help from their teachers, parents, and friends. A teacher can be of greatest help when that teacher is truly competent at fundamental instructional practices. Loving children, caring about their welfare, feeling warm and open, and so on are all desirable qualities—but not enough. Just as we all want a doctor who is an expert at helping us to recover from injury or illness, so in teaching, the educator must become a master of the methods and materials of instruction. This chapter has presented a number of considerations essential to the education of exceptional children. These considerations can be summarized as follows: First, teacher *attitude* is crucial. Working with an exceptional child often demands an obliviousness to what others may say about the child. A positive expectation that you can and will assist the child to develop new capabilities is the best posture for you to take. Secondly, the teacher must *plan* and prepare for excellence of instruction. This means surveying your resources, considering the opinions of others, selecting materials, preparing your assistants, designing the classroom layout, and selecting carefully the objectives and goals for each child. Third, the teacher must *interact expertly* with each child. Skill at teacher-child interactions includes competence in using materials, providing cues and reinforcers, modeling, and maintaining discipline. The methods of instruction and management must be mastered. Fourth, to be effective, the teacher must monitor and *record child progress*. Formative and summative evaluations, through formal and informal means, allow the

teacher to adjust and change instruction for optimum effect. Teaching without measurement is somewhat like building a house without checking levels, lengths, and stresses. Such construction—and teaching—is not to be trusted! Finally, the contemporary educator must *plan for the child's departure* and use techniques to enhance transfer of training, for example, generalization of skills to future settings. We want our efforts with children to last beyond our time with them and beyond our restricted setting. Teachers must involve parents and others who are or will be interacting with the children. It may seem like a mammoth task to be an excellent teacher, but any real professional must learn competence in the tools of the trade—and basic instructional practices are the keystone in the building of teacher competence.

Robert M. Smith
John T. Neisworth

CHAPTER 9
SETTINGS
AND SERVICES
FOR SPECIAL EDUCATION

(Courtesy of Chuck Zovko.)

The environment within which the special education program takes place is of utmost importance. After the relevant characteristics and educational needs of the child have been identified, a decision must be made as to where the child should be assigned for optimum progress. The personal and environmental arrangements needed for a child to function within a more normal context is at the heart of the placement issue in special education. This chapter will consider three related issues: the concept of normalization, the variety of placement alternatives, and the physical facilities required by exceptional individuals. We will close with a section on community services.

MAXIMIZING NORMALIZATION

Wolfensberger defines the principle of normalization as "utilization of means which are as culturally normative as possible, in order to establish and/or maintain personal behaviors and characteristics which are as culturally normative as possible" (1972, p. 28). Figure 9-1 describes the interrelationship of several key concepts associated with normalization. The model has two clusters of factors. At Level 1 a person interacting with the environment (here called "antecedent factors") results in some response ("behavior"). Behavior is always followed by some type of reinforcement or reaction ("consequences"). Of course, we would anticipate an increase or decrease in the future behavior of the individual depending on whether the consequences were positive or negative.

We also believe that it is possible to think of behavior as having qualitative and quantitative differences. This will be illustrated shortly.

Level 2 describes different degrees of usualness ranging from extremely atypical ("A") to very typical, natural, or normal ("G"). These degrees are pertinent for each of the major dimensions listed in Level 1. Every person

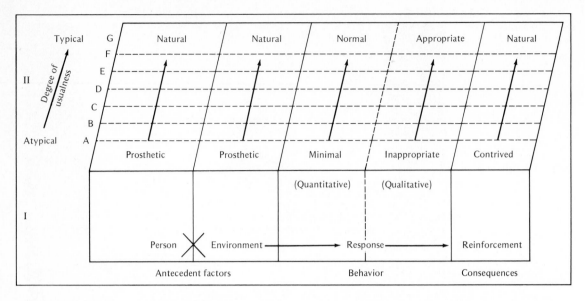

Natural	Natural	Normal	Appropriate	Natural
Prosthetic	Prosthetic	Minimal	Inappropriate	Contrived
		(Quantitative)	(Qualitative)	

Person ✕ Environment ⟶ Response ⟶ Reinforcement

Antecedent factors / Behavior / Consequences

Degree of usualness: Typical G F E D C B A Atypical

FIGURE 9-1
The interrelationship of
factors related to
normalization.

has different needs for special environmental arrangements and prostheses according to the extent and degree of performance deviation. Herb, for example, who needs glasses, an artificial arm and leg, and a hearing aid may have unusual prosthetic needs in contrast to others. His extreme needs might result in his being classified at the "B" degree of usualness. Less extreme prosthetic needs would be assigned to one of the levels closer to the typical or more natural circumstances. This same concept can be applied to the environmental category. We have also suggested that the environment will need to be arranged in certain ways according to an individual child's instructional requirements. An environment designed to accommodate prostheses might be illustrated by a special classroom for blind children in which braille readers and writers are present, special desks are needed, and other educational devices are required to promote progressively more appropriate behavior by the child.

We believe that it is possible to discern two characteristics of responses—quantitative and qualitative. In the first instance, one's response might range from "minimal" to "normal." To the question, "How are you today?", a child might respond, "Okay," or at the other extreme, "Fine, thank you; how are you?" Both are appropriate responses: one is adequate, but minimal; the other is quite normal, but relatively more complex. To the same question, another child might answer, "Mashed potatoes," an obviously inappropriate response.

Finally, differences exist in the degree of usualness of the reinforcer, or consequences of the behavior (see Figure 9-1). At the lower end, there are contrived, relatively unnatural reinforcers that are used with persons as a way of strengthening or decreasing behavior. Candies, trinkets, tokens, gold stars, and other types of tangible objects might fit into the contrived category if the setting within which they are used and the dispensing procedures fall outside the usual classroom routines. At the other end, there are natural reinforcers one typically uses to control behavior. A simple touch, a kind word, and a frown fall into this category if they are used in a natural way.

IMPLICATIONS FOR TEACHING

We will now turn to the implications that this model has for the concept of normalization. First and foremost, we want every exceptional child (whatever the type and level of disability) to respond to the environment in a fashion that approximates appropriate behavior within the child's cultural context. For the youngster to respond in a progressively more normal fashion, it may be necessary to provide certain types of individual prostheses, to modify the environment to accommodate children with prostheses, or to provide reinforcers that are unnatural or contrived. In short, teachers must be willing to provide whatever prostheses and artificial consequences are necessary to encourage development of a response repertoire that is progressively more normal.

As an example, suppose you were interested in helping Gloria learn to follow verbal directions that require some movement on her part. Assume that Gloria has some motor problem and a significant visual defect: Your goal for her is that she follow directions in ways which are normal and appropriate. To aid her in achieving this normal level of functioning it may be necessary to provide magnification for her as well as some type of apparatus to aid her in getting around, such as a standing walker. It may also be necessary to create an environment that will make it possible for her to accomplish the expected behavior. For example, a special ramp, carpets on the floor, a room with open space, desks that are secured to the floor, and frosted window glass might be used to minimize the negative features of her environment. These will make it possible for her to function as desired. And finally, you may have to begin your instructional program with Gloria by providing motivation—immediate, continuous, and tangible reinforcers such as small pieces of cracker—as she begins to develop skills in the target area. Later, as the tasks are accomplished, you may be able to restructure the type and delivery of the reinforcers. Helen, another girl with the same group of problems, may need an even greater modification of the environment than Gloria. But Helen may require fewer prostheses in order to acquire the very same group of competencies.

We are saying, then, that the primary factor in fostering normalization is absolute focus on the individual. Do not lose sight of the fact that as behaviors change and situations vary, you will need to change the types of alterations required to maintain and upgrade the skills that have been established.

Notice, however, that the first part of Wolfensberger's definition stresses that the means that are used to establish and encourage normal behavior should be as culturally normal as possible. To normalize certainly means to focus on behavior, but you must also consider what types of procedures you

Early social integration of handicapped and nonhandicapped children may be the best way to maximize normalization and minimize social stigma. (*Courtesy of Jim Lukens.*)

must use in order to try to normalize behavior. In most cultures it is unusual for a person to have certain types of prostheses, to operate within a highly artificial environment, or to be constantly reinforced with tangible objects. These unusual circumstances, individually and collectively, call attention to the exceptional children, can result in a negative attitude toward the child on the part of others, and ultimately will cause drops in the youngster's performance. Moreover, such circumstances result in the child's exhibiting lowered self-esteem and abnormal behavior. Thus, normalization ultimately means that teachers must strive to reduce the atypical character of the visible prostheses by slowly and meticulously moving in the direction of a natural and normal situation without appreciably compromising their goals for the child or allowing regression in behavior to earlier levels of performance. Further, the concept of normalization also suggests that reinforcement programs must gradually but systematically move toward a natural, more typical situation. The more contrived, the less normal the situation.

Complete normalization involves the physical and social integration of the exceptional individual into the normal environment. Ultimately, integration can be said to have occurred when an exceptional individual lives with members of the cultural group in a normal domicile within the community, when there is access to all of the privileges and services that are available to others, when there is the respect of fellow citizens, and when the exceptional person is accepted unreservedly by peers and other persons in the culture. In order for this to occur, physical integration is necessary, but not sufficient in itself. Once the individual has been integrated physically, social and cultural normalization are largely dependent on the attitude and actions of the members of the community. Thus, legislation cannot guarantee the complete integration of the handicapped. Instead the impact of such legislation is to increase the probability of complete normalization by ensuring the first steps towards that ideal.

Physical Integration

Wolfensberger (1972) has defined four factors in the physical integration of a facility and, ultimately, of an exceptional person into the community:

1. The services needed by an exceptional person should be located in the community, so that the individual can be provided for within a normal and natural context. Isolation is to be avoided in every instance.

2. The services to be provided should fit into the appropriate area; that is, halfway houses ought to be in residential areas, and sheltered workshops should be in industrial settings.

3. Transportation should be readily available among all of the components of the system.

4. Exceptional persons in a community should be organized and provided for in such a way that they can become amalgamated into the total fabric of the community. Normalization will not occur if exceptional individuals tend to cluster, group, or become congregated. This principle strongly suggests the need to diversify services throughout the community, supporting the use of small residential centers as opposed to large institutions, and providing services to all members of the community within the same facility.

Social Integration

The social integration of the exceptional person into the community depends on a number of factors: the attitudes of members of the community concerning the value of all human beings and their rightful place in society, and the attitudes of the members of the community toward integration of the handicapped into the community; and the extent to which physical integration of services has been realized according to these attitudes.

How a program or service is labeled will dictate how the consumers of the services are viewed and accepted by all facets of the community. If a school, workshop, residence, school bus, or recreation center is identified as a facility for the mentally retarded or handicapped, the deviant or atypical, you can be sure that the community will not allow social integration of all people to take place. People will simply perceive the consumers and the place as deviant and something to be avoided. The building should not be set apart by either location or architecture. Services for exceptional individuals should be available within the context of all services provided within the community. For the good of all, educational programs for exceptional children should be located within the usual school facility, with ample opportunities provided for personal interaction among all who use the facility.

These children spend about half their school day in regular classes and half in a special class with a special education expert. (*President's Committee on Mental Retardation.*)

BENEFITS OF NORMALIZATION

When the physical and social integration of exceptional children into the community is possible—when appropriate prostheses are provided for the person and the environment is modified appropriately, and when the process of integration is continually monitored and revised—numerous benefits accrue.

1. Members of the community begin to learn tolerance for those with deviations, they relate to exceptional individuals with increased frequency and commitment, they learn of the important contributions that each person can make to the advantage of all, and they become more willing to participate in the various aspects of community life. Respect for all is encouraged.

2. Interaction with the normal public provides the exceptional person with opportunities to:
   a. learn acceptable behavior within a natural context;
   b. practice making responses to actual problems and issues within a meaningful social context;
   c. learn to tolerate differences in performance, attitudes, appearance, interests, and aptitude of others;
   d. learn to accept themselves when they see that others accept them.

3. Integration promotes equal treatment and services for all citizens whenever needed.

4. The possibility will be reduced that exceptional persons will be placed in atypical environments and managed by individuals who frequently serve to exacerbate their handicaps.

5. Integration helps prevent the secondary emotional disabilities that result from physical and social isolation in the community.

6. Integration reduces the possibility that exceptional persons will be blamed for a deviant performance by placing the responsibility for enhancing the level of function of all citizens on the citizens themselves.

7. Integration is completely compatible with the entire philosophy of habilitation and rehabilitation. Neither can be realized without physical and social integration.

8. Integration signals the end of an era when the community felt obliged to provide separate services to separate groups who were classified according to artificial criteria. With an integrated system, it will no longer be logical to have separate community counseling programs, medical services, or fund-raising drives for each of the many types of handicaps that are represented in a community.

9. Not only is integration functionally efficient, but it has multiple advantages from a cost-benefit point of view.

10. Integration suggests that the fundamental principles involved in identifying, understanding, and effectively managing the problems of human beings are appropriate for all types of people and their problems and needs.

ALTERNATIVES IN EDUCATIONAL PLACEMENT

SEGREGATED EDUCATION

Only since the late 1960s have educators become especially concerned about normalization. Before then special educators seemed to be more concerned about providing an instructional environment that would increase the academic performances of children with educational problems and be economical for school systems. Thus, during the post–World War II era most programs were developed with the belief that special schools and special classes within regular schools could best serve both the children and the schools. Additionally, the belief prevailed that placing exceptional children apart from other youngsters would promote more rapid acquisition of skills, satisfy parents that the schools were providing an appropriate program of instruction, and provide an environment in which instruction could be delivered efficiently by a teacher who was presumed to possess special skills and understanding of the needs of exceptional children—all at no apparent expense to the children and teachers in the regular classes.

This organizational plan for the delivery of education to exceptional children quickly became instituted throughout the country and was supported by practitioners, academicians, school administrators, parents, psychologists, national organizations, and various funding agencies. This plan became tradition, the deficiencies were virtually overlooked or ignored, and a sense of satisfaction and accomplishment became evident among special educators. Regular educators felt good about the approach as well. Their nagging and most recalcitrant instructional problems were presumably being taken care of somewhere else. The schools were now providing for children who could profit from special educational programming. Presumably, those who were not enrolled in either special schools or special classes could not be helped through this unique instructional intervention and thus should be excluded. Further, it was argued in certain quarters that public education did not have the responsibility to train or educate the "uneducable." This belief resulted in the systematic and arbitrary exclusion and suspension of children. Many public institutions for the mentally retarded and mentally ill chose not to provide educational programs because their patients were viewed as being uneducable.

Sporadically, questions were raised about the wisdom of cloistering children away from their normal peers. However, the issue received special attention when it was revealed that children who were judged mentally retarded did no better academically when placed in special classes than in regular classes (Cassidy & Stanton, 1959; Mullen & Itkin, 1961; Thurstone, 1960). Immediately the ardent separatists took exception to the conclusions of these studies by noting the potential weaknesses in the design of this research, emphasizing that one should not look at academic programs alone in conducting such an assessment, and pointing out that wide discrepancies between the performance of exceptional children and normal children could only lead to rejection and further academic and psychosocial difficulties for the exceptional children (Engel, 1969; Harvey, 1969; Kidd, 1970).

Attempts were made to conduct well-controlled studies on the benefits of special versus regular classes for the mildly retarded (Goldstein, Moss, & Jordan, 1965). Basically, the findings suggested that at the end of their fourth year of schooling the groups did not differ in measures of intellectual performance, academic achievement, and social knowledge. The validity of the conclusions that were reached in this study was itself called into question (Guskin & Spicker, 1968), and the arguments for and against placement in special classes went on and on (Blatt, 1960; Christoplos & Renz, 1969; Dunn, 1968; Heber and Dever, 1970; Johnson, 1962; Jones, 1971; Kolstoe, 1972; MacMillan, 1972; Meyerowitz, 1962; Sparks & Younie, 1969).

FACTORS CAUSING REAPPRAISAL OF SEGREGATION
During the latter period of these debates, a number of events caused a relatively rapid reassessment of the philosophical bases for special education. Along with the uncertainty about the value of school systems that

1. Realization that isolation from any or all components of society not only is legally wrong but restricts the development of a person in many areas.

2. Concern about the unreliable and questionable bases on which children were identified as exceptional and were placed in special schools or classrooms without adequate justification or documentation.

3. Proof that many handicaps can be prevented and reversed, that their consequences can be minimized and managed without special equipment or unique settings, and that many of the methods which had been viewed as confined to the domain of specially trained teachers could be fully implemented with equal effectiveness by teachers of regular classes.

4. Belief that the community not only is required to provide instruction for the exceptional child but that its members should be understanding and interact with exceptional children, that is, learn about them. It was thought that this type of reciprocity should extend to all levels of society and that special education should be linked with all phases of the regular education systems.

5. Increased concern about the pressure by parents whose children were excluded from school, for reasons which in many cases were arbitrary and in spite of the clear suggestions in the literature that children with similar disorders could be helped.

6. A switch in emphasis by educators from organic characteristics, etiological patterns, and weird clinical syndromes to observable and measurable problems which are responsive to instructional intervention.

7. Demands by funding agencies for documented reports of results from recipients of funds for special education.

8. Dissatisfaction with the segmentation of services, the lack of articulation among service agencies, and the tremendous waste of resources among programs that lack comprehensiveness.

9. Belief that all children should be provided a free public school education and have equal access to the full range of resources available to everyone.

10. Realization that the educational system can and should support more than the simple alternatives of special or regular classes, that a continuum of educational programming should be provided.

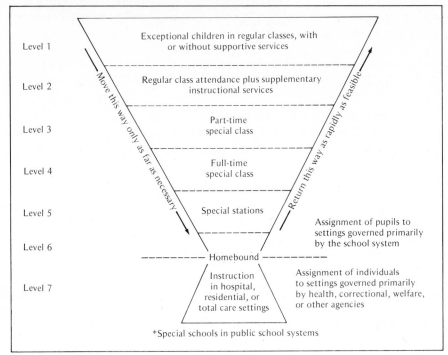

FIGURE 9-2
The "cascade" system of
special education service.
(Reprinted from Deno, E.
Special education as
developmental capital,
Exceptional Children,
1970, 37, 229–237. By
permission of The Council
for Exceptional Children.)

11. Cognizance that special education classes differ, that it is a distortion of reality to assume that special classes and regular classes can be fairly compared because of the multiple variables on which each differs within its separate category, that the behavior of the special education teacher within the classroom is of more fundamental significance than the administrative organization, and that the field has not yet identified or agreed upon what skills are required for a competent teacher of exceptional children.

A MODEL FOR EDUCATIONAL OPTIONS

Deno (1970, 1971) and her colleague Reynolds (1971) have suggested an educational framework in which instructional services for exceptional children might be organized, administered, and delivered. Dunn (1973) has elaborated on Deno's basic model. Fundamentally, Deno's cascade model suggests a range of settings within which each specific level emphasizes a unique instructional character (see Figure 9-2). Presumably, there is more commonality within each level on this continuum than among the various levels. The degree to which the environment is structured varies, with the greatest degree of special prostheses at Level 7. As one moves toward Level 1, the number, types, and complexity of special environmental arrangements decreases. In complete agreement with our concept of normalization, the Deno model emphasizes that (1) relatively fewer youngsters will be found at each succeeding level as one progresses from Level 1 to Level 7;

(2) children should not be moved downward in the system unless clear documentation is available to warrant such a move; and (3) each child should be moved upward in the system as far and as quickly as possible. In the following sections we briefly highlight the unique characteristics of each of the levels in the system.

LEVEL 1: REGULAR CLASS ASSIGNMENT

At this most integrated level, children attend regular classes with other youngsters of the same age. Because they may have functional disorders of various types and degrees, the children may require minimal adjustments in their environment that exceed the usual demands of their peers. An extra large desk, more space, a ramp into the classroom, a stairway elevator, an amplification system, special instructional materials, a braille writer, low-vision aids, a special type of chair, modifications in curricular targets, and slight alterations in instructional procedures all illustrate the kinds and degrees of supportive services that may be found in the Level 1 classes. In addition, regular-class teachers may need to consult with someone within or outside the schools to gain a better understanding of special problems that pertain to a certain child. Consultation with an educational diagnostician, special resource teacher, supervisor, reading consultant, or school psychologist should take place as often as necessary.

The key to success for an exceptional child located in a regular classroom is, of course, the teacher. The teacher attributes that will help a child in the regular classroom to succeed include:

1. Teacher's judgment of the child's capacity for progress, teacher's attitude toward having exceptional children in the classroom with other students, and the way in which they act and react toward the child.

2. The procedure the teacher uses in forecasting and dealing with inevitable problems of peer acceptance between the exceptional child and other youngsters.

3. The efforts of the teacher to maintain a reasonable and normal environment for the exceptional student while at the same time providing the unique methods and materials necessary to help the child perform better.

4. The skill of the teacher to deal with the emotional behavior and problems of the exceptional child that result from not being able to compete with other youngsters in those areas which the youngster considers to be important. The teacher must also be aware of and skillful in handling jealousies of other students when special attention is given to the exceptional child.

You can see that the regular-class teacher has a difficult and awesome responsibility, for most such classrooms will have one or more exceptional

Homebound instruction can be provided to permanently or temporarily handicapped students who are unable to attend center-based programs. (*Courtesy of Paul J. Quinn.*)

children. In addition to the teaching of routine academic skills, the regular-class teacher will usually confront a very difficult social situation. The teacher must deal with issues in a straightforward way, seek to maintain a mentally and socially healthy environment, and be alert to potential problems that could undermine the entire program and ruin the school year. In preparation for the placement of exceptional children in regular classrooms, regular-class teachers are increasingly seeking special education training as a way to prepare themselves to deal effectively with this ever-increasing range of responsibilities.

LEVEL 2: REGULAR CLASS ASSIGNMENT WITH SUPPLEMENTARY INSTRUCTIONAL SERVICES

This program option has become quite popular in the United States as a way of dealing with the instructional needs of those children who exhibit mild disorders in functioning. Such youngsters have their home room in a regular class, remaining there for most of the day, but certain portions of their instruction are provided in a resource room, which is usually located within the same school building. A trained specialist or a resource-room teacher delivers the special instruction to each child or to groups of children. As soon as a particular lesson has been completed, the child returns to the regular classroom. The special skills of the resource-room teacher may vary according to the instructional needs of the children within a given school. To a lesser degree, reading specialists, speech therapists, or counselors are like itinerant resource-room specialists or consultants.

Whatever the programming organization or emphasis a school decides upon, the whole idea behind this plan is to allow exceptional children to receive as much instruction in the regular program as possible but at the same time to provide for their individual educational needs without calling undue attention to their handicaps. Assignment to instruction by the resource-room specialist is based on performance differences and not on IQ. Thus, at any moment during a school day, children with a wide range of disabilities or disorders may well be receiving instruction at the same time, and in an identical way, *if their functional level and instructional needs are the same.*

Since most resource-room teachers are specialists in the assessment and remediation of instructional difficulties, the regular-class teachers in the school will find it helpful to ask about alternative approaches in dealing with functional exceptionalities that occur from time to time. At the very least the resource-room and regular-class teachers should share ideas and strategies that are appropriate to the children for whom they have mutual responsibility. Agreement on these matters by the teachers should be reached before and continuously throughout the program. Accurate performance data must be maintained in all settings. Types of reinforcement, alterations in the goals, and procedures of instruction should be discussed and agreed upon by all concerned. Do not assume that adequate coordination will take place without planning—the resource-room teacher should take the leadership in assuring that productive relationships occur among all teachers.

LEVEL 3: PART-TIME SPECIAL CLASS
There are certain children in every school system whose educational problems require an instructional setting that is highly specialized. When the complexity of the child's problems exceeds the expertise of the regular instructional staff in the resource room, the child may be a likely candidate for a part-time special class. A portion of the school day might be spent in either the regular class or even in a resource room.

A part-time special class will differ dramatically among school districts, and even within a given school system, according to the unique character of the population of children. It is risky for an administrator to plan for a certain number of part-time special classes and whatever unique focus each might have without knowing a great deal about which children might best be served in that type of setting. Moreover, special classes vary greatly. Differences exist among teachers in their philosophy, talents, orientation, approach, attitudes, cooperativeness, and so on. In practice, then, not only must a special education administrator be skilled in assigning children to the setting in which maximum benefits will accrue, but teachers should be matched to settings according to their own unique skills and interests. This is best exemplified in a part-time special-class program in which one teacher might specialize in language arts, another focus on social and occupational instruction, and still another emphasize the development of motor and mobility skills. Large school systems can usually afford specialization of this sort. From year to year, then, the character of the part-time special

Community centers can provide a place for meetings, workshop activities, and other social programs that serve handicapped and nonhandicapped citizens. (*President's Committee on Mental Retardation.*)

classes will change according to the children's needs and the teachers' skills.

LEVEL 4: FULL-TIME SPECIAL CLASS

School personnel are justifiably hesitant to assign children arbitrarily to full-time special education classrooms because of the possible serious consequences, some of which have been alluded to in earlier sections of this book. Among the most obvious is that in many school systems children who are assigned to special classes are left there without ever being considered for an alternative placement. Then there is always the problem that special classes do not provide an adequate level of integration with other segments of the school and community. This stifles normalization. It is difficult to conceive of a child learning to function properly in an environment that is totally different from the surroundings in which the training takes place. This is one of the main hazards of a full-time special education class.

Yet there are certain groups of children who are so disabled or handicapped that a very comprehensive and intensive specialized environment must be provided in order to increase their functional level in certain areas and decrease the frequency of undesirable behavior. These youngsters often have significant multiple disorders with associated maladaptive social and emotional behavior that further exacerbates their problems.

Teachers in full-time special education classes must be highly skilled professional people if they are to be successful in changing the performance of children in those classes. Such teachers deal with the most stubborn and resistant types of educational problems; even under the most desirable circumstances they can expect to encounter frustrations, minimal progress by the children, resistance from other teachers, questioning glances from parents, and token support by school administrators. Too frequently children placed in full-time special classes are at the court of last resort. In this case, the teacher often becomes both advocate and mentor for the child. Teachers frequently find themselves in a situation of having to justify not only their program but the child's presence in school. Then teachers must try to achieve as much integration with other phases of the school program, in order to foster as much of a normal experience for the children as possible. You can see, then, that full-time special education teachers must be among the most capable and effective professionals in the schools.

LEVEL 5: SPECIAL STATIONS OR SPECIAL SCHOOLS

There are a number of possibilities that could be included under Level 5 in this system. School districts have special day schools for children with moderate, severe, or profound deviations. In certain districts the special school is used to parallel the full-time special class setting, with, for example, all trainable retarded children being placed in the special school and educable mentally retarded assigned to special classes. Obviously, this type of arbitrary assignment is difficult to justify. Not only does it militate against normalization, but it fails to recognize that children should be assigned to an instructional setting according to their functional level and the most appropriate situation that can be provided. Assignment by medical-clinical syndrome is an inappropriate criterion for deciding on the best educational setting for a child.

It is most unfortunate to observe large school systems, county programs, or intermediate units that years ago decided to deliver special education services to all exceptional children through special schools. There are a great number of programs of this type in the United States. They are, indeed, very efficient because services can be centralized. But they are also very isolated and provide an extraordinarily abnormal, unnatural, and biased instructional environment for children who are and will continue to be functioning members of the open community. After World War II and into the 1950s, some school directors decided to pool their capital resources and develop a network of special schools, which, quite naturally, are virtually impossible to phase out. The result has been a continuation of the special-school plan in those school districts. Buildings exist, and it becomes difficult to change programs in those buildings regardless of the strength of the prevailing mood of the school personnel, the state of contemporary thought, or the persuasiveness of research on these matters.

These cautions notwithstanding, we emphasize that special schools for certain types of functional disorders may be entirely appropriate for specific children. For example, Baltimore has an outstanding school for children with serious orthopedic disorders. Comprehensive physical and occupational therapy, as well as educational programs, are offered within that unique school. Youngsters are usually assigned to the special school on a temporary basis and reassessed periodically from medical, social, psychological, and educational perspectives. At the appropriate time the young-sters are moved into other, more normal types of instructional settings.

The Pittsburgh schools have a special station within a psychiatric center for children who need intensive therapy at specific stages in their school career. A team of medical, behavioral, and educational specialists work with each child and the family in a form of crisis intervention. The youngsters attend the center until they are able to return to a more normal setting.

As emphasized earlier, the remedial character of a special station or school is especially important. Teachers who are involved in the programs in such settings must learn to deal with extremely deviant behavior and very difficult problems. They are usually trained to use powerful methods of behavior management. Such teachers typically have had years of experience dealing with children who have serious multiple disorders. They must be patient, able to tolerate slow rates of behavioral change in their students, not become upset by regression to previous levels of function, and be able to approach their duties with an optimistic attitude.

LEVEL 6: HOMEBOUND INSTRUCTION

Schools are legally required to provide free public education to all children, whatever their types of deviations or levels of functioning. This means that children who are unable to attend school and who are not residents of an institution or a residential center must have a school program brought to them. This is a very expensive form of instruction because a single teacher can handle but a few children. Moreover, the logistics involved in traveling from house to house and the expensive equipment that each teacher of the homebound must have available further complicates the situation.

There may be a problem with the lack of comprehensiveness and often weaker caliber of instruction that is provided in the homebound program. Especially with older children whose level of performance in various subject areas is fairly mature, the child may well know more about a subject than the teacher. This can be restricting for the student as well as a source of anxiety for the teacher. The problem becomes more complex and significant when the teacher has children of various ages, disabilities, levels of func-tioning, and diffuse interests. But there is a definite trend toward providing more homebound instruction for children with severe handicaps—young-sters who have either been excluded from public school programming or who were institutionalized and not provided for educationally. Currently their education is the responsibility of the public schools.

LEVEL 7: RESIDENTIAL OR INSTITUTIONAL ASSIGNMENT

The courts have decreed that all children of school age must be provided with a free public school education. This means that schools have the man-date to plan and deliver educational programs to children who live in resi-dential centers within the community. Departments of public welfare, who previously were responsible for providing special education to institutional residents, have been relieved of this duty. This change caused a measure of trepidation among institutional administrators because an outside agency was given responsibility for a service that had been within the institution's sphere of influence for decades. Institutional directors of education and training now must coordinate services with other clusters of professionals. Teachers in the institutions were nervous because the diagnosis of their students, which was required by law, revealed how uninfluential their program of education and training had been over the years. On the other hand, teachers in the community were now responsible for educating groups of children about whom they knew little, and they lacked the skills required to formulate and deliver an effective instructional program.

You can see from Figure 9-2 that Level 7 is the most segregated from the normal environment. The drawbacks are even more pronounced if the residential center itself is isolated from the community, as is true of many institutions for the mentally retarded in the United States. (As discussed later, the Swedish and Danish residential centers are exemplary models of the way in which articulation can take place among all facets of the community.)

APPROPRIATE APPLICATION OF THE CASCADE MODEL
The provision of these various levels of administrative programming is not the complete story for the establishment of a successful system. The exceptional children who are part of a school system that adopts an approach such as Deno's cascade model will be successful only if: (1) administrators identify the specific instructional focus to be delivered in each setting; (2) teachers are assigned to a setting on the basis of their individual instructional strengths and interests; (3) children are assigned according to their individual instructional needs; and (4) the system is flexible and allows for easy coordination among the various levels and segments.

MOBILITY IN PLACEMENT
In the past one of the most unfortunate facts about special education was the likelihood that the children, once assigned to a class, would remain there throughout their school career. The child and his parents have had no recourse or chance for due process until recently. The passage of P.L. 94-142 has provided legal relief for parents of handicapped children. A cornerstone of the philosophy we have presented is that all children can do better than their present level suggests, that the main mission of education is to structure the educational environment accordingly, and that children should be moved from one level to another according to where the most appropriate instructional situation exists. We have already indicated that normalization implies the fading out of contrived, special arrangements and the movement of the child toward more normal circumstances without compromising or fostering a regression of the youngster's behavior. A special school is more contrived (and abnormal) than a special class, a special class is more atypical than a part-time special class, and so on up the ladder. Remember, you must keep in mind the need to graduate children to more normal environments when appropriate.

We strongly support, then, the belief that entrance and exit criteria be developed for each of the different classrooms, levels, and settings within the cascade system. Everyone should know what it takes to move up, including the child's parents. This matter should not be left to chance. Patients in a hospital are told that they can move on to a more normal environment as soon as their temperature is normal for three successive days, the scar has healed, the stitches are removed, or whatever. When someone is present to bring their meals, they may go home to their own bedroom; other criteria are established for extending their movements to the rest of the house, and so on. This same plan is needed for the cascade system—or any other system of pupil placement or ladder assignment—to work effectively. Another thought on this issue is that specific criteria for the levels, settings, and classrooms probably cannot be transferred easily from one school system to another. Variations exist among school systems. Students' needs, teachers' characteristics, physical facilities, financial resources, and the number of levels of the cascade system that any school district can reasonably support may well differ from one setting to another.

Finally, while it is awfully important for special educators to be optimistic, it is important to recognize that some children, a minority, are not going to progress because of profound multiple disabilities. These children will need lifetime custodial care, and it is foolish to think that they can progress to more normal environments.

COMMUNITY SERVICES AND RESOURCES

People with significant physical or functional disorders often require services beyond special education in order to progress toward normalization. Aside from the disabled and their families, few other people recognize this need as much as those who work in special education. There is frequently a paucity of services and resources within reasonable distance of many communities. Those that exist are often poorly coordinated and overwhelmed by paperwork problems and bureaucracy. Some community service agencies often seem to operate at cross-purposes with each other, duplicate efforts, and at times compete for clients and financial support. These conditions cause frustration among community leaders, divide the local and state resources in ways that make for less than optimum productivity, confuse potential clients, and generally lead to a diminution of professional effectiveness and community service.

HUMAN RIGHTS FOR ALL

Our society currently has the scientific, managerial, and fiscal capabilities to design and deliver excellent programs of community service to all who are in need. Other countries, notably Denmark and Sweden, provide excellent prototypes of the provision, organization, and delivery of various forms of community services. The philosophy that underlies the provision of services in these countries is instructive.

Denmark and Sweden first affirmed the proposition that "all of the human family, without distinction of any kind, have equal and inalienable rights of human dignity and freedom" (Bank-Mikkelesen, 1969). The central beliefs of that philosophy state that people who are considered handicapped have:

1. The same basic rights as other citizens of the same country and age

2. The right to proper medical care and physical restoration, and to whatever education, training, habilitation, and guidance is needed to enable them to develop their abilities and potential to the fullest extent possible, whatever their degree or type of disability

3. The right to economic security, to a decent standard of living, and to involvement in a productive and meaningful occupation

4. The right to live with their families or in foster homes, full participation in all aspects of community life, involvement in appropriate leisure-time activities, and reasonable proximity to normal community opportunities and facilities

5. The right to have a qualified guardian when necessary to oversee their personal rights and interests

6. The right to protection from exploitation, abuse, and degrading treatment

7. The right to be protected by appropriate safeguards, in instances when modification of the preceding rights is necessary or appropriate

Whether community services are provided for everyone is dependent on the community's view of the worth of each person, regardless of personal character and station in life, and the priority people give to community programs that require some expenditure of time and money.

These issues can be illustrated by an example from the public schools in America. Many high schools in this country devote a great deal of their human and fiscal resources to the football program. Special coaches are employed, equipment is purchased, stadiums are constructed, parents organize booster clubs to provide fringe benefits to the players, football fever strikes the student body and community, employers close down during the times the games are played, students and players are bused to other states for special events and games, and so on.

Why do the debating teams or the chess teams in the same high schools not receive the same type and level of support and interest? Obviously, we support those things that we value or that have personal meaning to us.

Scandinavian countries have provided full community-based totally financed services to exceptional children and adults because this reflects their individual and social philosophy and priorities. The point we emphasize is that effective, adequate, and comprehensive community programs for all people cannot be expected to occur without personal commitment. Scientific knowledge, ability to organize and deliver a service program, and financial resources are not in and of themselves enough to make a community program possible or workable. These are necessary conditions, but more fundamental is the need for individual commitment to the concept, if it is to work at all. One indicator of the degree of commitment is the amount of financial support a society is willing to allocate for social services. For example, Denmark, with a population of less than 5 million in an area of approximately 17,500 square miles, spends 40 percent (1970) of the national income on public expenditures, the biggest item of which is social services, followed by health, education, and defense, in that order.

RANGE OF POSSIBLE SERVICES

The variety of services available in a given community will differ a great deal according to local conditions. The section following this will consider some of the prominent circumstances that dictate the extent to which a community is able to provide a range of programs. Here we will describe an ideal configuration of supporting services.

There are a number of ways to classify supporting services that are directed toward exceptional children and adults in the community. Certain services are evaluative or diagnostic in focus. Diagnostic centers of a multidisciplinary character, certain rehabilitation centers, medical diagnostic facilities, and special types of programs in vocational evaluation place emphasis on obtaining an accurate assessment of an individual's disability and the services needed to improve his or her level of functioning. These agencies rarely provide more than diagnostic and evaluative services.

A second group of community agencies offers habilitative and rehabilitative services to clients. Their primary role is to work with exceptional individuals—to train them in the use of prostheses, if necessary, and to provide an appropriate environment so that clients can improve their functional level. In most instances such services are of short-term duration. That is, the agency and the client anticipate certain habilitative or rehabilitative goals that will allow the person to progress to a higher level of functioning in a social or vocational context. For example, speech therapy, auditory training, mobility instruction, or physical therapy illustrate areas of service that are usually of specific duration.

Some community services have a long-term character. Sheltered workshops, community housing arrangements or youth hostels, health insurance programs, out-patient consultations, and adult education opportunities are examples of services that are provided to clients for whatever duration the services are required. Community agencies are also interested in providing programs and services that both prevent disabling conditions and reduce the probability of secondary disorders.

Another way to classify community agencies and services is according to whether they provide primarily physical, psychosocial, or vocational support. These are arbitrary classifications: in reality many agencies provide combinations of these services. The following list summarizes the main focus of the most prominent types of agencies.

1. Physical
   a. Medical
   b. Dental
   c. Nursing
   d. Physical therapy
   e. Speech and hearing therapy
   f. Braille reading and writing
   g. Mobility instruction
   h. Home care and homemaker assistance

2. Psychosocial
   a. Psychiatric and psychological counseling
   b. Rehabilitation counseling
   c. Therapeutic recreation
   d. Social casework
   e. Social welfare programs

3. Vocational
   a. Special education
   b. Sheltered workshops
   c. Work-study programs
   d. Vocational rehabilitation and training
   e. Employment placement, counseling, and evaluation
   f. Occupational therapy

CONDITIONS DICTATING THE EFFECTIVENESS OF A SERVICE

Numerous factors determine the extent to which community services find their way into the fabric of our society and are used by those who really need them. Optimum delivery is important. Community leaders must be aware of the factors to be considered in the development and provision of such services.

The most important aspect for the successful provision of community services is the *community's attitude* toward exceptional individuals. Success requires a commitment, a spirit that reflects individual and collective responsibility toward those with special needs. The old adage "Out of sight, out of mind" has enormous implications. Deviant people have been cast into institutions and other residential centers far from major population centers, only to be forgotten except during the annual review of the budget. And then it was (and still is) only too easy to reduce the fiscal requests of those agencies that are not within easy view.

Services will be supported and provided in direct relation to the attitude of the people. Are people willing to spend whatever it takes to initiate and maintain community agencies? Will those who provide financial and spiritual support use the services themselves if the need arises? The answers to these two questions indicate the degree to which a community is willing to provide for the needs of exceptional people. A neutral or negative response suggests that community attitudes must first be changed in a more positive direction.

The needs of communities differ greatly. Moreover, the type and range of agencies and services provided within a given community will change from time to time as the prospective clientele changes. It is important that planners have a fairly accurate indication of *demand* before a program to initiate community support is mounted. This information will serve to support the arguments used in mobilizing community interest. It is a key step in the process.

After a tentative decision has been made regarding the nature of community needs, a status assessment should be conducted in three primary areas. First, the *existing community agencies* should be carefully analyzed; this analysis should include their service functions and modes of delivery, the types and numbers of clients they currently serve, their interest in participating in a coordinated service approach, their attitudes toward expanding their services to populations that are currently not served, their financial policies, and the kinds of professionals available.

Second, some attention should be given to the *available human resources* in the community. Staff will be needed to plan, provide, and maintain services in the community. Part-time and full-time workers will have to be mobilized on a continuous basis, and it is important to gain some appreciation for the size and commitment of this group before an expansion and coordination of services takes place.

Third, the *financial resources* in a community must be evaluated. Federal and state funds are often available to supplement certain segments of most community service programs; however, there is no question that the local districts will have to provide some funds to support a program of services. An adequate system of services should involve diversified sources of fiscal support, including state, federal, local, and private resources. The magnitude and availability of such funds should be determined before plans are established.

Another important factor is the *general organization of the community*. This includes the political bases of power and influence as well as the physical layout. In addition, one must consider such factors as the cultural characteristics of the community, the predominant religious beliefs, the major socioeconomic levels represented, ethnic characteristics, political persuasions and inclinations, and labor-management issues that might influence the establishment and functioning of service agencies.

A final consideration is the need to gain some estimate of the *power base and boundaries* of existing and proposed community programs. It is natural for well-established groups, agencies, or individuals to be hesitant to turn over any control, power, influence, responsibilities, or funding sources to others who are less well established. Doing so often results in relinquishing control over their own destiny. This is a difficult problem, but it is one that must be faced by the established and emerging units. Before interagency war breaks out and territories are established, it is important to evaluate the degree to which boundaries have been established around agencies and what they consider to be their responsibility and base of operation. Launching into the development of a program before making such assessment will simply delay the establishment of a coordinated effort, cause hard feelings among potential contributors, and serve to make more rigid the lines of communication, which should be open for maximum effectiveness.

SUMMARY

Along with the scientific approach, the principle of normalization is the most important philosophic position of the contemporary educator. This chapter has detailed the implications of normalization and the options available for children in America's educational system. Movement from more to less contrived settings and methods should be a continual goal. Certainly, not all exceptional youngsters can move into the everyday, normal environment; yet, every child can move progressively closer to this goal. Teachers must arrange goals, methods, and settings that successively approximate cultural normalcy. The cascade of services described in the chapter provides the array of settings available. Adjustments of materials and teaching strategies can be made to complement each setting.

The modern educator realizes that education does not take place solely in the classroom. Rather, the child learns from interacting in a total context, including the home and community. The teacher must be aware of the resources and potential for learning that are available. It is the orchestration of resources inside and outside the classroom that permits the teacher to create a powerful learning arrangement for the child. Each child must be seen as a member of the community, with the school as the focal—but not exclusive setting—for learning. More and more, teachers, especially special educators, will be coordinators of services made available through a variety of community agencies and facilities.

John T. Neisworth
Robert M. Smith

CHAPTER 10
SPECIAL EDUCATION PROSTHESES

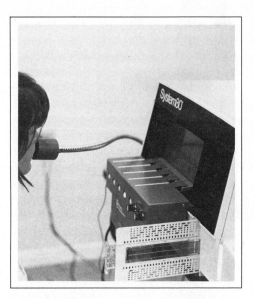

(*Borg-Warner Corp.*)

Handicap results from Person × Environment—it is a *product*. The product can be changed by altering the person (prosthetic devices) or the environment (modifying to make behavior easier). Earlier we discussed the implications of viewing behavior as the result of a person's interaction with the environment. We emphasized that behavior will be faulty when the person, the environment, or both are significantly deviant. This is a distinct philosophical and theoretical departure from the traditional view in special education, namely, that only the person is disabled. The position we advance, then, is that modifications must be made in the child, in the environment, or in both as a means of encouraging behavior changes in desired directions. Prostheses help to normalize interaction between the person and the environment and thus facilitate appropriate and normal behavioral development.

Whether the individual should be fitted with a prosthesis or the environment should be modified is a very important decision. To illustrate, assume that a child is born with both hands missing. All the doors in a school could be designed to open in such a way that the child could simply bump them with an elbow. This expensive but effective environmental modification may be appropriate to some restricted settings but will not help the child in others. We could choose to fit the child with artificial hands that would allow for opening a standard door. This solution would require specific training but have wider generalizability. We could, finally, train the child to grasp a doorknob with both elbows and thereby open doors without benefit of either a prosthesis or a modified environment.

The type of program that is most appropriate is a very individual matter. Modifying the environment usually requires little training for the disabled person. Typically it demands a great deal of technology. The major disadvantage is that such approaches usually have little generalizability. For children who will likely be institutionalized for long periods modifying the environment may be the best option. A prosthesis, such as an artificial leg,

requires individual training and has potential psychological implications. It increases the visibility of the deficiency, unless, of course, it is a cosmetic prosthesis. The big advantage to using a personal prosthesis is that its use generalizes outside of a protective environment, such as a special class or school. Compensatory training, such as using the elbows to open doors, involves teaching alternative ways to deal with a problem. It is less expensive from a technological point of view, but it may require much more training than the other two options. If at all possible, a combination of personal prostheses and compensatory training should be provided. Situations must be anticipated in which one would need to open a door quickly but may not have time to strap on the prosthetic appliance. In such a case the individual would have profited by having been trained to use compensatory back-up procedures.

In this chapter we will present a sample of the technology that is available for minimizing handicaps. We cannot explore in detail all of the many types of advances that have been made within the past few years. Our purpose is to survey the environmental modifications and prostheses that are available to foster progressively more normal behavior on the part of exceptional children. The material is organized under broad classes of function: locomotion, life support, personal grooming, communication, and household aids. There is a brief section on advanced technology in which very elaborate and sophisticated apparatus is discussed. A final section discusses environmental barriers characteristic of public facilities that amplify handicaps.

LOCOMOTION

CRUTCHES

Crutches (Figure 10-1) are used by relatively normal children during periods of temporary disability, such as after an operation or when the child has broken a leg or sprained an ankle. When the disability is permanent or of long duration, however, crutches and canes can be designed for comfort by reducing the weight the legs must bear as well as providing for stability and support. Numerous considerations enter into the design of such prostheses. Many times people who require crutches and canes have other types of disabling conditions. The range of movement and strength of the person's shoulders, elbows, and wrists must be considered in the design of crutches. Equilibrium, head balance, and involuntary motion of various body parts are also important considerations.

No opportunity should be lost for increasing the utility of crutches, not only in terms of their primary functions (balance, locomotion, and reducing weight on the lower extremities), but it is also important to think of other possible purposes which all prosthetic devices can serve. Crutches aid movement of the lower extremities, but they may reduce the amount and range of functioning of the arms. It is difficult to carry items when one uses

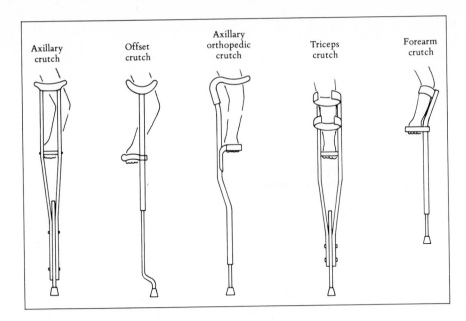

FIGURE 10-1
Crutches.

crutches. To offset these liabilities, attachments can be designed to increase the independence of the person (Figure 10-2).

The surface on which the person with a crutch will be functioning must be considered. If it is slippery, rubber-tipped ends, spiked ends, or tripod legs should be provided. Other surfaces will not require these attachments.

WALKERS

Walkers constitute another category of upright devices to assist and support movement. They can be modified in various ways according to each individual's unique needs. Some have casters, wheels, seats, handlebars, and var-

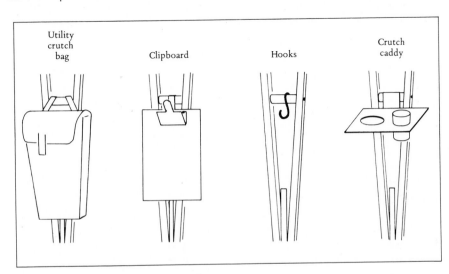

FIGURE 10-2
Attachments for crutches.

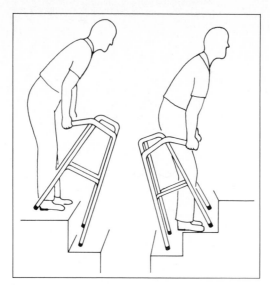

FIGURE 10-3
Stair-climbing walker.

ious types of grips. To illustrate, we have chosen a stair-climbing walker, and a more complex apparatus for individuals with problems of uncontrolled or involuntary motion during ambulation. Trays, bags, and baskets can also be attached to the walker as needed or desired.

Stair-climbing Walker
This apparatus (Figure 10-3) makes stair climbing possible by providing excellent support and stability. It is especially useful for persons who have excellent control of upper extremities.

Multiple Walker
This device (Figure 10-4) is specifically for persons with involuntary movements, as is true in some forms of cerebral palsy. The features restrain spas-

FIGURE 10-4
Multiple walker.

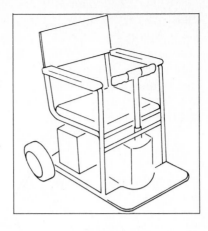

FIGURE 10-5
Motorized wheelchair.

tic movements and help to support the trunk of the body. Skids can be placed over the rear wheels to support movement of the walker.

WHEELCHAIRS
Wheelchairs are available in an amazing range of variations and models. They can be motorized with front-wheel drive, recline in various directions, have different types of seats (including commodes), be adapted for stair-climbing and curb hopping, be collapsible, and be equipped with numerous types of attachments, including straps, supports, cushions, grips, safety devices, and convenience adaptations.

Motorized Wheelchair
This battery-operated wheelchair (Figure 10-5) is moved by the control of a knob placed in the best position for the handicapped individual. It is a means of independent transportation for people who cannot use a standard

FIGURE 10-6
Stair-climbing wheelchair.

wheelchair because of significant motor disability or loss of range and strength of the arms or hands.

Stair-climbing Wheelchair

This ingenious wheelchair (Figure 10-6) is equipped with caterpillar treads; it is able to traverse rough territory and even climb steps like a tank. The seat tilts to maintain an upright position during climbing. During level transit, the treads clear the ground. Everything is operated by battery-powered push-button controls.

Stand-up Wheelchair

By locking the main wheel brakes and releasing the seat from its attachment, the individual can lean forward and swing into an upright position. Adjustments can be made according to the individual's weight and a 10 percent positioning from the vertical can be effected. This prosthesis is useful to individuals with a wide range of physical disorders, but it is especially useful to paraplegics (Figure 10-7).

Adaptations for Wheelchairs

Some of the ancillary attachments and adaptations for use on wheelchairs are shown in Figure 10-8.

Recliners

People with certain types of disability must remain in a reclining position. Devices have been developed to provide for self-propulsion or assisted pro-

FIGURE 10-7
Stand-up wheelchair.

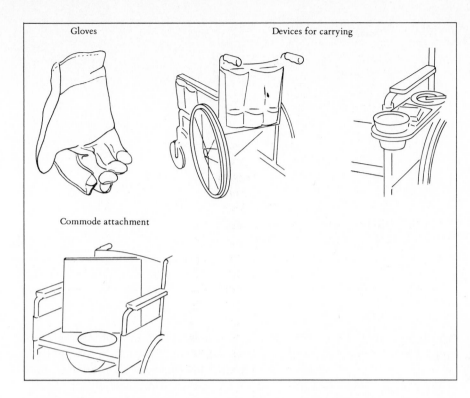

Gloves

Devices for carrying

Commode attachment

FIGURE 10-8
Attachments for
wheelchairs.

pulsion while in this position. These range from a simple creeper to elaborate hydraulic stretchers. (Figures 10-9, 10-10, and 10-11).

Figure 10-11 shows how a prosthetic device may enhance functioning (locomotion) without limiting one's performance in other areas (reading).

VERTICAL LIFTS
These devices provide assistance to the individual for movement from one location to another, e.g., from a bed to a wheelchair or to a toilet. The ramp

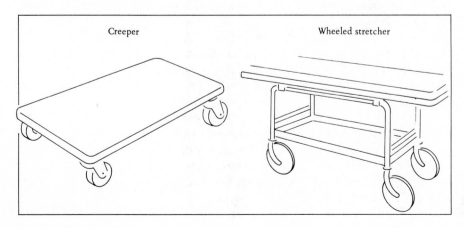

Creeper

Wheeled stretcher

FIGURE 10-9
Recliners.

182

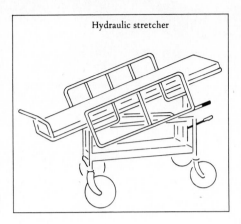

Hydraulic stretcher

FIGURE 10-10
Hydraulic stretcher.

is the simplest form of the various transfer devices. Other types of lifts are much more complex (Figures 10-12.) Other devices have been developed to aid the less handicapped driver, several of which appear in Figure 10-13.

LIFE-SUPPORT AIDS

Prosthetic aids that are presented in this section are amazingly similar to those that have been developed to help astronauts function in a weightless environment. There is impressive variation in the types of adaptations found in life-support aids. Friction, counterbalance, suction, leverage, manipulation of weight, pressure, and rotation are all used as principles in the development of aids to enhance a person's level of functioning.

EATING AND DRINKING

The adaptive equipment used for eating and drinking should increase independence, provide for ease in the act of eating, and be as normal in appearance and function as possible. Some feeding devices have been developed which deliver the food by mechanical means to the operator's mouth. The user initiates a mechanical feeding arm by pushing a knob or lever or by electric or fluid control. In most situations some form of special-

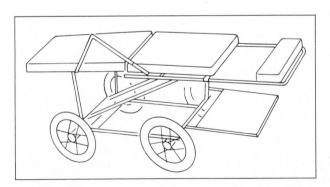

FIGURE 10-11
Self-propelled stretcher.

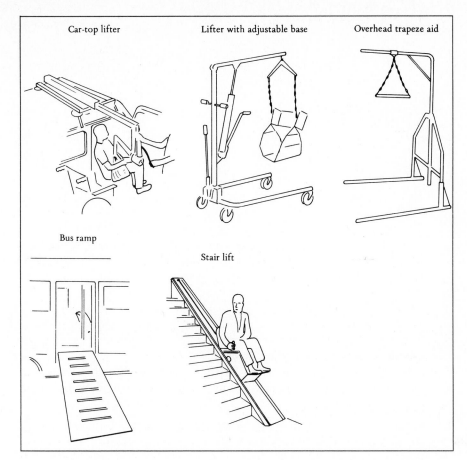

Car-top lifter   Lifter with adjustable base   Overhead trapeze aid

Bus ramp

Stair lift

FIGURE 10-12
Vertical lifts.

ized training will be required to gain competence in the use of the aids. Figures 10-14 to 10-25 illustrate devices used in three major functional areas: containing solids and liquids, holding and manipulating food, and delivering food to the mouth.

ELIMINATION
For handicapped persons the bathroom is not only inconvenient but a potential hazard. The prosthetic devices shown in Figures 10-26 to 10-30 illustrate the range of possible adaptations, from improvisations of existing fixtures to totally new apparatuses.

PERSONAL GROOMING
Being well-groomed reduces the potential somatopsychological complications of disability. Unpleasant odors, dirty appearance, and untidy clothes all alienate the disabled from others. Every attempt should be made to reduce the stereotype that the handicapped cannot take care of personal grooming needs and do not care about their appearance.

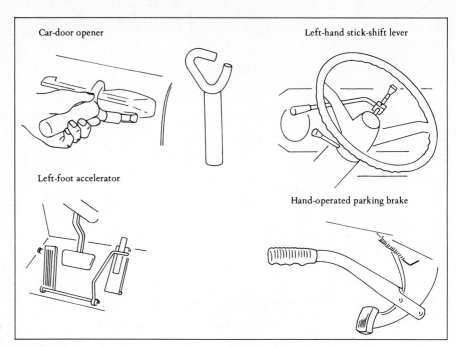

Car-door opener

Left-hand stick-shift lever

Left-foot accelerator

Hand-operated parking brake

FIGURE 10-13
Devices for automobiles.

PERSONAL APPEARANCE AND HYGIENE

The aids shown in Figures 10-31 to 10-40 illustrate some approaches that have been used to make grooming a more independent and likely behavior.

CLOTHING ADAPTATIONS

In addition to using various types of devices for dealing with the task of dressing and undressing, it is helpful to have clothing adapted in whatever

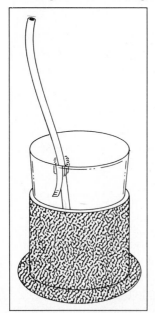

FIGURE 10-14
Suction cup. This cup will
work only on surfaces that
are flat and nonporous
and thus permit the
formation of a suction.

way is necessary, especially during early stages of teaching dressing skills. Some examples of alterations that might be made include the following:

1. Openings should be wide enough to allow ease of entry and exit (Figure 10-41).

2. Fastenings must be made in such a way that they can be easily ma-

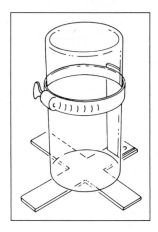

FIGURE 10-15
Glass holder—a stable base for a cup or glass that prevents spilling. This is an alternative to the suction cup.

FIGURE 10-16
Vacuum cup. This container allows one to drink while lying down; because it requires sucking, it controls spills.

FIGURE 10-17
Cup with detachable handle. (The handle can be adapted for any grasp.)

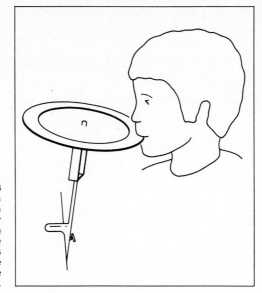

FIGURE 10-18
Rotating plate. This works like a lazy Susan; children with paralysis of arms or upper extremities can rotate the plate with the mouth. The food is arranged along the edge of the plate so that the child can choose.

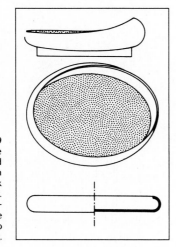

FIGURE 10-19
"Easy-scoop" dish. The rim is rounded and turned upward so that one can find a spoon or fork without spilling the food. A suction cup or high-friction base can be placed on the bottom to control slipping.

nipulated (e.g., Velcro-fasteners and zippers such as those shown in Figure 10-42).

3. Garment materials should be considered to minimize snagging, wrinkling, pulling, tearing, and soiling.

COMMUNICATION

This area focuses on devices that improve the reception and expression of information. Amplification and magnification of stimuli, whether coming in or going out, are important considerations in designing prosthetic communication devices; however, there are conditions for which increasing the

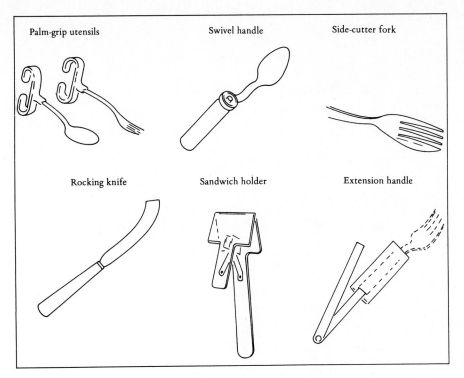

Palm-grip utensils   Swivel handle   Side-cutter fork

Rocking knife   Sandwich holder   Extension handle

FIGURE 10-20
Utensils.

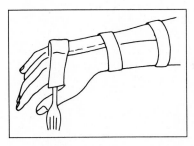

FIGURE 10-21
Feeding splint.

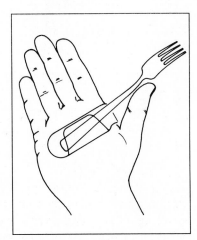

FIGURE 10-22
Utensil holder.

FIGURE 10-23
This feeding device can
be used by individuals
who have limited control
of the upper extremities.
To operate, the user
depresses the knobs
which position the food,
move the spoon on the
plate, and raise the spoon.
(Cerebral Palsy Feeder,
Ontario Crippled
Children's Center,
Ontario, Canada.)

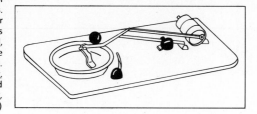

FIGURE 10-24
This electric feeder is
operated by fluid control.
The user presses the
control pad and the spoon
rotates to pick up food to
the mouth. (Abbey
Medical Rehabilitation
Equipment, Automatic
Feeder, Model AM 13-
1273.)

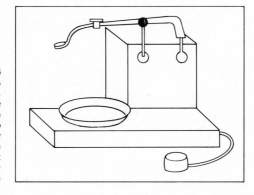

FIGURE 10-25
This battery-powered
device requires no arm
movement to operate. The
user pushes food onto the
spoon with a head-wand
and then pushes the
operating level which
causes the feeder arm to
move up to the user's
mouth or back to the
plate. (Preston Automatic
Feeding Device.)

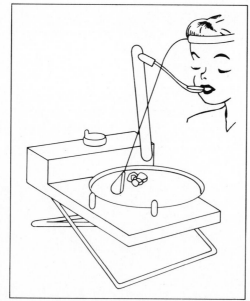

FIGURE 10-26
Portable safety frame.

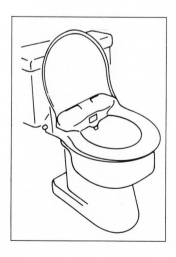

FIGURE 10-27
Portable commode and
skewer chair.

FIGURE 10-28
Cleansing apparatus
(bidet).

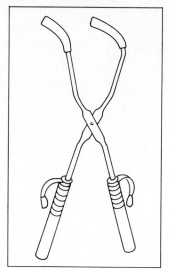

FIGURE 10-29
Toilet wiping aid.

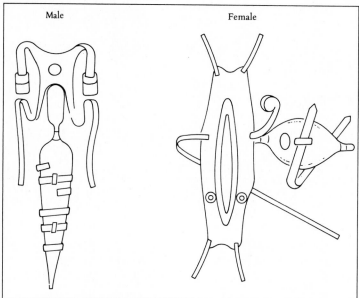

Male   Female

FIGURE 10-30
Urinals.

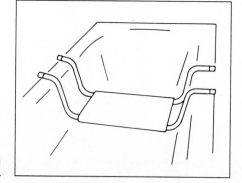

FIGURE 10-31
Hanging bathtub seat.

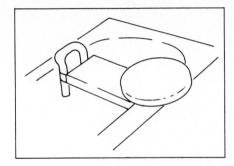

FIGURE 10-32
Swivel bathtub seat.

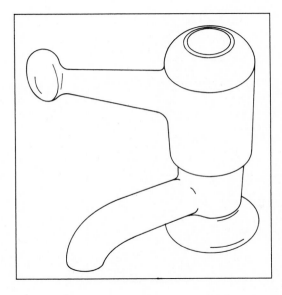

FIGURE 10-33
Faucet lever. This
ingenious device fits over
a standard faucet handle.
Its single lever can be
nudged by any part of the
body to control the flow
of water without grasping
the handle.

FIGURE 10-34
Suction-mounted sponges
and brushes.

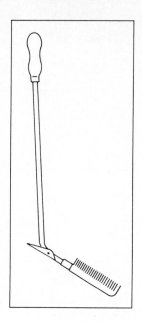

FIGURE 10-35
Comb on extended
handle.

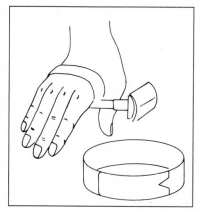

FIGURE 10-36
Razor handle.

stimulus level alone is not enough. Few areas of a technical nature have received more attention and support than those involving communication. We have tried to identify some examples of the range of possible aids in this important area (Figures 10-43 to 10-54).

HOUSEHOLD AIDS
Household aids, such as those shown in Figures 10-55 to 10-58, increase the independence of the disabled person in the home.

ADVANCED TECHNOLOGY
Research and development in many of the nation's scientific programs, especially in aerospace, have resulted in extraordinary technological ad-

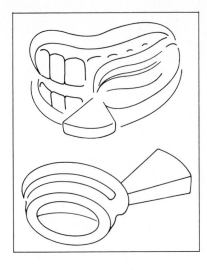

FIGURE 10-37
Oral hygiene device.
Toothpaste is applied to
the rubber mouthpiece,
which is inserted into the
mouth; a simple chewing
motion cleans the teeth
and stimulates the gums.

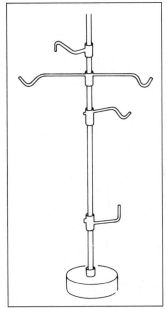

FIGURE 10-38
Dressing aid for
amputees. Clothing
(shirts, coats, pants, and
socks) is positioned on
the rods so that the
person can slip into it.

vances. This technology has drawn upon numerous disciplines, and the application of the principles and discoveries that have come from these research-and-development activities have considerable pertinence to the practical problems encountered by the handicapped. Control mechanisms, sensory devices, alarm systems, new materials, powered apparatus, portable equipment, stimulus detectors, unique processes of fabrication, implantable devices, sensitive measurement techniques, economical recording and playback mechanisms, and ingenious training procedures represent broad categories of technology which are applicable to habilitation and rehabilitation.

CHAPTER 10
SPECIAL EDUCATION
PROSTHESES

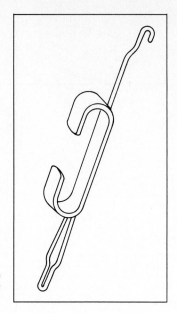

FIGURE 10-39
Button hook and zipper
pull.

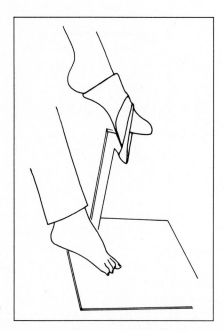

FIGURE 10-40
Shoe and sock hook.

Many of the prostheses that have resulted from these discoveries are still in the developmental stage and have not been widely advertised or discussed. In this section we want to alert you to examples of some unique technological accomplishments.

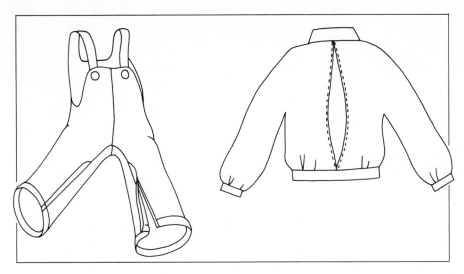

FIGURE 10-41
Openings in clothing.

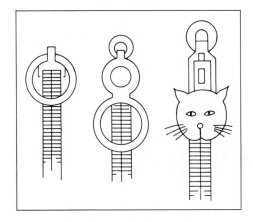

FIGURE 10-42
Zippers.

FIGURE 10-43
Telephone signal control.
A lamp of some sort is
plugged into the
telephone and lights up
when the telephone rings.
This device can be used in
other situations, as with a
doorbell.

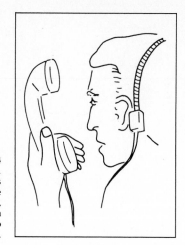

FIGURE 10-44
Bone conductor receiver.
A sound vibrator is
connected to the
telephone receiver,
allowing a person with a
conductive hearing loss to
hear.

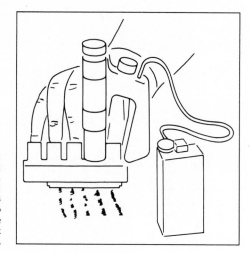

FIGURE 10-45
Sound-tactile reading
machine. This device,
which requires special
instruction, converts
written letters into
separate tones or unique
tactile sensations as it
passes over a line of type.

FIGURE 10-46
Larynx transmitter, an
apparatus for people
whose voice-box is
inoperative or has been
removed. The transmitter
is held against the throat,
speech is mouthed, and
the device amplifies and
transmits the natural vocal
vibrations.

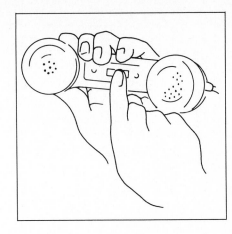

FIGURE 10-47
Voice-control handset.
With this apparatus,
persons with impaired
voice volume can make
their voices louder or
softer.

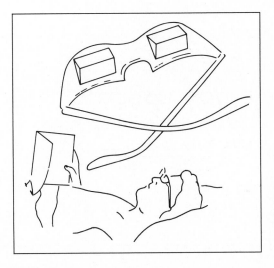

FIGURE 10-48
Prism glasses. These can
be adjusted to any angle
and worn over ordinary
eyeglasses. They allow
people with limited head
movement to read while
lying down.

FIGURE 10-49
Braille typewriter. This
conventional electric
typewriter, which can be
used by both the blind
and the sighted, has a
standard keyboard but
transcribes into braille.

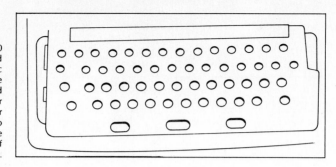

FIGURE 10-50
Typewriter keyboard
shield, a metal or plastic
plate that fits over the
standard electric keyboard
and prevents the user
from striking two keys or
the wrong key. It can also
be used, without the
typewriter, as a means of
pointing communication.

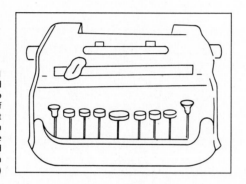

FIGURE 10-51
Braille-writer, for blind
persons who want to
make single copies of
braille. It has six keys that
are used in combination
to emboss forty possible
braille cells. (A slate and
stylus can serve as an
alternative.)

FIGURE 10-52
Braille receiver. By means
of this device, a deaf-
blind person who
understands braille can
communicate through
tactile sensations. A
standard alphabet
keyboard is used. The
deaf-blind person receives
the braille configurations
by holding his finger over
the receiver button at the
back of the machine.

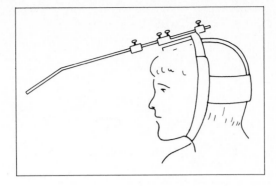

FIGURE 10-53
Pointer. A pointer attached to the head is a communication device for children without speech and with impaired upper-extremity functioning. Along with a typewriter keyboard shield (see Figure 10-50), it can be used to operate an electric typewriter.

FIGURE 10-54
Page turner, a suction device which turns a page in either direction. It is operated by a remote-control device that can be triggered according to the disabled person's needs.

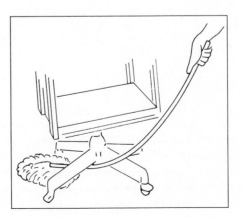

FIGURE 10-55
Mop with flexible handle. This allows someone in a wheelchair to dust under furniture without bending or stooping.

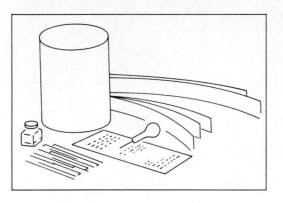

FIGURE 10-56
Marker kit. Plastic labels
embossed either in braille
or in ordinary letters can
be used to identify
shelves, canned goods,
learning materials, etc.

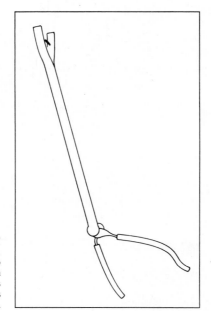

FIGURE 10-57
Squeeze-handle retriever.
This reacher has two
curved fingers and a
squeeze handle; it allows
the user to reach items
within 30 to 40 inches.

OPTACON

This device, which is about the size of a college textbook and weighs 4 pounds, is a unique reading aid for the blind. A miniature camera mounted on rollers is moved across a line of print. Connected by a small cable to the main chassis, the camera picks up an image and transmits the signal to an electronic section in which conversion of the visual image to a tactile image is accomplished. Each of 144 rods, vibrating independently according to the received pattern, protrudes through a plastic cover and touches the blind

FIGURE 10-58
Keyless lock, to replace a
conventional door or
ignition lock. It is a
pushbutton combination
lock that can be operated
with a reacher or mouth
stick and thus makes
using a key unnecessary.

person's finger in the same configuration as the stimulus received by the
camera. Differences in type size are handled by a zoom lens on the camera.

LASER CANE
This is an electronic apparatus to assist in mobility for totally blind persons.
The device has the appearance of a normal cane, but it emits pulses of

The portability of the
Optacon allows it to be
used almost anywhere.
(*Telesensory Systems Inc.*)

infrared light. Pulses reflected from an object in front of it are detected by a receiving mechanism, which in turn warns the traveler. The cane emits three beams simultaneously. By a low-pitched tone the downward beam warns the traveler of a drop from the cane tip to any distance larger than 9 inches. A second beam focuses straight ahead, approximately 2 feet high and 10 feet in front of the cane tip. Any obstacle detected within this range will actuate an index-finger stimulator. The third beam focuses upward from the cane top and activates a high-pitched tone when detecting objects at head height.

SONIC GLASSES

These special frames for glasses utilize an ultrasonic transmitter that scans a 55° angle and receives bounce-back signals from two receivers that are embedded within the spectacle frames. These signals are converted to an audible frequency level and are conveyed to the user through earphones. The power supply is located in a shirt pocket.

SIGHT SWITCH

Another advance to reduce response limitations is a control device operated by eye movements. It was developed by NASA for astronauts. Designed to be worn on standard spectacles, the device activates electrical control mechanisms by sensing variations in light reflected from the white portion of the eye. The light source for this reflection is a low-intensity beam. As the eye is moved in different directions, the control device is activated. The mechanism can be used to control battery-powered wheelchairs, turn pages, position and reposition beds, answer telephones, activate self-feeding devices, control fans or heaters, and in general give paralyzed people greater control over their environment.

VOICE-CONTROLLED WHEELCHAIR

A mechanism attached to a wheelchair can pick up packages, open doors, turn a television knob, and perform a variety of other functions. A possible boon to paralyzed and other severely handicapped persons, the chair-manipulator system responds to thirty-five one-word voice commands, such as "go," "stop," "up," "down," "right," "left," "forward," and "backward." The heart of the system is a voice-command analyzer which utilizes a minicomputer. Commands are taught to the computer by the patient's repeating them a number of times; thereafter the analyzer recognizes commands only in the patient's particular speech pattern. The computer translates commands into electric signals which activate appropriate motors and cause the desired motion of chair or manipulator. Based on teleoperator and robot technology for space-related programs, this voice-controlled system has been tested widely in various prosthetic centers.

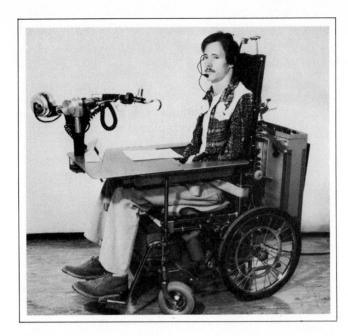

A quadraplegic can operate this NASA-developed voice-controlled wheelchair and its manipulator, which can pick up packages, open doors, turn a TV knob and perform a variety of other functions. (*NASA.*)

NASAL AIRFLOW METER

Fortunately, this device offers an impressively accurate measuring system for assessing inappropriate nasal emission in children with cleft palates. Heretofore, it has been virtually impossible to evaluate accurately the nasal airflow in such children because all of the available procedures altered normal nasal emission. This NASA-built device makes use of heated thermometers that rest beneath the person's nostrils. The temperature of the thermometers is changed as a result of the person's nasal airflow and thus allows for inexpensive but effective evaluation. By attaching meters to each of the thermometers, the individual can observe the degree of nasal emission as various sounds are made and thus seek to reduce the airflow through successive practice sessions.

BIOLOGICAL ISOLATION GARMENT

Hospital patients who are highly vulnerable to infection can leave their sterile habitat for several hours, carrying their germ-free environment with them. The garment was designed originally to be worn by astronauts returning to earth until their arrival in a quarantine facility aboard the recovery ship. It was meant to protect the earth from unknown microorganisms from the moon. The suit is coverall-like with attached mittens and slippers. The penetration-resistant fabric has a separate hood with a transparent face mask. Air is supplied through a diffuser at the top of the head by way of a flexible tube. Positive pressure is maintained to prevent unfiltered air from entering the suit.

This biological isolation garment was a spinoff from the astronauts' biological garment. (*NASA.*)

ADVANCED COSMETIC PROSTHESES

Although cosmetic prostheses have been constructed for centuries, it has only been since World War II that major advances have been made in materials and fabrication. Indeed, only in the last decade have scientists and technicians learned how to handle effectively the new vinyls, acrylics, and silicone rubber in a way that allows for naturalness in the appearance of face, hand, or body prostheses. Realistic face and body restoration in plastics is truly an art. The construction of a hand, an eyelid, a breast, an ear, a nose, or a limb prosthesis requires enormous technical skill, time, patience, and experience.

A wide range of powered limb prostheses has been developed. Elaborate control mechanisms of various forms have been designed to allow an amputee to perform a very complex series of tasks ranging from those that necessitate the greatest degree of delicacy to activities that require the operation of heavy and complex machines and tools. People formerly unable to function in such ways now have the potential for controlling many aspects of their surroundings.

MINIMIZING ACCESS BARRIERS

We have repeatedly made the point that a handicap does not reside in the individual, but rather is a result of the interaction of the person with the environment. This consideration is most crucial when we are discussing the nature of public architecture, transportation, and other aspects of community design. Characteristics of public facilities can be so handicapping that no amount of education, training, or therapy can surmount the obstacles. In other words, handicaps cannot be minimized simply by focus on the handi-

The biological isolation garment allows hospital patients who are highly vulnerable to infection to leave their sterile habitat for several hours, carrying their germ-free environment with them. (*NASA.*)

capped person; in addition, we must modify critical aspects of the public environment. What good is vocational training if the person cannot get to work? Of what consequence are incentive programs for building strong and worthwhile personal goals if the individual is thwarted at every attempt to achieve some measure of independence by an environment that is oblivious to anyone but the "average" ablebodied person? Teachers, rehabilitation counselors, physicians, and therapists may all do an excellent job, but their efforts can be frustrated by community barriers—in architecture, in transportation, and elsewhere—that restrict or preclude access by millions of individuals to opportunities for a fuller life.

Imagine, for a moment, the problems you would face in going to work, getting on the subway or bus, visiting the library, or just going to the shopping center if you required the use of a wheelchair. In the absence of a ramp or an elevator, even one step can bring your attempts to a dead end. Doorways are too narrow; public restrooms will not accommodate your wheelchair; you cannot get into the telephone booth; taking a bus is almost impossible; water fountains are inaccessible—there is little reinforcement but much punishment for your attempts to function independently. Such barriers to independence do not operate exclusively against the wheelchair-bound citizen. The dim lighting, lack of shelters at bus stops, and long flights of stairs prevalent in public settings produce enormous impediments for the aging, the sensorily limited, persons with heart conditions, and millions of people with temporary limitations.

TABLE 10-1
Providing an Environment without Barriers

BARRIERS TO MOVEMENT	RECOMMENDATIONS
Doors	Sufficient depth between inner and outer doors to prevent wheelchair from being trapped Adequate clear opening for all doors Light pressure to open Easily gripped and well-placed handles Protected windows in all swinging doors
Passageways	Sufficient width (minimum of 5 feet) Minimum slope Nonslip surface No steps, or at least one pathway without steps connecting vital facilities Adequate lighting
Stairways	Low risers, without projecting nosings Nonslip treads Well-placed handrails on both sides Landings of contrasting color and texture Adequate lighting
Elevators	Controls accessible from sitting position Cab size to accommodate wheelchair Elevator and building floors meet exactly at stops Doors equipped with sensor to prevent premature closing

BARRIERS TO USE OF FACILITIES	RECOMMENDATIONS
Drinking fountains	Location and height for easy use Controls located at front
Telephones	Location and height to accommodate wheelchairs
Vending machines	Convenient controls, easy operating tension
Toilets	At least one conveniently accessible for each major area or floor At least one stall large enough for a wheelchair, with doors opening out Grab bars on both walls of stall
Sinks	Unobstructed space below, to permit room for legs Faucets easy to operate
Floor, room identification	Raised symbols conveniently located for use by visually limited
Miscellaneous	Convenient placement of light switches Warning signals should be both auditory and visual Special parking facilities nearby

The environmental defects that produce handicaps are manifested most dramatically in the area of employment. While 71 percent of the nondisabled population between the ages of 17 and 64 work, only 36 percent of the disabled population are employed (U.S. Department of Transportation, 1970, p. 19). Fortunately, something can and is beginning to be done about the grossly unequal opportunities perpetuated by our handicapping public facilities. In 1959, architects, business managers, community leaders, and legislators organized a committee of the American Standards Association (ASA) devoted to the study of the restrictive effects of public facilities. The efforts of this committee resulted in the approval and publication of the *American National Standard Specifications for Making Buildings and Facilities Accessible to, and Usable by, the Physically Handicapped* (American National Standards Institute, 1961).

Naturally, it is important that the architectural characteristics of a facility contain those arrangements that will be required by its clientele. At the same time, it is unquestionable that the more a facility stands apart from its environment, the more likely it is that a negative connotation will be assigned to the facility as well as to the clients served. One can control such bias by (1) not setting the facility apart from other similar forms of service in the community; (2) designing the structure so that it fits into the surroundings in a natural way; (3) not naming the facility by handicap (e.g., School for the Blind; Farm for the Chronically Ill, etc.) for the types of people who are its clients; and (4) encouraging an open-door policy throughout periods of design, construction, and use.

We have stressed that the types and degree of environmental arrangements at each level of service must vary as do those illustrated by Deno's cascade system. This range of complexity, of course, is inextricably related to the needs of those who are being served. It is clear that the architecture and the types of furnishings that are contained in a facility, center, or classroom may be quite specialized. Therefore, they cannot be excluded from the planning if one desires maximum use and control of the instructional environment. The kind of special arrangements will differ greatly, depending mainly on the kinds of problems exhibited (for example, blindness, deafness, or motor problems) and the types of behavior to be focused upon within the setting (for example, social, mobility, speaking, academic, or vocational).

CONSIDERATIONS IN DESIGNING FACILITIES

We will not review all of the nuances one must consider in designing a facility; suggestions on this subject have been reviewed in great depth in numerous publications (Abelson & Berenson, 1970; Birch & Johnstone, 1975; Cruickshank & Quay, 1970; Gordon, 1972; Gunzburg, 1972; Muller, 1970; Nellistch, 1970; Wolf, 1968). Instead, we will simply summarize the areas to which an environmental designer must give attention when providing an appropriate instructional setting. Again, the extent to which one must exhibit concern about any of these dimensions is directly related to the needs of the clientele and the goals of the facility.

LOCATION

When a new unit is being considered for construction, the following issues are relevant:

1. The degree to which the site is accessible to the center of community services and activities

2. The extent to which the location is free from noise, dust, fumes, thick traffic, and other types of hazards

3. The adequacy of transportation, natural amenities (such as plant life, water, open space), outdoor conveniences, schools, and recreation possibilities

4. The local codes, ordinances, and zoning regulations that pertain to the construction and anticipated use of the facility

QUESTIONS CONCERNING THE USE OF THE FACILITY

Whenever a new structure is being planned or an existing building, classroom, or residence is undergoing remodeling for use by exceptional children, certain factors should be examined and programmed into the unit when and where appropriate. The decisions one makes concerning each of these factors will in large measure be dependent on the kinds of activities that are expected to take place in each area, the number and types of youngsters to be served in the different settings, the kind of general atmosphere desired in the various sections of the unit (for example, lively, cheerful, active, or sedate), and the flow of activities from one center to the others. Decisions will depend on the answers to certain questions:

1. What kinds of space will be needed within each of the various subunits of the facility?

2. What kinds of interior surfaces will best serve the children and provide the most effective instructional setting? For example, the hearing-impaired will need a classroom in which the surfaces are soundproofed as much as possible, the visually limited a setting in which glare is minimized, and motor-disordered children a classroom in which surfaces are stable and skidproof.

3. What unique characteristics should be included in the facility to foster greater independence on the part of children? For example, specially constructed toileting areas, ramps, and elevators, therapeutic pools, specially controlled areas for humidity and temperature, unique seating arrangements, or rooms which are electronically arranged for dealing with certain hearing and communication problems might need to be included in a unit.

4. To what extent should special lighting, acoustics, and climate control be considered?

5. What furniture and equipment will be required for the facility, and to what extent and how will the unit have to be remodeled to accommodate this unique requirement?

6. In what manner will the staff's needs be considered within the context of the unit or facility? What unique requirements do they have in the preparation of teaching materials?

7. If a food center, health room, professional offices, or community facility is required, in what manner will these needs be provided for, and how can these various segments of the program articulate with the others?

These few questions are but a brief sample of the large number of concerns that professionals must consider in the planning, design, and development of a special education environment. To a very large extent, the question of developing a facility really boils down to issues that pertain mainly to its location, physical context, size, access, appearance, and internal design (Wolfenberger, 1972). When each of these major dimensions is considered fully in light of the concept of normalization, we could expect progress in serving the instructional needs of exceptional children.

SUMMARY

Handicap can be reduced or eliminated through altering features of the person or the environment. Prostheses are devices or arrangements designed to substitute or compensate for features that are important for optimal functioning. Prostheses can be personal (e.g., eye glasses, hearing aids, artificial legs) or environmental (e.g., ramps, automatic doors, amplified sound). Additionally, prostheses can be of a functional or cosmetic nature. Teachers and therapists must be sensitive to the possible advantages of appropriate prostheses for promoting student progress. Sometimes a simple device or alteration in the environment can immediately change failure to success and frustration to elation.

While prosthetic arrangements can maximize success in certain contexts, they can also sometimes contribute to denormalized appearance and dependencies. Teachers and therapists must use expert judgment in deciding when prosthetic intervention is introduced, maintained, and faded.

Russell T. Jones
Janell I. Haney

CHAPTER 11
SOMATOPSYCHOLOGICAL INTERVENTION – A BEHAVIORAL APPROACH

(Courtesy of Jim Lukens.)

Somatopsychology is the study of some of the relationships between body and behavior. Some of the earlier definitions of somatopsychology include: "the study of problems and variables concerned with atypical physique as it relates to psychological status" (Barker, Wright, Meyerson, & Gonick, 1953, p. 1); "the study of some of the relationships that bind physique and behavior" (Meyerson, 1971, p. 2); and "those variations in physique that affect the psychological situation of a person by influencing the effectiveness of his body as a tool for actions or by serving as a stimulus to himself or others" (Hamilton, 1950, p. 2).

Somatopsychology is not to be confused with the similar term, "psychosomatics." Both words are derived from "soma" (meaning "body") and "psyche" (meaning "mind" or "soul"). However, psychosomatics is the study of the influence of the mind (emotions) on the body (physical disorders), and somatopsychology is the study of the influence of the body (physical characteristics) on the mind (behavior).

Both the benefits and the problems that individuals reap from their physical characteristics have been included in the study of somatopsychology, but the present chapter will focus on the negative side of this relationship—the problems. These problems include those resulting from (a) the cuing action of atypical physique itself, such as loss of a limb, facial or bodily deformity, or blindness, and (b) the behavioral characteristics potentially resulting from atypical physique, such as rocking, drooling, talking too loud, or avoiding others, which are viewed as somatopsychological problems.

The relationship between individuals' bodily characteristics and their behavior has been a matter of interest for centuries. As early as 425 B.C., Hippocrates grouped people into two basic physical types, each with a different temperament. During the middle of the nineteenth century, many areas of study focused on character reading. For example, physiognomy was an at-

tempt to determine inner character from outer appearance, especially facial features (Lavater, 1848). Phrenology, on the other hand, held that personality could be determined by the contours of the skull (Spurzheim, 1908). In the 1940s Sheldon and his colleagues (Sheldon, 1942; Sheldon, Stevens, and Tucker, 1940) developed a classification system that was based on three basic components of physique. Endomorphy was characterized by softness and roundness; mesomorphy was identified by predominance of muscle, bone, and connective tissue; and ectomorphy was associated with linearity and fragility. Sheldon then attempted to correlate these various components of physique with three temperament types. He found that endomorphy was associated with comfort and sociability. In contrast, ectomorphy was associated with restraint and secretiveness. Mesomorphy was associated with physical activity and risk taking. Although this work has been criticized on the basis of methodology (Humphreys, 1957), the large number of related studies points to the significance of this contribution to psychology.

Several investigators have more recently discussed the relationship between physique and behavior (Barker et al., 1953; Lindzey, 1965; Meyerson, 1971). These discussions present a number of possible explanations for any given interaction between physique and behavior: (a) there is no relationship; (b) behavior (for example, diet) determines physique, (c) physique (for example, height) determines behavior, or (d) a third variable (such as Down's syndrome) influences both physique and behavior. Whereas each relationship may be used to explain some of the relationships between physique and behavior, none of them totally explains observed phenomena. As a result, it has been concluded that conceptualization of behavior as a function of *person-environment interaction* could be used to explain adequately the relationship between physique and behavior (Meyerson, 1971). That is, physique (as one of a person's characteristics) may be viewed as one factor in determining behavior.

Theories on the nature of the interaction between an individual and the environment have been proposed by a number of theorists with varying views on development. From a behavioral point of view, the behavior of a person with an atypical physique would be described as a product of both past interactions and the present stimulus situation (Bijou & Baer, 1961). A similar position, suggested by Neisworth, Jones, and Smith (1978), has been applied to the somatopsychological problem. Organismic theorists have emphasized the individual's active role in the interaction between person and environment and point out the circular effect of the child acting on the environment and the environment providing feedback to the child (Erikson, 1964; Lerner, 1976; Lerner, Karabenick & Meisels, 1975; Schneirla, 1957). From a dialectical viewpoint, the emphasis has been on the continuing changes in the individual as a result of conflicts between any two dimensions of development (i.e., inner-biological, individual-psychological, cultural-sociological, and outer-physical) in both short-term situational changes and long-term developmental changes (Riegel, 1975). It is clear that an adequate conceptualization of somatopsychological problems must recognize the role of both the child, who possesses various physical characteristics and behaviors, and the environment. Given the complexity of this interaction, the necessity for thorough assessment of both the child and the environment is apparent.

The need for knowledge and understanding of somatopsychological problems is becoming increasingly evident to educators, parents, and others involved with exceptional persons as they push for the integration of these individuals into the mainstream of society. This chapter has been written to provide an understanding of both the problems that may result from having atypical physical characteristics and some techniques that may prevent or reduce these problems. It is hoped that this conceptualization of the somatopsychological problem will help those who work with exceptional children to achieve the goal of maximum normalization for each child.

DEVIATION, DISABILITY, AND HANDICAP

Somatopsychological problems cannot be discussed without reference to "deviation," "disability," and "handicap." Unfortunately, these terms (the last two terms in particular) have contributed to past confusion through their use as synonyms. To those who educate and rehabilitate exceptional individuals, "deviation," "disability," and "handicap" do not have the same meaning. These distinctions are important because of their implications for intervention.

First, it must be pointed out that a deviation is a characteristic that is different from the norm or average for that characteristic. Differences from the norm in height and weight; in length of nose, fingers, arms, and hair; and in degree of attractiveness, freckling, and deformity are all deviations. It must be noted that whether a difference or deviation results in negative, positive, or neutral consequences will be environmentally determined.

Smith and Neisworth define the second term, "disability," as "an objectively defined deviation in physique or functioning that, through interaction with a specified environment, results in behavioral inadequacies or restrictions for the person" (1975, p. 169). They refer to the last term, "handicap," as "the burden imposed upon the individual by the unfortunate product of deviation and environment" (1975, p. 169). Disability refers to actual, measurable impairment; handicap describes the physical and social problems that the individual encounters because of the disability. Blindness, then, may be a disability, but not being able to drive a car and not being able to observe facial expressions during conversation are handicaps. The educator's task is to lessen the extent of the environmental consequences—the handicap.

SOMATOPSYCHOLOGICAL PROBLEMS

As has been noted, individuals may deviate from the average on any number of physical characteristics. To determine whether a physical deviation results in a somatopsychological problem, both the individual's physical deviation and the environment need to be examined.

INDIVIDUAL DEVIATION IN PHYSIQUE

Two factors determine others' perceptions of deviations as different in a negative fashion: (a) the prominence of the cues (or signals) of deviation; and (b) the ability of the observers to perceive the cues as deviant (Goffman, 1963; Neisworth et al., 1978).

Prominence of Cues

Deviations in length of fingers and toes, for example, are not readily apparent (or prominent) and are therefore not likely to be perceived as deviant. Loss or deformity of fingers and toes would be seen as deviant, but, because of lessened prominence, would not likely be considered as deviant as the loss of an arm or leg. Deafness, while not readily apparent upon sight, is highly visible through conversation and thus reacted to as a deviant characteristic.

Observer's Perception of Cues

Additionally, because focus tends to be on the face, deformity of a finger is less likely to be noticed than deformity of the nose. Deformity of a toe is yet less obvious because people tend to place more emphasis on the hands than on the feet. People will observe that which experience has "taught" them to pay attention to (that with which they are familiar).

A deviation is not perceived as deviant unless: (a) it is prominent to such a degree that it is likely to be seen by others, and (b) others, through experience, have been taught to think of it as deviant.

ENVIRONMENTAL VARIATION IN PERCEPTION OF DEVIANCE

The perception of certain physical and behavioral characteristics as deviant is not uniform from situation to situation. Deviance varies with both the physical and the social environments.

Not being able to walk, hear, or see are not disabilities unless they are needed for a particular situation. Is inability to whistle, snap your fingers, or roll your tongue a disability? Only if the situation requires it. Because Tom cannot walk does not necessarily make his physical functioning deviant. In his office, from which he controls a large corporation, Tom's paralysis is of little importance. However, Tom does have difficulty when he attempts to shop, especially when he encounters revolving doors. While shopping, Tom may be perceived as deviant.

Socially, one group may consider moles, dimples, or chubbiness to be characteristics of beauty while another may consider the same features unbecoming. Down's syndrome characteristics, for example, are not necessarily significant in a person's social environment. At school, Sue has Down's syndrome like many of her classmates, and she is accepted as being simply another student. On the bus going home, however, students from another school will not talk to her because she looks "different" and behaves "strangely." Sue is perceived as deviant by the students on the bus. Hence, deviance—both actual and perceived—varies from situation to situation.

Physique is simply one factor in a complex person-environment relationship, whether we use a behavioral, organismic, or dialectical approach. We must also consider others' perceptions, attitudes, and reactions vis-à-vis a particular physical characteristic.

Research in this area indicates that peers are less apt to like a child who is either not attractive (Dion & Berscheid, 1974; Kleck, Richardson, & Ronald, 1974; Salvia, Sheare, & Algozzine, 1973) or not "normal" (Richardson, Goodman, Hastorf, & Cornbusch, 1961) in appearance. The closer the handicap is to the face of the stimulus child, attraction to the child declines (Richardson, et al., 1961). Children also respond more positively to a child who appears normal than to a child who appears retarded, regardless of the stimulus child's competence (Siperstein & Gottlieb, 1977). The significance of these attitudes toward atypical physical characteristics is demonstrated by the effect that atypical characteristics have upon both perceptions and reactions. Studies suggest that negative perceptions and evaluations result from low physical attractiveness or unattractiveness (Clifford & Walster, 1973; Dion, 1972; Lerner & Lerner, 1977), and that physical deformity negatively influences judgments of normality (Aloia, 1975) and ability (Siperstein & Gottlieb, 1977). Compliance (Levitt & Kornhaber, 1977); variability of response, truthfulness of expressed opinions, and termination of interaction (Kleck, Ono, & Hastorf, 1966); and distance kept from a person (Worthington, 1974) are some reactions that appear to vary as a result of presence or absence of disability.

Given the knowledge that children who differ in appearance are likely targets for negative attitudes, perceptions, and reactions, educators may be alerted to potential somatopsychological problems. Verbalized attitudes toward the disabled have been found to be positive, even though nonverbalized attitudes may frequently be negative (Barker & Wright, 1954); therefore, the teacher should rely on observations of actual behavior rather than verbal reports in determining whether there is a need to intervene. Attitudes toward one form of deviancy have been shown to be generalized to a whole group of deviancies (Wolfensberger, 1972), and studies of preschool children suggest a tendency on the part of nonhandicapped children to reject handicapped peers (Thurman & Lewis, 1979). This highlights the importance of early intervention.

In summary, attitudes toward and perceptions of individuals with physical disability may tend to be negative; people appear to react differently toward disabled individuals, and observation of actual behavior and early intervention appear to be important considerations in altering behavior. The possibility that cues to deviance (Shushan, 1974) and others' attitudes toward individuals with disabilities (Rapier, Adelson, Carey, & Croke, 1972; Sadlick & Penta, 1975) may be altered is suggested by recent research. One approach to intervention involves the use of behavioral techniques, a method that will be discussed in detail.

A BEHAVIORAL MODEL

Given the amount of success of operant conditioning techniques with children over the past two decades, their potential for modifying a host of behaviors is evident (see Drabman, 1976; Jones & Kazdin, 1981; O'Leary & O'Leary, 1976 for reviews). Through use of these techniques, the frequency of a given behavior may be increased (if followed by a positive consequence) or decreased (if followed by a negative consequence). By viewing body-behavior problems from a behavioral perspective, substantial gain is made in terms of explaining the relationship between body and behavior as well as providing assessment and treatment strategies for intervention.

ADVANTAGES OF A BEHAVIORAL MODEL

One advantage of a behavioral approach is that it allows the therapist, parent, or special educator to focus on behavioral rather than personality variables (which are often assumed to cause behavior). For example, when directing attention to personality variables, the physically disabled child may be said to interact little with other classmates because of "shyness." When viewing this situation from a behavioral perspective, however, the child's lack of interaction may be viewed as resulting from a lack of social or behavioral skills with which to interact appropriately with classmates in a positive, reinforcing manner. Furthermore, this lack of skill could result from other children choosing not to talk with the child because of the deviation. The behavioral explanation serves to specify the variables that are operating to cause the observed behavior.

A second advantage is the emphasis on direct assessment. Unlike many approaches to problem behavior, where emphasis is placed on indirect forms of assessment (for example, self-report inventories and projective tests) and behavior is assumed to result from the individual's underlying traits, the behavioral model emphasizes a direct approach in which samples of the individual's behavior are obtained. Rather than assuming, as a result of indirect measurements, that the child with a disability would exhibit certain behaviors, direct observation is carried out to assess the frequency with which the responses of interest are emitted. For example, Henry, who has a deformed arm, was observed to engage in "aggressive" behavior (defined as hitting, kicking, or spitting at other students) an average of five times per hour. This assessment provides more practical and usable information than the knowledge that, on a projective test, he demonstrated possession of an "aggressive trait."

A final advantage of the behavioral model is the approach to intervention. Can Henry be helped to decrease the amount of inappropriate interactions with his classmates? Through behavioral techniques, which may consist of controlling the child's environment, helping him to control his behavior, or both, desired behaviors may be increased and undesired behaviors may be reduced or eliminated. Henry could be taught not to hit, kick, or spit, and the other students could be taught both to interact with him when he is behaving appropriately and to walk away when he starts to hit, kick, or spit.

APPLICATION OF A BEHAVIORAL MODEL

Borrowing from the behavioral model described by Neisworth et al. (1978), and further developed by Jones and Haney (1981), the effects of the cuing properties of bodily deviation may be explained in terms of differential reinforcement. As described in the model, bodily deviations may be considered as "discriminative stimuli" or cues because they set the occasion for differential reactions from others. A person's appearance might serve as a DS (discriminative stimulus) in that it signals that a particular response is likely to be reinforced and brings about that response, or it might serve as an S__ in that it signals that the response will not be reinforced and does not bring about that response. The type of response that individuals receive as a result of their appearance is called feedback. This feedback may be reinforcing (in that it serves to increase the frequency of a response) or punishing (in that it serves to decrease the frequency of a response).

An example of the discriminative stimulus function, as applied to the child who appears physically different, is seen when this child's appearance occasions teasing and ridicule by classmates. In the reverse situation, the child who is perceived as being normal may be neither teased nor ridiculed but, rather, may receive friendly responses from classmates. Punishing consequences of deviation (teasing and ridicule), neutral consequences (avoidance) and reinforcing consequences (teacher or parent reactions to hitting, kicking, or spitting) may result in new or strengthened inappropriate responses on the part of the child.

Meyerson (1971) supported this notion in pointing out that, as a result of social reactions to deviations in physique, children with disabilities as a group often experience more frequent and more severe psychological problems. A behavioral model may be applied to explain, assess, and treat these psychological problems as they are manifested in behavior.

Given the differential patterns of responding to children with disabilities, special educators, therapists, and parents should be equipped with both the knowledge of behavioral principles and the skills with which to modify and prevent the development and the maintenance of inappropriate responses on the part of the individual who is physically different and others in the environment.

IMPLICATIONS FOR INTERVENTION

So what if Johnny wears a leg brace, Susan has a badly scarred arm, and Freddie has a deformed ear? What difference does that make to them or those around them? Why might they benefit from a more normal appearance?

A number of researchers have shown that the physical characteristics of a child often serve as cues for differential reactions. Oftentimes, as has been noted, the reactions to atypical physical characteristics are negative (Kleck et al., 1966; Richardson et al., 1961; Worthington, 1974), and this may produce a great deal of misery for exceptional children. Indeed, the label of deviance, whether it refers to mental illness, mental retardation, or hyperkinesis, has been shown to have a negative influence on reactions (Farina & Ring, 1965; Jaffe, 1967; Neisworth, Kurtz, Jones, & Madle, 1974). The numerous studies on physical attractiveness and the findings concerning racial characteristics (Dion & Berscheid, 1974; Kleck et al., 1974; Salvia et al., 1973) give further evidence of the social handicap resulting from reactions to atypical physical characteristics. Inasmuch as some researchers have stated that an individual will behave as expected (Merton, 1948; Rosenthal & Jacobson, 1968), the negative expectations that may accompany these negative reactions—and their possible fulfillment—increase the desirability of intervention.

How, then, can the decreased popularity and the negative expectations and reactions (and the consequent distortions of a child's development) which result from the interaction of environment and atypical physique be prevented or reduced? What can teachers, therapists, and parents do to help the different-looking child? Three possible forms of intervention are: manipulation of the deviation, manipulation of consequences, and manipulation of environment.

CHANGING THE DEVIATION

Neisworth et al. have stated that "one's physical appearance may be considered as a set of cues that set the occasion for certain behaviors of others" and that "these behaviors act to alter the behavior of the person presenting the cues" (1978, p. 266). Manipulation of discriminative stimuli or cues, as described by Smith and Neisworth (1975) and Neisworth et al. (1978), refers to the elimination or reduction of the visibility of those stimuli or characteristics (such as facial features, body build, deformity or absence of limbs, and style of dress) that cause an individual to be perceived (and reacted to) as deviating from the norm. Methods of eliminating or reducing the prominence of discriminative stimuli include actual removal of deviation, reduction of deviation, and reduction of the visibility of deviation.

Removal of the Deviation

The most straightforward method of intervention is simply to remove the deviation. Presently, methods of removing deviation include plastic and corrective surgery, orthodontics, appropriate grooming, and diet. Removed scars, closed cleft palates, artificial noses and ears, straightened or replaced teeth, well-groomed appearances, and weight loss are some of the results of efforts in these areas. Lack of deviation implies normality.

Often, however, removal is not possible. Lack of finances may be an obstacle to plastic surgery, lack of technology may prevent corrective surgery, and lack of motivation or "willpower" may interfere with dieting. In these and other situations, either reduction of the actual deviation or reduction of the visibility of the deviation may be useful methods of intervention.

Reduction of the Deviation

Reduction of actual deviations may be brought about through use of substitutive learning and functional prosthetics. In *substitutive learning,* the individual learns a substitute skill that may reduce a deficit in functioning. Through this approach, a person might learn to read braille as a substitute for print, to use lipreading in place of hearing, or to use toes instead of fingers. Other skills that might serve as substitutes include learning to attend to environmental sounds (if blind), utilize residual vision (if some vision remains), and use the functional prostheses to be described later. Through this mode of intervention, the disability may no longer result in a handicap. The individual with a disability may no longer be prevented from participating in a normal activity in the mainstream.

Use of substitutive learning is illustrated in the situation of Joanne, a 25-year-old client at a sheltered workshop. Joanne was born deaf, and her IQ test scores indicated an intellectual functioning within the educable mentally retarded range. Being deaf, she never learned to communicate clearly with others except in writing. Joanne was always proud of her handwriting and through this method communicated her needs well (substitutive learning)—at least, until she was involved in an accident and lost her right arm (she was right-handed). Joanne was in a situation where she again needed substitutive learning: she had to learn either to write or type with her left hand. An alternate method of performing a common task (typing or writing with the left hand) was to be substituted for the original normal method (writing with the right hand). Since Joanne discovered that a lack of coordination caused her writing to be illegible, she learned to type and began practicing diligently. As a result of this simple substitution, she continues to communicate her needs well.

Reducing functional deviation through the attachment of an artificial device or prosthesis is called *functional prosthetics.* Such a device may actually replace a missing body part or enhance the functioning of an individual in some other way. Through functional prosthetics, individuals may overcome visual, auditory, motor, or other impairments that prevent them from adequately performing normal activities. Glasses and contact lenses, hearing aids, canes and laser canes, wheelchairs, crutches, walkers, braces, and artificial limbs are some prosthetic devices that are commonly used to reduce deficiency or deviation of functioning.

Actual use of functional prosthetics is demonstrated in the case of Carl, a 9-year-old educable mentally retarded boy who was mainstreamed into a regular class. There had been some doubt about whether Carl would be accepted by his new classmates because he had a history of epileptic seizures and was required to wear a functional prosthesis, a head protector. Prior to Carl's entry into the class, however, the students were shown the purpose of the head protector along with the proper things to do if Carl had a seizure at school. Carl himself explained the problems which he encountered because of the seizures and how his head protector allowed him to participate in normal activities without fear of injuring his head. With the understanding that Carl needed the head protector to permit him to function in school, just as some of them needed glasses and one of them needed a hearing aid, the students accepted their new classmate with little hesitation.

Reduction of the Visibility of Deviation

When reduction of functional deviation is insufficient, cosmetic prosthetics and compensatory learning may be used to reduce the visibility of the deviation. Individuals with facial or body deviations may profit from *cosmetic prosthetics,* which makes use of artificial devices (cosmetic prostheses) to conceal or draw attention away from a deviation in appearance. Subtractive cosmetic prostheses are those that conceal, while additive cosmetic prostheses draw attention away from a deviation by providing an attractive, added feature (Neisworth et al., 1978). Wigs, makeup, contact lenses, artificial limbs, and artificial eyes are subtractive if they conceal a deviation. Jewelry, fingernail polish, false eyelashes, and fashionable clothing are additive in that they place emphasis on another, added feature. Cosmetic prostheses such as these attempt to prevent a disability from resulting in a social handicap and to permit participation in normal activities through increasing acceptance.

Techniques that have been shown to be effective in recent research studies may be applied by teachers, therapists, and parents to normalize the appearance of exceptional individuals. For example, a recent study found that cosmetic prostheses such as makeup, complimentary eyeglass frames, sunglasses, wigs, and complimentary necklines significantly reduced the number of perceived appearance deficits in mentally retarded subjects (see Shushan, 1974). Use of these methods with students, clients, and children may result in similar improvements.

Complimentary wigs may be used to conceal unattractive haircuts or baldness and abnormal facial expressions or characteristics. Hairstyling (an artificial device in an extended sense) may be used to cover protruding ears and to frame faces in a flattering manner. Complimentary eyeglass frames may do much to normalize the appearance of children with Down's syndrome, while dark sunglasses may conceal the eyes of a person with an inward-turned eye.

Elimination or reduction of the visibility of the deviating features may also be achieved through *cosmetic learning.* This means that the person learns new ways of behaving that obscure, reduce, or eliminate the deviating features. Like cosmetic prosthetics, cosmetic learning may be either subtractive or additive. Cosmetic learning that reduces the visibility of deviation by eliminating inappropriate, stereotypic behaviors is subtractive, while cosmetic learning that increases normal behavior through the addition of normalized mannerisms is additive (Neisworth et al., 1978). Proce-

A change in hairstyle, eyeglass frames, and clothing help to improve this young woman's appearance. (*Courtesy of Paul J. Quinn.*)

dures to eliminate rocking and drooling are subtractive; procedures to promote good posture and appropriate smiling are additive. Normalization may be enhanced through the reduction of behaviors that serve as cues to deviance and the promotion of behaviors that serve as cues to normalcy. Learning what to do and what not to do in social situations may go a long way toward building a positive, normalized repertoire of behaviors that interacts favorably with the social setting.

Again generalizing from research, students may be told how to hold their heads and how to normalize the expression around their eyes and mouths (additive cosmetic learning). Physical prompting and tension-easing discussion have been shown to assist subjects in normalizing expressions and may be helpful in similar efforts with students and clients (see Shushan, 1974).

For example, Sandy, a 15-year-old trainable mentally retarded girl with cerebral palsy, had lived in an institution for ten years prior to her parents' decision to care for her at home. After living at home for a couple of months, Sandy seemed to be enjoying her new life. Often, however, Sandy was found rocking all by herself in a corner, both at home and at school. She generally did this when she was not receiving attention. Both her teachers and parents decided to stop this rocking through reinforcing Sandy (constantly at first, and then less frequently) when she was not rocking and ignoring her while she was rocking. The other students at school cooperated in this effort. Sandy received praise, a pat on the back, and sometimes a token for sitting still. By the end of the school year, Sandy had ceased rocking altogether (subtractive cosmetic learning).

Teaching Substitutive and Compensatory Learning

As in any learning situation, the teacher should first determine the objectives. In this case, the objectives involve attainment of those behaviors that enhance normalization. The teacher should then:

1. Assess the student's needs, as related to the objectives. (What behaviors need to be learned or unlearned?)

2. Determine priorities. (Which behavior should be learned or unlearned first, if there is more than one behavior?)

3. Decide upon an objective. (How should the individual behave after intervention?)

4. Operationally define the behavior. (How can the behavior be measured?)

5. Measure present occurrence. (How frequently and in which situations does the behavior occur?)

6. Intervene. (Use a method appropriate for the individual.)

7. Have students repeatedly rehearse appropriate behavior. (Train under varying conditions and during daily activities to increase generalization of responding to other settings.)

8. Fade intervention to increase maintenance of responding. (When the goal has been reached, stop teaching.)

9. Withdraw intervention, and continue measurement. (Check occasionally to see if the normalized behavior is still occurring.)

MANIPULATING CONSEQUENCES

Functional and cosmetic learning may be facilitated by manipulating the consequences of performing the desired behavior to increase the likelihood of its occurrence. For example, manipulation of consequences may be used to promote subtractive cosmetic learning by assisting in elimination of those behaviors that are frequently associated with physical deviance (such as aggression, withdrawal, rocking, and head banging). This third and final method of intervention involves the use of behavioral techniques, such as token and social reinforcement and self-control procedures (see Jones & Kazdin, 1981), which may increase the occurrence of appropriate behaviors. Individuals are contingently reinforced for cleanliness and normal behavior; individuals do not receive reinforcement for slovenliness and deviant behavior.

Environment manipulation has been described as including those alterations that permit ease of physical access and social acceptance in order to promote the process of normalization (Smith & Neisworth, 1975). There are several ways the environment may be changed in order to minimize deviance.

Alteration of the Physical Environment

Currently, much attention is being given to removal of access barriers. Narrow doorways, steps, and other barriers are giving way to wide entrances, ramps, and other arrangements that permit individuals with disabilities to go about their daily activities more freely.

Kathy, a 15-year-old whose legs were paralyzed, had learned to use a wheelchair (functional learning with a functional prosthesis), to skillfully cover a facial scar with makeup (subtractive cosmetic prosthetics), and to style her hair and dress fashionably in order to detract attention from the facial scar and motor problems (additive cosmetic prosthetics). Kathy had average intelligence and wanted more than anything to attend the public school in her town. Unfortunately, the three-story school building was equipped only with stairs, a formidable obstacle to Kathy's wish. Situations such as this are being resolved through environmental improvements, which make physical access possible.

Spacious, well-lit rooms and hallways; wide, easily opened doors; level, nonslip floors; railed, slowly rising stairways and ramps; and elevators, escalators, and stair lifts may provide for ease of movement within buildings. Buses with ramps, adequate seating, and storage space for wheelchairs and other equipment facilitate use of public transportation, while nearby parking may increase access to public places. Lowered light switches, doorknobs, drinking fountains, and sinks and toilet stalls large enough for wheelchairs may permit use of public facilities.

Special chairs, cut-out tables, bookracks, automatic page turners, and pencil holders may enhance functioning within an academic environment. Special eating utensils, modified buttons, zippers, and snaps, and altered doorknobs, locks, and light switches may assist performance in the home.

Alteration of the Social Environment

Although difficulties may be encountered, changing the social acceptance of individuals with disabilities by educating the public may be a dramatic, effective way to reduce the stigma of being different.

In Richardson's (1970) study, young children were found to rank individuals according to how much their overall appearance differed from that of a nonhandicapped child (with liking decreasing as difference in appearance increased), indicating that unfamiliarity leads to decreased liking. It was suggested that early and frequent contact with individuals of differing appearances might increase liking for children with disabilities by decreasing

Selection of flattering
eyeglass frames can be an
important step in reducing
the visibility of some
socially negative
deviation. (*Pennsylvania
Department of Welfare,
Office of Mental
Retardation.*)

their strangeness. Inasmuch as increased proximity has been shown to be more likely to result in attraction or positive attitudes toward an individual (Berscheid & Walster, 1978), the notion that contact with individuals with disabilities might increase liking appears to be supported.

Where contact with exceptional individuals is limited or negative, awareness may be increased through films, lectures, simulation of deviations, role playing, public discussion, dissemination of information through the media, and other public relations efforts. Increased awareness of and exposure to differences may enhance the normalization process through reduction of sensitivity to differences. In the classroom, a teacher might focus on modifying the behavior of those children who exhibit extremely negative reactions to a child with a deviation, or those who have high status among the group, or the whole class. In this effort, the previously described procedure for enhancing cosmetic and substitutive learning would be utilized.

The earlier example of Carl, the child with a head protector, demonstrated some techniques for increasing acceptance. There are also examples of more radical social change, as illustrated by one community living arrangement (CLA) in Utah. Doug, the administrator at an institution for the mentally retarded, had three residents who he thought would benefit from a homelike situation within a quiet community. The community *was* quiet until its citizens learned about the CLA. Rumors describing how dangerous mentally retarded individuals are were passed around, petitions were started to prevent the opening of the group home, and the CLA issue made headlines in the local paper. Doug was able to get his CLA, however, by going to town meetings, making himself available so that people could voice their concerns, showing movies and asking audience members to participate in role playing (to discover how it feels to have a disability), and inviting people to visit his institution in order to become acquainted with the residents and to see what institutionalized living is like. Increased contact and awareness succeeded in providing a more normalized environment for Doug's residents.

CHOICE OF INTERVENTION

Given that alternatives for intervention do exist, selection of an intervention becomes important. Smith and Neisworth (1975) mention important factors that should be considered in selection, including available technology, required modification, expense, learning, generalizability, and psychological implications:

1. *Available technology.* Alteration of the physical environment or enhancement of functioning and appearance through prostheses may be prevented simply because the required technology does not exist. Some deviations cannot be easily eliminated or obscured with existing devices or procedures.

2. *Required modification.* The technology may be available, but the amount of modification needed may not be considered justifiable. Should elevators and ramps be installed for one individual? Many public buildings, universities, and other institutions face this problem.

3. *Expense.* Again, the technology may be available, but the expenses may be prohibitive to either individuals or localities.

4. *Learning.* The amount of learning required for an intervention may be beyond the capabilities of the individual to be taught.

5. *Generalizability.* An intervention may not be generalizable to all of the individual's situations.

6. *Psychological implications.* An intervention may enhance functioning but at the same time increase the visibility of deviation. Use of a hook to replace a hand may improve an individual's functioning, but it may also produce excessive negative reactions.

Because the type of intervention that may be appropriate in one environment (an institution, for example) may not be appropriate in another (such as the community), intervention should, perhaps, include a combination of all three methods. In this way, the individual has an alternative method for achieving a goal in an emergency.

School psychologists, teachers, parents, and others must be alert to the numerous possibilities for improving the exceptional student's social impact. Reduction of deviation and its consequent stigma as part of the curriculum or program for exceptional persons may contribute to optimal individual development.

SUMMARY

In view of the increasing integration of exceptional individuals into the mainstream, studies are needed which further clarify both the perception of deviance and the consequent reactions of the individual. Recent research has been carried out largely in the areas of attitudes and reactions of other individuals toward individuals with deviations. Clarification of the somatopsychological relationship from a behavioral perspective will assist in understanding, predicting, and controlling behavior generated by this interaction. Study of the development, maintenance, and modification of reactions to disabilities should serve as goals for future research.

Furthermore, studies on the effectiveness of intervention techniques may promote application of this understanding of somatopsychological problems. Such studies need to research: (a) the specific appearance characteristics that determine whether an individual is perceived as deviant, (b) the consequent behaviors on the part of the individual that increase the likelihood of his or her perception as deviant, (c) the methods of intervention that will remove or reduce the amount of deviation or perceived deviation, and (d) the methods of intervention that will reduce the negative reactions of others to deviation.

Continued research in the area of somatopsychological problems may facilitate mainstreaming by providing teachers, therapists, and parents with both an understanding of the negative attitudes, perceptions, and reactions which the exceptional child may encounter and the techniques with which to reduce or prevent them.

P. David Kurtz

CHAPTER 12
WORKING
WITH THE FAMILY

(*Courtesy of Jim Lukens.*)

A New Role For Families

The role of the family of the handicapped individual has shifted dramatically. Wolfensberger's review of the literature revealed that prior to the mid-1940s "very little mention was made of parents, of their feelings and sensibilities, or of the impact of the diagnosis on them" (1967, p. 379). A trickle of literature in the late 1940s and 1950s focused on parent dynamics and the trend to institutionalize handicapped children. The question was often not *whether* but *when* to institutionalize the child. One article, for example, bore the title, "When should the seriously retarded infant be institutionalized?" (Jolly, 1953). Aldrich wrote convincingly that children with Down's syndrome "are happiest when allowed to grow up in situations where they compete with their peers, in institutions." (1947, p. 45).

More recently a number of studies show that severely handicapped children brought up in their own homes are more advanced in their development than those who are reared in institutions (Carr, 1970; Centerwall & Centerwall, 1960; Lyle, 1960; Stedman and Eichorn, 1964). Partly as a result of these findings and the shift in emphasis to normalization, parents are under increased pressure to keep the handicapped child in the home, to assume the primary role for care and management during the early years, and to facilitate their children's integration into the broader community during adolescence and early adulthood. While normalization offers the handicapped person an opportunity to maximize development and involvement in society, it also exposes the individual and persons in the environment to risks. There are many unanswered questions about the impact a handicapped child has on the family as a whole and on the individual development of each member.

FAMILY INFLUENCE ON THE INDIVIDUAL

Every day, every hour, children with disabilities are born. Cerebral palsy or spina bifida will prevent a child from running, riding a bike, and dancing. If

the child is blind, the opportunity to see the rising and setting sun will be denied. Mental retardation will preclude children from following in the footsteps of their parents. Although birth defects are a major source of handicap, accidents also account for many disabilities. In an unguarded moment a child may fall from a tree or skateboard, be hit by a car, or ingest a toxic substance—all of which may result in permanent disability. No family is immune from possible disability, regardless of wealth, education, religious persuasion, race, composition, or physical and mental health.

No matter what form the family assumes, whether nuclear, single-parent, or extended, it is a powerful factor in determining behavior, moral development, and social evolution. The family is an interdependent social system composed of various subsystems, depending on its composition and roles. The complex interrelationships influence the individual development of each member as well as the development of the whole family. Any change in one member's behavior will affect individual members, subsystems, and the family unit. Most families have relatively clear and stable norms, role definitions, communication networks, and decision-making patterns. The occurrence of a serious, unexpected event such as a financial crisis, natural catastrophy, or a prolonged illness, even in the healthiest of families, will result in substantial and in some cases even drastic changes in the family's lifestyle. Roles are redefined, adjustments in norms and values occur, and expectations for the future are altered. The impact of a handicapped member may be even more dramatic. Families form exceptionally high expectations for their members, and many disabilities are not transitory but remain throughout life. Society's attitude intensifies the family's plight: "Society creates handicaps. While most disabilities are products of birth and accident, the debilitating impact on the person's life often results not so much from the 'disability' as from the manner in which others define or treat the person" (Gordon, 1974, p. 7).

Pearl Buck (1950) provided a moving account of her life in China with her severely retarded daughter. She observed that her daughter was not singled out because of her handicap: the Chinese accepted such disabilities as a simple fact of life and treated her daughter as they would any child. However, when she returned to Western culture, she noted the stigmatization and prejudice toward the handicapped. Even she gradually began to perceive her daughter as different and to treat her as such. Handicap is, indeed, socially defined and imposed.

The study of the handicapped individual in the context of the family requires an examination of the three-way interaction among individual members, the family, and society.

1. Each member's development affects the development of other members.

2. Each member's development affects the development of the family, and the family affects members' development.

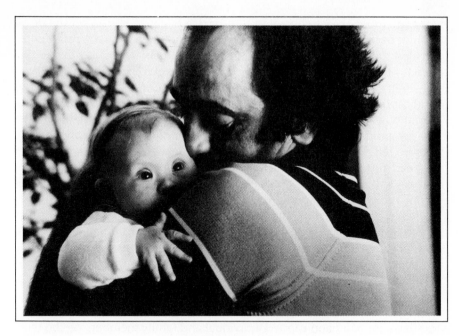

Contrary to the beliefs of most parents, infants can and do control parent behavior. (*National Down Syndrome Society.*)

3. Society affects the development of the family and its members, and they in turn affect social evolution.

Through interaction with the family environment, members learn a broad range of behaviors, roles, norms, and values. The powerful contingencies used by family members are a major variable in shaping members' behavior, both functional and dysfunctional. Support now exists for the idea that social reinforcement from parents is sufficient to maintain deviant behavior in children (Patterson, 1971a). Furthermore, just as parents are rewarded by feelings of pride and joy that result from the normal development and functional behavior of their children, children's antisocial or deviant behavior has an aversive affect on them: they feel guilty, embarrassed, frustrated, and angry when their children display behavior which society deems deviant.

EARLY INTERACTION
Each infant and parent must learn sucking and feeding skills respectively. Success in feeding is often central to feelings of competent parenting. The difficulties a parent encounters in feeding a handicapped infant—as, for example, a cerebral palsied infant with poor sucking and swallowing mechanisms—may be frustrating and even frightening. These apprehensions may be intensified by society's expectation that feeding should be a rewarding time for both parent and child.

Certain behavior patterns, such as excessive passivity, placidity, or hyperactivity, may be a direct result of the handicap. The excessive demands of handicapped children can be exasperating, and family members may acquire negative interaction patterns to deal with the aversive situation. The family members' reaction may in turn have a negative impact on the development of the handicapped child. A study conducted in Israel, for example, revealed that mothers of children with cerebral palsy failed to provide their children toys that would facilitate cognitive development (Shere, 1971).

A dramatic example concerns a mother whose fourth child was multi-handicapped owing to rubella (Freedman, Fox-Kalenda, & Brown, 1970). Even though she had successfully reared her first three children, the mother was not prepared for the complications of caring for a handicapped child. His care fell exclusively on her. He persisted in keeping his back arched and his head retracted and thus was difficult to fondle and cuddle. Since his senses were impaired, he experienced a reduction in environmental stimulation and was correspondingly less responsive to interaction with his mother. He was often ill, and because of his poor feeding mechanisms he required frequent feeding. Although she spent a considerable amount of time with him, the care was carried out in a very mechanical manner. When he failed to respond to her ministrations or opposed them with irritation, she was quickly discouraged.

INAPPROPRIATE USES OF REINFORCEMENT
The behavior of a handicapped individual and family members can be reciprocally reinforcing in positive or negative ways. Often family members do not possess the reinforcement skills that facilitate development and encourage appropriate behavior. Rather, they resort to aversive methods such as threats, demands, yelling, and physical punishment (Patterson and Reid, 1970). To avoid the aversive stimuli, children comply. Compliance reinforces the use of the aversive methods and, thus, a spiraling of coercive interactions. On the other hand, parents tend to *reinforce* a wide variety of undesirable behaviors (Patterson, 1971b). The reinforcement can be quite subtle and thus easily overlooked, such as a fleeting warm facial expression. However, modification of these contingencies is essential to eliminating problems in child-parent interactions. Intervention focuses on replacing coercive interaction with consistently positive methods. Rather than attending to or giving in to inappropriate demanding behavior, such as begging and temper tantrums, parents must learn to dispense their reinforcement only when the child makes a request in a sociably acceptable manner.

As children grow older their behavior is increasingly influenced by a wide spectrum of people: peers, teachers, neighbors, and so on. However, in the early years parents and other family members are the main source of influence.

LIFE-SPAN DEVELOPMENTAL VIEW

THE FAMILY LIFE CYCLE
Various approaches exist for conceptualizing the family life cycle. Perhaps the most common approach is the chronological cycle, such as Duvall's eight stages. The stages are based on family patterns, age and school place-

ment of the oldest child, and functions and statuses of families prior to the presence of children and after they leave. The stages are: (1) married couples, (2) childbearing families, (3) families with preschool children, (4) families with school children, (5) families with teenagers, (6) families launching young adults, (7) middle-aged parents, and (8) aging family members. The middle stages revolve around the children. Clear delineation of stages occurs only in families with one child. When more children are present, the stages overlap. In reality, few families move through the eight stages in the "typical" fashion.* According to Farber (1975), the presence of a mentally retarded member may initially slow down movement in the family cycle and eventually prevent or arrest the development of later stages in the cycle.

WHAT FACTORS AFFECT FAMILY LIFE-CYCLE DEVELOPMENT?
It is important to note that certain factors impinge on family interaction and affect the course of events. Generally, it is assumed that family functioning is adversely influenced; however, Fotheringham and Creal (1974) stress, "It must be reiterated that a reduction in family functioning is *not* the inevitable consequence of having a handicapped child" (p. 360). Each family must be evaluated on its own merits.

The short- and long-term impact depends on notable factors which influence family adaptation over time, including: severity of the handicap, sex of the retarded individual, family socioeconomic status, family religious practice, degree of help the family receives, stability of marital and filial ties, discrepancy between the handicapped person's presence and the family goals and aspirations, and the manner in which the community perceives and reacts to the situation.

THE HANDICAPPED CHILD AND THE FAMILY LIFE CYCLE
This section focuses primarily on the family of the mentally retarded individual for two reasons: there is more literature regarding this population than any other, and the retarded individual's handicap often affects the family throughout its life span. The impact of other handicaps on the family may vary considerably or be quite similar to that of mental retardation.

MARRIED COUPLE
The family life cycle actually begins with the husband-wife dyad. Building the relationship involves learning to nurture and satisfy each other, negotiating differences and conflicts, defining one's roles and assuming responsibility for them, and resolving unrealistic expectations. "Intimacy is based on a realistic perception of the partner as a whole person, as opposed to the idealization of one's partner as a romantic image, or disillusionment with one's partner as unresponsive" (Rhodes, 1977, p. 303). The marital pair is constant throughout the family life cycle and is the backbone of its devel-

---

*The family as conceived in this section is limited to the two-parent nuclear family of varied socioeconomic status, which has several children, one of whom is mentally retarded.

opment. Therefore, the developmental task of achieving marital integration is seen as being one of the most important in the family's development; unsuccessful achievement of this task influences all others. Our rising divorce rate forecasts increasing risks for positive child development.

While it is often assumed that the presence of a retarded child in the family disrupts marital integration, it is not necessarily the case. Farber (1960), Fotheringham and Creal (1974), and Fowle (1968) compared families in which the retarded child was kept at home with families who institutionalized their retarded child. They concluded that: (1) the presence of a severely retarded child does not adversely affect marital integration; (2) families who institutionalized their children were functioning at such low levels prior to the children's birth that they could not cope with their presence; and (3) while institutionalization does not solve the family's problems, it does remove an aspect of the problem. In some families, marital ties may have been fragile even prior to the child's presence and the birth of a retarded child could easily exacerbate an already shaky relationship. Farber (1975) states that adaptation to a retarded child "seems to require that the family bonds be fairly strong to begin with." Similarly, Ross (1964) claims that couples who successfully achieve marital integration can more easily make decisions about their retarded child's future such as training, siblings, and placement.

CHILDBEARING FAMILY

During the childbearing years, the major developmental tasks encountered involve nurturing offspring, adapting to the physical and emotional needs of preschool children, and sustaining the development of the marital relationship. The triad replaces the dyad. Individual roles must be redefined to include both marital and parental responsibilities. Couples must consciously assume their parental roles without relinquishing their marital responsibilities. While the parents must adapt to the needs of children, they must guard against losing marital integration. The married couple must continually replenish their relationship.

Parental Reactions

The birth of a handicapped child is a traumatic event. Parental reactions to the diagnosis that their child is retarded are highly individualistic. The type and intensity of the response varies widely, depending on a range of factors: how parents handle crisis situations in general, stability of the marital relationship, parental aspirations, social class, and so on. Some of the more common reactions include guilt, disappointment, shame, grief, anger, and disbelief.

Informing parents of their child's disability requires great sensitivity and skill (Bennett, 1981; Wolfensberger, 1967; Wurm, 1981). Key factors in the initial interviews are its timing, what information is given, and how it is told. Typically, parents prefer to be informed as early as possible (Carr, 1970). After the initial shock of hearing that their child is handicapped, most par-

The young parents of a retarded child usually must resolve their feelings and thoughts about "Why me?" and "What will happen next?" (*Courtesy of Paul J. Quinn.*)

ents request detailed information and advice regarding the child's limitations, expectations they should have for the child, and methods for caring and helping. Frequently, more than one interview is needed to enable parents to absorb the information. The informant's method of communication is critical to parents' understanding and acceptance of the situation. An empathetic informant who is willing to take the time to fully answer parent questions communicates sympathy, understanding, and concern to the parent. Parents often resent the person who abruptly informs them and who seems uncaring.

Despite the difficulties, parents usually wish to keep their mentally retarded children at home. The family's acceptance of the disabled child is in part dependent on the parents' (particularly the mother's) response. If the mother is reasonably optimistic and willing to integrate the child, the family will reflect her reaction. On the other hand, if she is despondent and disappointed, the family is more likely to respond negatively to the child.

Infants use the smile, the cry, and contented babbling to be responsive to initial social responses from others. Excessive crying and lack of smiling and verbalization, which often typify handicapped infants, may make it difficult for parents to relate to the child. This problem may be compounded since the handicapped child often remains at this stage much longer than the normal child. It is not clear whether impoverishment of social relationships has more detrimental consequences at one age level or another. "There is good evidence of the existence of sensitive periods for the establishment of primary social bonds in many species. Studies in humans in which the mother-child relationship did not develop or was disrupted provide evidence in support of the basic contention for sensitive periods during which the human infant is maximally sensitive to social contracts with its mother, contracts that will lead to the cementing of an "affectional bond" (Marinelli & Orto, 1977, p. 57). In a study of forty families of "failure to thrive" children, none of the parents experienced a sense of fulfillment in the parental roles (Evans, 1980). The "emotional symbiosis," the confidence of the mother in her role and in the child did not occur. In most instances mothers experienced frustration, anger, and poor self-image owing to their perceived inadequate mothering.

In the traditional family reactions also appear to be linked to sex roles, with mothers assuming expressive roles and fathers instrumental roles (Gumz & Gubrium, 1972; Tavormina, Boll, Dunn, Luscomb, & Taylor, 1981). Fathers are usually concerned about the retarded child's impact on the family budget, the child's ability to learn a trade and become an independent adult. A handicapped child is often a financial hardship and places the father under considerable strain to find a better-paying position or to seek a second job. Because occupational roles require that the father be absent from home during most of the day, fathers "characteristically have fewer opportunities to do something directly helpful for their handicapped child, something which provides concrete evidence of their loving, caring, and benevolent concern" (Cummings, 1976, p. 253). Nor do fathers have much opportunity to express their feelings of frustration and anger.

Mothers, on the other hand, are more often concerned with the emotional strain of caring for the child, the additional time involved, the ability to maintain harmony within the family, the child's ability to make friends, and the child's future happiness. All children at this stage require nurturing, but the severely retarded child requires an inordinate amount. The preschooler may not be able to walk, may possess few if any self-help skills, and may have problems in self-management. The parents, particularly the mother, are under constant pressure to provide for the child's needs. If the mother is almost completely responsible for the child's care, she may respond in a variety of ways. She may simply provide routine care in a perfunctory manner. At the other extreme, she may develop an unnaturally close relationship, in which she receives fulfillment through the child's dependence.

In a study comparing everyday rearing problems of Down's syndrome children with normal children, Carr (1975) found that at 15 months the handicapped group experienced less trouble over sleeping, cried less, and had significantly fewer temper tantrums than the nonhandicapped children. By age 4 these differences had disappeared. Over half the mothers in *each* group reported the children were easy to manage. Approximately 12 percent of the parents in each group found the children so difficult to manage as to constitute a problem. Differences were noted between the groups in behaviors involving independence. In particular, Down's syndrome children were more difficult to feed and dress and were slower to walk and be toilet-trained. Furthermore, they experienced more ill health than normal children.

In some cases handicapped children are treated as if they are sick (Richardson, 1969). Parents give the child less responsibility, place fewer restrictions on behavior, and are more tolerant of undesirable behavior and personal whims, often at the expense of siblings. Furthermore, total care of the disabled child may result in parents' unintentional neglect of other children. Siblings may react to an impoverishment of parent-child interaction by withdrawing from the family or by protesting and acting out (Adams, 1967). Parents must walk a tightrope to avoid arousing sibling resentment while at the same time providing for the special needs of the handicapped child.

The special responsibility of rearing a disabled child can intensify existing parental problems. It is not uncommon for parents to gradually become isolated from one another and for their mutual respect, affection, and compassion to diminish. A parent expresses his unresolved feelings:

> I think the problems of parent reaction do not fit into any progressive pattern that assumes that people will "get over it." I loved Diana as much as I could love any other person. It satisfied me deeply to hold her and to feed her (even though she would not cooperate) and to play with her. . . . Yet in spite of that love I resented her at times. She kept me home too much. We could not get out when we wanted to . . . she tired me out and put me under intense stress. I knew that her life depended upon me. . . . I never resolved either the depth or the complexity of such conflicting feelings (Searl, 1978, p. 129).

Under these circumstances, opportunities for couples to replenish and enhance their marital relationship may be diminished. Respite care for the retarded is a relatively new service in this country and is not available to all parents. Baby-sitters are often as reluctant to care for a retarded child as parents are to leave their child with an inexperienced person. Extended family members may or may not be tolerant of the child.

Cultural Expectations

Society's reaction to abnormality has a substantial impact on the development of the family unit and each of its members. Family members are conditioned to certain social expectations and myths. Marriage is idealized by some as "eternal bliss," and from this blissful union beautiful and perfect children will be conceived. In our culture we are continually exposed to reminders of such attitudes. Physical and mental standards are constantly being defined and demonstrated. For instance, ads depict the tall, slim female and the macho male as being the epitome of what we should strive for. Failure of parents to produce a perfect replica of themselves and thus fulfill society's expectations can result in feelings of guilt, shame, and inferiority.

Some couples attempt to maintain their social relationships and actively help their relatives and friends understand the situation. On the other hand, frequently couples withdraw from social activities and even avoid relatives and friends. The tendency toward isolation is often negatively reinforced by outsiders, who don't know how to respond to the family in a sensitive and facilitative manner. Family members' problems can be compounded by people who shun them. A mother of a handicapped child wrote, "Last summer I met a woman who really did not *want* to know Jim. She came up to me at one of Jim's brother's ball games and said 'We almost bought the house next to yours, then we saw him (pointing to Jim sitting beside me) and decided not to.' " (Michaelis, 1974, p. 30.)

FAMILIES WITH SCHOOLCHILDREN

After parents have passed through the early childrearing years, they face the developmental task of facilitating children's movement from a dependent to a quasi-dependent role. The major task of this stage is for all family members to form identities which are not defined by their roles within the family. Grade-schoolers must feel secure and free to develop relationships outside the family. As mothers gradually relinquish their predominant roles as caretakers, they may also begin to venture into new nonfamily roles such as returning to school or seeking employment. Fathers are in the process of evaluating their success and making decisions regarding their vocational and avocational interests. The ability of the family to support individuation (personal identity) at this point is an important aspect of a healthy family. The family who keeps its children dependent or whose mother lives for her children runs the risk of developing a falsely mutual relationship among its members. Such a family fears autonomy and individuation but disguises this fear by claiming to be very close. The success or failure of previous developmental tasks, such as separation from the family of origin, attainment of marital integration, and the separation of parenting and marital roles, influences how well a family will achieve the individuation of all its members.

At the same time as they are pursuing individual interests, couples are faced with the continuing task of replenishing and enhancing the marital relationship. It is during this period that marital satisfaction is found to be at a low ebb (Burr, 1970). The excessive demands of children, conflictive relationships between siblings, and the problems children encounter in their new experiences with the community heavily tax parents. Wives express negative emotions, such as feelings of resentment and not being needed, more often while dependent children are in the home than during any other period of their marriage (Rollins & Feldman, 1970). Parents of the retarded have the added responsibility of providing substantial care while facilitating the transition of siblings from the family to the larger society. The constant care required may inhibit parents from pursuing their own individuation. The mother, for instance, may have neither the time nor the inclination to pursue career interests or social activities. Often mothers become buried in the child's care to the point of exhaustion. The predominant role as caretakers is an obstacle to their progressive independence and individuation (West, 1981).

Individuation is also important to the development of the disabled child. A critical dilemma which confronts many parents is whether to smother the child in an overprotective environment or to provide a more normal environment, which involves risk. The world in which we live is not always safe, secure, and predictable. But it is the world—the world that parents must face, the world that the disabled child must learn to live in as well. Parents must appreciate the critical developmental role that people outside the family play in the child's life. They must learn to balance security with the freedom necessary to encourage the child to develop relationships outside the family.

School-related Stigma

When the child enters school, the family members must be prepared to deal with outsiders' evaluations of their child-rearing practices, the goals they have for the child, as well as the child's abilities. Parents have many apprehensions. How will the teacher provide for the child's needs? Will the teacher be understanding? How will my child get along with the other kids? Will they tease my child? Can my child meet the school's expectations? A troubled parent of a handicapped child reported, "I overheard some mothers at the first PTA meeting talking about how they feel their children have been cheated because Jean has captured so much of the teacher's attention" (*The Exceptional Parent,* 1976, p. 22).

The unique needs of the handicapped child mean that parents are expected to take on yet another function—that of being actively involved in their children's education. Their ability to assume this responsibility varies depending on how well they have resolved their feelings and dealt with problems in the home. School social workers can play a crucial role in preparing and supporting parents to participate in relevant school tasks such as an IEP conference (Schafler, 1980).

Sibling Problems

With increased age the differences between retarded children and their siblings become more apparent. How a normal child reacts to having a retarded sibling depends a great deal on the reactions of the parents (Wolfensberger, 1967). A family in which retardation is openly discussed is likely to foster healthy acceptance, but a family which denies problems is likely to foster fantasies. Siblings wonder about such things as the origin of the child's retardation, whether the same fate will befall them, whether curiosity about retardation is bad, and whether sibling anger or jealousy caused the child's retardation (Grossman, 1972). Siblings frequently feel guilty for merely being normal, a factor which may hinder their progress in school as well as their overall individuation from the family (San Martino & Newman, 1974).

What are some of the problems normal siblings encounter? Parents may be overly involved with the special needs of the disabled child. Siblings may have unmet needs, or parents may have unrealistically high aspirations for them to compensate for the limitations of the handicapped child. Also impeding the development of the normal child is the expectation to share in the responsibility for the retarded sibling by substituting for the parents or by requiring the sibling to take the handicapped child along in peer group activities. Since female siblings frequently serve as mother's helpers, they are more affected by the presence of a retarded child in the family than are male siblings (Adams, 1967; Farber, 1960; Fowle, 1968; Grossman, 1972). Another concern is that the normal child may have only a small peer network because of the stigma of having a retarded sibling. From a study of 240 families with a severely retarded child Farber (1960) concluded:

> The retarded child's siblings were adversely affected by his high degree of dependence, which adversely affected the siblings' relationship with their mother. When the children were young, interaction between the normal and retarded brothers and sisters tended to be on an equalitarian basis. As they grew older, the normal siblings frequently assumed a superordinate position in the relationship. However, siblings who did not interact frequently with their retarded brother or sister generally were affected less than those who interacted frequently (p. 159).

Regardless of birth position, eventually the retarded child acquires the status of the youngest child in the family. Conversely, young siblings assume a superordinate position. Apparently, older siblings bear the impact better than young ones. Carr (1974) cautions that many of the sibling studies suffer from methodological drawbacks. He concludes, "What emerges from the studies (apart from Holt's) is a consistent lack of support for the widely held view that normal children will necessarily suffer from the presence of a retarded child in the home" (p. 829).

FAMILIES WITH TEENAGERS

Much activity outside the family is emphasized in the fourth stage of the family life cycle when the children are teenagers. An important developmental task at this stage is one of balancing freedom with responsibility, as teenagers mature and strive for autonomy. It is a time of budding sexuality for the children and of renewed sexual feelings between the parents. Family members attempt to deal with the dichotomous struggle of companionship through revitalization of the marriage as well as through new interests outside the family. Sexual themes and separation themes prevail and new parent-child relationships need to be established to adapt to these themes. The ability of the marital couple to unite in providing appropriate limits and responsibility will enable teenagers to experiment with autonomy while remaining reasonably dependent on the family. The middle years may also be a time of identity crisis for parents. While they are evaluating their lives and beliefs, the teenagers are challenging those beliefs and experimenting with new lifestyles.

Accomplishing these tasks is often difficult for families with a handicapped adolescent. Because many retarded adolescents never achieve a significant degree of autonomy, the marital relationship is affected. Instead of increased emancipation and separation, the parent-child relationship remains constant. A parent of a mentally retarded adolescent stressed: "Whatever Andy does involves me, my husband and all the other members of our immediate family" (Hamilton, 1977, p. Y26). Since parents are bound to the needs of an eternal child, their relationship has little opportunity to grow and be replenished. The conflict in parental and marital roles occurs at a time when most couples experience a gradual increase in freedom from their parental responsibilities and have additional opportunities for individual development. This newfound freedom is not available to many couples of handicapped children.

The presence of a child who has been handicapped from birth often hinders couples' sexual interaction and restricts their desire to reproduce. Holt (1958) discovered that out of 160 families with retarded children, 101 did not want more children and 90 families reached this decision because of the retarded child. Similarly, Tizard and Grad (1961) found a tendency for such families to avoid having additional offspring. Parents report that they fear and dread the thought of giving birth to another such child. Such apprehension can have an adverse effect on the marriage. One such wife confided, "I'm afraid to have another child. . . . Last week John threatened to end our marriage. He said that if we weren't going to have children, there was no sense in our staying together." (*The Exceptional Parent*, 1977b, p. M21). A small number of couples, however, have additional children as a compensation for bearing the disabled child (Tizard & Grad, 1961).

It seems that restriction of fertility may be passed on to the siblings of the retarded. Adams (1967) claims that adolescent siblings often question their ability to procreate normally. They also profess to difficulty dating owing to the embarrassment of having a retarded sibling. They often continue to harbor the fantasy of being similar to their handicapped brother or sister. Adolescents tend to have great self-awareness; the fantasy of "Am I also retarded?" is also magnified (Grossman, 1972). They experience ambivalent feelings, at times wanting to defend their sibling from community ridicule and at other times wanting to dissociate themselves from the handicapped child for fear that they may be perceived as similar. Adolescents are concerned about their retarded sibling's ability to understand retardation as well as sexuality. Some have guilt feelings about their own increasing autonomy, realizing that their retarded sibling will never be able to achieve the same level of accomplishment.

The family of the severely retarded adolescent must also deal with the sexuality of the child. This can be a very difficult problem for parents who have been nurtured to believe in conventional standards of sexual expression but who also want their budding adolescent to enjoy sexual relationships as part of a full life. Freedom to enjoy and express one's sexual potential is a right denied many handicapped people. Society imposes restrictions, such as perpetuating the myth that retarded people have strong or unnatural sexual desires. Families are fearful that their handicapped member may give birth to a child they cannot be responsible for. There is, as well, the threat that the offspring of the handicapped person may be disabled. The threat of fertility without maturity places pressure on the parents to control and in some cases inhibit the adolescent's sexual freedom. Increasingly, parents and professionals are advocating the use of various methods of birth control to avoid unwanted parenthood and suggest masturbation as a normal sexual outlet. However, for many parents these options are in conflict with their basic moral values. They are torn between what is best for their child and their own entrenched beliefs.

While the normal adolescent has some latitude for sexual expression, the handicapped youth has few. In part, lack of opportunities to learn appropriate sexual behavior may result in deviant sexual responses, which only furthers the negative stereotype. Fotheringham and Creal (1974) and Farber (1975) both believe that a child's institutionalization is often related not so much to IQ or to the degree of handicap but rather to "disruptive behavior." Granted, such disruptive behavior could occur at any age; however, Poznanski (1973) speculates that while it is rarely talked about, "One suspects that the adolescent's sexuality plays a role in the timing of the institutionalization" (p. 326).

FAMILIES LAUNCHING YOUNG ADULTS

When children are ready to leave the family and establish their own lives apart from the parents, a major developmental task is to achieve disengagement without sacrificing intimacy. Recomposition can be a time of intense conflict. A smooth transition depends on the degree of marital satisfaction and the strength of the sibling and peer support systems. The family's history of fostering individuation and intimacy relates to its ability to adjust to the separation of a family member. Prolonged antagonism between parent and adolescent can lead to premature expulsion of the adolescent, while overprotection may stymie individual development and bind the young adult to the family.

The principle of normalization stresses that the handicapped should be integrated into the mainstream of society to the maximum extent possible. For young adults this may mean placement in a residential setting, group home, or foster home in which they can maximize their independence. Even if they remain at home, opportunities now exist for retarded adults to participate in work, social, and recreational activities apart from their families. Unfortunately, not all mentally retarded adults are involved in age-appropriate activities. Stanfield (1974) interviewed families of 120 graduates of special education programs and found that 94 percent of the graduates were living at home. Of this group 40 percent worked in sheltered workshops, 11 percent attended activity centers, and 44 percent were not involved in any program.

Throughout the retarded member's life, parents are confronted with the dilemmas of independence-dependence, overprotection-overexpectation, and acceptance-rejection. Often parents are reluctant and fear to let go despite desires to launch their children. Yet, when a group of twenty-five retarded adults living away from home were asked, "What is the best thing that has happened to you since living independently?" twenty-one answered, "Living on our own and making our own decisions." Their desire for independence offset what appeared to be a situation in which they had a lower standard of living, more difficulty in traveling, faced more rejection, and appeared to be lonelier than they did in previous, more protected home environments (Lusthaus & Lusthaus, 1978, p. C30).

Parents who have had a commitment to care for the retarded member as long as they are able must make readjustments if the decision is made to seek alternate living arrangements. They must deal with their apprehensions about the capacity of the placement to provide for their member's needs. It is not an easy decision for parents who have been led to believe that such settings are snake pits.

A less frequently encountered but equally important dilemma is marriage. A mother of a retarded daughter describes her reaction when a mentally retarded adult proposed marriage to her daughter:

> The marriage for Judy meant colossal reversal of everything we had planned for her. . . . We consulted a professional counselor, who warned us of the possible psychological trauma Judy would suffer if she were not allowed to marry. . . . Neither Judy nor Robert understood the full responsibility of marriage (Consteria, 1977, p. M4).

Out of necessity the parents looked after the newlyweds. Although they were happy for their daughter, they wondered how the couple would survive without them.

It is often thought that the siblings of a retarded adult refrain from dating and marriage possibilities. To the contrary, Grossman (1972) found that college-age siblings were fairly well adjusted individuals and that the female students had experienced more responsibility for their retarded sibling than the male students. Roughly half of the students interviewed claimed to have benefited from the experience of having a retarded sibling. Farber (1968) speculates that "Normal siblings who act as parent-surrogates apparently internalize welfare norms and turn their life careers toward the improvement of mankind, or at least toward the enhancement of goals they believe will enhance social welfare" (p. 164). He further suggests that siblings would only marry an individual who could tolerate the mentally retarded sibling.

In an effort to discover whether or not Farber's suggestion is indeed true, Cleveland and Miller (1977) attempted to determine if the life commitments of adults had been influenced by having a mentally retarded sibling. The results indicate that: (1) most families coped with having a mentally retarded member and provided a sound environment for the development of normal siblings; (2) sex roles in the family determined the amount of information the subjects knew about the mentally retarded sibling and also the subject's relationship with the sibling; (3) when there was only one normal sibling in the family, much attention was given to that sibling, and the family had high expectations of him or her; and (4) when the only normal sibling was female, she became a parent to the handicapped child and experienced conflict with her parents. Unfortunately, the results do not indicate how life commitments such as marriage choice, size of family, and career selection were influenced.

AGING FAMILY MEMBERS

Little is known and written about the impact of the retarded adult on the elderly couple and on adult siblings. The field of gerontology is a relatively new discipline and our knowledge of the normal aging process is very scant compared to that of child and adolescent development. There is an even greater void in our understanding of retarded adults, their needs, and the process of aging in mentally retarded individuals (Kriger, 1976).

This stage is the second postparental phase and the last stage in the family life cycle which spans the parents' retirement to their death. According to disengagement theory, the elderly tend to become withdrawn and dissociate from others and from activity: "Many older people, perhaps most older people, at some point in their lives direct their attention to themselves and away from others—they grow less responsive to the larger world about them; they narrow their social world. At the same time, the world of people and institutions pushes them out" (Botwinick, 1973, p. 50).

The couple are now grandparents, and their children are parents. During this stage role reversal may occur. The elderly couple may become dependent on their children and experience feelings of helplessness, obligation, and uselessness. An important developmental task is to develop mutual aid between the elderly couple and their children to reduce generational disconnectedness and the couple's feeling of uselessness. To maintain their dignity, the couple needs to feel that there is a mutual reliance between themselves and their children.

In contrast, the couple with a retarded child must continue with longterm care and management. The couple's tendency to become increasingly introverted and less responsive, combined with reduction in health and financial resources, heightens the probability that the handicapped member will be a burden. Physically as well as psychologically it is increasingly more difficult to meet the member's exceptional needs. On the other hand, it is possible that the continued responsibility and dependency adds to the elderly couple's sense of their value and reduces the feeling of loss of loved ones. Reliance of the handicapped member may give parents a feeling of mission and contribute to the life of the family.

From interviews with eighteen parents with retarded adult offspring, Kriger (1975) found that after years of effort on behalf of their child, parents reported they were seeking to lead quiet lives rather than continuing to struggle for their child. Specific problems mentioned included difficulty finding a sitter who could and would handle an older retarded individual, the expense involved in the handicapped member's care, lack of respite-care facilities for retarded adults, difficulties with physicians and dentists, and problems in locating lawyers who were knowledgeable of the best way to legally secure the adult's future. Most parents were preoccupied with the future of their retarded adult and stated outright that they did not want to be separated from the member except through death. They had negative perceptions of the institution as a placement. Generally they felt helpless and hopeless in finding a suitable placement for their adult. Only one set of parents had separated from their adult by placing him in a community facility.

Even if retarded adults are placed in a community living center, they are more likely to participate in the community if parents or relatives are available (Kriger, 1975). Unfortunately, the older retarded people become, the less likely they are to receive visits from family members (Stotsky, 1967).

Parents worry that when they are no longer able to care for the retarded member the burden may fall on the shoulders of the siblings who have established their own families. However, some siblings appear to have strong feelings toward their retarded brother or sister and want to provide care (Kriger, 1975). The manner in which the sibling family accepts and adapts to the presence of a handicapped adult member will depend in part on the previous relationships between the individual and the sibling family members. After the death of her sister, one woman describes her feelings about assuming responsibility for her retarded brother, whom she barely knows:

My oldest sister had the responsibility of looking out for my brother or worrying about him for the last fifteen years—ever since my mother died. . . . We never discussed my brother. I barely remember him. I have not seen him since I was five. He left for the state hospital about the time I started school. He must be almost 60 by now. . . . When I got the letter raising the possibility of moving my brother out of the state hospital, all sorts of thoughts rushed through my mind. At first I had the terrible idea that he had somehow gotten money from my sister in her will that he didn't deserve, and now he was going to get money that belonged to me and my family. I began to dream that my sister wanted me to take care of my brother, and I would be damned forever if I didn't. Maybe he would be happier outside the state hospital, but who would take care of him if we didn't? And then I began to be angry at the government. What a terrible new business to force people on families, whether they wanted them or not or can afford them or not. I thought that we were going to lose everything we'd saved. . . . I don't know whether I need a lawyer or a psychologist. There's a part of me that feels we should do more . . . and there's a part of me that's angry and wants to resist this new state policy. (*The Exceptional Parent,* 1977C, p. Y21–Y22)

Other considerations in planning for the handicapped member's future include practical matters such as guardianship and insurance. A study of twenty health insurance companies revealed that 75 percent did not provide coverage for mentally retarded dependents (Warner, Golden, & Henteleff, 1972).

FAMILY INTERVENTION

It is clear that a handicapped member has an impact on the family. The impact need not necessarily be adverse, but some modification in roles, communication networks, norms, power structure, decision-making patterns, and the relationship of the family to the community is inevitable. The exact form these changes take differs among families over time depending on a range of variables such as the type and severity of the handicap, the stability of marital and filial ties, and the reaction of friends and relatives.

Parents and siblings encounter problems and adjustments which can often be met more adequately if they receive help from sources outside the family. The developmental approach points out the importance of a continuum of services tailored to the needs of the family at each stage of development. A wide range of programs and services are available to assist families with disabled members, such as genetic counseling, psychotherapy, parent counseling, training, and education groups, group therapy, and family counseling. Other services include counseling for siblings, homemaker's services, nutritional planning, and respite care. The fields of health, mental health, and education assume primary responsibility for the delivery of services to families.

A SHIFT IN TREATMENT APPROACH

It is generally assumed that the reciprocal influence between an individual's development and family functioning suggests the need for the family to be the treatment unit of choice.

This shift from individual to family treatment is reflected in the study of the family with a mentally retarded individual. Adams (1967) states that "Mental retardation has to be viewed as a 'total family handicap'" (p. 312). Not only does the mentally retarded individual fail to meet role expectations and behave in ways which may disrupt the functioning of other family members, but the behavior of other members may also influence the manner in which the retardation is manifest. Farber's (1965, 1968, 1975) pioneering work analyzed the dynamics of families containing severely retarded children. Of particular importance are investigations dealing with husband-wife integration, general family integration, and parent-child interaction. Farber's studies and related works (such as Birenbaum, 1970; Cummings, 1976; Wolfensberger and Kurtz, 1969) have expanded our knowledge of the influence of the retarded child on the family constellation. The current literature, however, has significant limitations. First, it focuses largely on the development of the mentally retarded individual, with relatively few studies examining the impact of the retarded person on the roles and positions of family members. Second, although there is increasing concern about the retarded individual throughout the life cycle, most investigations focus on only the child and adolescent. Third, the vast majority of studies of the family with a retarded individual are cross-sectional rather than longitudinal.

WHY TREAT THE FAMILY?
The unique contribution of the developmental approach is that it permits an analysis of family interaction on a time dimension. As in individual development, familial developmental tasks arise at critical periods. According to Havighurst, an individual developmental task is a "task which arises at or about a certain period in the life of an individual, successful achievement of which leads to his happiness and to success with later tasks, while failure leads to unhappiness in the individual, disapproval by the society and difficulty with later tasks" (1953, p. 2). It is assumed that the developmental task is something the individual must actively participate in and must accomplish in order to be a fully developed person. Developmental tasks are normative expectations which arise over time from two primary sources: (1) physical and psychological maturation present in both children and adults, and (2) social pressures to perform expected roles and assume appropriate positions.

GENETIC COUNSELING
After parents have dealt with their initial reaction to the news that their child is handicapped, many of them are worried about bearing additional offspring. Genetic counseling, a relatively new service, is becoming increasingly available to parents in medical settings, public health clinics, and even mental health clinics.

In the past, the geneticist, either a Ph.D. or M.D., has assumed the primary role in genetic counseling. The focus has been largely on determining the etiological diagnosis and probability of recurrence and transmitting this information to the parents. However, there is a growing realization that genetic counseling is more than simply diagnosis of the genetic disorder and the imparting of information to the couple. The couple also needs to be educated regarding the nature of the genetic defect, its course of development, and possible treatment. They need a clear understanding of their options; the advantages and risks of each as well as support in making the decision of whether or not to have another child. The stress of an unfavorable diagnosis may aggravate existing individual and family problems, which may require more in-depth intervention such as marital counseling. Murray (1976) even advocates that the genetic counselor help the family adjust to the presence of the handicapped child and identify and obtain services from appropriate public and private agencies. Typically, social workers, and in some cases nurses, work with the geneticist to provide comprehensive genetic counseling.

PSYCHOTHERAPY
The presence of a handicapped member can aggravate existing problems and create new ones (Bernstein, 1979). The added strain may intensify the

reactions of an already unstable parent and lead to a pathological reaction. The main cause of such parental reactions is not the presence of the handicapped individual per se but the severe psychological state of the parents themselves (Baroff, 1974; Hutt and Gibby, 1976; LaVietes, 1978).

Psychotherapy is based on the assumption that in order to help the handicapped member, the parents must first resolve their own problems. Traditional psychotherapy is based on the psychoanalytic (Freudian) model. It is a long-term process which attempts to help parents resolve intrapersonal and interpersonal conflicts by changing their personality structure. This approach to solving or remediating parental problems was popular in the 1950s, but its use as the exclusive means of intervention has diminished.

COUNSELING

In a survey of parents of handicapped children, the foremost needs expressed by parents were for counseling for themselves and special education programs for their children. Parents are primarily seeking information about their children's capacities and advice about how to manage and facilitate their children's development rather than counseling for their emotional concerns (Barclay, Goulet, Holtgrieve, & Sharp, 1962). Although professionals often prefer to provide therapy, parents usually request guidance on child rearing and the nature of the disability (Cummings & Stock, 1962; Nadal, 1961).

Counseling programs encompass a range of approaches. Therapeutically oriented methods focus on psychological problems stemming from adjusting to the presence of a disabled person. Concrete and rational counseling attempts to explain the nature of the handicap, principles of child development and parent-child relationships, methods for effective management of the child, and information about community resources. Buscaglia (1975) stresses lifelong counseling for the exceptional person and the family that includes both information and self-discovery.

PARENT EDUCATION

There is a growing awareness that parents play *the* crucial role in facilitating and maintaining developmental gains in disabled children. Although traditionally parental involvement in their children's educational program has been encouraged, typically they play a peripheral role. Teachers were thought to be the primary change agent. However, Bronfenbrenner (1974b) has indicated that programs in which parents serve a central role were most effective in maintaining long-term developmental gains.

Unlike the psychotherapeutic approach, which deals with personality restructuring, and the counseling approach, which helps parents cope with daily living and make important decisions, the educational approach teaches parents how to enhance their child's development. The emphasis is on what parents and other family members can do to assist the child's development. Family members, particularly the parents, are partners in the continuing education of the handicapped member. A wide range of innovative parent education programs have been implemented with the common goal of enhancing the child's development by helping the parents to become educational change agents.

Some programs are home-based, some center-based, and others combine home and residential training. The Portage Project (Shearer and Shearer, 1972) is an example of an operant-oriented, home-based program which serves rural, multihandicapped preschool children and their parents. A teacher who visits the home on a weekly basis uses a structured curriculum to train parents to enhance their handicapped children's physical, self-help, social, academic, and language development. The Regional Intervention Program (RIP) is a behavior modification–oriented program which serves families of handicapped children under 5 years of age who manifest a variety of problems ranging from mild disorders to severe developmental delays (Regional Intervention Program, 1976). Under the supervision of the professional staff, parents teach other parents what to do at home to facilitate their children's development and manage their children's behavior. The family-training-center model assumes that the home is the handicapped person's primary living environment, but the residential center provides a program for enabling family members to learn to interact with one another in a positive manner and solve problems through precise use of behavior modification (Ray, 1974). The residential setting serves as a temporary placement for the children and a source for parents to learn to manage their children.

Programs such as the Community-based Transitional Program (Farseth, Hynes & Sorem, 1981) promote successful adjustment of trainable mentally retarded youths from life at school to adult life in the community. A major component of such programs is to increase the ability of parents to train their children in skills of community living.

SUMMARY

With the growing emphasis on deinstitutionalization, normalization, and the benefits of home care for the handicapped person, families are assuming greater responsibility for the care and development of exceptional members. Although in many cases the family is thought to be the optimum environment for the development of handicapped individuals, the addition of a disabled member usually results in substantial adjustments in the roles, norms, goals, and communication patterns of the family. The type of adjustments required vary from one family to the next. The adjustments do not necessarily have an aversive impact on the development of the family. However, frequently the presence of a handicapped member does precipitate a range of problems which may hinder the functioning and development of the family unit as well as individual members, including the disabled person. Adjustments and problems are not static but change throughout the course of the life of the family. Success at an early stage increases the likelihood of successful adjustment at a later stage.

While in most cases the family appears to be the best environment for the development of the handicapped, families often need psychological support and concrete services to aid in making adjustments, solving problems, and enhancing the development of its members. With the family assuming a more active role in rearing the handicapped member, more services are needed to assist the family in carrying out its role. The developmental approach points out the need for a life-cycle continuum of services designed to assist families at each stage of development.

Frances M. Hunt
Elizabeth A. Llewellyn

CHAPTER 13
EARLY
SPECIAL EDUCATION

(*Courtesy of Elizabeth A. Llewellyn.*)

As we have learned more about strategies for working with handicapped individuals, it has become evident that the *earliest* intervention is by far the most effective. Many of the most severe problems handicapped children and their families face can be prevented or at least minimized if services are provided to the *preschool* child instead of waiting until that child enters school. This newest approach to special education has gained support in recent years as professionals from many disciplines collaborate to develop efficient, comprehensive systems for delivering early intervention to young handicapped children.

THE EVOLUTION OF EARLY SPECIAL EDUCATION

Early special education or early intervention is a relatively new approach to education for exceptional individuals—one which has been influenced by developments and trends in many fields. American leaders with varied backgrounds—psychologists, human development specialists, preschool and kindergarten teachers, labor representatives, and leaders of parent-teacher associations—have all made important contributions. Most recently, leaders from the field of special education have influenced our understanding of how young children develop and of techniques and strategies that can shape that growth. As we trace the development of this new field of early special education, we can see dramatic changes in our understanding of child development and how that development can be shaped. Just as with other technologies though, we will also see that answers to the old questions produce many new and challenging puzzles for the future.

AGE-OLD QUESTIONS AND OLD-WORLD PRACTICES

Preformationism
Education in America has long been influenced by the philosophies of Western Europe and Great Britain. During the Middle Ages, preformation-

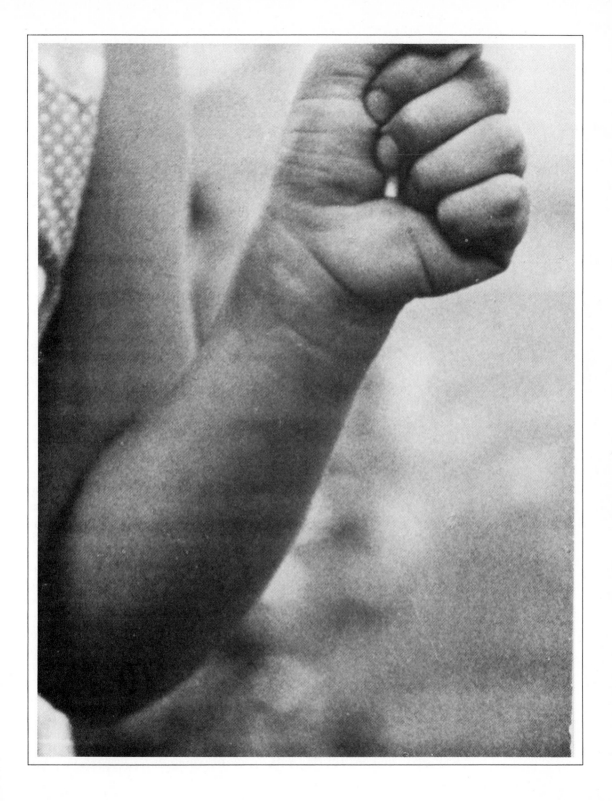

ism—the position that the environment has no influence upon the development of the child—was perhaps the most dominant position. Doctors, priests, parents, and teachers all believed that the infant's characteristics were fixed before birth. Thus it followed that remediation or special intervention could be neither useful nor reasonable. Intervention would be contrary to nature's planned or predetermined course. The disabilities and problems of the young child were not questioned. Though parents probably attempted to help their children with simple homemade prosthetic equipment and folk medicines, the role of the environment was never formally addressed by the philosophical and ruling class leaders of that period. Handicapped children seldom fared well.

Predeterminism

Not until the 1700s did a theory emerge which attributed to the environment a small but active role in the development of the infant and young child. Through the philosophy of predeterminism the environment was seen as a place in which the determined characteristics of the individual could "unfold." The normal environment was thought to provide a trigger for the release of hereditary traits. Deficient environments were responsible for less-than-optimal development. This philosophy of child development was most ably advocated by Rousseau (1962) in his text *Emile*. Children best thrive in an unstructured environment, asserted Rousseau, one where natural characteristics can mature. His message was that a good environment allows nature to "take its course"—not to change or better it.

However, support for beliefs such as "determinism" was not unanimous. Many others before and after Rousseau gave *more* credit to the environment. They believed that the environment could play an active role in directing and shaping development, rather than simply releasing or distorting it. A group of "sense empiricists," inspired by John Locke (1964) and others began to experiment with providing sensory stimulation to alter development. With Victor, the "Wild Boy of Aveyron," Itard demonstrated behavior changes brought about by careful use of multisensory stimulation and crude reinforcement techniques (Itard, 1962).

Seguin maintained that curiosity in one's environment was another behavior which promoted a child's development (Ball, 1971). To teach curiosity, the senses were stimulated: a typical lesson by Seguin would involve the classification of materials by their texture. Seguin left his native France for the United States in 1850 and later founded the American Association of Mental Deficiency (Talbot, 1964).

The works of Seguin and Itard stimulated many in both the Old and the New World. Dr. Maria Montessori (1870–1952), the first woman to earn a medical degree from the University of Rome, was influenced by the work of Seguin and Itard (Josephina, 1967) and pioneered in establishing preschools based on these theories. In 1906 she was commissioned by the city planners of Rome to establish an educational preschool center for the city's disadvantaged children. The students, many of whom were delayed in one or more areas of development, attended daily sessions and participated in motor, sensory, and language-education experiences (Orem, 1969). The Montessori preschool programs that have subsequently been established in American communities have been some of the most popular of early education programs available to young children in the United States.

New World Influences

While European theorists debated the influences of the environment on child development, parents in the United States became interested in the normal development of young children, and established organizations such as the *Society for the Study of Child Nature* and publications such as *Mother's Magazine* and *Mother's Assistant.* Parents debated ethics, religion, and child management, as well as the ideas proposed by Locke, Rousseau, and Seguin. The notion that children benefit most from a structured learning environment was perhaps the most popular trend. Espousing this view, Elizabeth Palmer Peabody established the first American kindergarten, based on providing learning experiences in a structured environment. Finally, after the Civil War, G. Stanley Hall established the study of child development as a legitimate academic field. Hall's work focused on applying learning technologies to the development of young children.

After the Civil War, children became more visible to the public as they joined the swelling labor force of the industrial revolution. In their travels to and from work, as well as work itself, it became evident that these children had received little assistance in their early years of development. In 1909, the first White House Conference on Children was held to review management techniques used by big business and to define and establish remedial programs for special children. Now a tradition, the White House sponsors such studies every ten years to establish goals for improving the quality of life for children in the next decade.

National and international developments continued to influence child-care practices throughout the first half of this century. During World War I many of the war-related industries provided child-care services for working mothers. Nursery schools were again popular during the great depression and World War II as mothers increasingly worked outside of the home.

Some of the nursery schools, child-care centers, and kindergartens became research sites and vehicles for disseminating new information about child development. Parents and teachers began to objectively observe and record the activities of the children for whom they cared and use this information to screen and identify children with special needs. Theories of early intervention, such as Montessori's, and theories of learning such as Watson's, influenced many of these early intervention efforts. A young child's potential was thought to need cultivation. Cultivation requires an organized environment: "A farmer does not haphazardly plant his crops nor should a teacher haphazardly plan lessons" (Watson, 1925).

After World War II, rehabilitation for returning soldiers provided another major breakthrough for meeting the special needs of citizens. New medical techniques, therapeutic methods, and prosthetic devices were more and more frequently applied to young handicapped children. In the 1950s young children with sensory impairments (blind and deaf children) began to receive not only medical but also educational services. Federally and privately funded schools were established to meet the medical and educational needs of sensorially impaired children. However, children with other types of handicaps related to learning difficulties were not receiving many special services in the home or local school setting. Severely and profoundly retarded children, once identified, were usually placed in state or privately owned institutions, along with many children who displayed similar behavior patterns. "Trainable" children were either placed in state institutions or private day schools if parents could afford the expense, or remained at home with little professional intervention.

ANSWERS THROUGH RESEARCH

Only in the last fifty years have we attempted to empirically answer the age-old question, "Does the environment play an important role in the development of the child?" Research and demonstration programs of the past half-century have made substantial contributions to our present understanding that the environment does, indeed, play a crucial role in the development of young children. Bloom (1964), Hunt (1961), and Kirk (1958), for example, produced now-classic works establishing the importance of the first three or four years of life. They suggested that intervention during this period of rapid development is more likely to be effective than intervention at the traditional school age. Skeels (1966) reported dramatic findings of his longitudinal study of the effects of the environment on development. He documented over a period of thirty years the differential progress of children who, at about the age of three, were removed from unstimulating orphanages and placed in stimulating environments and a control group of similar children who remained in the orphanage. After nearly three decades the differences between the groups were striking.

> All 13 children in the experimental group were self-supporting, and none was a ward of any institution. In the contrast group of 12 children, one had died . . . and 4 were still wards of institution.
>
> The contrast group completed a median of less than the third grade. The experimental group completed a median of the twelfth grade. Four of the subjects had one or more years of college work, one received a B.A. degree and took some graduate training. (Skeels, 1966, p. 55)

Other longitudinal studies have also reported positive findings. Most studies evaluated the effects of preschool programs on a number of characteristics of disadvantaged, low socioeconomic status, and at-risk children (e.g., Heber & Garber, 1975; Klaus & Gray, 1968; Schweinhart & Weikart, 1980). Some more recent projects have produced similar findings with handicapped infants (e.g., Moore, 1979; Stedman, 1977). Some of the bene-

The first few years are critical to lifelong development. The elaborate stimulus and response opportunities of these children will forever contribute to their development. (*Courtesy of Chuck Zovko.*)

fits of early intervention for both at-risk and handicapped children include the following:

1. Increased cognitive ability for entrance to school.

2. Greater student commitment to learning and to school.

3. Higher achievement in academic subjects.

4. Lower frequency of placement in special education classes.

5. Increased parent involvement in the schools.

6. Decreased behavioral problems of the student in the school setting.

7. Positive economic results: money required to fund a single child for one year of preschool or early intervention is often recovered completely by the decline in funds required for services by special education departments in the public schools.

SUMMARY

For centuries people have debated how the environment affects the development of children. *Preformationists* argued that the environment had no influence on the development of children: that all attributes of the child, his behavior, personality and abilities, were determined before the child entered the world. Thus, few efforts were made to remediate or compensate for disabilities.

By the eighteenth century, a new philosophy called *determinism* emerged which recognized a limited influence of the environment on human development. The normal environment was thought to "trigger" the release of individual traits. Soon, however, this view was questioned by philosophies and writers such as Locke and Itard, who recognized a much more significant role for the environment. Recognition of the importance of the environment provided the foundation for most contemporary intervention strategies, and provided the rationale for early intervention.

Despite isolated efforts to provide early intervention in the New World, it was not until the middle of this century that the role of environment was investigated empirically. The research of the 1950s and 1960s demonstrated that manipulation of the environment can dramatically alter child development. Bricker and Sheehan (1980) describe the evolution of early special education in the 1970s and define the puzzles of the 1980s:

> Originally, the focus (of research in early special education) was on the feasibility of initiating early intervention programs. The subsequent developmental phase was focused on the exploration of the form and context of early intervention efforts. Today the field is moving into a third phase which is concentrating on the impact or effectiveness of these programs on a broad range of young handicapped infants and children. (Bricker & Sheehan, 1980, p. 1)

We know that early intervention can be effective. Our goals for the future are to identify the best early intervention strategies and make quality early intervention available to all those who could benefit from it.

CONTEMPORARY EARLY SPECIAL EDUCATION

FEDERAL PROGRAMS

Some of the first research on the effects of early interventions generated great concern that disadvantaged children would, even before beginning grade school, fall so far behind their middle-class peers that they could never have equal opportunities in this country. Many of these underprivileged children were minorities, and the civil rights movement of the 1960s played a vital role in establishing the first early intervention efforts. Project Head Start (1965) and the Early and Periodic Screening, Diagnosis, and Treatment Program (EPSDTP) (1966), were targeted to provide services for very young disadvantaged children. Many exceptional children, primarily at risk or with mild and moderate handicaps benefited from these programs.

It was not until 1968, however, that the first major program targeted specifically at young handicapped children was established. The Handi-

Center-based programs can provide early socialization experiences. (*National Down Syndrome Society.*)

capped Children's Early Education Assistance Act (HCEEAA) launched the field of early special education. Each of these programs will be reviewed.

Head Start
Project Head Start, which originated in 1965 as part of the Equal Opportunity Movement, was intended to provide compensatory programs for economically disadvantaged preschool children. Services are provided for both the child and immediate family, including

1. *Educational intervention:* center-based instruction, home-based instruction, or a combination.

2. *Medical intervention:* identification of physical and mental health problems and intervention, often totally free. Nutritional education is stressed.

3. *Family services:* information concerning all of the available social services for families of the enrolled preschooler and parent-training programs.

Since the early 1970s, Project Head Start has served as a model for mainstreaming the handicapped child. In fact, Head Start programs must enroll at least 10 percent of handicapped preschoolers. With expected funding reductions in programs for early intervention Head Start will probably begin to serve more and more handicapped preschoolers. Early special educators of the 1980s will probably work more closely with local Head Start programs than any other service delivery network.

The CDA Trainer from a local university (left) is observing a lesson conducted by one of many CDA candidates at this rural Head Start. (*Pennsylvania Department of Welfare, Office of Mental Retardation.*)

In anticipation of the expanding responsibilities Head Start professionals will assume in the 1980s, many Head Start programs are providing special training opportunities for their workers. According to the Administration for Children, Youth and Families (ACYF), over 7,000 Head Start employees are working toward a special certification, the *Child Development Associate* (CDA) *Credentials* (ACYF, 1981). Universities and colleges throughout the United States are offering special courses to help these professionals develop a number of competencies related to early education:

1. Establish and maintain a safe and healthy environment.

2. Advance physical and intellectual competence.

3. Build positive self-concept and individual strength.

4. Promote positive functioning of children and adults in a group.

5. Bring about optimal coordination of home and center child-rearing practices and expectations.

6. Carry out supplementary responsibilities related to programs.

EPSDTP

One of the major obstacles to early intervention is identifying children who need such services. Often parents may not recognize delays in development or problems such as mild sensory deficits. Parents who do suspect that a problem exists are often ill-advised that "the child will grow out of it." In 1967, Title 19 of the Social Security Act was amended to provide screening for all Medicaid children under 21 (Hayden & Edgar, 1967). This amendment, called the Early and Periodic Screening, Diagnosis, and Treatment Program (EPSDTP) has enabled services to be provided to about 1.3 million eligible families since screening efforts began in 1972. These efforts must be continued, however, since over 13 million families are eligible for these services (Report on Preschool Education, May 20, 1980).

HCEEAA

Recognizing the great need for special services at the earliest possible age, and the dearth of trained professionals, materials, and program models, Congress in 1968 established the Handicapped Children's Early Education Assistance Act (P.L. 90–538), which is sometimes referred to as the "First Chance Program." The purpose of the First Chance Program was to initiate activities in the following areas:

Research—to provide a sound base knowledge of the preschool handicapped child upon which to base programs.

Development—to develop curriculum and techniques designed to meet particular needs of the preschool handicapped.

Demonstration—to create programs of excellence from which other communities and schools are able to pattern their activities, using the best of current wisdom and skills.

Training—to develop a cadre of well-trained professional and supportive personnel to head new programs.

Implementation—to develop quality programs dispersed throughout all areas of the country. (LaVor & Krivit, p. 381)

In just a little more than a decade, hundreds of model programs have been developed throughout the country. Grants have been provided to colleges and universities, hospitals, schools, and child-care agencies to develop effective models for early intervention.

This investment is now paying off; a variety of early special education models, each with field-tested components such as curriculums, parent and paraprofessional training methods, behavior management guides, and child find-and-screen procedures are available. Innovative professionals in early special education can "mix and match" components of these models to provide the most individualized appropriate combinations for any given community.

LEGISLATION: THE RIGHT TO EARLY INTERVENTION

P. L. 94–142 presently has the most positive influence on the education of young handicapped children. By September 1, 1980, states were to provide free appropriate public education for all children ages 3 through 21. But this does not guarantee all 3- to 5-year-old preschool children early intervention. States are required to provide services to preschool children *only* if this section of P.L. 94–142 does not conflict with state law, practice, or order of any court (*Federal Register*, 8/23/77, p. 42481). Table 13-1 lists the eligibility ages for each state (as of May 1, 1980). Unfortunately, economic considerations have caused some programs to be curtailed. States which were moving to provide early programs are now being forced to scratch these plans because of lack of funding. Many school administrators cannot foresee funds to cover existing special education programs. The states' reimbursements for each preschool child served as insufficient to cover the cost of an effective program. Continued progress toward quality early intervention depends on the priorities of each community and the foresight of state legislatures.

COMPONENTS OF EARLY INTERVENTION PROGRAMS

Identification

The identification of children who may need early intervention typically occurs through either *referral* or *screening.* Conditions such as cerebral palsy or spina bifida are likely to be identified and referred by the physician or the child's parents because the problems are so obvious. However, very severe handicaps constitute only a small percentage of all handicapping conditions. Identification of less obvious but equally severe problems is complicated by several issues. Individuals who typically have the most contact with young children—that is, parents and child-care workers—tend to have little or no training in normal child development and may not be cognizant of less obvious signs of a problem. Parents who do express concern are all too often advised that their child will "outgrow" the problem.

Obviously, the referral system is not adequate if we are interested in providing early intervention to all children who need it. Children with unnoticed or unreported problems can be identified through a *screening* process. Screening involves examination of large numbers of children for characteristics which indicate that the child *might* need special services. The purpose of screening is *not* to document that children have handicaps; rather screening provides a cost-effective method of sorting out those children who should have more thorough assessments. Screening tests that are frequently used at the preschool level and the behaviors they sample are described by Johnson & Kapp (1980) in a booklet available through Project Reach, UCLA Department of Education.

A number of different screening approaches have been developed and field-tested by Handicapped Children's Early Education Project (HCEEP) programs. The HICOMP Project at University Park, Pennsylvania, for example, has developed a step-by-step guide for organizing and conducting child-find efforts in rural communities. Some of the options recommended in the COMP-Ident Find/Screen Planning Package (Laub, Kurtz, & Worobey, 1978) include offering a free developmental checkup at community fairs, distribution of "Jotty Giraffe" (a quick check of child development that parents can use), and systematic screening done by volunteers within each community. New research is reporting on the relative merits of various approaches to finding and screening youngsters (Kurtz & Laub, 1976).

Assessment

When the screening procedure indicates that the child may have problems, a follow-up assessment or evaluation is conducted to examine more carefully the areas of concern. Assessment may include evaluation of sensory functions (for example, tests for vision or hearing dysfunctions), development of gross and fine motor skills, and level of communication (for example, speech and language development). Self-care skills such as eating, dressing, and toileting and abnormal behavior patterns such as evidence of self-injurious behavior, severe tantrums, or withdrawal are also checked. The purposes of these evaluations are to identify specific skills the child *can* and *cannot* do, and to identify the specific ancillary services (for example, speech therapy, physical therapy) or behavior-change programs (for example, modify tantrum behavior) the child may require.

A variety of assessment devices have been used to evaluate children on these dimensions. Some programs have developed their own assessment devices. For example, the Learning Accomplishment Profile, Diagnostic edition (Sanford, 1973), is used by the Chapel Hill Training-Outreach Project to establish individual learning objectives for children. Other projects, such as the Infant Stimulation/Mother Training Project at the University of Cincinnati (Badger, 1977) use the Brazelton Neonatal Behavorial Assessment Scale, 1973, and the Bayley Scales of Infant Development (Bayley, 1969) to evaluate children in the clinic and at home. Table 13-2 provides a brief description of some assessment devices which are commonly used at the preschool level.

Intervention

When it is determined that the child is in need of special services, an IEP is developed using the information obtained from the assessment, parent-provided information, and direct observation. The general goals of intervention should be to increase the child's repertoire of appropriate behaviors and decrease maladaptive behaviors. To facilitate generalization and maintenance, parents and siblings may receive training and assume active roles in the intervention process.

Many curriculums have been published in the past decade to help parents and teachers identify appropriate learning objectives and activities. These curriculums vary in format and scope, and can help both the experienced and the novice. Table 13-3 describes several popular curriculums which can be used with preschool handicapped children. Sample pages from a few of these are included in Figures 13-1, 13-2, and 13-3.

The IEP also includes recommendations for services from a speech therapist, physical or occupational therapist, optometrist, audiologist, and nutritionist. Plans for use of special prosthetic devices and environmental arrangements are also delineated in the IEP.

TABLE 13-1
A synopsis of state education policies as they relate to ages of eligibility for special education and related services (Smith, 1980)

State	LAW Ages of Eligibility	LAW Permissive Ages	REGULATION Ages of Eligibility	REGULATION Permissive Ages	STATE PLAN Ages of Eligibility	STATE PLAN Permissive Ages
Alabama	Between 6 and 21			Preschool	6 through 21	3—D, B, MH
Alaska	At least 3		Legal school age 3 to 19		3 to 19 inclusive	
Arizona	Lawful school age[1]				Between 6 and 21 If K-5	
Arkansas	Between 6 and 21 If K-5	Below 6 if SHC			Between 6 and 21 If K-5	Below school age if SHC
California	Between 3 and 21 C	Younger than 3	4.9 to 21 C	Birth to 4.9[2]	4.9 to 18 with exceptions[3]	Under 3
Colorado	Between 5 and 21	Under 5			Between 5 and 21 C	3-5
Connecticut	Over 5 under 21	Under 5	School age and preschool		HI—3 to 21st birthday or C— All others 4 to 21st birthday or C	

State						
Delaware	4 through 20 inclusive		Between 4 and 21 HI & VH—0 to 21		Between 4 and 21	
Florida*	5	Exceptional children—3 Below 5 D, B Severely PH TMR			13 consecutive years of instruction 5-18	0 to 4 18 and above
Georgia	6 to C if K-5⁴	0-5 if SHC necessitates early intervention	Between 5 and 18	0-4 If enrolled can continue 19-21	5 to 18	0 to 4 19 to 21
Hawaii	Under 20				9/1/80 Between 3 and 20	
Idaho	School age⁵	To 21	School age Between 5 and 21		Between 6 and 18 inclusive, if K-5, if 18 and has not graduated through 21	Between birth and 4 or 5 inclusive
Illinois*	Between 3 and 21	0 to 2	Between 3 and 21		9/1/80 Between 3 and 21	
Indiana	Over 6 and under 18	D-6 mo. 3 to 5 18 to 21	6 to 18	3 through 5 HI—18 through 21 6 mo.	6 to 18	

continued on following page

CHAPTER 13
EARLY SPECIAL
EDUCATION

TABLE 13-1 (continued)

State	LAW		REGULATION		STATE PLAN	
	Ages of Eligibility	Permissive Ages	Ages of Eligibility	Permissive Ages	Ages of Eligibility	Permissive Ages
Iowa	Under 21		Between birth and 21		9/1/80 Birth through 20	
Kansas	Subject to regulations school age[6]		If K then 5 through 21 C, otherwise 6 through 21 C		Same age as nonhandicapped to school year student reaches 21	Preschool
Kentucky	Under 21		School attendance age pursuant to law		5 through 17	Birth to 4 18 to 21
Louisiana	3 to 21[7]	Below 3—Serious handicapping condition	3rd birthday to 22nd birthday		Not less than 3 or more than 21 inclusive	SHC—under 3
Maine	5 to school year student reaches 20. If 2-year K, 4		5 to school year student reaches 20		5 until year reaches 20	
Maryland	As soon as child can benefit and under 21[8]		Birth through 20—children under 5 will be phased in as required by law		9/1/80 Birth through 20	

Massachusetts	3 through 21		3 through 21—3 and 4 year olds must have substantial disabilities[9]		3 through 21	
Michigan	Under 26		Not more than 25—if turns 26 after enrollment, may complete year		0 through 25 C	
Minnesota	4 to 21	TMR—through school yr. student is 25, if attended public school less than 9 years.	4 to 21		4 to 21	Before 4
Mississippi	6 and under 21	Under 6	Under 21		9/1/80 6 through 20	3 to 5
Missouri	5 and under 21	Under 5	School age	3 and 4	5 through 20	Under 5
Montana	9/1/80 Between 3 and 21	9/1/80 0 to 2	9/80 between 3 and 21		9/1/80 Between 3 and 21 inclusive	0 to 2
Nebraska	From diagnosis to 21		5 to 21 (school age) MH—birth to 21 C		From diagnosis to 21	

continued on following page

TABLE 13-1 (continued)

State	LAW		REGULATION		STATE PLAN	
	Ages of Eligibility	Permissive Ages	Ages of Eligibility	Permissive Ages	Ages of Eligibility	Permissive Ages
Nevada	5 and under 18	MR—3 G—4 D & VH—under 5			5 or 6 to 18	Outside eligible age range
New Hampshire	3 to 21 C		Up to 21		3 to 21	0 to 3
New Jersey	Between 5 and 20	Under 5 and over 20	Between 5 and 20	Under 5 and over 20	Between 5 and 20	
New Mexico	School age[10]		Legal entry age until age 18	Over 18		
New York	Over 5 and under 21		Under 21		Between 5 and 21[11]	
North Carolina	Between 5 and 18		5 through 17	Birth through 4 18 through 21	Between 5 and 17	Birth to 4 18 to 21
North Dakota	6 and under 21	3 to 6	6 to 21		6 to 21	3 to 6
Ohio*	Between 6 and 18 If K—5	Other ages	Legal school age		Compulsory school age	
Oklahoma	4		4 eligible for a minimum of 12 years[12]		4 through 18 minimum period of 12 years	19 to 21

Oregon	Superintendent establishes eligibility		6 to 21 inclusive If K-5 to 21 If preschool 3 to 21		6 through 20 If K—5
Pennsylvania	6 to 21	Below 6	6 to 21 below 6 if regular programs below age 6		Policy is same as regulations and law
Rhode Island	3 to 21		3 to 21 C		9/1/80 3 to 21
South Carolina	Lawful school age[13]				Between 6 and 21 HI 4 to 21
South Dakota	Under 21		Under 21[14]		Under 21
Tennessee	Between 4 and 21	D—3	4 through 21 D—3		4 through 21 D—3 through 21
Texas	Between 3 and 21		Between 3 and 21 inclusive. Auditorily, visually handicapped— between birth and 22		Between 3 and 21. Auditorily, between birth and 22
Utah	Over 5 (if K) under 21		5 through 21		5 through 21

continued on following page

CHAPTER 13
EARLY SPECIAL
EDUCATION

270

TABLE 13-1 (continued)

State	LAW Ages of Eligibility	LAW Permissive Ages	REGULATION Ages of Eligibility	REGULATION Permissive Ages	STATE PLAN Ages of Eligibility	STATE PLAN Permissive Ages
Vermont	Under 21	Over 21 to C	Under 21		6 to 21 C If K—5	3 to 5
Virginia	2 and under 21 VH—birth to 21		2 to 21		Between 2 and 21	
Washington	Common school age[15]	Preschool	5 to 21[16]		5 to 21 common school age	3 to 4[17]
West Virginia	Between 5 and 23	3-5	Between 5 and 23		Between 5 and 23	
Wisconsin	3 under 21	Under 3	3 to 21		3 to 21	
Wyoming	Over 6 and under 21 If 5-K		School age		Between 6 and 21 If K—5	
District of Columbia			Between 3 and 21		9/1/80 Not less than 4 or more than 21. 4 year olds when provided to regular children	

Prepared by the
Policy Research Center
The Council for Exceptional Children
for
The Policy Options Project (POPs)

Key

K — Kindergarten
C — Completion of Course
D — Deaf
B — Blind

PH — Physically Handicapped
TMR — Trainable Mentally Retarded
HI — Hearing-Impaired
VH — Visually Handicapped

MH — Multiple Handicap
MR — Mentally Retarded
G — Gifted
SHC — Serious Handicapping Condition

Footnotes

[1] Arizona—Lawful school age is between 6 and 21.
[2] California—3-4.9 identified as requiring intensive special education.
[3] Georgia—Exceptions include: 3-4.9 for those identified as requiring intensive services; 19-21 if enrolled before 19 and have not yet completed a course.
[4] Georgia—3 and 4 year old children who are physically, mentally, or emotionally handicapped or perceptually or linguistically deficient are eligible.
[5] Idaho—Services of public schools are extended to any acceptable person of school age (defined as between 5 and 21).
[6] Kansas—school age is 6 or 5 if kindergarten is available.
[7] Louisiana—Legislation has been passed extending eligibility to 25 in certain circumstances.
[8] Maryland—Effective 7/1/80 Senate Bill No. 734 provides for compensatory education over 21 in certain circumstances.
[9] Massachusetts—Substantial disabilities are defined as intellectual, sensory, emotional or physical factors, cerebral disfunctions, perceptual factors or other specific learning impairments or any combination thereof.
[10] New Mexico—School age is at least 5 and for children in special education a maximum of 21 years of age.
[11] New York—Blind, deaf, or severely physically handicapped children in state schools between 3 and 21; deaf children less than 3 years of age in approved educational facilities.
[12] Oklahoma—No set minimum age is specified for blind and partially blind, deaf, hard of hearing, or low incidence severely multiple handicapped children.
[13] South Carolina—Lawful school age is over 5 and under 21.
[14] South Dakota—Programs for children under the age of 3 years shall be provided only to those children who are in need of prolonged assistance.
[15] Washington—Common school age is between 5 and 21.
[16] Washington—0 to 1 and 1 and 2 year old children with multiple handicaps, gross motor impairment, sensory impairment, moderate or severe mental retardation are eligible for services.
[17] Washington—Services are permissive for children 0-2 if they have a multiple handicap, gross motor impairment, sensory impairment, or moderate or severe mental retardation.

Comments

* Florida—According to Florida State Department of Education officials, there is no maximum school age.
* Ohio—According to Ohio State Department of Education officials, Ohio's mandated age range is 5 through 21.
* Illinois—Permissive ages are listed in § 10-22-38 rather than in Special Education Law.

CHAPTER 13
EARLY SPECIAL
EDUCATION

TABLE 13-2
Assessment devices for preschool children

ASSESSMENT DEVICE	BEHAVIORS SAMPLED	PUBLISHER
A Social Maturity Scale for Blind Preschool Children	Adaptive behaviors of blind children	American Foundation for the Blind 15 West 16th Street New York, N. Y. 10011
Vineland Social Maturity Scale (1965); (revision available 1982)	Adaptive behaviors	American Guidance Service Publishers' Building Circle Pines, Minn. 55014
Wisconsin Behavior Rating Scale	Adaptive behaviors (for use with multihandicapped children)	Central Wisconsin Center for Developmentally Disabled 317 Knutson Drive Madison, Wis. 53704
Denver Developmental Screening Test	Screening of developmental levels	University of Colorado Medical Center Boulder, Colo. 80302
Battell Developmental Inventory	Development of normal and/or handicapped preschool children	Walker & Company 720 Fifth Avenue New York, N. Y. 10019
Bayley Scales of Infant Development	Infant behavior record; motor scale; mental scale	Psychological Corporation 757 Third Avenue New York, N. Y. 10017
Developmental Programming for Infants and Young Children: Assessment and Application	Fine motor, gross motor, cognition, language, social/emotional, and self-care skills	University of Michigan Press, University of Michigan Ann Arbor, Mich. 48106
Gesell Developmental Schedules	Motor, adaptive, language, and self-help skills	Psychological Corporation 757 Third Avenue New York, N. Y. 10017
Developmental Potential of Preschool Children: An Evaluation in Intellectual, Sensory, and Emotional Functioning	Development of multi-handicapped pre-schoolers	Grune & Stratton 381 Park Avenue South New York, N. Y. 10016

TABLE 13-2
(continued)

273

ASSESSMENT DEVICE	BEHAVIORS SAMPLED	PUBLISHER
Cattell Infant Intelligence Scale	Intellectual functioning	Psychological Corporation 757 Third Avenue New York, N. Y. 10017
Hiskey-Nebraska Test of Learning Aptitude	Intellectual functioning of normal and hearing-impaired children	Union College Press Lincoln, Nebr. 68501
Leiter International Performance Scale	Nonverbal intellectual functioning of normal and hearing-impaired children	Stoelting Company Chicago, Ill.
McCarthy Scales of Children's Abilities (MSCA)	Intellectual functioning and achievement	Psychological Corporation 757 Third Avenue New York, N. Y. 10017
Perkins-Binent Intelligence Scale	Intellectual functioning of blind preschool children	Perkins School for the Blind Watertown, Mass. 02172
Pictorial Test of Intelligence (PTI)	Intellectual functioning for use with multi-handicapped children	Riverside Publishing Co. 1919 S. Highland Avenue Lombard, Ill. 60148
Wechsler Preschool and Primary Scale of Intelligence (WPPSI)	IQ	Psychological Corporation 757 Third Avenue New York, N. Y. 10017
Curriculum HICOMP	Criterion-referenced test of developmental domains	HICOMP Outreach Project 307 CEDAR Building Pennsylvania State University University Park, Pa. 16802
Learning Accomplishment Profile-Diagnostic (LAP-D)	Criterion-referenced test of developmental domains	Chapel Hill Training-Outreach Project Lincoln Center Chapel Hill, N. C. 27514
Stanford-Binet Intelligence Scale Form L-M	IQ	Riverside Publishing Co. 1919 S. Highland Avenue Lombard, Ill. 60148

TABLE 13-3
Curriculums for preschool children

CURRICULUM AND AUTHOR	FOCUS OF INTERVENTION	POPULATION
The Cognitively Oriented Curriculum. Weikart, D. P. HI*Scope Foundation, 1971.	Relationships & representations of objects & events in the environment, attention skills & language skills.	3–4 year olds culturally disadvantaged, educably mentally retarded.
COMP Curriculum. Willoughby-Herb, S., Neisworth, J. T., & Laub, K. W. The Pennsylvania State University, 1980.	Twenty-one subskill areas are organized within four general areas of development: communication, own care, motor, and problem solving.	Birth to five years handicapped and non-handicapped.
Curriculum Programming for Young Handicapped Children. Bos, C., University of Arizona, 1980.	Five skill areas: body management, self-care, communication, pre-academics, & socialization.	2–6 year olds non-sensorially handicapped.
Distar Language I: An Instructional System. Englemann, S., & Osborn, J. Science Research Associates, Chicago, 1976.	Language instruction.	4–6 year olds language delayed and non-English speaking.
The EMI Curriculum Pool Materials. Elder, W. B., & Swift, J. N., University of Virginia Medical Center, 1977.	Five areas of development: gross motor, fine motor, social, cognitive, and language.	Birth–24 months multihandicapped.
Learning Accomplishment Profile. Sanford, A. R., Kaplan Press, 1974.	Six areas of development: gross motor, fine motor, social, self-help, cognitive, & language.	Birth to six years handicapped.
Portage Guide to Early Education. Bluma, S. M., Shearer, M. S., Frohman, A. H., & Hilliard, J. M. The Portage Project, 1976.	Six areas of development: infant stimulation, cognitive, language, self-help, motor, & socialization.	Birth to six years multi-handicapped.
Programmed Environ-ments Curriculum. Tawney, J. W., Knapp, D. S., O'Reilly, C. D. & Pratt, S. S. Charles-Merrill, 1979.	Eight areas: receptive language, expressive language, cognitive, fine motor, gross motor, eating, dressing, & grooming.	All ages moderately to profoundly handicapped.
Project Memphis. Quick, A. D., and Campbell, A. A. Kandall/Hunt Publishing Company, 1976.	Five areas: personal-social, gross motor, fine motor, language, and perceptual-cognitive.	Birth to five years handicapped.

Infant stimulation 10

Title: Indicates sensitivity to body contact by quieting, crying, or body movement

What to do:

1. When baby cries, hold him snugly wrapped in light blanket. Walk around the room with him in your arms.
2. Gentle rocking motion of your arms may quiet baby.
3. Gentle rubbing of head may sooth.
4. It is not always necessary to pick up child. Try gently patting or stroking him while you talk quietly as child lies in crib.
5. Turn baby over and try to sooth him by rubbing his back or tummy.

 PortageGuide

The specific approach to intervention—the theoretical basis of the program—varies depending on the philosophy of the administrator and, to an extent, the viewpoints of the parents of the handicapped children. Karnes and Zehrbach (1977) have identified six general theoretical approaches which describe the models in the first-chance network:

> open education; precision teaching with a heavy emphasis on language development; precision teaching based on developmental guidelines in the areas of gross and fine motor development, self-help and social skills, and cognitive language development; behavior modification; cognitive developmental instruction based especially on the work of Piaget; and the creation of a learning environment with particular emphasis on the physical aspects of that environment. (Karnes & Zehrbach, 1977, pp. 21-22)

There has been, as yet, no definitive evidence on the relative effectiveness of the different theoretical orientations.

MODELS FOR SERVICE DELIVERY

Home-based

Because most preschool children are cared for by their parents, many of the first-chance projects provide services in the home. These home-based delivery systems focus on training parents how to manage the child's environment to maximize learning and prevent complications secondary to the handicap.

Perhaps the most widely known home-based program is the model developed by Shearer & Shearer (1976) called the Portage Model. The objec-

PERSONAL–SOCIAL SKILLS

Raw Score	Years	Months	Pass	Fail	PERSONAL–SOCIAL SKILLS
60	5.00	60	P	F	Plays competitive exercise games.
59			P	F	Dresses self with attempts at tying shoes.
58			P	F	Spreads with knife, partial success.
57	4.75	57	P	F	Uses play materials constructively; builds, does not tear down.
56			P	F	Dresses self except tying shoes.
55			P	F	"Picks up" some after playing with no coaxing.
54	4.50	54	P	F	Attends well for short stories.
53			P	F	Uses paper straw appropriately without damaging.
52			P	F	Washes face well.
51	4.25	51	P	F	Separates from mother easily.
50			P	F	Distinguishes front from back of clothes.
49			P	F	Completely cares for self at toilet, including cleaning and dressing.
48	4.00	48	P	F	Plays with others with minimal friction.
47			P	F	Buttons medium-sized buttons.
46			P	F	Goes on very short distance errands outside the home.
45	3.75	45	P	F	Performs for others; i.e. performs a simple rhyme or song.
44			P	F	Washes hands well.
43			P	F	Brushes teeth adequately.
42	3.50	42	P	F	Attempts help at little household tasks; i.e. sweeping, dusting.
41			P	F	Completely undresses for bedtime.
40			P	F	Removes clothing for toileting.
39	3.25	39	P	F	Buttons large buttons.
38			P	F	Performs toilet activities by self (not dressing, cleaning).
37			P	F	Plays cooperatively, interacts with others
36	3.00	36	P	F	Puts on shoes and socks (tying not required).
35			P	F	Feeds self with little spilling, both fork and spoon.
34			P	F	Shares upon request.
33	2.75	33	P	F	Avoids simple hazards (hot stove, etc.)
32			P	F	Puts on a coat (buttoning not required).
31			P	F	Dries hands well.
30	2.50	30	P	F	Is not overly destructive with household goods, toys, etc.
29			P	F	Gets a drink unassisted from fountain or sink.
28			P	F	Sucks from a plastic straw.
27	2.25	27	P	F	Eats with fork but spills some.
26			P	F	Recognizes self in mirror.
25			P	F	Uses single words or likenesses to show wants.
24	2.00	24	P	F	Minds—does as told generally.
23			P	F	Removes coat or dress (unbuttoning not required).
22			P	F	At least asks to go to toilet—day and night.
21	1.75	21	P	F	Does not place objects on floor in mouth.
20			P	F	Eats with spoon, spilling little.
19			P	F	Voluntarily "slows down" to take naps or rest.
18	1.50	18	P	F	Plays around other children effectively.
17			P	F	Drinks from cup or glass unassisted.
16			P	F	Pulls off socks, but not necessarily shoes.
15	1.25	15	P	F	Follows simple commands or instructions.
14			P	F	Feeds self with a spoon—some spilling allowed.
13			P	F	Holds out arms to assist with clothing.
12	1.00	12	P	F	Temporarily responds to "no," "stop."
11			P	F	Cooperates with dressing—does not resist.
10			P	F	Chews food.
9	.75	9	P	F	Places food in mouth with hands.
8			P	F	Grasps small objects with thumb and index finger.
7			P	F	Desires personal attention and contact beyond just holding.
6	.50	6	P	F	Drinks from a cup or glass with assistance.
5			P	F	Occupies self with a toy for a short period of time.
4			P	F	Grasps foot or brings hand to mouth.
3	.25	3	P	F	Pulls at clothing with hands.
2			P	F	Sucking and swallowing are present.
1			P	F	Reaches for and wants to be held by familiar persons.

Chronological Age _____

Developmental Age _____

Date of Evaluation _____

Name _____

Date of Birth _____

Source: Quick, A.D., Little, T.L., & Campbell, A.A. Project MEMPHIS: Enhancing developmental progress in preschool exceptional children. Belmont, CA: Fearon Publishers, 1974b. Reprinted with permission.

FIGURE 13-2
Memphis Comprehensive
Developmental Scale.
Reprinted with
permission.

This scale reprinted with permission of Fearon Publishers, Inc.,
6 Davis Drive, Belmont, Calif. 94002

PROBLEM SOLVING

Objective Number	General Objective	Pretest	Date Begun	Date Ended	Strategy	Evaluation Technique	Comments: Activities: Materials:
P-1-1	Attention						
P-1-1.1*	Responds to sound				1, 4, 5, 6, 7	3/7	
P-1-1.2*	Briefly sustains gaze at speaker				1, 4, 5, 6, 7	5	
P-1-1.3	Focuses on object				1, 4, 5, 6, 7	5	
P-1-1.4*	Shuts down response to repeated sounds				1, 6	6	
P-1-1.5	Focuses on object and follows its movement briefly				1, 4, 5, 6, 7	5	
P-1-1.6	Shifts eyes toward sound				1, 4, 5, 6, 7	3/7	
P-1-1.7	Focuses on and follows an object, finding it again when it is momentarily lost				1, 4, 5, 6, 7	3	
P-1-1.8	Smoothly follows with eyes a horizontally moving object				1, 4, 5, 6, 7	5	
P-1-1.9*	Head turns to sound				1, 4, 5, 6, 7	3	
P-1-1.10	Follows horizontally moving object with head and eyes				1, 4, 5, 6, 7	5	
P-1-1.11	Visually inspects objects				1, 4, 5, 6, 7	5	
P-1-1.12	Follows vertically moving object briefly				1, 4, 5, 6, 7	5	
P-1-1.13	Head turns to sound followed by visual inspection				1, 4, 5, 6, 7	3	
P-1-1.14	Follows vertically moving object with head and eyes				1, 4, 5, 6, 7	5	
P-1-1.15	Visually follows object through circular movement				1, 4, 5, 6, 7	5	
P-1-1.16*	Responds favorably to pleasant smells				1, 4, 5	7	
P-1-1.17	Responds differentially to pleasant and unpleasant smells				1, 4, 5, 11	3	
P-1-1.18*	Responds differentially to pleasant and unpleasant tastes				11	3	

tive of the Portage Project was to provide early intervention to children from birth to 6 years of age. Because the target area was rural Wisconsin, where families were separated by great distances, the primary focus of intervention was to train parents to assess their child's behavior repertoire, identify skills which needed to be developed or modified, and effect those changes by using behavioral management and teaching strategies. "Home teachers" were trained to work with parents and help them develop these skills. Teachers then visited the homes of handicapped children for 90 minutes each week.

The materials which were developed by project staff are now available commercially. They include the *Portage Guide Kit,* the *Portage Parent Program,* and the *Parent Guide to Early Education.* The kit includes a card-file box of developmentally sequenced skills and activities parents can use to help teach children these skills, a manual of instructions, and a checklist to record progress.

Center-based

A second model for service delivery is the center-based program. These programs are typically for older preschool children and children who can benefit from specialized personnel, such as medical specialists and physical therapists, or special equipment which is difficult to transport such as orthopedic equipment or electronic equipment (Karnes & Zehrbach, 1977). Although children receive intervention in a center, parents maintain an active role in the intervention process and are encouraged to participate in activities at the center. Parents may serve as teacher aides or therapy assistants. Follow-up activities are often encouraged so that the skills parents acquire through experiences in the center are carried over into the home environment.

The Seattle Model Preschool Center for Handicapped Children offers several different types of programs for children from birth to 6 years of age (Karnes & Zehrbach, 1977). These include special programs for Down's syndrome infants, at-risk infants, children with communication problems, intermediate and advanced programs for older Down's syndrome children, a mainstreaming program which integrates handicapped and nonhandicapped preschoolers, and a program for severely handicapped preschoolers.

The preschool program uses systematic behavior modification procedures to help children develop skills necessary for effective participation in regular activities. A preschool profile is developed for each child to establish programming priorities and maintain an ongoing record. Progress is measured by direct, systematic observation of the child.

Parents are encouraged to participate actively in the intervention process. At regular meetings, parents can share information and support as well as receive training in behavioral management techniques and specific procedures for developing social, cognitive, communication, and other skills.

Home- and Center-based

The third model for early intervention is the home- and center-based model. This approach combines the advantages of the other two models by offering a combination of center-based activities ·(such as three days per week of classes) and home visiting. Although this model is more expensive than either approach alone, there are numerous advantages. The home visitor can identify aspects of the child's natural environment that may be critical to the intervention process and enlist the support of siblings and parents to make necessary changes in that environment. Patterns of family interactions, nutrition habits, and type and degree of appropriate stimulation are more easily and accurately monitored by such programs as the *COMP-Parent: A Training Program for Parents* (Peters et al, 1977). Additionally, parents and siblings of the handicapped are often in need of emotional support, and the home visitor can make this support seem more personalized and private.

The numerous advantages of a center-based program are also realized in this combination approach. The handicapped child can receive the specialized services that are needed, instruction time may be greater and of better quality, children have the opportunity to interact with peers, and parents may benefit from the free time away from the demands of their child.

The *COMP-Parent* (Peters et al., 1977) is part of the HICOMP project, one of the many combination home-and-center models which has been developed through HCEEP programs. The four components of the HICOMP model include:

COMP-Ident: Procedures for early identification of handicapped preschoolers.

COMP-Curriculum: Over 800 developmentally sequenced child-behavior goals, each with suggested teaching strategies based on principles of errorless learning, and methods of evaluating mastery of objectives.

COMP-Parent: Procedures for training parents to be active "teachers" for their children; for both group and individualized training.

COMP-Training: Field-test workshop sessions to train teachers to arrange the environment for maximum achievement and development.

In the home-and-center model, children attend center-based activities three days each week and receive home-based instructions on one or two remaining days. The home visitor suggests follow-up activities for the home which complement classroom activities, modifies program goals based on parent feedback, trains parents and siblings to use behavior-modification techniques, and provides feedback, support, and encouragement to the families. Parents also serve as classroom aides several days each month.

Mix-and-Match Components

These projects have developed materials and procedures which have successfully and efficiently established and provided early-intervention services to communities throughout the country. These models do not have to be replicated identically: instead, many can be "mixed and matched" to find the most appropriate combination for a particular community. To obtain more information on these programs, contact: Technical Assistance Development System, 500 NCNB Plaza, Chapel Hill, N. C. 27514; and Western States Technical Assistance Resource, 215 University District Building, 1107 NE 45th Street, Seattle, Wash. 98105.

BENEFITS OF EARLY INTERVENTION

Research aimed at evaluating the effectiveness of early intervention, though extensive, reflects the relative newness of the field. While a review of the specific limitations of the research is beyond the scope of this text, dramatic positive findings have been reported in the research literature (e.g., Bissell, 1970; Lazar, 1979; Skeels & Dye, 1942; Weikart, Bond, & McNeil, 1978). These studies have been criticized primarily on methodological grounds. For example, in a review of seven early-intervention projects, Bronfenbrenner (1974) criticized the use of changes in IQ scores as the primary measure of effectiveness of early intervention. This heavy emphasis on cognitive development may be due to the fact that the procedures for assessing cognitive development (standardized tests of intelligence) are the most reliable, technically adequate methods available (Ramey & Campbell, 1974).

Most experts agree that there are, in fact, numerous advantages to providing early intervention to handicapped and at-risk children, despite the present limitations in measuring them. Smith (1980) delineates four kinds of positive effects: benefits to the child, the family, and society, and the economic value of early intervention.

Benefits to the Child

Early-intervention efforts have documented dramatic increases in all areas of development—cognitive, motor, language, social-emotional, and self-help (Bissell, 1970; Lazar, 1979; Ramey & Smith, 1975; Skeels & Dye, 1942; Weikart, Bond, & McNeil, 1978), and may prevent the development of secondary handicapping conditions (Garland, Stone, Swanson, & Woodruff, 1980). While the *persistence* of these positive effects on the child have been questioned (Clarke & Clarke, 1976), additional benefits of early education have not been as harshly criticized and point to the need for such early services.

Benefits to the Family

The difficulties and problems experienced by families of young handicapped children are extensive and serious (see Chapter 12). Early-intervention programs have helped families to focus on their children's capabilities (rather than disabilities), learn to deal with and prevent the grief and disruption associated with having a handicapped child, and develop advocacy skills to work toward insuring the best services possible (Hayden & Pious, 1979). Lillie (1978) reports improved personal attitudes of parents about themselves and their child when parents received support through early intervention. Other positive effects resulting from programs which emphasize parent training include generalization of improved parenting skills to younger siblings. This is sometimes called the *diffusion effect.*

Benefits to Society

Early intervention for children and families in need of special services is consistent with one of the most important social values: that every individual has a right to prosper and develop his or her own potential (Smith, 1980). Early intervention benefits society in other ways as well. Our quality of life is improved when handicapped individuals and their families are accepted and supported by family and friends. When handicapped children make progress, this acceptance and support increases (Hess, Block, Costello, Knowles, & Lergery, 1971).

Economic Benefits of Early Intervention

"The case for early intervention may eventually rest on its economic good sense" (Hayden & Pious, 1979). Early intervention can in many cases prevent the need for special education services and costly institutionalization. Several researchers have attempted to quantify the long-term economic benefits of providing early intervention. Haring, Hayden, & Beck (1976) reported the *monthly* cost of institutionalization in 1975 to be $1,400; Rothschild (1977) more recently reports an average monthly cost equal to $1,800. In contrast, Swan (1980) reports that the *annual* per pupil expenditure for projects of the HCEEP ranges from $1,080 to $4,822. Clearly, the annual cost of early intervention is substantially less than that of institutionalization, which may span a lifetime.

Of course, all handicapped preschoolers are not likely to face institutionalization, but it is likely that many will require special education services. Weber, Foster, and Weikart (1978) report that children who participated in the Perry Preschool Project were significantly less likely to require special education services in their later public schooling than control-group children. The authors summarized the economic advantages of early intervention as follows:

1. A substantial portion of the total costs of the preschool projects was recovered from savings which resulted because students who had preschool education required less costly forms of education as they progressed through school than comparable students who did not have preschool — they required less special education and no institutional care.

2. Students who had preschool education had higher projected lifetime earnings than students who did not have preschool education. (The lifetime-earnings projections were based on students' educational progress in school, family background, and IQ scores.)

3. The value of a parent's time released as a result of the child's attending preschool was considered an economic benefit.

To summarize, there are numerous advantages to providing early intervention to handicapped children and children at risk. The direct effect of early intervention is to improve the cognitive, motor, social, communication, and self-help skills of the child who receives the intervention. The indirect effects include benefits to the family and society, as well as the

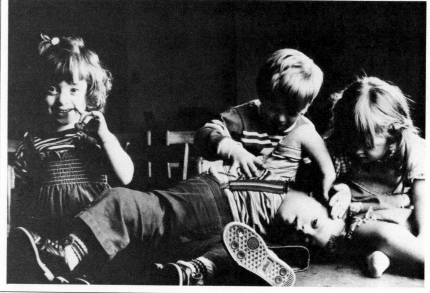

It is hoped that all children and families will some day benefit from the many advantages of early intervention. (*National Down Syndrome Society.*)

cost-effectiveness of preventing the need for more expensive remediation at a later point in the child's life. Hopefully, as these findings receive more attention, taxpayers will recognize the advantages and more actively support early-intervention programs.

EARLY INTERVENTION: THE FUTURE

Early intervention is a field which is still evolving. As we learn more about young children, it becomes necessary to coordinate the efforts of diverse professionals and agencies that have been created to meet the needs of young children. In the 1980s, the roles of agencies and professionals will expand as they begin to work together to provide a more coordinated, efficient system of service delivery. As early intervention is perceived as a necessity rather than a luxury, many changes will occur.

If progress is to continue, these changes will include modifications in legislation so that full services for children from birth to school age will be available to all children who need them. Although financial support for early intervention may appear to be on the decline in the immediate years, we are *confident* that these services, as well as preventive services (such as prenatal services) will be deemed essential. The questions for the future, then, do not focus on the existence or nonexistence of early-intervention services but ask instead, What directions will early education take?

In the future early education will take the following course:

Preschool education for handicapped youngsters will become mandatory through continued legislation at local, state, and federal levels.

Each state will develop effective means for identifying preschool handicaps.

Intervention models, curriculums, and methods will be evaluated to prove which are optimal for different kinds of problems.

Various agencies will work together effectively to form a coordinated system of delivery.

It will be determined if programs for training early-childhood specialists will be primarily provided through the education establishment or multidisciplinary training approach.

Early education will become available for all children rather than just handicapped youngsters.

Research concerned with accountability will become sufficiently refined so that the most effective and efficient programs are delivered.

To succeed in these areas special education must attract ambitious, hardworking, and creative professionals devoted to early intervention.

SUMMARY

While early special education is just now evolving as one of the newest branches in the field of education, its roots have been well established by the earliest leaders such as Seguin and Montessori. In the past twenty-five years, the importance of the preschool years and early intervention were demonstrated by ambitious researchers such as Schweinhart and Weikart, and Heber and Garber, and Karnes, whose longitudinal research findings served as the impetus for establishing the Handicapped Children's Early Education Assistance Act. Sometimes called the First Chance Program, this act established research, development, demonstration, training, and implementation components throughout the country.

The programs developed through the First Chance network have provided models for early intervention including methods, products, and materials which have been field-tested and found to be effective. Several models and materials have been reviewed to give an overview of the array of components that can be combined to meet the needs of different communities.

During the past decade, the energies of early special educators have focused on developing and field-testing components of early intervention. The future efforts of early interventionists will involve disseminating these programs so that quality early intervention will be available to all children who need these services. This goal can be accomplished by carefully documenting the benefits of early intervention and by disseminating the findings to the public. We hope that the public will recognize the many advantages of early intervention and take steps to guarantee its availability to those who will benefit from it.

L. Allen Phelps

CHAPTER 14
VOCATIONAL AND
CAREER EDUCATION

(Courtesy of Paul J. Quinn.)

Work-related education for handicapped individuals has become a priority in recent years. There is an exciting and expanding job market for professionals in vocational and career education. The employment problems of disabled individuals represent a serious lack of vocational preparation opportunities for this population. The magnitude of the problem is seen in several important research findings, which have been articulated in the results of the following studies.

1. The President's Committee on Employment of the Handicapped (1975) noted that only 42 percent of the handicapped are employed, compared with 59 percent of the total population.

2. The average weekly wages of employed disabled males in one study were found to be 22 percent lower than those of their nondisabled counterparts (U.S. Department of Health, Education, and Welfare, 1978).

3. The disabled who find employment tend to be concentrated in the worst jobs. Accounting for one-tenth of the work force, the disabled were one-sixth of all service workers, laborers, and farmers and more than one-third of all private household workers (Levitan and Taggart, 1977, p. 5).

4. Nearly 30 percent of those not in the labor force—without jobs and not looking for work—are disabled (Levitan and Taggart, 1977, p. 5).

Effective participation in career and vocational education programs is a critical factor for helping exceptional individuals secure employment. To insure that students achieve and maintain optimal success in the work

force, the school curriculum must include both labor market and societal trends.

The career education concept has gained recognition over the past several years as an integral part of all educational activities. Not surprisingly, many parents, employers, and educators have difficulty distinguishing between the awareness mission of career education and the occupational preparation mission of vocational education. The interface between career education and vocational education, which will be described later in this chapter, is critical to the development of a comprehensive program of education that prepares exceptional individuals for work.

A number of common themes appear in federal legislation pertaining to career education, vocational education, and special education. These themes address such key issues as mainstreaming, nondiscrimination in educational programs and employment, individualization, full educational opportunity, and cooperation among educators and key agencies in the delivery of vocational and career education to the handicapped. To function effectively, vocational and special educators must recognize the implications of the federal legislation recently enacted to assure disabled students access to an appropriate comprehensive vocational education.

In most communities several delivery systems exist to provide training for the world of work. In addition to vocational-education programs at the secondary and postsecondary level, Vocational Rehabilitation Services and Comprehensive Employment and Training Act (CETA) agencies provide job preparation programs and support services for exceptional youth and adults. Through the 1980s the continued operation of these programs will depend upon changing federal-state relationships. As the federal government's support for these programs declines, state agencies and communities will be required to assume much of the responsibility for their operation.

There is a growing need for trained personnel who are knowledgeable and trained in meeting the vocational and educational problems of exceptional youth and young adults. Traditionally special education personnel have been trained to work almost exclusively with elementary-school students. As the need for elementary special education personnel has gradually been met, increased attention has been given to older exceptional students. Approximately eighty-six colleges and universities now offer courses and degree programs and options that prepare individuals to specialize in the vocational preparation of special students. A number of states have created new certification requirements to respond further to this need (Brock, 1979). Recent developments in personnel preparation programs and several of the new options open to individuals desiring to specialize in this field will be discussed later in this chapter.

CHANGING RELATIONSHIPS BETWEEN EDUCATION AND WORK

Within the past five years several occupational and social changes have had a major impact upon the vocational preparation of disabled students.

AFFIRMATIVE ACTION

For many years employers were encouraged to hire the handicapped because it was a charitable thing to do. Society in general no longer believes that the best jobs and educational opportunities should be reserved for white, able-bodied males (Hoyt, 1978, p. 4). The civil rights movement of the 1950s and 1960s has spread to include minorities, women, and handicapped individuals. Laws have been enacted to eliminate bias and stereotyping on the basis of race, sex, and handicap in all government-supported contracts and activities. Section 503 of the Rehabilitation Act of 1973 states that employers who receive federal contracts of more than $2,500 cannot discriminate against an otherwise qualified handicapped person in any employment practice. The President's Committee on Employment of the Handicapped (1975) estimates that this covers approximately half of the private businesses and industries in the United States.

It would certainly be presumptuous to suggest that all employers, including the federal government, have initiated positive affirmative-action efforts to employ handicapped individuals. It is apparent, however, that employers are more seriously considering employment options for the full range of exceptional persons than at any time in the past. Social and employment stereotypes regarding the handicapped worker appear to be dissolving. As a result of conservative influences regarding the role of the federal government in employment, it is somewhat speculative as to whether or not this trend will endure through the 1980s.

CONCERN FOR EMPLOYABILITY

In America we have emphasized the value of academic and general education. Only limited value has been attached to vocational education. Unfortunately for many individuals, the pursuit of general and academic education was not focused on the eventual selection of an available job. The result has been that 25 to 33 percent of American workers feel they are overqualified for their jobs (Konizsberg, 1978, p. 48). Many college graduates find themselves performing tasks for which a high school diploma would suffice. Society can no longer assume that general education alone is the best preparation for work. The mismatch between the occupational needs of society and the qualifications of the available work force is a growing concern. Education for and about work at all levels must reflect curriculum content that will enable students to make realistic and appropriate decisions about a future occupation. Greater resources must be devoted to career guidance and counseling services, career exploration and orientation experiences, and current occupational information.

OCCUPATIONAL CHANGE

Hoyt (1977) notes that today's youth faces uncertainty regarding rapid and frequently unpredictable changes in occupations. Technological advancements, automation, and the introduction of new materials are among the major causes of occupational change. Occupations also change as a result

Students in this program are learning direct and indirect work skills as part of their IEP. (*Pennsylvania Department of Welfare, Office of Mental Retardation.*)

of shifts in management-worker relationships. Assembly-line boredom and increased concern about quality control have resulted in several experimental and innovative changes in the work place. Major experiments in job sharing, rotation, redesign, and flexible working hours are likely to reshape the nature of many jobs in the 1980s.

Like other students, the handicapped must be prepared to engage in life-long learning. To adapt to changes in the work place successfully, future workers must be capable of managing content and structural changes in their jobs. In an occupationally mobile society, individuals must be prepared to cope with change, establish helpful relationships with supervisors and other employees, seek appropriate retraining experiences as needed, and obtain assistance in job transition and relocation.

VOCATIONAL EDUCATION AND CAREER EDUCATION

There are important differences between career education and vocational education. The basic distinction lies in the fact that *vocational* education represents a program that is implemented at the secondary or postsecondary level. *Career* education, on the other hand, is a concept that is presumed to permeate the curriculum at all levels of instruction. Both have been defined by the U.S. Office of Education. *Vocational education* comprises organized educational programs which are directly related to the preparation of individuals for paid or unpaid employment, or for additional preparation for a career requiring other than a baccalaureate or advanced degree (*Federal Register,* Oct. 4, 1977). *Career education* means the totality of experiences through which one learns about, and prepares to engage in, work as a part of one's way of living, and through which one relates work

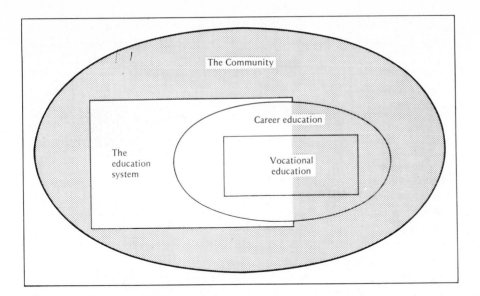

values to other life roles and choices, such as family life (*Federal Register,* Dec. 18, 1978).

Vocational education can be characterized as an integral part of career education. Through vocational education students should:

1. Acquire career decision-making skills, work-seeking skills, and work-evaluation skills

2. Perfect skills in communication, computation, and human relations

3. Acquire additional saleable skills which apply more to some types of work than to others (Evans, 1975, p. 7)

The major goals of vocational education, then, include meeting the labor needs of society, increasing individual options related to work, and conveying knowledge of the relevance of general education in work.

Figure 14-1 describes the functional relationship of career education and vocational education. Both occur in school as well as in the community. Community-based vocational-education experiences are generally in the form of part-time employment in a specific occupation for the purpose of developing entry-level or technical-level job skills. The community also supports career education activities which are focused on awareness and exploration of career options. Visits to local industries and short-term job observation are two of the most popular community-based career education activities.

RELEVANT LEGISLATION

Since 1975 the federal government has enacted five pieces of legislation that have implications for the education and employment of exceptional individuals. These five pieces of legislation are as follows:

1. Vocational Education Amendments of 1976 (P.L. 94-482, Title II)

2. Education for All Handicapped Children Act of 1975 (P.L. 94-142)

3. Career Education Incentive Act of 1977 (P.L. 95-207)

4. Comprehensive Employment and Training Act of 1978 (P.L. 95-524)

5. Section 503 and 504 of the Vocational Rehabilitation Act of 1973 (P.L. 93-112)

Vocational Education Amendments

Federal legislation for vocational education has existed since 1917; however, it was not until 1968 that the legislation established a specific purpose for serving handicapped and disadvantaged students. In 1982 $653 million was appropriated by the U.S. Congress to be spent on state programs of vocational education. Under the law each state is required to spend 10 percent of its funds ($653 million nationally) specifically for the excess costs (e.g., special instructional materials, resource teacher, etc.) involved in providing vocational education for handicapped students. Similarly, 20 percent of the funds are set aside for vocational students who are economically, academically, and/or culturally disadvantaged. To the maximum extent possible, the students served with these funds are to be enrolled in regular vocational education classes. In addition, each handicapped student that is served in vocational education programs is to have his or her vocational education program described in the Individual Education Program required under P.L. 94-142.

Education for All Handicapped Children Act

P.L. 94-142 mandates that a free and appropriate education be provided to every handicapped individual between the ages of 3 and 21. Each handicapped student is to receive appropriate special education and support services that will maximize his or her educational growth. The regulations which implement the law (*Federal Register*, August 23, 1977) define special education to also include vocational education. Thus, access to vocational education is considered an essential part of the full educational opportunities that are to be provided to *all* handicapped youth and adults. Funds provided under this law can be used to provide prevocational and vocational education, including industrial arts and consumer and homemaking education.

A written IEP must be developed for each handicapped student. If vocational education is considered appropriate for the student, a plan must be prepared describing annual goals, short-term instructional objectives, special-service requirements, and the student's present level of vocational performance. Development of the plan requires a great deal of communication between the vocational educator and special education personnel in areas such as selected instructional objectives and appropriate procedures to be used in vocational classes.

Employability is a main concern of vocational-career educators. (*Pennsylvania Department of Welfare, Office of Mental Retardation.*)

Career Education Incentive Act

The Career Education Incentive Act of 1977 (P.L. 95-207) was designed to "increase the emphasis placed on career awareness, exploration, decision-making, and planning, and to do so in a manner which will promote equal opportunity in making career choices through the elimination of bias and stereotyping in such activities, including bias and stereotyping on account of race, sex, economic status, and handicap" (U.S. Congress, *Career Education Incentive Act,* December 13, 1977).

State departments of education, local school districts, and postsecondary institutions receive funds for such activities as:

Developing comprehensive career guidance, counseling, placement, and follow-up services utilizing counselors, teachers, parents, and community-resource personnel

Developing and implementing work experiences for students whose primary purpose is career exploration

Providing in-service education for educational personnel, especially teachers, counselors, and school administrators designed to help them understand career education

Conducting seminars for members of boards of local educational agencies, community leaders, and parents concerning the nature and goals of career education

While no funds were earmarked directly for exceptional students, the act did assure that handicapped students would have full access to participation in any program or service funded under this legislation.

Comprehensive Employment and Training Act

Providing employment and training opportunities for unemployed, underemployed, and economically disadvantaged individuals was the primary focus of CETA. The program was to be administered through a network of local prime sponsors; that is, political subdivisions in communities of 100,000 population or greater. Depending on local unemployment data and other economic factors, each local prime sponsor was to receive funds from the Department of Labor in order to provide eligible clients with on-the-job training, vocational classroom training, career counseling, occupational information, transportation, day-care services, and subsidized public-service employment that are designed to enhance their employability. The 1978 Amendments to CETA (P.L. 95–524), which were to expire in FY 1982, show an increased concern for the problem of youth unemployment. Funds were provided to assist public schools in providing career exploration, counseling, occupational information, and summer and part-time work experience for economically disadvantaged youth. During FY 1981 and 1982 significant cuts were made in several of the CETA titles, especially those which offered public service employment. Funds were retained, however, for youth training programs and private sector training services of CETA clients. It is anticipated that new legislation will be enacted replacing CETA which focuses heavily upon training programs and job placement for youth who are currently, or likely to become, dependent on state/federal income support or welfare programs. These new programs will deliver basic skills and skill training for available jobs, and will be monitored closely by state and local governments and private-sector employers. (*Manpower and Vocational Education Weekly,* January 14, 1982, p.2)

Rehabilitation Act of 1973

Section 503 of the Rehabilitation Act of 1973 requires employers who have contracts with government agencies of more than $2,500 to employ qualified handicapped persons. Such employers must establish affirmative-action policies and practices in recruiting, hiring, promotion, training, transfer, and termination (*Federal Register,* Apr. 16, 1976). Handicapped individuals who feel that they have been discriminated against in any of these areas can file a complaint with the U.S. Department of Labor. Such complaints are investigated and resolved on an individual basis. This important legislation assures that handicapped persons will be able to participate in the mainstream of the world of employment.

Section 504 provides assurances that handicapped individuals will not be discriminated against in any program that receives federal financial assistance, including direct grants, loans, or indirect support (*Federal Register,* May 4, 1977). Subpart D prohibits discriminatory practices in preschool, elementary, secondary, postsecondary, and adult education programs. Any school or agency receiving federal assistance is required to:

1. Provide opportunities, benefits, aids, or services for the handicapped equal to those provided the nonhandicapped, even though these

Work-study programs have helped thousands of students learn work skills while in school. (*Pennsylvania Department of Welfare, Office of Special Education.*)

opportunities do not produce the identical result or level of achievement

2. Provide aids, benefits, and services for the handicapped in the same setting as the nonhandicapped, except in cases where their effectiveness is jeopardized by doing so

3. Provide barrier-free environments to ensure program accessibility

4. Recruit, train, promote, and compensate handicapped and nonhandicapped individuals equally (Phelps, 1977)

Since vocational education is a federal grant program, it is subject to the nondiscrimination requirements of Section 504. In 1978 the U.S. Office of Civil Rights, the federal agency responsible for enforcing Section 504 of the Rehabilitation Act, issued specific guidelines about discriminatory practices in vocational-education programs. The guidelines assure equity for handicapped persons in: (1) distribution of vocational education funds, (2) counseling and prevocational services, (3) access to vocational instruction, (4) participation in work-study and job-placement programs, and (5) employment of faculty and staff in vocational-education programs (*Federal Register,* Dec. 19, 1978).

IMPLICATIONS FOR CHANGE
There are a number of implications for the career and vocational education of exceptional youth and adults as a result of the aforementioned legislation. They include the following:

CHAPTER 14
VOCATIONAL AND
CAREER EDUCATION

The mandate to protect the rights of the handicapped to education and fair treatment in employment calls for significant changes in the existing systems for vocational education, employment training, special education, vocational rehabilitation, job placement, and personnel management in business and industry. Several new personnel roles (for example, hearing officers and handicapped affirmative-action specialists) have been created, while other roles have become more prominent. To serve the handicapped effectively, all of these systems must provide services in a manner to accommodate each individual's handicap and, at the same time, not restrict the individual's constitutional right to receive optimum services in the least restrictive environment.

The range of individual differences in regular school programs will expand, as will the diversity of individuals in the nation's work force. A general attitude of acceptance, as well as organized programs of awareness and public information, are critical if the intent of the Congress is to be realized.

There continues to be a significant need for preservice and in-service education of all personnel in the job-preparation and placement process.

Increased cooperation between schools and business and industry will continue to be imperative if an appropriate supply of handicapped individuals who are trained and competent in needed occupations is to be reached and sustained. Expanded work-study programs, which provide handicapped students with a broad range of part-time occupational experiences in local businesses and industries while still attending school, will facilitate communication between employers and school personnel. Vocational-education advisory committees, which are composed of local business personnel, must begin to review more closely the needs of handicapped students enrolled in vocational-education programs.

DELIVERY SYSTEMS
Historically there have been three principal systems used to prepare exceptional individuals for work. These include vocational education, vocational rehabilitation, and employment training (CETA). Most vocational and special educators who are concerned about the career development of exceptional students will need to know something about each of these areas.

VOCATIONAL EDUCATION
Of the three delivery systems, vocational education is the one with the largest school-based responsibility for preparing individuals for work. Historically, vocational education has been offered in comprehensive high schools, area vocational schools, and community or junior colleges. The level at which vocational education is offered within a state is determined by the state board of vocational education. In states such as Colorado, Minnesota, and Wisconsin, the majority of the vocational-education programs

are offered at postsecondary vocational-technical institutes or community colleges because the view is held that students have more to gain from vocational training if it follows the high school year.

During 1978 and 1979 approximately 60 percent of the 17.3 million students enrolled in vocational education were at the secondary level (Galladay & Wulfsberg, 1980). Nationally, these programs offer vocational training in more than 400 occupational areas. The seven major areas include: agriculture, office and business education, distributive education, home economics, health occupations, technical education, and trade and industrial education. In some states, industrial arts and consumer and homemaking programs that have a prevocational purpose are also funded with vocational-education dollars.

The range of programs offered in local schools often depends on the occupational composition of the community. For instance, a suburban community in which the principal employers are large shopping centers will likely offer more vocational programs in distributive education, (sales, marketing, advertising) than in say, agricultural education. Specific vocational programs are usually based on employment and occupational data from local and state employment offices, student interest surveys, and advice from local employers and community representatives.

In addition to in-school vocational instruction, many local districts allow advanced students to work on a part-time basis and receive both pay and vocational education credit. Cooperative education provides students with opportunities to explore various career options, gain work experience, and develop advanced skills. Cooperative work programs are similar in design and purpose to special education work-study programs.

CETA

Under the Comprehensive Employment and Training Act of 1978, funds were made available to local communities to provide job training and employment opportunities for economically disadvantaged, unemployed, and underemployed persons. This legislation insures that training and other services will be made available in order to maximize employment opportunities and enhance economic self-sufficiency.

Funds are available to eligible prime sponsors and economically disadvantaged and handicapped youth to provide:

1. Useful work experience opportunities in a wide range of community betterment activities such as rehabilitation of public properties.

2. Productive employment and work experience in fields such as education, health care, neighborhood transportation services, preservation of historic sites, and so forth.

3. Outreach, assessment, and orientation.

4. Counseling, including occupational information and career counseling.

This handicapped woman is learning how to use adapted equipment in a special vocational school for the handicapped. (*Pennsylvania Department of Welfare, Office of Mental Retardation.*)

5. Activities promoting education-to-work transition.

6. Development of labor market information and information describing employment and training opportunities.

7. Job sampling, including vocational exploration.

8. Institutional and on-the-job training.

9. Transportation assistance.

10. Job restructuring to make jobs more responsive to the needs of economically disadvantaged youth. For example, job restructuring might involve developing job ladders or new job opportunities for youth in order to improve work relationships between employers and youth.

11. Job development, direct placement, and placement assistance to secure unsubsidized employment for youth.

12. Programs to overcome sex stereotyping in job development and placement.

13. Programs to increase the labor force participation of minorities and women (P.L. 95–524 Section 432).

VOCATIONAL REHABILITATION
Vocational rehabilitation plays a critical role in providing for the adjustment of handicapped individuals to the world of work. As a professional field of endeavor, rehabilitation began with the enactment of the Smith-Seara Act

of 1918, which provided federal rehabilitation assistance to physically handicapped veterans. The Vocational Rehabilitation Act of 1920 established the state-federal matching-fund system and included services to civilians. In subsequent rehabilitation legislation, the government specified a responsibility for assisting vocationally handicapped individuals, including the mentally retarded, disturbed, social offenders, and the disadvantaged. Persons are eligible for services if their physical, mental, or learning disability presents a substantial obstacle to employment but the potential for employment through vocational rehabilitation exists. Rehabilitation is a joint federal-state program, administered by the Rehabilitation Services Administration. Within the framework of federal rules and regulations, each state establishes its own array of services. As one might expect, programs and services vary considerably in quality from state to state.

At the state level, cooperative relationships are usually established with various agencies and organizations, including vocational education, special education, state employment offices, and state welfare agencies. In October 1978, the Commissioners of Education and Rehabilitation Services issued a joint memo to state officials encouraging the revision and updating of cooperative agreements among relevant state agencies. The memo outlined a number of services that should be provided either by contract or directly through state and local rehabilitation agencies:

1. Full evaluation services including assessments of medical and psychological problems, speech and language, vocational interest and aptitude, and work skills

2. Occupational skills instruction

3. Academic, personal, and vocational-adjustment counseling

4. Special aids and prosthetic devices

5. Job development and job placement

6. Family counseling and support services

7. Transportation

Generally, rehabilitation agencies attempt not to duplicate vocational or special education services provided by local agencies. For eligible in-school clients, extensive efforts are made to supplement on an individual basis the local school's services with needed vocational-rehabilitation services. The specific services available to in-school students will vary from community to community.

PROFESSIONAL DEVELOPMENT
The principal reason for the lack of vocational programming and services for exceptional individuals can be linked to the scarcity of in-service and pre-service personnel. Personnel training programs have prepared vocational-

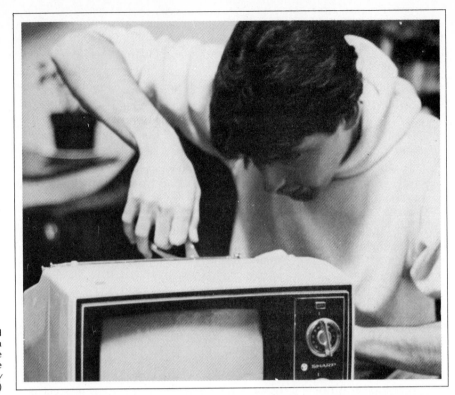

Vocational training should be thought of as a strategy for increasing the student's lifetime opportunities. (*Courtesy of Paul J. Quinn.*)

education teachers and special education teachers in separate programs. Effective program implementation simply requires more integration of effort, more intensive in-service training for teachers, and greater coordination among administrative staff from both fields. In-service professional development should address program arrangements, special students, and issues and problems that are specific to the district or program in which professionals are employed. Professionals and future professionals must continuously formulate plans to keep themselves up-to-date on legislation, emerging issues, special materials, in-service training opportunities, exemplary programs, and research outcomes.

LOCAL IN-SERVICE ACTIVITIES

Locally directed in-service activities have been productive in helping professionals to implement mainstreaming. Under P.L. 94-142 local districts are provided with in-service funds through state education agencies. These funds are to be used for implementing a comprehensive personnel development system, which includes providing in-service training for regular educators. Funds for local in-service activities are also available from state departments of vocational education.

A broad range of personnel from vocational education, special education, regular education, counseling, and administration require in-service training. Parents and employers are also important audiences. Once the specific in-service needs of various groups (for example, vocational teachers, work-study coordinators, building principals, counselors, and parents) are determined, any of several in-service activities may be implemented. Several models that have been effective include:

An area vocational school in the Chicago suburbs contracted with one of the state universities to offer a semester-long workshop in teaching methods for special education students. Vocational and special education instructors from the school met once a week for three hours. Working in teams, they developed projects to improve instruction in each of the vocational program areas. Some of the projects included developing slide presentations for use by special students, preparing vocabulary and math concept lists for each unit, revising curriculum materials and objectives, and developing diagnostic evaluation devices.

Several school districts have conducted one- or two-week curriculum development workshops. These are frequently held during the summer and are designed to enhance curriculum coordination for exceptional students in work-study programs and career exploration classes, as well as in specific vocational areas, such as automotive services or horticulture.

Groups such as the National Association for Industry-Education Cooperation have sponsored community resource workshops. Teachers and counselors develop procedures and survey instruments that are then used to identify and assess all of the available community resources (career speakers from industries, field trips, vocational rehabilitation services, occupational-aptitude testing services, and so forth). The results are compiled into an extensive community resource directory for use by teachers and counselors throughout the district.

Several universities and school districts have sponsored summer workshops which assist vocational and special educators, counselors, and parents in writing and developing IEPs for the forthcoming year.

In some instances, school districts that offer summer vocational programs for exceptional students have developed in-service programs for the teaching staff. In cooperation with a university, staff training sessions are held to assist teachers in developing teaching plans and perfecting techniques and materials that are immediately used with the special students. Such programs provide a much-needed opportunity for exceptional students to enhance or catch up on basic academic skills in a hands-on learning environment.

PROFESSIONAL ASSOCIATIONS

Several major professional associations have formed special-interest groups to focus on concerns associated with education and work for exceptional children. In 1976, the Council for Exceptional Children (CEC) established a division on career development. The National Association of Vocational Education Special Needs Personnel was formed in 1974 as an affiliate organization of the American Vocational Association. The National Rehabilitation Association has two affiliated organizations of interest—the National Rehabilitation Counseling Association and the Vocational Evaluation and Work Adjustment Association. Most of these organizations publish informative newsletters and journals, sponsor state and national conferences, and provide other professional services through state chapters.

SUMMARY

The civil rights movement in the United States now includes the right of the handicapped to both work opportunities and education. Through legislation and greater public acceptance, handicapped individuals can increasingly expect vocational and career education programs. Vocational education, vocational rehabilitation, and employment training are the three established means for delivering work-related training to handicapped individuals. These systems are available to those who have been handicapped since birth and those who acquire a handicap later in life. Because of the increasing demands for vocational preparation of handicapped people, strong new career opportunities are emerging for special educators, occupational therapists, counselors, and others who enjoy training people for vocational success.

PART FOUR
CATEGORICAL
CONCERNS
WITH SPECIAL
EDUCATION

Joseph L. French

CHAPTER 15
GIFTEDNESS

The ebb and flow of society's support for people who can and are capable of excelling has been dramatic. At least once in each of the last four decades, interest has increased abruptly only to wane, all along reflecting society's changing values. People support their values, and this is reflected in the manner in which they spend their money. If a community values a football team, the team will be supported. If citizens believe that law and order are important, the local police will be supported. If society feels a critical need to develop children's talents, then special educational provisions will be made at whatever the cost. Throughout the nation people pay more attention to the gifted in periods when anxiety is widespread.

Special education for gifted and talented students is an area in which tremendous vacillation has occurred. There is no question but that the quality of the future leaders of all societies is related directly to the quality of the educational experiences that can be provided. Yet it would be inappropriate to establish as a relatively high priority the educational needs of only one group—whether they are the gifted or disabled. Our society will not tolerate the presumption that one group is more valuable than the others. The challenge to all educators is to provide an opportunity for all children whatever their presumed potential or station in life. To that end, the very best schooling possible must be a prominent goal within the context of programs that require social support.

This chapter will describe characteristics and unique needs of gifted and talented children and the contemporary approaches which schools have developed to meet these needs.

DEFINING GIFTEDNESS

Changing conceptions of the scope of intelligence have expanded the definition of giftedness. Early definitions were based on IQ, with a score of 130 or 140 or higher considered the gifted category. Following World War I,

intelligence as indicated by IQ was thought to be indicative of native ability, which was determined primarily by heredity. Not only could school success be predicted, but IQ was thought to be directly related to a person's moral character and future position.

Subsequent research on early child development contributed to the current view that intelligence is not fixed but can be influenced by the environment to a significant degree. Because growing up in a culture other than the dominant one upon which most tests are based may produce different abilities, standardized testing alone cannot insure identification of all children. Qualities other than the narrow range of abilities sampled by intelligence tests are part of human intelligence and should be taken into account in defining giftedness. More complex ways of conceptualizing intelligence demonstrate the degree to which the concept of intelligence has expanded to embrace a wider range of mental traits than has heretofore been the case. While intelligence tests measure verbal and quantitative skills, creative abilities and leadership qualities may also be legitimate components of giftedness, all of which are of obvious value to society.

With the numerous abilities that can be unique and valuable, it is not surprising that defining giftedness has produced conflicting and sometimes confusing results. The terms "gifted," "talented," "able," "superior," "genius," and "creative" are frequently used interchangeably in describing and discussing children who are capable of high performance. While there is no universally accepted definition of giftedness, the one most often used is contained in educational amendments of 1978, P.L. 95–561, Section 902:

> For the purposes of this part, the term "gifted and talented children" means children and, whenever applicable, youth, who are identified at the preschool, elementary, or secondary level as possessing demonstrated or potential abilities that give evidence of high performance capability in areas such as intellectual, creative, specific academic, or leadership ability, or in the performing and visual arts, and who by reason thereof, require services or activities not ordinarily provided by the school.

While the federal definition offers some guidelines for shaping the future direction of special education for the gifted by emphasizing "potential abilities" that "require services or activities not ordinarily provided by the school," it suffers from a major limitation, namely, our inability to measure creative thinking, leadership ability, or potential ability in the visual arts. To date there are no methods with reliability adequate for measuring several of the characteristics listed in the definition. The most reliable measures are student performance scores as measured by standardized tests of intelligence and achievements. Generally scores which are more than two standard deviations above the mean are considered to fall in the gifted range. Figure 15-1 illustrates the normal distribution of scores on standard intelli-

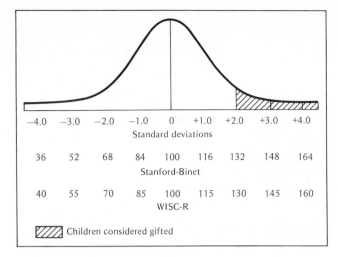

FIGURE 15-1
The normal distribution of IQ scores. The shaded area shows the theoretical number of children with IQs two standard deviations above the mean.

gence tests. On the two most frequently used measures of intelligence, the Stanford-Binet and the Wechsler Intelligence Scales for Children-Revised (WISC-R), scores of 132 and 130, respectively, are equivalent to two standard deviations above the mean.

HOW MANY ARE GIFTED?

The answer to this question is entirely dependent on the definition of giftedness one chooses. According to the federal definition, this would be the number of individuals who demonstrate high achievement or potential ability for high achievement. As we have mentioned previously, experts in the field have yet to operationalize the federal definition. We can estimate, however, the number of individuals who achieve high scores on standardized intelligence tests. According to traditional psychometric theory, 2 to 5 percent of the population can be expected to score within this range (see Figure 15-1).

But if we were able to select the most advanced 2 to 3 percent in each of the five areas outlined in P.L. 95–561 (intellectual, creative, specific academic leadership, visual, and performing arts), no one knows how much overlap would be found. In many programs participation is limited to those in the top 2 or 3 percent on nationally standardized tests of general intelligence and a few who have lower IQs but who are extraordinary when compared with their classmates in one or more of the other areas. Also, the federal definition limits involvement to those who are thought to be in need of differentiated educational programs. Many students who qualify for service by test score are (subjectively) judged to be progressing satisfactorily in the regular classroom, and therefore they receive no special program. Others receive nothing more than an occasional field trip or a few difficult extra assignments. No state education agency has reported identifying as many gifted as retarded students, even though a glance at Figure 15-1 indi-

Early evidence of intellectual ability well beyond peers is one of the best indicators of continuing giftedness. (*Courtesy of Elizabeth A. Llewellyn.*)

cates that, except for brain injuries, there is reason to expect as many gifted as retarded persons. Pennsylvania, one of the states which leads the country in providing funds for the gifted (Zettle, 1979), has identified four times more retarded than gifted children and youth. Estimates for the nation suggest that no more than 40 percent receive any special service at all.

HISTORY

As early as the 1800s some programs for the gifted existed in this country. The earliest schools and tutors in effect catered to the more able students, who were often from wealthy homes and preparing for college, while the majority of children did not receive formal education. In the 1920s education became more differentiated in order to meet the needs of a rapidly growing and diverse school population, and testing became instrumental in the development of a system of measuring both general cognitive development and achievement in specifically taught subjects such as reading, arithmetic, and so forth.

Giftedness as an area of study was legitimitized by Lewis Terman, who began his classic study of 1,000 gifted children after World War I. Selecting children who scored in the top 1 percent of the Stanford-Binet scales, he compared them with other groups of children on a variety of characteristics. The subjects were last followed up in 1972. From this study, many of the characteristics we now attribute to the highly intelligent individual are identified and defined. Although Terman's research has been invaluable in understanding giftedness, it is important to recognize that his sample was not randomly selected. Children in the study came mainly from middle-class schools in California, and minorities and children of foreign-born parents, except as they resided in the cooperating school districts, were excluded.

As American education has gone through many convolutions, so has the popularity of education for the gifted. Alternately, the victim and the beneficiary of educational policy, gifted programs have not been allowed to develop systematically but rather have experienced incremental changes in direct relation to national priorities.

During the depression, virtually no attention was given to gifted education. Following World War II, however, national leaders began to voice concern over the ability of schools to prepare persons to serve their country. At the same time, the nonacademic subjects, such as those advocated by the "life-adjustment" movement, prompted concern over education of the most able. Some claimed education was too important to leave to educators, and others urged the government to take education in hand if our country was to survive the cold war. Even before the launching of Sputnik in 1957, scientists and scholars were developing new science and mathematics curricula supported by government grants. After Sputnik the 1958 National Defense Education Act encouraged higher education in the sciences and vocational guidance to find and direct the talented into scholarly areas.

With the 1960s came disillusionment with academia and science as a result of the Vietnamese war and a growing alarm over environmental pollution. National priorities for education became increasingly egalitarian, focusing on racial integration and compensatory programs for the disadvantaged. As intelligence tests began to lose favor because of possible biases against the disadvantaged groups, giftedness defined by IQ began to seem elitist.

In the 1970s the Elementary and Secondary Education Act amendments (P.L. 93-380) marked the first substantial federal effort in the area of the gifted and talented. The first direct federal appropriation was for $50,000 in 1975. Although the authorization for 1976 was $12,250,000 only $2,560,000 was appropriated. The appropriation was increased to $3,780,000 in 1979, and to $6,280,000 in 1980. However, beginning in the 1982–1983 school year the budget for the gifted and talented was one of the few special education line items to be submerged in a block grant. Although no longer a special entitlement, unlike most categories in special education, the educational needs of the gifted were highlighted in the Elementary and Secondary Education Act and the definition remains essentially the same. With the advent of P.L. 94-142, however, schools turned their attention to developing mandatory programs for the handicapped. A national study in 1972 had set goals for gifted education, but implementation was not forthcoming. Nevertheless, many states now provide for gifted education in a variety of ways. National advocacy organizations are beginning to take up this cause, and even court cases demanding appropriate education for the gifted are beginning to emerge. Issues that remain to be solved deal with egalitarianism and defining least-restrictive environment as applied to the gifted.

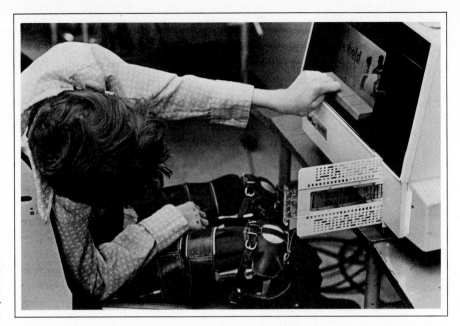

This boy with neuromotor dysfunctions is academically gifted and able to progress rapidly in school, thanks to technology. (*Borg-Warner Corp.*)

EDUCATIONALLY RELEVANT CHARACTERISTICS

Gifted individuals have long been stereotyped as socially inept, physically inferior, weak, unattractive, as well as prone toward emotional instability and a higher frequency of adjustment problems than is represented within the general population. In particular gifted children have been portrayed as belligerent, antagonistic, and difficult to manage. Yet descriptive studies of gifted children contradict these stereotypes. As a group, they tend to excel not only intellectually but in all other areas. They tend to be better adjusted, more attractive, taller, heavier, stronger, and healthier than average individuals. They also tend to have superior athletic abilities and special talents.

Of course, not every individual who is gifted will be superior in most areas. But as a group, gifted individuals tend to be above average in more areas than individuals who achieve average or below-average scores on intelligence tests.

CHARACTERISTICS OF ACADEMICALLY TALENTED CHILDREN

Teachers, particularly, should be familiar with the characteristics of academically talented children. As Freehill (1961) has pointed out, brightness is much less obvious than dullness. If people are capable of average achievement, as a result they may not show any easily identifiable indications that they are more than merely capable. In fact, gifted children themselves may be unaware of their superior ability simply because the opportunities to develop them have not been provided.

It is essential that teachers be aware of exceptional abilities and foster

these in all children. A composite list of typical characteristics of academically talented children would include such attributes as:

1. Learns rapidly, easily, and with little repetition

2. Learns to read sooner and continues to read at a consistently more advanced level than peers

3. Relies more on his or her own evaluation than on that of others

4. Asks more questions and wants to know the causes and reasons for things

5. Shows originality and often uses good but unusual methods or ideas to solve problems

6. Likes to study some subjects that are difficult because of the self-enjoyment derived from learning

7. Spends time beyond the ordinary on assignments and other school-related things that are of interest

8. Finds new ways to get attention

9. Knows about many things which other children are not aware of and is able to remember and understand information picked up incidentally

10. Gives a refreshing new twist to old ideas

11. Is able to organize self and ideas

12. Is often asked for ideas and suggestions, especially when the situation is difficult

13. Verbalizes opinions and ideas easily and spontaneously

14. Attempts to find easy ways out of difficult situations: in short, is parsimonious

15. Is able to adapt learning to various situations which are generally viewed as unrelated

16. Has diverse, spontaneous, and frequently self-directed interests

17. Recognizes relationships and comprehends meanings

18. Sees hidden meanings and cause-and-effect relationships that are not obvious

19. Quickly understands the idea in a joke or shades meanings to make things funny

Sometimes the boredom of the school can induce gifted children to look for challenge—and problems—in socially unacceptable ways. (*Courtesy of Paul J. Quinn.*)

20. Remembers facts about others

21. In writing a story or response uses diverse thoughts

22. Can judge the abilities of others with reasonable accuracy

23. Can reproduce accurately the correct sequence of happenings

24. Understands how machines work

25. Suggests to the teacher an alternate way of doing an activity

26. Has good motor and eye-hand coordination

27. Can pursue an activity in which he or she is interested for very long periods of time

As with health and height, few if any gifted children exhibit all of these traits. However, as a group, gifted and academically talented youth exhibit more of these traits and more exceptional behavior than do other pupils.

GIFTEDNESS IN MINORITY GROUPS

Many of the characteristics commonly used to describe gifted individuals are based on experiences with children from the dominant culture. Occurring in all cultures, giftedness may be displayed in ways that are unique to a particular background. Bernal (1979) has pointed out that no society is likely to develop all of the 120 abilities hypothesized in Guilford's (1959) structure-of-intellect model, so it seems reasonable that every culture selectively reinforces a limited number of those abilities. Unfortunately, children have been judged on the abilities prevalent in the dominant culture rather than those highly regarded in the Mexican American or black cultures, for example. Cognitive strengths of various cultures are being investigated, and for the present, caution should be used in applying standard measures to those of different cultures.

IDENTIFICATION AND ASSESSMENT

Acceptance of various facets of giftedness has prompted the use of a wide range of methods for identifying the gifted. The Council for Exceptional Children undertook a nationwide survey in 1977 which included compiling information on state definitions of gifted and assessment techniques used by the various states. Here is a summary of the results (Zettel, 1979).

1. Intellectual ability was included in the definition of thirty-eight states. While some states used broad definitions of children capable of high intellectual performance, leaving specifics to the local schools, the most common criteria was an IQ of 130, or two standard deviations above the mean on an intelligence test.

2. Academic aptitude was included in the definition of thirty-eight states. Standardized achievement tests were the most common means of identification in this area, with a 95th percentile the most commonly accepted criteria.

3. Creative and productive thinking abilities were included in the definitions of thirty-two states; however, there was no consensus on how to measure these characteristics. Maryland was described as using a combination of staff recommendations, performance, and a behavioral checklist for screening aptitudes in the areas of creative and productive thinking.

4. Leadership ability was considered important in only twenty-six states, reflecting the difficulty one has in attempting to quantify this ability. Idaho recommended using specific tests for this area; however, this was not an approach used in the majority of other states.

5. Visual and performing arts were part of the gifted definition in twenty-eight states. While Idaho again recommended specific tests, the most common method of assessment was evaluation of the student's creative performance or product by experts.

6. Psychomotor ability was included in the definition in only twenty-three of the states, and CEC identified only two that were actually providing programs at the time of the survey. Criteria for giftedness in this area seemed to be controversial, and inclusion of athletes in gifted programs based on this ability was often avoided. While man-

ual dexterity and motor tests were recommended in Idaho, most states looked for gross or fine motor abilities in mechanical, artistic, or medical areas rather than athletics.

To make the problems of identification and assessment even more complex, even the most commonly used methods of assessment posed special problems in identifying the gifted. Some of the standard procedures, such as teacher nomination, intelligence testing, and tested creativity, have come under enormous criticism for a number of reasons. The upshot of this dilemma is as the CEC study identified—different people used diagnostic approaches with which they are most comfortable and in which they have greatest confidence. To be sure, the basis for determining how best to identify and assess gifted children within the schools rests directly on one's philosophical viewpoint concerning the nature of giftedness, the types of instrumentation in which one has greatest confidence, and one's perception of the relative strengths and weaknesses of various approaches. But as one can see, there is no unanimity of thinking among those professionals, who are clearly viewed as experts in this particular area.

CONTEMPORARY EDUCATIONAL INTERVENTION

SOCIAL CONSIDERATIONS
Special education for the gifted has not enjoyed the full, consistent support of society. Problems in defining and conceptualizing giftedness have been compounded by sharply conflicting social values. Newland (1976) described three social concerns (not necessarily supported by evidence) that may be related to this lack of commitment.

1. Special education of the gifted would contribute to intellectual snobbishness.

2. The gifted themselves would be deprived of the social benefits of association with the nongifted.

3. Nongifted children would be deprived of the experience of learning from the gifted—the stimulus to learn more and the example of their learning styles (p. 36).

PROGRAMS FOR THE GIFTED
While there are many different approaches to providing services to the gifted, programs can generally be described as enrichment or acceleration. Enrichment is to find as many means of providing information or instruction over and above that which would be offered in the regular curriculum. Special classes, special schools, resource and itinerant programs, independent studies, and mentor programs may be classified as enrichment in the broadest sense of the term. They usually provide the traditional number of grades or years of schooling. Pressey (1949) defined acceleration as advancing through the total school program more rapidly than the average. Accel-

eration can take the form of early school admission, grade skipping, subject matter acceleration, and early college admission. However, grade skipping implies omissions and is recommended only when it is clear that the child will not miss vital content.

For the most part gifted education has relied on enrichment, but there is much disagreement as to which approach is most beneficial. The Johns Hopkins Study of Mathematically Precocious Youth began in 1971 under the direction of Dr. Julian G. Stanley. His work has provided new support for the concept of acceleration.

Daurio (1979), a proponent of acceleration, described two types of enrichment—lateral enrichment (which Stanley has called "irrelevant enrichment") and relevant academic enrichment, which includes special schools, special programs within schools, and fast-paced classes. It is Daurio's view that there are three sources of bias against acceleration: (1) traditional age-grade progression in American schools; (2) bias against using standardized tests for identifying precocious intellectual ability; and (3) selective recall of the social adjustment of accelerated students (that is, remembering the few failures as opposed to the many successes).

Even advocates of enrichment have criticized it as being without substance. Providing periodic activities, however interesting, without building a systematic program directed toward goals appropriate to the individual does little to improve education for the gifted student. Renzulli (1979) developed a model for integrating the various types of enrichment into a more balanced program. In his model, Type 1, General Exploratory Activities, and Type 2, Group Training Activities, are designed to expand a student's interests and develop thinking and feeling processes—activities which would be beneficial to all students. Type 3, Individual and Small Group Investigations of Real Problems, is the core of the gifted program in which students use their skills to investigate problems and communicate their ideas about their work. In summary, it is clear that both acceleration and enrichment are currently found in American schools. Enrichment leads to acceleration. Acceleration requires enrichment. Various modes of service delivery are being employed, and each strategy has its own strengths and weaknesses.

ACCELERATION

Acceleration programs, of which there are a variety, move a gifted child through the school program more rapidly than the conventional rate. Here are four illustrations of different types of acceleration programs.

Early School Admission

Early school admission usually refers to the practice of admitting the preschool child to kindergarten or first grade before the usual age rquirement. Concerns usually focus on whether the child will be able to adjust emotionally and socially. Some research has suggested that children who were admitted to school early tended to be exceptionally well adjusted. Decisions to place young children in school early should be made after careful evaluation of the child's development in all areas, not just academic skills, and efforts should be made to insure that the child is placed appropriately in the classroom that will meet his or her individual needs.

Grade Skipping

Some schools attempt to meet the special needs of gifted students by allowing the student to progress through the grades faster than usual. Again, concerns have been expressed that detrimental consequences may result if socially and emotionally immature students are grouped with older children. Some believe that grade skipping creates a gap in the child's education; however, Newland (1976) has concluded that the limited research on this type of program consistently reports it as being a favorable approach. Moving a child from second to third grade in January and to fourth grade in September minimizes the "gaps." Klausmeir (1963) recommends a summer school program to cover omissions expected in moving directly from second to fourth grade (or third to fifth, and so forth).

Subject Matter Acceleration

There are a number of ways the curriculum can be altered to accommodate the special needs of the gifted students. Students can carry extra credit loads, take courses from more than one school, apply for exceptions from some of the requirements, take proficiency tests, or progress through independent study modules.

Early College Admission

Students can begin early their college studies in a number of different ways. Some programs allow students to complete high school requirements during one part of the day and attend local college classes for the remainder. The student attends high school and college classes simultaneously in this case. In other programs, students complete the high school curriculum as rapidly as possible and begin college full time, but at an early age. The research on both academic and social adjustments of students who achieve early college admission has generally been favorable.

ENRICHMENT AND ABILITY GROUPING

Most schools attempt to meet the special needs of gifted students by enriching or supplementing the regular curriculum as well as by grouping together children with similar intellectual aptitudes. Here are several ways in which these strategies have been used by school systems concerned about providing special attention to the gifted.

Tracking

Children can be segregated into groups based on ability within single classrooms, grades, or entire schools. Tracks can be organized for each subject area or for entire grades. Placements are typically based on achievement and/or IQ. The instructional variables across tracks are usually pacing, intensity of rehearsal or practice, and style of presentation. For example, tracks for brighter students are likely to cover material more rapidly, devote less time to drilling, and spend more time manipulating and experimenting with materials. Without differential instruction tracking is of little value. The research on achievement gains from tracking only is negligible. With differential instruction comparison of groups is biased. One criticism of this method is that tracking may result in racial or class segregation.

Cluster Grouping
Similar to tracking, gifted children are grouped according to their abilities. Rather than placing all bright children in one class, however, a smaller number of students is placed in a regular class. Such an arrangement provides a peer group of gifted individuals with whom they can share advanced instruction while simultaneously allowing important social contacts with regular students.

Special Resource Classes
Groups of gifted students may attend special classes part-time on a daily basis or for several days each week. Special or supplementary topics are studied and may complement the lessons covered in the regular classroom. Children spend most of the day with their peers but spend one or more hours in the special classroom.

Special Schools
It has generally been unpopular to serve gifted students in special or segregated schools—separate from the mainstream of their peers. However, a few schools, primarily in large cities, offer special segregated programs for exceptionally able children. Placement decisions must be very carefully considered. The potential advantages, such as the unique opportunities for highly individualized appropriate curriculum, must clearly outweigh the possible disadvantages before one can legitimately justify such placement. Some well-known special schools include the Julliard School of Music, the Bronx High School of Science, and Hunter College Elementary School. About thirty-five special schools for adolescents emphasizing the visual and performing arts exist.

Resource or Itinerant Programs
Providing a resource teacher who serves one school or an itinerant teacher who serves the gifted in several schools are arrangements that allows schools with small numbers of gifted students or specially trained teachers to cope. Students are placed in regular classes, meeting with a special teacher periodically for small-group sessions or for planning individual programs. These programs often rely on independent study and consultation with the regular teacher about ways to enrich the program. In the early 1980s, these programs and independent study enrolled the most students.

Independent Study

Independent study is a common factor in almost all programs for the gifted, taking a variety of forms. Fox (1979) described several approaches to independent study. Self-paced study using programmed materials is perhaps the least creative form, best suited for teaching lower-level skills. Correspondence courses can provide instruction unavailable within the school, although the time lapse for receiving feedback on work is a disadvantage. Self-directed independent study projects which may involve the consultation of a mentor or a resource person can be quite rewarding. The final form of independent instruction described by Fox is the diagnostic-prescriptive model, in which students with advanced skills may be tested in order to determine areas in which they are lacking specific skills or concepts. Students can remediate their deficiencies and move on to more difficult levels of instruction or to advanced classes by participating in this form of instruction.

Mentors

Very precocious students may often be able to work on a level beyond that which their teacher, whether a regular teacher or a teacher of the gifted, can provide guidance. Expert assistance from a person in the community who has a high degree of competence in the student's area of interest can be an effective means of facilitating the student's progress. Also, mentors can extend the breadth of a school curriculum. Programs involving mentors can be administered in conjunction with conventional work-study or release-time programs.

SUMMARY

At this point we have come full circle. To implement any of the special programs which have been mentioned as being appropriate for the gifted requires a significant level of financial support. Whether or not a community is willing to provide such support depends entirely on its priorities. The development of an important natural resource, such as bright and talented children, ought to be one of the top priorities within every community. Unfortunately, this is not a generalized view in America. Educators at all levels have an important responsibility to constantly remind community leaders of the need to give more sustained attention to providing for intellectually superior children in the schools, handicapped or nonhandicapped.

Ronald A. Madle

CHAPTER 16
MENTAL RETARDATION: GENERAL LEARNING DYSFUNCTION

(President's Committee on Mental Retardation.)

In a complex society that is oriented toward the independence and achievement of its members, a very highly valued characteristic is the general ability to learn. However, for a number of reasons—biological, environmental, and social—there are individuals who are unable to learn as rapidly and spontaneously as most others in the society. When learning performance falls significantly below the average, the individual has typically been labeled "mentally retarded."

Who are the mentally retarded, and what causes this learning dysfunction? What are the goals of intervention, and how are they achieved? This chapter will consider these and other questions and provide a closer look at mental retardation.

DEFINING MENTAL RETARDATION

Before we can study and develop intervention strategies for the mentally retarded, it is necessary to agree on a common definition for the term *mental retardation*. Several definitions are currently used in the United States (Filler, Robinson, Smith, Vincent-Smith, Brecker & Brecker, 1976; Wilson & Spitzer, 1969), but the definition of the American Association on Mental Deficiency (AAMD) is widely accepted in special education. It specifies that two kinds of deficits must be present for an individual to be considered mentally retarded: (1) *below-average intellectual functioning,* as assessed on standardized tests of intelligence; and (2) *deficits in adaptive behavior,* those everyday behaviors necessary for survival in society (Grossman, 1977).

Most previous definitions have focused predominantly on either the intellectual or the biomedical abnormalities present in the mentally retarded. The AAMD definition integrates both and adds specific emphasis to the notion of deficits in adaptive behavior. This emphasis is a primary criterion for assigning the mentally retarded label to an individual. The relationship

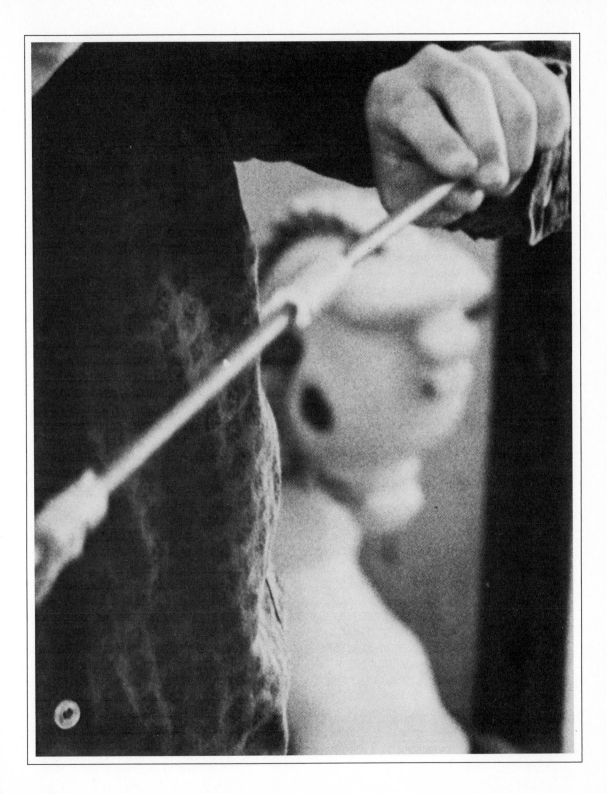

322

A child must demonstrate deficits in both adaptive and intellectual functioning to be labeled "mentally retarded." (*President's Committee on Mental Retardation*.)

between intellectual functioning, adaptive behavior, and mental retardation is illustrated in Figure 16-1. It should be noted that the classification and labeling of an individual as "mentally retarded" can change as the individual's functioning changes.

CAUSES OF MENTAL RETARDATION

Many theories or models have been proposed to explain mental retardation. The causes can be *internal* or *external* and can be *observable* or *hypothetical* (Neisworth & Smith, 1973). In up to 85 percent of all cases professionals are unable to identify with certainty the specific cause of retardation, although there may be speculation about "faulty mental processes" or "brain damage."

FIGURE 16-1
Relationship of intellectual functioning and adaptive behavior in the dual AAMD system of definition. An individual is not labeled as "mentally retarded" unless deficits are indicated in *both* adaptive and intellectual functioning. (Adapted from Grossman, 1977.)

Adaptive Behavior	Intellectual Functioning	AAMD "Label"
Not retarded	Not retarded	Not retarded
Not retarded	Retarded	Not retarded
Retarded	Not retarded	Not retarded
Retarded	Retarded	Retarded

BIOLOGICAL CAUSES

Biological causes of various handicaps, including mental retardation, are discussed in Chapter 4. Observable, pathological causes of retardation, account for probably no more than 15 percent of all cases. Major otological causes have been identified by the AAMD as follows:

1. Infections and intoxications

2. Trauma and physical agents

3. Metabolism and nutrition

4. Gross postnatal brain damage

5. Unknown prenatal influence

6. Chromosomal abnormalities

7. Gestational disorders

BIJOU'S BEHAVIORAL MODEL

Bijou (1966) has proposed a behavioral model of retardation, in which the causes of retardation are considered to be the observable antecedents and consequences of the behavior in question. The behavioral approach to retardation does not include any hypothetical, internal constructs to explain behavior because behaviors are always the end-product of observable environmental events. Rarely, if ever, is a person labeled mentally retarded from this perspective. In fact, the use of the term "mental" is inappropriate from this viewpoint (Bijou, 1966). What is retarded is *not* the mental functioning of the person, but the development of behaviors which are needed in our society.

This model was primarily developed as an approach which could be used to identify specific ways in which retarded behaviors (not people) could be caused and then to suggest methods by which remedial and preventive programs could be designed to develop the necessary behaviors. The behavioral definition of retardation offered by Bijou indicates that: "From this point of view a retarded individual. is one who has a limited repertory of behavior *shaped by the events that constitute his history*" (1966, p. 2, italics added).

In detailing the specifics of this model, Bijou described four factors in an individual's history which may cause retarded behavioral development.

1. Retardation may be caused by abnormal bodily structures which alter the person's ability to receive stimuli, respond, or both.

2. The individual may have never been properly reinforced for those behaviors which need to be learned.

3. The person may have been severely punished for specific behaviors, causing an overall suppression of behavior.

Many children may be functionally retarded in an academic setting, but have average social and personal abilities. (*President's Committee on Mental Retardation.*)

4. The person may have actually been reinforced for dysfunctional behavior patterns.

While the behavioral model stresses the causes of retarded development, they are causes which can be manipulated by special educators. Consequently, the behavioral model lends itself directly to the development of intervention programs designed to either build new behaviors or eliminate undesirable ones.

CLASSIFYING RETARDED PERSONS

The task of classifying the mentally retarded person does not end with the overall determination of retardation. More refined classification systems exist for further subdividing the population into smaller, more homogeneous groups. Generally, classification systems are based on either the degree of impairment, the cause of retardation, or the cluster of symptoms exhibited by the individual.

Selection of the kind of classification system to be used should be based on the relevance of the characteristics by which the group is subdivided. As educators, we are primarily concerned with increasing the functional levels of our students. For this reason, we will focus on only one classification system (degree of impairment). Other approaches to classification were presented in Chapter 3.

In this type of classification scheme, individuals are considered to exist along a continuum of abilities in certain areas of functioning. Intelligence and adaptive behavior are measured and individuals are identified as belonging to a specific *level* of impairment based on their measured performance. The American educational system has classified individuals on three levels: *educable, trainable,* and *custodial.* The AAMD classification scheme is slightly different, with four discrete levels of severity: *mildly, moderately, severely,* and *profoundly retarded.*

INTELLECTUAL FUNCTIONING

To measure intellectual functioning, school psychologists or clinical psychologists administer one or several standardized tests, such as the Stanford-Binet or the WISC. The results are scored and interpreted by the psychologist, who can then classify the child according to one of the levels of impairment. Table 16-1 shows the IQ scores of two popular tests of intelligence, and the corresponding levels of severity based on the AAMD system. (More information on the nature and uses of intelligence tests can be found in Chapter 7.)

ADAPTIVE BEHAVIOR

Recall that the AAMD definition of mental retardation requires that an individual must have deficits in *both* adaptive and intellectual functioning for the label "mentally retarded" to apply. Just as with intellectual functioning, adaptive behavior is assessed and an individual is classified by the degree of impairment using the same four classification levels. While in principle this system seems to be adequate, one of the most frequent criticisms of the AAMD definition and classification system is that in practice, there is no highly reliable method of classifying individuals by adaptive behavior level (Baumeister & Muma, 1977). Although many tests and scales have been developed (Walls, Werner, Bacon, & Zane, 1977), there is no simple, quantifiable, and reliable method of assigning individuals to levels of adaptive behavior as is the case with intelligence.

The AAMD, however, does offer a manual which provides a number of

TABLE 16-1
Levels of Intellectual Retardation on Two Standard Types of Intelligence Tests

LEVEL OF IMPAIRMENT	OBTAINED INTELLIGENCE QUOTIENT	
	Stanford-Binet*	WISC†
Mild	67–52	69–55
Moderate	51–36	54–40
Severe	35–20	39–25‡
Profound	19 and below	24 and below‡

* Standard deviation = 16
† Standard deviation = 15
‡ Extrapolated.

TABLE 16-2
Examples of AAMD Adaptive Behavior Levels*

AGE AND LEVEL INDICATED	ILLUSTRATIONS OF HIGHEST LEVEL OF ADAPTIVE BEHAVIOR FUNCTIONING
6 years: MILD 9 years: MODERATE 12 years and above: SEVERE 15 years and above: PROFOUND	*Independent functioning:* Feeds self with spoon or fork, may spill some; puts on clothing but needs help with small buttons and jacket zippers; tries to bathe self but needs help; can wash and dry hands but not very efficiently; partially toilet trained but may have accidents. *Physical:* May hop or skip; may climb steps with alternating feet; rides tricycle (or bicycle over 8 years); may climb trees or jungle gym; play dance games; may throw ball and hit target. *Communication:* May have speaking vocabulary of over 300 words and use grammatically correct sentences. If nonverbal, may use many gestures to communicate needs. Understands simple verbal communications including directions and questions ("Put it on the shelf." "Where do you live?"). (Some speech may be indistinct sometimes.) May recognize advertising words and signs (Ice cream, STOP, EXIT, MEN, LADIES). Relates experiences in simple language. *Social:* Participates in group activities and simple group games; interacts with others in simple play ("Stone," "House,") and expressive activities (art and dance).

SOURCE: Grossman, 1977, p. 29. Copyright 1977 by the American Association on Mental Deficiency. Reprinted with permission.

tables describing the functioning of individuals at different ages and adaptive behavior levels (Grossman, 1977). An example of one of these tables is presented in Table 16-2.

A revised version of the AAMD Adaptive Behavior Scale, has been developed (Nihara, Foster, Shellhaus, and Leland, 1974) which covers the ages from 3 to adulthood. This scale is extremely comprehensive and covers both developmentally critical skills, such as eating, dressing, and peer relations, and fourteen areas of maladaptive behavior such as violence, hyperactivity, and withdrawal. This and most other scales are completed by individuals familiar with the person being evaluated—teachers, family members, attendants—rather than by a psychologist.

Adaptive behavior scales are useful in the process of sampling and itemizing the person's level of functioning in a number of behavior areas. One of the earliest tests of adaptive behavior was the Vineland Social Maturity Scale (Doll, 1953). This has long been used as a way of characterizing a

THE DEVELOPMENTAL RECORD-LAURELTON CENTER ADAPTATION

Level of Function -- Degree of Independence

CLUSTER	ITEM	SCORE	GOAL	1	2	3	4	5	6	7	8	9
SELF-CARE	Eating	4		Fed	Assisted	Fingers	Spoon	Fork	Serves	Knife	Manners	Public
	Toileting	5		Diapers	Trip Trn	Commands	Bowel	Bladder	Night	Lavatory	Restroom	Unsupvsd
	Grooming	4		Dressed	Assists	Undresses	Pulls	Fastens	Ties	Chooses	Approp.	Style
	Hygiene	3		Bathed	Aware	Helps	Attempts	Supervised	Showers	Changes	Cleans	Launders
	Mean 4.0											
PERCPT-MOTOR	Fine	5		Waves	Grasps	Pinches	Handed	Builds	Assembles	Copies	Tools	Dexterous
	Gross	4		Moves	Crawls	Walks	Runs	Climbs	Skips	Balances	Games	Skillful
	Perceptual	4		Reflexes	Acts	Investig.	Experim.	Invents	Sequence	Relaxes	Rules	Integrate
	Mean 4.3											
SOC.	Peer	5		Uninvolvd	Solitary	Acknowlgs	Parallel	Cooper	Teamwork	Friends	Dates	Civic
	Authority	3		Uninter.	Recognize	Request	Two-step	Complex	Assists	Friend	Approp.	Utilizes
	Mean 4.0											
COMMUN-ICATION	Verbal	2		Cries	Noises	Babbles	Words	Phrases	Sentence	Describes	Grammar	Converses
	Concepts	3		Minimal	Changes	Forms	Discrim.	Polars	Position	Time	Concrete	Abstract
	Reading	3		Unrespon.	Responds	Attention	Pictures	Names	Words	Functnal	Leisure	Fluent
	Writing	3		Undevelpd	Smears	Scribbles	Colors	Copies	Name	Words	Phrases	Writes
	Mean 2.75											
SELF-DIRECTION	Travel	3		Moved	Vehicle	Residence	Outside	Grounds	Off-grnds	Bus	Long Trps	Plans
	Recreation	3		Inactive	Alone	Play	Group	Games	Attends	Camping	Sports	Self
	Domestic	4		Unable	Minimal	Picks-up	Dusts	Bed	Chores	Room	Cooks	Apartment
	Vocational	3		None	Potential	Untrained	Repetit.	Pre-voc	Daywork	Formal	OJT	Competit.
	Shopping	2		Uninvolved	Looks	Unskilled	Supervised	Consultan	Quantity	Useful	Plans	Quality
	Economics	3		Unaware	Primary	Edibles	Trades	Tokens	Money	Denom.	Change	Budget
	Health	3		Depend.	General	Compliant	Cooper.	Indicates	Safety	Prevent.	Self-care	Community
	Mean 3.0											

TOTAL 69

	ITEM	SCORE	GOAL	1	2	3	4	5	6	7	8	9
SPECIAL	Non-Verbal	4		Movement	Points	Tugs	Gestures	Signs	Chains	Commun.	Fingersp.	Strangers
	Prosthetic	NA		Moves	Crawls	Propped	Bars	Walker	Crutches	Limp	Free	Graceful
	Wheelchair	NA		Supported	Sits	Lifts	Inside	Maneuvers	Hi-Lo	Outside	Lo-Hi	Independent
	Aggressive	8		Dangerous	Assaultve	Combative	Hits	Obnoxious	Quarrels	Sulks	Adequate	Construct.
	Withdrawn	5		Total	Cyclical	Resists	Hides	Passive	Particip.	Interacts	Initiates	Confident
	Bizarre			Constant	Intermitt.	Periodic	Infrequnt	Occasional	Interfrrs	Tolerable	Rare	Adequate
	Delinquent	7		Uncontrol	Vandalism	Breaks-in	Steals	Runs away	Follows	Lies	Control.	Respons.

DEPENDENT — SEMI-INDEPENDENT — INDEPENDENT

*Special items which do not apply should be marked NA under the SCORE column.

RESIDENT	CASE NO.	DATE	COTTAGE	EXAMINER SIGNATURE
SALLY JONES	4189	7-25-79	LYNN	JOHN Q. GLEEN, SCHOOL PSYCHOLOGIST

FIGURE 16-2
Example of a completed profile of a moderately impaired individual on an adapted version of the Developmental Record. (Adapted from Hutton and Talkington, 1974. Used with permission of Laurelton Center.)

person's level of social development. The Vineland relies primarily on parent and other significant-adult reports.

Another useful behavior rating scale is the Developmental Record (Hutton & Talkington, 1974). Five major behavioral domains are covered: self-care, perceptual-motor, social, communication, and self-direction. The scale has been designed to be administered in about twenty-five minutes by an individual familiar with the child; it provides information on the degree of impairment in each area. An example of a completed profile of a moderately impaired individual on an adapted version of the Developmental Record is shown in Figure 16-2.

After the adaptive behavior of the individual has been assessed, it must then be compared with the tables in the AAMD manual to determine an overall level of adaptive behavior.

EDUCATIONALLY RELEVANT CHARACTERISTICS

This section will briefly cover the characteristics of individuals at the four levels of mental retardation of the AAMD system. Table 16-3 shows the typical levels of adaptive behavior for individuals at each level during major periods of their life.

MILD RETARDATION

General Characteristics

Individuals classified as being mildly retarded deviate only to a relatively minor degree in their level of functioning from normal individuals of the same chronological age (Mercer, 1973). According to the AAMD criteria, individuals with a mild degree of retardation will score between 55 and 69 on standardized intelligence tests. As far as adaptive behavior is concerned, the mildly retarded are able to develop social and communication skills, can learn academic skills to approximately a sixth- or seventh-grade level, and are usually able to master social and vocational skills well enough to support themselves at a minimal degree of subsistence. During the periods of early childhood and adulthood, the mildly retarded frequently differ so little from others of the same age that they are often not identified and labeled as mentally retarded at all.

The mildly retarded do not typically show physical abnormalities or deformities. Their appearance and behavior are closer to the norms expected for their age and sex groups but are comparable to those persons of limited socioeconomic status. Their knowledge of general information, comprehension, and interest patterns are somewhat childlike. Their capacity for abstract thinking is limited and their concepts tend toward the concrete.

The developmental progress of the mildly retarded is somewhat slower than average throughout infancy and childhood. They learn to walk, talk, eat, and toilet themselves about eight or nine months later than the average

TABLE 16-3
Developmental Characteristics of the Mentally Retarded

DEGREE OF MENTAL RETARDATION	PRESCHOOL (AGE 0–5) MATURATION AND DEVELOPMENT	SCHOOL (AGE 6–20) TRAINING AND EDUCATION	ADULT (21 AND OVER) AND VOCATIONAL ADEQUACY
Profound	Gross retardation, minimal capacity for functioning in sensorimotor areas; needs nursing care	Some motor development present; may respond to minimal or limited training in self-help	Some motor and speech development; may achieve very limited self-care; needs nursing care
Severe	Poor motor development; speech minimal; generally unable to profit from training in self-help; little or no communication skills	Can talk or learn to communicate; can be trained in elemental health habits; profits from systematic habit training	May contribute partially to self-maintenance under complete supervision; can develop self-protection skills to a minimal useful level in controlled environment
Moderate (trainable)	Can talk or learn to communicate; poor social awareness; fair motor development; profits from training in self-help; can be managed with moderate supervision	Can profit from training in social and occupational skills; unlikely to progress beyond second grade level in academic subjects; may learn to travel alone in familiar places	May achieve self-maintenance in unskilled or semi-skilled work under sheltered conditions; needs supervision and guidance when under social or economic stress
Mild (educable)	Can develop social and communication skills; minimal retardation in sensorimotor areas; often not distinguished from normal until later age	Can learn academic skills up to approximately sixth grade level by late teens; can be guided toward social conformity	Can usually achieve social and vocational skills adequate to minimum self-support but may need guidance under unusual social or economic stress

SOURCE: Sloane & Birch, 1955, pp. 258–264.

Individualized, appropriate instruction can greatly increase the chances for academic success. (*Courtesy of Jim Lukens.*)

child. Socially they often continue to engage in solitary play after their age-mates have acquired sharing and participatory play.

Special Concerns

One outstanding feature of the mildly retarded is that they frequently lack motivation to be completely independent. One of the greatest problems in working with this group is in motivating them: great numbers of failure experiences throughout life have left them with a motivational pattern which is based primarily on avoiding failure rather than achieving success (Zigler, 1971). This group also shows a higher prevalence of emotional problems than normal individuals, since they have difficulty in developing solutions to the social and nonsocial stresses that are imposed upon them.

MODERATE RETARDATION

Moderately retarded individuals are those who typically score between 40 and 54 on IQ tests. Most moderately retarded individuals will also display rather clear-cut deficits in adaptive behavior. Signs of delayed development occur very early in life but sometimes they are not recognized by unsuspecting parents. The child is delayed in virtually all areas of development. They may not begin to walk or talk until two or more years after the usual age. They also are more likely than normal to have various physical and physiological abnormalities and deformities.

During the preschool period, moderately retarded persons generally exhibit poor motor development, a lack of social awareness, and delays in learning self-care skills such as eating and toileting. They are capable, however, of benefiting from structured training in self-care skills.

During the school years the moderately retarded show extreme difficulty with academic subjects and can usually not progress beyond the second- or third-grade level. The focus of training for these children is on social and vocational skills, which will reduce their dependence in adulthood. As the moderately retarded grow up, the progressive widening of the developmental gap tends to make their retardation more obvious. This is in contrast to the mildly retarded, where the differences become less obvious in adulthood.

During the adult years the moderately retarded are often able to achieve some measure of semi-independence by performing unskilled or sometimes semiskilled work in sheltered workshops. They are also quite capable of living in community-based group homes with supervision and assistance from live-in residence managers.

SEVERE RETARDATION

Severely retarded individuals obtain IQs between approximately 25 and 39 and show rather marked deficits in adaptive behavior. In most cases, but not all, severe impairment will be evident almost at birth. The frequency and severity of medical problems are generally so great that many severely retarded individuals do not survive childhood. Most of these children have pronounced difficulties in the area of motor development. They generally show minimal speech and language development until they attain school age.

During the school years the severely retarded will usually be able to develop minimal communication skills. At this point they are most likely able to learn basic health and self-care habits through systematic instruction. As adults these individuals may be capable of partially contributing to their support by doing highly supervised, unskilled work in sheltered workshops. They may also live in group homes in the community, but many are still institutionalized.

PROFOUND RETARDATION

The profoundly retarded are some of the most seriously impaired of all disabled people. The nature and degree of their handicaps are so great that without various forms of intensive training and therapy they will exhibit virtually no adaptive behaviors. In almost all cases the profoundly retarded will be identifiable at birth or within several weeks. In addition to the frequent presence of observable anatomical abnormalities, they will have low birth weight and require incubation and other life-sustaining assistance for some period of time after birth. The death rate of these children in infancy is extremely high. Those who do survive require comprehensive care for the remainder of their lives. By the time they reach adulthood, some of the profoundly retarded may have gained some minimal speech abilities or more likely have learned a minimal substitute of speech, such as using a communication board to communicate basic wants and needs. If they have been provided with intensive, systematic instruction they may have also acquired some of the most basic self-care skills, such as self-feeding and toileting on a schedule.

These individuals have only recently been admitted to services other than institutional care. Most of them still live in institutions which, owing to limited availability of highly trained staff, are often only able to provide custodial care. This, of course, further impairs the individual's development. This most common alternative to institutional care, which is still quite rare, is a Developmental Maximization Unit based in a community setting, where a wide array of intensive, multidisciplinary services are available.

Chapter 23 deals specifically with severely and profoundly retarded individuals.

PREVALENCE OF MENTAL RETARDATION

"Prevalence" refers to the number of cases there are per 1,000 people in the overall population. Theoretically, the prevalence of mental retardation can be predicted when IQ scores alone are used as the criterion for labeling an individual as mentally retarded. In this situation, according to traditional psychometric theory, approximately 3 percent of the population will score an IQ of less than 70 and therefore be labeled retarded. The number of individuals at each of the four levels can then be estimated, based on the United States population of 220 million people, as shown in Table 16-4.

There are a number of problems with such prevalence figures, however. MacMillan (1977) has indicated that when a multidimensional definition such as the AAMD's is used, the actual prevalence of retardation is around 1 percent. Studies which use IQ alone as the criterion spuriously identify a large number of mildly intellectually retarded individuals who display adequate adaptive behaviors and should not be labeled "mentally retarded." IQ cannot be used as the sole criterion.

Another problem with the prevalence estimates based on IQ alone was noted by Dingman and Tarjan (1966). They identified a "bulge" at the low end of the tail of the normal curve. That is, there were actually more individuals scoring in the low-IQ range than had been expected. This phenomenon has been attributed to the presence of relatively more individuals with

TABLE 16-4

Expected Prevalence of Mental Retardation Based on a Population of 220 Million

LEVEL OF RETARDATION	PERCENT OF TOTAL POPULATION	ESTIMATED NUMBER
Mild	2.6	5,720,000
Moderate	0.2	440,000
Severe	0.1	220,000
Profound	0.05	110,000

major genetic abnormalities or pathological deviations at the low end of the
distribution (Robinson & Robinson, 1976).

The prevalence of mental retardation can be influenced by age, race, sex, and geographical location (Robinson & Robinson, 1976). For example, the number of mentally retarded individuals shows a rather drastic increase during the school-age years. It appears that relatively large numbers of individuals are able to successfully avoid the label "mentally retarded" during both the preschool and postschool years. These are largely mildly impaired people who, while not having major deficits in adaptive behavior, are quickly identified as mildly retarded because of the academic demands placed upon them in school.

"Incidence" refers to the number of new cases per 1,000 births in the population. The incidence can also vary, depending on factors such as the quality of health care received by the mother during pregnancy or the nature of child-rearing practices. Factors influencing prevalence and incidence of mental retardation are discussed in more detail in Chapters 4 and 6.

HISTORICAL AND CONTEMPORARY SERVICES

Historically there have been several different approaches to the problem of mental retardation (Kolstoe & Frey, 1965). During the earliest era, the goal of our primitive ancestors was survival. The weak and physically abnormal, which included many of the severely and profoundly retarded, were either destroyed or abandoned to die. They could not be allowed to consume resources needed for survival of the human race.

As the fight for survival became less pressing, a somewhat more humanitarian trend emerged. While most were no longer destroyed, the mentally retarded were often ridiculed. Some became slaves. Others were taken in by beggars and deliberately maimed so they could solicit alms. Some of the more fortunate were taken in by wealthy families and kept as a source of amusement for family members and guests (Kanner, 1964). Even later a select few were employed as court jesters or companions for wealthy individuals. Still, most did not fare well.

During the Middle Ages, religion brought a more humanitarian attitude toward and treatment of the mentally retarded. They were often taken in as wards of the church and cared for in monasteries and asylums (Kaufman & Payne, 1975). The same era, however, showed throwbacks to the earlier times when the mentally retarded were destroyed. One notable example comes from the pronouncements of Martin Luther. Believing that the retarded were possessed by demons, Luther advocated throwing them in the river to perish (Kanner, 1964).

Concern for custodial care gradually evolved into concern for education. The beginnings of this trend date from the theories of John Locke who, in 1690, attempted to distinguish between the mentally retarded and the mentally ill (Hutchins, 1978). Locke, with a remarkable anticipation of modern views, felt that the capabilities of human beings were a function of the environment they lived in rather than innate, biologically determined characteristics of the person. Since each person is the product of the environment they are raised in, this brought a new optimism that the mentally retarded could be educated and rehabilitated rather than simply cared for.

There is a rather fundamental difference in the way services are now provided to the mentally retarded from that which was common as few as ten years ago. The shift in service delivery is the turning from the custodial model to a more positive habilitative approach which offers greater hope for the mentally retarded and their families (Joint Commission on the Accreditation of Hospitals, 1977). This shift is a considerable change in the way the mentally retarded person is viewed. Changes have occurred in the way one looks at, treats, and structures an environment around the individual. The mentally retarded individual now emerges as a person with discrete handicaps deserving of evaluations which stress strengths and potentials, rather than weaknesses and limitations, and a position on a continuum of functioning, differing from the average person on some measurements and dimensions—but not necessarily on all.

This, of course, is the basic position of this entire book; that is, in spite of the labels applied to people, they have strengths in some areas and limitations in others. Each individual, whether retarded, learning-disabled, visually impaired, emotionally disturbed or whatever, is a person with many characteristics as well as problems in defined areas of human functioning which must be detailed and dealt with.

Before looking at educational intervention, it must be pointed out that mentally retarded individuals require many types of support and habilitative programs. They need more, perhaps, than almost any other category of exceptional individuals owing to the pervasiveness of their handicaps. These services have been detailed by Baroff (1974) as consisting of:

1. *Preventive:* During gestation and early childhood, services such as prenatal care, genetic counseling, medical screening, immunizations, stimulation, training, and education are needed to prevent or lessen the severity of mental retardation.

2. *Identification:* Mostly during infancy and early childhood, services such as screening, diagnosis, and medical management assume importance.

3. *Training and education:* Training and educational services are needed at all ages, although they assume less importance in adulthood.

4. *Residential:* Many forms of residential services, such as natural, foster, and adoptive homes, community living arrangements (group homes), and various types of institutions are needed at all ages.

5. *Recreational:* Beginning during the school years, various forms of organized recreational and leisure-time services become important.

6. *Vocational:* Once adulthood is reached, the mentally retarded individual needs access to various types of vocational settings, such as

prevocational, vocational, and on-the-job training, sheltered employment, and competitive employment.

7. *Legal and advocacy:* At all stages of life these individuals require services to assure the protection of their rights. During the early and school years this is often done by parents, but later formal advocates or guardians may assume this role.

Turning from the more general service needs of the mentally retarded, we now look somewhat more closely at educational services.

EDUCATIONAL INTERVENTION

CURRICULUM CONSIDERATIONS

Children with general learning dysfunction progress through the same curriculum areas that normal children do. The primary differences are *when* the retarded youngster is taught a certain skill and *how far* in a given sequence the child progresses. The teacher must identify what skills the child has, specify the next objective in the particular sequence, and utilize a variety of teaching methods to facilitate the child's acquisition of skills. For example, one sequence might include the following skills which most children acquire by 2 or 3 years of age.

1. Child holds own bottle.

2. Child holds cup and drinks from cup.

3. Child uses spoon to feed self.

The teacher identifies that the child can hold a bottle but cannot hold and drink from a cup. The teacher then specifies the next appropriate objective in the sequence for the child (child holds cup and drinks from cup) and lists a variety of teaching methods to help the child acquire the target skills. When the child learns to hold and drink from the cup, the teacher will begin to work on the *next* objective. This process is repeated again and again as the child progresses through the sequences of objectives. *Where the child begins* in the sequence is not determined by the child's age, IQ, grade level or other characteristics. Rather, the specific skills the child *does* or *does not* have determine the starting point for the child in the individual sequences.

Since the implementation of P.L. 94-142, the Bureau for the Education of the Handicapped has sponsored a variety of projects to develop sequences of objectives for use with the retarded based on the normal sequences of development. The special educator can review these products and select sequences for a variety of skill areas which the child lacks. Typical skill areas include communication, self-help, motor, problem-solving, reading, social skills, arithmetic, science, and vocational areas, to name a few. An overview of skill areas is presented here, from basic to more complex.

Basic and Compliance Skills

The earliest and most basic skills include compliance behaviors such as establishing eye contact when called by name, following simple instructions, imitating simple behaviors, basic communication skills (both expressive and receptive), early self-care skills such as toilet-training, self-feeding, simple dressing and undressing skills, care and use of prosthetic devices, and elimination of self-stimulatory and self-injurious behaviors (if they are exhibited).

While moderately and mildly retarded individuals usually acquire these skills spontaneously, the severely and profoundly retarded may not.

In summary, the curriculum for the severely or profoundly retarded individual is comprised primarily of basic and compliance skills.

Self-care Skills

Once a child has mastered basic and compliance skills, he or she will move on to skills, habits, and characteristics which will contribute to reducing dependence on other people. These skill clusters include objectives such as brushing teeth, tying shoelaces, zipping and buttoning clothing, using eating utensils properly, combing hair, and functional academic skills such as reading their own names, repeating addresses, simple counting, recognition of survival words and actions (stop, go, restrooms, using the telephone in an emergency, and so forth). At this level the curriculum should also include skills related to social behaviors such as appropriate interpersonal skills, how to shop for groceries, how to use community transportation. Motor skills are also emphasized.

Individuals who are considered profoundly retarded do not usually progress to objectives such as those described at this level. However, a curriculum for the moderately retarded will most likely focus on objectives in this level.

Intellectual and Social Skills

Cognitive, affective, and psychomotor development are skill areas which are important for preparing individuals for the responsibilities of a job and self-sufficient living in the community. This third level of skill area includes readiness activities, such as reading, writing, and arithmetic, and functional skills such as balancing a checkbook and completing a job application. Other curriculum areas which are stressed at this functional level are related to social adjustment and vocational skills. Usually, the mildly retarded individual will receive instruction at this skill level and will not progress into the more abstract and complex curriculum level of the nonretarded child.

WHAT TEACHING METHODS ARE USED?

The teacher of children with general learning dysfunction uses the same generic teaching strategies which are discussed in Chapter 8. The severity of the learning dysfunction determines the degree to which objectives are broken down into steps (task analysis), the reinforcement schedule to be used (that is, how many responses must be emitted before the child is reinforced), and the structure of the lessons. When objectives are selected from the basic and compliance skill areas, the teacher working with these children will generally work with them in one-to-one settings. Some current research also indicates that small-group instruction may be effective (Favell, Favell, & McGimsey, 1978). Individuals who do not spontaneously master skills at this level very frequently have a variety of complications and usually receive special services from ancillary personnel such as physical therapists, occupational therapists, physicians, nurses, and speech and hearing specialists. Teachers must be able to function as part of a well-coordinated interdiscipinary team.

Teachers working with children on self-care and social-behavior skill levels again use precision-teaching methods: task analysis and other methods based on the operant-learning approach. Teachers of children functioning at these levels must demonstrate an ability to identify realistic competencies and then methodically employ precision-teaching methods to attain them.

SUMMARY

Since the 1960s the field of mental retardation has been changing significantly. The services provided to the retarded have been expanded and improved. There is now a greater array of services available to the retarded person than ever before—both educationally and in other areas. Just as significantly, services are now being provided to the more severely retarded individual who, until recently, received little more than medical and custodial care. There appears to be little slackening of the demand for more professionals in the field. More importantly, however, the mainstreaming movement is demanding that regular classroom teachers learn many of the basic skills needed to provide services for the retarded. The mentally retarded are no longer a group who can be segregated into specialized services and ignored by the majority of teachers, psychologists, social workers, and physicians. They are citizens who require and deserve help and opportunities to develop.

Linda L. Varner

CHAPTER 17
LEARNING DISABILITIES: SPECIFIC LEARNING DYSFUNCTION

(Courtesy of Jim Lukens.)

The study of learning disabilities or specific learning dysfunction is perhaps one of the most controversial, dynamic, and significant areas in special education. Even though the term "learning disability" is relatively new, as early as the nineteenth century, professionals in many disciplines have been concerned with individuals who might have been considered to be learning-disabled. The field of learning disabilities is distinctly multidisciplinary, a fact which has historically influenced the controversy surrounding every aspect of the field, from defining the learning-disabled to planning intervention strategies. The disciplines which have had the strongest influence on learning disability include medicine, speech and language, psychology, and education.

DEFINING LEARNING DISABILITIES

Historically, definitions of "learning disability" have emphasized some internal, biological, or pseudo-medical condition related to the brain (Clements, 1966; Stevens & Birch, 1957; Strauss & Lehtinen, 1947). However, the education profession has been moving toward a functional approach to defining or labeling individuals as "exceptional." This movement away from nonfunctional definitions and classification systems based on inferred and hypothetical causes is striking in the field of learning disabilities.

ANALYSIS OF P.L. 94-142 DEFINITION

The most recent definition of specific learning disability (SLD) is that included in P.L. 94-142. The *Federal Register* (December 24, 1977, Part 3) states:

"Specific learning disability" means a disorder in one or more of the basic psychological processes involved in understanding or in using language

spoken or written, which may manifest itself in an imperfect ability to listen, think, speak, write, spell, or to do mathematical calculations. The term includes such conditions as perceptual handicaps, brain injury, minimal brain dysfunction, dyslexia, and developmental aphasia.

It goes on to outline the regulations for defining and identifying students with SLD.

1. The child does not achieve commensurate with his or her age and ability levels in one or more of the areas listed in the paragraph . . . below . . . when provided with learning experiences appropriate for the child's age and ability levels; and

2. The team finds that a child has a severe discrepancy between achievement and intellectual ability in one or more of the following areas: oral expression; listening comprehension; written expression; mathematics calculations; or mathematics reasoning.

The team may not identify a child as having a specific learning disability if the discrepancy between ability and achievement is

primarily the result of visual, hearing, or motor handicaps of mental retardation, or of environmental, cultural, or economic disadvantages.

Additionally, observation is an important procedure.

(a) At least one team member other than the child's regular teacher shall observe the child's academic performance in the regular classroom settings.

(b) In the case of a child of less than school age or out of school, a team member shall observe the child in an environment appropriate for a child of that age.

In order to evaluate a specific learning disabiity, a multidisciplinary team approach must be utilized. This team must include

1. The child's regular teacher or qualified replacement, if the child does not have a regular teacher.

2. For the preschool child, an individual qualified by the state educational agency to teach preschool children.

3. At least one individual qualified to conduct individual diagnostic examinations of children (for example, school psychologist, speech and language specialist, learning disability specialist).

These children need special instruction to help overcome specific learning problems, although they are neither retarded, disturbed, nor sensorially impaired. (*Courtesy of Jim Lukens.*)

In practice, then, a child is usually identified as learning-disabled if the child's achievement is eighteen months to two years below the level the child could be expected to achieve.

As Salvia and Ysseldyke (1978) point out, careful statistical evaluation of this procedure reveals a number of problems with this labeling system. Yet, despite these problems, the P.L. 94-142 definition is the most reliable.

PREVALENCE OF LEARNING DISABILITY
Some estimates of the prevalence of learning disabilities have ranged from 1 to 30 percent of the school-age population. The 1975 Department of Health, Education, and Welfare estimated that 3 percent of children from 0 to 19 years of age were learning-disabled. In 1978, the Bureau for the Handi-

TABLE 17-1
Prevalence of SLD by Degree of Severity and Type of Program

SEVERITY	SETTING OR PROGRAM	% OF TOTAL PROGRAM POPULATION
Mild	Regular classroom	5–10
Moderate	Resource room program with regular classroom	2–5
Severe	Special class placement	1–2

SOURCE: Valett, 1970, p. 69.

capped identified almost 2 percent of children from age 3 to 21 years as learning-disabled. According to Valett (1970), special class programs are recommended for only a small number of the children thought to have specific learning disabilities (1 to 2 percent). The prevalence of learning disabilities by degrees of severity and type of programs required are shown in Table 17-1.

HISTORICAL AND CURRENT VIEWS

Wiederholt (1974) divides the history of learning disabilities into three distinct periods of development. The foundation phase, beginning about 1800, was influenced primarily by individuals from the medical profession, who developed theories of brain function and dysfunction based on their observations of brain-injured adults. Then, during the transitional phase, dating from roughly 1920, psychologists and educators attempted to translate the theoretical formulations of the first phase into diagnostic tests and remedial practices for children with learning problems. The integrative phase (1963 to the present) depicts a time period where many different approaches are being used and evaluated in order to determine their effectiveness for children with learning disabilities.

FOUNDATION PHASE

During the foundation phase, medical practitioners and researchers developed theories of learning disabilities by observing adults who acquired brain damage primarily through injury or as a result of a stroke. Various learning problems were observed clinically and the cause was then inferred to be the result of the patient's brain damage. Similarly, in the area of language problems, researchers extended this clinical approach to tie certain types of language problems to damage in certain localized parts of the brain. At this time, little use was made of experimental manipulation of variables or statistical techniques.

Word blindness, or dyslexia as we know it today, was first described by James Hinshelwood (1917). He defined dyslexia as a "condition in which, with normal vision and therefore seeing the letters and words distinctly, an individual is no longer able to interpret written or printed language" (p. 2). In further advancing his theory, Hinshelwood hypothesized about a condition labeled "congenital word blindness" which caused reading disorders in school-age children. This condition was defined as a congenital defect which occurred in children with otherwise normal and undamaged brains. Hinshelwood also speculated that this condition could be explained by disease, injury at birth, or faulty development.

Disorders of perceptual-motor processes have strongly influenced the field of learning disabilities and were also first noticed during the foundation phase. As with disorders of spoken and written language, much of the research pertaining to perceptual-motor processes involved the study of brain-injured adults (World War I soldiers). Goldstein (1939) published a book theorizing several aspects of the effect of brain damage upon humans.

This was followed by a series of investigations which tried to determine whether the characteristics of brain-damaged adults would be present in brain-damaged children.

During this phase, medical causes were most frequently postulated. Strauss (Strauss & Lehtinen, 1947), hypothesized a medical cause for behavioral characteristics which resulted in varied learning problems, claiming they were manifestations of brain injury received either before, during, or after birth.

TRANSITION PHASE

Professionals in the transition phase shifted their emphasis from etiological or causal concerns to the development of remedial intervention strategies. The primary focus of attention was *children* with minimal brain damage. Psychologists and educators extended the theoretical research of the first phase into psychoeducational principles. Perhaps the greatest controversy associated with the field of learning disabilities is rooted in this extension of unsubstantiated theories into practice. Intervention programs—designed and implemented on a large scale—were based on theories which were never actually documented! This issue has damaged the entire field of learning disabilities considerably. Unfortunately, despite the harsh criticism of these programs and the lack of evidence to support their effectiveness, many schools continue to use these as the basis for intervention programs for children with learning disabilities.

Many theories and associated training activities have been developed for learning-disabled children. A popular but unsubstantiated approach emphasizes practice of perceptual-motor skills. (*President's Committee on Mental Retardation.*)

Some of the better-known professionals in the transition phase included Charles Osgood, Joseph Wepman, Marianne Frostig, Samuel Kirk, and Newell Kephart. These and many other individuals developed psychoeducational constructs which they then translated into both assessment instruments and remediation programs. Similar models of communication were developed by Osgood (1953, 1957) and Wepman (1960). Two of the assessment instruments most commonly used to identify learning disabilities are the Illinois Test of Psycholinguistic Abilities (ITPA) by Kirk, McCarthy, and Kirk (1968) and Frostig's (1963) Developmental Test of Visual Perception (DTVP). Both of these instruments identify process (that is, modality) areas of strength and weakness, which are assumed to be the underlying causes of the specific learning disability. This cause-and-effect relationship has led to the belief that a specific learning disability can be cured if the underlying process area is properly restored.

The Osgood and Wepman models of communication were utilized by Samuel Kirk in the development of the ITPA. This test, according to the authors, was to be employed as a diagnostic tool and not as a classification instrument. It was purported "to delineate specific abilities and disabilities in children in order that remediation may be undertaken when needed" (Kirk et al., 1968, p. 5). According to Kirk (1972, p. 55), the ITPA measures the following general abilities:

1. The ability to receive and understand what is seen and heard

2. The ability to make associations and understand interrelationships of what is seen and heard

3. The ability to express oneself by verbal and motor responses

4. The ability to grasp automatically the whole of a visual pattern or verbal expression when only part of it is presented

5. The ability to remember and repeat visual and auditory sequences of material

Furthermore, Kirk and Kirk (1971) have indicated that teaching should not only be directed toward the specific abilities identified by the ITPA; it should also be an integrative process.

> Activities which promote the development of verbal expression for example, also involve the use of auditory reception, memory and association as well as visual and other functions. It is the task of the teacher to integrate verbal expression activities with these other functions and thereby draw verbal expression into the mainstream of the child's functioning. (p. 121)

Multisensory Approach

While many of the individual programs and approaches designed during this period had unique features, the one common denominator was the emphasis placed on multisensory approaches to teaching. One example of a program which relied very heavily on the multisensory approach was that developed by Grace Fernald and Helen Keller (1921) for specific written language disorders. Called the visual-auditory-kinesthetic-tactile approach, it has become part of an acceptable and desirable approach to teaching children with learning disabilities today.

Integrative Phase

The integrative phase is characterized by the rapid expansion of school programs for children with learning disabilities. While there is still considerable interest in building theories and gaining an in-depth understanding of learning disabilities, the present focus in the schools is directed toward developing remediation programs. Since this phase is currently in progress, the remaining section will briefly summarize the diverse occurrences within the present area of learning disabilities.

The designation of learning disabilities as a distinct and separate area in special education came in 1963, stimulated by a speech from Samuel Kirk:

> I have used the term "learning disabilities" to describe a group of children who have disorders in development in language, speech, reading, and associated communication skills needed for social interaction. In this group, I do not include children who have sensory handicaps such as blindness or deafness, because we have methods of managing and training the deaf and the blind. I also exclude from this group children who have generalized mental retardation. (pp. 2–3)

Shortly thereafter, the Association for Children with Learning Disabilities was formed. The ACLD was established primarily as a forum for parents of children with learning disabilities and became a powerful force in lobbying for appropriate educational services. A number of government-sponsored projects, studies, and surveys were established, which resulted in significant advances and legislative mandates. A brief description of some of the more important events are listed:

1966 *Task Force 1* The report focused on identifying the most common characteristics of children with learning disabilities.

1968 *The First Annual Report of the National Advisory Committee on the Handicapped* led to subsequent legislative action.

1969 *Amended Title IV,* which was part of ESEA, was amended to include programs for children with learning disabilities.

1969 *Division for Children with Learning Disabilities* (DCLD) was established in the Council for Exceptional Children for professionals interested in learning disabilities.

1969 *Task Force II* reported on identification, assessment, and evaluation procedures, programs, professional preparation, and legislation for education of children with learning disabilities.

1969 *Task Force III* reported on central processing (neuropsychological) dysfunctions in children.

1970 *The Advanced Institute for Leadership Personnel in Learning Disabilities* was developed to train specialists in the field.

1971 *Bureau for the Education of the Handicapped* (BEH) awarded grants to state educational agencies for the purpose of developing child service demonstration projects (CSDP). These projects have resulted in model programs for children with learning disabilities.

1975 *Education for All Handicapped Children Act* (P.L. 94-142) was a legislature mandate which contained a definition of specific learning disabilities.

1978 *P.L. 94-142* was fully implemented at all levels.

EDUCATIONALLY RELEVANT CHARACTERISTICS

Many different characteristics have been identified in children thought to have learning disabilities. Traver and Hallahan (1976), identified eleven characteristics typically associated with the phenomenon. These characteristics and a brief description of each are listed in Table 17-2. It is interesting

TABLE 17-2
Characteristics of Children with Learning Disabilities

1. *Hyperactivity:* constant motion
2. *Perceptual-motor impairment:* the inability to identify or discriminate
3. *Emotional lability:* emotional instability
4. *General coordination defects:* physical awkwardness of some children
5. *Attention disorders:* the inability to remain on tasks
6. *Impulsivity:* the tendency to act quickly and/or inappropriately
7. *Memory disorders:* in general, the inability to remember past experiences
8. *Specific learning disabilities:* the inability to perform in specific academic areas (e.g., reading)
9. *Speech and language disorders:* deficient skills in oral expression, listening comprehension, and written expression
10. *Neurological soft signs:* minimal signs of central nervous system dysfunction
11. *Behavioral disparity:* wide performance differences across domains of functioning

to note that the first ten characteristics were initially identified by Task Force I as those most frequently cited in the literature (Clements, 1966). The eleventh characteristic reflects the trend in the last fifteen years toward observable, quantifiable characteristics and the P.L. 94-142 definition of specific learning disabilities.

VARIED CHARACTERISTICS

In examining the list of characteristics, keep in mind that the population of children with learning disabilities is an extremely diverse one. Identifying certain associated characteristics only provides a frame of reference in the phenomenon of learning disabilities. Children with learning disabilities may exhibit difficulty in one of these areas and not another. The range of combinations of various characteristics is tremendous. We should also be aware that *all* children may exhibit many of these same characteristics, and because of this we must be able to discriminate a specific learning disability from a transient characteristic. For this reason, it is necessary to consider the variable of time: the characteristics must be *persistent*.

To avoid subjective judgments about whether a child displays persistent characteristics or just transient behaviors, professionals—teachers and others working with the child—should specifically describe the behaviors in question and obtain objective data, such as the frequency or duration of the behavior. For example, a teacher may note that a particular child seems to be hyperactive and impulsive. Rather than refer to the child as such, the teacher should specify or describe the child's behaviors: "Shane does not sit still: he is always moving at his desk, tapping his pencil, and fidgeting. He stops working after several seconds; quits games and fights with friends without any obvious reason." This type of information is more useful in planning intervention strategies, because it provides information that is unique to the particular child.

ACADEMIC ACHIEVEMENT PROBLEMS

Without a significant discrepancy in a specific academic area, a learning disability does not exist. According to all definitions, academic problems must be present in order for any individual to be diagnosed learning-disabled. By and large, the most prevalent academic problem is reading. However, some children have deficits in more than one subject. In order to determine the existence of a discrepancy, we must evaluate the student's potential and actual levels of performance. Lerner (1976) supports the use of these questions:

1) What is the individual's potential for learning?

2) What is the individual's present achievement level?

3) What degree of discrepancy between potential and achievement is significant?

All of these questions relate to *measuring* and *assessing* the child's potential and achievement.

ASSESSMENT AND CLASSIFICATION

Philosophically, the field of SLD has progressed primarily from explaining the inborn causes and effects to the present focus of remediating the academic deficits. By focusing on academic remediation, professionals are much less concerned about many of the other related characteristics. Currently, specialists in the field feel that many of the related characteristics merely point to the existence of the learning disability. This is particularly true for characteristics like sensory perception and perceptual-motor process areas. Because of this, a basic philosphical shift has occurred in how we conceptualize SLD, especially in the areas of assessment and individualized educational programming.

Special education has provided the impetus for the development of various formal and informal assessment instruments and techniques. Recently, Salvia and Ysseldyke (1978) described the state of the art.

> Testing may be part of a larger process known as assessment; however, testing and assessment are not synonymous. Assessment in educational settings is a multifaceted process that involves far more than the administration of a test. . . . Assessment is the process of understanding the performance of students in their current ecology. . . . Assessment is always an evaluative, interpretative appraisal of performance . . . it provides information that can enable teachers and other school personnel to make decisions regarding the children they serve. (p. 4)

Generally, the field of learning disabilities has had the greatest impact on the development of testing and assessment instruments. Psychoeducational assessment of children with learning disabilities is presently geared toward obtaining meaningful information that can be used to generate specific educational recommendations. Lawrence Peters (1965) was instrumental in formulating the idea of "diagnosis for teaching" rather than "diagnosis for identification." In addition, current legislative mandates also provide the legal basis for sound, purposeful, and responsible assessment procedures.

Assessment instruments and techniques in the field of learning disabilities basically include the use of standardized achievement tests, process (modality) tests, informal teacher-made tests, criterion-referenced tests, and behavioral assessment techniques. The following section will provide a brief explanation and description of several assessment instruments and techniques.

STANDARDIZED ACHIEVEMENT TESTS

The most commonly used assessment device with children thought to have learning disabilities is the standardized achievement test. Achievement tests are instruments that directly assess the students' skill levels in specific areas.

They are measures of both formal and informal educational experiences which are compared to other individuals of the same age or grade levels.

Academic achievement instruments are classified as either screening or diagnostic devices. Screening devices are used to ascertain the students' global level of functioning. The diagnostic devices are constructed to pinpoint areas of skill strengths and weaknesses. Achievement tests that reflect the content of the school curriculum are most efficient and beneficial. The results from this type of achievement test can be directly incorporated into the child's IEP. A list of standardized achievement tests most commonly used by professionals in the field of learning disabilities is presented in Table 17-3. Most of the instruments are relatively easy to administer and moderately inexpensive to purchase. Several of these devices were specifically designed for classroom teachers to administer and to interpret. In addition, there is currently more attention and emphasis on error analysis and test interpretation, with training provided at both the preservice and in-service levels.

PROCESS TESTS

Perceptual theory is based upon the concept that certain modalities (processing pathways) are functioning adequately before successful learning occurs. The most important modalities, for educational purposes, include auditory, visual, and motor channels (Reger, Schroeder, & Uschold, 1968). Within the perceptual-theory framework it is believed that children develop different abilities or preferential modalities in order to be successful learners. By ascertaining the child's preferred modality (style of learning), the teacher can achieve more efficient educational programming. Therefore, most of these perceptual or process assessment devices are geared toward determining the adequacy of the auditory, visual, and motor modalities.

It is generally agreed that for a test to be educationally useful it is extremely important that it has relatively good predictive validity. However, several literature reviews (Hallahan & Cruickshank, 1973; Hammill & Larsen, 1974; Newcomer & Hammill, 1976) indicate that many of the most popular instruments used in the process area have failed to demonstrate adequate predictive validity for academic achievement.

TEACHER-MADE TESTS

Unlike formal standardized tests, informal tests are administered almost exclusively by the classroom teachers. Otto, McMenemy, and Smith (1973) suggest the use of informal teacher-made tests when specific data are not available from standardized tests or to supplement information obtained from standardized tests. Advantages of using informal tests include:

1. *Similarity to teaching programs.* Informal tests often approximate the skills and objectives of classroom teaching programs.
2. *Teacher involvement.* Ongoing direct work provides more information for the teacher in formulating a successful program for students.

TABLE 17-3
Standardized Achievement Tests Commonly Used by Professionals in the Field of Learning Disabilities

ACHIEVEMENT TEST	SCREEN-ING	DIAG-NOSIS	GROUP ADMINIS-TERED	INDIVID-UALLY ADMINIS-TERED	NORM-REFER-ENCED	CRITE-RION-REFER-ENCED
California Achievement Test	X		X		X	
Criterion Reading		X		X		X
Diagnostic Reading Scales		X		X	X	
Durrell Analysis of Reading Difficulty		X		X	X	
Gates-MacGinitie	X		X		X	
Gates-McKillop		X		X	X	
Gilmore Oral Reading Test		X		X	X	
Gray Oral Reading Test		X		X	X	
Iowa Tests of Basic Skills	X		X		X	
Key Math		X		X		X
Metropolitan Achievement Test	X		X		X	
Peabody Individual Achievement Test	X			X	X	
Silent Reading Diagnostic Test		X	X		X	
Stanford Achievement Test	X		X		X	X
Stanford Diagnostic Reading Test		X	X	X	X	X
Wide-Range Achievement Test						
Woodcock Reading Mastery Test		X		X	X	

3. *Simplicity of design.* Informal tests are usually easy to administer, score, and interpret.

4. *Broader range of pupil progress.* Frequent use of informal tests over time provides the teacher with an ongoing evaluation of both specific materials and individual achievement (Wallace & Kauffman, 1978).

It is important to note that careful planning, administration, and interpretation are necessary for effective informal assessment; otherwise, the results are of little value to either the teacher or the student.

CRITERION-REFERENCED TEST

Criterion-referenced tests (CRT) are designed to assess the student's performance in terms of an absolute or specific criterion that has been established for the individual student. The purpose of CRT is to help educators determine whether or not a student has certain skills or knowledge. After determining what a student should be taught, immediate instruction can begin. Since CRTs do not lose reliability if given every day, the student can be evaluated daily in order to determine when to end instruction (Howell, Kaplan, & O'Connell, 1979). Hallahan and Kauffman (1976) have indicated that if a student does not achieve the criterion set, then the teacher should consider that either an inappropriate criterion was established, or additional work is necessary for the student to complete the required task.

Proger and Mann (1973) have specified four major advantages of CRTs.

1. Flexibility in using this type of test for various individual requirements

2. Continuous assessment for noting individual student progress

3. Adaptability to any commercially available curriculum

4. Judgment of the student relative to his or her own strengths and weaknesses and not to any normed group performance

Criterion-referenced tests are usually easy to integrate into the student's individual program. Testing becomes an integral component of the individualized program, focusing only on what skills the child needs to acquire. However, one difficulty with this type of testing involves the potential danger of establishing inappropriate criteria. Without appropriate criteria the student's instructional program can result in wasted time and effort, as well as frustration for both the teacher and the student.

BEHAVIORAL ASSESSMENT TECHNIQUES

Behaviorists use a technique of measurement which is direct, continuous, and precise. The behavior itself is observed and recorded. Within the area of learning disabilities, behavioral assessment has been gaining credibility as one of the most effective and efficient techniques available for sound educational programming. Hallahan and Kauffman (1976) have found that advocates of behavior modification or applied behavior analysis are "interested in the teaching of specific skills to children with specific learning problems . . . and seek to determine precisely the teaching procedures that are responsible for improvement" (p. 57).

One approach to behavioral assessment developed by Deno and Mirkin (1977) is Data-Based Program Modification (DBPM). This program consists of a set of procedures for evaluating alternative solutions to the learning problems of most students facing school difficulties. The following is a summary of features included in Deno and Mirkin's DBPM.

1. The student's academic and social behavior is always assessed in relation to the regular classroom, as organized by the teacher and acted on by peers, and to explicit expectations for performance (by teachers, parents, and school).

2. The importance of the "problem" (i.e., the discrepancy between expectation and actual student performance) is determined through interpersonal negotiations among concerned parties (i.e., student, parent, professionals), and the actual observation of academic and social behaviors on the priorities which have been established in these negotiations.

3. Intervention plans are developed which are consistent with the doctrine of "least restrictive alternative" and the right to due process.

4. Special educational interventions (program changes) are evaluated; systematic attempts to obtain cumulative benefits occur through making progressive modifications in the physical environment, instruction, and motivation.

5. Programming recommendations focus on "what works" for the individual child, and content validity is obtained by making the diagnostic process and the teaching process the same.

6. Programs are responsive to changes in performance through a process of frequent reviews and evaluations. Decisions are data-based.

7. Because evaluation of student progress is based on the summation of changes in performance on curriculum tasks, it is possible to determine if the special intervention is more successful than the regular program in reducing the discrepancy between student performance and expectations. (p. 29)

EDUCATIONAL INTERVENTION AND TREATMENT APPROACHES

APPROACHES

Several theoretical models have evolved into different educational training approaches. Three of the most widely used programs are ability training (process-oriented, multisensory training, and skill development training (task analysis).

Ability Training

The ability training approach is based on the assumption that performance deficits or learning problems are caused by a weakness or deficit in an *ability* which is thought to be prerequisite to learning in a particular subject area. For example, a child's inability to read is assumed to be caused by a visual-perception disorder. Remediation, therefore, focuses on strengthening or improving the child's visual perception. According to this approach, learning disabilities can be caused by deficient abilities in any or all of the following: perceptual motor processes, sensory processes, or psycholinguistic processes.

Intervention focuses on improving these "underlying" deficits. Examples of programs which are based on remediating these faulty underlying processes include: visual-perceptual training (Frostig & Horne, 1964); psycholinguistic training (Kirk et al., 1968); and perceptual-motor training (Kephardt, 1960). The remedial activities proposed within these programs include bead stringing, balance-beam exercises, bean-bag throws, and other body-awareness activities, puzzles, coloring books, pegboards, and nursery rhymes among others.

Multisensory Training

The multisensory training approach is based on the assumption that disabilities are the result of faulty sensory processing, and intervention focuses on providing stimulation across multiple sensory modalities. Tasks emphasize the use of visual-auditory-kinesthetic-tactile inputs, which theoretically allow the child to capitalize on any areas of strength while also improving areas of deficit. For example, a program for a child who has difficulty recognizing a specific word in reading would involve practice in tracing the word in sand (tactile) while saying the word aloud (auditory).

Evidence of Instructional Effectiveness

Little research evidence supports ability training programs or multisensory training programs. Hammill & Larsen, (1974) and Hammill, Goodman, and Wiederholt (1974) reviewed forty-two studies on the effectiveness of these programs. Most of these studies did not meet acceptable research criteria—that is, the results were confounded by insufficient research controls. Of those studies that were reliable, results indicated that use of motor training procedures did not significantly improve readiness skills, academic achievement, intelligence, or perceptual-motor performance (Lerner, 1976). Yet despite the ineffectiveness of these approaches, many schools continue to use these programs as the basis for intervention for children with learning disabilities. Special educators today must be accountable: that is, as professionals and experts, they must select strategies and programs of intervention which are most effective in meeting the needs of the students.

Skill Development Training

The skill development training approach is based on the underlying assumption that the student's demonstrated performance deficit is the problem. It is *not* the sign of any underlying disability or process problem. Rather it is received as the result of inappropriate opportunities for the student to learn the skills. Skill development training involves the use of:

1. Precise operational definitions of the specific behaviors or skills to be acquired

2. Task analysis to break down complex skills into small units

3. Direct teaching methods requiring the student to practice

4. Direct daily measurements to monitor the student's progress

Within the skill development model more emphasis is placed on the use of nonstandardized informal teacher-made tests, direct observations, and criterion-referenced tests. Considerable evidence supports the direct instruction approach (Bijou, 1973; Haring and Phillips, 1972; Lovitt, 1973; Mann, 1971).

While considerable advances have been made in the field of learning disabilities, some of the same problems found in the previous phases are also evident in the integrative phase. One major problem which has consistently plagued the field of learning disabilities is that of establishing the efficacy of its current assessment procedures and educational training programs. While we have seen the increased use of empirical research during the integrative phase, many more studies are needed to establish credibility within the field. Several research reviews by Mann and Sabatino (1973), Myers and Hammill (1969, 1976), and Hallahan and Cruickshank (1973) have not been able to substantially prove the efficacy of current practices in the field of learning disabilities.

PLACEMENT OPTIONS

Recent legislation and changing societal attitudes concerning the handicapped have resulted in the principle of least restrictive environment in educating exceptional children. While this principle applies to all handicapped individuals, it is especially relevant in respect to determining the educational settings and instructional programs for children with learning disabilities. Fortunately, public schools offer the entire range of service delivery and placement alternatives required for children with learning disabilities. The most common arrangements, from least restrictive to most restrictive, for children with learning disabilities include: regular classroom, consultant teacher and itinerant teacher, resource room, self-contained special classroom.

Regular Classroom

The courts and P.L. 94-142 require that children should be educated in the least restrictive environment. The general attitude is that all students should begin their formal education in the regular classroom and remain there if possible. Many children with learning disabilities can receive an appropriate education with their normal peers if the regular classroom is properly planned, staffed, and equipped. However, there are some children with learning disabilities who are not going to receive an appropriate educational program in the regular classroom. Wallace and McLoughlin (1979) point out:

> The practice of considering the regular classroom as a realistic service delivery system is also one aspect of the intention to prevent learning disabilities. Instructional factors may cause or at least compound the learning difficulties of some children. By including the regular classroom setting as one of the key delivery systems, we may be channeling the necessary information and skills where they are most needed. (p. 365)

The Consultant Teacher and Itinerant Teacher

The consultant teacher provides support services to regular classroom teachers and other related school staff who work with learning-disabled students. The consultant teacher delivers no direct service to the students, but rather helps the regular classroom teacher design appropriate programs, locate appropriate materials, and coordinate special services. The role of the consultant teacher requires general skills, such as an ability to work with other teachers, and specific technical skills, including precision teaching strategies, materials, and evaluation techniques.

The itinerant teacher is actually a combination consultant teacher and learning-disabilities specialist. This teacher travels to several locations providing direct services to children with learning disabilities. In addition, the itinerant teacher also provides supportive services to regular classroom teachers. This approach was developed to meet the need for a service delivery model appropriate for schools with few students with learning disabilities or in districts in sparsely populated areas. This model allows the children with learning disabilities to receive special help in the regular classroom setting.

Resource Room

A current and popular trend in the field of learning disabilities has been the development of the resource room for children with various learning problems. Wiederhold (1974) explains that a resource room is a specially staffed and equipped classroom where learning-disabled children come for one or more periods during the school day in order to receive individualized instruction.

The resource-room teacher is a highly trained specialist whose primary role is to provide direct educational services to children with learning disabilities. Services also involve educational assessment and continuous evaluation of student progress. In addition to providing direct service to children with learning disabilities, the resource-room teacher may act as a consultant to other teachers in the school and be responsible for in-service training of school staff.

Mayhall and Jenkins (1977) list some advantages of the resource-room model.

1. The children do not lose their identity with their peer group, which results in a better self-concept.

2. Individualized instruction helps remediate the learning deficit so the child can function more appropriately in the regular classroom.

3. Flexible scheduling allows the resource room to service a greater number of children.

Success of the resource room depends upon the skills of the teacher as well as the administrative practices used by the school. The resource room must include techniques that will help facilitate generalization of skills learned in the resource room, so that students can function more appropriately in other less restrictive settings.

Self-contained Special Class
Self-contained special classes for the learning-disabled usually consist of six to twelve students. Within this setting the teacher has the major responsibility for the total educational program of the learning-disabled children. The intended purpose of the self-contained classroom is to provide intensive small-group instruction for the entire day. Placement in self-contained special classes should not be considered permanent. Furthermore, it should only occur after all other less restrictive alternatives have been tried and found to be inadequate.

SUMMARY

The field of learning disabilities has been the most controversial in special education. The trend in the past ten years has been away from unsubstantiated theories of brain injury, faulty mental processes, and permanent restrictive labels to pragmatic, individualized intervention which focuses on the use of precision teaching methods and the child's specific problem.

Federal agencies estimate that approximately 3 percent of the school-age population have specific learning disabilities, although the accuracy of this estimate has been questioned. A careful analysis of the best definition of learning disabilities indicates the many difficulties in documenting "a significant discrepancy between ability and achievement."

Skill development training or task analysis has been the most effective model of intervention. Implementing this model requires expert understanding and use of precision teaching methods. Services are provided to children with learning disabilities along a continuum which includes special services in the regular classroom, use of consultant and itinerant teachers, resource rooms for more individualized instruction, and finally, self-contained classrooms.

Paul T. Sindelar

CHAPTER 18
EMOTIONAL DISTURBANCE: SOCIO–EMOTIONAL DYSFUNCTION

(Courtesy of Paul J. Quinn.)

Emotional disturbance is one of the most diverse categories in special education. Labels such as "emotional disturbance," "social maladjustment," and "behavior disorder" are used to describe a group of children who also may be gifted, mentally retarded, learning-disabled, multiply handicapped, blind, deaf, and average. Although terms such as "emotionally disturbed" and "socially maladjusted" suggest that a clear distinction can be made between social and emotional problems, it is difficult to imagine a child who is emotionally well adjusted but socially inept: socio-emotional dysfunctions pervade all aspects of the child's life.

How do the behavior characteristics of emotionally disturbed children affect the learning process and the educational experience? What are the educational characteristics to be considered when providing special education for children who are socially maladjusted? How are behavior disorders treated? This chapter attempts to provide answers to these and other questions about socio-emotional dysfunction. Indeed, this area of dysfunction is one of the intriguing and challenging behaviors that educators and other professionals deal with.

DEFINITION OF EMOTIONAL DISTURBANCE

LIMITATIONS OF A DEFINITION

Differing Perspectives
Emotional disturbance is a difficult handicap to define for a number of reasons. First, there are many ways of thinking about these problems, each with its own assumptions and concepts. According to a behaviorist approach, problem behavior is a learned set of responses, subject to change

through the manipulation of environmental events. Alternately, the psychodynamic view emphasizes personality development and the role of personality structure in determining behavior. From one perspective, causation lies in the individual's environment; from the other, within the individual's personality structure. From the behaviorist perspective, treatment involves restructuring the environment; from the psychodynamic point of view, the personality.

Nature and Measurement of Disturbance

A second problem which contributes to the difficulty of defining behavior disorders involves the nature and measurement of social and emotional behavior. For one thing, there is no measure of emotional disturbance which parallels the intelligence test for widespread use, acceptance, and technical quality (at least for certain populations). As a consequence, we cannot rely upon test performance to help define social and emotional problems. Moreover, many deviant behaviors appear in the repertoires of normally developing children. Lapouse and Monk (1958), for instance, reported the frequency with which mothers identified problem behaviors in the repertoires of their children. Nearly half of these children were described as overactive, while a similar proportion had temper tantrums at least twice a week. Fully 43 percent were described as having at least seven specific fears. Many other fairly serious behavior problems were reported by these mothers, though somewhat less commonly. These results are not unusual. Recently, Werry and Quay (1971) and Rubin and Balow (1971, 1978) have described the overlap in the behavior of disordered and normal children.

Wide Variety of Behavior Patterns

Finally, the wide variety of problem behavior patterns also contributes to the problems of definition. A comprehensive definition must encompass both the acting-out, aggressive child and the socially withdrawn child, whose behavior is far less obtrusive. Furthermore, a comprehensive definition must encompass disorders at all degrees of severity. Both the socially withdrawn child and the more severely withdrawn autistic child must be incorporated in the same definition. With obstacles as serious as these, it is not surprising that a universally acceptable definition of behavior disorder has yet to be written.

DEFINITIONS

The U.S. Office of Education uses Bower's (1969) descriptive definition in its rules and regulations (*Federal Register,* August 23, 1977). An emotionally handicapped child has one or more of the following characteristics: (1) an inability to learn which cannot be explained by intellectual deficits or differences in cultural background; (2) an inability to establish or maintain relationships with either peers or adults; (3) immature behavior, feelings, or interests which appear under normal circumstances; (4) a mood of unhappi-

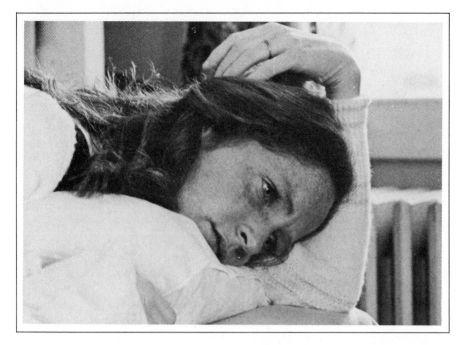

Transitory depression does not constitute emotional disturbance, although such states, if frequent, may become a pattern that does qualify for the label. (*Courtesy of Paul J. Quinn.*)

ness; and (5) a tendency to develop physical symptoms in stressful situations. According to Bower, children must exhibit these characteristics to a marked extent for a prolonged period of time before the designation "emotionally handicapped" is justified.

Of course, the Bower definition presents problems of its own. On the basis of more current attempts to define disturbance, two problems may be identified: first, it fails to consider the problem in a social context; and second, it fails to operationalize such terms as "marked extent," and "prolonged period of time."

Graubard (1973), by contrast, defines the problem as a reaction by individuals in the child's environment to the child's misbehavior. Here, the environmental determinants of maladjustment are as important as the child's behavior. Algozzine, Schmid, and Conners (1978) attempt to operationalize criteria for a definition of emotional disturbance. For example, they suggest measuring the length of time a behavior has been a problem, or determining either its pervasiveness across social situations or its frequency.

DISTINCTION BETWEEN SOCIAL AND EMOTIONAL DEVELOPMENT

SOCIAL DEVELOPMENT

Social behaviors are those used in interactions with other individuals. In a most general sense, the process of socialization prepares children to function effectively in the social groups to which they belong. Patterns of interaction are first established within the family. As toddlers, children begin interacting with their peers in play situations. Throughout childhood, the peer group grows increasingly important and assumes more and more of the functions originally served by the family. A 4-year-old boy seeks consolation from his family following an upsetting argument with the 4-year-old girl next door. A 16-year-old is more likely to seek consolation from his peers when he quarrels with the same girl twelve years later. Of course, the family remains extremely important to the developing child. Separation from the family is at best a difficult process, for both the young adults and their parents. Nevertheless, successful socialization increases the chances that the young adult has acquired the skills necessary to function effectively in society.

EMOTIONAL DEVELOPMENT

Emotional behaviors, as opposed to social behaviors, are internal or private events and are frequently inaccessible to others. Emotional development is not as well ordered as social development. Infants have a limited range of responses which might be described as emotional. Infants cry, smile, and coo but do not communicate more subtle emotions. Emotional development might be described in a very general sense as the process through which individuals come to recognize a wide range of feelings, attitudes, and sensations. The development, or more correctly, the elaboration of fears during the preschool years, demonstrates this point explicitly. Before the age of 3 or so, children's fears are limited. During the preschool years, fears of strange persons, strange objects, loud noises, and sudden movements (to name a few) decrease. Fears of imaginary creatures, the dark, animals, and other imaginary threats become increasingly prevalent. Thus, the child with developing verbal facility communicates a more elaborate set of fears than the preverbal infant for whom fears must be inferred from nonverbal behavior.

PREVALENCE OF EMOTIONAL DISTURBANCE

INCIDENCE: TWO CLUSTERS

Considering these problems, we might anticipate a wide range of estimates, each based upon different definitions. In fact, estimates of the incidence of behavior disorders do range widely, from .05 percent (Schultz, Hirshoren, Manton, & Henderson, 1971) up to 40 percent at some grade levels in the Spivack, Swift, and Prewitt (1971) study of deviant behavior in regular classrooms. In spite of this wide range, Wood and Zabel (1977) noted that estimates clustered around two points: at 2 to 3 percent and again at 20 to 25 percent. These authors argued that the two clusters represent estimates of different operational definitions of behavior disorder. The low figures represent estimates of the incidence of severe disorders; the high estimates, less severe disorders. Low estimates were usually attributed to expert opinion, while higher estimates were made by teachers or others with direct contact with children. It is not surprising that teachers' estimates were so high, since they must deal with the transient behavior problems of otherwise normal children.

RELEVANCE FOR SPECIAL EDUCATION
Wood and Zabel also point out that these clusters do have relevance for special education. On the one hand, low estimates are useful for the purpose of program planning. An administrator might use a figure like 2 percent in estimating the number of children to be served by a new program for severely disturbed children. On the other hand, high estimates may be useful for teachers and teacher trainers. If up to one-fourth of the children in public schools present serious management problems to their teachers, then both regular-class and special-education teachers must be taught classroom management skills.

DISTRIBUTION

Onset
Mild behavior disorders appear to be a phenomenon of school-age children, although hyperactivity is often recognized by the parents before their child attends school (Cantwell, 1975a). The onset of the more severe disorders such as psychosis may occur at any age, although peaks appear during the preschool years and again in adolescence. Autism is unique in that an age of onset of less than 30 months is considered one of the cardinal symptoms of the disorder (Rutter, 1978a).

Sex
Independent of the severity of the disorder, behavior disorders are a predominantly male phenomenon. Spivack et al. (1971) noted that approximately two of every three children who are classified as underachieving, acting out, or both, were boys. Cantwell (1975a) reported boy-girl ratios of at least 4 to 1 among hyperactive children. Most recently, Rubin and Balow (1978) reported that a majority of the children considered consistent behavioral problems were boys. Among more severe populations, boy-girl ratios have ranged from 2.3 to 1 to nearly 10 to 1 (Werry, 1971).

Socioeconomic Status
With regard to socioeconomic status (SES), studies like the classic work of Hollingshead and Redlich (1958) have shown that families in which the father is employed as either an unskilled or semiskilled worker contribute disproportionately to the incidence of childhood behavior disorders. Not surprisingly, since racial minorities are disproportionately represented at lower SES levels, minority children are overrepresented among disordered populations. For instance, Spivack et al. (1971) reported that blacks were overrepresented in underachieving and acting-out groups.

Hyperactive children seem to get into everything. (*Courtesy of Chuck Zovko.*)

Intelligence

The intelligence of children with mild to moderate problem behavior falls slightly below average. The results reported by Rubin and Balow (1978) are consistent with the results of virtually all earlier studies; they reported an average IQ of 94 for children with "consistently identified problems." Not surprisingly, children with mild to moderate disorders function below grade level, even when mental age is taken into account. Most severely disturbed children function in the mildly to moderately retarded range, although the range of intelligence test scores among autistic children, at least, extends into the gifted range. However, the performance of autistic children on intelligence tests differs from the performance of retarded children, suggesting a more specific, language-related cognitive deficit (Rutter, 1978b). Severely and profoundly disturbed children typically function at a preacademic level. It is necessary to teach these children fundamental skills such as imitation, language, toileting, and appropriate play.

CAUSES OF PSYCHOSOCIAL DYSFUNCTION

Theorists have advanced many ideas or concepts to account for social and emotional disorders. No single concept has proven to be an adequate explanation for all or even most of these disorders. For this reason, four *different* concepts of emotional disturbance are reviewed in this section: the physiological, psychodynamic, behavioral, and ecological concepts. The discussion of each of these concepts includes two major topics. First, a general account of each model is presented, including a definition, an analysis of the problem, and implications for treatment. Second, a representative model or theory is presented which attempts to explain a particular behavior disorder.

Sociopathic delinquents are preoccupied with "partying" and aggravating others, and seemingly experience little or no guilt about their violations. (*Courtesy of Paul J. Quinn.*)

For example, following the general account of the behavioral perspective, Ferster's account of the development of autism appears as an instance of behavioral theory.

PHYSIOLOGICAL CONCEPTS OF EMOTIONAL DISTURBANCE

Behavior disorders may be thought to result from physiological disease or dysfunction. This perspective rests on the assumption that all behavior may be reduced to a biochemical or genetic base. Physiological disease presumably disrupts the functioning of the brain or central nervous system (CNS) and is expressed in disordered behavior. The site of the problem of emotional disturbance from this physiological perspective lies within the afflicted individual, in the brain or the CNS. Solutions to the problems of emotional disturbance are designed to rectify or cure the physiological basis of the disorder. Substances are introduced to, or eliminated from, the body with the intention of eliminating the underlying chemical imbalance.

Zentall's Model of Hyperactivity

Zentall (1975, 1977) has advanced a model of hyperactivity that is illustrative of physiological concepts of disturbance, (although somewhat unusual in the number of hypothetical constructs involved). In Zentall's model, the hyperactive child is thought to be understimulated; conventional thinking had relied upon overstimulation to account for hyperactivity. Zentall assumes that there is a basic human drive for stimulation, and that for each individual there is an optimal level of stimulation. Next, she hypothesizes a control mechanism which operates to increase the stimulation of an understimulated individual and to decrease the stimulation of an overstimulated individual.An understimulated individual can reestablish optimal levels of stimulation by increasing motor or verbal activity or by changing the orientation of the head in order to increase visual and auditory stimulation. These behaviors are characteristics of a hyperactive pattern, and this account portrays them as purposeful and adaptive.

Experimental Evidence Supporting Zentall's Model

Zentall supports her model with three kinds of experimental evidence. First, the relationship between environmental stimulation and activity level suggests that, for retarded and normally intelligent hyperactive children, increased environmental stimulation is associated with decreased motor activity. Moreover, in some cases, increased environmental stimulation results in improved task performance, though these effects are neither as extensive nor as consistent as the effects on motor behavior. Second, the research on sensory deprivation in normal adults suggests that when free to move about, adults in deprived environments increase their motor activity and restlessness; when constrained, they are disorganized and less able to concentrate. Zentall regards these effects as comparable to behaviors of hyperactive children. Third, Zentall believes that her model can account for the effect of stimulant medication on the activity level of hyperactive children. Stimulants serve to increase arousal to a more optimal level so that overactivity is no longer required to optimize stimulation.

Abnormalities in the Central Nervous System

Satterfield (1975) described a similar account of the effect of stimulant medication on activity level, implicating the CNS inhibitory system instead of an hypothesized sensory control mechanism. Satterfield argued that stimulant medication arouses the CNS inhibitory system, and as a result, motor behavior is controlled. Accounts of other usually serious disorders also involve CNS functioning to explain the development and symptomatology of the disorder. For example, Ornitz (1978) has attempted to account for autism on the basis of dysfunction in the vestibular area of the brain, which is thought to modulate the interaction of sensory and motor functions. Ornitz argues that faulty modulation of sensory input, as expressed in disturbances of motility and perception, is an intrinsic feature of the pattern of autistic behavior.

Ornitz's concept of autism points out several of the limitations of a physiological approach to behavior disorders. First, the account is highly speculative; it is not known for certain that the vestibular system modulates sensory and motor processes. Second, although a dysfunction in the vestibular system (given for the moment that it does modulate these processes) could account for certain features of the autistic pattern of behavior, it fails to adequately account for all the features. By emphasizing disturbances in mobility and perception, Ornitz has not accounted for what others regard as the central features of the disorder, such as deficient language and social withdrawal. Finally, the vestibular dysfunction model has not to date led to effective treatment of the disorder, although it theoretically could.

PSYCHODYNAMIC CONCEPTS OF EMOTIONAL DISTURBANCE

Personality Development: Freud and Erikson

From a psychodynamic perspective, emotional disturbance is thought of as disrupted personality development. Freud described stages of psychosexual development defined by a predominant source of gratification. Erikson expanded upon Freud's thinking and conceptualized development as being psychosocial in nature.

According to psychodynamic thinking, emotional disturbance lies in the personality structures which are the product of development: the id, ego, and superego. The id is the inherited source of instincts, drives, and desires. The ego, which begins to develop at the end of the oral stage, must cope with the drives of the id and mediate between them and constraints imposed first by society and later by the superego. The superego separates from the ego with the resolution of the Oedipus or Electra complex at the end of the phallic stage. At this point, the child begins to incorporate societal standards as represented by the same-sex parent. In mediating between the impulses of the id and the constraints of the superego, the ego establishes patterns of coping known as defense mechanisms. Some of these patterns are familiar: the frustrated employee who goes home and kicks the dog is thought to *displace* her hostility; the artist *sublimates* sexual desires into artistic expressions; or the forgetful individual *represses* particularly embarrassing incidents. The presence of defense mechanisms is not itself indicative of disturbance, though the exclusive reliance on a single coping strategy is. Also unresolved conflict of unusual stress may disrupt the development of the personality structures themselves, so that development is abnormal or too much energy is invested to compensate for deficiencies.

Solutions to the problems of emotional disturbance depend upon the severity of the disruption in development. Treatment of a mild or moderate problem involves helping the individual to understand the nature of the underlying conflict and teaching the individual better, more adaptive ways of coping with it. With children, treatment is designed to reestablish normal growth processes. For more severe disturbances, however, an individual might be allowed to regress, that is, to return to earlier developmental stages at which the problems arose. When regression has occurred, the individual recreates the initial conflict in the relationship with the therapist. Once the underlying conflict is resolved, the individual can recapitulate the usual developmental sequence and function in a more adaptive way.

Psychoanalytic Analysis of Aggressive Behavior

Redl and Wineman (1975) analyzed the behavior of aggressive children from a psychoanalytic perspective. They argued that the behavior of young, acting-out, aggressive boys could result from three different personality deficits: deficient superego, deficient ego, and delinquent ego. When the superego fails to develop adequately, aggression can occur without guilt or remorse—the usual negative feelings associated with antisocial behavior which limit its expression among children with normally functioning superegos. Redl and Wineman differentiated the deficient superego from a deficient ego, in which the child experiences guilt from aggressive acts but nevertheless cannot cope with the impulses from the id. In some cases, though, neither the ego nor the superego are deficient and aggressive behavior occurs. In this case, the ego, though intact, is delinquent; the child participates in antisocial behavior since it is the standard for the gang. Finally, Redl and Wineman note that the defenses used to compensate for these deficiencies can sometimes contribute to the severity of the child's disorder, as in the case of a child who denies any involvement in antisocial acts. When involved with an adult who refuses to accept the *denial,* the child may grow frustrated and express that frustration through additional aggressive acting out.

BEHAVIORAL CONCEPTS OF EMOTIONAL DISTURBANCE

Analysis of Deviant Behaviors

According to a behavioral perspective, all behavior is acquired according to the same principles, although not all behavior is regarded as useful or constructive. Behaviors which occur with excessive frequency or intensity, behaviors under poor stimulus control, and behaviors which compete with or prevent the acquisition of appropriate behaviors are considered maladaptive. A behavior problem results from unfortunate environmental contingencies (the relationships between behavior and its consequences). If a behavior is followed by rewarding consequences, then it is strengthened and more likely to occur in the future. If a behavior is followed by punishing consequences, then it is less likely to recur, but emotional side effects may occur under similar circumstances in the future. Thus, in the case of excessive patterns of behavior, reinforcement may follow increasingly frequent or intense forms of the behavior. In the case of behavioral deficits, reinforcement following appropriate behavior may be inadequate, if present at all. Emotional outbursts may arise in response to excessive punishment.

Although historical contingencies may account for the acquisition of deviant behaviors, current environmental contingencies contribute to their maintenance. Since existing environmental contingencies (unlike historical ones) can be manipulated for the purpose of treatment, these are the focus of behavioral therapies. Behavioral problems are solved when environmental contingencies are rearranged so that maladaptive responses are eliminated and competing and adaptive responses are established. Such manipulation involves the removal of reinforcements which follow maladaptive behavior (and perhaps the introduction of punishing stimuli contingent upon these responses) and the introduction of reinforcement following more adaptive responding.

Ferster's Analysis of Autistic Behaviors

Using behavioral principles, Ferster (1961) analyzed the development of the autistic behavioral repertoire. Ferster argued that the behaviors in the autistic repertoire were unique only in terms of the relative frequency with which they occurred. Autistic behavior was (1) *quantitatively* different from the behavior of normal children, but not *qualitatively* different. Furthermore, the autistic repertoire was characterized by (2) a narrow range of performance; behavior which has only slight effects on the environment makes up a large proportion of the entire repertoire. Third, there is little social control over the child's performance. Few behaviors are either conditioned or maintained by social rewards— smiles, hugs, or words of approval. The emergence of deficits in the child's early development results primarily from inconsistent reinforcement and extinction (the withholding of reinforcement). Speech and social behavior, the most vulnerable aspect of the child's repertoire, fails to develop because of the inadequate schedule of reinforcement. Ferster argues that the birth of a child, particularly a firstborn child, can disrupt the parental repertoire so that the child's initial social responses are not reinforced. Other responses which compete with parenting may be prepotent in the parental repertoire, or the child may provide no reward for the parent. Independent of the initial cause, behavioral deficits may be cumulative in the sense that the child loses opportunities to earn reinforcers because the child's behavior does not match expectations based on age and physical development.

ECOLOGICAL CONCEPT OF EMOTIONAL DISTURBANCE

Theory

From an ecological perspective, disturbance is thought to be an outcome resulting from a mismatch between the child's behavior and the demands of the child's environment. These demands may take the form of societal, parental, school, or peer group expectations. The severity of the disturbance is a function of the number (or importance) of mismatches or of the uniformity of the response which the child's behavior elicits. Since the core of the problem resides in the interaction of children and their environments, solutions might involve changing children's behavior, changing the nature of the environmental demands, or changing both.

One important contribution of ecological theory is its emphasis on the context in which deviant behavior occurs. Thus, some effort must be directed at changing the deviant aspects of the child's environment. A second strength of ecological theory lies in its eclectic approach to treatment. Unlike other perspectives, there are no treatments uniquely associated with ecological theory. Chemotherapy, behavior modification, or psychoanalysis are all compatible with this approach. Ecological theory is unique in emphasizing that these treatments may be directed toward significant adults in the child's environment. For example, an ecologically oriented therapist might prescribe medication for the parents of a hyperactive child, so that they, in their relieved state, grow more tolerant of their child's behavior.

Rhodes (1967) proposed two new goals to replace the exclusive focus on changing child behavior. The short-term goal of treatment is to enter into a disturbed situation and alter it. On the surface, this short-term goal does not differ significantly from traditional treatment goals, although changes are sought in elements of the child's environment. On a long-term basis, intervention focuses on modifying the socialization process. Rhodes advocates not only expanding the focus of our existing treatment efforts but also directing our efforts toward prevention as well. In order to accomplish the long-term goal of ecological intervention, Rhodes proposed a new educational institution in which instruction in social skills receives the same emphasis as academic instruction. In essence, he argued for a parallel institution, with separate personnel and administration, in which the child is educated to cope with a complex industrial society. Not only emotionally disturbed children but normal children as well would benefit from this long-term continued influence upon their lives.

CLASSIFICATION OF BEHAVIOR PROBLEMS

Specific patterns of deviant behavior have been identified. At the present time, however, differential diagnosis has not led to reliable treatments for specific disorders. For example, severe social withdrawal, language impairment, and compulsive behavior constitute an autistic repertoire, and the word "autistic" has come to communicate this pattern of behavior. One danger in using words like "autistic" or "autism" is that they may be misused to explain the behaviors which constitute the disorder. Thus, explaining that a child does not interact because he or she is autistic fails to account for why the child is autistic. In this section, patterns of disturbed behavior are described. Although many of these are commonly referred to with a single descriptive phrase (autism, hyperactivity), these descriptions are not regarded as explanations of the deviant behavior. Behavior problems in regular and special classes are described, as are more specific patterns of deviant behaviors: hyperactivity, severe emotional disorders, emotional disorders of later childhood, and delinquency.

In a large-scale descriptive study of the behavior of elementary school children, Spivack et al. (1971) reported three patterns of deviant behavior: underachievement, acting out, and a combination of school failure and antisocial behavior. The first two of these three patterns occurred at each grade level through sixth grade; the more pervasive pattern did not appear in grades one through four. For each pattern, boys outnumbered girls; between one-third and one-half of the children at each grade level fell into one of the deviant patterns.

The authors characterized children with the underachieving pattern as being unable to cope with the demands of the classroom. They had difficulty concentrating on the teacher and lacked the self-reliance necessary to operate independently. Not surprisingly, these children had poor self-concepts and low ratings on comprehension and initiative. By contrast, the acting-out group had average or better scores on achievement and intelligence tests; their teachers described them as attentive and interested in classroom activities. Nevertheless, teachers also characterized children in this group as obstreperous, interrupting, and uninhibited. Teachers acknowledged that the behavior of these children demanded a considerable amount of their time. Finally, major behavioral disturbances and poor achievement characterized the social and academic behavior of children in the third group. The authors described these children as being "estranged from the educational enterprise" (p. 270).

It should be emphasized that the children in this study were placed in regular classrooms and were not regarded as seriously disordered. Thus, disruptive, acting-out behavior, even in severe forms, does not necessarily result in special education interventions.

BEHAVIOR PROBLEMS IN SPECIAL CLASSES

Patterns of deviant behavior which lead to referral for special education services and placement in special classes were the subject of a study reported by Quay, Morse, and Cutler (1966). Quay et al. had classroom teachers in special classes for the emotionally disturbed complete behavior ratings for their students using the Behavior Problem Checklist (BPC). Behavior ratings on the BPC yield scores on four dimensions: conduct disorder, personality problem, inadequacy-immaturity, and socialized delinquency. The conduct disorder dimension was characterized by aggressive, defiant behavior and poor interpersonal relationships. Of the four dimensions, the conduct disorder dimension was most like the deviant behavior patterns of regular-class children. Sadness, anxiety, social withdrawal, and oversensitivity characterized the behavior of children with personality problems. The inadequacy-immaturity dimension was characterized by behaviors which were inappropriate for elementary-age children: distractibility, preoccupation, and indifference, among others. Finally, behaviors such as truancy, theft, and gang activities fell into the socialized-delinquent dimension.

CHAPTER 18
EMOTIONAL
DISTURBANCE:
SOCIO-EMOTIONAL
DYSFUNCTION

In previous research, Quay and his colleagues had established these dimensions and had documented the relative frequency with which each appears in a number of different populations. Among eighth-graders, adolescent delinquents, and preadolescent delinquents, conduct disorders and personality problems were the most clearly and consistently observed. However, in the sample of children in special classes, these two dimensions were relatively underrepresented, while the proportion of children receiving deviant scores on the inadequacy-immaturity scale was higher than expected. The authors concluded that children with immature patterns of behavior are more likely to be placed in special classes than children whose deviant behavior fits the conduct disorder and personality problem profiles.

The results reported by Spivack, Quay, and their colleagues suggest that a high proportion of children in regular classes are conduct problems. However, the presence of acting-out behavior is not a sufficient condition for special-class assignment. In fact, children exhibiting markedly immature patterns of behavior are more likely to be placed in programs for the emotionally disturbed than are acting-out or neurotic children. Interestingly, immaturity is also an important component of a behavioral pattern which has come to be known as "hyperactivity."

HYPERACTIVE BEHAVIOR SYNDROME

Cantwell (1975a) has enumerated the cardinal characteristics of the hyperactive behavior syndrome: (1) hyperactivity, (2) distractibility, (3) impulsivity, and (4) excitability. Hyperactive behaviors are present from an early age; parents report unusually high activity levels, (toys and clothes wear out faster) and less time spent sleeping. Later, teachers report fidgetiness and excessive talking. Distractibility is more evident in school than at home, since short attention span and attention to extraneous stimuli are more troublesome in structured settings. Hyperactive children seldom complete assignments at one sitting and often cannot sit through a game, story, or other rewarding activity. Impulsivity is seen in reckless behavior, while tantrum behavior and a low tolerance for frustration suggest excitability.

Although not always present in the pattern of hyperactivity, aggressive, antisocial behavior and learning problems sometimes occur. Finally, low self-esteem and depression can also occur with the syndrome. The belief that hyperactive behavior diminishes as children mature is not well established. Current research (Cantwell, 1975a) suggests that although the problem behaviors of hyperactivity grow less severe as children mature, other problems emerge in adolescence and sometimes persist into adulthood. It is not yet understood whether problems in adolescence and adulthood are products of hyperactivity in childhood or, rather, manifestations of the same disorder. There is considerable speculation about an organic basis for the hyperactive syndrome, though no definitive conclusion has been reached. In this way the hyperactive pattern may be likened to more severe early childhood disorders for which organic involvement is likely.

Psychoses, the most serious and debilitating form of emotional disorder, assume several forms in childhood: autism, childhood schizophrenia, and symbiosis (Kessler, 1966). The most familiar though still uncommon form is autism, a disorder first described by Kanner (1943). Among the primary behavioral characteristics are extreme social withdrawal, compulsive, self-stimulatory behavior, and the absence of prerequisite or basic social behaviors such as imitation. Although Kanner thought autism to be an *affective* disorder, current theorists (Rutter, 1978a) emphasize the deficits in language development and regard the social deficit as a secondary characteristic; that is, such children lack social skills because they lack language. Whether the primary disability is affect or communication, deficits in the social behavior of autistic children are pervasive and profound.

Symptoms of Autism

Rutter (1978a) has enumerated the universal and specific symptoms of autism. (Symptoms are universal and specific if they occur among all individuals with a particular disorder but among very few others without the disorder.) The four criteria are (1) delayed and deviant language development, (2) impaired social development, (3) compulsive patterns of behavior, and (4) early onset. Some autistic children never develop speech or any but the crudest forms of communicative behavior. When speech does develop, it is often echolalic; that is, the children simply parrot or imitate whatever they hear. Even among the most capable autistic children, inflection may be unusual and words and phrases may be idiosyncratic or metaphoric. Next to intelligence, the degree of speech development is the best indicator of adjustment in later life.

Most prominent among the social deficits is withdrawal, which appears in early infancy as a failure to develop attachment to another person. Eye-to-eye gaze apparently is not used by autistic children to initiate social interaction. Later, cooperative play fails to develop and personal friendships are uncommon. The compulsive patterns associated with the autistic repertoire include limited and repetitive patterns of play, attachments to unusual play objects, and sometimes a resistance to changes in the environment. Finally, the autistic pattern is characterized by an early onset; 30 months or earlier is a common diagnostic criterion. According to Rutter, the autistic syndrome can be reliably separated from other profoundly handicapping childhood disorders, including mental retardation, childhood schizophrenia, neurosis, and developmental language disorders.

Distinguishing Characteristics

Autistic children differ from mentally retarded children in two important ways. First, not all autistic children score in the retarded range on intelligence tests; in fact, up to 25 percent score in the average or above-average range. Moreover, when compared to retarded children of the same age, sex,

CHAPTER 18
EMOTIONAL
DISTURBANCE:
SOCIO-EMOTIONAL
DYSFUNCTION

and level of intelligence, autistic children show a cognitive deficit which involves language and other symbolic processes. Autism may be differentiated from schizophrenia on the basis of clinical picture (Kessler, 1966; Rutter, 1970) and course (Rutter, 1968). With regard to clinical picture, the social isolation of autistic children contrasts to the clinging dependence of childhood schizophrenics. Moreover, autistic individuals rarely develop the delusions or hallucinations in adulthood which characterize adult schizophrenia. The course of schizophrenia is frequently characterized by alternating episodes of remission and relapse; the course of autism, on the other hand, seldom assumes this variable pattern. Autism can be differentiated from the other serious emotional disorders of childhood on the basis of early onset and pervasiveness of the disability.

EMOTIONAL DISORDERS OF LATER CHILDHOOD AND ADOLESCENCE

Fears and Anxieties

Fears, anxieties, depression, and social withdrawal are common emotional problems in school-age children. Since these behaviors appear commonly in the repertoires of normal children, overly frequent or overly intense patterns constitute significant adjustment problems. Fears and anxieties peak in early childhood and again at puberty. Not surprisingly, the specific nature of the complaints differ at these times: younger children commonly fear animals, monsters, or other imaginary dangers, while adolescents fear social embarrassment and, on occasion, sexual maturity. A phobia is an acute, long-lasting, and irrational fear. A fairly common example among school-age children is school phobia, in which the child refuses to attend school and becomes upset when forced to do so. Needless to say, school phobia is a serious disorder which, if untreated, may seriously disrupt a child's development.

Depression

Depression in adults often involves unhappiness, loss of appetite (and loss of other interests), sleeplessness, social withdrawal, irritability, and sometimes physical complaints. Like fear and anxiety, depression does not in and of itself suggest serious emotional disorder since most individuals experience depression at some point in their lives. Problems arise when depression becomes pervasive and severe. Depression in this form is uncommon before puberty. In young children, depression is more situational, more transient, and less physically debilitating. Suicide is an uncommon problem among preteens, although recent evidence suggests that the scope of this problem may be greater than originally thought.

Social Withdrawal

Social withdrawal refers to low rates of social interaction. Strain, Cooke, and Apolloni (1976) differentiated between a deficient social repertoire and deficient social performance. A deficient social repertoire implies that the child has not learned or has not had the opportunity to learn the skills required in social interaction. The child with deficient social performance, on the other hand, has an adequate social repertoire but does not emit appropriate behaviors under all circumstances. In the latter case, social performance is disrupted because the child is fearful or because other competing responses, such as aggressive behaviors, are stronger.

Most people choose to spend some time alone, if not for solitude, then in order to get something done which is difficult to do with others around. Social withdrawal, then, does not become a problem until it occurs for prolonged periods of time or when interaction is restricted to a chosen few individuals. Although the importance of social withdrawal is frequently questioned, withdrawal is associated with delayed cognitive development and impaired academic performance. Moreover, a high proportion of schizophrenic adults are described in retrospective reports as withdrawn children. On the other hand, follow-up studies of withdrawn youngsters suggest that social withdrawal does not frequently lead to adult psychosis. In any case, a child with deficient social skills (or performance) will have more difficulty functioning as an independent adult than a child with an adequate repertoire. For this reason, social withdrawal may be regarded as a serious disorder worthy of structured intervention.

Obsessive-compulsive Behavior

Finally, obsessive and compulsive patterns of behavior occur occasionally among children. Obsessive thoughts are commonly linked to compulsive behaviors and, in children, frequently involve parents and siblings. A child who repeatedly asks the same question (or set of questions) and demands a stereotyped response engages in an obsessive-compulsive pattern of behavior. If the response is withheld, the child may tantrum until it occurs. Clearly, obsessive-compulsive patterns of behavior represent serious disturbances in emotional behavior. Serious disturbances of social behavior, by contrast, assume a markedly different form, as in the instance of juvenile delinquency.

JUVENILE DELINQUENCY

It has been argued by sociologists that delinquency involves no individual pathology; rather, the delinquent is socialized in the same way as other individuals in society. As it happens, the values and behavior of the delinquent gang—the group to which the individual is socialized—conflict with societal values and expectations. The deviant behavior of the delinquent gang is familiar: truancy, immorality, theft, aggression, and drug and alcohol abuse. In general, the problem behavior of the delinquent gang may be said to involve breaking society's moral and legal standards.

Frequency

The frequency of delinquent conduct peaks during adolescence, although delinquency has an early onset and younger children are more and more likely to commit serious offenses. The ratio of boys to girls among adjudicated delinquents has been dropping for twenty years, to about 6 to 1 according to current estimates. Delinquents come from disorganized if not broken families and at least in urban areas, are likely to come from low socioeconomic strata. Blacks, Puerto Ricans, Mexicans, and American Indians are overrepresented among delinquent populations, in part because they are disproportionately represented at low SES levels and in part because delinquency is predominantly an urban phenomenon.

Neurotic and Sociopathic Delinquency

Some delinquency may involve individual disturbance. A neurotic delinquent differs from the socialized delinquent by the tendency to act alone. The neurotic delinquent is more likely to come from a middle-class home and neighborhood. Antisocial behavior is thought to stem from a personality disturbance; getting caught supposedly relieves guilt and anxiety and sometimes punishes parents. The sociopathic delinquent, like the neurotic delinquent, forms no lasting bonds with a delinquent group, although unlike the neurotic, the sociopath may belong to a group. Sociopathic delinquents act in a rebellious, impulsive way. They experience little of the guilt or anxiety which normal teenagers experience around rule-breaking or which socialized delinquents experience around the violation of gang standards.

EDUCATIONAL INTERVENTION AND TREATMENT APPROACHES

PHYSIOLOGICAL

In a most general sense, treatments derived from physiological models involve the introduction or elimination of substances from the body in order to reestablish normal bodily functioning. Occasionally, environmental variables can be manipulated in order to reestablish physiological balance. Zentall (1975) for instance, suggests that optimal levels of stimulation may be achieved in three ways, only one of which (stimulant medication) involves the introduction of substances to the body. The same effect may be achieved by increasing environmental stimulation and motor activity, which is the adaptation made by hyperactive children.

Stimulant medication is among the most familiar treatments derived from physiological models, although other drugs are used in the management of emotional behavioral problems. For example, tranquilizers are commonly prescribed in cases of debilitating anxiety, and lithium has proven useful in the management of severe depression. Treatments like the Feingold diet involve the elimination of substances (salicylate-like compounds found naturally in some foods and introduced as artificial colors and flavoring in others) from the diets of afflicted individuals. Finally, megavitamin therapy for the management of hyperactivity and nicotinic acid in the management of schizophrenia are other examples of physiological treatments.

Of most relevance to teachers are treatments designed to control hyperactive behavior. The research investigating the efficacy of stimulant medication is voluminous and has been comprehensively reviewed elsewhere (Adelman & Compas, 1977; Sprague & Werry, 1974). Although estimates of the proportion of children who benefit from stimulant medication range from 25 to 50 percent or more, not everyone agrees that the research is definitive. Adelman and Compas argue that the widespread use of stimulant medication is premature, given methodological shortcomings of existing research and the little that is known about the possible seriousness of side effects, both long- and short-term. Similarly, the research investigating the effectiveness of elimination diets in the management of hyperactivity offers little in the way of conclusive support. Connors and his colleagues (1976) and more recently Rose (1978) have presented evidence suggesting that some children may respond positively to the K-P Diet, as it is known. On the other hand, Connors's group results are difficult to interpret, and Harley and his colleagues (1978) were unable to obtain a significant effect for groups of hyperactive children.

PSYCHODYNAMIC

The classical psychotherapies with adults—group, family, and individual therapy—rely heavily on the adult's ability to verbalize his or her inner feelings. Because young children lack the verbal facility, and most probably the insight, classical therapy is generally not the treatment of choice. It is believed that inner conflicts can be expressed symbolically as well as verbally through activities which are intrinsically rewarding. Probably the most common form of expressive therapy used with children, though by no means the only form, is play therapy (Axline, 1947). In play therapy, children are allowed to play with a variety of toys of their choosing. The therapist does not direct the child's play but rather reflects the child's thoughts and feelings with the intention of clarifying these expressions. Assuming that play is the child's natural medium of expression, the child can express underlying conflicts, producing a sense of relief and, through the reflections of the therapist, a better understanding of feelings and attitudes. Other expressive therapies commonly used with children include art therapy, music therapy, dance and movement therapy, and mutual story telling. With the exception of mutual story telling, these therapies provide for the expression of underlying conflicts but do not allow for the construction of adaptive coping strategies.

Classroom Management

Redl has described a set of principles for managing the surface behavior of children (Long & Newman, 1976) without contributing to the child's discomfort. Redl suggests that behavior be either tolerated, permitted, prevented, or interfered with. Behavior indicative of a developmental stage, or symptomatic of a particular disorder, is best tolerated. On the other hand, teachers might avoid situations in which children test limits by specifying exactly what is permissible in the classroom. Certain strategies can effectively prevent the occurrence of certain problem behaviors, as when a sixth-grade class eats lunch with a first-grade class in order to preclude the rowdiness which results when the sixth-grade classes eat lunch together. Finally, under certain circumstances, the teacher must interfere with misbehavior. Interference techniques range from presenting subtle, nonverbal cues to a child (placing a hand on the child's shoulder, or scowling) to physical restraint. Interfering is allowed when the child or other classmates are in physical or psychological danger or when the behavior of an individual child jeopardizes the involvement of other children in some classroom activity.

How Effective Are the Psychodynamic Treatments?

For many years the effectiveness of psychotherapy for adults (Eysenck, 1952) and children (Levitt, 1957) was doubted. It was thought that individuals who received psychotherapy were no more likely to improve than individuals who did not receive psychotherapy. Recently, Smith and Glass (1977) have reviewed psychotherapy outcome research and have subjected this information to an analytical process referred to as meta-analysis. They suggest that psychotherapy is effective, in that individuals in treatment are better off than 75 percent of individuals who receive no treatment. No systematic differences were observed among various kinds of therapy, even when as general a comparison as behavioral versus nonbehavioral therapies was made. Thus, the issue of the effectiveness of psychotherapy is certainly open to more debate than the early reviews would have us believe. However, with regard to children few researchers have studied the effects of the educational approaches advanced by psychodynamic theorists. No generalization about the effectiveness of psychoeducational approaches can be made at this time.

BEHAVIORAL

Behavior modification and behavior therapy are two similar treatments derived from a behavioral perspective. According to Ross (1972), behavior therapy includes procedures for the establishment of behavior missing from the child's repertoire, for the elimination of maladaptive behavior, and for the elimination of avoidance behavior. Avoidance behavior is established and maintained by the elimination of contingent aversive stimulation. Although this reinforcement process is quite different from positive reinforcement in which rewards are introduced, the effect of the removal of aversive stimulation is the same—behavior is strengthened. Thus, a child who complains of an upset stomach in order to avoid a distressing reading class is reinforced for having stomach distress.

Among the techniques that behavior therapists have developed for dealing with avoidance behavior are *emotive imagery* and *desensitization*. Emotive imagery involves training children to evoke pleasant images, while gradually introducing representatives of the distressing stimulus. It is thought that the child cannot be both fearful and pleased at the same time and that even as the stimuli become increasingly anxiety provoking, the child will maintain the pleasing images. Ultimately, the child remains relaxed in the presence of the most distressing version of the stimulus. Presumably, this ability generalizes to real-life situations, where avoidance behavior is preempted. *Desensitization* involves a similar but *in vivo* approach. The child is exposed to increasingly more intense doses of the actual distressing stimulus. In the treatment of a school phobia, for example, gradual approaches to the anxiety-provoking circumstances are made in an order probably unique to each case. Thus, a child may first return to an empty classroom, then to the hall outside the occupied classroom, to the classroom for short periods, and finally remain for increasingly lengthy periods.

How Effective Are the Behavioral Treatments?
The experimental method used by behavior modifiers and behavior therapists involves the establishment and demonstration of experimental control over the behavior of individual subjects. A treatment is introduced, removed, and reintroduced, while the effects of these manipulations are observed. Thus, behaviorists can claim to have changed specific problem behaviors of specific samples. The generality of these treatments, however, has not been well established, largely because of the experimental emphasis on individual cases. Nonetheless, control has been demonstrated over a wide variety of responses: disruptive classroom behavior, aggressive and verbally aggressive behavior, social isolation, delusional talk, excessive crying, self-injurious behavior, self-stimulatory behavior, echolalia, hyperactivity, truancy, theft, oppositional behavior, and enuresis. Emotionally disturbed and conduct-disordered children have been taught certain adaptive skills using the principles of behavior modification: conversational skills, attention, self-management, speech, and appropriate play, among others. These are not meant to be all of the behavior problems which have been effectively handled by behavior therapists. Rather, they should be regarded as representative of the kinds of problems which behavior modifiers have successfully solved.

ECOLOGICAL
The Project Re-Ed schools (Hobbs, 1966; Lewis, 1967) typified the ecological approach to the treatment of emotionally disturbed children.

The Project Re-Ed teacher-counselors were trained, in a relatively short period of time, to work effectively with disturbed children in both school and cottage settings. Treatment in the Re-Ed schools focused upon making *adjustments in the child's behavior,* and was not designed to effect pervasive changes in the child's personality or behavior. *Adjustments in the child's environment* were also sought. Thus, work was done with the family,

CHAPTER 18
EMOTIONAL
DISTURBANCE:
SOCIO-EMOTIONAL
DYSFUNCTION

the school, and the peer group, in addition to work done with the child. Modest adjustments in each were sought in order to allow the child to function effectively in natural settings.

Re-Ed schools were residential schools, at which the children lived five days a week for a period of four to six months. The children returned home on the weekends in order to maintain ties to family and the neighborhood peer group. While enrolled in Re-Ed schools, the children lived with seven other children and were cared for by two teacher-counselors: one who functioned as a teacher and the other as a cottage parent. Additional staff—liaison teachers and social workers—worked simultaneously with parents and teachers to modify the ways in which these individuals interacted with the children. In this regard, Project Re-Ed can be seen as representative of an ecological approach to the treatment of deviance.

Other researchers have taken a more limited ecological approach and have focused on teaching children skills which would promote more positive involvements with adults in their environments. For instance, Graubard, Rosenberg, and Miller (1971) taught special-class children to modify the frequency of positive and negative interactions with regular-class teachers. These children were taught to maintain eye contact, to ask for help, to sit up straight, to make positive comments to teachers, and to ignore provocations, such as scoldings. The children acquired these skills and as a consequence their interactions with the regular-class teachers became increasingly positive. Similarly, Seymour and Stokes (1976) taught work skills to delinquent girls with the hope of generating increased social praise in the vocational program in which they were enrolled. Although the girls acquired the responses and emitted them in the work setting, the amount of social praise did not increase until the girls were taught to prompt the staff to evaluate their work. More recently, Stokes, Fowler, and Baer (1978) reported a program in which preschoolers were taught to prompt feedback and praise from their teachers.

Advantages Inherent in the Ecological Approach

These studies raise two important points. First, they demonstrate that children can be taught to effect changes in the way individuals in their environments interact with them. The behavioral approach has long been criticized for failing to specify what behaviors to teach. The ecological approach compensates for this shortcoming by suggesting that we teach those behaviors which produce desired effects on the environment—behaviors which have a normalizing effect on adult-child interactions. Second, these studies illustrate how behavioral strategies are compatible with an ecological approach to intervention.

How Effective Are Ecological Approaches?

Weinstein (1969) reported the results of an evaluation of the two original Project Re-Ed schools but her results are of limited usefulness because of weak experimental methodology. The significantly higher posttest scores of the Re-Ed children on measures of social maturity and classroom conduct can be attributed as validly to maturation as to the Re-Ed intervention.

The research conducted by Stokes and his colleagues, on the other hand, included an experimental demonstration of treatment effects. However, these studies used single-subject research designs, like the behavior therapy research discussed in the previous section. Thus, although Stokes has demonstrated that the observed effects were attributable to his treatments, he has not yet shown that his approach will be successful when applied to groups of children. The ecological concept has only recently evolved. It is not surprising that research has failed to keep pace with the advance of theory (it seldom does). The absence of empirical research derived from the ecological model is most probably attributable to the recent development of this theory and not to its failure to generate testable hypotheses.

ALTERNATIVE EDUCATIONAL PLACEMENTS

Any of these four concepts of emotional disturbance can be used to develop the content of an educational program and each would be different from the other. On the other hand, the provision of special education service is an administrative concern, and theory contributes little to the way in which service is provided. Following the cascade model of Deno (1970), from most to least restrictive, the alternative placements available within the educational system are homebound, special schools in public school systems, full-time special classes, part-time special classes, and regular class attendance, with and without supplementary services. In this section, examples of programs at each level of the cascade are presented, and where available, the effectiveness of these programs is discussed. First, however, we shall discuss the appropriateness of the cascade of services for behaviorally disordered children.

The logic of the cascade requires that movement down the cascade to more restrictive environments proceeds only as far as necessary, and movement up the cascade, to less restrictive placements, occurs as rapidly as is feasible. By implication, then, changes in placement should represent one-step changes. For example, a child who makes no progress in a part-time special class might be correctly placed in a more restrictive environment, such as a full-time special class. Alternatively, a child making exceptional progress in a special school might be more appropriately placed in a full-time special class in a regular school building. On the other hand, for behaviorally disordered children, an appropriate step from Level 1 (regular-class attendance with no supplementary services) may well be Level 4, full-time special-class placement. From an ecological point of view, problem behaviors may be conceptualized as resulting from the interaction of environmental and child variables. Removing the child from the environment in which the problem exists might eliminate the problem behavior without providing the child a way of coping in the original setting. Resource programs and part-time special classes for behaviorally disordered children may preclude the occurrence of problem behavior without resolving the basis of the problem. The child may still display disturbed behavior in the regular classroom but not in the resource room or part-time special class.

If problems persist after repeated attempts to change the behavior of the teacher and the child, then a change in placement is indicated. In short, if a child in a regular classroom presents a problem which defies the school staff's best efforts, then the appropriate placement may well be a full-time special class. But even though logic may not fully support the use of resource programs for behaviorally disordered children, research has. One of the more successful approaches to the education of behaviorally disordered children is a resource program (Glavin, Quay, Annesley, & Werry, 1971).

SPECIAL SCHOOLS

The lowest or most restrictive point of the cascade at which public schools are responsible for providing services is the residential or special school. The behavior problems of children at this level are so serious that they cannot be managed in self-contained special classes. Two outstanding and well-known examples of programs at this level are the previously described Project Re-Ed (Hobbs, 1966; Lewis, 1967) and Achievement Place (Phillips, 1968). While Re-Ed derived from an ecological theory base, Achievement Place represents an application of behavioral technology to the treatment of predelinquent adolescent boys.

Achievement Place is a residential treatment program. The boys participate in a token economy, which is enforced throughout the day. Points are awarded for such appropriate behaviors as helping with chores, maintaining a neat appearance, doing well in school, and watching television news. Points are withdrawn when inappropriate behaviors such as verbal aggressiveness, lying, cheating, or stealing occur. Back-up reinforcers are those naturally available in the home setting: after-school snacks, late bedtimes, riding a bicycle to school, and watching television, for example. The economy is designed so that a child who accomplishes what is expected of him and who loses a minimal number of points may purchase all of these privileges for the next week. The currency of the Achievement Place token economy is checkmarks entered in (or removed from) a 3-by-5 card which each child carries.

The boys at Achievement Place attend the neighborhood school, where points are available for appropriate behavior and achievement. As the child's behavior improves, privileges are awarded on the basis of global behavioral evaluations, which replace the point system. Each child's family is taught to use management principles similar to those used at Achievement Place in order to promote the generalization of behavior change to the home. In directing some effort at changing the behavior of parents, the Achievement Place program is comparable to Re-Ed.

SELF-CONTAINED CLASSROOMS

Self-contained classrooms represent a less restrictive placement than residential treatment settings, since children placed in special classes live at home and not in a specially designed treatment environment. Nevertheless, because children in special classes are physically segregated and because the effectiveness of special-class placement is not well established for mildly retarded children (Cegelka & Tyler, 1970), this placement must also be regarded as a restrictive one. Interestingly, more emotionally disturbed children are placed in special classes than at any other point on the cascade. One of the most widely known and highly regarded special-class programs is Hewett's (1968) engineered classroom.

Like Project Re-Ed, the engineered classroom represents an educational solution to the problems posed by emotionally disturbed children. Hewett (1968) argued that maladaptive behavior can be modified in the classroom using resources unique to the school and skills unique to the teacher. The fundamental task for the teacher is to provide the child appropriate instructional tasks; that is, tasks at the appropriate developmental level. Hewett proposed a seven-stage developmental sequence of educational goals to facilitate finding appropriate educational tasks.

Hewett's Sequence of Educational Goals
The first four levels in this sequence—attention, responding, ordering, and exploration—are prerequisite skills which prepare the child for learning. The developing child is taught first to attend and then to respond to environmental cues; subsequently attending and responding occur in an orderly way before the child learns to explore the environment in pursuit of additional stimuli. At the fifth or social stage, the child acquires the skills for dealing effectively with peers and teachers. Social skills complement children's existing repertoires so that they may engage in the kind of interactions with their teachers that are essential to learning. At the sixth level of the sequence, the mastery level, children acquire the cognitive and adaptive skills which allow them to function independently. Finally, at the achievement level, children acquire self-motivation in learning and pursue intellectual and adaptive skills in depth.

Hewett's Teaching Strategies
Hewett also provides teaching strategies for children functioning at the various levels. For example, at the attention level, he recommends reducing distracting stimuli, increasing the vividness of instructional stimuli, and breaking instructional materials down into small, discrete units. The nature of the task is determined in part by the nature of the child's attention deficit. Thus, if a child seemingly prefers fantasy to reality, the teacher is advised to use neutral subject matter in order to preempt flight from reality. At the social level, by contrast, all learning tasks are communication-oriented. The teacher is advised to take advantage of a child's unique skill or to provide other opportunities for increased recognition.

Physical Arrangements of the Engineered Classroom
The physical arrangement of the classroom is such that activities at certain levels occur in certain areas of the room. There are three centers: the ex-

ploratory center, the mastery center, and the order center. The level at which children function determines not only the appropriate instructional task but also the area within the classroom at which they work. The rewards available to children in the engineered classroom vary with developmental level as well, though most children begin at a stage where tangible rewards predominate. A checkmark system is used with new children and with children functioning at lower developmental levels. Points are available every fifteen minutes for beginning promptly, working steadily, and completing assignments.

RESOURCE-ROOM PROGRAMS

Improvement in academic and social skills established in a resource-room program must generalize to the regular class. With regard to the social domain, generalization is an especially difficult problem because the social environment in a resource room is different in many important ways from the social environment in a regular class. For example, the adult-student ratio in a resource room is significantly greater than it is in a regular classroom. As a consequence, the density of social reinforcement is likely to be higher, as is the amount of individualized instruction. Competition among classmates (in which handicapped children seldom succeed) may be eliminated totally in a resource-room program. Because of these differences, behavior change established in resource rooms may fail to generalize to the regular class. The program described and evaluated by Glavin, Quay, Annesley, and Werry (1971), although regarded as one of the more successful resource-room programs reported in the literature, suffers in its inability to establish generalized behavior change.

Evaluations of this resource-room program were reported in the literature for four consecutive years (Glavin, 1973, 1974; Glavin et al., 1971; Quay, Glavin, Annesley, & Werry, 1972). The final two represented follow-up research. Any differences in academic achievement and improvements in behavior failed to generalize from the resource setting to the classroom setting. Perhaps careful programming for transfer of behavior to classroom settings would have resulted in significant changes in the follow-up evaluation.

MAINSTREAM SETTING

To avoid the need for programming for transfer, management problems may be dealt with in the environment in which the problem occurs. Most commonly, that environment is the regular classroom. The Vermont Consulting Teacher Program (Fox, Egner, Paolucci, Perelman, & McKenzie, 1973) represents one approach to dealing with the problems of handicapped children without removing these children from their regular-class placements.

Although not specifically designed for work with children with behavior disorders, such a program can be used for management as well as instruction. When a problem exists, the teacher and consulting teacher arrange for a more effective educational (or management) program, which is then carried out by the regular-classroom teacher. Fundamental to this approach are the principles of applied behavior analysis and the emphasis on individualizing instruction. Before the involvement of the consulting teacher, each problem is operationalized by the referring teacher, and objective measures of the behavior are obtained. The teachers develop a treatment program and evaluate the program on the basis of data collected after treatment is begun. The consulting-teacher program is therefore an empirical, problem-solving approach to special education. Its applicability to the management of classroom behavior problems is obvious—especially as an alternative to resource-room programs, where success has been limited.

SUMMARY

None of the theoretical concepts of emotional disturbance adequately accounts for all the phenomena associated with behavioral disorders, although each accounts for some. Nor does any one of the concepts surpass the others in its ability to account for problems in emotional and social behavior. With regard to treatment, on the other hand, behavior modification and behavior therapy rest on more solid data than treatments derived from any of the other perspectives. Of course, the fact that behavior therapy has proved effective does not preclude the effectiveness of other treatment modes. Nor does the effectiveness of behavior therapy imply that the behavioral concept for the cause of behavior disorders is more valid than the others. Reasoning from treatment to cause is a logical fallacy.

The cascade of special education services includes two levels at which behaviorally disordered children may be misplaced. Problems in the social and emotional domains are context-bound, and removing a child from the environment in which a problem occurs does not guarantee that the problem in that situation will be eliminated when the child returns—regardless of the changes in the child's behavior. Resource rooms and part-time special classes, at least for children with emotional and social disorders, violate ecological principles by directing all efforts for change toward the child and ignoring deviant aspects of the child's environment. Much remains to be done in developing the theories and treatments necessary to help behaviorally disordered children. Special educators can do great service in studying, applying, and evaluating approaches and by adding to the data so necessary in this field.

Ralph L. Peabody

CHAPTER 19
VISUAL
DYSFUNCTION

Children and youth who are visually handicapped cannot readily be grouped into a precise category for educational purposes; there are no fixed and predetermined ways to teach all "blind" students. Instead, a number of factors must be considered in developing appropriate individual programs for each student. We will focus on some of these factors and provide some general curriculum considerations.

(NASA.)

DEFINING VISUAL DYSFUNCTION

"More people are blinded by definition than any other cause" (Greenwood, 1949, p. 111). Many attempts have been made to define visual limitations adequately and to identify those persons of our concern. Invariably, these definitions come from a public or private agency, serve a limited purpose, and are not particularly useful for educational planning and programming.

SOCIAL SECURITY ACT DEFINITION

To determine eligibility for many public and private services and benefits, the Social Security Act of 1935 defines blindess as: "central visual acuity of 20/200 or less in the better eye with correcting lenses, or contraction of the visual field to 20 degrees or less if central visual acuity is greater than 20/200." This definition of blindness excludes many who could benefit from specific programs and includes others often not requiring services. It complicates research and confuses the public by creating misunderstanding and misconceptions about blind and visually handicapped persons (Schloss, 1963).

What the figure 20/200 means is that the person considered blind can see at 20 feet the same amount that the person with normal or average vision

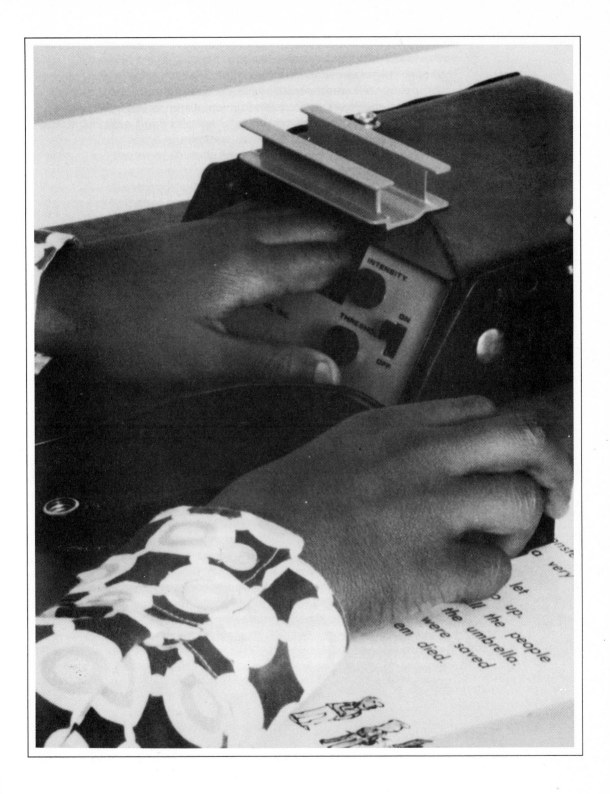

(20/20) can see at 200 feet. Therefore, for many environments and tasks, such an individual is a seeing person.

It might be more useful to know the near-visual acuity (usually measured at 14 inches) than the far-visual acuity (measured at 20 feet). Also, it has been shown that there is not a direct relationship between these measures and a person may have poor distance vision and good near vision or vice versa (Birch, Tisdall, Peabody, & Sterrett, 1966).

PREVALENCE OF VISUAL DYSFUNCTION

As with other areas of dysfunction, the estimates of the prevalence of individuals with visual dysfunction vary depending on the definition of blindness that is used.

ASSESSING AND IDENTIFYING VISUAL DYSFUNCTION

Our purpose in assessing and identifying students who are visually impaired is to find those who require and can profit from special education services. To this end we must seek out information that is educationally relevant to the student's visual functioning.

The word "blindness" means to most people a total inability to see, a total absence of vision, but the issue is more complex. Gruber (1966) has spoken of blindness as occurring when one is "unable to manage life by visual means." This is rather understandable when the person is totally blind, which is rare among schoolchildren as most have some useful residual vision. Gruber's statement implies that persons with limited vision will be able to manage their lives by visual means in some environments or for some tasks and unable to do so for others. Therefore, the totally blind person lives with a visual constant and the person with limited vision lives with a visual variable. This is important in understanding the person and appreciating that in essence he or she may be blind at one moment and not the next, depending on the context. It is also extremely important to consider this visual variability in educational assessment and planning.

Examine the continuum of visual function in Figure 19-1. Think of the areas within the broken lines as a bubble in a carpenter's level, always moving from end to end depending on the circumstances. The bubble (the visual functioning of the individual) moves as the person goes from task to task and environment to environment.

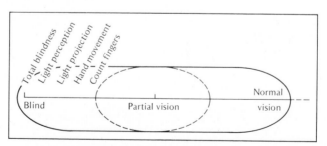

FIGURE 19-1
Continuum of visual
functioning.

Another important factor—one which affects many aspects of development, learning, and functioning—is whether the person is congenitally or adventitiously blind. When did the visual condition occur? This question merits careful consideration, as the person who was born blind (congenitally blind) will have no visual memory or references. Everything must be learned assuming no previous visual experiences. Therefore, all concepts the person forms will have to be carefully constructed, learning small parts and putting them into a whole concept. On the other hand, the person who has once seen (adventitiously blinded) may be able to visualize new learning tasks based on previous experience. The amount of experience, of course, will vary with the age of the person at the time of onset of the visual problem.

The visually impaired population is extremely diverse (despite some acceptable definitions) even when we consider only the age at onset and the continuum of visual functioning.

Additional information from the medical profession can contribute to our understanding. We should use this information in both identification and educational planning. Many causes of visual dysfunctions have some similar characteristics. Figure 19-2 gives some examples of these characteristics.

The schools also play an active role in the identification process. Routinely within our schools, trained volunteers or health personnel screen preschool and school-age children and refer for examination those whom they identify. A well-planned and supervised screening program with trained personnel is extremely important. We cannot rely on the children to identify their own condition. The most common method used is the Snellen eye chart or its variations at 20 feet.

Teachers and parents also play a role in identifying children who need attention. Through sensitive observation they note children's behavior which might be indicative of visual problems: squinting, rubbing the eyes, distractibility, and holding close work to the eyes (Faye, 1970).

CAUSES OF VISUAL DYSFUNCTION

Causes of visual dysfunction can be categorized into two groups: common problems, which can be corrected with glasses or contact lenses; and more serious problems not optically correctable.

CORRECTABLE VISUAL IMPAIRMENT

DeMott (1974) has identified refraction errors as the most frequent cause of visual problems in school-age children. Three common refraction problems are:

Myopia: The child experiences difficulty in focusing on objects which are far away. The child with myopia, or nearsightedness, may be inattentive during tasks which require distance focusing.

Characteristics of Eye Diseases

Category

I Congenital or hereditary
  A. Nonprogressive
  B. Progressive
  C. Secondary complications

II Adventitial
  A. Nonprogressive
  B. Progressive
  C. Secondary complications

Functional Characteristics

a. Peripheral field loss
b. Central field loss
c. Defective night vision
d. Defective color vision
e. Bright light preferred

f. Average light preferred
g. Dim light preferred

Physical Needs

h. Distance glass or aid
i. High-plus reading spectacle
j. Hand-held lens preferable
k. Can read without glasses
*l. Physical activity may be restricted
*m. May be on eye treatment
   or medication

*Check with physician
 or ophthalmologist

Diseases	Category	Functional	Physical
Achromatopsia	I A	d g	h i
Albinism, Complete	I A	f g	h i
Ocular	I A	f	h i
Amblyopia ex anopsia	II B	b f	h i m
Aniridia	I C	f g	i m
Aphakia, Surgical	II A C	f g	h i l m
Cataract	I A B	f g	i m
	II A B	f g	h i j m
Chorioretinitis	II A	a or b, e f g	i m
Coloboma of iris, choroid or disc	I A	a e f	i j
Corneal dystrophy	I A or B	e f	i
Corneal graft, recent	II A	f g	h i l m
Corneal scarring (trauma, keratitis, leucoma)	II A	e f	i
Detachment of retina Surgically treated	II A B	a or b, c e f	h i l m
Diabetic retinopathy	II B C	b c e f	h i j l m
Dislocation of lens	I A C	f g	h i l m
Glaucoma	I B	a c e f	i j m
	II A or B	a c e f	h j m
Hypertensive retinopathy	II B	b e f	i j l m
Keratoconus	II B C	a e f	h i k
Macular degeneration Juvenile	I A	b d f g	h i k
Senile	II A or B	b de f g	i j
Marfan's Syndrome (see Disl. lens)			
Myopia, Degenerative	I B C	a or b, c d e f	h k l m
Axial	II A	f g	h i k
Nystagmus (A reflex associated with eye disease)	I A		
Primary Optic atrophy, Congenital	I A	b c d e f	i j
Neurological	II A B	a c d e f	i j l m
Retinitis pigmentosa	II B	a c e f	h i j
Retrobulbar neuritis	II A B	a b d f g	i j m
Retrolental fibroplasia	II A C	a or b, e f	h i k l
Uveitis	II A B C	e f	i j m

FIGURE 19-2
Characteristics of eye diseases. (Source: Fay & Hood, 1969.)

Hyperopia: The child has difficulty focusing on objects which are close at hand. The child with hyperopia, or farsightedness, may be restless and inattentive during tasks which require close work. Farsighted children frequently have difficulty with distance vision as well.

Astigmatism: The child has blurred vision at all distances. The child may complain of dizziness and headaches.

MORE SERIOUS CAUSES
The most prevalent causes of serious visual dysfunctions are problems in the retina, lens of the eye, optic nerve, and other nerves and muscles.

Diabetic Retinopathy: Some individuals who have diabetes may experience this condition. This loss of vision is caused by interference of the blood supply to the retina of the eye.

Retinitis Pigmentosa: This hereditary condition is caused by the progressive degeneration of the retina. The individual first loses peripheral vision, and gradually central vision decreases. Common symptoms include color blindness and night blindness.

Retrolental Fibroplasia: The loss of vision resulting from this condition (RLF) is caused by the formation of scar tissue at the back of the lens of the eye. This condition has been linked to the concentration of oxygen administered to the child at birth in the incubator (Chase, 1974).

Cataracts: The amount of light received by the retina is reduced by a clouding of the lens of the eye. Vision loss depends on where the cataract is located on the lens and how dense the clouding is. Treatment (surgery and eyeglasses or contact lenses) can be effective.

Glaucoma: This is a condition in which the normal fluid of the eye (aqueous humor) does not drain properly. This causes pressure within the eye, which may damage the optic nerve and result in severe loss of sight or tunnel vision (the person sees only the center of the visual field). If detected early enough, glaucoma can be treated by controlling the pressure in the eye.

Strabismus: This is a condition in which the eye is turned inward or outward or squints because of weak or malfunctioning muscles. The child may use one or both eyes alternately. Treatment includes patching the stronger eye, corrective lenses, and surgery.

Nystagmus: This condition results in involuntary, rapid, rhythmic eye movements, usually side to side and continuous. This condition usually occurs in combination with other severe visual problems and may indicate certain brain malfunctioning and inner-ear problems. Effects may include dizziness and nausea.

EDUCATIONAL INTERVENTION

ECOLOGICAL-SYSTEMS MODEL

As we have discovered, our student—whether termed blind, visually impaired, visually handicapped, partially seeing, or whatever—is a unique individual whose needs are also unique. Therefore, to provide optimum services and appropriate programs, we must seek a model for consideration. The ecological-systems model proposed by Hobbs ". . . consists of the child and the settings that are a part of the child's daily life. All parts of the system influence all other parts of the system. Physical and psychological as well as social factors are involved. Thus assessments and interventions focus on the exchange between the child, the settings in which he participates, and the significant individuals who interact with him. Each child's ecological system is unique. The objective is not merely to change or improve the child but to make the total system work. Change in any part of the system, or in several parts, may accomplish this purpose. And changes may be brought about through interventions affecting physical, psychological, or social functioning or one or more of the components of the system." (1976, p. 114)

We are well on our way to building our ecological system; we need now to look at the ever-changing components of the system and, finally, to determine our educational interventions. Our system begins for the visually handicapped child at the time of diagnosis. Not only are medical personnel such as pediatricians, ophthamologists, nurses, physical therapists, and others a part of the system, but other support personnel as well. As indicated in other chapters of this book, parents, siblings, and other members of the extended family may require the professional services of a social caseworker, psychologist, or counselor.

THE TEACHER'S ROLE
In many parts of the country it is becoming more and more common for the professional teacher of the visually handicapped to provide educational services to the newborn infant and parents in the home, the familiar setting referred to in Hobbs's definition. Educators in this system often have to define new role dimensions and become valuable referral sources as well as teachers as they increase their environment with the child and family. Teachers must be sensitive to all factors affecting the system, yet not take on the role of another professional, such as counselor, for which they are not prepared (Hull & Ross, 1979). Other members of the team change according to the needs of the person, and as the teacher is frequently the one member of the ecological team to have continued contact over a long period of time with the child, he or she functions more and more as a case manager interrelating with all parts of the system.

As the child progresses into a neighborhood day-care center or preschool, the teacher, aware of the demands of a new environment on the child, becomes involved with new teachers and other children's parents who may never have had previous experience with the child who is visually handicapped. Not only does this involve an instructional role, but one of advocacy as well. For as the student's environment continues to expand throughout the school period, so does the number of persons in the ecological system in both the school and community.

PLACEMENT OPTIONS
An array of administrative plans exists for the education of the visually handicapped. These range from total support of the child to consultant assistance, depending on local resources and the ability of the individual student to function independently.

Organizational patterns for the education of the visually handicapped have been quite clearly defined. These include the residential school, the special class, the resource room, the cooperative plan, the itinerant-teacher plan, and the teacher-consultant plan (Jones & Collins, 1966). Today, many programs function in combination, depending on the needs of the individual child. Therefore, we will discuss in a more generalized sense the residential school, the resource room, and the itinerant teacher.

RESIDENTIAL SCHOOLS

Historically, the residential school was the only alternative. Such schools were first built in the eastern United States in the early 1830s. However, there did exist among some leaders a philosophic opposition to this arrangement. "Of the three great men who founded residential schools for the blind—Hauy, Klein, and Howe—the last two mentioned and seriously considered the education of blind children in regular schools. As early as 1810, Johann Wilhelm Klein advocated that places be reserved for the seeing" (Lowenfeld, 1973, p. 13–14). In this country the great leader, Samuel Gridly Howe, founder of the present-day Perkins School for the Blind in Boston, spoke out against the residential schools at various times.

Since their inception, residential schools have played an important role in the education of the visually handicapped and still do play a strong role today. Over the years many have altered their services as the population has changed. They are now accepting many more multihandicapped visually-impaired students, who a few short years ago would have been denied any training. Many have developed programs for the deaf-blind since the rubella epidemic of the 1960s. New personnel were trained as aides and new professional personnel began providing services.

A continuum of services exists, as the children usually range in age from about 5 to 21, although some schools provide limited preschool services. Some children attend on a day basis, commuting to home, while others live at the school and attend a public day school on a limited or full-time basis. In most instances the students live at the school and receive their education there. The schools must, therefore, provide a twenty-four hour program to meet all the recreational, social, educational, and personal needs of their students.

THE RESOURCE ROOM

The resource room changes functions on a daily basis as the demands of the children and the teachers in the regular classrooms change. The resource-room teacher may have children over a wide range of ages and visual and academic abilities. Therefore, the teacher may at one time be spending a great deal of time with a particular child, and at another time the same child may be spending the majority of the time in the regular classroom. This instructional plan is in compliance with P.L. 94-142—education in the least restrictive environment, yet individualized for each child. The resource teacher must be extremely versatile as each child's ecological system is different from every other child's in the same program. The teacher must alter systems affecting the child where misunderstanding about visual handicaps occurs among teachers and children and where program modifications are indicated. It is important for the resource teacher to be consid-

Perhaps this comparison will help you to appreciate the educational difficulties presented to children whose vision is limited. Sometimes corrective measures can greatly improve vision, but often the child must use quite limited visual capabilities. (*Courtesy of Paul J. Quinn.*)

ered a *resource,* and not to be confused or identified with the older concept of a special class teacher in an isolated self-contained classroom. Corn and Martinez have aptly described this resource teacher.

> Permanently based in your school, she is available throughout the school day for consultations, specialized instruction, and provision of materials especially adapted for the visually handicapped. The resource room may be likened to a library where the student does not spend the whole day but rather goes there for information and some instruction. (1977, p. 3)

THE ITINERANT TEACHER

This is another organizational plan which permits the student to remain in the community school and receive special instruction, materials, and other appropriate services from a teacher traveling to the school on a regular basis. The amount of special education instruction the child will receive will depend upon the child's requirements at the time.

It appears rather evident that no two itinerant teachers could describe their positions as similar at any one time. The itinerant programs also vary owing to geographic demands, administrative philosophy, local resources, and the individual teacher's perception of the role. Inasmuch as such variance does exist, it appears helpful to determine a functional description of the itinerant teacher of the visually handicapped. One study involving over 75 percent of the itinerant teachers in Pennsylvania found the following:

> Itinerant teachers reported an average of approximately 59 percent of their time in direct instruction of children, 11 percent in consultation relating to the children, and 16.5 percent driving. The remaining 13.5 percent of their time was utilized in administrative duties such as procuring materials, record keeping, meetings, reviewing referral materials, and screening referrals. (Moore & Peabody, 1976, p. 48)

ROLE PERCEPTIONS

As has been indicated, resource-room and itinerant teachers are highly involved with other professional and lay persons as they work within each pupil's ecological system. In essence, as the teachers collect information about the pupil, not only are they functioning as a part of a team effort, but they are likely to have to assume responsibilities as the team leader or case manager. Many teachers are not prepared for this role and must develop new skills and role perceptions. As pointed out by Ducanis & Golin:

> Each team is a unique blend of the professional and personal characteristics of its members, its effectiveness determined in large part by the dynamics of that configuration. The similarities, differences, and areas of overlap among the various professionals provide a source of potential conflict and misunderstanding. (1979, p. 9)

As various children are capable of participating in integrated or mainstreamed programs, the degree of participation affects the educational decision-making process. As the amount of integration becomes greater, from 0 to 100 percent, this results in a greater responsibility for making educational decisions on the part of the regular teacher and less by the teacher of the visually handicapped, as shown in Figure 19-3. If we wish to think in terms of the role of the teacher of the visually handicapped in each of the types of instructional settings, we can superimpose on the figure the wavy lines to indicate the educational decision-making responsibility in the various educational settings. Therefore, it is imperative to perceive clearly role expectations of the teacher in terms of the pupil's individual program and in terms of the instructional setting.

In a similar manner, as the child enters or moves along the continuum of independence or integration from 0 to 100 percent, that pupil's need for

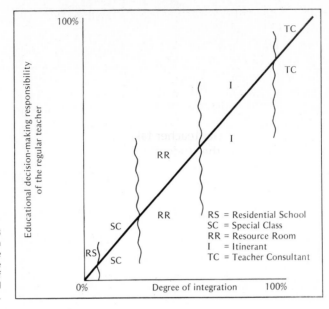

FIGURE 19-3
The relationship between responsibility of the regular teacher and the degree of integration of the visually handicapped student.

support services decreases, as shown in Figure 19-4. Similarly, the amount of support services to be supplied by the special teacher varies among the different educational settings as indicated within the wavy lines.

THE CURRICULUM

It must be clearly understood that visually handicapped students must have the same educational opportunities as all students. They will eventually be entering professions and trades representing a broad array of occupations

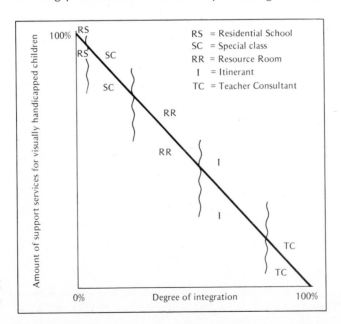

FIGURE 19-4
The relationship of support services to the degree of integration.

commensurate with their individual interests and abilities. There are no stereotypic occupations for visually handicapped persons. Yet in addition to the normal school curriculum, teachers of visually handicapped students do find it necessary to teach additional skills, adapt, and develop different methods of teaching, and utilize special materials.

The residential school must provide all curricular opportunities for its students through its own professional faculty. In the day-school programs, where much of the actual learning occurs in the regular classroom, the instructional responsibilities of the special teacher take on a different emphasis. The special teacher responds to the student's requirements in terms of the environment and task as it relates to the visual handicap, without the usual emphasis on curricular content which is more frequently the domain of the regular teacher.

A recent study by Scholl (1979) has contributed to answering the important question of what the teacher of the visually handicapped in day-school programs should teach. The study reported the following eighteen curricular areas:

- Abacus
- Braille
    Skills readiness
- Optacon training
- Visual-efficiency training
- Sensory-awareness training
- Map reading
- Reference material skills
- Auditory-aids training
- Physical education
    Gross to fine motor movement
    Rhythm and games
- Vocational training
- Orientation and mobility training
    Safety awareness
- Daily living skills
- Typing
- Concept development
    Spatial relations
    Categorization
    Identification
- Leisure-time activities
    Recreation
- Human sexuality
- Social skills
- Communication skills
    Speech
    Handwriting

Of further interest, this study also reported the appropriateness of each area in terms of degree of vision and level of intellectual functioning at three educational levels.

The next determinant in deciding what to teach depends upon the learner and his or her personal characteristics. This can in part be determined by continual informal and formal assessment. First, the teacher must appropriately answer such questions as what should be assessed and why. There must always be a reason and a plan for using the data collected. Merely to assess as an end in itself is an exercise in futility. Results must have a predetermined purpose. Second, the teacher must ask what assessment instruments should be used. Does the instrument fit the child and the task? An inappropriate assessment procedure can be discriminatory, and children are protected from this under P.L. 94-142. Merely to transcribe a test into braille, large type, or tape does not necessarily make it appropriate if the items do not correspond to the child's background of experiences and capabilities.

A serious case in point relates to the assessment of young blind children. Several classic research studies have shown the normal development of the blind infant is at a different rate than that of the seeing child. Vision and imitation based on vision is an important component to growth and development. For the seeing child, vision affects all early developmental areas. When the effects of sensory deprivation (blindness) are understood, parents and professionals alike can accept the fact that we can expect our blind children to progress normally at a different rate than the seeing child.

Warren (1978) points out the dangers of comparing sighted and blind children, and using instruments developed for the sighted. A solution may be to look instead at each child in a longitudinal manner. Two examples of assessment instruments with curricular suggestions for visually handicapped children are provided by Croft and Robinson (1976) and O'Brien (1976).

SPECIAL CONSIDERATIONS

Two implications have emerged from the previous discussion which merit examination prior to reviewing some of the unique curriculum areas. First, *it takes extra time when you are blind.* This is true in early growth and development. It is also true for many other tasks. For example, reading rates are reduced owing to the amount of information a person can process. In tactile reading (braille) the amount of information a person can process at an exact moment is that symbol under the fingertip at that moment. This may account for average braille reading rates of 90 to 110 words per minute. Partially seeing persons also have reduced reading rates owing to the limited amount of visual information they can process in a specific time frame. For this reason, research has shown the necessity of relaxed time limits in achievement testing (Birch et al., 1966). The teacher must be sensitive to the time demands upon the person for many tasks.

Second, we must assure the individual of maximum learning opportunities. It is not enough to recognize only that the development of the young blind child is at a different rate; it is imperative that the child and parents have the services of the professionally prepared educator to promote maximum growth starting at the birth of the child. The teacher of the visually handicapped not only gives direct training to the child and demonstrates to parents activities they may use to ensure growth, but also can assist in environmental modifications for the child.

SELECTED CURRICULAR AREAS

In a general discussion of specific curricular areas, selection must be exercised, as each of the eighteen areas previously listed are in themselves content areas requiring understanding and knowledge in depth. This discussion, therefore, must be brief and in some instances combine areas from the previous list.

Reading

Reading per se is not included in the original list. This does not mean initial reading skills are not taught by the teacher of the visually handicapped. Rather, beginning reading is taught using the tactile, visual, and auditory modes depending upon the most appropriate mode or combination of modes for the particular pupil. Thus in the tactile mode we pursue the teaching of reading using braille or the Optacon. In the auditory mode reading is accomplished through listening, using auditory-aids training, and in the visual mode using visual-efficiency training.

Braille

Braille is a tactile symbol system representing the letters of the alphabet with additional symbols in the literary code for certain words and letter combinations. Codes for mathematics, science, foreign languages, and music are also produced in braille.

Optacon

The Optacon is a portable electronic reading aid. It is an optical-to-tactile converter.

> To read with the Optacon, the reader with one hand scans the print with a small camera about the size of a pocketknife and perceives with the forefinger of the other hand a vibratory image of exactly what the camera sees. . . . The tactile array upon which the image appears has a window width of a single letter space and the text travels across the reader's finger one letter at a time. This rather resembles that procedure used by a visual reader when he is reading a "Times Square" display of writing. (Moore & Bliss, 1975, p. 15)

Auditory-aids Training

The auditory mode of reading is a valuable asset to the visually handicapped, as this mode can transmit more information in a shorter period of

An individual who is proficient in braille can take notes and later read them—without depending on another person to transcribe them. (*Courtesy of Perkins School.*)

time than either the tactile or visual means. Printed material is often read to blind persons by the sighted. In addition, textbooks and leisure-time reading—including current magazines—are available on both tapes and records. Machines are available to accelerate or slow down the delivery, and multi-track tape records are increasing the versatility of the presentation of materials. Listening skills, therefore, must also be learned by the visually handicapped person.

Visual-efficiency Training

Research has shown that the functional use of vision can be improved, as the use of vision is learned. Objectives for learning and materials have been developed for teachers of the visually handicapped to assist their pupils in developing greater visual efficiency.

Any rationale for improvement of efficiency in visual functioning may consider several variables, including: (a) the basic visual functions related to use of the eye and the visual system, (b) the selection of progressively more difficult visual tasks in keeping with perceptual/cognitive developmental milestones, and (c) the diversity in visibility of indoor and outdoor environments.

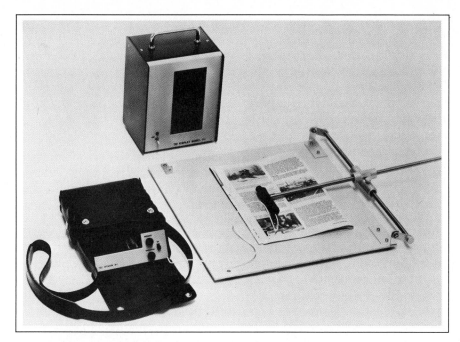

The Optacon raises the print—a tactile stimulus quite different from braille. (*Telesensory Systems Inc.*)

Visual functions seem to develop in a pattern which may be influenced by three primary factors: (a) the type and scope of visual stimulation and experiences available to promote looking, (b) the variety of visual tasks actually performed under all environmental conditions, and (c) the motivation and capacity for consistent, progressive development both perceptually and cognitively. (Barraga & Collins, 1979, p. 21)

In all instances the use of residual vision should be encouraged and developed, as any vision whatsoever is useful in certain environments and for certain tasks.

Orientation and Mobility Training
Orientation and mobility training involves learning skills which will enhance a person's independence. For the child it is a continuous learning process as he or she learns about enlarging the environment and controlling it as an independent traveler.

Orientation is the process of establishing an awareness of one's position in relation to the environment and significant objects within the environment by utilizing the remaining senses, including any useful vision.

Mobility is the ability to move safely, efficiently, effectively, and comfortably from one place to another within the environment by utilizing the remaining senses, including any useful vision. (Illinois Office of Education, 1974, p. 260)

Other authors (Hill & Ponder, 1976) have included in their general definition the importance of the person's psychological self-concept. Often one hears that in the process of gaining independent mobility, the person moves out psychologically as well as physically. This important aspect of the student's education will lead to the individual's being able to use clues from the environment in traveling safely and independently with either a guide dog or a long cane.

Sensory-awareness Training
Like orientation previously discussed, the student must on a continuous basis use all senses to learn realistically about the environment.

> Sensory training for the blind is concerned with the understanding and use of non-visual stimuli. Its purpose is to provide a structure in which a blind person can develop self-confidence in his/her sensory abilities, and use these abilities in establishing and maintaining a functional awareness of the environment.
>
> Vision is a person's primary method of gaining information about the environment. It also acts as a counter-check for all other sensory information. When vision is lost in any significant degree, confidence in the remaining senses is also lost and this tends to result in total disorganization of the sensorium. Subsequent to the onset of blindness, reorganization of the sensorium does not automatically occur. The remaining senses do not automatically "compensate" for the loss of vision . . . .
>
> It is further recognized that, while no one sense can substitute for vision, the reorganization, training, subsequent integration, and confidence in the use of non-visual stimuli can convey valid and dependable information needed to be functional within one's environment. (Kimbrough, Huebner, & Lowry, 1976, p. 9)

Without careful consideration of the use of the senses the visually handicapped student can be deprived of basic knowledge and can form misconceptions about the environment.

SUMMARY
It is difficult to group visually handicapped individuals into precise categories for educational purposes because of educationally relevant factors which vary from individual to individual. Some of these factors are visual variability, time of onset of visual problems, visual acuity, visual versatility, and visual capacity.

Identification of individuals with visual problems can be made by a medical examination, school screening operations, and the sensitive observation of teachers and parents who are alert for symptoms of visual problems.

Students with visual dysfunctions have traditionally been educated in residential schools. More and more, residential schools are opening their doors to severely multihandicapped, visually impaired students, since the traditional population has been moving to the more normal and less restrictive public school classrooms. Students in these classes receive special services from the resource room or itinerant teacher. These special facilities function to supplement the visually handicapped child in areas such as efficient use of braille, the Optacon reading aid, and auditory training aids, visual-efficiency training, orientation and mobility training, and sensory-awareness training.

These teachers are different, however, in more than the curriculum areas they specialize in. Many times, the itinerant and resource-room teacher serve as the child's case manager and the ancillary service team leader. They are highly involved with other professionals and lay persons as they work within each pupil's ecological systems; they therefore benefit from a broad background in course work and experience in other areas of special and regular education.

Donald F. Moores

CHAPTER 20
AUDITORY
DYSFUNCTION

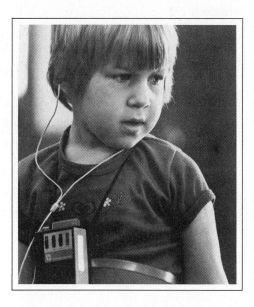

(*Courtesy of Chuck Zovko.*)

As in so many areas of special education, the field of education of children with auditory dysfunctions has undergone fundamental and profound changes in the past twenty years. The impetus for such changes has come from a variety of sources. At the present time the profession is in a state of flux, and permanent trends are difficult to identify. It is the purpose of this chapter to discuss the characteristics and needs of children with impaired hearing, to describe the resources presently available to them, and to project possible future developments. Throughout the chapter it must be remembered that the needs of any group must be considered within the context of the larger population in which they function. For example, education programs of 100 years ago might have been adequate in preparing people to function well within an agrarian society. That same education today would be inadequate for people with normal hearing and impaired hearing alike. Thus, the basic characteristics of hearing-impaired children may be the same within two separate cultures, but the environmental demands, and therefore the educational needs, may be quite diverse.

DEFINING AUDITORY DYSFUNCTION

In dealing with auditory dysfunctions, as with other conditions, care must be taken to differentiate among the terms *impairment, disability,* and *handicap* (Moores, 1982). Briefly, a hearing impairment refers to a physical condition, for example, the destruction of parts of the hearing mechanism because of a high fever, or the lack of development of organs of hearing because of maternal rubella. A hearing disability can be quantified and is measured by the child's reception of sound at certain levels of intensity and frequency. A handicap is not so easily observed or measured. It refers to the extent to which a person's ability to function is affected by the impairment and should be considered in behavioral terms. (Refer to Chapter 11 for a review of these distinctions). Most definitions of hearing impairment are

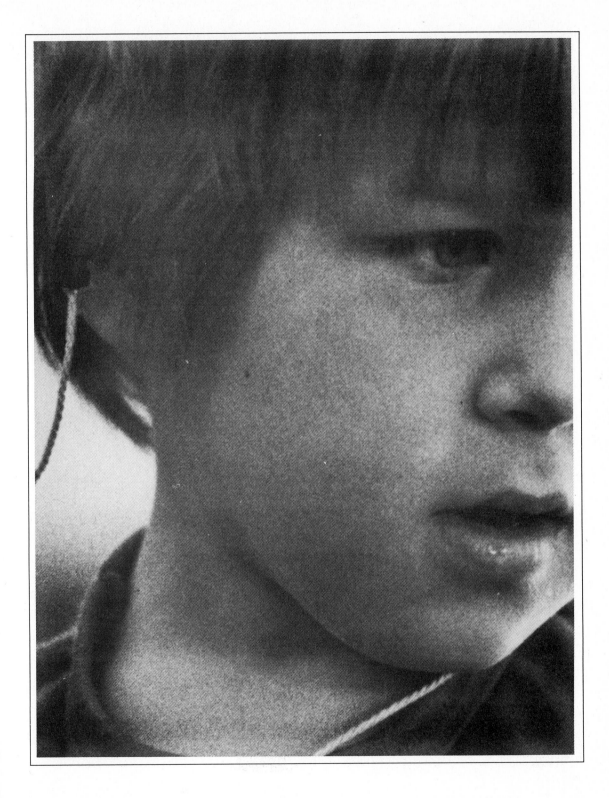

written in terms of quantifiable measures, that is, in relation to disabilities. As such, the impairment and the handicap receive somewhat less attention. The situation can best be understood by considering the classification of hearing loss recommended by the Conference of Executives of American Schools for the Deaf (Frisina, 1974).

> **Level 1:** *35 to 54 decibels.* Individuals in this category do not usually require special class or school placement; routinely they do require special speech and hearing assistance.

> **Level 2:** *55 to 69 decibels.* These individuals occasionally require special class or school placement; they routinely require special speech, hearing, and language assistance.

> **Level 3:** *70 to 89 decibels.* Students in this category of deafness occasionally require special class or special school placement; they routinely require special speech, language, and educational assistance.

> **Level 4:** *90 decibels and beyond.* These individuals routinely require special class or school placement and special speech, hearing, language, and educational assistance.

For convenience sake, we will refer to Levels 1 and 2 as signifying hard of hearing and Levels 3 and 4 as signifying deaf. The first thing to notice about this classification method is that the children are classified according to audiometric measurements that are quantifiable, that is, according to disability. The classifications clearly show an awareness that the resulting handicaps may be quite different from individual to individual. Two children may have very similar patterns of hearing loss and they may appear on the surface to have the same needs. However, the hearing loss itself is only one dimension of a very complex picture. One child may be able to receive much more benefit from a hearing aid than another. The development of English skills, speech, academic achievement, and social maturity may be quite different between the two. The different patterns of growth may be affected by such factors as age of onset of the hearing loss, age of identification, type of training provided, presence of other conditions, and even hearing status of parents, with deaf children of deaf parents being superior in English and academic achievement to deaf children of hearing parents.

Perhaps the greatest confounding variable is the presence of other conditions which can place restrictions on development. Approximately 30 percent of children in the United States in programs for the hearing-impaired have additional handicapping conditions, such as cerebral palsy, visual dysfunction, and learning disabilities (Gentile & McCarthy, 1973). Some of the most common causes of severe hearing losses at birth or in young children, such as maternal rubella, mother-child blood incompatability, and spinal meningitis, are of such a nature that the chances of additional handicaps are great.

As might be expected, most of the educational programs that have been established for children with auditory dysfunctions have been oriented to those with more severe hearing losses. For this population we have a body of knowledge extending back for more than a century and a half in the United States and as far back as 400 years to the beginning of education of the deaf in Spain (Moores, 1982). Thus we can specify many of the speech, language, academic, and social characteristics of this deaf population and can point to large areas of knowledge regarding the deaf. We must be aware, however, that there are larger numbers of children with mild and moderate handicaps, those who would be classified traditionally as hard of hearing. The speech, language, academic, and social characteristics of these children have not been studied to any substantial degree and we are less sure of the needs of such children. The major portion of this chapter deals with children with severe and profound hearing losses because their needs may be greater and because we have more information on these children. However, it must be noted that a majority of children with severe and profound hearing losses are receiving educational services, while a majority of those with mild and moderate losses are presently in general education programs but have not been detected as in need of additional help.

One of the problems we encounter when we consider the development of educational programs is that hearing loss is relatively common in the general population, but for most individuals the effect of a hearing loss on educational achievement may be slight. For example, most people experience a loss of hearing acuity with age. This is not of concern for the present chapter which is directed to early hearing loss, which might place restrictions on linguistic and educational development.

A national study conducted by Schein and Delk (1974) reported that more than 13 million Americans had hearing impairments. Of this number less than 2 percent, or 200,000, were classified as prelingually deaf; that is, they suffered from a severe to profound hearing loss at birth or prior to 3 years of age. The incidence of prelingual deafness in the United States is approximately 1 in 1,000. The incidence of all hearing impairments is approximately 66 per 1,000. In most cases the loss is acquired after childhood. Those classified as prelingually deaf typically need intensive services. What is not clear at present is the number of children with mild and moderate hearing losses who may also need services and the type of service that may be required.

Recent investigations suggest that between 65,000 and 70,000 hearing-impaired children are receiving special educational services, with perhaps another 40,000 to 50,000 receiving speech therapy but not special education. The Gallaudet College Office of Demographic Studies identified a total enrollment of 60,231 students and estimated that the total national enrollment was about 69,000 (Rawlings & Trybus, 1978). The Bureau for the Education of the Handicapped (BEH) estimated that 377,000 children in the school-age population had educationally relevant hearing losses (Sontag, Smith, &

Deaf children grow up and relate to the culture in basically the same way as hearing children. (*Courtesy of Paul J. Quinn.*)

Certo, 1977). Of this number approximately 50,000 would be considered deaf and the remainder hard of hearing. More than 45,000 of the deaf children were receiving special education services. Only 20 percent, or approximately 65,000, of those classified as hard of hearing were receiving services, with the majority of them participating in speech therapy but no other special programs.

CAUSES OF AUDITORY DYSFUNCTION

Hearing impairments are generally classified as conductive, sensorineural, and mixed hearing losses. Conductive hearing losses result from a malfunction or inability of the organs of the outer ear to transfer sound along the conductive pathway. Sensorineural problems result from problems of the inner ear, and mixed hearing losses are caused by combinations of outer- and inner-ear problems.

The most frequent outer-ear problems which cause hearing impairments include the presence of foreign objects (young children may place small objects into the ear canal), external otitis (swimmer's ear), build-up of ear wax or cerumen, and perforation of the ear drum. These problems typically result in minor hearing loss and can be treated.

Problems of the middle ear are more serious, although most are correctable. The most common cause of hearing impairment associated with the middle ear is otitis media, or infection of the middle ear. Other causes, though less frequent, include tumors, congenital defects, blows to the head, and bone disease of the middle ear (ostosclerosis).

Inner-ear problems usually cause the most severe hearing loss. The child may experience annoying ringing noises, balance difficulties, and most importantly, difficulties in understanding speech. Hereditary causes include degeneration of the organs of the inner ear, ostosclerosis, and Rh incompatibility. Viral infections, bacterial infections, anoxia (lack of oxygen), and prenatal infections are all nonhereditary causes which may result in serious inner-ear problems.

EDUCATIONALLY RELEVANT CHARACTERISTICS

DEFICIENCY MODEL

In formulating an approach to hearing loss, the pathological or deficiency model has most commonly been adopted. Under this orientation the individual with a disability is considered in terms of deviance, of being somehow below a norm or a standard. Under such a philosophy persons with hearing losses are considered inferior to persons with normal hearing, and the goal of education is to make them as much like hearing people as possible. Success is judged by the extent to which they speak and act like people without hearing losses. Such an approach concentrates on a *condition* and not on the human being per se. It is true that people with severe and profound hearing losses have serious difficulties with speech, English, and academic achievement. These difficulties are documented and will be discussed within the present chapter. It is also possible—but less extensively documented—that individuals with mild and moderate hearing losses also face substantial problems. A point to remember, however, is that many of the difficulties are not caused by hearing loss alone. Of more importance is the inadequate response of the larger society to the condition of the hearing loss. Inappropriate parent counseling, inadequate educational programming, job discrimination, and the ignorance of the general public are some of the major forces which combine to make a hearing disability a handicap.

THE ROLE OF THE PARENTS

Speech

Parents of young deaf children tend to make two basic mistakes. First, they look at the problem as an inability to speak rather than an inability to hear. Second, they think of the condition as a temporary one which may be cured or outgrown (Meadow, 1981). Thus when a diagnosis is made parents frequently will search for a cure. At the same time, they will ask, "Will my child be normal? Will my child speak?" It is at this point that well-meaning educators, audiologists, speech pathologists, and pediatricians fail the parents and their children. In order to reassure parents, many will answer, "Yes. Your child will speak if you follow our guidelines."

Such an attitude constitutes a disservice. Professionals must help parents come to terms with the fact that the hearing loss will probably be a lifelong condition. The deaf child will become a deaf adult. They must also help parents to understand that the major problem is a lack of hearing, not a lack

Hearing tests with children can be more difficult to conduct than most people realize, but they are an important part of a good screening program. (*Courtesy of Jim Lukens.*)

of speech. Even with perfect speech, the person will still deal with the world as a deaf person. The most honest—and most effective—answer for parents is to tell them that, given our present techniques, we are not able to say if a particular young child will develop understandable speech but that the parents can be effective in helping the child develop in all areas, of which speech is only one.

Dealing with the World as a Deaf Person

Most people outside of the field are surprised when they discover that deaf children of deaf parents are superior in academic achievement, English, and social adjustment to deaf children of hearing parents (Meadow, 1981; Stuckless & Birch, 1966; Vernon & Koh, 1970). Those with deaf parents have equivalent speech even though the clarity of parental speech is not always good. One of the reasons for the superiority may be due to the fact that the deaf parents are not overwhelmed by its appearance in their children. They know that deafness itself is but one aspect of an individual, that deafness occurs across all races, ethnic groups, and social classes, and that deaf people reflect tremendous variability in intelligence, academic achievement, occupational status, psychological adjustment, and speech. They are aware of the existence of deaf lawyers, dentists, and professors, as well as computer technicians, painters, and factory workers. They know that even among the most successful deaf professionals, there is a range in terms of speech intelligibility.

In short, despite discrimination and inadequate educational programs, deaf Americans tend to deal with the world in much the same way as hearing Americans. They go to school, work, marry, pay taxes, raise children (mostly hearing), and socialize in a manner similar to that of the society in general. Deaf parents, being aware of this, can be comfortable and relax with their deaf children. They can respond to the child first and foremost as a child who, because of a hearing loss, has some unique characteristics and needs. In other words they primarily respond to the child and not to the hearing loss.

Parent Education

Unfortunately, 95 percent of deaf children have hearing parents, and educators have not helped these parents cope with the realities of lifelong deafness (Moores, 1982). The majority of hearing parents have never had any real previous exposure to deafness, and the diagnosis usually comes after a long, emotionally draining process (Moores, 1973). Parents frequently are unaware of the cause of the deafness, and feelings of guilt may be close to the surface. The natural strain surrounding the presence of a young child in a family may be increased by recriminations between husband and wife.

At the time of diagnosis the *family* is most vulnerable. The parents are dealing with a condition they do not understand that threatens to overwhelm them. They are trying to work through their feelings of grief and helplessness. They are trying to respond to each other at a time when they do not know if they will be able to either understand or react to the unanticipated demands of a deaf child. The conflicting pressures are obvious. The parents need time to work through their own feelings and accommodate to deafness in their child.

Among the accommodations is the development of a realistic acceptance of the deafness and a realization of the potential for development of the child. At the same time the child should receive services as soon as a diagnosis is made. This would include fitting for a hearing aid and initiation of communication training in speech, sign language, auditory training, finger spelling, and lip reading. The needs for parent counseling and parent training must be balanced sensitively with the immediate needs of the child for the development of communication skills. This is an extremely difficult situation, and most educational programs have yet to develop the capability of providing adequate support both to parents and to the deaf child during this adjustment period.

ASSESSMENT AND CLASSIFICATION

As described earlier in the chapter, classification is based on the location of the problem in the ear: problems in the outer ear, the inner ear, or both. The

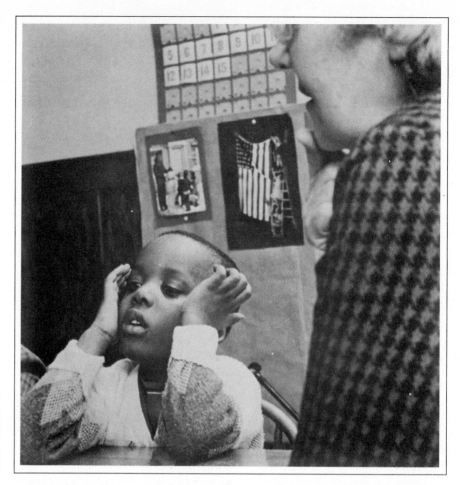

Already discriminated against because of race, an additional hearing handicap can evoke inappropriate classification as mentally retarded. (*President's Committee on Mental Retardation.*)

purpose of assessment is to identify the location of the problem in the ear and to specify the severity of the problem. Professionals who specialize in the detection and remediation of hearing losses (audiologists) generally use three kinds of hearing tests to achieve their objectives: pure-tone audiometry, speech audiometry, and other specialized procedures for children who present special testing problems.

The pure-tone audiometry tests assess the intensity of sounds which are audible at different frequencies. Speech audiometry tests assess the person's ability to detect and understand speech presented at different frequencies and intensities. Both types of assessment require that the individual be able to understand and follow the directions of the audiologist. Since these criteria may not be met for younger children or children with other dysfunctions such as retardation or severe motor impairments, other tests have been designed which rely on the use of reflexes (Davis & Goldstein, 1970; Downs & Sterritt, 1967), classical conditioning of galvanic skin responses (Wiley, 1971), and electroencephalograph or brain wave activity

(Martin, 1975). The latter two methods have become more sophisticated and reliable in recent years, and offer promise for accurate early identification of hearing impairments.

HISTORY

It is difficult to establish precisely when education of the deaf first began. The first known school for any handicapped children was a program for young deaf aristocrats established by the monk Ponce de León in a monastery in Spain around 1550 (Chaves & Solar, 1974). The work of Spanish educators led to the establishment of schools for the deaf in France in the eighteenth century. These schools, in turn, provided the model for the first schools for the deaf in the United States.

Special education in the United States began with the establishment of schools for the deaf in the early 1800s. The first permanent school was the American School for the Deaf, which opened in Hartford, Connecticut, in 1817. As might be expected, this school and those established later in the nineteenth century did not serve children with a complete range of hearing losses but was primarily designed for children with severe to profound impairments, those who are traditionally labeled "deaf".

The techniques and methods employed at the American School were based on those used in schools for the deaf in France. The first teacher at the American School, a man by the name of Laurent Clerc, had been a teacher in a school for the deaf in Paris. He modified the French sign language to accommodate to English. He also utilized the basic principles of a highly structured, analytic system to teach English to deaf children. The techniques were based on ones used to teach French to deaf children in Paris, again modified to accommodate to the properties of English.

THE MANUAL SYSTEM

With few exceptions, the schools established in the fifty-year period from 1817 to 1867 used what was known as the Manual Sign System. The manual system relied on signs and finger spelling without the accompanying use of speech. Instruction usually followed a three-step sequence. First a subject was presented purely by means of signs. The major concern was to get concepts across to the students, and the order of signs did not necessarily follow English word order or use all elements of English such as plurals, verb tenses, or many function words ("by," "the," "of"). This mode of communication was known as *natural sign language* and was considered separate from English. The second step involved the presentation of material following English word order and illustrating all elements of English. This was done by using both signs and finger spelling, with finger spelling employed to spell out the letters of function words and to spell word endings to show such grammatical aspects of English as plurals and verb tenses. This was considered a manual representation of English and was known as *methodical sign language*. The final phase involved the children reading related material and being able to demonstrate knowledge of content through written English.

Advantages and Limitations

Such a system had many benefits. It enabled children to be exposed to a range of concepts despite their problems with English. At the same time, the academic material was used in such a way as to develop English skills. The aspect of the system most open to criticism was the fact that it ignored the auditory-vocal channel completely. Little or no attention was paid to the use of residual hearing or to the development of speech. By the middle of the nineteenth century a reaction had set in against manual-only instruction, and the beginning of a split in the field appeared. In 1867 two oral-only schools were established: the Lexington School for the Deaf in New York and the Clark School for the Deaf in Northampton, Massachusetts. Education of the deaf split into two warring factions—oral only versus manual only. Despite attempts to reconcile and integrate the two approaches, the majority of educators of the deaf were aligned with one of the extremes and refused to consider any modifications of viewpoint. As might be expected, each philosophy had its successes, but each also was inadequate for large numbers of children. The children had to adjust to the system; the system would not adjust to the children. It was not until the 1970s that a majority of programs for hearing-impaired children in the United States had the flexibility to provide combined oral-manual education to children as needed.

EDUCATIONAL INTERVENTION

Even if we include those receiving speech therapy only, only about 110,000 children—less than one-third of the children with educationally relevant hearing losses—are receiving services. On the positive side, the large majority of those classified as "deaf", those who probably need intensive help, are identified and served. In terms of issues such as classification and labeling, the identification of such children with severe and profound hearing losses is beneficial. A much more complex issue involves the larger group of children who fell under the category "hard of hearing," according to BEH definitions. Should we identify and label all of the estimated 327,000 hard of hearing children in the public schools? Should we establish distinct separate programs for such children? Should we develop special teacher-training programs and certification requirements? The author's position is a cautious no. At present we have very little information on how hard of hearing children function. The evidence suggests that many of them have been sitting in regular classrooms and their needs have been ignored. Many of these children also have identifiable speech, language, and academic difficulties. But perhaps many do not. A much more careful evaluation of the needs of the hard of hearing school-age population is required before satisfactory special education procedures can be developed.

P.L. 94-142 is discussed in detail elsewhere in this book. The act was written to assure that all handicapped children from ages 3 to 21 receive appropriate educational services. The impetus has been to develop programs for children with the greatest handicaps and for children who previously have received no services. P.L. 94-142 has also stressed the concept of least restrictive environment and, as such, has been identified in some quarters with the mainstreaming movement.

As mentioned previously, BEH estimates that 80 percent of hard of hearing children receive *no* special services at all. Thus, the issue of mainstreaming itself is irrelevant because they always have been mainstreamed. Davis (1977) has claimed that hard of hearing children are the most mainstreamed of all handicapped children, but that they have not received the special help they need. Ross (1977) echoed this sentiment: "Although physically put in the mainstream, they have been . . . simply drowning there" (p. 5). In this context, the impact of P.L. 94-142 for the hearing-impaired is closely tied in with the mandate to provide services to children who have received none in the past.

PLACEMENT OPTIONS
Of the children identified by Rawlings and Trybus (1978), approximately one-half were in part-time or full-time public school classes. Of the remaining half, most attend residential schools for the deaf. The remainder either attend day schools for the deaf—public schools in large cities in which all students are deaf—or separate facilities for the multiply handicapped.

The public school classes followed a number of patterns. The most common arrangement is for a number of classes for the deaf to be established in a school in which the majority of children have normal hearing. Depending on the children's needs, they might spend varying parts of the school day in regular classrooms. The second model is a resource room in which there might be one or two classes for the deaf in a school. The children spend large amounts of time in regular classrooms and return to the resource teacher for special work in English, speech, and selected academic areas. A third model is that of the itinerant teacher, who might work with children in several different schools, providing individual instruction on a daily or weekly basis.

Many large school districts or regional programs have developed all three alternatives—self-contained classes, resource rooms, and itinerant services—to serve children with different needs. Traditionally those in itinerant programs tended to have better hearing than those in self-contained classes. The pattern exists today, but there are some beginnings of change. The author has worked with some public school programs in which deaf elementary and secondary school students are integrated into regular classes with the aid of a sign language interpreter. The results suggest that this can be very effective: children who have previously been assigned to self-contained classes can compete in a partially integrated program and function with resource or itinerant teachers.

SCHOOL PLACEMENT AND LEVEL OF HEARING LOSS

Across the wide range of hearing loss the question of segregated and integrated placement is difficult to address. As might be expected, those in segregated programs have less hearing or tend to be multiply handicapped. The children in different settings have different characteristics. The best example of this is provided by an extensive study of the school placement of more than 45,000 hearing-impaired children by Karchmer and Trybus (1977). They reported that almost two-thirds of children in residential schools for the deaf would be classified as profoundly deaf (Level 4), as compared to 18 percent of children in integrated programs. On the other hand, only 1 percent of children in residential schools had mild losses (Level 1), as compared to 18 percent in integrated programs. In addition, 13 percent of children in integrated programs had postlingual hearing losses (after age 3) compared to 4 percent in residential schools. Karchmer and Trybus stated that "it is clear that the integrated programs are generally serving a group of hearing-impaired children who are very different in many educationally critical dimensions" (1977, p. 3).

The differences in characteristics of children with different patterns of placement should be neither surprising nor alarming. The goal of special education is to provide services appropriate to the individual needs of children. To accomplish this a number of options should be available. For the hearing impaired, this calls for a range of placements, oral-language training techniques, modes of communication, and curriculum modifications. Beginnings have been made to develop more flexibility, and it is hoped that future developments will stress a sensitivity to the needs of a particular child at a particular point of development.

Deaf Teachers

One interesting aspect of the mainstreaming issue has caused some concern among deaf educators of the deaf. Throughout the nineteenth and twentieth century public schools have discriminated against deaf teachers. Even today, there are states in which no deaf teachers of the deaf have been hired to work in the public schools. As a result, deaf teachers have taught predominantly in residential schools. Because of federal legislation and recent litigation, the situation has begun to change. A few public school programs have even hired deaf administrators. However, change is slow. It is clear that many school districts and states have not actively recruited deaf teachers. Many deaf teachers are developing the position that mainstreaming should not be limited to children: if deaf children are to be taught in mainstream environments, then deaf adults should be employed to teach in these very same environments. It is harmful for deaf children not to interact with deaf adults in educational settings.

Traditionally, public school programs have not hired deaf teachers of the

All three of these children have learned manual communication at an early age from their parents. (*Courtesy of Frances M. Hunt.*)

deaf. In the residential schools there has been a traditional policy of restricting deaf teachers to work with secondary-age students but not at preschool and elementary school levels. Jensema and Corbett (1981) report that 14 percent of teachers of the deaf are themselves deaf. They still tend to be employed mostly at the secondary level in elementary schools, but a growing number are now finding employment in public school programs and with younger children in both day and residential settings.

It would be a disaster if a result of the mainstreaming movement entailed a restriction on the employment of handicapped adults who possess skills and insights no hearing person could ever have.

AREAS OF EXPANSION
Beginning in the early 1960s programs for the hearing-impaired began to grow significantly in the numbers of children served. To a large extent, of course, this reflected an increase in the national school-age population. Of equal importance was the establishment of programs in new areas, such as at the preschool and postsecondary levels, and the spread of programs for multiply handicapped children. Programs also began to serve children in greater numbers from ethnic-minority populations. Finally, the development of integrated programs increased the number of children served with mild and moderate hearing losses.

PRESCHOOL PROGRAMS
The biggest impetus for the establishment of preschool programs in public and residential schools was the rubella epidemic of the early 1960s. This epidemic doubled the number of children with hearing loss, many of whom were multiply handicapped. Prior to this time, most preschool programs

were operated by private agencies, not public school programs. Over the past two decades, service has expanded to the extent that most large metropolitan areas have free, public preschool programs for hearing-impaired children. Outside of metropolitan areas, most states have established regional services for parents and preschool children.

POSTSECONDARY EDUCATION

As with preschool programs, the number and type of programs at the postsecondary level have grown tremendously, with the beginning traced back to the 1960s. Prior to 1965, Gallaudet College, which was established in 1864, was the only substantial program available for deaf college students. The only exceptions were a few small technical-vocational programs. Deaf students had a choice between Gallaudet, a liberal arts college, and attempting to make it through college programs designed for students with normal hearing with no supporting services. The difficulties in the second choice are pointed up by the results of a survey by Quigley, Jenne, and Phillips (1968). The joint efforts of the Alexander Graham Bell Association, the National Association of the Deaf, and the U.S. Institute for Research in Exceptional Children were able to identify only 113 prelingually deaf individuals who had graduated from colleges and universities other than Gallaudet during the period 1910 to 1965.

In 1965 the National Technical Institute for the Deaf (NTID) was established as part of the Rochester (New York) Institute of Technology. Offerings range from self-contained programs specifically designed for deaf students to attendance in integrated classes for students with normal hearing. Support services include counseling, note taking, sign language interpreters, and tutoring. Shortly after the establishment of NTID, three regional technical-vocational programs were established in Seattle, New Orleans, and St. Paul, Minnesota. In each case the programs were developed in settings in which the majority of students had normal hearing. As with NTID, services involved counseling, interpreters, note taking, and tutoring.

In 1964, California State University at Northridge (CSUN) first accepted deaf graduate students into a special program for administrators of programs for the deaf. The students were successful, and it was decided to develop comprehensive programs to include deaf undergraduate and graduate students in all areas of the college. By 1979, 240 deaf individuals had received graduate degrees from CSUN alone, and 80 received undergraduate degrees.* In other words, more deaf individuals received master's degrees in a fifteen-year period from one university than Quigley et al., (1968) were able to identify as graduating from college over more than fifty years in the United States.

The results from NTID, CSUN, and three regional programs have been impressive. They indicate that a modest commitment toward counseling,

*Personal communication, Dr. Ray Jones, Director of CSUN Programs in Deafness, March 1979.

interpreter services, and note taking can have profound benefits for postsecondary training for deaf individuals in colleges, technical institutes, and vocational-technical schools.

MULTIPLY HANDICAPPED

Once again, the expansion of services can be traced to the 1960s and, like the spread of preschool programs, perhaps the major impetus can be traced to the effects of the rubella epidemic. Over the past several years the trend has been to establish programs in large metropolitan areas to accommodate children and adults previously living in institutions for the retarded. As the multihandicapped children representing the "rubella bulge" have matured, efforts have been made to develop adequate programs and services. The biggest challenge at present—one that has never been faced systematically before—is the development of comprehensive appropriate life education services for severely multihandicapped individuals who will be moving through adult life cycles but who will have very different needs than most individuals.

AUDITORY DYSFUNCTION IN MINORITY GROUPS

Following general trends in America, education of the hearing-impaired is beginning to pay closer attention to the needs of minority group children. As might be expected, substantial information is being developed regarding Hispanic and black hearing-impaired children, the two largest identified minority groups in the United States. Much less is known about the needs of Asian American and Native American hearing-impaired children. It is hoped that a more complete understanding of these populations will be developed in the near future.

BLACK HEARING-IMPAIRED CHILDREN

Throughout most of the history of the United States it has been assumed that deafness was less common among blacks than among whites. Census figures as far back as 1830 suggest a far smaller incidence of deafness in the black population (Best, 1943). School enrollment was also much smaller than would be estimated on the basis of general population figures. Data summarized by Moores and Oden (1977) indicate that more than 15 percent of the school-age hearing-impaired population is black, a figure somewhat greater than representation in the general school-age population. Part of the difference may be due to the relatively large number of school children whose hearing loss may be traced to meningitis (Gentile & McCarthy, 1973)—a condition that may be related to sickle-cell anemia, which is more common in the American black population.

Black deaf children are more likely to be misdiagnosed as mentally retarded than white deaf children and are less likely to secure preschool training (Moores & Oden, 1977). In addition, the economic status of black deaf adults has been below that of white deaf adults (Best, 1943; Furfey & Harte,

1968), and black deaf adults have faced discrimination from social clubs consisting primarily of white deaf adults (Anderson & Bowe, 1972). Because the size of the deaf black population has been underestimated, the needs have been minimized.

HISPANIC HEARING-IMPAIRED CHILDREN

The term "Hispanic" will be used in this chapter although the author is aware that labels such as Spanish-surnamed, Latin, and Latino also have been utilized. The three largest groups of Hispanics in the United States are Chicanos (Mexican Americans), Puerto Ricans, and Cubans. Other substantial elements can be traced to South and Central America. The Hispanic population has great ethnic and cultural diversity. The common characteristics include the Spanish language, a legacy of Spanish colonial rule, and a number of common cultural traditions.

If the black hearing-impaired population has been slighted, the Hispanic hearing-impaired population has been ignored. In the most recent attempt at a census of the deaf population (Schein & Delk, 1974), the Spanish-surnamed population was not enumerated.

In 1973, Gentile and McCarthy reported that of children in programs for the hearing-impaired for whom information existed, 7 percent would be classified as Spanish-surnamed, using this term in much the same way the present author utilizes "Hispanic." Most recent information indicates that almost 9 percent of children in programs for the hearing-impaired are Hispanic, a percentage likely to increase dramatically for a number of reasons.* First, the American Hispanic population tends to be young, with a projected high rate of increase. Second, the figures are for the 1970s, a period in which a large number of unregistered Hispanic aliens entered the United States, mostly from Mexico but also from Central and South America. It is certain that large numbers of parents did not request services for their children because they were unaware of the existence of services, they did not speak English, or they were afraid to call attention to themselves.

There continues to be a lack of sensitivity toward the needs of Hispanic deaf children. There has been little or no attention devoted to phonemic (sound) and grammatical distinctions between English and different Spanish American dialects and their implications for educating hearing-impaired children. As in the case of the black population, there are relatively few Hispanic educators of the deaf with the necessary sensitivity to sociocultural values. The fact that one-fourth of the American hearing-impaired population in school is identified as either Hispanic or black indicates that the necessity for meeting the needs of these children and training Hispanic and black professionals—both hearing and hearing-impaired—should receive highest priority.

*The author would like to express his appreciation to Dr. Michael Karchmer of the Office of Demographic Studies for making this information available.

COMBINED ORAL-MANUAL COMMUNICATION

One fundamental change, which again can be traced to the 1960s, has been the shift to combined oral-manual communication in classrooms. As previously discussed, there was considerable debate in the nineteenth century between oral-only advocates and manual-only advocates, a debate in which oral-only education gained the upper hand. With few exceptions, this situation continued in the United States into the 1960s. Work by the linguist Stokoe, which first appeared in 1958, had the effect of dispelling bias concerning sign languages in general and American Sign Language, which is used by a majority of the adult deaf population in the United States and Canada, in particular. Stokoe demonstrated that sign languages could be subject to the same kind of linguistic analysis as oral languages. Sign languages have the same potential for grammatical complexities as spoken language and, despite traditional myths, are not concrete: they have the same potential for treating philosophy, religion, biology, or psychology as spoken languages. One of the biggest breakthroughs was the growing evidence that a majority of highly educated deaf adults used sign comfortably and still retained oral skills. Thus, it is not uncommon for a deaf adult to communicate orally with a hearing person ignorant of sign, to speak and sign simultaneously with a hearing person who understands sign, and to sign without speech with a deaf adult. Stokoe (1958) was able to demonstrate that even as spoken languages have building blocks called phonemes, sign languages have building blocks, which he named cheremes.

RESEARCH ON DEAF FAMILIES

At the same time that the results of Stokoe's work were being circulated in the fields of linguistics, psychology, and education, the evidence was accumulating, as mentioned in a previous section, that deaf children of deaf parents, who were exposed to early manual communication in the home, were superior linguistically and academically to deaf children of hearing parents, who did not receive early manual communication. The results constituted a shock to educators of the deaf who for generations had repressed sign language in the classroom and had even resorted to physical punishment to stamp it out. For the first time data were becoming available. The results clearly indicated that the dominant thrust in education of the deaf actually was harmful and prevented young deaf children from developing to their fullest potential.

FAILURE OF PRESCHOOL PROGRAMS

A third major influence in the reorientation of education of the deaf was the apparent failure of the preschool programs which had been established in the early 1960s. Outside evaluations of many of the programs indicated that early intensive preschool programs limited to oral-only communication

422

had no lasting benefits. Deaf children who had gone through such training were indistinguishable from matched children with no preschool experience; and both types of children were academically and linguistically retarded in comparison with deaf children of deaf parents with no preschool experience (see Moores, 1978, for a complete treatment of the topic).

FOREIGN RESEARCH

A fourth factor which influenced American educators of the deaf was a series of reports from the Soviet Union, which had modified its oral-only methods by adding finger spelling. Children were instructed by simultaneously speaking and spelling, using a manual alphabet (Moores, 1972; Morkovin, 1960). Results suggested that by using this system, labeled neo-oralism, children went through preschool at an accelerated pace and developed a far better command of Russian.

TOTAL COMMUNICATION

Fortunately, changes in the mode of instruction did not regress to the nineteenth-century debate of oral-only versus manual-only instruction. The change was to establish manual communication as an integral part of programs for the deaf along with the very best possible training in speech, speech reading, and utilization of residual hearing. The term used to describe this addition is "total communication." Although there are different definitions, total communication essentially refers to reliance on all modes of communication; speech, speech reading, reading, writing, finger spelling, and signs, depending upon the needs of the child.

The magnitude of the shift to total communication is highlighted to Joron, Gustason, and Rosen (1976), who found that by 1975 total communication was used in the majority of programs for the deaf at all levels—preschool, elementary, and secondary. During the period 1968–1975, a total of 333 programs had changed to total communication. During the same period only five changed to an oral-only method. The same phenomenon has been observed at the postsecondary level. Rawlings, Trybus, Delgado, and Stuckless (1975) reported that in 1975 there were more than forty postsecondary programs for the deaf. With the exception of Gallaudet College, all were incorporated within facilities for students with normal hearing. Of these programs, one—which was designed for hard of hearing students—utilized oral-only instruction. All others employed combined oral-manual communication. The evidence is clear that the revolution in methodology extends across the complete range from preschool to college and from residential schools to public school self-contained classes to integrated programs.

SUMMARY

Since 1960 a number of fundamental advances have been made in the education of hearing-impaired children. Most of these advances have been in relation to the improvement and extension of services to individuals falling within the traditional category of deaf. Needs of children who would be classified as hard of hearing are less well defined, and it is more difficult to identify patterns in this area with certainty. At present, a majority of the school-age population with mild or moderate hearing losses are not receiving appropriate special educational services. It is probable that at least some of them are misdiagnosed as learning-disabled, educable mentally retarded, or developmentally delayed and may be receiving inappropriate special education remediation. A much closer analysis of the characteristics and needs of this population should be a top educational priority.

In education of the deaf there have been significant developments in the expansion of programs down to the preschool levels and up to postsecondary training. Also, the number of programs for multiply handicapped deaf children has multiplied. Educators are beginning to develop sensitivity to the needs of deaf children from minority groups. The situation may not be good, but it is improving, and there is reason for guarded optimism. Another fundamental development has been the rise of public school programs and the availability of legitimate options for deaf children in terms of school and class placement. Finally, there has been the growing acceptance of sign language by the general public and professionals and the incorporation of simultaneous oral-manual communication in a majority of programs in the United States.

Along with all of the changes may be perceived the development of a different attitude towards deafness and deaf individuals. This may be characterized by a willingness to accept the fact that it is more advantageous for deaf people to develop to the extent of their potential rather than be placed in a restricted world by which the sole criterion of success is the extent to which they become pale copies of their hearing sisters and brothers.

Edward Klein

CHAPTER 21
COMMUNICATION
DYSFUNCTION

(*Courtesy of Elizabeth A. Llewellyn.*)

Most people tend to see communication as a fairly simple process—one person speaks and the other responds in some way. However, this simplistic view doesn't even begin to account for all the events that must take place in order for appropriate communication to occur. Communication is by no means a singular or solitary event. Instead, the communicative process entails a physiological and learned chain of events so complex that even with our most sophisticated technology, we can today only *begin* to explain and measure it.

Intervention for children with communication dysfunctions is designed and implemented by a speech pathologist. In this chapter we will discuss the assessment and intervention techniques this specialist uses to remediate the communication dysfunctions which are most prevalent among school-age children. The teacher may be responsible for three important aspects of the intervention: identification and referral, follow-up classroom activities, and generalization of new behaviors and skills to nontherapy settings.

Characteristics of the most prevalent areas of communication dysfunction are described in this chapter to familiarize the regular and special educator with problems which may indicate the need for referral and assessment. The follow-up and generalization activities are usually recommended by the speech pathologist: they reflect the individual therapy goals and specific intervention strategies unique to each case. The assessment and intervention techniques described in this chapter should help to familiarize you with the theoretical bases and activities used by the speech pathologist.

The content areas we will discuss include articulation, language, voice, and stuttering dysfunctions. For each area we will consider the criteria for assessment and classification and the treatment approaches. Following this discussion, three specific categories of speech and language problems will be addressed: acquired language dysfunctions (aphasia), communication dysfunctions in autism, and speech dysfunctions in cleft palate.

Because the exact criteria for communication dysfunctions are difficult to

agree on, the prevalence data have been criticized by speech and language professionals as highly unreliable. For our purposes, it is more functional to remember that communication problems are the most frequent school-age disorder. Without a doubt, articulation is the most prevalent communication dysfunction in children. Language dysfunction is the next most prevalent category, followed by voice and stuttering dysfunctions, which are seen the least often. This chapter is written with these relative prevalences in mind.

ARTICULATION DYSFUNCTIONS

DEFINING ARTICULATION DYSFUNCTIONS
Individuals who experience articulation dysfunctions have difficulty in producing certain speech sounds. Perkins (1971) states that articulation is defective if either the speaker or the listener considers it so. But this definition might include as defective incorrect pronunciations that are actually encouraged by a subculture and are part of a regional dialect. For example, for many years it was standard practice to view black English as defective. This led to some ill-advised attempts to teach black children general American English and created in some cases an implicit discrimination against black culture.

Today, it seems more valuable to define dysfunction in terms of the need for and desirability of intervention. In this way, a person can evidence what is technically an error without being labeled defective or dysfunctional.

An articulation dysfunction, then, is defined as a variation from the norm in speech sound production for which intervention is feasible.

CRITERIA FOR DETERMINATION OF ARTICULATION DYSFUNCTIONS
There are five aspects a speech pathologist will consider when deciding if a significant articulation dysfunction exists.

Intelligibility of the Speaker
This is perhaps the prime and overriding consideration. How intelligible is the child or adult? How well can you understand the person? If a person's speech is unintelligible or contains so many errors that communication is impaired, then articulation dysfunction exists and some intervention is usually warranted.

Effect of Any Given Speech Variation on a Person's Life
Articulation errors can have an adverse effect on a person's life even if there is no problem with intelligibility. For example, a 10-year-old child who says, "My thithter wath thick today" might only be exhibiting a "th" for "s" substitution (also referred to as a *lisp*), but this error can and often does lead to teasing, scorn, and humiliation from others. Therefore, it is vital for a

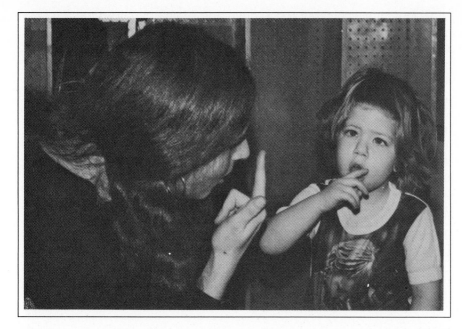

This child is repeatedly practicing correct usage and is motivated to do so by the reactions of the teacher. (*HICOMP Preschool Project.*) *

teacher not only to be able to recognize articulation errors but also to become sensitive to any effects of that error, and to undertake intervention if a child's social development is in jeopardy.

Unfortunately, not all of the impact of an articulation dysfunction is immediately apparent. A 7-year-old child might be relatively unaffected by a lisp and yet by the age of 10 might have undergone enough negative experiences that the lisp has now become a significant social problem. By the age of 20, that same "th" for "s" substitution could affect vocational prospects.

In short, professionals—teachers and specialists—must use some judgment when determining whether a child's speech variations necessitate intervention. What may not be a problem today may become a problem eventually.

Speaker Sensitivity

There may be instances in which a particular speech problem is not prominent, yet the student will indicate a desire to improve her speech. This will tend to occur most often with adolescents and adults. Sensitivity to a speaker who claims to have speech difficulties but overtly exhibits only minimal speech variation is then essential because your perspective may not appreciate the problems the individual is facing.

Age

Obviously a person's age is a vital factor in determining whether an articulation dysfunction exists. The speech of a 2-year-old child is not going to be particularly intelligible, but this is quite normal and no intervention is necessary. Likewise a 4-year-old child who misarticulates an "s" sound is behaving normally and is exhibiting only an articulation variation. However, if that same variation persists until the child is 10 years of age, it may then be viewed as dysfunctional.

Culture

For many years, any child (or adult, for that matter) speaking with a non-standard American dialect was thought to have defective speech worthy of intervention. This has changed in the last decade, however. A person speaking with a foreign, black, Spanish, or even regional American dialect is regarded as having *different* rather than *incorrect* speech. This is as it should be, since the child's dialect is adaptive in his particular environment.

CONSIDERATIONS FOR ARTICULATION ASSESSMENT

After considering the five factors discussed above, the speech pathologist or teacher can determine whether or not intervention is warranted. If the child appears to have an articulation dysfunction, several strategies can be used to analyze it. These include functional, process, and etiological strategies.

Functional Strategy

Until recently, this was the most popular way to characterize articulation dysfunctions. This method involves analysis of the specific sound errors made by the client. If an "s" sound is misarticulated, then the child has an "s problem," and intervention involves trying to establish that sound. If a child misarticulates "s" and "f," then there are two sounds to work on. These errors are unrelated, and often the error sounds are remediated quite independently of each other. According to this strategy, there are four types of articulation errors which can occur (Perkins, 1971).

Sound substitution occurs when one standard phonetic sound is substituted for another. For example, if a child says "dite" for "light," she is substituting a "d" for the "l." Similarly, "pid" for "pig" is a "d" for a "g" substitution.

In a *distortion,* the child is substituting a nonstandard phonetic sound for the normal sound. Distortions are really a form of substitution and can occur on almost any sound and in many different ways. Perhaps the most common distortion errors involve "s" and "r." For example, an "s" distortion occurs if the child attempts to make the "s" sound with his tongue in the "l" position.

An *omission* occurs when a person simply leaves out part of a word. For example, in the next sentence, the "s" is omitted in all positions: "I ee omething mall itting nect to the hor" ("I see something small sitting next to the horse").

Additions involve an extra speech sound in a word. Care should be taken when analyzing this form of error because many additions are due to cultural factors. For example, in Boston you would probably hear "ideeuh" for "idea." In New York, a common way of articulating "elm" (tree) is "elum," with an addition not only of the sound but also of a syllable.

When using the functional strategy, the child's speech is recorded and then analyzed using the above four categories. The focus for intervention is on changing one error at a time. Obviously, for children who have many problems intervention could take a very long time.

Process Strategy

This strategy focuses on identifying a pattern of errors that will collectively indicate what the child is doing incorrectly. Winitz (1975) suggests that this approach may be more useful than the functional strategy because it focuses on the articulatory processes the child is using to make different sounds. Assume a child has trouble with the following sounds: "s," "z," "sh," "zh" (as in "closure"), "f," "v," soft "th" (as in "thick"), and hard "th" as in ("then"). What is the common denominator of these sounds? They are all "blowing" sounds. This child has a pattern of errors that indicates a dysfunctional blowing process. Intervention would focus not on teaching specific sounds but on teaching this deficient blowing process.

Process strategies have often used devices called distinctive-feature systems (Chomsky & Halle, 1963; Jacobson, Fant, & Halle, 1952). *Distinctive features* are those acoustic, physiological, and anatomical features of the speech sounds that distinguish one sound from others. For example, "t" is made in the front of the mouth and "k" in the back. Thus, one feature might be front versus back. Another, as described above, might be blowing versus nonblowing. What is important to realize is that by analyzing a child's errors according to this process approach, one can often find patterns to the child's errors and thus speed up intervention by teaching the pattern, rather than separate sounds one at a time. Although advantages may include more rapid progress—and in some cases more effective intervention—there are also some limitations to the process approach. First, most systems use terms that are abstract. In addition, the distinctive-feature approach has been criticized on the grounds that the analysis provides only a limited picture of the child's speech because it is based only on substitution errors without consideration of meaning, phonetic context (the effect of neighboring sound on the articulation of a word), or word length (Weiner, 1979a). The omissions and distortions of a person's speech are likewise ignored.

A few people have attempted to overcome these problems while at the same time retaining the benefits of a process strategy. Ingram (1976) has described a number of articulation processes or rules which are less ambiguous than the distinctive-features processes because they describe what the child *is doing* in her speech rather than assuming what the person *might be* doing. Hopefully, within the next few years, process theory will become even more sharply defined, so that better use of it can be made in the classroom setting.

Etiology Strategy

In much educational practice, looking at the cause of behavior is irrelevant to selecting the best treatment. However, when considering speech, voice, or language problems, the etiology (cause of the variation) might indeed be relevant not only to intervention but also ultimately to prognosis for improvement. For example, speech distortion as the result of muscular paralysis will require different therapy techniques than the same speech distortion which occurs for functional reasons.

There are four basic articulation dysfunctions for which cause or etiology is a factor highly relevant to intervention. *Dysarthria* can be described as any disorder of articulation in which movement is impaired because of some neurological dysfunction (Carrell, 1970). Dysarthria occurs when there is paralysis or paresis of the muscles used for speech. There are many physiological conditions which can cause dysarthria of varying degrees and forms. Perhaps the most widespread of these conditions is cerebral palsy.

Apraxia is the partial or complete inability to execute voluntary, preplanned movements of the articulators in the absence of any weakness or paralysis which might explain this inability (Brookshire, 1973). Thus, there is no impairment in the ability to use the speech muscles; in fact, all speech sounds *can* be made at selected times. What is impaired is the ability to make these movements *voluntarily* or *purposefully*.

Deaf and hard of hearing speech results when a child has a sensorineural hearing loss (a hearing loss resulting from inner ear or auditory nerve dysfunction). Reception and perception of all sound, including speech, will be impaired; this impairment will often cause some articulation problems, especially with higher pitch sounds like "s" or "sh."

In cleft palate and other conditions involving *structural defects* (anatomical problems), articulation may be adversely affected. For example, many children with cleft palate have difficulty building up the air pressure needed to make some consonants.

When assessing a child's articulation, the major goal is to obtain a large enough sample of the child's speech, such that a comprehensive analysis can be made, regardless of whether a functional, process, or etiological approach is used. Teachers and speech pathologists typically elicit the desired speech sample by one of the following methods: (1) using pictures which are structured to elicit certain sounds, (2) using written sentences which are loaded with the sounds being assessed, and (3) using the individual's conversational speech. The method used will depend on the age, ability, and personality of the child.

ARTICULATION INTERVENTION

The type of intervention used by the teacher or clinician will, of course, depend on the type of articulation analysis that has been undertaken. For example, if the functional strategy has been used to assess the child's speech, then intervention will take the form of training specific sounds.

Alternately, if a process strategy has been used, then a pattern (such as "blowing") will be taught.

Functional

Many procedures have been described using this approach. Following is a simplified version of four of the most popular methods.

1. *Phonetic placement* trains the child in the specific placement or posture of the articulators for the production of each sound. The child is shown where the positions of his articulators are incorrect and how to change position of the tongue and other articulators in order to produce the sound correctly.

2. *Auditory stimulation* refers to the use of auditory cues to help the child produce the target sound. These cues can take many forms, from speaking directly into the child's ear to using speech that is broadcast through earphones at louder than normal volumes.

3. *Proprioceptive-tactile-kinesthetic methods* include those techniques which attempt to teach the child to "feel" the correct positioning of the sounds.

4. *Visual techniques* use visual cues (such as a mirror) to help the child produce the more visible sounds correctly.

Process

Since this strategy is a young, albeit growing, method for analyzing articulation dysfunctions, the development of intervention procedures is only in its beginning stages. As one example of a process approach to speech therapy, McReynolds and Bennett (1972) described a distinctive feature procedure in which the children are taught to produce two sounds: one that has the given feature and one in which the feature is absent. If the child can learn these feature contrasts, the authors assume, she should then be able to generalize the correct feature production to other sounds in which that feature is in error.

Etiological

If a child has some physiological involvement affecting his articulation, normal articulatory treatment procedures will often prove futile. Instead, procedures have to be developed which minimize or compensate for the effect of the physiological dysfunction. The specific procedure used will depend on the dysfunction. For example, in dysarthria, much attention will be given to muscle strengthening exercises and increasing the precision of the articulation. In apraxia, a much greater use of visual and auditory cues will be needed to help the person develop voluntary control over the articulators.

DEFINING LANGUAGE DYSFUNCTIONS

Individuals who are unable to understand or communicate effectively with others are considered to have a language dysfunction. The study of language development and dysfunctions of child language is really only a very recent phenomenon. Most of what we know about child language has been learned in the last ten to fifteen years. Until the mid-1970s speech pathologists worked primarily with speech and articulation disorders. Formal language measures were few in number and inadequate in content. What early investigators and testers didn't account for was that there are four components of language: *phonology, morphology, syntax* and *semantics.* Also, there are two channels for communication: *receptive,* the input from another person or the environment; and *expressive,* the output or what is communicated to another person. Each of these aspects of language will be addressed in this section.

Two Channels of Communication

The first thing you want to find out when studying a child's language dysfunction is whether the problem is one of language input (reception), output (expression), or both. Usually children with language deficits have problems with both reception and expression, although expression is usually the more impaired of the two.

Analysis of expressive language is relatively easy and involves a judgment made by the speech and language specialist as to whether the output or expression is appropriate. Receptive language, however, is much more difficult to analyze, because it cannot be measured directly. Receptive language can only be inferred. Failure to respond may be the result of failure to understand—or of other problems such as lack of motivation or physical inability to respond in a given way.

Four Components of Language

As stated previously, investigators have come to realize that language is composed of four somewhat separate but interrelated components. In order to get an accurate picture of a child's language abilities, each of these components must be studied, both receptively and expressively.

Phonology is concerned with speech sounds and how they are produced. Thus it is technically the same as articulation. However, linguists and other investigators prefer the term phonology, because articulation has historically been considered separate from language, whereas phonology is considered part of the structure of language. In fact, phonology is the foundation upon which other aspects of language (morphology and syntax) are built. *Phonemes* are the units of speech studied in phonology and are defined as the *smallest units of sound, which have no meaning by themselves but contribute to word meaning.* For example, in the word "fine," there are three phonemes: "f," "i," and "n." Because the "e" is silent, it is not considered a phoneme. Each of these phonemes has no meaning by itself, but each contributes to the word meaning. (For example, "f" doesn't mean anything by itself, but if "f" were changed to "l," the word meaning would change).

Morphology is the study of how sounds are put together to have meaning, and how words are composed of units of meaning, called morphemes. *Morphemes* are the smallest combination of sounds that have meaning. For example, the word "books" would have two morphemes—the root word "book" and the plural morpheme "s."

Syntax is synonymous with the term grammar. There are three major components of syntax: word class, word order, and transformations. *Word class* refers to the function of the word in a sentence (for example, noun, verb, adjective). *Word order* refers to rules of the language which dictate order of the words. (In English, for example, the basic word order in a sentence is subject-verb-object). *Transformations* refer to rules which allow us to alter the basic subject-verb-object word order.

Semantics refers to the inherent meanings in words, and more specifically, vocabulary, categorization, ability to define words and detect ambiguity and absurdities.

In summary, then, the four components of language are phonology, morphology, syntax, and semantics. All of these components are interrelated, and a child's language dysfunction might include problems in more than one component. Thus, in order to conduct a valid analysis of a child's language abilities, all components must be studied in each of the channels of communication, both receptive and expressive.

CRITERIA FOR DETERMINATION OF LANGUAGE DYSFUNCTION

As with articulation dysfunctions, there are several aspects to consider when deciding if a child has a language dysfunction requiring intervention:

1. *Success in communicating intent* (expressive ability). How successful is the child's communication? Can she communicate what she wants to?

2. *Comprehension ability* (receptive ability). How well does a child understand the intended communication?

3. *Culture.* As in articulation, a child might have language variations which are appropriate to the culture but technically incorrect. For example, in central Pennsylvania it's not unusual to hear the phrase, "My car needs fixed" rather than the more typical "My car needs to be fixed." Although this is a language variation, it is not a dysfunction, owing to its appropriateness within the culture.

4. *Age.* Again, as in articulation, age is a factor to consider when deciding on the existence or nonexistence of a language dysfunction. For example, "I store" might be a very appropriate utterance for a 2-year-

old child, whereas a 6-year-old with the same utterance would be rushed into some therapy program.

CLASSIFICATION OF LANGUAGE DYSFUNCTIONS

There has been much argument and disagreement as to the best way of classifying language dysfunctions. Some have argued for a classification system based on etiology, or cause. However, this type of system is usually inappropriate because for the most part we really don't know the cause of many language problems. Below is a more descriptive type of classification system:

Level 1: *Failure to acquire any verbal language.* This is self-explanatory, referring to children who are mute, that is, exhibit no verbal language abilities.

Level 2: *Delayed language acquisition.* Children at this level are those whose language levels are below those of their age peers, for whatever reason. Delayed language acquisition may occur in all, one, or some combination of the four components of language.

Level 3: *Acquired language dysfunctions.* Children at this level have or should have developed normal language, but because of external or physiological factors (trauma, stroke, tumor, sensory deprivation) have lost their capability for language. Usually these children exhibit proven and demonstrated brain damage.

LANGUAGE ASSESSMENT

Generally, there are two methods of language assessment: informal and formal.

Informal

Most informal assessment techniques involve making a tape recording of a sample of a child's speech. From this tape, the therapist or teacher listens for the phonological, morphological, syntactic, and semantic components of language. The speech sample is usually obtained through conversation, playing with toys, or looking at pictures. Generally, about 50 to 100 utterances are necessary for an adequate assessment.

These informal assessment techniques usually refer only to language expression. Most assessment of language reception has been confined to the formal mode.

Formal

Formal appraisal of a child's language dysfunction is complicated by the fact that all testing devices assess different areas of language, but no one test has been developed which assesses all important areas adequately. In Table 21-1 below, a number of the better and more popular language tests are listed, along with some helpful summary information.

TABLE 21-1 435
Some Frequently Used Language Tests and Summary Information on Each

TEST AND AUTHOR	PUBLISHER	CHANNEL OF COMMUNICA-TION ASSESSED	AREA OF LANGUAGE ASSESSED
Carrow Elicited Language Inventory (Carrow, 1974)	Learning Concepts, Austin, Tex.	Expressive	Morphology, syntax
Assessment of Children's Language Comprehension (Foster et al., 1973)	Consulting Psychologists Press, Palo Alto, Calif.	Receptive	Mostly vocabulary, single- and multiword
Test for Auditory Comprehension of Language (Carrow, 1973)	Learning Concepts, Austin, Tex.	Receptive	Vocabulary, morphology, syntax
Peabody Picture Vocabulary Test (Dunn, 1965)	American Guidance Service, Circle Pines, Minn.	Receptive	Single-word vocabulary
Illinois Test of Psycholinguistic Abilities (Kirk, et al., 1969)	University of Illinois Press, Urbana, Ill.	Receptive and expressive	Perhaps some word-class syntax, otherwise difficult to determine
Northwestern Syntax Screening Text (Lee, 1971)	Northwestern University Press, Evanston, Ill.	Receptive and expressive	Syntax
Berko Test of English Morphological Rules (Berko, 1958)	Unpublished; for source see Berko	Expressive	Morphology
Zimmerman Preschool Language Scale (Zimmerman, 1979)	Charles Merrill, Columbus, Ohio	Receptive and expressive	Phonology, morphology, and some syntax
Utah Test of Language Development (Mecham, 1967)	Communication Research Associates, Salt Lake City, Utah	Receptive and expressive	A bit of this and a bit of that
Vocabulary Comprehension Scale (Bangs, 1976)	Learning Concepts, Austin, Tex.	Receptive	Some morphology; mostly vocabulary

Most of the intervention procedures for teaching language to children can be grouped under one of the following three categories: (1) informal treatments, (2) commercial kits, (3) instructional approaches advocated by certain individuals.

INFORMAL PROCEDURES

Since language problems are usually particular to the child, informal procedures created by the teacher often allow for more attention to a child's individual problem than do formal procedures.

Semantics

The teaching of semantics involves instruction in the following skills (Wiig & Semel, 1976).

1. *Verbal production and fluency.* Does the child have a sufficient number of words readily available so that production of phrases and sentences is easy and appropriate to the age level?

SAMPLE TEACHING ACTIVITIES

(a) Teach the child names of a wide variety of items, using concrete objects that can be manipulated rather than pictures. (b) Demonstrate the use of an object and include that demonstration as an extra cue until the child has learned the name (for example, for "toothbrush," show brushing movements). Once the child has learned the name for the object, begin fading the cues.

2. *Ability to retrieve words.* Does the child have enough familiarity with the words that he knows; does he use them often enough so that they are easily retrievable?

SAMPLE TEACHING ACTIVITIES

(a) Speech drills are usually very effective in increasing the speech of word retrieval. (b) Sentence completion tasks which have answers from a restricted word set can help speech retrieval (Wiig & Semel, 1976). For example, in "On my head, I wear a _____, only a limited number of words (hat, wig, etc.) would be considered appropriate.

3. *Semantic relations.* Beyond just knowing what a word means, does the child know how a given word relates to another word? This involves analogies, opposites, object-action relationships, categories, and other areas.

SAMPLE TEACHING ACTIVITY

> Exercises involving object-action relationships might take this form: "I fly a plane; I drive a _____."

4. *Originality.* Are the child's responses stereotypical, or does she produce an adequate type and number of unusual responses?

SAMPLE TEACHING ACTIVITY

> Present the child with a sentence and ask her to say the same thing in a different way.

5. *Elaboration.* Does the child demonstrate adequate attention to the description of details as well as to the embellishment of verbal responses?

SAMPLE TEACHING ACTIVITY

> Use an active picture with much going on and ask the child, "What is happening? What else? Why do you think they _____?" and so on.

Morphology and Syntax

The teaching of morphology and syntax is less prevalent but just as important. Muma (1978) lists the following techniques for teaching syntax to a child with a language dysfunction. Note that the first four are child-initiated and the final four are teacher-initiated.

1. *Correction technique.* This model is widely used in schools and at home by parents. Unfortunately, its effectiveness has been questioned (Mellon, 1967). In this method, the clinician or teacher tells the child that his production has been incorrect and then corrects him.

EXAMPLE

Child: "I comed back yesterday."

Teacher: "No, not 'comed back.' You *came* back yesterday."

2. *Expansion technique.* In this model, there is no attempt to tell the child that she is wrong. Instead, an alternative but expanded utterance is provided. Again, research has indicated that the expansion technique has not been effective when utilized by itself (Brown, 1973).

EXAMPLE

Child: "Daddy go store."

Teacher: "Daddy is going to the store."

3. *Expatiation technique.* This technique requires the teacher not only to expand on the child's original utterance but to extend the entire topic. Cazden (1965), as cited in Muma (1978), found that children exposed to this model made significantly more progress than those children in the control or expansion groups.

EXAMPLE

Child: "Daddy go store,"

Teacher: "The boy needed some food for dinner. Daddy is going to the store. He likes to drive."

4. *Alternatives technique.* In this technique, the teacher agrees with the child's statement (whether correctly stated or not) and then asks questions about it. Although this technique seems valuable, Muma (1978) warns that the teacher must be wise when using it because it disrupts the flow of communication.

EXAMPLE

Child: "Daddy go store."

Teacher: "Right. Why do you think Daddy went to the store? What will he buy?"

5. *Completion technique.* This is a clinician- or teacher-initiated model in which an incomplete sentence is given to the child, who analyzes what is needed and supplies the appropriate words. Ideally, the teacher omits the parts the child should work on. The incomplete sentence can be presented just verbally or with a picture cue.

EXAMPLE

Teacher: "The boy is _____."

Child: "The boy is eating."

6. *Replacement technique.* In this method, the teacher gives the child a sentence which includes the syntactic structures being worked on. Then the teacher tells the child to take one word out and replace it with another word.

EXAMPLE 439

Teacher: "The boy is eating."

Child: "The boy is playing."

7. *Combination technique.* The teacher using this method presents two or three separate short sentences and instructs the child to combine the sentences in any way desired. This allows the child to explore alternative syntactic structures as well as to learn the usage of transformations.

EXAMPLE

Teacher: "The boy is eating. The boy is hungry. The boy's name is Jack."

Child: "Jack is eating because he is hungry."

8. *Revision technique.* This method is an extension of the combination technique. The teacher presents a short one-paragraph story loaded with the syntactic structures the child is working on and instructs the child to revise and retell it.

EXAMPLE

Teacher: "The boy is eating. He is crying. Father is making him eat his rutabaga. The steak is burning. Jack is not eating steak, but he is hungry."

Child: "Jack is hungry and he is eating. But he is not happy because the steak is burning, so he can't eat steak. Jack hates rutabaga, but his father is making him eat it anyway."

Finally, one more method of teaching syntax should be mentioned because it is effective in teaching otherwise difficult-to-teach syntactic structures (such as the verb "is"). It is especially helpful for children with poor language abilities. The *over-practice imitation technique* forms the basis for the Monterey Language Program (Gray & Ryan, 1972) but its basic format is generic enough such that it can be utilized apart from the standardized program.

In order to use the over-practice imitation technique, the clinician or teacher selects a syntactic form to teach (for example, the verb "is") and, beginning with just the target word and some extra stimulus (picture or object), has the child imitate her. (Teacher shows the picture and says, "The grass is green." "Is," after which the child imitates the word "is.") Slowly, the response is enlarged until the child is imitating a phrase ("boy is big"). Then, by altering and slowly fading the model, the child eventually produces the phrase in response to appropriate teacher-contrived situations and questions.

EXAMPLE

Teacher: Is	Child: Is.
Teacher: Is happy.	Child: Is happy.
Teacher: Girl is happy.	Child: Girl is happy.
Teacher: Girl _____.	Child: Girl is happy.
Teacher: Who is happy?	Child: Girl is happy.

Each stage is practiced numerous times while varying the pictures or objects, so that the child has practice using different words. This continues until the teacher is certain the child has learned the required step. Again, the overpractice-imitation technique seems to be effective with some low-functioning children or when trying to teach difficult syntactic structures.

COMMERCIAL KITS

There are numerous materials on the market which purportedly teach language skills to children. Unfortunately, most of them spend much time on general-concept language stimulation and little or no time training morphology and syntax. Also, many of these language kits are loaded with general activities but are lacking in structure and direction. For these reasons, it is important to be cautious in using any commercially prepared program. Make sure any program you use is able to fulfill the following criteria:

1. The activities must relate directly to the structure or concept being taught. General language stimulation is fine but its effectiveness in treating language dysfunctions is questionable.

2. Activities should be somewhat integrated and lead toward a specific goal.

3. There must be a way of measuring progress as the child proceeds toward the goal.

4. Contingencies should be provided for the child who doesn't learn using the regular procedure.

Despite the reservations implied above, a well-developed commercial program can be valuable. First, the structure already has been created. Thus, the teacher need not spend a great deal of time in program preparation. Second, the teacher need not spend time creating stimulus materials, because materials are often provided with the kit. Third, a well-prepared program is often the culmination of months and even years of theorizing, field-testing with children, and constant revision. This often represents more than a single teacher in a classroom can accomplish in the short time allowed to prepare a child's program. For these reasons, don't be shy about using com-

Programs for Language Intervention

PROGRAM	PUBLISHER	COMPONENTS OF LANGUAGE TAUGHT
Distar Language (1970)	Science Research Associates, Chicago, Ill.	Expressive: some vocabulary, some morphology and syntax
Peabody Language Development Kit (1966)	American Guidance Service, Circle Pines, Minn.	Receptive and expressive vocabulary
Developmental Syntax (Coughran-Liles Syntax Program) (1976)	Learning Concepts, Austin, Tex.	Expressive morphology and syntax
Fokes Sentence Builder (1975)	Teaching Resources, Boston, Mass.	Expressive morphology and syntax
Wilson Initial Syntax Program (1973)	Educators Publishing Service, Cambridge, Mass.	Some receptive syntax
Semel Auditory Processing Program (1976)	Follett, Chicago, Ill.	Receptive morphology and syntax
Monterey Language Program (Programmed Conditioning for Language) (1972)	Monterey Learning Systems, Palo Alto, Calif.	Receptive vocabulary: expressive phonology, morphology, syntax, and vocabulary
Interactive Language Development Teaching (1975)	Northwestern University Press, Evanston, Ill.	Expressive morphology and syntax

mercial language materials, just be careful. A listing of some of the more familiar language kits appears in Table 21-2.

OTHER INSTRUCTIONAL APPROACHES

There are some professionals in the field who have developed their own instructional approaches to teaching language but haven't developed and marketed them commercially. Some of these approaches are valuable and widely used and thus deserve mention here. Whereas space limitations prevent a total explanation of any of these programs, brief descriptions are given for each.

1. *Feigenbaum's English Now Program* (1970). This presents a method of teaching standard English to people who speak nonstandard English (Spanish dialect, black dialect, and so on). The program is based on Feigenbaum's belief that there is no reason to get rid of nonstandard English. Instead, standard English can be taught as a second dia-

lect in the same way that English is taught as a second language to persons in foreign countries.

2. *Kent's Language Acquisition Program for the Retarded or Multiply Impaired* (1974). This is an extremely structured program, one of the few that teaches language to severely handicapped children. It includes sections on attending, motor imitation, and reception and expression of morphological, syntactic, and semantic aspects of language. The program also contains a section on the use of sign language and other procedures for severe communication handicaps.

3. *McGinnis's Association Method* (1963). This is a highly structured technique for language learning which includes training in three units of language: (1) work on individual sounds; (2) combining sounds into words and using nouns, questions, and simple sentences; and (3) developing complex syntactical structures. The program also has four other "correlative programs" which include visual-motor exercises and number and calendar work. This program was developed for preschool children, and a major objective is to enable the children to be mainstreamed into normal classrooms as soon as possible.

4. *Lee, Koenigsknecht, and Mulhern's Interactive Language Development Teaching* (1974). This program is based on the model of grammar described in Lee's *Developmental Sentence Analysis* (1974). Its purpose is to teach syntax in a setting that approximates as closely as possible the conversational setting that occurs in normal language development. As such, teachers don't ask for imitation but talk to the children and ask questions to which the child has to respond using the correct morphological or syntactic structure. The program consists of sixty-two stories or lessons at two levels of difficulty, as well as instructions on writing other stories to meet a child's individual needs.

VOICE DYSFUNCTIONS

DEFINING VOICE DYSFUNCTIONS

Sometimes a child will have no difficulty either with articulation or with language but instead will exhibit a variation from the norm in quality, pitch, or loudness of voice. If this variation is great enough, the child might have a voice dysfunction requiring intervention. Voice dysfunction, then, is loosely defined as an extreme variation in the quality, pitch, or loudness of voice.

The incidence of voice problems in school-age children is not high. Eisenson and Ogilvie (1971) report that the ratio of children with defective articulation or stuttering to those that have voice disturbances is between 10 and 15 to 1. Still, voice dysfunctions do occur, and it is important for the teacher to be aware of what can and should be done in a given case.

CAUSES OF VOICE DYSFUNCTIONS

There are two main causes of voice dysfunctions in children and adults: *vocal abuse* and *physiological disturbances.* Vocal abuse is probably the prime cause of voice disturbances and can take many forms. Yelling, singing, smoking, drinking, and pollution can cause voice problems. For example, continuous yelling will often result in growths on the vocal cords causing breathiness, hoarseness, and sometimes, in severe cases, aphonia (no voice at all).

The other cause of voice dysfunction—physiological disturbance—includes any infection, disease, paralysis, or other insult affecting the optimum workings of the vocal cords. In instances of physiological disturbance, usually the physician (rather than the teacher or clinician) will direct intervention. However, it is vital for the teacher to be sensitive to the physiological problems that can affect the vocal cords, because usually the teacher will be the first person to notice any deviations from the child's normal voice pattern. With physiological problems of the vocal cords, time can be an important factor.

CLASSIFICATION OF VOICE DYSFUNCTIONS

There are two methods of classifying voice dysfunctions: physiologically and acoustically.

Physiological System

The physiological classification system looks at where in the vocal tract the voice dysfunction is and describes that dysfunction by indicating abnormality of the vocal structure. For example, with this system a voice dysfunction might be described as "improper closure of the vocal cords."

Within the physiological system three categories of voice problems can occur:

1. *Phonation problems.* Phonation refers to the production of voice as a result of vocal-cord movement. If there is some disturbance of this vocal-cord movement, a voice dysfunction can occur.

2. *Resonance problems.* Sound that is produced at the level of the vocal cords is like a low-pitched, soft squeak. The ability to produce the type of voice that we end up hearing is owing to the resonance of this soft squeak throughout the throat, mouth, nasal cavity, sinuses, and even bones of the head and chest. If any of these structures are deficient, voice dysfunctions can occur.

3. *Structural deviations.* If there is some structural deviation of the vocal cord, for example, if the person has a growth on one of the cords, a voice problem may result. This is because a growth on one cord doesn't allow for the two vocal cords to come together as optimally as possible. Thus, some breathiness might occur. Figure 21-1 shows two normal vocal cords coming together while the person is speak-

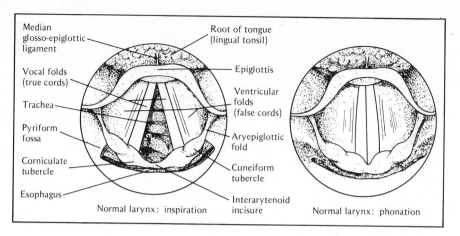

FIGURE 21-1
Normal and abnormal
vocal cords.

ing, and these same two cords coming together when one of the cords has an ulceration or an excess growth, such as a vocal nodule (to be described shortly). Notice the space between the vocal cords in the latter two conditions, allowing for air escape and, thus, breathiness.

Acoustic System

The acoustic system describes a voice dysfunction by referring to its acoustic and perceptual characteristics. The acoustic system for classification of voice dysfunctions is simpler to comprehend because it basically relies on what is heard by the listener. There are three parameters by which a voice dysfunction can be determined and described according to this system:

1. *Loudness.* A dysfunction occurs where a person's voice level is too loud or too soft.

2. *Pitch.* An individual's habitual pitch level might be inappropriate to his or her sex or physical build. For example, some men trying to make their voice seem "professional" speak with too low a pitch. This can in turn cause contact ulcers on the vocal cords, which can then affect voice quality even further.

3. *Quality.* This last acoustic parameter refers to the tonal quality of the voice. Hoarseness, breathiness, harshness, denasality (not enough nasal resonance, which occurs when people have colds), and hypernasality are the dysfunctions that are considered when assessing voice quality.

Usually, both of the above classification systems are used simultaneously when describing voice dysfunctions—one helps to describe the cause, and the other aids in describing the feature of the voice that is abnormal.

Numerous conditions exist which can create a voice dysfunction in an individual. Perhaps the most common cause of voice problems in children is *vocal nodules.* Vocal nodules are small, rounded beads of hardened tissue occurring on the front portion of the vocal cords. Because of this excess tissue, the vocal cords can't close properly and hoarseness and breathiness will be the result, in addition to excess throat clearing.

Another very prevalent voice dysfunction is *hypernasality.* In hypernasality, there is too much air escaping from the nose during sound production. The possible causes of hypernasality are many. For example, a short or paralyzed soft palate or a cleft palate can cause hypernasal speech. But it can also be learned, for example, if the child has a hypernasal mother and father.

There are many other voice dysfunctions which occur in children, and intervention will depend on the specific condition or cause. What is most important for teachers to realize is that *both* structural and functional factors are possible contributors to the development of voice dysfunctions. Thus, it is imperative that the initial step of any voice treatment program be a medical (laryngoscopic) examination administered by an otolaryngologist (a doctor specializing in throat problems).

Initial diagnosis of whether an individual has a voice problem deserving of further study and treatment can be difficult because our culture tolerates a wide variety of different and atypical voices without calling them deviant. Marlo Thomas, the actress, has a low-pitched voice with a hoarse-sounding quality and pitch breaks, while Wayne Newton, the singer, has a high-pitched voice. Yet not only are their voices accepted, but both performers are making money, at least partly as a result of those vocal characteristics.

The decision of the teacher to refer a child who is suspected of having a voice dysfunction should be made after considering the following factors:

1. *Persistence of the inappropriate voice.* For what length of time has the voice variation persisted? A day or even a week is no real cause for concern, but if the inappropriate voice lasts much longer than this, a medical referral would probably be appropriate.

2. *Other concurrent medical events.* Has the child been sick lately? Does the child have allergies which may be affecting his or her voice? Is the child on any current medication? If the answer is yes to any of these questions, a change in voice quality might be expected and nonsignificant.

3. *Voice models.* What are the child's voice models like, especially at home? Perhaps the parents might have a specific voice quality which the child has imitated.

4. *Concurrent physical symptoms.* Sometimes a child will manifest some other physical symptoms, such as extreme muscle tension in

the neck area or excessive constriction of the jaw, along with the voice disturbance. This is often indicative of the need for further investigation.

INTERVENTION

Numerous techniques have been developed which help in the treatment of voice dysfunctions. For example, Boone (1977) describes no less than twenty-four intervention techniques which can be used in voice therapy. All of these techniques fall into one of the following three categories: medical, behavioral-structural, and behavioral-functional.

Medical

These procedures are performed by a physician and usually involve some minor surgery to alter a physiologically deficient vocal tract. For example, the doctor will often remove surgically an individual's vocal nodules. The problem with this treatment for nodules is that since nodules are caused by vocal abuse (yelling, smoking), they generally will reoccur after surgery unless there is also some behavioral intervention to alter speaking habits. Another example of a medical treatment might be injection of teflon into a paralyzed vocal cord to try to help the cords come together more easily.

Behavioral-structural

Sometimes there will be structural problems which have no medical cure. In these cases, some behavioral techniques are necessary in order to help the individual make optimum use of the existing structures. As an illustration, in a person with a short palate who will not benefit from further surgery, a technique called overarticulation is used. Using overarticulation, the individual is instructed to strongly exaggerate every articulatory movement while speaking. This will result in decreased hypernasality.

Behavioral-functional

When medical intervention is not necessary, behavioral techniques are used most often to alter a person's vocal behavioral. In cases of vocal abuse especially, even when some structural abnormalities have formed (as in vocal nodules), the ultimate goal is to retrain the child to speak without that abuse, without the yelling, or low-pitch, or tension. Thus, behavioral techniques will most often be used. Most of these techniques involve either relaxation of the speech musculature or alteration of pitch.

For example, Froeschels (1952) described his *chewing technique,* the major purpose of which was to relax the muscles of the jaw, tongue, and larynx (voicebox) and produce a sound at the optimum pitch level. The chewing technique consists of four steps: First the individual drops his jaw and moves his head very slowly in a circular manner a number of times. Second, the sound "ah" is voiced while the head is rotating. Third, the person starts chewing with a wide open mouth, with the tongue moving around and in and out of the mouth in a very exaggerated fashion. Finally, while still chewing and moving the head, the individual puts some sound to the chewing.

Finally, one more intervention procedure deserves mention: *vocal rest.* The idea of vocal rest (refraining from any talking) certainly seems a promising method for ending vocal abuse. And indeed, many physicians request vocal rest from their voice patients. Unfortunately, the beneficial effects of vocal rest are usually short-lived because after the period of vocal rest is over, most persons go back to their original mode of speaking. Also, vocal rest is inappropriate for children for obvious reasons. In short, *vocal rest is not a therapeutic technique at all.* A person who has developed a vocal nodule because of vocal abuse needs to learn new speaking habits. As stated above, even if a physician surgically removes the nodule, the chances are very great that it will recur unless vocal abuse is ended.

STUTTERING

Stuttering refers to the phenomenon in which individuals speak with occasional to very frequent involuntary disruptions or breaks in their speech. Stuttering has been around for many thousands of years. It has existed in every civilization and in every country. Many supposed "cures" have been promoted, most of them bogus or false. For example, Demosthenes put stones in his mouth to cure his stuttering. And it probably worked—try to stutter with a mouth full of rocks. What is surprising is the persistence of these pseudo cures. Only a little more than twenty years ago, a U.S. patent was issued for a device called the Freed Stammercheck (Freed, 1957, cited in Robinson, 1964). This device was put in the mouth, restricted tongue movement, and thus cured stuttering, if properly fitted (and speaking also, one assumes).

Although stutterers can be taught strategies to control their stuttering, *there is no cure for stuttering.* In fact, there has been *no* well-controlled study which has been able to prove the long-term success of *any* intervention strategy with a high percentage of stutterers.

One problem is that there are many mysteries surrounding the act of stuttering. Many charlatans and well-meaning but misled professionals have utilized some of these "mysteries" in their therapy and have "cured" a stutterer for a short period of time, only to have the same stutterer turn up again six months later at another clinic across town, stuttering as badly or worse than ever. Another, sometimes more frustrating problem is that any competent professional can make a stutterer fluent in a therapy room in a very short period, but generalizing this fluency to other settings over time has proven difficult.

CRITERIA FOR DETERMINATION OF STUTTERING

Everybody is dysfluent at one time or another. Indeed, normal developing children are especially prone to breaks in fluent speaking. For example, many young children tend to repeat their words when relating an exciting story or event. Thus, the task of determining what is normal dysfluency and

CHAPTER 21
COMMUNICATION
DYSFUNCTION

what is a stuttering dysfunction is extremely difficult, especially in young children.

Still, some things are known about stuttering which suggest at least two aspects to consider when determining if intervention is necessary or desirable.

Age

If a child is below the age of about 5 (maybe even later in some cases), it is likely that stuttering will consist of simple *whole-word repetitions* with no other accompanying problems. As long as stuttering is at this elementary stage, it may disappear spontaneously. In fact, Van Riper (1971) indicated that perhaps as high as 80 percent of all children show stuttering behavior for some period of time during their speech development but eventually recover spontaneously. Therefore, if a child has some word repetitions with no other more severe forms of stuttering, it may be better to give his or her speech a chance to improve without any intervention.

Awareness

The child's awareness of a speech problem is probably the most vital factor to consider when contemplating intervention. Simple word repetitions are nowhere near as damaging as the learned negative emotions many stutterers develop concerning their speech. When stutterers are aware of and upset with their speech behavior, they will attempt to avoid stuttering. This avoidance and fear will usually result in an increase of simple stuttering behavior and the development of secondary stuttering behaviors such as excess jaw movement or filler words like "ah" and "you know." Therefore, if a child has no knowledge of speech dysfluency and no secondary stuttering behaviors, it seems better to ignore the stuttering.

If the above two conditions, age and awareness of the problem, are not satisfied according to these criteria, then assessment and intervention are recommended.

TYPES OF STUTTERING BEHAVIOR

Repetitions

There are three types of repetitions: (1) phoneme or sound repetitions ("p-p-p-pot"), (2) syllable repetitions ("an-an-animal"), and (3) whole-word repetitions ("I want want want to come"). Usually young children exhibit whole-word repetitions, but as the stuttering becomes more severe, phoneme and syllable repetitions are noted with increasing frequency.

Prolongation

In a prolongation, some sound in the word, usually at the beginning of the word, is prolonged ("s-s-s-soap" or me-e-e-t"). Of course, prolongations can only occur on vowels or continuant sounds (*f, v, s,* etc.). Also, the stutterer might demonstrate a rise in pitch during the prolongation.

Gaps or Silent Pauses

Perkins (1971) calls these pauses hesitations. Instead of one word flowing normally into the next, there may be pauses between the words. These pauses may or may not be accompanied by struggle, for example: "I" (pause) "want to" (pause) "come."

Postponements, Stalling Words, or Interjections

Postponements occur when words such as "like," 'uh," "well," and "you know" are used as fillers in between content words. We all do this to some extent. However, stutterers exhibit this behavior to a much greater degree than nonstutterers; for example: "I, uh, well, you know, I, uh, want to, uh, you know, uh, come."

Substitutions

Sometimes stutterers want to say something but can't get it out. In order not to struggle for too long a time, they will probably search for another word of similar meaning that they can use instead; for example: "Let's go to my c (pause), uh, automobile."

Secondary Behaviors

Finally, stutterers exhibit a number of learned secondary behaviors, including facial grimaces and contortions, poor eye contact, lip tremors, struggle, jaw jerks, gasping for air, and even limb movement. How have these behaviors developed? It is generally thought that they've been learned through negative reinforcement, that is, these behaviors have been learned because at one time they helped the stutterer escape the stuttering.

In addition to the above overt behaviors, stutterers will often undergo some covert reactions which accompany and help to reinforce the stuttering behavior. These covert reactions include shame, embarrassment, guilt, frustration, anger, avoidance of speaking situations and words, social isolation, specific word fears, and anxiety. For further discussion of the covert aspects of stuttering, see Van Riper (1971).

THE "MYSTERIES" OF STUTTERING

There are certain conditions which have consistently been shown to affect the stuttering behavior of the majority of stutterers. For the most part, we don't know the reasons that these effects exist—if we did, we might better understand the cause of stuttering and be better able to treat it. Still, these conditions or effects have stimulated a host of bogus therapy procedures (as well as some legitimate ones), and knowledge of them should help to understand the limitations of some forms of intervention which might be observed some day.

Rhythm Effect

Almost no stutterers will stutter when utilizing any type of rhythmic base for talking, such as in singing, unison talking (saying aloud the same thing at the same time as someone else), and when talking in synchrony with a rhythmic beat. This explains somewhat the longstanding use of metronomes or other rhythmic-beat counters. The obvious limitation is that people can't talk to a beat in most nontreatment settings.

Automaticity Effect
Stutterers rarely stutter when using automatic phrases. This includes behaviors such as swearing, getting angry and yelling, talking without thinking about it, and talking with animals or self.

Adaptation Effect
Stuttering decreases with successive speaking or reading of the same passage or phrases. (Many bogus therapy programs which required stutterers to read the same things over and over again were based on this phenomenon.)

Consistency Effect
There is a tendency for stuttering to occur on the same words or sounds in successive readings or speakings of the same or similar passages. (Even though stuttering decreases with the adaptation effect, the words that are still stuttered on are the same as in previous readings.)

Effect of Punishment
Stuttering will decrease if punishment is made a contingent variable. In other words, if a person is sure that punishment will follow the stuttering, stuttering will decrease. This finding has important ramifications for cause. For example, if stuttering is a neurosis, as some investigators have conjectured, then wouldn't the threat of punishment increase rather than decrease anxiety and stuttering?

Distraction Effect
For some reason, if a person is distracted, no stuttering will occur.

Effects of Altering Auditory Feedback
Much research in this area has been undertaken in the last ten years. It has been found that when the auditory feedback (how stutterers hear what they are saying) is delayed by a certain interval, many stutterers stop stuttering. There is a machine called DAF (Delayed Auditory Feedback) which does just this, that is, delays self-hearing by up to 250 milliseconds. Many stutterers who have been put under conditions of DAF with earphones have stopped stuttering. As with other techniques, the problem is in fading the DAF. Interestingly, when normal speakers are put under conditions of DAF, they begin to show stuttering behavior.

Another altered condition of self-hearing concerns noise. When a certain high level of noise is presented to the ears of the stutterer, stuttering ends.

There are, of course, many other conditions which affect the severity of stuttering, such as the size of the audience, the time of day, and the status of the listener. However, the above "mystery" conditions are those which have led to the I-can-cure-your-stuttering-quick schemes and thus are the most important for teachers and clinicians to be aware of.

THE CAUSES OF STUTTERING

The cause of stuttering is unknown, although we are probably closer to an answer today than ever before. Since there is no agreement as to what causes stuttering, many investigators eventually promote their own theories and provide interventions which are outgrowths of these theories. Therefore, in order to better understand the wide variety of popular treatment procedures and their underlying theoretical bases, a brief discussion of stuttering causation follows.

Since the beginning of the twentieth century, four basic theories of stuttering etiology have arisen: (1) stuttering as a psychogenic problem, (2) stuttering as a learned behavior, (3) stuttering as a result of an organic problem, and (4) stuttering as a result of a perceptual problem.

Stuttering as a Psychogenic Problem

Neurotic behavior usually presents three major characteristics: unpleasant feelings, inability to understand these feelings, and symptoms or patterns of behavior that symbolize and maintain them (Van Riper, 1971). Many stutterers fulfill these three criteria. However, is neurosis the *cause* of the stuttering or just a *consequence* of the stuttering? Many speech clinicians and psychoanalysts have believed that stuttering is symptomatic of conflicts which have been resolved by fixations or neuroses (Barbara, 1954; Coriat, 1931; Fenichel, 1945; Glauber, 1958; Murphy & Fitzsimmons, 1960; Travis, 1957). As a modern example of this type of theory, Freund (1966) described the most common form of stuttering as an *expectancy neurosis,* a category including writer's cramp, stage fright, and certain forms of impotence. After a person has failed in the attempt at communication, this expectancy neurosis arises, and because the person is afraid that he or she is going to stutter, the stuttering inevitably does occur.

Psychogenic theories of stuttering are understandably not very popular at present. First, no adequate research data have been presented to show that stuttering is at its core a neurosis. As Van Riper (1971) states, "Neurosis in stuttering [seems to] represent the end result of a learned process. . . . Most stutterers [do not] begin as neurotics." Second, research on punishment seems to contraindicate neurosis as the basis for stuttering. As stated previously, if stuttering were indeed a neurosis, wouldn't the threat of punishment increase the fears and the stuttering rather than decrease them?

Stuttering as a Learned Behavior

Much of the current thinking about stuttering etiology reflects the influence of learning theory. Few investigators will deny that learning plays at least some part in determining the patterns of behavior shown by advanced stutterers. However, there is much disagreement about the extent of the role that learning plays in developing and maintaining stuttering.

Shames and Sherrick (1963) view stuttering as an operant behavior. They believe that every child has normal dysfluencies during early childhood. If these dysfluencies have no positive consequences, they feel, the child is and will remain a normal speaker no matter how dysfluent he or she may seem at the time. If, on the other hand, these normal dysfluencies produce desired consequences (such as gaining parental attention), they will increase in frequency until the child is a stutterer. Then, if after parents lose patience, these dysfluencies now get punished through frustration or rejection, the child will start doing things to avoid them—these become the secondary behaviors.

Many investigators feel that stuttering is too complicated a phenomenon to be explained solely through operant conditioning. They point out that there are many children whose normal dysfluencies *are* reinforced but do not become stutterers.

Brutten and Shoemaker (1967) have proposed a two-factor learning theory of stuttering. Stutterers, they feel, show two classes of learned behavior. The first class, and the core of stuttering behavior, they call *classically conditioned negative emotions*. The stutterer has built up anxiety to the act of speaking. This response has become conditioned and becomes a stimulus for dysfluent speech. The second class of behavior is escape or *avoidance devices* such as head-jerking, eye-twitching, and so forth. This second class of learned behavior is operantly developed through negative reinforcement (escaping the stuttering). In their therapy, Brutten and Shoemaker try to weaken the learned negative emotion. By doing this, they feel that the secondary behaviors will also disappear.

The preceding learning theories seem attractive. The major problem is that if stuttering were caused solely through learning, then we should be able to arrange consequences that would eliminate the stuttering behavior. This has not been accomplished for any length of time.

Stuttering as a Result of an Organic Problem

Theories of organic involvement have been around longer than any of the other categories. Perhaps the most well known and, for a long time, widely accepted organic theory was the *cerebral dominance theory* (Orton, 1927). According to this hypothesis, stutterers lack a dominant hemisphere for speech. In normal speakers, the dominant hemisphere acts as a sort of a computer station, where messages are organized and integrated. Because stutterers lack this, their motor sequences are disorganized or interrupted, hence stuttering. Recently, this theory has lost its popularity because research has cast doubt on the supposition that stutterers demonstrate mixed dominance for language.

Organic theories for stuttering still abound. For example, Schwartz (1976) believes that outside stress on the stutterer results in a laryngeal spasm (total locking of the vocal cords). This spasm then supposedly causes the stuttering behavior that we observe.

Stuttering as a Result of a Perceptual Problem

Although this topic rightfully belongs as a subset of the organic theories, enough interest has been shown recently that it would benefit from some extra attention.

A number of investigators have theorized that stuttering results from a dysfunctional system of auditory perception. For example, Stromsta (1962), cited in Robinson (1964), compared stutterers and nonstutterers in their self-hearing or auditory-feedback abilities and found that stutterers had distorted and delayed self-hearing compared to normal speakers.

Stutterers and nonstutterers were then compared on a machine (DAF) which artificially delayed self-hearing. The results were interesting: normal speakers demonstrated stuttering behaviors (Black, 1951; Lee, 1951) whereas stutterers showed improved fluency while under the artificially delayed self-hearing condition (Soderberg, 1969).

Investigators then thought that stutterers had a deficient auditory feedback system. But recently findings suggest that the stutterer's auditory perceptual problems stretch to other areas also. For example, Klein (1976) and Hall and Jerger (1978) assessed varied areas of central auditory processing and found that stutterers performed significantly poorer than nonstutterers on many of the auditory tests.

Current Thinking

Presently most investigators agree that a majority of the behaviors that we see in stutterers, such as repetitions and facial grimaces are learned, but that there is a core of stuttering that is physiologically determined. This is why we can control stuttering (the learned behaviors) but we cannot cure it (the physiological core).

ASSESSMENT OF A STUTTERING DYSFUNCTION

The major purpose of assessment is to get a baseline measurement of stuttering behavior, so that the effectiveness of intervention can be evaluated. A baseline measure should include the following information:

1. Average number of syllables per minute

2. Average number of dysfluent syllables per minute

3. Listing and description of all stuttering behaviors

4. Baseline count of frequently observed stuttering behaviors

Both reading and conversational speech modes should be assessed. Obtain a 3- to 5-minute sample for each mode so that the measure is not biased by chance fluctuation. Some clinicians suggest administration of an attitude-toward-stuttering questionnaire, so that changes in the stutterer's self-concept can be documented.

INTERVENTION

Many techniques for the treatment of stuttering have been developed. It cannot be overemphasized that no single technique has been effective with all stutterers. However, for a small minority of stutterers some have been highly successful.

The therapeutic technique used by a given clinician will usually depend on his or her theoretical orientation: a clinician who believes that stuttering is a psychogenic problem will use a different technique than one who believes that stuttering is learned. In all, the therapeutic techniques for stuttering can be divided into four categories: altering the psychological state, preplanning of motor movements, rate control, and alteration of motor posture.

Altering the Psychological State

Using this approach, stutterers attempt to alter the negative feelings they have to stuttering. Van Riper (1973), for example, describes *desensitization,* in which the attempt is to find the sources of emotional arousal, desensitize the stutterer to listener reaction, and increase the stutterer's threshold of tolerance for speech blocks and tremors.

Preplanning of Motor Movements

A number of techniques are included in this approach. All of them involve concentrating on the motor movements of the tongue and stress tactile, kinesthetic, and proprioceptive cues. Sometimes the stutterer will even make purposeful pauses in speech in order to plan the upcoming motor movements.

Rate Control

Rate control has been used for many years in many different ways. For example, having the stutterer talk with a metronome (to a beat) is one form of rate control which has been quite prevalent. Unfortunately, there are three problems with a metronome approach. First, tick-tock speech results. Second, the change from the metronomic tick-tock speech to normal speech is not clearcut or easy. Third, secondary behaviors, for example tapping a knee to the beat, can occur and generalize to nonmetronomic speech.

Another form of rate control has involved greatly slowing down the stutterer's speech (to about fifty or sixty syllables per minute) while prolonging the vowels. Finally, rate control and prolonged speech have been used in a technique called "continuous phonation." In this procedure, the stutterer is instructed to continue voicing of all sounds in a sentence, without stopping the phonation or vocal-cord movement.

Perhaps the most prevalent technique in this category is light contacts. In this procedure, stutterers are instructed to concentrate on making very soft articulation contacts. Then they compare hard and soft contacts to "feel" the difference. Finally, when they get to a stuttering block they should remember the feel of the soft contact, use it, and be able to get over the block with little problem.

There are also therapy programs based totally on operant-learning principles (Ryan, 1972), as well as some commercial programs for stuttering (Cooper, 1976). In short, practically everybody has tried to come up with an answer to stuttering. Thus far, nobody has. However, a recent study by Andrews (1979) has finally addressed the issue of which therapy techniques are most effective in reducing stuttering behaviors. Using a newly developed statistical technique called meta-analysis, Andrews studied all published data describing provision of stuttering therapy (forty-two studies in all) and, regarding the dozen or so therapeutic techniques studied, concluded:

1. Gentle onset and prolonged speech were the most effective techniques for reducing stuttering.

2. Desensitization was shown to be totally ineffective in the reduction of stuttering.

3. Other therapy procedures were shown to have some degree of effectiveness, but much below gentle onset and prolonged speech.

APHASIA

DEFINING APHASIA

Aphasia refers to a *loss of previously acquired speech and language abilities as a result of some traumatic incident which has disturbed normal brain function.* This loss of language can be in either the receptive or expressive channels of communication, or in both, depending on the extent of the disturbance.

Most individuals exhibiting aphasic dysfunctions are older adults who have sustained strokes, brain tumors, brain infections, or traumatic injuries such as a blow to the head, fracture, or gunshot wound. Thus, it is not surprising that aphasia has been rarely, if ever, discussed in texts dealing with handicapped children. This is an unfortunate oversight, because children also are subject, albeit less frequently, to those same conditions which cause brain damage in adults. Yet most teachers, having read little or nothing about aphasia, are ill-equipped for working with children who exhibit this language dysfunction.

Causes of Aphasia in Children

Aphasia in children is usually caused by one of the following:

1. Injuries sustained in a car accident

2. Any other blow to the head, especially if the child has lost consciousness at any time

3. Stroke

4. Brain tumor

5. Any virus invading the brain, including encephalitis and meningitis

SPEECH AND LANGUAGE BEHAVIORS IN APHASIA

Severe
A number of language and other difficulties may be present in children with severe aphasia. These include: (1) comprehension problems, (2) fluent (no articulation problems) but meaningless speech, (3) echolalia, (4) no speech at all, and (5) difficulty imitating gross motor movements.

Residual
After some intervention the child may experience: some apraxic (coordination) problems; difficulty reading aloud, although comprehension is intact; or some word-finding problems, with the need to rely too much on gestures. The child may need some extra time to answer questions because of difficulty in finding words; in other words, the child knows what she wants to answer but can't find and program the words for it. The child will often talk more slowly, and writing and spelling might show some apraxiclike errors. For example, complicated words might be spelled correctly, with some simple words spelled incorrectly. The words most likely to give reading and writing problems are the less concrete words, such as "the," "and," "it," "if," "do," and so on. Finally, voice level might be low with some slurring evident.

Associated Complications
There will often be a paralysis, paresis, or apraxia of the right side of the body. Writing might have to be done with the left hand. The child may also have some visual problems.

TEACHING SUGGESTIONS
The following suggestions may be helpful in working with a child who has aphasia.

1. The child has probably not lost the capacity to learn. For the most part, aphasia is not a learning problem, it is instead a problem of input and output of information. Therefore, *don't immediately assume that the child cannot learn at the previous rate.*

2. The child has not necessarily totally lost all that was previously learned. Although there will be some loss of ability, reteaching should take into account the fact that the child has once learned the

material. Make ample use of cues, rather than spending much time explaining, as if the material were new.

3. Measure reading ability through comprehension tasks rather than by oral reading. Oral reading may never be totally normal in a child who has had aphasia, owing to the physiological insult. Thus, it is counter-productive to penalize the child for having poor oral reading skills.

4. Apraxic errors (leaving out letters, writing letters incorrectly) will occur in writing. It is therefore a good idea to have the child check his or her work a second time, and even take the word out of the sentence, prior to assuming an inability to spell. Often, the child will recognize and be able to correct an error if it is pointed out.

5. Often children with aphasia will respond to a question from the teacher with silence. Usually the teacher will assume that they don't know the answer, but this is not necessarily true. Instead, they may know the answer but be unable to program the sounds to produce the word for a period of time. Therefore, try not to place a time limit on the child's response; also, whenever possible, provide a multiple-choice format.

6. Expect the child with an acquired language dysfunction not to finish a written assignment or test as quickly as others.

In summary, readjustment of some of the normal teaching routines is necessary for a child with aphasia. Speed must be deemphasized in favor of accuracy. Also, one can't assume immediately that a child's responses are necessarily indicative of his or her abilities. Thus, a teacher must be ingenious in the development of assessment strategies for a child with aphasia. Still, with this readjustment of teaching routines, a child with an acquired language dysfunction can accomplish much, including college.

SPEECH AND LANGUAGE DYSFUNCTIONS IN AUTISM

Although autism is discussed in the chapter on emotional disturbance (Chapter 18), the speech and language patterns of children with autism are strangely unique and atypical and thus merit further consideration here.

Many investigators now believe that a language dysfunction constitutes the central component of the autistic syndrome (Bartak, Rutter, & Cox, 1975; Churchill, 1972; Hermelin & O'Connor, 1970; Rutter, 1978). However, the exact nature of this language dysfunction is unclear. Nonetheless, it can be said that the speech and language characteristics of autistic children are unique and do not represent just another form of aphasia or delayed language development.

DESCRIPTION OF SPEECH AND LANGUAGE BEHAVIORS

The many speech and language behaviors which characterize the autistic syndrome are presented below. It should be noted that the given autistic child may or may not exhibit *all* of these behaviors.

Echolalia

This refers to the parrotlike echoing or repetition of what the child has just heard. The following example illustrates a possible conversation with an echolalic child.

EXAMPLE

Teacher: "Johnny, come over here and sit down."

Child: (not moving): "Sit down."

Teacher (gesturing strongly, touching Johnny's shoulder): "Here—come sit down."

Child (sitting down): "Sit down."

Teacher: "OK, what do you want to work on today?"

Child: "Today."

Teacher: "Yes, today. What do you want to work on?"

Child: "Work on?"

Teacher: "Do you want to work on colors?"

Child: "Colors."

Teacher: "OK, good."

Child: "OK, good."

Pronoun Reversal

This is very probably a function of the child's echolalia. The child will very rarely, if ever, use the pronoun "I" but will replace it with "you." (For example, "You want to eat" rather than, "I want to eat," in response to the question, "Do you want to eat?").

Stereotyped Phrases

Sometimes autistic children will produce stereotyped or automatic utterances which are inappropriate to the verbal interaction. This may include musical jingles, advertising slogans, swearing, or other inappropriate stereotyped sequences of words.

Jargonlike Language

Often, an autistic child will produce a phrase or group of phrases that sounds appropriate but not to the given situation. For example, a boy sitting at his table, working on counting skills, might suddenly say, "But I really like the birds and how they fly over the trees. Aren't the birds nice, so near the sun? They fly and fly."

Metaphorical Language

Sometimes autistic children will use metaphors, rather than the appropriate content words, to express their meaning (Rutter, 1978). For example, "Gas tank is low, have to stop at station and fill up, for I'm hungry and would like to eat."

Deficient Prosodic Patterns
Prosody can be defined as the rate, rhythm, stress, and melody of speech. We all speak with pauses, accents, and a variety of tonal patterns (for example, "i" in "bit" is a short vowel, whereas "ee" in "beet" is a long vowel). If we were to change our normal prosodic patterns, for example by changing our vowel length or stressed syllables, our speech would sound quite strange. The sounds would be correct, but the tone or melody would sound foreign. Many autistic children, if they learn speech at all, demonstrate atypical and strange-sounding prosodic patterns.

Impaired Understanding of Spoken Language
Almost all autistic children have some problems in the area of language comprehension (Rutter, 1978). Usually simple directions are followed without any difficulty, especially if some cue, such as a gesture, is given. However, more difficult instructions, containing fewer cues, are often incorrectly followed (for example, "Bring me the red ball that is on the small chair, and then close the door").

Lack of Appropriate Gesture
Many autistic children do not communicate their needs even by the use of gesture. Often, the sole nonverbal language behavior will be taking the teacher's or parent's wrist (not the hand) and leading him or her to the object of concern (Rutter, 1978).

Again, not all autistic children who have speech exhibit all of the above characteristics. Also, some of the characteristics, such as prosodic deficiencies, are typical of autistic children with advanced speech development, while other characteristics, such as stereotyped or automatic phrases, are typical of autistic children demonstrating little or no speech development. Finally, it should be kept in mind that approximately 50 percent of all autistic children, especially those who are also mentally retarded, never develop any speech at all (Kauffman, 1977).

CLEFT PALATE
Cleft palate is a condition in which the child's upper oral cavity has not formed normally during the first twelve weeks of embryological development. The result is a hole or opening in the child's lip, hard or soft palates, or both. This opening must be closed surgically in order to avoid the following speech problems associated with cleft palate.

1. *Hypernasality.* This is due to an escape of air from the hole in the oral cavity to the nasal cavity or to deviations in the structure and function of the soft palate.

2. *Poor articulation.* Since there is air escapage through the opening in the palate (usually) or lip, it is difficult for a child with an open cleft to build up enough air pressure to produce some high-pressure sounds, such as "p," "t," "k," and "ch."

Ten or twenty years ago, a chapter on speech and language dysfunctions such as this one would inevitably include many pages of discussion on various aspects of cleft palate. However, such an extended discussion is no longer necessary. As a result of better prenatal care and improved surgical procedures, deficient speech secondary to cleft palate is becoming increasingly uncommon, especially in children with no other handicaps. Nonetheless, multiply handicapped children do sometimes exhibit cleft palate as part of a syndrome of physical and mental abnormalities. In many of these children there is a greater risk inherent in any surgery. Thus, physicians will often not attempt a surgical correction until the child is at least 5 or 6 years old. Even in these children, however, numerous artificial devices, or prostheses, are available; these help to alleviate most, if not all, speech problems which are due to the cleft. For further information in the area of cleft palate, see Morley (1970).

SUMMARY

Most children who need special services for speech and communication problems will receive those services from a speech pathologist. The teacher's role in the intervention process is critical: teachers may refer children for speech and language assessments and intervention or conduct classroom activities which reinforce the therapy. Finally, activities may be suggested by the speech therapist which are designed to help these children generalize their progress to settings outside of the speech therapy sessions; teachers may coordinate and participate in these activities. For these reasons, it is important for educators to be familiar with the most common speech and language problems and the different intervention approaches used to modify them.

Several strategies or approaches are currently used by speech pathologists to remediate the most common communication impairment—articulation dysfunctions. These include the functional strategy, process strategy, and etiological strategy. More research needs to be conducted to evaluate the conditions for which each is most effective.

The area of language is extremely complex, and one in which intervention will very likely involve the teacher. The area of language involves two channels (expressive and receptive) and four components (phonology, morphology, syntax, and semantics). A variety of approaches have been developed, some available commercially as kits. As with interventions for articulation dysfunction, the approaches to language dysfunction are just beginning to be evaluated and compared for effectiveness.

Voice dysfunctions and stuttering have each stimulated an array of intervention strategies. While those used to treat voice dysfunction have generally been based on the cause of the dysfunction and have generally been effective, the same cannot be said for stuttering. To date, we still know very little about the causes of stuttering or modification techniques which are effective and enduring.

Finally, three less frequently encountered problems which have received a great deal of attention are acquired language dysfunction, language problems associated with autism, and cleft palate. Each problem is described and intervention strategies are discussed.

Greg Reid

CHAPTER 22
NEUROMOTOR
DYSFUNCTION

General forms of physical dysfunction include clumsiness, poor physical fitness, obesity, and deviations in posture. These problems can be manifested by nonhandicapped and handicapped children alike. Specific forms of motor dysfunction usually constitute disabilities in themselves, whether or not they are associated with another handicap. The specific dysfunctions to be discussed are cerebral palsy, epilepsy, spina bifida, poliomyelitis, arthritis, and muscular dystrophy. Before detailing either general or specific motor problems, we will first consider

(Courtesy of Jim Lukens.)

the importance of motor skills and the features of normal motor development.

THE IMPORTANCE OF MOTOR SKILLS

In Chapter 17 on learning disabilities, several programs of intervention were described that were highly influential to the general field of education throughout the 1960s and the early 1970s. The prominent feature of these programs was the view that certain motor behaviors are prerequisites to academic competence in writing and reading. These programs allege that motor development is an important foundation to other areas of functioning.

Recent trends in the literature, however, view motor development as important in its own right and not just as a prerequisite for other higher skills. Movement provides the infant and child with opportunities to interact with the environment. Through such exploratory movement the infant begins to learn cause-and-effect relationships as well as various spatial and temporal dimensions. During the preschool years much of the child's social and emotional learning occurs through play situations (Frank, 1968). Social stature among peers becomes related to movement proficiency for the school-age child (Smoll, 1974). Psychomotor development, then, appears related to emotional and intellectual attributes of human behavior. Our present knowledge does not allow us to state that motor abilities necessar-

Poor coordination may limit the opportunity for normal social interaction as well as physical activity. (*President's Committee on Mental Retardation.*)

ily *cause* the other attributes to develop or change in any direct manner. The contemporary educator, therefore, believes that motor development and performance are important components in the total educational program of children, and especially so for those children who suffer some form of motor dysfunction.

FEATURES OF NORMAL MOTOR DEVELOPMENT
Many educators and other child-care workers find it useful to be aware of the characteristics of normal motor development. Knowledge in this area helps to provide a frame of reference for understanding and working with neurological and motoric abnormalities. Many physical therapists, occupational therapists, and child development experts urge that teachers become aware of the fundamentals of motor development because of the high incidence of motoric delays and distortion in the school population.

DEVELOPMENTAL SEQUENCE OF MOTOR SKILLS
Motor development is sequential and orderly because each new skill or behavior is built on previously acquired skills and behaviors. Each new behavior utilizes, integrates, and refines abilities which the child has already accomplished. For example, walking up stairs constitutes a complex skill which emerges in most children between 18 months and 2½ years (Chandler, 1979). Such complex behavior integrates the following motor skills:

1. Walking forward

2. Standing and balancing body weight

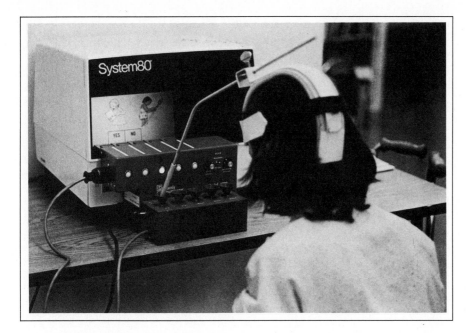

Children who cannot control their arms or hands can use a prosthetic device such as this head wand. (*Borg-Warner Corp.*)

3. Extending legs

4. Balancing head

5. Voluntarily controlling movement of limbs

The child must practice and refine the individual prerequisite skills before they can be integrated and used to perform a new motor behavior.

When can we expect specific motor skills to emerge? Child development specialists have delineated the ranges within which most children acquire specific motor skills, but many factors affect the acquisition of new skills—for example, the physical size of children, the maturity of the musculoskeletal system, the maturity of the nervous system, and the availability of opportunities to practice prerequisite skills. While many children pull themselves to a standing position at 8½ months, a great many infants do not acquire this skill until 1 year of age. Child development specialists urge that parents not become concerned about what they perceive to be slow development because the average age range for acquiring such skill may be quite wide.

Gross Motor Development

1. *Cephalocaudal direction:* As the infant matures, control of movement proceeds from head (cephalo) to foot (caudal). Infants acquire control of their head before they control their arms and legs.

2. *Flexion and extension:* The newborn infant's muscles are flexed or contracted. Control and refinement of muscle movement occurs

gradually as the young child develops extension movements. The child does not lose the flexion skills: instead the flexion and extension controls become integrated to allow for mature and smooth movement. For example, reaching for food and bringing it to the mouth involves deliberate extension of the arm away from the trunk to obtain the food and then deliberate contraction or flexion of the arm toward the body to deliver the food to the mouth.

3. *Reflexive-to-volitional control:* Movement in the infant is controlled much of the time by reflexes—automatic responses to various stimuli. Many reflexes, such as the sucking reflex, are important to the infant's survival. As the infant develops, however, many of the reflexes fade, and the infant begins to control body movements voluntarily. Failure to develop volitional control over certain responses can be an indication of certain motor problems.

Fine Motor Skills

Fine motor development involves movement of the hands and fingers, as opposed to gross motor movements, or movements of the body. Fine motor skills involve the coordination of vision, reaching, and grasping behaviors. As with gross motor development, there are several trends or patterns which emerge during the developmental process.

1. *Proximodistal direction:* The proximodistal direction of muscle control refers to the developmental patterns in which the child acquires more and more control of muscles which are progressively farther away from the trunk. Initially, the youngster has greater control of the shoulder and gradually develops control of the muscles which are more distant. A child is able to reach before grasping because of the principle of proximodistal direction.

2. *Pronation and supination:* Very young children complete fine motor activities with their palms facing down. This position is called pronation. As children develop motorically, they gradually acquire the skill of manipulating objects with the palm in the supine position, or facing upward. The gradual maturation of fine motor skills involves the integration and coordination of pronation and supination. Examples of skills which require this integration and coordination are holding a spoon for feeding, brushing teeth, and manipulating a ball.

3. *Ulnar-to-radial direction:* Initially, infants try to use the side of the hand farthest from the thumb to pick up and manipulate objects. For example, to pick up food the infant sweeps the tray and attempts to catch food between the palm and the little finger. Gradually, however, the young child begins to use the opposite side of the hand near the thumb to grasp objects. The most refined radial grasp is the pincer, which involves the use of thumb and index finger in juxtaposition.

Four categories of motor dysfunction seem to occur with many exceptional children: clumsiness, low physical fitness, obesity, and postural abnormalities. Children who demonstrate one or more of the four disorders frequently have been diagnosed as learning-disabled (Bruininks & Bruininks, 1977), mentally retarded (Rarick, Dobbins, & Broadhead, 1976), emotionally disturbed (Shoemaker & Kaplan, 1972), visually handicapped (Buell, 1973), or hard of hearing (Lindsey & O'Neal, 1976). The regular-class teacher, special educator, and psychologist should become acquainted with these dysfunctions and understand the role that professionals can play in helping children cope with and overcome such physical problems.

Although children who are clumsy, unfit, obese, or have poor posture are also found in traditional categories employed in special education, it does not follow that all mentally retarded or learning-disabled children are clumsy or unfit. Conversely, there are children who show no signs of learning impairment in the classroom but who are clumsy and unfit. This complex relationship between motor dysfunction and other types of handicap does not pose a problem to the teacher if the child's behavior is dealt with directly rather than categorically. A program to help children with general motor dysfunctions should be considered an integral part of individual programs in special education. Whether or not a label categorizing the learning characteristics of the individual has been attached is totally irrelevant.

CLUMSINESS

The child who is clumsy or uncoordinated is a child who experiences repeated failure in play situations owing to an inability to perform typical motor skills adequately (Arnheim & Sinclair, 1975; Cratty, 1975; Grosse & Bechere, 1975). This child may continually bump into obstacles or people on the playground or demonstrate an inability to throw and catch a ball. Climbing skills are ineffective, and jumping is generally uncoordinated or lacking in power.

It is not clear why children are clumsy. It has been proposed that many of the factors that result in mental retardation, epilepsy, and cerebral palsy can also produce physical clumsiness (Arnheim & Sinclair, 1975). Despite a host of potential causes for motor impairment, it should be remembered that clumsiness is ultimately a product of the person and the environment. As Morris and Whiting (1971) have stated, "the problem of motor impairment is one that has been created by the demands made upon the individual to learn certain skills that are regarded as important, or at least desirable from a normal developmental viewpoint" (p. 37).

It has been estimated that as much as 9 percent of the school-age population may be described as clumsy (Keogh, Sugden, Keynard, & Calkins, 1979). It is also believed that there are more clumsy boys than girls. In general, the identification of clumsy children lacks clear direction.

Motor clumsiness is often associated with other problems in children and adults. The clumsy child, for instance, does not usually score well on tests

FIGURE 22-1
Clumsy children require
many positive movement
experiences.

purporting to measure peer status or socialization (Smoll, 1974). To the
elementary school child in particular, proficiency in game skills is an important means to gain social prestige and friends. The motorically awkward
child must search for status in avenues other than games. As a result these
children shy away from physical activities as much as possible, creating a
cycle of inactivity. This planned avoidance of activity prevents the unskilled
child from improving already deficient motor skills. When the child does
engage in a game, social punishment is likely to occur and thereby further
reduce the probability of future participation.

Clumsy children report that their playmates make fun of them. Expressed
attitudes toward awkward children such as this may lead to moderate or
severe emotional problems (Cratty, 1975). Data suggest that clumsy children
express lower self-concepts than their more physically adroit peers.

There is a tendency for adults to participate in physical activities they
learned and practiced as children. If clumsy children do not develop essential motor skills, they may become clumsy adults who do not engage in
regular exercise and thereby avoid one very important dimension to healthy
living.

No specific system or technique for instruction of clumsy children has
evolved (Arnheim & Sinclair, 1975). Regardless of the system of remediation
selected, several principles of instruction have been advocated. Motivation
of the clumsy child is particularly important. The youngster has probably
developed a "failure syndrome" as a result of repeated failures and thus has
a lowered level of aspiration and motor skill achievement. Consequently,
the instructor must motivate the child to establish and work toward realistic
goals. The instructor must also create a learning environment that initially is
free from stress. Poorly learned motor skills demonstrate disruptive performance under high-stress situations. Stress should be gradually introduced so
that the performer learns to tolerate it. Learning ball-handling skills on a

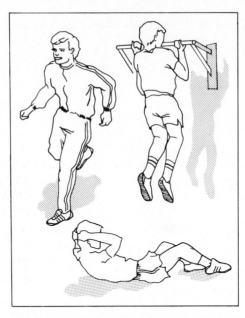

FIGURE 22-2
Some components of
physical fitness.

one-to-one basis is important but not particularly functional unless the student becomes relatively proficient in a game situation which does not contain more stress.

The final and possibly most critical principle of dealing with clumsy children is the no-failure concept. Gym programs are geared toward competitive games which train a few "stars" and while individual instruction may be vital, it is usually not possible. Awkward children must be afforded movement programs in which they experience success. This means individual programs when at all possible. The cliché, "Success breeds success" is accurate in this situation. The types of activities usually considered appropriate for clumsy children are basic locomotion (jumping, hopping, and running), balance, throwing and catching, climbing, exploring objects with various spatial restrictions, rhythmical activities, trampolining, and specific play skills such as rope jumping and bicycle riding.

PHYSICAL UNFITNESS

Physical fitness has been defined as "the ability to carry out daily tasks with vigor and alertness, without undue fatigue, and with ample energy to enjoy leisure pursuits and to meet unforeseen emergencies" (Clark, 1967, p. 14). This definition acknowledges that one's occupation will dictate to a certain degree the level of physical fitness required by the individual. Indeed, there is no universally accepted level of physical fitness which all people should attain. Yet, as indicated by the definition, a physically fit person can work with vigor and remain active in the enjoyment of recreational pursuits.

The components of fitness usually include strength, muscular endurance, cardiovascular endurance, and flexibility. Strength is the ability of selected muscle groups to exert force during one contraction, while muscular endurance is the ability of muscles to continue contracting over a period of time. Cardiovascular endurance is the ability of the body to supply oxygen to the tissues during work. This is a function of the heart, lungs, and circulatory system. Flexibility is the range of movement about a joint.

The health-related factors of physical fitness begin in the elementary and high school years. Although many children are active, some simply lack a minimum level of physical fitness. Actually, the physical-fitness levels of children may begin to decline during the school years (Bailey, 1972). Although a heart attack will not be a direct result, certain cardiovascular diseases such as atherosclerosis have been found in teenagers and young children (Thornton, 1976; Vitale, 1973). Atherosclerosis is a form of arteriosclerosis (hardening of the arteries), in which fatty deposits such as cholesterol become attached to the linings of arteries and interfere with blood circulation. In order to help avoid atherosclerosis and other diseases associated with older persons, regular and remedial exercise programs should be considered an important element of special education programs.

Fait (1978) contends that several factors contribute to subnormal physical fitness: physical defects or disorders, faulty nutrition, poor health practices, psychological weakness, inherited factors, lack of activity, and illness are among the most predominant. Improvement in the physical fitness of exceptional children may depend a great deal on taking care of these particular factors for a given child.

OBESITY

It is generally acknowledged that obesity is a major health problem in adults. Obesity increases susceptibility to a number of diseases, including coronary heart disorders, atherosclerosis, and gall bladder disorders. Mayer (1968) has claimed that if the adult population in North America were to avoid obesity, the average gain in life expectancy could be four or five years. Such an increment is twice what the cure of cancer could bring!

Obesity is also a malady of childhood which affects 10 to 15 percent of the school-age population in the United States (Sherrill, 1976). Contrary to the assumption that obese children will grow out of their condition, convincing evidence exists that obese children will become obese adults (Corbin, 1973). Also, obesity frequently results in somatopsychological problems (see Chapter 11). Obesity, therefore, is a major concern for special educators.

Determining desirable weight is most accurately predicted through formulas which consider the ratio of fat tissue to body weight. Common height-weight tables are not valid measures of obesity because they ignore the person's body build. Professional football players are often obese according to such tables but in terms of body fat content they may actually be thin. The "extra" weight they carry is usually attributed to well-developed muscles. Indeed, obesity is not so much a problem of how much one weighs as it is a problem of how much fat one carries around.

There are a number of methods for assessing the amount of fat on the body. Perhaps the optimal procedure is the skin-fold method. With a skin-fold caliper, the skin and subcutaneous layer of fat are pinched and measured at appropriate sites on the body and these data are converted into estimates of percentage of body fat. The average percentage of weight in fat for males age 20 is approximately 12–13 percent, while the average for females is 20–21 percent (Hockey, 1973). Using this percentage of body fat as the unit of measurement, obesity is defined as 20 percent of more of body weight in fat tissue for males and 27 percent or more for women (Vitale, 1973).

Most causes of obesity have been identified. Mayer (1968) suggests that a genetic factor in the susceptibility of obesity should be acknowledged. A recently identified physiological factor related to obesity is the increased number of fat cells which apparently characterize obese persons. It is believed that infants who are overfed will develop large numbers of fat cells which will never disappear and thus make weight control very difficult in future years (Hirsh, 1975). Although weight and fat gain are expected in the first year of life, excessive caloric intake is apparently not wise.

A host of environmental factors can also cause obesity. The fallacy that a fat person is healthy is still upheld in some cultural groups which promote overeating. The nature of the diet and the method of cooking of food are also critical factors in determining the food value of the ingested calories. Two forces often coexist in the obese person: inactivity and overeating. These two factors are usually considered the prime causes of obesity, but it is an oversimplification to assume they might not interact with other genetic or physiological factors. Viewing the obese person as simply one who is too sedentary, overindulgent, and lacking in self-control is not a sound foundation for treatment.

Inactivity is considered by Mayer (1968) to be the most significant culprit in causing obesity in our North American culture. His studies have identified adolescents who do not overeat but who are obese owing to extreme sedentary lifestyles.

Obesity management programs for children should be conducted in collaboration with a physician. Ultimately the program is the responsibility of the medical doctor. It is the physician's role, for instance, to determine the nutritional requirements of the growing child. Reduced caloric intake is generally part of the total program, but such intake must be determined by the doctor in light of the child as a growing organism. Weight reduction programs also include a nutritional reeducation section. Sherrill (1976) suggests that both child and parents be part of the overall program. This strategy is especially important for the nutritional component, which teaches the participant to select healthy foods with minimal calories. Treatment of obesity must also be conducted in a nonaversive, motivating manner. A final component in programs for the management of obesity is increasing the activity level of the child. Regular, graded exercise is considered by most authorities essential in the reduction and prevention of obesity. Ultimately, weight gain is prevented by keeping caloric intake equal to caloric output.

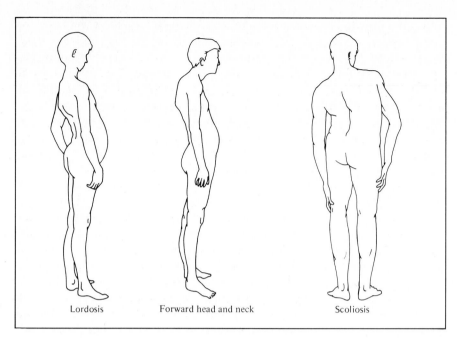

FIGURE 22-3
Examples of postural
abnormalities.

Lordosis   Forward head and neck   Scoliosis

It is important that obesity be treated in childhood. Sensible food habits and regular exercise must be established and maintained by children who are predisposed toward obesity. The treatment of adult obesity by programs described in the preceding paragraph have not met with great success. Weight reduction programs as part of special education might in part alleviate this poor record of accomplishment.

POSTURAL DEVIATIONS

Physical posture refers to the alignment of body segments. Obtaining good posture is desirable because it aids appearance, allows for optimal efficiency of musculoskeletal activity, and benefits health. Postural disorders increase susceptibility to backache or may even impair respiratory capacity (Lindsay, Jones, & Whitley, 1974).

Postural abnormalities can be categorized as structural or functional. A structural deviation is caused by skeletal damage and usually can be ameliorated only through surgery. Functional deviations are the result of weak or imbalanced muscle development. Therapeutic exercise and occasional braces can aid a functional postural abnormality. Some of the causes of poor posture classified by Arnheim, Auxter, and Crowe (1977) are environmental, such as improperly fitting clothing; overwork and fatigue; psychological, such as shyness or depression; pathological, such as faulty vision, tuberculosis, or arthritis; growth handicaps resulting in weakness of the skeletal structure; congenital defects, such as amputations and bone deformities; and nutritional problems, such as under- or overweight.

Standing posture can be assessed by the teacher using a postural grid or plumb line. A postural grid is a grid composed of 2-inch squares on the wall. The grid extends all the way to the floor. The lines of the grid are used as reference points to ascertain the alignment of the body parts. A plumb line is simply a long string which is suspended from the ceiling to the floor. A weight on the bottom of the line keeps it taut. The plumb line is also used as a reference to determine any faulty alignment of body parts. Common deviations of the spinal column include: forward head and neck, lordosis, kyphosis, flat back, and scoliosis. When the head is not balanced above the cervical vertebrae, a forward head and neck is obvious. It has been estimated that as many as 70 percent of American school children have some degree of forward head and neck owing to the great emphasis on early book learning (Sherrill, 1976). Kyphosis (hunchback) is an excessive convexity in the thoracic region of the spinal column. Lordosis (sway or hollowback) is an excessive curve in the lumbar vertebra. Flatback is the opposite of lordosis. Scoliosis is a lateral or sideways curvature of the spine.

The special educator, physical educator, or nurse should be responsible for initial screening of posture deviations. If a disorder is suspected, a follow-up examination by a physician should be requested. The physician can confirm or reject the original diagnosis, determine if the problem is structural or functional, and make any appropriate prescription of exercises or braces.

CEREBRAL PALSY

Cerebral palsy is a recent term which encompasses a number of motor dysfunctions. The historical antecedents of cerebral palsy, however, appear rich in years. The sculptured monuments of Egypt include drawings of individuals who appear to have cerebral palsy and the scriptures describe persons apparently so afflicted (MacDonald & Chance, 1964). An English physician, William John Little, was the first to report clinical descriptions of these individuals in 1843, and the condition soon became known as Little's disease. In the 1930s Phelps popularized the term "cerebral."

PREVALENCE AND CAUSES OF CEREBRAL PALSY

Cerebral palsy (CP) is a group of conditions caused by damage to the brain (cerebral) and manifested in motor disorders (palsy). Incidence studies of cerebral palsy vary, with a range of approximately 1 to 7 per 1,000 school children afflicted with the condition. Most reports are closer to 2 per 1,000. The ratio of males to females is about 55 to 45 (Capute, 1975).

Prenatal causes associated with cerebral palsy include rare inherited conditions, infections, the Rh blood factor, and irradiation of the mother during pregnancy. Causes related to the birth process include anoxia and direct trauma as a result of mechanical injuries from a difficult birth. Postnatal factors which are frequently cited as offenders in cerebral palsy are trauma such as skull fractures, infections such as meningitis and encephalitis, poisons, and anoxia. It is believed that approximately 50 percent or more of the cases of cerebral palsy have their origin during the birth process.

ASSOCIATED DISORDERS

Problems which commonly accompany cerebral palsy include mental retardation, learning disabilities, emotional problems, seizures, visual impairments, auditory and speech disorders, and orthopedic difficulties. Approximately 50 to 60 percent of cerebral palsied children are mentally retarded.

The children who are not retarded are usually considered capable of achievement within regular school programs. Many of these children, however, demonstrate certain behaviors suggestive of learning disabilities. These behavioral characteristics include hyperactivity, short attention span, perseveration, low frustration to tolerance, impulsivity, and distractibility.

Emotional problems are often exhibited at various times in the life span of the cerebral palsied individual. During adolescence, it is frequent for the youngster to lose some acquired skills. A spurt of bone growth without concomitant muscular development may temporarily prevent walking. Depression and withdrawal may occur as the teenager anguishes over the loss of skills which demand so much energy to obtain initially.

Seizures occur in 25 to 35 percent of individuals with cerebral palsy. A similar proportion of these people also demonstrate strabismus, a squinting resulting from imbalance of the eye muscles. Refractive errors such as nearsightedness or farsightedness are also common. Prevalance figures for speech defects as high as 70 percent have been reported for cerebral palsied children. Orthopedic problems are also common and often the result of continual muscular contractions. These contractions produce skeletal deformities by the constant pressure the muscles inflict on the bones.

ASSESSMENT AND CLASSIFICATION

The nonambulatory cerebral palsied adult is obviously handicapped. Impairment is seldom diagnosed at birth because there are so few meaningful abnormal neurological signs at that time (Bobath & Bobath, 1975; Denhoff, 1976). The hyperirritability or excessively listless infant is watched carefully for further evidence of brain damage, but such characteristics do not guarantee cerebral palsy. Signs evident during the first few weeks of life which are suggestive of neuromotor disturbance include cyanosis, excessive startle reflex, strabismus, and jaundice. The diagnosis of cerebral palsy continues, however, as the child grows and develops.

The neurological examination of infants and children includes an assessment of reflexes and observation of muscle tone and quality of movement. Infants and children are also diagnosed by developmental progress. Developmental diagnosis involves an evaluation of the onset of certain behaviors, many of which are motor. In the earlier discussion of motor development it was pointed out that the ability to sit without support was normally achieved at 7 months. It is considered abnormal if the child cannot sit alone

Spastic gait

FIGURE 22-4
Spastic gait.

by 10 months; however, the average age of acquiring independent sitting by cerebral palsied children is estimated at 20.4 months.

A number of methods of classifying cerebral palsied individuals have been offered (Denhoff, 1976). The two systems most frequently used are the clinical method and the topographical method.

Clinical Classification
This system classifies on the basis of deviations in motor capabilities. The American Academy of Cerebral Palsy has recommended six subcategories for the clinical classification system.

1. *Spasticity* An exaggerated stretch reflex (when the arm reaches forward it is pulled backward by the stretch reflex), poorly coordinated and jerky movements, and hypertonicity. Accounts for 50 to 60 percent of the total cerebral palsied population.

2. *Athetosis* Slow, irregular, uncontrollable, and twisting movement, particularly in the fingers and wrist (involuntary movement occurs with voluntary exertion). When calm and well rested, the athetoid's gait may be surprisingly coordinated. Accounts for about 20 percent of cerebral palsied individuals.

3. *Ataxia* Poor motor coordination and balance (high steps, stumbling, lurching). It is estimated that 1 to 10 percent of cerebral palsied victims are ataxic.

4. *Rigidity* Increased resistance to passive movement through the complete range of the movement (both flexor and extension muscles contract simultaneously). About 4 percent of all cerebral palsied are afflicted with rigidity.

5. *Tremor* Involuntary shaking movements. About 2 percent of individuals with cerebral palsy are afflicted with tremor.

6. *Mixed type* About 15 to 40 percent of all cerebral palsied individuals exhibit more than one type of cerebral palsy. For example, spasticity and athetosis often coexist in some body parts. Also, rigidity and ataxia are occasionally combined.

Topographical Classification

Topographical classification is often used with clinical designations. The part of the body affected by the neuromotor disability is the basis of the topographical system. *Hemiplegia* refers to motor dysfunction, which is confined to one side of the body. It accounts for 35 to 40 percent of cerebral palsy cases. *Quadriplegia* is the term used to denote disability in all four limbs and represents 15 to 20 percent of cerebral palsied individuals. *Diplegia* is also a condition involving the four extremities but the legs are more involved than the arms. Between 10 and 20 percent of all cerebral palsied persons are diplegic. Paraplegia refers to dysfunction only in the legs and is implicated in 10 to 20 percent of cerebral palsy cases.

EDUCATIONAL INTERVENTION AND TREATMENT APPROACHES

Medical Treatment

Since cerebral palsy has been considered an aggregate of handicaps, it follows that effective management of the condition has an interdisciplinary focus. The neurosurgeon is occasionally involved in attempts to relieve severe rigidity or spasticity. The procedures usually include creating lesions within the basal ganglia of the brain in order to destroy certain groups of nerve cells which control motor functioning. The use of drugs in the management of cerebral palsy motor disorders is in the formative stages, but much energy has been directed toward this type of treatment for athetosis and spasticity. Surgery may be appropriate if one of three objectives can be realized: (1) cosmetic improvement, (2) reduced contractions which prevent subsequent structural deformity, or (3) improvement in motor performance. If surgery is not appropriate, bracing may be prescribed in order to provide support to the individual, prevent or remedy deformities, or to regulate involuntary movements.

Speech Therapy

An integral part of the total treatment in the management program for cerebral palsy is speech therapy. This is necessary since good oral communication greatly enhances successful habilitation. Occupational therapy is also fundamental to the interdisciplinary nature of programs for the cerebral palsied. Occupational therapists focus on manipulative skills as a prelude to self-help skills such as toileting, eating, dressing, and undressing. The cerebral palsied individual might also be aided in managing a typewriter or alphabet word board by the occupational therapist.

Physical Therapy

A substantial portion of treatment programs for cerebral palsy is devoted to physical therapy. The physical therapist emphasizes posture and locomotion skills such as walking. This therapist in particular works closely with the orthopedic physician in the overall muscle education program, which might include surgery or bracing. Contemporary physical therapists are eclectic and borrow from several prominent theories of therapy.

EPILEPSY

Epilepsy has been defined as a "recurrent loss or impairment of consciousness which may be accompanied by muscular movements ranging from a simple twitching of the eyelids to a convulsive shaking of the entire body" (Argangio, 1978). Epilepsy is derived from the Greek word meaning "to be seized." The direct cause of an epileptic seizure is a disturbance in the normal pattern of an electrical discharge in the brain cells. The disturbance arises and spreads to other areas of the cortex, producing motor abnormalities. Major and minor seizures have been described in the writings of Hippocrates in the fifth century B.C. Among famous people thought to have been epileptic are Alexander the Great, Julius Caesar, Buddha, Napoleon, and Tchaikovsky.

PREVALENCE AND CAUSES OF EPILEPSY

The figures for epilepsy are unclear, although a common estimate is 0.5 percent of the population (Haslam, 1975). Epilepsy is usually evident in childhood. About 90 percent of all patients develop their first symptom prior to age 20.

The causes are not clear. Indeed, the largest category of epilepsy in terms of causes is the ideopathic or unknown group. A genetic factor in epilepsy has been a matter of some debate, but most experts recognize this possibility. It has been shown repeatedly that convulsive disorders do seem to run in families, a finding which supports but does not prove the genetic basis of epilepsy.

RELATIONSHIP TO INTELLECTUAL DEVELOPMENT

There are no specific common intellectual characteristics of persons with epilepsy. Although there is a higher incidence of mental slowness in the epileptic than in the nonepileptic population, there is simply no universal relationship between the two phenomena. Mental retardation exhibited by some individuals is not a result of the accompanying epilepsy, but it may well be related to the brain damage which was present prior to the epilepsy.

478   Neither the severity nor the frequency of seizures correlates appreciably with IQ scores. A child with as many as 100 attacks a day may still have normal or even superior intelligence. Other individuals with only one or two seizures a year may be institutionalized for mental retardation. Some cognitive deterioration may occur in patients with severe and frequent major epileptic attacks because of repeated insults to the brain as a consequence of the seizures.

ASSESSMENT AND CLASSIFICATION

When epilepsy is suspected, the physician initiates a comprehensive medical examination. This examination consists of a detailed medical history, neurological examination, assessment of blood cell counts and chemistry, blood sugar determination, x-rays of the skull, and an EEG study (Livingston, 1972). Behavior features of the seizures are also described. The EEG results are used as a part of a total examination and are not regarded as the only diagnostic methodology. The incidence of normal EEG findings in young children with grand mal epilepsy is exceedingly high.

The classification used by educators is based upon the clinical observations of the seizure as well as the EEG findings. The forms of epileptic seizures are:

1. *Grand mal.* Major motor seizures which account for 80 percent of all epileptic seizures. Three stages may occur: the aura, or period of warning that precedes the seizure, the tonic phase (loss of consciousness during which the muscles become contracted), and the clonic phase (convulsive phase of violent contractions).

2. *Petit mal.* Characterized by a brief loss of consciousness from five to thirty seconds. This may occur in as many as 23 percent of all epileptic children. The simple petit mal consists of sudden vacant staring and occasional rolling of the eyes back into the head. The clonic petit mal seizure involves minor jerky movements of the head and upper limbs. Petit mal spells with automatisms include repetitions such as smacking of the lips, chewing, and swallowing movements.

3. *Psychomotor epilepsy.* Characterized by behaviors ranging from blank stares to varied bizarre psychic and motor performances. The person does not lose consciousness but appears to be unaware of the behavior.

Epileptic seizures do not occur randomly. There are several factors which are acknowledged precipitants of seizures for individuals. For instance, some persons have almost all their seizures during sleep, while others are characterized by daytime seizures. The physiological changes which occur during the menstrual cycle are also considered precipitants of seizures. Many women have their seizures just before or during the menstrual flow. Sudden exposure to light may also elicit a seizure. Other factors which are related to the onset of seizures in known epileptics are hyperventilation, the sudden withdrawal of antiepileptic drugs, fever, fatigue, and allergies. Epileptic seizures do not appear to be precipitated by vigorous physical activity or focused concentration.

EDUCATIONAL INTERVENTION AND TREATMENT APPROACHES

Drug Therapy

The most common procedure for the treatment of epileptic seizures is drug therapy. Although a wide variety of anticonvulsant drugs have been employed, the two agents used most often are phenobarbital and Dilantin. Richens (1976) has indicated that for the majority of epileptics long-term drug therapy is the only practical form of treatment. Drugs do not remove the basic cause of the seizure but rather free the individual from the attacks. In approximately 50 percent of epileptics, full control of seizures is realized with anticonvulsant drugs, and 20 to 30 percent achieve significant control although not elimination of all seizures.

The Role of the Educator

The educator may play a significant role in the management of epilepsy. The dispensing of midday anticonvulsant medication must be ensured. The teacher can also report a number of observations regarding the child's behavior which might be important to the physician. If the child is excessively drowsy, it is necessary to determine whether or not it is the result of too much medication. Also, the teacher must be aware of the first-aid procedures for a grand mal seizure. Furthermore, frank discussion of seizures, if they occur during the school day, can result in educational gains for nonepileptic children, since the stigma associated with epilepsy is often the greatest handicap for the individual.

TABLE 22-1
First-aid Procedures for Grand Mal Seizures

1. Don't move the patient to a new location; just see that he can't hurt himself.

2. Loosen clothing around neck.

3. If possible, patient should be on side to allow mucus and saliva to flow from mouth.

4. Insertion of object into mouth is not necessary unless patient has a history of tongue biting. If object is indicated use a firm blunt object such as folded leather belt.

5. If patient's behavior in postconvulsive phase can be harmful to others or themselves, restraint may be necessary.

6. If seizure was brief, regular activity can be resumed.

7. If seizure was long and/or patient is drowsy, allow rest.

SOURCE: Livingston, 1972, pp. 133.

Behavioral Intervention

Epilepsy may also be managed by behavioral techniques. Mostofsky (1978) has stated, "It is now possible to state as a matter of fact that epileptic seizures respond to behavioral intervention." The four categories of therapeutic strategies highlighted by Mostofsky include traditional psychotherapy, reward management, psychophysiological procedures, and cortical biofeedback.

Social Normalization

Epilepsy constitutes a motor dysfunction only when a seizure is actually occurring. The day-to-day problems faced by an epileptic are often associated with the psychological parameters of the disorder and may prove to be a greater burden than the seizures. Epileptics have reported discrimination associated with the stigma of epilepsy. They have difficulty finding employment and are often not insurable under workers' compensation. Until several years ago, many states maintained laws forbidding marriage for the epileptic.

Parents must create an atmosphere of natural and relaxed affection for such children. Children may interpret other attitudes of misguided parents as meaning they are unwanted and different. Overprotected epileptics are not likely to experience optimal growth socially and emotionally. It has been argued that for most epileptics with controlled seizures, even body contact sports are not associated with additional risk (Livingston & Berman, 1974). To prohibit such participation may have detrimental ramifications in terms of psychological adjustment. It appears that if the total therapy program, medical and psychological, is adequate, the majority of epileptic individuals can be rehabilitated to the extent that they live essentially normal lives.

SPINA BIFIDA

Spina bifida are Latin words which mean "spine split in two." It is a generic term for a group of congenital malformations of the central nervous system. More specifically, spina bifida is an abnormality of spine development characterized by the failure of the spinal cord to close at the lower end.

PREVALENCE AND CAUSES OF SPINA BIFIDA

Spina bifida was originally described in 2000 B.C. (Anderson & Spain, 1977). Until very recently the majority of infants born with the condition died within weeks of birth, either from infection of the central nervous system or from hydrocephalus. The present incidence figures are approximately 2 to 3 per 1,000 births, a frequency slightly greater than cerebral palsy.

The brain and spinal cord begin as a single sheet of cells in the normally developing human embryo. By the end of the third week of pregnancy the sheet has enlarged and forms a longitudinal groove. In the fourth week, the groove deepens and folds over. The sides of the groove will eventually fuse, forming a closed tube rather than an open groove. The newly formed elongated tube is called the neural tube and will eventually become the brain and the spinal cord. It is somewhat later that the meninges (the covering tissue) and bony spinal column develop.

With spina bifida, a section of the developing neural tube fails to close at its lower end. The spinal cord and the surrounding tissues at that point remain immature and improperly formed. Often associated with spina bifida is a second problem, hydrocephalus. Hydrocephaly refers to a fluid buildup within the cavities of the brain. If left unchecked, this will result in brain damage and mental retardation.

The etiology of spina bifida is even less clear than cerebral palsy and epilepsy. The available evidence suggests a complicated interaction of genetic and environmental factors (Allum, 1975). Support for a genetic cause comes from a number of sources. Sex differences in spina bifida are striking; three girls are born with the problem for every boy (Anderson & Spain, 1977). Ethnic variations also are suggestive of a genetic component in spina bifida. There is a high incidence in the United Kingdom, northern India, and northern Egypt, while a low frequency is reported in Japan and among blacks (Anderson & Spain, 1977). These data support a genetic factor rather than environmental influences because migrants tend to retain the incidence of the areas from which they originate. Finally, family studies provide some evidence for the influence of genetics in spina bifida, since a sibling of an affected child is 7 to 15 times more likely to be affected than is an unrelated child (Anderson & Spain, 1977).

ASSESSMENT AND CLASSIFICATION

The classification of spina bifida has two main divisions, spina bifida occulta and spina bifida cystica. Spina bifida cystica is further subdivided into meningocele and myelomeningocele.

Spina Bifida Occulta

This is a failure of the vertebral bones to fully close, but the spinal cord and membranes are usually normal. At the site of the spinal defect there is sometimes a slight swelling, a dimple, or patch of hair. This condition is very common, occurring in 10 percent of the population, but it is rarely associated with any disability.

Spina Bifida Cystica

The spinal cord tissue protrudes through an opening in spina bifida cystica. In the meningocele condition, the cord is usually not impaired as it remains in its normal position. The meninges (nerve covering), however, bulge through a gap in the spine and form a cystic sac, which is usually covered by normal skin. Approximately 15 to 25 percent of the children with spina bifida cystica demonstrate this variety.

In the myelomenigocele variety, both the meninges and the spinal cord have protruded through unfused vertebrae. The cord not only protrudes but is not formed adequately, remaining a permanent and irreversible neuro-

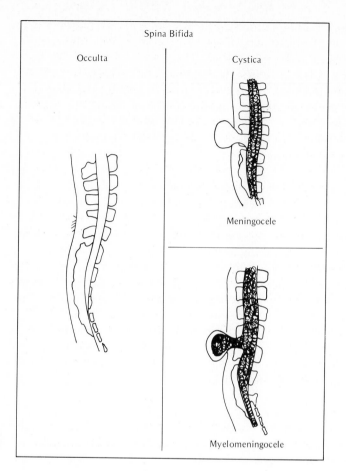

FIGURE 22-5
Spina bifida occulta and
spina bifida cystica.

logical problem. Weakness or paralysis of the lower limbs is associated with this condition. With weak muscles, braces may allow the child to walk, but total paralysis necessitates the use of a wheelchair. Other problems which can be associated with this form of spina bifida include sensory loss of the skin, urinary and bowel control difficulties, kidney infections, hydrocephalus, and accompanying mental retardation.

EDUCATIONAL INTERVENTION AND TREATMENT APPROACHES
Surgical techniques are available for controlling hydrocephalus. A shunt is installed in the head to drain off excessive cerebrospinal fluids. This prevents the fluid buildup and returns the fluid to the brain and spinal column.

As far as repair of the myelomeningocele, little can be done. Since the spinal cord is not formed adequately, there is permanent dysfunction—often paralysis, and lack of control of elimination. Braces, wheelchairs, and other prosthetic devices are helpful in management, but normal function is usually not possible.

The management of children with spina bifida is expensive, frustrating, and time-consuming (Myers, 1975). Among others, the professional skills of the neurosurgeon, neurologist, pediatrician, urologist, general surgeon, orthopedic surgeon, physical therapist, nurse, and social worker are required. Surgery is necessary for spina bifida meningocele, since the sac is usually removed. In the case of myelomenigocele, prompt surgery is required to close the skin defect in order that infection not arise. Orthopedic surgery is often necessary to lengthen, shorten, or transplant tendons in order to avoid deformity. Physical therapists help affected children use their limbs as effectively as possible with braces, if necessary. Pressure sores can develop because of a reduced sensitivity of the skin. Padded chairs, for example, should be used. If pressure sores are not treated, infection will occur. The child also faces the full ramifications of problems associated with bowel and bladder disorders. The physical problems have been treated by urinary diversions via surgery, applications of devices such as catheters, diet, or special medication.

The intellectual development of children with spina bifida tends to be below average but does not necessarily vary with the severity of the physical handicap. There are, of course, children with this disorder who score well above average on intellectual measures. Spina bifida children can thus profit from schooling appropriate to their intellectual, social, and emotional abilities. Such children also require support from teachers, parents, counselors, and social workers in order to cope effectively with physical disabilities and accompanying inconveniences.

POLIOMYELITIS

The deformed limbs of Egyptian mummies provide evidence of the possibility that poliomyelitis may have occurred nearly 6,000 years ago (Huckstep, 1975). In 1559 a painting by Brueghel depicts a crippled beggar who may have suffered from polio. The first known description of poliomyelitis was provided by Underwood in 1789. One of the most famous persons affected by polio was Franklin D. Roosevelt.

Poliomyelitis is an infectious disease caused by one of three types of ultramicroscopic viruses. The virus destroys the motor cells of the spinal cord and results in temporary or permanent paralysis of the muscles. The muscles affected depend on the level of the spinal cord involved but lower limbs tend to be paralyzed more often than upper limbs.

Although major epidemics of polio in the early twentieth century and again in 1952 left thousands of people paralyzed in the United States, the disease is virtually eradicated today in North America. Polio vaccines developed in the 1950s by Salk and Sabin resulted in large-scale immunization programs. Sherrill (1976) has indicated the general prognosis for polio as follows:

1. About 6 percent of polio victims die.

2. About 14 percent have severe paralysis.

3.   About 30 percent have mild after-effects.

4.   Complete recovery occurs in about 50 percent.

For example, the number of severely paralyzed persons with polio in Uganda is about 30,000 and the number of untreated patients in Nigeria has been estimated to be between 200,000 and 300,000 (Huckstep, 1975).

JUVENILE RHEUMATOID ARTHRITIS

Rheumatism is a general term for a group of disorders affecting muscles and joints. It includes arthritis, meaning an inflammation of the joints. Rheumatoid arthritis is the number one crippler in the United States, affecting over 3,000,000 persons. It may strike at any age and is referred to as juvenile rheumatoid arthritis when it affects children and adolescents. The average age of onset of juvenile rheumatoid arthritis is 6 years and affects three to five times as many girls as boys. The etiology is generally unknown, but estimates of the number of children in the United States with the disease range from 100,000 to 300,000 (Miller, 1975).

The symptoms of this type of arthritis are variable, since the joint involvement may be sudden and severe with painful swelling, or it may begin gradually with joint stiffness and limited movement particularly in the morning. Only one joint or several joints may be affected. Commonly accompanying symptoms include fever, irritability, poor appetite, anemia, and rash. In addition, complications with the heart, liver, and spleen do occur with children. Inflammation of the eyes is also a possibility which must be treated to prevent blindness.

Management of juvenile rheumatoid arthritis includes medication, such as aspirin and gold salts. Cortisone is also prescribed but should be a last resort, since side effects may result in the cessation of growth, obesity, and brittle bones. Physical therapy is also important to maintain an improved joint flexibility and muscle strength. When the disease is in the active phase, the child will voluntarily restrict painful movement. In severe cases the child may be confined to bed. With less severe pain, teachers should be aware that arthritic children may wish to get up and walk around the classroom periodically to relieve the discomfort created by prolonged immobility. In general, the child should be encouraged to participate in school activities to the greatest extent possible. The psychological management of the arthritic child is also essential, since they are often depressed.

The prognosis for full recovery in children is good, particularly if only one or two joints are involved. About 60 to 70 percent of the children will be free from the disease after a period of ten years and only 10 percent will be left with any significant functional limitations.

MUSCULAR DYSTROPHY

Muscular dystrophy is a group of disorders that is characterized by the following features:

1. Increased weakness and wasting of the muscles

2. Progressively debilitating disorders which may cease but will not improve spontaneously

3. A hereditary familial condition which is usually transmitted by females who are not themselves affected (Milhorat, 1967)

Approximately 250,000 people in the United States suffer from the muscular dystrophies, which were reported in medical literature in the early part of the nineteenth century (Walton, 1963).

Although a number of types of muscular dystrophy have been identified, the most common and severe form is Duchenne muscular dystrophy. Although this disease may occur as late as the third decade of life, the onset is usually in the first three years of life. The victims are almost always boys (Bleck, 1975).

The earliest symptoms are decreased physical activity, clumsiness in walking, a tendency to fall frequently, and difficulty in climbing steps. An awkward side-to-side waddling gait will soon develop. The child may actually appear to gain in muscular development as fat and connective tissue replace degenerating muscle fibers. Within ten years of the first symptoms the child will be forced to use a wheelchair. Death usually occurs in the late teens as the result of respiratory infection or cardiac failure.

Management of the Duchenne type of muscular dystrophy is particularly frustrating because there is no known cure and death is inevitable. Drug therapy has been employed, but success has been limited to the treatment of respiratory ailments. Physical activity throughout the course of the disease, to the extent possible, is believed to slow the process somewhat, but once the child is confined to a wheelchair or bed, deterioration appears particularly rapid.

A second type of muscular dystrophy, and the most common form in adults, is facioscapular-humeral muscular dystrophy. It affects males and females equally, and the onset is usually during adolescence. The major symptom of this disease is a progressive weakness of the shoulder and face muscles, which result in difficulties lifting the arms above the head and produces dropping cheeks and pointing lips. Hip and thigh muscles are occasionally affected, and this creates the characteristic waddling gait. The prognosis is good compared to other forms of muscular dystrophy, since deterioration is slow and many sufferers live until normal old age. In some cases the disease may arrest itself.

A third form of muscular dystrophy is called juvenile or limb girdle muscular dystrophy. The onset is generally in adolescence or early adulthood, and again both sexes are equally affected. Muscular degeneration follows a similar course to Duchenne muscular dystrophy but is slower. Death results from cardiac failure or respiratory infection, but the person is much older at death than the typical victim suffering from the Duchenne variety.

SUMMARY

Motor development, while not necessarily a foundation to other areas of functioning, is viewed by most professionals as important in its own right. Most authorities believe that young children initially act, interact, and react to environmental demands through movement. The sequence of motor development is generally consistent across children, with new skills emerging for the first two years, and subsequent development consisting primarily of qualitative changes.

Four generic forms of motor dysfunction were identified: clumsiness, physical unfitness, obesity, and postural deviations. Special educators should be aware of these conditions in order to adequately program for individualized instruction.

Specific forms of motor dysfunction include cerebral palsy, epilepsy, spina bifida, poliomyelitis, juvenile rheumatoid arthritis, and muscular dystrophy. An important skill for the special educator is the ability to work cooperatively with an interdisciplinary educational team, which may include physicians, physical and occupational therapists, speech therapists, and counselors. Educational goals include the careful integration of these services, and classroom and home carry-over to ensure maximum development is essential.

James W. Tawney

CHAPTER 23
SEVERE, PROFOUND, AND MULTIPLE DYSFUNCTION

(Courtesy of Chuck Zovko.)

P.L. 94–142 has, perhaps, had its greatest impact on those who have severe, profound, and multiple handicaps. This group has been given top priority for educational services and in many cases will experience great changes in how and where they will be educated. Until recently, custodial care, rather than educational programming, was provided to these individuals. Fortunately, things are changing rapidly. Contemporary special education for this group is the antithesis of custodial services: highly structured educational programs focus on training skills that will lead to independent living. This chapter will discuss the nature of severe, profound, and multiple handicaps and the emerging roles of teachers in this context, and we will explore the implications for the training of teachers and delivery of service.

DEFINING THE SEVERELY HANDICAPPED

As in most areas of exceptionality, there is no single definition that serves everybody's purpose. "Severely handicapped" includes persons with diverse characteristics but who have in common certain severe limitations in sensory response mechanisms that require special arrangements if they are to progress at all. Two selected definitions should suffice to illustrate the common dimensions of severe handicap.

Sontag, Burke, and York (1973) describe the severely handicapped as

> those who are not toilet trained; aggress toward others; do not attend to even the most pronounced social stimuli; self-mutilate; ruminate; self-stimulate; do not walk, speak, hear, or see; manifest durable and intense temper tantrums; are not under even the most rudimentary forms of verbal controls; do not imitate; manifest minimally controlled seizures; and/or have extremely brittle medical existences. (p. 22)

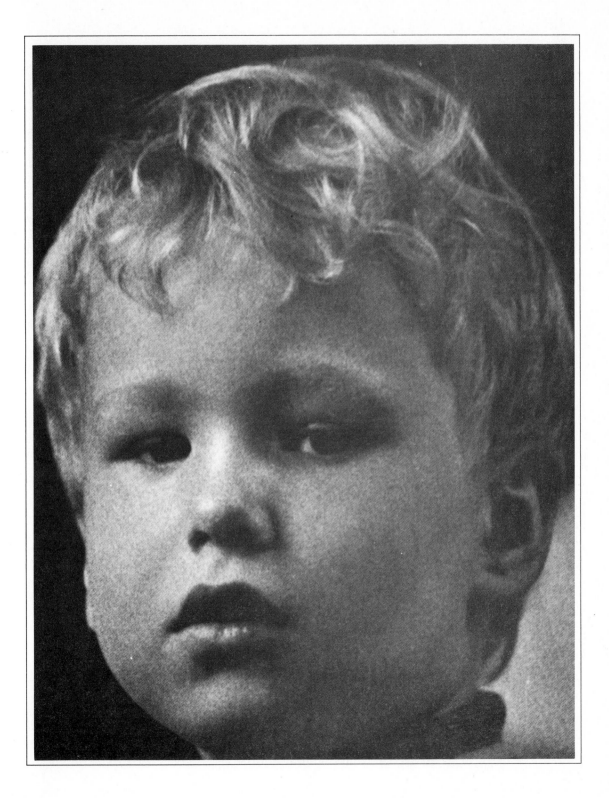

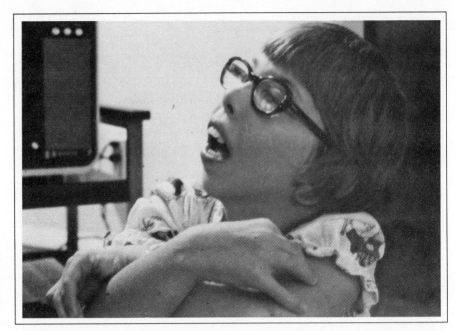

P.L. 94-142 mandates a free appropriate public education to severely and multihandicapped children. (*Pennsylvania Department of Public Welfare, Office of Mental Retardation.*)

The Office of Special Education in the U.S. Department of Education has proposed this definition for the severely handicapped:

> The severely handicapped child is one who because of the intensity of his physical, mental, and emotional problems, or a combination of such problems, needs educational, social, psychological, and medical services beyond those which have been offered by traditional regular and special educational programs, in order to maximize his full potential for useful and meaningful participation in society and for self-fulfillment. Such children include those classified as seriously emotionally disturbed (schizophrenic and autistic), profoundly and severely mentally retarded, and those with two or more serious handicapped conditions such as the mentally retarded deaf and the mentally retarded blind.
>
> Such children may possess severe language and/or perceptual cognitive deprivations, and evidence a number of abnormal behaviors including: a failure to attend to even the most pronounced social stimuli, self-mutilation, self-stimulation, durable and intense temper tantrums, absence of even the most rudimentary forms of verbal control, and may also have an extremely fragile physiological condition.

PREVALENCE AND CAUSES OF SEVERE HANDICAP

As with the other categories of exceptionality, estimates of how many individuals are considered severe, profound, or multiply handicapped vary depending on the definition and methods used to estimate prevalence. The U.S. Office of Education has reported that approximately 0.8 percent of the school-age population falls into the moderate and severe range of retardation: Kauffman and Payne (1975) estimate the severe-profound incidence to be 0.1 percent.

It should be evident that "severe handicap" does not really refer to a separate kind of disorder but rather to the *degree* of handicap. Retardation, emotional disturbance, blindness, and so forth all suggest different types of handicaps, whereas severe handicap refers to pronounced deficits in one or several areas of functioning. Thus, the causes of severe handicaps include the causes of each of the handicapping conditions presented in previous chapters.

Generally speaking, severe handicap results from relatively extreme problems in the following:

1. Hereditary and congenital defects resulting in marked problems in the development of the central nervous system, sensory apparatus, or response mechanisms.

2. Pronounced complications before or during pregnancy, including drastic deficits in the mother's nutrition, exposure to drugs or radiation, prolonged and difficult labor, and damage caused by physical trauma and disease.

3. Damage incurred after the birth of the child caused by accident, poisoning, or extremes in nutrition and environmental deprivation

As stated earlier, severe handicap may refer to marked problems in one or more areas of functioning, for example, motoric or sensory capabilities. In the case of multiple handicap, the problems in the several areas may be relatively less pronounced when separately considered. However, several moderate handicaps in combination can produce a severe handicap. Many of the children considered severely handicapped have limitations across several areas and thus experience great developmental and behavioral difficulties.

CHARACTERISTICS AND CLASSIFICATION
For purposes of classification, severe and profound handicaps can be grouped into four main clusters: developmental retardation, behavior disorders, motor and sensory handicaps, and multiple dysfunctions. Each of these is briefly discussed here. Notice the commonality of behavioral limitations among the groups. When the handicap becomes severe, even in one area, there is a "spread" of dysfunction and many complications arise. Thus, severe limitations in motoric functioning can produce related difficulties in communication, social functioning, and even intellectual development. Thus, handicap is seldom pure.

DEVELOPMENTAL RETARDATION
The term "developmental retardation" is derived from Bijou's (1966) functional analysis of retarded behavior, which focuses on observable character-

istics rather than hypothetical underlying conditions. Tawney (1972) proposed the following descriptive behaviors of severe developmental retardation:

1. Little or no vocal behavior

2. Limited motor gestural behavior

3. Limited self-help skills

4. Inconsistent or no bowel or bladder control

5. No obtained score on a standardized test because none has ever been administered or because these persons are nontestable in the testing situation

6. Limited social interaction with other children and adults

7. No reciprocal social reinforcement of others in their environment

8. High rate of stereotyped behaviors

9. High rate of disruptive social behavior

10. Low rate of "constructive play behavior"

11. Attendant multiple handicaps

BEHAVIOR DISORDERS

Kauffman (1977) lists these attributes which generally distinguish severe emotional problems from ones that are mild or moderate in degree. He describes severely disturbed children who

> exhibit an identifiable cluster of clinical symptoms, bizarre or grossly inappropriate behavior, self-injurious behavior, self-stimulation or preoccupation with manipulating objects, stereotyped movements, severe disorders or absence of speech or language, disturbances of biological function, avoidance of eye contact, and unresponsiveness or unrelatedness to other people, whose intelligence is in the retarded range and are functionally retarded, although they may exhibit a few very remarkable skills that lead one to believe that they have normal or even superior intelligence. (p. 29)

Thus, to the observer, the behaviors of severely developmentally retarded or severely disturbed children will be apparent. The verification of intellectual functioning will, in most cases, be suspect—a factor which is incorporated into Tawney's (1972) set of descriptors.

MOTOR AND SENSORY HANDICAPS

The behavioral attributes of these children are described in previous chapters. These youngsters, whose primary handicapping condition is not severe

Intervention for the multihandicapped includes strategies to compensate for severe sensory impairments, such as blindness and deafness. (*Courtesy of Elizabeth A. Llewellyn.*)

developmental retardation, are presently served by public education, either in community public day classes in large population centers or in regional residential schools. The least restrictive environment provision of P.L. 94-142 applies to these settings. It is sufficient here to note that many institutionalized children will be returned to their local communities and will be the responsibility of present and future generations of public school teachers.

EDUCATIONAL INTERVENTION AND TREATMENT APPROACHES

PLACEMENT OPTIONS

Institutional Settings

The plaintiffs in *Pennsylvania Association for Retarded Children v. Commonwealth of Pennsylvania* included residents of the state institution, Pennhurst. That suit was not directed at conditions in Pennhurst but toward the exclusionary policy which did not allow such children to attend community-based public school programs. That outcome, then, established public education programs. Recent developments in another case, *Halderman and the United States v. Pennhurst State School and Hospital,* strengthen the basis for community-based educational services, for the decision challenges the justification of large residential institutions. Ferlenger (1978) reports that in the December 23, 1977 decision, the presiding judge ruled that the very existence of the institution violated federal and state laws and set into motion steps to close Pennhurst. While it may take many years to completely phase out this institution, and many more years to influence the closing of other large institutions, the court decision should ensure that young children will never again be institutionalized in large public facilities.

P.L. 94-142 permits states to contract with private residential and community-based school programs. The state education agency is responsible for those programs which must offer services equal to those provided in the public system. The continued existence of these programs is questionable at this time, since it is reasonable to expect that wherever feasible the public schools will provide services rather than contract with these outside agencies. Thus, public education (within the local school district) is and should continue to be the predominant setting for programs for the severely handicapped.

Special-Class Placement

While nearly all professionals support public education for the severely handicapped, there is not a consensus on the maximum extent of effective integration of severely and nonhandicapped students. Smith and Arkens (1974) present representative arguments for special-class placement:

1. Needed special environments to house prosthetics and other apparatus

2. Requisite and expensive alterations of the physical environment in regular schools to accommodate the needs of these children

3. Centrally located space for the therapists who provide supporting services

4. Inability of teachers in regular classes to attend to the needs of severely retarded students

5. Inability of resource rooms to provide a number of additional services for the severely retarded

6. Loss of intervention by therapists who must serve children dispersed throughout the school system

7. Need for highly trained teachers who demonstrate skills not emitted by regular teachers

8. Lack of data to verify that integration will result in positive outcomes in social acceptance by nonhandicapped persons

9. Curriculum needs for the severely handicapped are divergent from the regular curriculum

Brown, Wilcox, Sontag, Vincent, Dodd, & Gruenewald (1977) state that "educational service delivery models for severely handicapped students must closely approximate the best educational service delivery models used for nonhandicapped students" (p. 195). They note that the most severely handicapped students are served in self-contained residential and day schools, both private and public, residential facilities, self-contained units and classes within public schools, and regular classes in regular schools.

They reject all but the last two options. Their criterion for a least restrictive environment is "settings that encourage and support extensive long-term interaction between handicapped and nonhandicapped students (p. 196). Further, they suggest that:

1. Maximum interaction between handicapped and nonhandicapped should be facilitated.

2. The concentration of handicapped in a school should be no greater extent than in the population.

3. Interaction should occur among chronological-age peers.

4. Ratner than the public schools' financing extensive architectural barriers, severely handicapped students should be taught to adapt to existing barriers.

5. Severely handicapped students should share the same facilities, including transportation.

These two perspectives focus attention on the special class. Smith and Arkens (1974) give priority to special environments which enable highly trained teachers and supportive service personnel to serve children efficiently, and presumably, effectively. Brown et al. (1977) emphasize integration of handicapped and nonhandicapped students and agree with Smith and Arkens on the need for a coordinated and functional curriculum and access to requisite support personnel.

CURRICULUM CONSIDERATIONS

Educational services for the severely handicapped are based on the premise that these people will, as adults, assume a role as independent and economically productive members of society. Curricula developed for use with these individuals typically focus on objectives which are designed to achieve such independence. While this may seem a Utopian view, those professionals who are responsible for the education of these persons consider that independence is within the realm of possibility.

Coordinated Life Curriculum

Brown et al. (1977), have suggested, as have many others, that the severely handicapped require a coordinated life curriculum. Today, while curriculum and intervention programs exist for infants and preschoolers, for school-age students, and for vocational education adults, a coordinated sequential curriculum does not exist. Instead, programs have been developed in selected areas such as language development (Bricker, Dennison, & Bricker, 1976; Guess, Baer, & Sailor, 1976–1977; Kent, 1974; Tawney & Hipsher, 1970). Curriculum guides abound (Ohio Department of Mental Health and Mental Retardation, 1977). Task analyses and instructional strategies have been developed (Fredericks et al., 1976). One recently developed program (Tawney, Knapp, O'Reilly, & Pratt, 1979) integrated instructional procedures and programs of direct instruction in many areas of concept and skill development.

Functional Skills

Common to the majority of programs is an emphasis on the development of functional skills, that is, those necessary for adults to live independently in society. The most comprehensive curricula cover a broad range of behavior from basic attending skills such as eye contact and observable responses to sounds through complex skill acquisitions such as concept development and preacademic skills. Existing curricula vary in the degree of specificity in instructional programs. Some present general strategies to follow; others are highly sequenced, that is, instructional tasks are broken into very small component parts, which are taught in highly programmed steps.

The content of instruction for severely handicapped children, particularly those whose primary handicapping condition is developmental retardation, is likely to include:

1. Basic attending skills

2. Basic motor response development as a mode for discrimination learning, for example, "Touch" or "Pick up"

3. Concept acquisition, discrimination, and generalization

4. Receptive language, for example, motor responses to verbal commands, for example, "Bring me the ball."

5. Expressive language, for example, consistent use of speech sounds, vocal identification of objects, such as "What is this?" "Ball."

6. Social-skill acquisition, for example, appropriate peer interaction, reciprocal play

7. Gross and fine motor development, for example, walking unassisted, beginning writing skill

8. Preacademic instruction in math and reading

9. Self-help skill development, for example, eating, grooming, and toileting

For older students or those who have mastered communication, self-management, and social development, curricula will typically include:

1. Appropriate use of community transportation systems

2. Cooking and home management

3. Vocational preparation

4. Age-appropriate social interaction skills (dating, sex education, and so forth)

INSTRUCTIONAL PROCEDURES

Systematic Instruction
Direct, or systematic, instructional procedures have emerged as the dominant method of teaching. These procedures have been derived from the experimental laboratory and, in part, from the direct instruction model for preschool education for disadvantaged students (Bereiter & Englemann, 1966). Systematic instruction materials and texts for the severely handicapped have been developed by Haring and Gentry (1976), McCormack, Chalmers, and Gregorian (undated), Snell (1978), and Tawney and Hipsher (1970). Systematic instruction incorporates many or all of these attributes:

1. List of instructional materials required for teaching sessions

2. Detailed analysis of learning tasks

3. Procedures for maintaining a high degree of instructional control

4. Expected child responses stated in behavioral terms

5. Planned, sequential instruction

6. Defined consequences for correct responses

7. Planned correction procedures to reduce the probability of error responses

8. Systematic use of selected instructional procedures such as fading, shaping, and prompting

9. Data-based decision making

BENEFITS OF EDUCATION TO SEVERELY RETARDED
In one court case after another, experts have testified to the educability of the severely retarded. What data have been provided to support this testimony? A complete answer to this question is not presently available.

Since educational programs were not established until 1972, no substantial data base yet exists on the academic performance of severely retarded students in public education settings. Instead, data on the educability of these students is based on single-subject research studies, a program of skill development, a longitudinal study of Down's syndrome children, studies on vocational-skill acquisition of severely disabled persons, parents' anecdotal reports (Lipman & Goldberg, 1973), and a recently completed curriculum validation project (Tawney, in press).

SINGLE-SUBJECT STUDIES

Single-subject studies report the behavior of one or a small number of students on clearly defined learning problems. These studies are conducted in experimental laboratories or in a laboratory setting in a school or institution. The studies described here have been selected because they illustrate the application of behavioral learning theory to communication skill.

Expressive and Receptive Language Production

Guess (1969) trained two institutionalized retarded subjects, ages 13.10 and 13.8 with IQs of 40 and 42 respectively, to point correctly to singular or plural objects, then to expressively label singular or plural sets. The children were trained to point to single or plural sets and reinforced for reversed labeling. The objective of this study was to determine whether receptive and expressive language production are interrelated. Both children, when taught to point to reverse-labeled pairs, continued to correctly label objects vocally, demonstrating independence in receptive and expressive repertoires. While this study left unanswered many questions concerning the facilitating effect of training one mode or the other, in either order (expressive, then receptive or vice versa), it demonstrated acquisition of a critical language function. In a subsequent study utilizing a different training mode (Guess & Baer, 1973), three of four children showed independence between receptive and expressive modes while a fourth youngster demonstrated a high degree of generalized ability.

ADAPTIVE SKILL DEVELOPMENT

Brown and his students at the University of Wisconsin, in conjunction with the Madison public schools, have reported a series of instructional program development activities conducted with moderately and severely handicapped students. A representative program (Certo, Schwartz, & Brown, 1975) taught ten students with an average IQ of 50 and an average chronological age of 17 to ride the Madison public bus system. This complex program was designed to teach independent use of the bus system in four phases: (1) riding a simulated bus in the classroom; (2) teaching students about the community, for example, places to get food, clothing, recreation, health services, and how to identify the appropriate bus to reach a selected place; (3) riding the bus to specific destinations on prepared bus route cards; (4) and riding the bus to destinations not on bus route cards. They report that all students acquired some degree of bus-riding skill; two were unable to ride without adult supervision, four were able to ride to specific destinations with a small group of peers, and four were able to ride without adult or peer assistance. This project is important in that it focuses on a specific functional skill, demonstrates a systematic training program, and demonstrates that some participants were able to acquire skills enabling them to become more independent. While some parts of the program are idiosyncratic to the Madison bus system, the general methodology provides a framework for others who wish to attempt a replication in their community.

THE DOWN'S SYNDROME PROJECT

The Down's Syndrome Project, initiated in 1971 at the Experimental Education Unit at the University of Washington, has received international attention. The project is notable in two respects: it has developed a behaviorally based long-term educational intervention program, and it has systematically assessed the development of groups of Down's syndrome children for an extended period of time.

The purpose of the intervention program is to accelerate the developmental growth of students and then to test periodically to determine the extent to which developmental gains are maintained over time. This question is of particular interest because historically it has been presumed that Down's syndrome persons show a decrease in intelligence and development as they increase in age.

Experimental Design

The academic program for the first group of students and for the infants currently entering the program is located in a model preschool at the university. When the first group of students reached school age, a class was created for them in the Seattle public schools (the primary program). To compare developmental growth, four groups of children are evaluated periodically:

1. Students once enrolled in the model preschool, now enrolled in the public schools

2. Students presently enrolled in the model preschool who will transfer to the public schools

3. Students never enrolled in the model preschool (but perhaps enrolled in another preschool program) and now enrolled in the public school primary program

4. Students never enrolled in the model preschool and not served in the Seattle primary program but enrolled in other programs in the state of Washington

These groups allow comparisons between children who have received early and continuous intervention with those who have not, and comparison of age-matched students. The subjects are periodically evaluated on standardized intelligence measures and the Down's Syndrome Performance Inventory and academic skills checklist, which was developed at the University of Washington.

Tentative Conclusions

Hayden and Haring (1976) report tentative conclusions from comparisons obtained during the 1974–1975 and 1975–1976 school years. Across all groups of subjects a decline in performance with increasing age was observed. However, when single subjects' performances are analyzed they indicate that children who were enrolled in their preschool program show increases in development as they grow older; that most children past preschool age continue to grow at or above normal rates, whether enrolled in a preschool program or not; and that model preschool graduates level off at about 95 percent of regular developmental rates while nonmodel preschool enrollees level off at about 61 percent of development.

Educational Impact

Again, the authors stressed the tentative nature of the conclusions they have drawn. However, if these students maintain high levels of functioning as they progress through adolescence into adulthood, and if present and future students (who will have the advantage of an increasingly sophisticated instructional technology) demonstrate an even higher level of performance, the persistent myth that Down's syndrome persons are retarded in life functioning will have been dispelled.

GOLD'S VOCATIONAL ASSEMBLY TASK STUDIES

Gold (1969) initated a research program to teach complex assembly tasks to retarded persons. His first study trained sixty-four retarded adolescents (experimental group IQ means of 46.31–48.06) to complete a fifteen-piece and a fourteen-piece assembly task (a bicycle brake) under different experimental conditions. These subjects, across all groups, learned the task to criterion (six out of eight consecutive correct responses) in 25.53 trials. Estimated time to criterion for each person was approximately two hours. Gold indicated that one of the most important outcomes of the study was the discrepancy between the subject's performance and the expectations of workshop personnel. Further, he indicated that prior to the implementation, workshop directors stated that the most capable of their employees would be incapable of completing the task. A subsequent study (Gold, 1976) utilized the same tasks with blind retarded subjects. Each of the 22 subjects learned the task in a mean of 59.5 trials (range 9–194) and produced the assembled brake at a mean rate of 12.38 (range 4.9–17.4) units per hour, with a mean number of 4.23 errors. This study, conducted with persons institutionalized for an average of 21.73 years, provides dramatic evidence of the learning capability of a severely and multiply handicapped population once they are taught to perform a task in a systematic way and with precisely defined procedures.

PROGRAMMED-ENVIRONMENTS CURRICULUM

The Study

Tawney (in press) reported the results of a process used to document the performance of students who were taught skills by teachers who were trained to criterion on the Programmed-Environments Curriculum. Data were collected daily by classroom teachers who were frequently observed by on-site trainers and periodically observed by a field coordinator. This project involved teachers located in four states and was conducted over a two-year period. Results were reported on every instructional program taught during the validation process. Program usage was variable across programs. Some programs were used only one time, but others were used up to forty-eight times. Three types of data were collected on different types of programs: rate (number of responses during a ten-minute lesson); parts completed (on task analysis programs, for example, putting on a hat); and percent of correct responses. For the 1977–1978 validation year, the data showed that the percent of correct responses for all programs ranged from 65 to 100 percent. The average, calculated for each program, ranged from 78 to 100 percent. Across all programs, the mean percent correct responses were 91.35.

The Implications

This large-scale study demonstrates that teachers trained in direct instructional procedures, who use these procedures daily as they present highly programmed instructional tasks, can produce a high percentage of correct responses in their students. The study also indicates great importance of teachers adhering to instructional procedures that are precisely specified if progress is to be realized in such severely retarded students. Staff in each participating system were responsible for observing teachers regularly and recording data on teacher and child performance. This procedure enabled the researchers to determine the extent to which teachers maintained their skill in the utilization of the procedures they had learned and demonstrated to criterion. These data have significant implications for the future direction of the inservice retraining of that first generation of teachers employed to meet right-to-education mandates, as well as for emerging graduate programs for the next generation of teachers.

THE ROLE OF THE TEACHER

A basic description of the role of the contemporary special education teacher is described in earlier chapters of this book. Given the broad framework of behaviors that are required in any teaching environment, what are the specific functions of teachers of children with severe and multiple handicapping conditions? These functions seem to fall into three general areas: management, direct instruction, and communication skills.

MANAGEMENT OF THE EDUCATIONAL ENVIRONMENT

Teacher-child ratios may be as small as 1 to 3, 1 to 4, or 1 to 5. Children may be served in classes of six or eight, managed by a teacher and one or two aides. During the course of the school day each child may be served by one or more supportive-service personnel, including physical, speech, or occupational therapists. In a typical day, the teacher may coordinate and supervise aides, schedule and coordinate the development of supportive services, analyze data from existing child performance records, specify modifications in existing educational programs, or develop new programs that build on the terminal objectives of programs that have been taught to criterion. With or without computer support systems, the teacher will summarize child performance data so that it can be retrieved in a case history or other record that will describe students' skill acquisitions over time and on increasingly more complex tasks. Further, the teacher must schedule each child's working day, so that a high percentage of time is spent in academic instruction and very little time is spent on unsupervised activities.

DIRECT INSTRUCTION

Many first-year college students view the instructional function of a classroom teacher from the context of their personal experiences in regular classes—verbal instruction and directions from a teacher in the "front and center" of the classroom. Some may recall small-group activities led by a teacher who corrected students' errors as they took turns reading or responding in other content areas. Teachers of children with severe and multiple handicapping conditions will do very little of this type of instruction. Instead, direct instruction, either individually or in groups of two or three children, will be the dominant teaching mode.

Children who are nonambulatory, whose activity is limited by wheelchairs, leg braces, or other prostheses, or whose movements are restrained by cerebral palsy, will almost certainly require direct physical manipulation when they first begin to receive academic instruction. That is, teachers may, in the early stages of the direct instructional task,

1. Gently place their hands on a child's face and position it so that the child's gaze falls on a set of stimulus materials.

2. State an attention cue such as "Mary, look." This verifies that the child is attending and provides an opportunity for the teacher to mark a data sheet with a code to verify that attending was established.

3. State a request, for example, "Mary, touch the fork." Depending upon the child's level of motor functioning, the teacher may:
   a. physically manipulate a hand into a fist, with the index finger extending to touch or point to;

b. physically direct the child to complete an arm motion that will enable her to touch.

4. Physically intercept a self-initiated incorrect response and guide the child's hand to the correct response.

5. Place an edible reinforcer in the child's hand. If the child is unable to grasp it, the teacher may place it in the child's mouth directly.

6. Repeat the sequence of events with decreasing amounts of assistance until the child can complete the task independently.

With the students who are more physically involved, teachers may seek assistance to determine the most efficacious position for the child to respond, then position the child appropriately before the instruction begins.

Direct physical assistance may be extended to self-help skills, such as dressing, feeding, and personal hygiene. Whether direct instruction is provided on an individual basis or with small groups, the teacher will carry out a sequence of tasks to instruct and verify the outcomes of instruction. These might include:

1. Carefully selecting instructional materials so that the concept to be taught is isolated and clear; that is, if a child is to discriminate colors, then make sure that he is not expected inadvertently to learn size.

2. Determining the consequences of a child's correct or incorrect responses.

3. Preselecting positive consequences from among an array of items or events known to be preferred by the child.

4. Instructing according to a written plan.

5. Responding immediately and consistently to the child's responses.

6. Recording responses continuously, or on a programmed-behavior sampling sequence.

7. Utilizing the written record or product of instruction to modify the next sequence of instruction.

Data-based Instructional Models

Data collection is considered an integral component of instructional technology (Smith & Snell, 1978; Tawney et al., 1979; White & Liberty, 1976). In one comprehensive instructional program (Tawney et al., 1979) a child's responses may be recorded on a trial-by-trial basis and error-pattern analysis done in order to lead to program revision. In this program children progress from step to more complex step with a minimum of errors. Data collection and data-based decision making must form an even more important component of the contemporary teacher's function than ever before, and parents

Focusing
Attention

Rate Data

Cycle

Skill:

In this program the child increases the frequency with which he focuses his attention on a single aspect of his environment, looking directly at a particular sound, object, or person. This skill enables the child to respond to a variety of stimulus events and to sustain his attention for longer periods to increase the awareness of his surroundings.

Entry Behaviors:

1. S will look at (1-2 second glance) an identifiable target. Although S has demonstrated that he can attend to an object, he rarely does so. Rather, his usual eye movements appear random or nondirected, and he demonstrates little visual-motor coordination, such as directed reach or movement, and little sustained attention. If S has a visual disability, adapt by using other behaviors in addition to eye contact to define attention; behaviors such as a specific change in body position, head turning, or arm extension. Use only those cycles that are appropriate. Note that the intent of this program is to increase any focused attention at all. For sustained attention (over 2 seconds), refer to programs containing the word attending in their titles.

2. S turns his head slightly. Or, adapt by always keeping the target in a position so that he need only move his eyes (not head) to look at it.

Objective:

S looks at different targets. S must initiate his response correctly to at least five different targets a total of 25 times anytime during a 10-minute session.

looks at = moves eyes to AND fixates 1-2 seconds on a specific point. S may also make other responses (reaching for or holding the target) as long as he fixates.

target = a specific point of focus.

Cycle:

Different cycles increase S's focus on different targets.

1. Varied Targets: S looks at any target.

2. Objects: S looks at objects.

FIGURE 23-1
An example of a highly programmed instructional model from the work of Tawney and his colleagues (1979).

3. Eye Contact: S looks at a person's face, preferably making eye contact. Note that S need only focus on one person rather than on five different targets.

4. Sound: S looks at any target that is making sounds.

Cycles may be taught in any order, although Cycle 1, Varied Targets, usually occurs first.

Follow-Up:

Continue to work on S's attention throughout the day. Give individual trials on a regular basis, taking data to insure that S's performance is or becomes consistent in a variety of natural situations. Demand S's attention whenever presenting a target. This follow-up is extremely important.

Continue to present S with a variety of types of stimulation to increase his awareness. Require S to attend for longer intervals than the brief fixation period that meets the criterion for this program. Later introduce Attending to Voice and Attending to Objects. Encourage S to turn his head to look at different stimulus events. Use the Controlling Head Movements program if S does not have sufficient head and neck control. Later encourage S to look at, then reach for, the target, using Reaching if S does not have sufficient arm and hand control. Also, have S look directly at his hands as he holds or manipulates objects to develop fine motor coordination.

Program for Cognitive Skill 1

Materials:

Select materials appropriate to the cycle.

Chart:

Stimulus Chart (for events), page 467.

GENERAL STRATEGY

Arrangement:

In a play situation, position several objects where S can easily see them. Include mobiles and pictures, but do not clutter the area. You should be able to identify the object at which S is looking.

Stimulus Event:

Use suggestions from the Stimulus Chart to structure interactions with S. The same object may be used in different ways to attract S's attention so that he will focus (e.g., an object may be held out, shaken, moved, and so on). Conduct the event in S's range of vision (6 to 36 inches away, to the side, upward, downward) but not directly in his line of sight. (S must move his eyes and fixate according to Objective definitions.) Continue the stimulus event up to 30 seconds.

Latency:

None. Anytime S looks at (focuses on) the target, he has made a correct response.

Correction:

Anytime S does not look, bring the target closer, directly in front of his eyes. Attract S's attention for up to 5 seconds with the target in this position. Then begin a new stimulus event.

Natural Consequence:

Anytime S fixates on a target, continue the stimulus event until he breaks attention. After the initial focus (1-2 seconds), you may reinforce S to sustain his attention. However, this sustained attention is not required and does not count as a new response. Note: If S usually sustains attention for more than a brief interval, reconsider the justification for teaching this program.

Other Trials:

Repeat the strategy. Vary stimulus events during the 10-minute session. Vary the distance and position of the target (up to 3 feet, to the sides, upward, downward).

Modification:

S has not met step criterion after four sessions.

	CONDITIONS	BEHAVIOR	CRITERIA
		S moves his eyes and fixates 1-2 seconds on a target...	during a 10-minute session
PRE	Present the stimulus event. Present the natural consequence.	unassisted	25 times, 5 different targets (of the appropriate cycle)
S/1	Present the stimulus event. Correct if needed. Present the natural consequence.	unassisted	5 times, any target
S/2	Present the stimulus event. Correct if needed. Present the natural consequence.	unassisted	10 times, 2 different targets
S/3	Present the stimulus event. Correct if needed. Present the natural consequence.	unassisted	15 times, 3 different targets
S/4	Present the stimulus event. Correct if needed. Present the natural consequence.	unassisted	20 times, 4 different targets
S/5	Present the stimulus event. Correct if needed. Present the natural consequence.	unassisted	25 times, 5 different targets on each of 4 days
POST 1	Same as PRE	unassisted	25 times, 5 different targets for each test
POST 2	New Targets		
POST 3	New Setting		

MODIFICATIONS

Gradually increase the distance and/or direction in which S can focus. At first when the target is a short distance away (6 to 8 inches) and almost in S's line of sight, then, when the target is farther away (12 to 15 inches) and more out of his line of sight, increase S's rate of responding to the target. Gradually S will be moving his eyes/head varied amounts. Continue to increase the distance (up to 3 feet) and direction in which S is to respond, as well as his rate of responding.

must become more sophisticated in the evaluation of their children's programs.

Here is an example of a highly programmed instructional model from the work of Tawney et al. (1979). This program is presented in extraordinary detail because it is important to appreciate all of the ramifications of teaching the severely and multiply handicapped even the most fundamental skills.

LIAISON, COMMUNICATION, AND ADVOCACY

Prior to the enactment of P.L. 94-142, teachers were generally expected to recommend changes in placements for children, to communicate with their district administrators upon request, and to confer with parents about their children's progress. The new law and the current regulations require certain communication skills and, further, dramatically change the dynamics of this interaction.

Placement Committees

Parents must be notified of plans to change a child's educational placement and are expected to participate in that decision. When a placement is recommended or an individual plan is developed, the decision making must be collective and not individual. That is, it is no longer permissible for a teacher to recommend a change in placement, discuss it with the teacher who is recommended to receive the child, and, in effect, accomplish a teacher-to-teacher transfer. Instead, teachers are required to meet as part of a committee, and then to provide objective information that can be used in the decision-making process.

Due Process Hearings

When parents and schools disagree on an individual placement or program, the new law requires that due process hearings be held. While the first level of these hearings is often held in the schools, the structure of the proceedings follow the courtroom model. Both parents and the schools may be represented by legal counsel and can request the support of expert witnesses. Testimony is taken and recorded, and both sides may examine and cross-examine witnesses. If the issue is not resolved locally, either side may request an administrative review from the state education agency. If the issue is not resolved at that level, the case may proceed into the state or federal civil court system. Teachers who participate in these hearings, and their numbers will surely grow, will be expected to communicate factual information and present their professional opinions. They will be expected to present reasoned arguments and to have their information challenged in cross-examinations.

Communication with the School System

Theoretically, within the new law, the local education system must transmit data to the state education agency to verify that each child has an individual educational plan developed according to law and regulations. In turn, the state must transmit data and assurances to the federal government to confirm that the local plans exist. These regulations place a heavy burden on teachers to communicate requests for adequate resources to their immediate supervisors and to verify that instructional programs exist in fact as well as on paper. Moreover, they must demonstrate under the law that these programs are effective. Having analyzed the management skills required of a teacher of students with severe and multiple handicaps, one can now better understand the emphasis on planning and documenting the performance of the students. Teachers must organize and report that information within the system in order to demonstrate compliance with the law.

Communication with Parents

The transition of the concept of an equal right to education into law has fundamentally changed the nature of interactions between parents and schools. It is entirely possible that parents and schools will be legal adversaries until all the present issues are resolved. On a personal basis, teachers can expect that the nature of their interactions with parents will change. The law requires that parents approve their child's individual educational plan, and the law permits them to evaluate it on their request. While the law does not require accountability (that the child demonstrate behavior change as stated in long- and short-term objectives), the mechanism is set into place to allow parents to challenge any aspect of a child's program and to reject the teacher's contention that the child is performing satisfactorily.

The intent of the law is to bring into effect what has always been considered "best practice" in educational programming, that is, that the parent and teacher would sit down amicably and share information so that the student's program is based on complete information, and that parents would cooperate in the instructional process by carrying out selected activities at home. Now the teacher is required to arrange periodic meetings with parents to listen to their descriptions of the student's at-home behavior, to incorporate that information into instructional plans, and to document the progress that the child is making for the parent's edification. Teachers will be expected to share information, to provide documentation on student progress on many discrete steps or programs, to provide a rationale for the instructional program they have selected, and to prove that the strategies they are employing bring about behavioral changes in the students. Successful teachers will be able to communicate objectively and dispassionately.

Professional Advocacy

Educational change proceeds within two parameters: the ideal state on one hand, and the practical constraints of the real world on the other. Within these parameters, it is also the case that, in some systems, the minimum effort is expended while in others there is a constant striving to achieve the status of exemplary practice. In the parlance of the new law, systems might be said to be in hostile noncompliance or acting to demonstrate full-compliance efforts. Acknowledging that many sources of influence are needed to bring about change in educational practices, certain types of hot lines have been authorized. People who are aware of a handicapped child who is not presently being served may call a toll-free number and suggest that the child's candidacy for special education be determined. This confidential information will then be acted on and set into motion a chain of events that will eventually lead to a decision on special education placement. Similarly, other advocacy offices are being established. It may well be within teachers' advocacy role to report situations that deny equal-education opportunities to the handicapped students. If, for example, a school district does not supply the materials necessary to carry out instructional programs, and if internal appeals are not effective, then it may be necessary to utilize these external resources. Or, if a school district falsely states that child evaluations have been conducted, when in fact they have not, this is a violation of the law that may need to be reported. The area of advocacy is one of great delicacy, requiring objectivity, sound judgment, and a considered analysis of professional responsibility.

Professional Preparation of Teachers

Much of what a teacher must know is implicit in the functional tasks described in the previous section. It is apparent that management skills predominate. For this reason, among others, graduate-level programming is requisite. At this time, the nature of preparation is extensive. Two-year M.A. programs which include an extensive practical requirement may emerge as the primary training pattern.

Focusing again upon the severely retarded, the prospective teacher should expect to master course content that includes:

1. A core of course work in:
    a. Behavioral attributes of persons who manifest deficits in functional abilities and attendant sensory deficits
    b. Curriculum design and development in areas specific to the functional needs of students
    c. Direct instructional procedures incorporating behavioral and instructional technologies
    d. Program planning and management, including classroom management and the coordination and management of adults providing direct and supportive services to students

2. Basic content in supportive fields:
    a. Physical therapy
    b. Speech therapy
    c. Language development
    d. Motor development
    e. Adapted physical education and recreation
    f. Social-service delivery

3. Concentration in areas that are age-appropriate to the career goals of the teacher:
   a. Infant learning
   b. Early childhood education
   c. Career education
   d. Vocational management

4. Practical research skills:
   a. Single-subject research design
   b. Research-based curriculum intervention strategies

5. Related areas:
   a. Civil rights of the handicapped
   b. Parent interaction
   c. Specialized child assessment devices and procedures
   d. Prosthetics

PREPARATION FOR THE FUTURE

What does the future hold for a profession that did not exist ten years ago? Much of the answer to this question is linked to the impact of P.L. 94-142 and the extent to which its provisions are weakened or strengthened in successive Congresses. Other critical factors are the extent to which technology and wide-scale reforms are introduced into educational settings. Teachers in the twenty-first century should look forward to:

1. Increased use of technology in a classroom, including computerized response-recording and report-writing systems; teaching computers which talk, listen, consequate correct and incorrect responses appropriately, record child performance, and branch to appropriate instruction through the delivery of alternative sequences; space-age prostheses, such as the Kurzweil reading machine, which reads print and translates it into spoken sentences for blind persons.

2. Increased emphasis on the analysis of the quantity and quality of instruction in the classroom. The parent-participation and external-monitoring components of P.L. 94-142 have the potential to transform the classroom into an open arena where educational practices receive extensive scrutiny.

3. Increased emphasis on a research-oriented instructional technology. The need for a data base on the academic performance of severely handicapped students has been described. Documentation of academic performance, under conditions which permit the results to contribute to a national data pool, will enhance the growth of programs.

4. Increased emphasis on early intervention, from birth to traditional school entry years. While preschool and infant education is permis-

sive within most state laws, growth of programs in this area should create a demand for specially trained interventionists.

5. Increased coordination of educational programming from birth through adulthood. Current efforts to develop a curriculum are aimed at different age levels, designed for different settings and developed with little attention to an extended skill-acquisition period. Future efforts will undoubtedly focus on coordination among existing products and expansion of skill-acquisition programs in the areas where gaps occur.

6. Increased emphasis on the legal and human rights of handicapped persons, and on increasing sensitivity to the full range of human variation. P.L. 94-142 and its governing regulations, the normalization movement, and the right-to-education movement are significantly altering the scope and nature of community services to handicapped persons. Future teachers should expect to behave in ways that ensure that their students experience equal-education opportunities in fact. By virtue of their membership in the community, as professionals, they can expect to show by example respect for and sensitivity to problems faced by persons who are significantly disabled.

SUMMARY

Legal opinions and professional judgments suggest that severely handicapped children will be served in community-based programs in special classes in regular school settings. Whether children are concentrated in large numbers or dispersed throughout the school system, their environment will be structured to enable them to receive requisite supporting services. Local educational philosophy is likely to determine the extent to which handicapped children are integrated with nonhandicapped students. Current professional opinion suggests that maximum feasible integration will be practiced. Severely handicapped students who are served in large urban systems are likely to have access to a full array of educational and supportive services in environments which afford maximum interaction with nonhandicapped students. In smaller school systems options may be limited for severely handicapped children. Students who reside in remote or sparsely populated areas pose a dilemma for educational planners, for there may be no best alternative for them. Initially it may be necessary to provide extensive technical assistance to the teacher and to the local school system personnel so as to develop an adequate individual educational program. As renewed child-find efforts and community awareness grow, other children are likely to be identified and sufficient numbers may be found to start a special class. Clearly, many years will pass before special educators grapple with each aspect of this problematic situation and establish exemplary services in all regions of the state.

Curricula for the severely handicapped are based on the premise that these persons will, as adults, assume a role as independent and economically productive members of society. Content progresses from functional skills for younger students to social and adaptive vocational skills for the older. Systematic, data-based instructional models are used to provide highly structured, empirically individualized instruction. Single-subject studies and several group studies imply that these methods can be highly successful with the severely handicapped.

Teachers of the severely handicapped manage the educational environment through direct instruction. Communication skills which include participation in placement committees, due process hearings, communication within the school system, with parents and with child advocacy groups. These activities differ greatly from the traditional responsibilities and routines of the regular educator, and for these reasons, a two-year M.A. program is emerging as the primary training pattern.

Teachers in the twenty-first century should anticipate increased use of technology in the classroom, increased emphasis on accountability, early intervention, and development of a coordinated life curriculum. Above all, teachers will focus on individually appropriate curricula for both the handicapped and nonhandicapped individuals.

GLOSSARY

Ability training An instructional approach based on the assumption that a learning problem is due to a deficit in a general ability, and that this more general ability can be trained for a particular subject.

ABO system Classification scheme for blood typing to indicate the presence of A or B antibodies. Thus, an "A" individual has anti-B; a "B" individual has anti-A; an AB individual has neither A nor B antibodies; and an "O" individual has both antibodies.

Acceleration Advancement through a school program that is more rapid than the average. It may take the form of early school admission, grade skipping, subject matter acceleration, or early college admission.

Acculturation The modification of one culture by contact with another culture.

Achievement tests Devices that directly assess a student's skill development in a particular content area. They can be group administered or individually administered and must reflect the content of the curriculum.

(ACLD) Association for Children with Learning Disabilities Organization established as a forum for parents of children with learning disabilities, it became a powerful force for lobbying for appropriate educational services.

Adaptive assessment   Evaluation of the degree to which individuals meet the demands and expectations of their environment. Included are aspects of motivation, social behavior, physical abilities, intellectual functioning, and others.

Adaptive behavior   The effectiveness and the extent to which any individual meets the standard of self-sufficiency society expects of his or her age or cultural group or both.

Adventitiously blind   Refers to an individual who has once seen, but is now unable to see; not blind at birth.

Advocate   A person who argues for a cause—supporter or defender—and pleads on another's behalf.

Affectional bond   An emotional tie, usually developed during infancy, between mother and child.

Affective   Pertaining to feelings or emotions rather than thought.

Affirmative action   Positive action to rectify some inequalities in hiring or placement.

Amniocentesis   A procedure for analyzing factors in the amniotic fluid that may indicate the presence of problems for the offspring.

Analgesia   Inability to feel pain while conscious.

Anecdotal report   A written account of behavior as it occurs.

Anoxia   Lack of oxygen or the disturbance of bodily functions resulting from lack of oxygen.

Apgar scores   An assessment technique designed to evaluate the newborn's status. Observations are made in five areas: heart rate, respiratory effort, muscle tone, reflex irritability, and skin color.

Aphasia   Loss of symbolic formulation and expression owing to a brain lesion.

Aphonia   Loss or absence of voice as a result of the failure of the vocal cords to vibrate properly.

Apraxia   The loss of the ability to execute simple voluntary acts, especially the loss of the ability to perform elementary units of action in expressive language.

Articulation   The movement or placement during speech of the organs which serve to modify the voiced or unvoiced airstream into meaningful sounds.

Assessment   The informal and formal evaluation of performance in a variety of settings and activities.

Assessment/curriculum linkage   Refers to the relationship between testing and teaching which forms the basis of a child's Individual Educational Program (IEP).

Ataxia   A form of cerebral palsy marked by an impairment of muscular coordination which makes it difficult to walk or maintain balance.

Athetosis   A form of cerebral palsy marked by involuntary, wormlike movements.

Audiologist   A person who has studied the entire field of hearing, normal and disordered, and is concerned with the nature and conservation of hearing and the identification, assessment, and rehabilitation of those with a hearing impairment.

Autism   A psychological aspect of schizophrenia; in childhood the chief symptoms of autism are withdrawal behavior, reduction or absence of socialization, bizarre play activity, echolalia, lack of verbal communication, purposeless activity.

Autosome   An ordinary chromosome as opposed to a sex-determining chromosome.

AVE   American Vocational Education Association.

Aversive stimulus (punisher)   Stimulus having the effect of decreasing the strength of a behavior when it is presented contingent upon that behavior.

Behavior Problem Checklist   An instrument listing behaviors thought to be indicative of disturbed behavior. Rating scores lie on four dimensions: conduct disorder, personality problem, inadequacy/immaturity, and socialized delinquency.

Behavioral checklist   An observational tool listing specified behaviors to facilitate check-off and assessment of behaviors.

Behavioral objective   A precise specification of the goal, including the behavior expected, the conditions under which it is to occur, and the criterion for successful attainment.

Behaviorial objectives   A precise, measurable statement of expected student performance, including the conditions under which the student will perform and the criteria for measuring performance.

Behaviorism   A field of psychology which holds that all behavior is learned through previous experiences.

Bilirubin   Compound produced by the breakdown of free hemoglobin in the blood stream. In large amounts, bilirubin causes jaundice as well as tissue and brain damage in infants.

Blind Learning Aptitude Test   Device which was developed especially for blind individuals to assess learning aptitude.

Blindness   Central visual acuity of 20/200 or less in the better eye with corrective lenses or contraction of the visual field to 20 degrees or less if central visual acuity is greater than 20/200.

Braille   A tactual symbol system representing the letters of the alphabet. A system of writing and printing for the blind in which varied arrangements of raised dots represent letters and numerals and can be identified by touch.

Career education   The total experiences through which one chooses a role and engages in work as a part of his or her life.

Career Education Incentive Act   Legislation enacted in 1977 to place increased emphasis on career awareness, decisionmaking, and planning.

Cascade of Services   A descriptive hierarchy of services available to exceptional students with the least restrictive placement occupying the lower level and with the most restrictive placement (residential facility) at the highest level.

Cataracts   Vision loss due to clouding of the lens.

Ceitar International Performance Scale   Device which samples intellectual abilities of children with hearing and language problems through the use of pantomime directions.

Center-based program   Program designed for older preschool children and delivered through day-care centers, group centers, or nursery schools.

Cephalocaudal   Referring to the development of movement control in infants which proceeds from head (cephalo) to tail (caudal).

Cerebral palsy   A paralysis or muscular incoordination due to lesions in the brain. The term is applied to a group of cerebral afflictions in children, including Little's disease, spastic paralysis, and many others.

Cerumen   Waxlike secretion found in the external canal of the ear.

CETA   Comprehensive Employment and Training Act, which created an agency to provide job preparation programs and support services for exceptional youth and adults.

Child find   State-organized strategy or strategies for identifying handicapped children in order to provide appropriate educational services.

Chromosomes   Very small bodies in the nucleus of a cell which carry the genes or hereditary factors.

Class action suit   Legal action occurring when a group of people file against an individual or organization to change unsatisfactory conditions.

Cleft palate   Congenital fissure of the soft palate and roof of mouth, sometimes extending through the premaxilla and upper lip.

Cloning   Producing genetically identical cells from a single common ancestor through an asexual process.

Clubfoot   A congenital deformity of the foot marked by an appearance often resembling a club.

Clumsiness   Uncoordination; the failure to perform typical motor skills adequately.

CNS (central nervous system)   A series of small cavities at the beginning of a canal, that is, ear, nose, or aorta.

Coercive behaviors   Those actions which result in a specified outcome though they are socially unacceptable (that is, tantrums, yelling).

Communication   The process of imparting to one another ideas, feelings, thoughts, or opinions by means of signs, signals, and symbols expressed consciously or unconsciously.

Compensatory learning   Learning which reduces the visibility of deviation either through the elimination of inappropriate behaviors or the addition of normalized mannerisms.

Compensatory training   Teaching alternative ways to deal with a problem. An example would be training an amputee to use an automatic feeding device.

Comprehensive diagnostic assessment   An approach that requires a team of specialists directing diagnostic work on the various areas of functioning, including development, intellectual, language, perceptual-motor, personal-social, and educational functioning.

Comprehensive Employment and Training Act of 1978 (CETA) An act designed to provide employment and training opportunities for the underemployed, unemployed, and economically disadvantaged.

Compulsion A type of neurotic behavior involving uncontrollable and repetitive actions.

Conductive hearing loss An impairment of hearing due to damage or obstruction of the ear canal, the drum membrane, or the ossicular chain in the middle ear; a failure of vibrations to be adequately conducted to the cochlea.

Congenital Existing at birth but not hereditary.

Congenitally blind An individual who is born blind and therefore has no previous visual experiences.

Conjugate gaze Movement of eyes simultaneously in the same direction.

Consultant teacher One who provides support services to regular classroom teachers and school staff, but delivers no direct service to the students.

Contingency The dependency between a behavior, its antecedent, and its consequence.

Contingent reinforcement The consequence attached to behavioral events.

Cosmetic prosthetics Refers to the use of artificial devices to conceal or draw attention away from a deviation in appearance. These may be either subtractive or additive.

Cretinism A thyroid deficiency caused by decreased activity of the thyroid gland characterized by dry skin, swelling around the lips and nose, mental deterioration, and a subnormal basal metabolic rate.

Criterion-referenced assessment An approach that measures the student's performance against a set of specific instructional objectives. Such measures sample that development of skills over time and serve as the measurement criteria for determining the extent to which the student is meeting the curriculum objectives.

Cultural deprivation Deficient environments for stimulating normal development in children.

Custodial model A formerly popular trend in caring for the handicapped which emphasized doing all self-care or other tasks for the exceptional person.

Cystic fibrosis A hereditary disorder producing a generalized malfunction of the pancreas leading to numerous organic and functional deficiencies.

Cytomegalic inclusion disease Disease similar to rubella. The infant may have severe involvement of the brain and eye, but other organ systems are usually not involved.

Decibel A unit of sound intensity.

Delusion An unrealistic belief which is strongly held and defended.

Deno's cascade A model of instructional services for exceptional children in which organization, administration, and delivery are set up on a continuum from least to most restrictive.

Descriminative stimulus A stimulus which tends to occasion a response, as behaviors completed in its presence are more likely to be reinforced.

Desensitization Masking or weakening stimuli by reducing their potency or visibility so that responses to which they have been conditioned will occur less frequently.

Developmental period The time period during which major, relatively stable characteristics of the individual are established, frequently designated as the interval between conception and 18 years of age; the time span between birth and adulthood during which physical and intellectual growth occurs.

Developmental task A normative expectation that the individual must accomplish before he or she may be considered a fully developing person.

Developmental view View of exceptionality based upon an understanding of normal intellectual, emotional, and physical development and of what constitutes deviance in the course of normal development.

Deviation From a social view, any departure from the norm sufficient to produce differential social consequences.

Diabetic retinopathy A loss of vision caused by interference in the blood supply to the retina common in diabetics.

Diagnosis The identification of component skills or steps of a learning task missing from the learner's repertoire; assignment to a clinical category.

Diagnostic prescriptive teaching Individualized instruction based upon student strengths and weaknesses. Prescribed activities are designed to remediate deficits and develop strengths.

Diagnostician A person who identifies a disorder by studying its nature, origin, development, and symptoms.

Diplegic Paralysis affecting similar parts of both sides of the body.

Direct instruction An instructional technique most often used which takes place on an individual or small-group basis, often using manual, verbal, and visual cues, brisk pacing, and continual feedback.

Disability A deviation in body or functioning that results in functional inadequacy in view of environmental demands.

Displacement A defense mechanism in which responsibility is shifted from oneself to another.

Distar A programmed reading instruction kit intended for use with children who are below grade level in their achievement.

Distinctive feature A linguistically distinguishable articulatory adjustment by which phonemes are produced and differentiated.

Distortion An alteration of the target sound resulting in a phoneme which is usually not regarded as a standard English sound (e.g., a lateral lisp for "s").

Down's syndrome A chromosomal abnormality characterized by a small skull, slanted eyes, stubby fingers, and a short, stocky hypotonic body.

Down's syndrome is associated with moderate to severe mental retardation.

Due process hearing   A review of an exceptional student's placement, identification, or evaluation by professionals initiated by parental complaint.

Duration recording   Recording of the time elapsed while an event occurs. This recording method is most appropriate for uninterrupted behaviors.

Dysarthria   A disorder of articulation owing to impairment of the central nervous system, which directly controls muscles of articulation.

Dyslexia   Inability to read characterized by associate learning difficulty; a form of dysphasia.

Early education   Programs serving a preventive as well as a corrective function which design environments to maximize the acquisition of appropriate behaviors.

Early intervention   Describes the delivery of services to high-risk preschoolers and their families.

Echolalia   Involuntary or automatic repetition of words or phrases spoken by others.

Ectomorphy   A body type which is characteristically tall and thin, fragile and thin-muscled.

Educable mentally retarded   Label applied to those who score between 52 and 68 on the Stanford-Binet test while concurrently demonstrating deficits in adaptive behavior.

Egalitarian   Advocating equal political, economic, and legal rights for all citizens.

Ego   In psychoanalytic theory, the reality-oriented region of the mind which involves perception, reasoning, learning, and all other activities necessary to interact effectively with the environment.

Electroencephalograph   An instrument for graphically recording electrical currents developed in the cerebral cortex during brain functioning; often abbreviated EEG.

Elitism   A sense of being part of a superior or privileged group.

Emotive imagery   The simultaneous presentation of pleasant and anxiety-producing stimuli. As each conflicting stimulus becomes stronger, it is expected that the individual will retain the pleasant images.

Empathy   An important factor in a successful counseling relationship, involving the counselor's complete understanding of the client's feelings.

Employability   Making use of someone's time advantageously and for wages or salary.

Endogenous   Originating within an organ or part.

Endomorphy   A body type which is characteristically soft and round, with relatively underdeveloped bone and muscle tissue.

Enrichment   Providing information or instruction over and above that which would be provided in the regular curriculum.

Enuresis   Involuntary urination.

Environmentalism   An approach which views development as the result of the physical environment—a nonbiological approach.

Epilepsy   A chronic functional disease characterized by convulsions and loss of consciousness for short periods; the mild form is called "petit mal" and the severe form is called "grand mal." It is related to disorders in the brain's electrical activity and may be present at birth or developed after illness or injury.

Equilibrium   Balance.

Etiology   The cause or origin of a condition as defined by medical science.

Eugenics   A movement initiated in the nineteenth century stressing that unfit individuals should not be allowed to reproduce because this would weaken the human species genetically. The study of the improvement of heredity, especially of human improvement by genetic control.

Event sampling   Provides a detailed description of behaviorial events.

Exceptional individual   Any person whose characteristics are so different from the norm that special environmental or personal arrangements are needed.

Expressive language   Actions or words which communicate to others what the individual thinks or feels.

External otitis   Inflammation of the outer ear.

Extinction   A behavioral procedure aimed at decreasing the frequency of an undesirable behavior; it involves the discontinuation of reinforcement for a previously reinforced response.

Fading   The gradual removal of discriminative stimuli such as directions, imitative prompts, or physical guidance.

Fetal monitoring   Refers to the use of technical apparatus to monitor fetal heart rate and intrauterine pressure during labor.

First Chance Network   Group of programs designed to demonstrate services to children from birth to age five, including prenatal instruction and assistance to parents and family members.

Formative evaluation   An assessment procedure based on the specification of competencies for each individual and the frequent progress checks made on each. These checks provide feedback as to the effectiveness of a program and indicate when or if an adjustment becomes necessary.

Foundation phase   Wiederholt's first phase in the history of learning disabilities, characterized by contributions from the medical profession.

Frequency data   The number of times a given behavior occurs during a predetermined time period.

Functional prosthetics   Refers to the use of devices designed to replace a missing body part or enhance the functioning of an individual in some way, for example, glasses, hearing aids, and crutches.

Functional skills   Those skills necessary for an adult to live independently in society.

Galactosemia   Disorder of carbohydrate metabolism in which the absence of a particular enzyme prevents the normal transformation of galactose to glucose, resulting in damage to tissue.

Gargoylism   *See* Hurler's syndrome.

Genetic disorder   A disorder attributed to heredity.

Genitalia   The reproductive organs, especially the external sex organs.

Germ cell   The male sperm or female ovum, carrying genetic materials.

Germfree environment   A sterile habitat that is essential for patients who cannot fight infection and germs that are encountered in everyday living.

Glaucoma   Vision loss caused by pressure buildup in the eye which damages the optic nerve.

Grand mal seizure   Epileptic seizure consisting of several phases in which the person loses consciousness, thrashes about, stiffens, and goes into a deep relaxed state.

Guilford's Structure of Intellect Model   An expanded conceptualization of intelligence addressing a wide range of mental traits.

Guthrie test   Simple blood test available for the diagnosis of PKU in the newborn period.

Habilitative approach   A recent trend in caring for the handicapped which places emphasis on teaching behaviors that will enable them to function as independently as possible in society.

Halderman vs. Pennhurst State School and Hospital   A case resulting in a 1977 decision which called for the closing of Pennhurst School and Hospital and challenged the justification of large residential institutions.

Halfway house   A housing facility located in the community for those who have left residential institutions and who will eventually return to live independently in the community.

Hallucination   A visual, auditory, or tactual experience which has no external stimulus correlate.

Handicap   The burden imposed socially on an individual because of a behavioral or somatic deviation.

Hemiplegia   Motor dysfunction which is confined to one side of the body.

Herpes   Virus which occurs in two forms—one is most commonly associated with cold sores or fever blisters around the mouth and nostrils; the other causes ulcers on the genitalia and is liable to affect the infant as it passes through the birth canal.

Heterogeneous   Having dissimilar elements.

High-risk environment   An environment deficient in stimulating development.

Hiskey-Nebraska Test of Learning Aptitude   Device which contains a separate norm group and response format for deaf individuals.

Hoarseness   The sound of the voice that is breathy, hoarse, and relatively low in pitch.

Home-based program   The delivery of educational services to the disabled preschooler by development specialists making home visits. In addition, they train parents to understand and work with the child's handicapping condition.

Homebound instruction   Refers to educational instruction provided in the home.

Home/center-based program   Approach combining the advantages of both models by combining center-based activities with home visits.

Homogeneous   Having similar elements

Hurler's syndrome   An inherited disorder characterized by a stunted and deformed body as well as by mental retardation.

(Hxe)xe   A formula illustrating a product of heredity and the environment through the continuous accumulation of new characteristics from a continuous interaction in the environment.

Hyaline membrane disease   Disease caused by the formation of a membrane between the long capillaries and the alveoli which interferes with the passage of oxygen into the blood and of carbon dioxide out of the body.

Hyperactivity   A condition characterized by excessive motor activity, inattention, and impulsivity.

Hypernasality   A vowel quality characterized by the presence of excessive resonance of the voice in the nasal cavity usually due to varying degrees of functional or structural inadequacy of velopharyngeal incompetency.

Hyperopia   Visual dysfunction characterized by the individual's having difficulty focusing on objects which are close to him.

Hyperplasia   Type of fetal growth which involves an increase in the number of body cells.

Hypertrophy   Type of fetal growth which involves an increase in cell size.

Hypothyroidism   A pathological condition resulting from severe thyroid insufficiency, especially myxedema or cretinism.

Id   In psychoanalytic theory, the totally unconscious region of the mind which strives for immediate personal pleasure and satisfaction.

Impairment   Actual tissue damage.

In service   Educational, career development activities provided while someone is fully employed.

Incidence   Refers to the number of new cases per 1,000 births in the population.

Individual Educational Program (IEP)   A provision of PL 94-142 that requires a written program of educational services which serves to link individualized methods of assessment with individualized methods of instruction. The IEP must include a statement of the child's current level of educational performance, short-term instructional objectives, specific services to be provided, information and dates by which services are to be provided, and criteria for evaluation.

Individuation   The movement from total dependency on a caretaker or caretakers toward independence.

Integrative phase   Wiederholt's third and final phase in the history of learning disabilities, characterized by the development of remediation programs in the school.

Interactionism   The view that the development of a child is a cumulative and progressive product of the continuous interaction between heredity and environment.

Itinerant programs   Those which provide a teacher who serves several schools' special programs. Counseling may include suggestions for programming, conducting small-group sessions, or planning individual programs.

Itinerant teacher   A teacher who travels to several locations to provide services to students.

Jargon   Personalized utterances without meaning to others; technical language.

Jaundice   Disorder of the liver resulting in yellowish pigmentation of the skin, tissue, and body fluids.

Kernicterus   Damage and pigmentation of the basal ganglia and other portions of the brain caused by the same pigments related to jaundice.

Kyphosis   Excessive convexity in the thoracic region of the spinal column.

Language   Any means, vocal or other, for expression or communication.

Larynx   The cartilagenous and muscular structure situated at the top of the trachea and below the tongue roots; the organ of voice consisting of nine cartilages connected by ligaments.

Lasar cane   An electronic apparatus which aids in the mobility of totally blind people by signaling the presence of individuals and objects.

Lean reinforcement   Contingent reinforcement that is delivered too infrequently or in too small quantities or both.

Learning accomplishment profile   A curriculum-based assessment instrument designed to measure developmental age functioning. This device also provides a breakdown of specific objectives.

Least restrictive environment   An environment which is based on a continuum of services sensitive to one's diverse needs and on placement in environment whenever it is appropriate.

Lens   Convex structure lying behind the pupil opening of the iris which changes shape to focus light on the retina.

Lesion   An injury or wound in any part of the body; deficit of tissue.

Longitudinal study   A research design entailing data collection on one or several individuals over an extended period of time.

Lordosis   Excessive curve in the lumbar vertebrae.

Low birth weight   A newborn who weighs less than 5-½ pounds regardless of the length of gestation.

Mainstreaming   Giving handicapped individuals the opportunity to participate in every activity that is available to all other individuals.

Manual communication   A method of instruction for the hearing impaired with communication by means of finger spelling and sign language.

Meningitis   Inflammation of the meninges.

Meningomyelocele   A severe form of spina bifida in which a sac containing cerebral-spinal fluid, coverings of the spinal cord, and the spinal cord protrude through an open area of the spinal column.

Mesomorphy   A body type characterized by developed muscles and bones, which is strong and resistant to injury.

Metabolic disorders   Hereditary (congenital) errors or glandular dysfunctions that prevent the proper breaking down of one or more nutritive elements such as protein, carbohydrates, fats, lactose, and so on.

Metabolism   The use of energy by the body; all the physical and chemical processes needed by the organism for its maintenance.

Mills vs. Board of Education   Litigation resulting in the ruling that all school-age children are entitled to a free, appropriate public education regardless of the severity of their handicap.

Mixed hearing loss   A combination of a sensorineural loss and a conductive hearing loss.

Mongolism   *See* Down's syndrome.

Morpheme   A basic unit of meaning composed of one or more phonemes. There are two types of morphemes: a free morpheme, a unit which can stand alone to convey meaning ("kitty"), and a bound morpheme, a unit which must be attached to a free morpheme ("ed").

Morphology   In linguistics the rules of word formation.

Multidisciplinary team   A panel of professionals representing various fields whose purpose is the comprehensive assessment of individual functioning.

Multiple handicapped   A label applied to those individuals who have two or more severe handicaps.

Multiple walker   A device designed to resist spastic movements and aid in the ambulation of individuals with involuntary movements, as in cerebral palsy.

Multisensory approach   An approach based on the premise that for some children learning is facilitated if content is presented by several modalities.

Multisensory training   Multisensory programs that focus on tracing, hearing, writing, and seeing are often referred to as VAKT (visual, auditory, kinesthetic, tactile).

Muscular dystrophy   One of the more common primary diseases of the muscle, characterized by weakness and atrophy of the skeletal muscles with increasing disability and deformity as the disease progresses.

Mutism A condition characterized by an individual's refraining from speaking or inability to speak.

Myopia (nearsightedness) Visual dysfunction characterized by the individual's having difficulty focusing on objects which are distant.

Nasal airflow meter A device which measures nasal airflow emission, used especially with children who have clefts of the palate.

National Association of Vocational Education Special Needs Personnel Founded in 1974 as an affiliate organization of the American Vocational Association.

Neonatal Referring to a time period, considered by some to last up to two weeks.

Neuromotor dysfunction In general, this type of dysfunction includes clumsiness, poor physical fitness, obesity, and postural deviations.

Neurotic delinquent One who tends to act alone and demonstrates guilt and anxiety concerning his or her behavior.

Nondiscriminatory testing Assessment methods that must reflect the learners' variations in ability and cultural background. Tests must be administered in the native language, be culture-fair, and allow those with handicaps to respond through alternative modes.

Norm-referenced assessment A test that provides a standard for comparing a child's performance with that typical for the age or grade in school. Intelligence tests and achievement tests are norm-referenced measures.

Normalization Making available to the mentally retarded patterns and conditions of everyday life which are as close as possible to the norms and patterns of mainstream society.

Normative evaluation An evaluation which compares the performance of a given child with that of other children of his or her age.

NTID National Technical Institute for the Deaf.

Nuclear family A family consisting of husband, wife, and children.

Nystagmus The involuntary, rapid, rhythmic eye movements, usually side-to-side and continuous.

Obsession A type of neurotic behavior involving uncontrollable and repetitive thoughts.

Occupational therapist One who specializes in prescribing creative activity for its effect in promoting recovery or rehabilitation.

Occupational therapy Refers to the development of educational, recreational, and creative activities for the handicapped.

Omission The absence of the target sound in a word (pronouncing "spill" as "pil").

Operational definition The product of breaking down a concept into its observable and measurable component behaviors.

Optacon A portable electronic reading aid which translates the printed letter into a vibratory image.

Optic nerve A structure extending from the back of the eyeball to the vision center of the cerebrum that carries the nerve impulses responsible for sight.

Oral manual communication   The process by which signs are accompanied by articulatory gestures.

Osteosclerosis   The formation of spongy bone in the labyrinth of the ear, especially such growth around the footplate of the stapes, impeding its movement in the oval window.

Otitis media   Inflammation of the middle ear.

Otologist   An expert on the anatomy, physiology, and pathology of the ear.

Paraplegia   Complete paralysis of the lower half of the body caused by disease or injury to the spinal cord.

Paraprofessional   A worker who is not a member of a given profession but who assists a professional.

Pathological   Related to disease.

Pediatrician   A physician who specializes in medicine that deals with the care of infants and children.

Perceptual motor approach   An approach to the problem of learning disabilities which attempts to coordinate perceptions with motor activities. Among the advocates of this approach are William Cruickshank, Newell Kephart, Raymond Barsch, and Gerald Getman.

Perinatal   Referring to a time period immediately surrounding actual delivery of the child.

Petit mal seizure   Mild and quite brief epileptic seizure in which there may be only a slight loss of consciousness.

Phenylketonuria (PKU)   A hereditary metabolic disease transferred through genetic action, resulting in a lack of the necessary enzyme for oxidizing phenylalanine, which in turn promotes the accumulation of phenylalanine with resulting mental retardation.

Phocomelia   Rare abnormality involving the absence of part of a limb. The remaining limb (or limbs) may be disfigured, resembling flippers. The condition is linked to the use of thalidomide.

Phonemes   A group or family of closely related speech sounds all of which have the same distinctive acoustic characteristics, in spite of their differences; often used in place of speech sound.

Phonology   The study of sounds of a language.

Phrenology   The determination of personality based on a study of skull contours.

Physical fitness   This refers to the ability to carry out daily tasks with vigor and remain active in recreational pursuits. The components of fitness usually include strength, muscular and cardiovascular endurance, and flexibility.

Physiognomy   The determination of character based on outward appearance, especially facial features.

Pictorial Test of Intelligence   An assessment device which uses oversized picture cards and requires only the use of simple gestural response to test simple learning capabilities of children with cerebral palsy and language disorders.

Pitch   Perceptions of highness or lowness of a sound determined by fundamental frequency.

PL 90-538   The Handicapped Children's Early Education Assistance Act, passed in 1968.

PL 94-124   The Education for All Handicapped Children Act of 1975.

Placement   The assignment of children to one or more specific instructional settings on a full-time or part-time basis.

Placenta   Membrane attached to the inside of the uterus and to the developing fetus during the pregnancy. The placenta connects the mother and the fetus by means of the umbilical cord.

Play therapy   A technique in which the therapist reflects the assumed underlying conflicts expressed in the child's actions during play.

Poliomyelitis   An infectious viral disease occurring in children and, in its acute form, attacking the central nervous system and producing muscular atrophy, paralysis, and other deformities.

Polygenic characteristics   Characteristics such as physical stature, skin color, and possibly intelligence that are dependent on information from many genes.

Positive reinforcement   The contingent presentation of a stimulus following a response which has the effect of increasing the rate of that response.

Postnatal   Existing or taking place after birth.

Precision teaching   A set of standard procedures for the measurement and change of educational behavior introduced by O. R. Lindsley in 1964. It consists of pinpointing a movement cycle, recording and charting rate data, and altering antecedents and consequences until a change occurs.

Predeterminism   A concept which holds the belief that if the environment is free and permissive, "innate" potentials, latent talents, and natural goodness will unfold as the child grows.

Preformationism   A view which states that all an individual is or ever will be is preformed at conception.

Prelingual deafness   Hearing loss occurring at birth or before the development of language.

Premack principle   A behavioral principle stating that contingent access to preferred activities serves as a reinforcer for the performance of less preferred activities.

Prematurity   In pregnancy, the period of time before the end of the normal gestational period in which a viable fetus is delivered. A premature infant is usually defined as a baby born at less than 37 weeks' gestation. In cases where the mother is uncertain about the last menstrual period, the determination is based upon physical examination of the infant.

Prenatal   Existing or taking place before birth.

Presentation of the fetus   This refers to the position of the fetus within the birth canal. Head first is the most common and safest presentation; the head should be positioned so that the top comes first. Breech presentation refers to a presentation in which the rump or the feet come first. "Transverse" refers to a presentation in which the long axis of the baby is at right angles to the outlet.

Prevalence Refers to the number of cases of a condition for every 1,000 people in the overall population.

Prevocational Given or required before admission to a vocational school.

Prognosis A prediction of the probable course and outcome of a condition.

Programmed material Educational materials which have been created and arranged on the principles of learning.

Project Re-Ed Residential schools attended by students five days a week. Weekends are spent at home in order to maintain ties with the family and peer group.

Prolongations Pertaining to syllables which seem to be arrested and terminated suddenly by an interrupted breath, which represents an overt stuttering behavior.

Prompting A change in, or addition to, the present discriminative stimulus presented in order to make the occurrence of a desired response more likely (that is, emphasizing certain words in a question as a "hint").

Prosody Stress, inflection, rhythm, the melody of speech.

Prosthesis An artificial replacement of an absent part of the body; adaptation of the environment to minimize sensory and response difficulties.

Prosthetics The study of the artificial replacement of a limb, tooth, or other part of the body.

Proximodistal Referring to the development of muscle control in which the child acquires control of muscles which are progressively farther away from the trunk.

Pseudomental retardation False, not genuine, mental retardation.

Psychologist A person trained to perform psychological analysis, therapy, or research.

Psychometric theory Theory which proposes that traits, such as intelligence, may be reliably measured through the use of standardized tests.

Psychomotor seizure A form of epileptic seizure consisting of purposeful but inappropriate acts. A difficult form to diagnose and control.

Psychosomatics The study of the influence of the mind on the body.

Punishment Removal of a positive reinforcer or presentation of an aversive condition contingent in a response followed by a decrease in frequency of that response.

Quadriplegia Disability in all four limbs.

Quality The resonance characteristic of the voice.

Rating scales/behavioral checklists Informal techniques involving predetermined lists or sequences of behaviors, skills, and problems that are rated according to their frequency, and level of attainment, or severity.

Receptive language The demonstration of comprehension of spoken or written words.

Recomposition A restructuring of interpersonal relationships between husband, wife, and other members of the nuclear family, once one member leaves.

Regression Moving from one's present stage of development to a previous, less mature stage.

Rehabilitation The act of restoring to a condition of health or useful functional activity.

Reinforcement A procedure for strengthening a response involving the immediate presentation of a consequence that acts to build the response frequency, duration, or intensity or all three.

Remedial Intended to correct.

Repetitions Pertaining to sounds, syllables, or words whereby the forward flow of speech is interrupted abnormally by tense, irregular reformulations of a word.

Repression A defense mechanism explained in psychoanalytic theory as the act of forcing into the unconscious any anxiety-producing mental image.

Residential school A facility in which an exceptional individual resides for 24 hours each day. This type of service is usually provided for the more severely handicapped.

Resonance The natural or inherent frequency of any oscillating system.

Resource room Any room in a school other than the regular classroom in which special education instruction is offered.

Resource room specialists A special educator employed to provide special assistance to exceptional children and others in regular and special classes through the use of specialized materials and methods.

Retina The expanded end of the optic nerve containing rods and cones.

Retinitis pigmentosa Loss of sight owing to a hereditary condition involving degeneration of the retina.

Retrolental fibroplasia A condition linked to the administration of high concentrations of oxygen administered to the child at birth. This loss of sight is due to the formation of scar tissue in the back of the lens.

Rh incompatibility Parental differences in a certain blood group factor (first discovered in Rhesus monkeys) that can result, for example, in an Rh-negative mother's producing antibodies against a father-contributed Rh-positive factor present in the fetus; this results in agglutination of blood with serious consequences for the baby and the mother.

Rigidity A diagnostic classification of cerebral palsy characterized by stiffness and immobility.

Role expectation Norms specifying the expected behavior of a person who holds a particular position in society.

Rubella German measles, especially hazardous to the fetus during the first three months of pregnancy.

Scoliosis Excessive curve in the lumbar vertebrae.

Screening General evaluation intended to identify potential problems.

Secondary behaviors Habitual, irrelevant movements used as devices to break up or conceal speech blockages in stuttering.

Self-contained special class A placement in which the special educator has the major educational responsibility for the education of the student.

Self-fulfilling prophecy A condition existing when individuals change their behavior in accordance with the expectations others have for them.

Self-injurious behavior Stereotypic action repeated over an extended period of time which results in pain or physical harm to the performer.

Self-stimulatory (stereotypic) behaviors Repetitive movements performed over extended periods of time without obvious purpose.

Semantic Relating to the study of meaning.

Sensitive period A time span during an individual's development in which he or she is more apt to establish primary social bonds with the caretaker.

Sensorineural A term applied to that type of hearing loss which is due to pathology in the inner ear, in the eighth cranial nerve, or both.

Severely or profoundly retarded Label applied to those who score between 0 and 35 on the Stanford-Binet test while concurrently demonstrating severe deficits in adaptive behavior.

Shaping A procedure through which new behaviors are developed by reinforcing successive approximations toward the behavioral objective.

Sheltered workshop A nonprofit rehabilitation facility utilizing individual goals, wages, supportive services, and a controlled work environment to help exceptional individuals achieve their maximum potential as workers.

Sheltered workshop A controlled supervised work environment designed for persons who cannot work in a competitive employment situation. Many of these workshops are under contract to private industries.

Sickle-cell anemia An inherited abnormality of the red blood cells (with cells shaped like "sickles" rather than spheres), resulting in severe anemia and predominantly, but not exclusively, found in persons of African ancestry. Parents who are "carriers" of the disorder may discover this through a sample test and receive counseling relative to treatment and the desirability of reproduction.

Sight switch Device developed by NASA in which the light source from eye movements can be activated and used to control wheelchairs, pages in a book, and an array of mechanical devices.

Skill development training A remedial approach based on the assumption that the deficit is the student's demonstrated performance on a particular skill. This involves an operationalized definition of the behavior, a task analysis of the skill, direct teaching methods, and daily measurement.

Snellen Chart A screening device for visual dysfunction requiring individuals to read letters of various sizes from a specified distance.

Social maladjustment A syndrome in which a person's behavior is sufficiently deviant that he or she cannot participate in normal activities with others. It usually involves violation of social norms and codes of conduct.

Social reinforcement A reinforcing stimulus mediated by another individual within a social context, that is, praise.

Social reinforcer A reinforcing stimulus presented by another individual in a social context, such as praise or a smile.

Socialized delinquent One who adheres to the values and expectations of the gang, acting with the group during the performance of delinquent behavior.

Sociopathic A person whose behavior is aggressively antisocial and who shows no remorse or guilt for his or her misdeeds.

Sociopathic delinquent One who acts in an impulsive rebellious way without subsequent guilt or fear.

Somatopsychology The study of the impact of bodily deviation on behavior and the effect of physical variations on behavior.

Sonic glasses Glasses which aid in the mobility of blind people by scanning the environment and transmitting auditory signals to the individual.

Spasticity Excessive tension of the muscles making control of the muscles difficult.

Special class An instructional alternative for exceptional children which involves the placement of children with similar educational needs in a class taught by a specially trained teacher.

Special education The profession concerned with the arrangement of educational variables leading to the prevention, reduction, or elimination of those conditions that produce significant defects in the academic, communicative, locomotor, or adjustive functions of children.

Speech Communication through conventional oral and vocal symbols.

Speech audiometry The measurement of hearing in terms of the reception of spoken words presented at controlled levels of intensity.

Speech-language pathology The study and treatment of all aspects of functional and organic speech-language defects and disorders.

Speech-language therapist A specialist in the study and treatment of all aspects of functional and organic speech defects and disorders.

Spina bifida A congenital defect characterized by a lack of closure at the base of the vertebral column which in severe cases may result in paralysis in legs and a lack of bladder or bowel control or both; a spinal defect in which the spinal cord tissue protrudes through an opening.

Spina bifida occulta A defect of closure in the posterior bony wall of the spinal canal that is not accompanied by associated spinal cord or meninges petrology.

Standardized achievement tests Achievement test standardized on a population.

Stereotype A conventional, usually oversimplified conception, opinion, or belief.

Stimulation The temporary increase of a functional activity or the efficiency of an organism or any of its parts.

Strabismus A visual defect in which one eye cannot focus with the other on any object because of imbalance of the eye muscles.

Stuttering A disorder of speech flow characterized by syllable disfluency; the abnormal timing of speech sound initiation.

Sublimation A defense mechanism in which one's energy is directed away from working toward undesirable goals and shifts to working on more desirable ones.

Substitution Replacement by one sound of another sound ("tite" for "kite").

Substitutive learning Acquisition of a substitute skill that may reduce a deficit in functioning, for example, reading braille as a substitute for print.

Success criterion A specification of an acceptable level of performance the client is to achieve (that is, 4/5 trials).

Summative assessment Single, end-of-sequence evaluation, for example, year-end achievement test and finals.

Summative evaluation An evaluative test administered to individuals only infrequently over large blocks of time in order to assess achievement gains.

Superego In psychoanalytic theory, that region of the mind which includes a view of ideal behavior and of right and wrong (conscience).

Superstitious behavior A response which has been accidentally reinforced on a single occasion and then persists owing to continuing intermittent reinforcement.

Supporting services Those services provided for the exceptional student which aid progress in areas related to his or her classroom education, such as speech or occupational therapy.

Syndrome A set of symptoms which occur together.

Syntax The way in which words of a language are arranged to create sentences.

Syphilis A contagious venereal disease.

Systematic desensitization A form of counter-conditioning in which positive feelings are substituted for fears and anxieties.

Task analysis The breaking down of a complex skill into its components; it is accompanied by criteria for success at each step.

Task-imbedded reinforcement Rewarding consequences which are inherent in the completion of the task itself.

Time sampling Recording of behavior only during a specific span of time. Data reveal the frequency and duration of a certain behavior pattern.

Token economy A contingency package which delivers tokens, contingent on the emission of target responses. These are later exchangeable for a reinforcing item or activity.

Toxemia Syndrome characterized by edema, hypertension, and protein in the urine during the last trimester of pregnancy.

Toxoplasmosis Infection which, although relatively mild in adults, may cause affected infants to be born with significant involvement of the brain and eye: serious mental retardation may result.

Trainable mentally retarded   Label applied to those who score between 36 and 51 on the Stanford-Binet test while concurrently demonstrating deficits in adaptive behavior.

Tremor   Involuntary shaking or unsteadiness, especially of the extremities.

Validity   Referring to whether a label, study, or the like does or names what it proposes to do.

Vestibular system   A series of small cavities at the beginning of a canal, that is, ear, nose, or aorta.

Vineland Social Maturity Scale   An instrument developed to assess social competency by ascertaining whether the child can complete tasks appropriate for his or her age level.

Visual acuity   The keenness or sharpness of sight.

Visual perception   The ability to make visual sensory stimuli meaningful.

Vocal abuse   Traumatization of the vocal cords or laryngeal area or both.

Vocal cords   The thyroarytenoid ligaments which produce sound when set into vibration.

Vocal nodules   Lesions caused by prolonged, vigorous use of voice; the precursor of polyps.

Vocal rest   The abstinence from phonation, including whispering, as a procedure to remediate vocal abuse; remaining silent.

Vocational education   Educational programs directly related to the preparation of individuals for paid or unpaid employment.

Vocational rehabilitation   A program in which the goal is potential employment for people whose physical, mental, or learning disability is a hindrance to employment.

Voice   Sound produced primarily by the vibration of the vocal bands.

Ward of the court   A child or incompetent person placed under the care of a guardian or court when parents are absent or unable to care for him or her.

Word blindness   *See* dyslexia.

REFERENCES

Abelson, A., & Berenson, B. *An interdisciplinary approach to research (final report).* Arlington, Va.: Council for Exceptional Children, 1970.

Adams, M. E. Siblings of the retarded: Their problems and treatment. *Child Welfare,* 1967, **46,** 310–316.

Adelman, H. S., & Compas, B. E. Stimulant drugs and learning problems. *Journal of Special Education,* 1977, **11,** 377–416.

Administration for Children, Youth and Families (ACYF). *Head Start: Directions for the next three years* (draft). Washington, D.C.: Office of Human Development Services, Department of Health and Human Services, October 22, 1981.

Affirmative action obligations of contractors and subcontractors for handicapped workers. *Federal Register,* April 16, 1976 (Section 503).

Aldrich, C. A. Preventive medicine and mongolism. *American Journal of Mental Deficiency,* 1947, **52**(2), 127–129.

Algozzine, B., Schmid, R., & Conners, B. Toward an acceptable definition of emotional disturbance. *Behavioral Disorders,* 1978, **4,** 48–52.

538

Allen, G. Patterns of discovery in the genetics of mental deficiency. *American Journal of Mental Deficiency,* 1950, **62**, 840-849.

Allum, N. *Spina bifida: The treatment and care of spina bifida children.* London: Allen and Unwin, 1975.

Aloia, G. F. Effects of physical stigmata and labels on judgments of subnormality by preservice teachers. *Mental Retardation,* 1975, **13**, 17-21.

Anastasi, A. *Psychological testing.* New York: Macmillan, 1976.

Anderson, E. M., & Spain, B. *The child with spina bifida.* Hampshire, England: Division Associated Book Publishers, 1977.

Anderson, G., & Bowe, F. Racism within the deaf community. *American Annals of the Deaf,* 1972, **117**, 617-619.

Andrews, R. J., & Andrews, J. G. A study of the spontaneous oral language of Down's syndrome children. *Exceptional Child,* 1977, **24**(2), 86-94.

Apgar, V. A. A proposal for a new method of evaluation of the newborn infant. *Current Researches in Anesthesia and Analgesia,* 1953, **32**, 260-264.

Arnheim, D. D., & Sinclair, W. A. *The clumsy child.* St. Louis: C. V. Mosby, 1975.

Arnheim, D. D., Auxter, D., & Crowe, W. D. *Principles and methods of adapted physical education and recreation.* (3d ed.) St. Louis: C. V. Mosby, 1977.

Arthur, G. *The Arthur adaptation of the Leiter International Performance Scale.* Chicago: C. H. Stoelting, 1950.

Ausubel, D. P., & Sullivan, E. V. *Theory and problems of child development.* (2d ed.) New York: Grune & Stratton, 1970.

Axline, V. *Play therapy.* Boston: Houghton Mifflin, 1947.

Badger, E. The infant stimulation/mother training program project. In B. Caldwell (Ed.), *Infant education.* New York: Walker & Co., 1977.

Bagnato, S. J., & Neisworth, J. T. Between assessment and intervention: Forging an assessment/curriculum linkage for the handicapped preschooler. *Child Care Quarterly,* Fall 1979a **(3)**.

Bagnato, S. J., & Neisworth, J. T. The Intervention Efficiency Index: An approach to preschool program accountability. *Exceptional Children,* 1980b, **46**(4), 264-269.

Bagnato, S. J., Neisworth, J. T., & Eaves, R. E. A profile of perceived capabilities for the preschool child. *Child Care Quarterly,* Winter 1978, **4,** 326-335.

Bailey, D. A. Exercise fitness and physical education for the growing child: A concern. Paper presented to the National Conference on Fitness and Health, Ottawa, Ontario, Canada, December 4, 1972.

Ball, T. Itard, Seguin, and Kephart: *Sensory education—A learning interpretation.* Columbus, Ohio: Charles E. Merrill, 1971.

Baller, W. R. A study in the present social status of a group of adults who, when they were in elementary schools, were classified as mentally deficient. *Genetic Psychology Monographs,* 1936, **18**, 165-244.

Bank-Mikklesen, N. E. Model service models: A metropolitan area in Denmark, Copenhagen. In R. B. Kugel & W. Wolfensberger (Eds.), *Changing patterns in residential services for the mentally retarded.* Washington, D.C.: President's Committee on Mental Retardation, 1969.

Barbara, D. A. *Stuttering: A psychodynamic approach to its understanding and treatment.* New York: Julian, 1954.

Barclay, A., Goulet, L. R., Holtgrieve, M. M., & Sharp. A. R. Parental evaluation of clinical services for retarded children. *American Journal of Mental Deficiency,* 1962, **67**, 232–237.

Barker, R. G., & Wright, B. A. Disablement: The somatopsychological problem. In E. D. Wittkower & R. A. Cleghorn (Eds.), *Recent developments in psychosomatic medicine.* Philadelphia: Lippincott, 1954.

Barker, R. G., Wright, B. A., Meyerson, L., & Gonic, M. R. *Adjustment to physical handicap and illness: A survey of the social psychology of physique and disability.* Bulletin 55. (2d ed.) New York: Social Science Research Council, 1953.

Baroff, G. S. *Mental retardation: Nature, cause, and management.* New York: Wiley, 1974.

Barraga, N. C., & Collins, M. E. Development of efficiency in visual functioning: Rationale for a comprehensive program. *Journal of Impairment and Blindness,* April 1979, **73**(4), 121–126.

Bartak, L., Rutter, M., & Cox, A. A comparative study of infantile autism and specific developmental receptive language disorder: 1. The Children. *British Journal of Psychiatry,* 1975, **126**, 127–145.

Baumeister, A. A., & Merna, J. R. On defining mental retardation. *Journal of Special Education,* 1975, **9**, 293–306.

Bayley, N. *Manual for the Bayley scales of infant development.* New York: Psychological Corporation, 1969.

Bayley, N. *Bayley scales of infant development: Birth to two years.* New York: Psychological Corporation, 1969.

Beach, F. A., & Jaynes, J. Effects of early experience on the behavior of animals. *Psychological Bulletin,* 1954, **51**, 239–263.

Beattie vs. State Board of Education, 172 N.W. 153 (1919).

Beery, K. E., & Buktenica, N. *Developmental test of visual-motor integration.* Chicago: Follett, 1967.

Beez, W. Influence of biased psychological reports on "teacher" behavior and pupil performance. Unpublished doctoral dissertation, Indiana University, 1970.

Bennet, J.M. The proof of the pudding. *The Exceptional Parent,* 1981, **11**(1), 21–26.

Bereiter, C., & Englemann, S. *Teaching disadvantaged children in the preschool.* Englewood Cliffs, N.J.: Prentice-Hall, 1966.

Bernal, E. M., Jr. The identification of gifted Chicano children. In A. Baldwin, G. H. Gear, & L. J. Lucito (Eds.), *Educational planning for the gifted: Overcoming cultural, geographic, and socioeconomic barriers.* Reston, Va.: Council for Exceptional Children, 1978.

540

Bernstein, B.   Social class and linguistic development: A theory of social learning. In A. H. Halsey, F. Anderson, & C. A. Anderson (Eds.), *Education, economy, and society.* Glencoe, Ill.: Free Press, 1961.

Bernstein, B.   Social structure, language and learning. *Educational Research,* 1961, **3**, 163–176.

Bernstein, B.   A sociolinguistic approach to socialization: With some reference to educability. In F. Williams (Ed.), *Language and poverty: Perspectives on a theme.* Chicago: Markham, 1970.

Bernstein, N. R.   Mental retardation. In S. I. Harrison (Ed.), *Basic handbook of child psychiatry.* Vol. 3. New York: Basic Books, 1979.

Berscheid, E., & Walster, E. H.   *Interpersonal attraction.* Reading, Mass.: Addison-Wesley, 1978.

Best, H.   *Deafness and the deaf in the United States.* New York: Macmillan, 1943.

Bijou, S.   Behavior modification in teaching the retarded child. In C. Thoresea (Ed.), *Behavior modification in education.* (72nd Yearbook of the National Society for the Study of Education.) Chicago: University of Chicago Press, 1973.

Bijou, S. W.   A functional analysis of retarded development. In N. R. Ellis (Ed.), *International review of research in mental retardation.* Vol. 1. New York: Academic Press, 1966.

Bijou, S. W., & Baer, D. M.   The laboratory-experimental study of child behavior. In Paul H. Mussen (Ed.), *Handbook of research methods in child development.* New York: Wiley, 1960.

Bijou, S. W., & Baer, D. M.   *Child development I: A systematic and empirical theory.* New York: Appleton-Century-Crofts, 1961.

Bijou, S. W., & Baer, D. M.   *Child development: Readings in experimental analyses.* New York: Appleton-Century-Crofts, 1967.

Birch, H.   Boldness and judgment in behavior genetics. In M. Mead, T. Dobzhansky, E. Tobach & R. E. Light (Eds.), *Science and the concept of race.* New York: Columbia University Press, 1968.

Birch, J. W., & Johnstone, B. K.   *Designing schools and schooling for the handicapped.* Springfield, Ill: Charles C. Thomas, 1975.

Birch, J. W., Tisdall, W. J., Peabody, R., & Sterrett, R.   *School achievement and effect of type size on reading in visually handicapped children.* Pittsburgh, Pa.: University of Pittsburgh Press, 1966.

Birenbaum, A.   On managing a courtesy stigma. *Journal of Health Soc. Behavior,* 1970, **11,** 196–206.

Black, J. W.   The effect of delayed sidetone upon vocal rate and intensity. *Journal of Speech and Hearing Disorders,* 1951, **16**, 56–60.

Blatt, B.   Some persistently recurring assumptions concerning the mentally subnormal. *Training School Bulletin,* 1960, **57**, 48–59.

Bleck, E. E.   Muscular dystrophy-duchenne type. In E. E. Bleck & D. A. Nagel (Eds.), *Physically handicapped children: A medical atlas for teachers.* New York: Grune & Stratton, 1975.

REFERENCES

Bloom, B. *Stability and change in human characteristics.* New York: Wiley, 1964.

Bloom, L., & Lahey, M. *Language development and language disorders,* New York: Wiley, 1978.

Bobath, B., & Bobath, K. *Motor development in the different types of cerebral palsy.* London: William Heinemann Medical Books, 1975.

Boehm, A. E. *Boehm test of basic concepts manual.* New York: Psychological Corporation, 1971.

Boone, D. *The voice and voice therapy.* (2d ed.) Englewood Cliffs, N.J.: Prentice-Hall, 1977.

Botwinick, J. *Aging and behavior.* New York: Springer, 1973.

Bower, E. M. *Early identification of emotionally handicapped children in school.* Springfield, Ill:. Charles C. Thomas, 1969.

Braginsky, D. D., & Braginsky, B. M. *Hansels and Gretels: Studies of children in institutions for the mentally retarded.* New York: Holt, Rinehart and Winston, 1971.

Bricker, D., & Sheehan, R. *Effectiveness of an early intervention program as indexed by measures of child change.* Paper presented at the HCEEP Directors' Meeting, Washington, D.C., December 1980.

Bricker, D., Dennison, L., & Bricker, W. *A language intervention program for developmentally young children.* Miami, Fla.: Mailman Center for Child Development, University of Miami, 1976.

Brigance, A. H. *Brigance diagnostic inventory of basic skills.* MS: Curriculum Associates, Inc. 1977.

Brock, R. J. *Preparing vocational and special education personnel to work with special needs students—State-of-the-art, 1977-79.* Menomonie, Wis.: University of Wisconsin-Stout, 1979.

Bronfenbrenner, U. *A report on longitudinal evaluations of preschool programs.* Vol. 2: *Is early intervention effective?* Washington, D.C.: U.S. Department of Health, Education and Welfare, Publication No. (OHD) 24-25, 1974.

Brookshire, R. H. *An introduction to aphasia.* Minneapolis: BRK Publishers, 1973.

Brown, L., Wilcox, B., Sontag, E., Vincent, B., Dodd, N., & Gruenewald, L. Toward the realization of the least restrictive educational environments for severely handicapped students. *American Association for the Education of the Severely/Profoundly Handicapped Review,* 1977, **2**(4), 195-201.

Brown, R. Development of the first language in the human species. *American Psychologist,* 1973, **18**, 97-106.

Bruininks, V. L., & Bruininks, R. H. Motor proficiency of learning disabled and nondisabled students. *Perceptual and Motor Skills,* 1977, **44**, 1131-1137.

Brutten, E. J., & Shoemaker, D. J. *The modification of stuttering.* Englewood Cliffs, N.J.: Prentice-Hall, 1967.

542

Buck, P. *The child who never grew.* New York: John Day, 1950.

Buell, C. E. *Physical education and recreation for the visually handicapped.* Washington, D.C.: American Alliance of Health, Physical Education and Recreation, 1973.

Burr, W. R. Satisfaction with various aspects of marriage over the life cycle: A random middle-class sample. *Journal of Marriage and the Family,* 1970, **32**, 29-37.

Buscaglia, L. *The disabled and their parents: A counseling challenge.* Thorofare, N.J.: Charles B. Slack, 1975.

Callahan, C. M. The gifted and talented woman. In A. H. Passow (Ed.), *Education of the gifted and talented.* Chicago: University of Chicago Press, 1979.

Cantwell, D. P. Clinical picture, epidemiology, and classifications of the hyperactive child syndrome. In D. P. Cantwell (Ed.), *The hyperactive child. Diagnosis, management, current research.* New York: Spectrum Publications, 1975a.

Cantwell, D. P. Natural history and prognosis in the hyperactive child syndrome. In D. P. Cantwell (Ed.), *The hyperactive child. Diagnosis, management, current research.* New York: Spectrum Publications, 1975b.

Capute, A. J. Cerebral palsy and associated disorders. In R. H. A. Haslam & P. J. Valletutti (Eds.), *Medical problems in the classroom.* Baltimore: University Park Press, 1975.

Career education incentive programs. *Federal Register,* December 18, 1978, **43**(243) (P.L. 95-207).

Carr, J. A comparative study of the development of mongol and normal children from 0-4 years. Unpublished Ph.D. thesis, University of London, 1975.

Carr, J. Mongolism: Telling the parents. *Developmental Medicine and Child Neurology,* 1970, **12**, 213-221.

Carr, J. The effects of the severely subnormal on their families. In Ann M. Clark & A. D. B. Clark (Eds.), *Mental Deficiency: The Changing Outlook* (3d ed.) New York: Free Press, 1974.

Carrell, J. A. *Disorders of articulation.* Prentice-Hall Foundations of Speech Pathology Series. Englewood Cliffs, N.J.: Prentice-Hall, 1968.

Cartwright, G. P. *Oversight hearing: Implementation of P.L. 94-142.* Presented to the Subcommittee on the Handicapped, Oct. 10, 1979.

Cartwright, G. P., & Cartwright, C. A. *Developing observation skills.* New York: McGraw-Hill, 1974.

Cassidy, V., & Stanton, J. An investigation of factors in the educational placement of mentally retarded children: A study of differences between children in special and regular classes in Ohio. U.S. Office of Education Cooperative Research Program, Project No. 043, Columbus, Ohio State University, 1959.

Cazden, C. *Environmental assistance to the child's acquisition of grammar.* Unpublished doctoral dissertation, Harvard University, 1965.

REFERENCES

Cegelka, W. J., & Tyler, J. L.   The efficacy of special class placement for the mentally retarded in proper perspective. *Training School Bulletin,* 1970, **67**, 33–68.

Centerwall, S. A., & Centerwall, W. H.   A study of children with mongolism reared in the home compared to those reared away from home. *Pediatrics,* 1960, **25**, 678–685.

Certo, N., Schwartz, R., and Brown, L.   Community transportation: Teaching severely handicapped students to ride a public bus system. In L. Brown, T. Crowner, W. Williams, and R. York (Eds.), *Madison's alternative for zero exclusion: A book of readings.* Vol. 5. Madison, Wis.: Madison Public Schools, 1975.

Chandler, H. N., & Utz, V. R.   PL. 94-142: Responsibility for the special education teacher. *Pointer,* 1979, **23**(2), 66–76.

Charles, D. C.   Ability and accomplishment of persons earlier judged mentally deficient. *Genetic Psychology Monographs,* 1953, **47,** 3–71.

Chase, H. C.   Perinatal mortality: Overview and current trends. *Clinics in Perinatology,* 1974, **1**, 3–17.

Chase, J. B.   Developmental assessment of handicapped infants and young children: With special attention to the visually impaired. *New Outlook for the Blind,* October 1975, 341–348.

Chaves, T., & Solar, J.   Pedro Ponce de Leon, first teacher of the deaf. *Sign Language Studies,* 1974, **5**, 48–63.

Chomsky, N., & Halle, M.   *The sound pattern of English.* New York: Harper & Row, 1968.

Christoplos, F., & Renz, P. A.   Critical examination of special education programs. *Journal of Special Education,* 1969, **3**, 371–379.

Churchill, D. W.   The relation of infantile autism and early childhood schizophrenia to developmental language disorders of childhood. *Journal of Autism and Childhood Schizophrenia,* 1972, **2**, 182–197.

Clark, A. M., & Clark, A. D.   *Early experience: Myth and evidence.* New York: Free Press, 1976.

Clarke, H. H.   *Application of measurement to health and physical education.* (4th ed.) Englewood Cliffs, N.J.: Prentice-Hall, 1967.

Clarren, S. K., & Smith, D. W.   The fetal alcohol syndrome. *New England Journal of Medicine,* 1978, **298**, 1063–1067.

Clausen, J. A.   Quo vadis, AAMD? *Journal of Special Education,* 1972, **6**, 51–60.

Cleary, T. A., Humphreys, L. G., Kendrick, S. A., & Wesman, A.   Educational uses of tests with disadvantaged students. *American Psychologist,* 1975, **30**, 15–41.

Clements, S. D.   Minimal brain dysfunction in children. NINDS Monograph No. 3, Public Health Service Bulletin No. 1415. Washington, D.C.: U.S. Department of Health, Education and Welfare, 1966.

Cleveland, D. W., & Miller, N.   Attitudes and life commitments of older siblings of mentally retarded adults: An exploratory study. *Mental Retardation,* 1977, **15,** 38–41.

544

Clifford, M. M., & Walster, E.   Research note: The effects of physical attractiveness on teacher expectations. *Sociology of Education,* 1973, **46,** 248–258.

Coburn, J.   Sterilization regulations: Debate not quelled by HEW document. *Science,* 1974, **183,** 935–939.

Connors, C. K., Goyette, C. M., Southwick, D. A., Lees, J. M., & Andrulonis, P. A.   Food additives and hyperkinesis: A controlled double-blind study. *Pediatrics,* 1976, **58,** 154–166.

Consteria, O.   Follow the rainbow. *The Exceptional Parent,* 1977, **7,** M6–M7.

Cooper, E. B.   *Personalized fluency control therapy (PFCT).* Austin, Tex.: Learning Concepts, 1976.

Corbin, C. B.   Physical fitness in children. In C. B. Corbin (Ed.) *A textbook of motor development.* Dubuque, Iowa: William C. Brown Company, 1973.

Coriat, I. H.   The nature and analytical treatment of stuttering. *Proceedings of the American Speech Correction Association,* 1931, **1,** 151–156.

Corn, A. L., & Martinez, I.   *When you have a visually handicapped child in your classroom: Suggestions for teachers.* New York: American Foundation for the Blind, 1977.

Corsini, D., & Rothschild, J.   *Parental approach for early intervention of learning disabilities (final report, 1972–1976).* Washington, D.C.: Bureau of Elementary and Secondary Education, No. EC 090565, 1976.

Cox, L. S.   Diagnosing and remediating systematic errors in addition and subtraction computations. *The Arithmetic Teacher,* 1975, **22,** 151–157.

Cratty, B. J.   The clumsy child syndrome: Some answers to questions parents ask. Unpublished manuscript, 1975.

Croft, N. B., & Robinson, L. W.   *Project vision-up curriculum, a training program for preschool handicapped children.* Boise, Idaho: Educational Products Training Foundation, 1976.

Cruickshank, W. M., & Quay, H. C.   Learning and physical design: The necessity for research and research design. *Exceptional Children,* 1970, **37,** 261–268.

Cummings, S. T.   The impact of the child's deficiency on the father: A study of fathers of mentally retarded and chronically ill children. *American Journal of Orthopsychiatry,* 1976, **46,** 246–255.

Cummings, S. T., & Stock, D.   Brief group therapy for mothers of retarded children outside of the specialty clinical setting. *American Journal of Mental Deficiency,* 1962, **66,** 739–748.

Dale, P. S.   *Language development.* Hinsdale, Illinois: Dryden Press, 1972.

Darwin, Charles.   *The descent of man.* (2d ed.) Philadelphia: McKay Publishers, 1874.

Daurio, S. P.   Educational enrichment versus acceleration: A review of the literature. In W. C. George, S. J. Cohn, & J. C. Stanley (Eds.), *Educating the gifted: Acceleration and enrichment.* Revised and expanded proceedings of the ninth annual Hyman Blumberg symposium on research in early childhood education. Baltimore: John Hopkins University Press, 1979. *Strategies for educating the gifted,* 1979.

Davis, H., & Goldstein, R. Audiometry: Other auditory tests. In H. Davis & D. R. Silverman, (Eds.), *Hearing and deafness.* (3d ed.) New York: Holt, Rinehart and Winston, 1970.

Davis, J. (Ed.). *Our forgotten children: Hard of hearing pupils in the schools.* Minneapolis: University of Minnesota, 1977.

Deinstitutionalization: "We never discussed my brother, I barely remember him." *The Exceptional Parent,* 1977a, **7**, Y21-Y23.

Dembo, T., and Tane-Baskin, E. The noticeability of the cosmetic glove. *Artificial Limbs,* 1955, **2**, 47-56.

DeMott, R. M. Reporting continuous progress. *Education of the Visually Handicapped,* 1974, **5**, 86-92.

Deno, E. N. Special education as developmental capital. *Exceptional Children.* 1970, **37**, 229-237.

Deno, E. N. Strategies for improvement of educational opportunities for handicapped children: Suggestions for exploitation of EPDA Potential. In M. C. Reynolds & M. D. Davis (Eds.), *Exceptional children in regular classrooms.* Minneapolis: University of Minnesota Press, 1971.

Deno, S., & P. Merken. *Data-based program modification.* Reston, Va.: Council for Exceptional Children, 1977.

Denoff, E. Medical aspects. In W. M. Cruickshank (Ed.), *Cerebral palsy: A developmental disability.* Syracuse, N.Y.: Syracuse University Press, 1976.

Deutsch, M., & Brown, B. Social influences on negro-white intelligence differences. *Journal of Social Issues,* 1964, **20,** 25-35.

Deutsch, M., Hatz, I., & Jensen, A. (Eds.). *Social class, race, and psychological development.* New York: Holt, Rinehart and Winston, 1968.

Dingman, H. F., & Tarjan, A. Mental retardation and the normal distribution curve. *American Journal of Mental Deficiency,* 1960, **64**, 991-994.

Dion, K. K. Physical attractiveness and evaluation of children's transgressions. *Journal of Personality and Social Psychology,* 1972, **24**, 207-213.

Dion, K. K., & Berscheid, E. Physical attractiveness and peer perception among children. *Sociometry,* 1974, **37**, 1-12.

Doll, E. A. *The measurement of social competence.* Minneapolis: 1955.

Doll, E. *Vineland social maturity scale.* Circle Pines, Minn.: American Guidance Service, 1965.

Doll, E. A. *Preschool attainment record.* Circle Pines, Minn.: American Guidance Service, 1966.

Downs, M. P., and Sterrett, G. M. Identification and training of a deaf child: Birth to one year. *Volta Review,* 1967, **70**(3), 154-158.

Drabman, R. S. Behavior modification in the classroom. In W. E. Graighead, A. E. Kazdin, & M. J. Mahoney (Eds.), *Behavior modification: Principles, issues and applications.* Boston: Houghton Mifflin, 1976.

Dubose, R. F., & Langley, M. B. *The developmental activities screening inventory.* New York: Teaching Resources, 1977.

Ducanis, A. J., & Golin, A. K. *The interdisciplinary team.* Germantown, Md.: Aspen Systems Corporation, in press.

Dunn, L. M. Special education for the mildly retarded: Is much of it justifiable? *Exceptional Children,* 1968, **35**, 5–22.

Dunn, L. M., & Markwardt, F. C. *Peabody individual achievement test.* Circle Pines, Minn.: American Guidance Service, 1970.

Dunn, L. M. Children with moderate and severe general learning disabilities. In L. M. Dunn (Ed.), *Exceptional children in the schools: Special education in transition* (2d ed.) New York: Holt, Rinehart and Winston, 1973.

Edgerton, R B. *The cloak of competence: Stigma in the lives of the mentally retarded.* Berkeley, Calif.: University of California Press, 1967.

Eisenson, J., & Ogilvie, M. *Speech correction in the schools.* (3d ed.) New York: Macmillan, 1971.

Engel, M. The tin drum revisited. *Journal of Special Education,* 1969, **3**, 381–384.

Erikson, E. H. (Ed.) *Insight and responsibility,* New York: Norton, 1964.

Evans, L., Rhinehart, J. B., & Succopi, R. A. Failure to thrive: A study of forty-five children and their families. In S. I. Harrison & J. F. McDerMott, Jr. (Eds.), *New directions in childhood psychopathology.* Vol. 1: *Developmental considerations.* New York: International Universities Press, 1980.

Evans, R. N. *Career education and vocational education: Similarities and contrasts.* Washington, D.C.: U.S. Government Printing Office, 1975.

Eysenck, H. J. The effects of psychotherapy: An evaluation: *Journal of Consulting Psychology,* 1952, **16**, 319–324.

Fait, H. F. *Special physical education.* (4th ed.) Philadelphia: W. B. Saunders, 1978.

Farber, B. *Family organization and crises: Maintenance and integration in families with a severely retarded child.* Monographs of the Society for Research in Child Development, 1960, **25** (1).

Farber, B. *Mental Retardation: Its social context and social consequences.* Boston: Houghton Mifflin, 1968.

Farber, B. Family adaptations to severely mentally retarded children. In M. Begob & S. Richardson (Eds.), *The mentally retarded and society: A social science perspective.* Baltimore: University Park Press, 1975.

Farber, B., & Ryckman, D. B. Effects of severely mentally retarded child on family relationships. *Mental Retardation Abstracts 2,* 1965, **1**, 1–17.

Farina, A., & Ring, K. The influence of perceived mental illness in interpersonal relations. *Journal of Abnormal Psychology,* 1965, **70**, 47–51.

Favell, J. E., & McGimsey, J. F. Relative effectiveness and efficiency of group vs. individual training of severely retarded persons. *American Journal of Mental Deficiency,* 1978, **83**, 104–109.

REFERENCES Faye, A. E. *The low vision patient.* New York: Grune & Stratton, 1970.

Faye, A. E., & Hood, C. M. *A worker's guide to characteristics of partial sight.* (rev. ed.) New York: New York Association for the Blind, 1969.

Federal Register, August 23, 1977, **42** (163), 42478.

Federal Register, December 29, 1977, **42**, 65083.

Feigenbaum, I. *English now.* New York: New Century, 1970.

Fenichel, O. *The psychoanalytic theory of neurosis.* New York: Norton, 1945.

Ferleger, D. The future of institutions for retarded citizens—the promise of the Pennhurst case. *Mental retardation and the Law.* Washington, D.C.: Office of the Assistant Secretary for Human Development, U.S. Department of Health, Education and Welfare Publication 78-21012, 1978.

Ferster, C. B. Reinforcement and behavioral deficits of autistic children. *Child Development,* 1961, **32**, 437-456.

Filler, J. W., Robinson, C. C., Smith, R. A., Vincent-Smith, L. J., Bricker, D. D., & Bricker, W. A. Mental retardation. In N. Hobbs (Ed.), *Issues in the classification of children.* Vol. 1. San Francisco: Jossey-Bass, 1976.

Foley, J. M. Effect of labeling and teacher behavior on children's attitudes. *American Journal of Mental Deficiency,* 1978, **83**, 380-384.

Forseth, S., Hynes, J., & Sorom, J. Helping retarded students reenter the community. *Social Work in Education,* 1981, **3**, 23-35.

Foster, G., & Keech, V. Teacher reactions to the label of educable mentally retarded. *Education and Training of the Mentally Retarded,* 1977, **12**, 307-311.

Foster, G. G., & Sabatino, D. A. *Non-motoric visual gestalt test.* State College, Pa: Model Learning Disability Systems, 1976.

Foster G., & Salvia, J. Teacher response to label of learning disabled as a function of demand characteristics. *Exceptional Children,* 1977, **43**, 533-534.

Foster, G., Ysseldyke, J., & Reese, J. I wouldn't have seen it I hadn't believed it. *Exceptional Children,* 1975, **41**, 469-473.

Fotheringham, J. B., & Creal, D. Handicapped children and handicapped families. *International Review of Education,* 1974, **20**, 355-369.

Fowle, C. M. The effects of the severely mentally retarded child on his family. *American Journal of Mental Deficiency,* 1968, **73**, 468-473.

Fox, L. The effects of sex role socialization on mathematics participation and achievement. In L. Fox, E. Fennema, & J. Sherman, *Women and mathematics: Research perspectives for change.* NIE Papers on Education and Work, No. 8. Washington, D.C., National Institute of Education, 1977.

Fox, W. F., Egner, A. N., Paolucci, P. B., Perelman, P. F., & McKenzie, H. S. An introduction to a regular classroom approach to special education. In E. Deno (Ed.), *Instructional alternatives for exceptional children.* Reston, Va.: Council for Exceptional Children, 1973.

Frank, A. A. Breaking down learning tasks: A sequence approach. *Teaching Exceptional Children.* Fall 1973, **6**(1), 16-19.

Frank, L. K. Play is valid. *Childhood Education,* 1968, 433-440.

Frankenburg, W. K., Dodds, J. B., & Fandal, A. W. *Denver developmental screening test.* Denver: Ladoca Project & Publishing Foundation, 1975.

Fredericks, H. D., Riggs, C., Furey, T., Grove, D., Moore, W., McDonnell, J., Jordan, E., Hanson, W., Baldwin, V., & Wadlow, M. *The teaching research curriculum for moderately and severely handicapped.* Springfield, Ill.: Charles C. Thomas, 1976.

Freed, G. H. *Anti-stammering device.* U.S. Patent Office, No. 2,818,065, December 31, 1957.

Freedman, D., Fox-Kalenda, B., & Brown, S. A multihandicapped rubella baby: The first 18 months. *Journal of the American Academy of Child Psychiatry,* 1970, **9**, 274–282.

Freehill, M. F. *Gifted children.* New York: Macmillan, 1961.

French, J. L. *The pictorial test of intelligence.* Boston: Houghton Mifflin, 1964.

Freund, H. *Psychopathology and the problems of stuttering.* Springfield, Ill.: Charles C. Thomas, 1966.

Friedlander, B. Z. The effect of speaker identity, voice inflection, vocabulary, and message redundancy on infants' selection of vocal reinforcers. Paper presented at the meeting of the Society for Research in Child Development, New York, March 1967.

Frisina, R. *Report of the committee to redefine deaf and hard of hearing.* Washington, D.C.: Conference of Executives of American Schools for the Deaf, 1974.

Froebel, F. W. A. *Die Menschenerziehung, die Erziehungsunterrichtung und Lehrkunst.* Leipzig: Weinbrack, 1826.

Froeschels, E. Chewing method as therapy. *Archives of Otolaryngology,* 1952, **56**, 427–434.

Frostig, M. Visual perception of the brain-injured child. *American Journal of Orthopsychiatrics,* 1963, **33**, 665–671.

Frostig, M., & Horne, D. *The Frostig program for the development of visual perception.* Chicago: Tollett, 1964.

Furfey, P., & Harte, F. *Interaction of deaf and hearing in Baltimore City, Maryland.* Washington, D.C.: Catholic University, 1968.

Gallagher, J. J., Forsythe, P., Ringelheim, D., & Weintraub, F. J. Funding patterns and labeling. In N. Hobbs (Ed.), *Issues in the classification of children,* vol. 11. San Francisco: Jossey-Bass, 1975.

Garland, C., Stone, N., Swanson, J., & Woodruff, G. (Eds.) *Early intervention for children with special needs and their families: Findings and recommendations.* Seattle, Wash: WESTAR, 1981.

Garrett, J. E., & Brazil, N. Categories used for identification and education of exceptional children. *Exceptional Children,* 1979, **45**, 291–292.

Gearheart, B. R. (Ed.). *Education of exceptional children.* Scranton, Pa.: International Textbook, 1972.

Gentile, D., & McCarthy, B. *Additional handicapping conditions among hearing impaired students, United States, 1971–1972.* Gallaudet College Office of Demographic Studies, Series D, No. 14, Washington D.C.: Gallaudet College Press, 1973.

Gesell, A. *Studies in child development.* New York: Harper & Row, 1948.

Gillung, T., & Rucker, C. Labels and teacher expectations. *Exceptional Children,* 1977, **43**, 464–465.

Ginzberg E., & Bray, D. W. *The uneducated.* New York: Columbia University Press, 1953.

Glauber, I. P. The psychoanalysis of stuttering. In J. Eisenson (Ed.), *Stuttering: A symposium.* New York: Harper & Row, 1958.

Glavin, J. P. Follow-up behavioral research in resource rooms. *Exceptional Children,* 1973, **40**, 211–213.

Glavin, J. P., Quay, H. C., Annesley, F. R. & Werry, J. S. An experimental resource room for behavior problem children. *Exceptional Children,* 1971, **38**, 131–137.

Goffman, E. *Stigma: Notes on the management of spoiled identity.* Englewood Cliffs, N.J.: Prentice-Hall, 1963.

Gold, M. Task analysis of a complex assembly task by the retarded blind. *Exceptional Children,* 1976, **43**(2), 78–85.

Gold, M. *The acquisition of a complex assembly task by retarded adolescents* (final report), Project 8–8060, Grant No. OEG-0-9-232021-0769 (032). Washington, D.C.: U.S. Office of Education, Bureau of Education for the Handicapped, 1969.

Goldfarb, W. Infant rearing as a factor in foster home replacement. *American Journal of Orthopsychiatry,* 1945a, **15**, 162.

Goldfarb, W. Psychological privation in infancy and subsequent adjustment. *American Journal of Orthopsychiatry,* 1945b, **15**, 247.

Goldstein, H. Construction of a social learning climate. *Focus on Exceptional Children,* 1969, **1**(2), 94–114.

Goldstein, H., Moss, J. W., & Jordan, L. J. *The efficacy of special class training on the development of mentally retarded children.* U.S. Office of Education Cooperative Research Program, Project No. 619, Urbana: University of Illinois Press, 1965.

Goldstein, K. *The Organism.* New York: American Book, 1939.

Golladay, M. A., and Wulfsberg, R. M. *The condition of vocational education.* (Review ed.) Washington, D.C.: National Center for Educational Statistics, September 17, 1980.

Goodman, H., Gottlieb, J., & Harrison, R. Social acceptance of EMRs integrated into a nongraded elementary school. *American Journal of Mental Deficiency,* 1972, **76**, 412–417.

Gordin, R. The design of a preschool therapeutic playground: An indoor learning laboratory. New York: New York University Medical Center, Institute of Rehabilitation Medicine, 1972.

Gordon, E. W. Methodological problems and pseudo issues in the nature-nurture controversy. In R. Cancio (Ed.), *Intelligence: Genetic and Environmental Influences.* New York: Grune & Stratton, 1971.

550

Gordon, S. *Sexual rights for people who happen to be handicapped.* Syracuse, N.Y.: Syracuse University, 1974.

Gordon, T. *Parent effectiveness training.* New York: Wyden, 1970.

Gottlieb, J. Attitudes toward retarded children: Effects of labeling and academic performance. *American Journal of Mental Deficiency,* 1974, **79** (3), 268–273.

Graham, F., & Kendall, B. S. Memory for designs test: Revised general manual. *Perceptual and Motor Skills,* 1960, **11**, 147–188.

Graubard, P. S. Children with behavioral disabilities. In L. M. Dunn (Ed.), *Exceptional children in the schools.* New York: Holt, Rinehart and Winston, 1973.

Graubard, P. S., Rosenberg, H., & Miller, M. B. Student applications of behavior modification to teachers and environments or ecological approaches to social deviancy. In E. A. Ramp & B. L. Hopkins (Eds.), *A new direction for education: Behavior analysis.* Lawrence, Kans.: Support and Development Center for Follow Through, 1971.

Gray, B. B., & Ryan, B. P. *Monterey language program.* Palo Alto, Calif.: Monterey Learning Systems, 1972.

Greenwood, L. H. Shots in the dark. In I. P. Schloss (Ed.), *Implications of altering the definition of blindness.* Research Bulletin No. 3. American Foundation for the Blind. New York: August 1963.

Grosse, S. J., & Becherer, M. C. *Physical education activities for the uncoordinated student.* West Nyack, N.Y.: Parker, 1975.

Grossman, F. K. *Brothers and sisters of retarded children: An exploratory study.* Syracuse, N.Y.: Syracuse University Press, 1972.

Grossman, H. J. (Ed.) *Manual on terminology and classification in mental retardation.* (7th rev. ed.) Washington, D.C.: American Association on Mental Deficiency, 1977.

Gruber, K. F. Self-concept of the visually impaired. Symposium presented at a meeting for the Special Education and Vocational Rehabilitation of the Visually Impaired, Teachers College, Columbia University, 1966.

Guess, D. A functional analysis of receptive language and productive speech: Acquisition of the plural morpheme. *Journal of Applied Behavior Analysis,* 1969, **2**(1), 55–64.

Guess, D., & Baer, D. An analysis of individual differences in generalization between receptive and productive language in retarded children. *Journal of Applied Behavior Analysis,* 1973, **6**(2), 311–330.

Guess, D., Sailor, W., & Baer, D. *Functional speech and language training.* Parts 1–4. Lawrence, Kans.: H & H Enterprises, 1977.

Guidelines for eliminating discrimination and denial of services on the basis of race, color, national origin, sex, and handicap in vocational education programs. *Federal Register,* Office of Civil Rights, December 19, 1978, **43** (244).

Guilford, J. P. Three faces of intellect. *American Psychologist,* 1959, **14**, 469–479.

REFERENCES

Guilford, J. P. *The nature of human intelligence.* New York: McGraw-Hill, 1967.

Gumz, E., & Gubrium, J. F. Comparative parental perceptions of a mentally retarded child. *American Journal of Mental Deficiency,* 1972, **77,** 175–180.

Gunzburg, H. C. The physical environment of the mentally handicapped. *British Journal of Mental Subnormality,* 1972, **28**(34), 48–57.

Guskin, S. L., & Spicker, H. H. Educational research in mental retardation. In N. R. Ellis (Ed.), *International review of research in mental retardation,* Vol. 3. New York: Academic Press, 1968.

Guskin, S. L., Bartel, N. R., & MacMillan, D. L. Perspective of the labeled child. In N. Hobbs (Ed.), *Issues in the classification of children,* Vol. 11. San Francisco: Jossey-Bass, 1975.

Haeussermann, E. *Developmental potential of preschool children: An evaluation in intellectual, sensory, and emotional functioning.* New York: Grune & Stratton, 1958.

Halderman and the United States v. Pennhurst State School and Hospital. Civil No. 74-1345 (E.D.Pa., December 23, 1977, and March 17, 1978).

Hall, J. W., & Jerger, J. Central auditory function in stutterers. *Journal of Speech and Hearing Research,* 1978, **21,** 324–337.

Hallahan, D. P., & Kauffman, J. M. *Introduction to learning disabilities: A psycho-behavioral approach.* Englewood Cliffs, N.J.: Prentice-Hall, 1976.

Hallahan, D. P. & Cruickshank, W. M. *Psychoeducational foundations of learning disabilities.* Englewood Cliffs, N.J.: Prentice-Hall, 1973.

Halsam, R. H. A. Teacher awareness of some common pediatric neurologic disorders. In R. H. A. Haslam & P. J. Valletutti (Eds.), *Medical problems in the classroom.* Baltimore; University Park Press, 1975.

Hamilton, J. Another view. *The Exceptional Parent,* 1977, **7,** Y26–Y28.

Hamilton, K. W. *Counseling the handicapped in the rehabilitation process.* New York: Ronald Press, 1950.

Hammill, D., & Larsen, S. The relationship of selected auditory perceptual skills and reading ability. *Journal of Learning Disabilities,* 1974, **7,** 429–436.

Hammill, D., Goodman, L., & Wiederholt, J. L. Visual-motor processes: Can we train them? *Reading Teacher,* 1974, **27,** 469–480.

Hammill, D. D., & Bartel, N. R. *Teaching children with learning and behavior problems.* Boston: Allyn & Bacon, 1978.

Haring, N. G., & Phillips, E. L. *Educating emotionally disturbed children.* New York: McGraw-Hill, 1962.

Haring, N., & Gentry, N. Direct and individualized instructional procedures. In N. Haring & R. Schiefelbusch (Eds.), *Teaching special children.* New York: McGraw-Hill, 1976.

Haring, N. G., Hayden, A., & Beck, R. General principles and guidelines in programming for severely handicapped children and young adults. *Focus on Exceptional Children,* 1976, **8,** 1–4.

Harley, J. P., Ray, R. S., Tomasi, L., Eichman, P. L., Matthews, C. G., Chun, R., Cleeland, C. S., & Traisman, E. Hyperkinesis and food additives: Testing the Feingold hypothesis. *Pediatrics,* 1978, **61**, 818–828.

Harlow, H. F. The development of affectional patterns in infant monkeys. In B. M. Foss (Ed.), *Determinants of infant behavior.* New York: Wiley, 1961.

Harlow, H. F., & Zimmerman, R. R. Affectional responses in the infant monkey. *Science,* 1959, **130**, 421–432.

Harvey, J. To fix or to cope: A dilemma for special education. *Journal of Special Education,* 1969, **3**, 389–392.

Hatch, E., Murphy, J., & Bagnato, S. J. Comprehensive evaluation of handicapped children. *Elementary School Guidance and Counseling Journal,* 1979, **3**, 170–187.

Havighurst, Robert J. *Human development and education.* New York: Longmans, Green, 1953.

Hayden, A., & Haring, N. Early intervention for high risk infants and young children: Programs for Down's syndrome children. In T. Tjossem (Ed.), *Intervention strategies for high risk infants and young children.* Baltimore: University Park Press, 1976.

Hayden, A. H., & Edgar, E. B. Identification, screening, and assessment. In J. Jordan, A. Hayden, M. Karnes, & M. Wood (Eds.), *Early childhood education for exceptional children: A handbook of ideas and exemplary practices.* Reston, Va.: Council for Exceptional Children, 1977.

Hayden, A. H., & Pious, C. G. The case for early intervention. In R. L. Edgar (Ed.), *Teaching the severely handicapped.* Seattle, Wash.: American Association for the Education of the Severely/Profoundly Handicapped, 1979.

Heber, R. A manual on terminology and classification in mental retardation. *American Journal on Mental Deficiency,* 1959. (Mimeographed supplement.)

Heber, R., & Dever, R. Education and rehabilitation of the mentally retarded. In H. D. Haywood (Ed.), *Social-cultural aspects of mental retardation.* New York: Appleton-Century-Crofts, 1970.

Heber, R., & Garber, H. The Milwaukee project: A study of the use of family intervention to prevent cultural-familial mental retardation. In Friedlander, B. G., Sterritt & G. Kirk (Eds.), *Exceptional infant: Assessment and intervention.* Vol. 3. New York: Brunner/Mazel, 1975.

Henshelwood, J. *Congenital word blindness.* London: Lewis, 1917.

Hermelin, B., & O'Connor, N. *Psychological experiment with autistic children.* Oxford: Pergamon, 1970.

Hess, R. D., Block, M., Costello, J., Knowles, R. T., & Lergery, D. Parent involvement in early education. In F. Grothberg (Ed.), *Day care: Resources for decisions.* Washington, D.C.: Office of Economic Opportunity, 1971.

Hewett, F. M. *The emotionally disturbed child in the classroom.* Boston: Allyn and Bacon, 1968.

Hill, E. & Ponder, P. *Orientation and mobility techniques.* New York: American Foundation for the Blind, 1976.

Hirsch, J. Cell number and size as a determinant of subsequent obesity. In M. Winick (Ed.), *Childhood obesity.* New York: Wiley, 1975.

Hirshoren, A., Schultz, E., Manton, A., & Henderson, R. A survey of public school special education programs for emotionally disturbed children, 1970, ERIC Document Reproduction Service No. ED 050 540.

Hiskey, M. *Hiskey-Nebraska test of learning aptitude.* Lincoln, Nebr.: Union College Press, 1966.

Hobbs, N. Helping disturbed children: Psychological and ecological strategies. *American Psychologist,* 1966, **21,** 1105–1115.

Hobbs, N. *The futures of children.* San Francisco: Jossey-Bass, 1976.

Hobson v. Hansen. 269 F. Supp. 401 (D.D.C., 1967).

Hockey, R. V. *Physical fitness: The pathway to healthful living.* St. Louis: C. V. Mosby, 1973.

Hollingshead, A. B., & Redlich, F. C. *Social class and mental illness: A community study.* New York: Wiley, 1958.

Holt, K. S. The home case of severely retarded children. *Pediatrics,* 1958, **22**, 744–755.

Hoyt, K. B. *Career education: What it is and how to do it.* (2d ed.) Salt Lake City, Utah: Olympus, 1976.

Hoyt, K. B. *An introduction to career education.* A policy paper of the U.S. Office of Education. Washington D.C.: U.S. Department of Health, Education, and Welfare, Office of Education, 1977.

Hoyt, K. B. *A primer for career education.* Washington, D.C.: U.S. Government Printing Office, 1978.

Huckstep, R. L. *Poliomyelitis.* London: Churchill Livingstone, 1975.

Hull, W., & Ross, M. The parent-teacher relationship in preschool programs. *Journal of Visual Impairment and Blindness,* 1979, **73**(3), 102–105.

Humphreys, L. G. Characteristics of type concepts with special reference to Sheldon's typology. *Psychological Bulletin,* 1957, **54**, 218–228.

Hunt, D. E., & Sullivan, E. V. *Between psychology and education.* New York: Dryden Press, 1974.

Hunt, J. McV. *Intelligence and experience.* New York: Ronald Press, 1961.

Hutt, M. L., & Gibby, R. G. *The mentally retarded child.* Boston: Allyn and Bacon, 1976.

Hutton, W. D., & Talkington, L. W. *The developmental record: A manual.* Corvallis, Oreg.: A Continuing Education Book, 1974.

Iano, R., Ayers, D., Heller, H., McGettigan, J., & Walker, V. Sociometric status of retarded children in an integrative program. *Exceptional Children,* 1974, **40**, 267–271.

Illinois Office of Education. *A curriculum guide for the development of body and sensory awareness for the visually impaired.* Springfield, Ill.: Illinois Office of Education, September 1974.

554

I'm afraid to have another child. *The Exceptional Parent,* 1977b, **7**, M21-24.

Ingram, D. *Phonological disability in children.* New York: American Elsevier, 1976.

Irwin, J. V., & Marge, M. *Principles of childhood language disabilities.* Englewood Cliffs, N.J.: Prentice-Hall, 1972.

Iscoe, I., & Payne, S. Development of a revised scale for the functional classification of exceptional children. In E. P. Trapp & P. Himelstein (Eds.), *Readings on exceptional children: Research and theory* (2nd ed.) New York: Appleton-Century-Crofts, 1972.

Itard, J. M. *The wild boy of Aveyron.* G. and M. Humphrey (Trans.). New York: Appleton-Century-Crofts, 1932.

Jacobson, R., Fant, C., & Halle, M. *Preliminaries to speech analysis.* Cambridge, Mass.: MIT Press, 1952.

Jaffe, J. What's in a name?—Attitudes toward disabled persons. *Personnel and Guidance Journal,* 1967, **45**, 557-560.

Jastak, J. F., & Jastak, S. R. *Manual: The wide range achievement test.* Wilmington, Del.: Guidance Associates, 1965.

Jensema, C., & Corbett, E. *Teachers of the deaf: Descriptive profiles.* Washington, D.C.: Gallaudet College Press, 1981.

Johnson, G. O. A study of the social position of mentally handicapped children in the regular grades. *American Journal of Mental Deficiency,* 1950, **55**, 60-89.

Johnson, G. O. Special education for the mentally retarded: A paradox. *Exceptional Children,* 1962, **29**, 62-69.

Johnson, G. O., & Kirk, S. A. Are mentally handicapped children segregated in the regular grades? *Exceptional Children,* 1950, **17,** 65-68, 87-88.

Johnson, K. L., & Kopp, C. B. *A bibliography of screening and assessment measures for infants.* (2d. rev.) Project REACH, 126 Moore Hall, U.C.L.A., Los Angeles, California, 90024.

Johnston, R. B., & Magrab, P. R. *Developmental disorders: Assessment, treatment, education.* Baltimore: University Park Press, 1976.

Joint Commission of the Accreditation of Hospitals (JCAH). *Manual for training surveyors in assessing active treatment.* Chicago: 1977.

Jolly, D. H. When should the seriously retarded infant be institutionalized? *American Journal of Mental Deficiency,* 1953, **57**, 632-636.

Jones, J. W., & Collins, A. P. *Educational programs for visually handicapped children.* Washington, D.C.: U.S. Department of Health, Education and Welfare, 1966.

Jones, R. L. (Ed.). *Problems and issues in the education of exceptional children.* Boston: Houghton Mifflin, 1971.

Jones, R. T., & Kazdin, A. E. Childhood behavior problems in the school. In S. M. Turner, K. Calhoon, & H. E. Adams (Eds.), *The handbook of clinical behavior therapy.* New York: Wiley, 1981.

Josephina, S. Research findings related to the Montessori method. *Education,* 1967, **88**, 139-144.

Kagan, J.   The determinants of attention in the infant. *American Scientist,* 1970, **58**, 298–306.

Kanner, L.   Autistic disturbances of affective contact. *Nervous Child,* 1943, **2**, 217–250.

Kanner, L.   Feeblemindedness: Absolute, relative, and apparent. *Nervous Child,* 1949, **7**, 365–397.

Karchmer, M., & Trybus, R.   *Who are the deaf children in mainstream programs?* Gallaudet College Office of Demographic Studies, Series R, No. 4. Washington, D.C.: Gallaudet College Press, 1977.

Karnes, M., & Zehrbach, R.   Alternative models for delivering services to young handicapped children. In J. Jordan, A. Hayden, M. Karnes, & M. Wood (Eds.), *Early childhood education for exceptional children: A handbook of ideas and exemplary practices.* Reston, Va.: Council for Exceptional Children, 1977.

Kauffman, J.   *Characteristics of children's behavior disorders.* Columbus, Ohio: Charles Merrill, 1977.

Kauffman, J. M., & Payne, J. S.   *Mental retardation: Introduction and personal perspectives.* Columbus, Ohio: Charles E. Merrill, 1975.

Kaunen, L.   *A history of the care and study of the mentally retarded.* Springfield, Ill.: Charles C. Thomas, 1964.

Kent, L. R.   *Language acquisition program for the retarded or multiply impaired.* Champaign, Ill.: Research Press, 1974.

Keogh, J., Sugden, D. A., Reynard, C. L., & Calkin, J. A.   Identification of clumsy children: Comparisons and comments. *Journal of Human Movement Studies,* 1979, **5**, 32–41.

Kephart, N. C.   *The slow learner in the classroom.* Columbus, Ohio: Charles E. Merrill, 1960.

Kessler, J. W.   *Psychopathology of childhood.* Englewood Cliffs, N.J.: Prentice-Hall, 1966.

Kidd, J. W.   Pro—The efficacy of special class placement for educable mental retardates. Paper presented at the 48th Annual Convention of the Council for Exceptional Children, Chicago, April 1970.

Kimbrough, J. A., Huebner, K. M., & Lowry, L. J.   *Sensory training, A curriculum guide: The Greater Pittsburgh guild for the blind.* Pittsburgh, Pa.: Davis & Warde, 1976.

Kirk, S. A.   *Early education of the mentally retarded: An experimental study.* Urbana, Ill.: University of Illinois Press, 1958.

Kirk, S.   Behavioral diagnosis and remediation of learning disabilities. In *Conference on exploration into the problems of the perceptually handicapped child.* Evanston, Ill.: Fund for Perceptually Handicapped Children, 1963.

Kirk, S. A.   Research in Education. In H. A. Stevens & R. Heber (Eds.), *Mental Retardation: A Review of Research.* Chicago: University of Chicago Press, 1964.

Kirk, S. A.   *Educating exceptional children.* (2d ed.) Boston: Houghton Mifflin, 1972.

Kirk, S. A., & Elkins, J. Identifying developmental discrepancies at the pre-school level. *Journal of Learning Disabilities*, 1975, **8**(7), 417-419.

Kirk, S. A., and Gallagher, J. J. *Educating exceptional children* (3d ed.) Boston: Houghton Mifflin, 1979.

Kirk, S. A., and Kirk, W. D. *Psycholinguistics disabilities*. Urbana, Ill.: University of Illinois Press, 1971.

Kirk, S. A., McCarthy, J. J., & Kirk, W. D. *Illinois test of psycholinguistic abilities* (Rev. ed.) Urbana, Ill.: University of Illinois Press, 1968.

Klaus, R., & Gray, S. *The early training project for disadvantaged children: A report after five years.* Monographs of the Society for Research in Child Development, 1968, **33**.

Klausmeier, H. J. Effects of accelerating bright older elementary pupils: A follow-up. *Journal of Educational Psychology*, 1963, **54**, 165-171.

Kleck, R., Ono, H., & Hastorf, A. H. The effects of physical deviance upon face-to-face interaction. *Human Relations*, 1966, **19**, 425-436.

Kleck, R., Richardson, S. A., & Ronald, L. Physical appearance cues and interpersonal attraction in children. *Child Development*, 1974, **45**, 305-310.

Klineberg, O. *Negro intelligence and selective migration.* New York: Columbia University Press, 1935.

Knobloch, H., & Pasamanick, B. *Developmental diagnosis.* New York: Harper & Row, 1974.

Kolstoe, O. P. Programs for the mildly retarded: A reply to the critics. *Exceptional Children*, 1972, **39**, 51-56.

Kolstoe, O. P., & Frey, R. M. *A high school work study program for the mentally subnormal student.* Carbondale, Ill.: Southern Illinois University Press, 1965.

Konigsberg, D. Laboring over the work crisis. *American Way*, December 1978, 47-50.

Koppitz, E. M. *Human figures drawing test,* New York: Grune & Stratton, 1968.

Koppitz, E. M. *The Bender gestalt test for young children.* Vol. 2: *Research and application, 1963-1973.* New York: Grune & Stratton, 1975.

Kriger, S. F. *Life styles of aging retardates living in community settings in Ohio.* Columbus, Ohio: Psychologia Metrika, 1975.

Kriger, S. F. Geriatrics. In J. Wortes (Ed.), *Mental retardation and developmental disabilities.* New York: Brunner/Mazel, 1976.

Kroth, R. *Communicating with parents of exceptional children: Improving parent-teacher relationships.* Denver: Love, 1975.

Kurtz, P. D., Neisworth, J. T., & Laub, K. W. Issues concerning the early identification of handicapped children. *Journal of School Psychology*, 1977, **2**, *136-140.*

Lachman, S. J. Psychosomatic disorders: A behavioristic approach. New York: Wiley, 1972.

Langley, B. Functional assessment of the brain damaged, physically handicapped child: cognitive, communication, and motor variables. *Diagnostique,* 1978, 31–37.

Lapouse, R., & Monk, M. An epidemiologic study of behavior characteristics in children. *American Journal of Public Health,* 1958, **48**, 1134–1144.

Laub, K. W., Kurtz, P. D., & Worobey, J. *The COMP-ident find/screen planning package: A descriptive manual and organizational guide for planning and conducting child find/screen efforts in rural areas.* University Park, Pa.: The HICOMP Preschool Project, 1978.

Lavater, J. C. *Essays on physiognomy: Designed to promote the knowledge and the love of mankind.* T. Holcroft (Trans.). London: William Tegg, 1848.

LaVor, M., & Krivit, D. The Handicapped Children's Early Education Assistance Act, Public Law 90-538. *Exceptional Children,* 1969, **35**, 379–383.

Lazar I. Does prevention pay off? *The communicator.* Council for Exceptional Children, Division of Early Childhood, Fall 1979.

Lee, B. S. Artificial stutter. *Journal of Speech and Hearing Disorders,* 1951, **16**, 53–55.

Lee, L. *Developmental sentence analysis.* Evanston, Ill.: Northwestern University Press, 1974.

Lee, L., Koenigsknecht, R., & Mulhern, S. T. *Interactive language development teaching.* Evanston, Ill.: Northwestern University Press, 1975.

Lerner, J. W. *Children with learning disabilities.* (2d ed.) Boston: Houghton Mifflin, 1976.

Lerner, R. M. *Concepts and theories of human development.* Reading, Mass.: Addison-Wesley, 1976.

Lerner, R. M., Karabenick, S. A., & Meisels, M. Effects of age and sex on the development of personal space schemata toward body build. *Journal of Genetic Psychology,* 1975, **127,** 91–101.

Lerner, R. M., & Lerner, J. V. Effects of age, sex, and physical attractiveness on child-peer relations, academic performance, and elementary school adjustment. *Developmental Psychology,* 1977, **13**, 585–590.

Levitan, S., & Taggart, R. *Jobs for the disabled.* Baltimore: Johns Hopkins University Press, 1977.

Levitt, E. E. The results of psychotherapy with children: An evaluation. *Journal of Consulting Psychology,* 1957, **21**, 189–196.

Levitt, L., & Kornhaber, R. C. Stigma and compliance: A re-examination. *Journal of Social Psychology,* 1977, **103,** 13–18.

Lewis, J. F. The community and the retarded: A study in social ambivalence. In G. Tarjan, R. K. Eyman, & C. E. Meyers (Eds.), *Sociobehavioral studies in mental retardation: Papers in honor of Harvey F. Dingman.* A monograph of the American Association on Mental Deficiency, 1973.

Lewis, W. W. Project re-ed: Educational intervention in discordant child rearing systems. In E. L. Cowen, E. A. Gardner, & M. Max (Eds.), *Emergent approaches to mental health problems.* New York: Appleton-Century-Crofts, 1967.

Liahy, A. M. Nature-nurture and intelligence. *Genetic Psychology Monographs,* 1935, **17,** 241–305.

Lillie, D. L. *Early childhood education: An individualized approach to developmental instruction.* Chicago: Science Research Associates, 1975.

Lindsey, D., & O'Neal, J. Static and dynamic balance skills of eight-year-old deaf and hearing children. *American Annals of the Deaf,* 1976, **121,** 49–55.

Lindsey, R., Jones, B. J., & Van Whitely, A. *Body mechanics.* (3d ed.) Dubuque, Iowa: William C. Brown, 1974.

Lindzey, G. Morphology and behavior. In G. Lindzey & C. S. Hall (Eds.), *Theories of personality: Primary sources and research.* New York: Wiley, 1965.

Lippman, L., & Goldberg, I. *Right to education: An anatomy of the Pennsylvania case and its implications for children.* New York: Teachers College Press, 1973.

Livingston, S. *Comprehensive management of epilepsy in infancy, childhood, and adolescence.* Springfield, Ill.: Charles C. Thomas, 1972.

Livingston, S., & Berman, W. Participation of the epileptic child in contact sports. *Journal of Sports Medicine,* 1974, **11,** 170–174.

Locke, J. *Some thoughts concerning education.* Woodbury, N.Y.: Barron's Education Series, 1964.

Long, N. J., & Newman, R. G. Managing the surface behavior of children in school. In N. J. Long, W. C. Morse, & R. G. Newman (Eds.), *Conflict in the classroom: The education of children with problems.* Belmont, Calif.: Wadsworth, 1976.

Louttit, C. M. *Clinical psychology of exceptional children.* New York: Harper & Row, 1957.

Lovitt, T. C. *Applied behavior analysis techniques and curriculum research.* Report submitted to the National Institute of Education, 1973(a).

Lowenfeld, B. History and development of specialized education for the blind. *Exceptional Children,* 1956, **23,** 53–57, 90.

Lowenfeld, B. *The visually handicapped child in school.* New York: John Day, 1973.

Lusthaus, E., & Lusthaus, C. The dignity of risk. *The Exceptional Parent,* 1978, **8,** C30–C32.

Lyle, J. G. The effect of an institution environment upon the verbal development of imbecile children. III: The Booklands residential family unit. *Journal of Mental Deficiency Research,* 1960, **4,** 14–23.

Macdonald, E. T., & Chance, B. *Cerebral palsy.* Englewood Cliffs, N.J.: Prentice-Hall, 1964.

MacMillan, D. C. Special education for the mildly retarded: Servant or savant. In E. L. Meyer, G. A. Vergason, & R. J. Whelan (Eds.), *Strategies for teaching exceptional children.* Denver: Love, 1972.

MacMillan, D. L. *Mental retardation in school and society.* Boston: Little, Brown, 1977.

MacTurk, R. H., & Neisworth, J. T. Norm- and criterion-based measures with handicapped and non-handicapped preschoolers. *Exceptional Children,* 1978, **45** (1), 34–39.

Madden, R., Gardner, E. R., Rudman, H. C., Kavisen, B., & Merwin, J. C. *Stanford achievement test.* New York: Harcourt, Brace Jovanovich, 1973.

Madle, R. A. Alternative residential placements. In J. T. Neisworth, & R. M. Smith, (Eds.), *Retardation: Issues, assessment and intervention.* New York, McGraw-Hill.

Mainstreaming—Is it right for Jean? *The Exceptional Parent,* 1976, **6**, 22–26.

Mann, L. Psychometric phrenology and the new faculty psychology: The case against ability assessment and training. *Journal of Special Education,* 1971, **5**(1), 3–14.

Mann, S. *The first review of special education.* Vol. 1. Philadelphia, Pa.: Journal of Special Education Press, 1973.

Manpower and Vocational Education Weekly, January 14, 1982, **13** (2).

Marinelli, R. P., & Orto, A. E. *The psychological and social impact of physical disability.* New York: Springer. 1977.

Marquis, D. P. A study of frustration in newborn infants. *Journal of Experimental Psychology,* 1943, **32**, 123–138.

Martin, F. N. (Ed.), *Introduction to audiology.* Englewood Cliffs, N.J.: Prentice-Hall, 1975.

Maxfield, K. E., & Buchholz, S. *A social maturity scale for blind preschool children.* New York: American Foundation for the Blind, 1957.

Mayer, J. *Overweight: Causes, cost and control.* Englewood Cliffs, N.J.: Prentice-Hall, 1968.

Mayhall, W. F., & Jenkins, J. R. Scheduling daily or less-than-daily instruction: Implications for resource programs. *Journal of Learning Disabilities,* 1977, **10**(3), 159–163.

McClearn, G. E. Genetic influences on behavior and development. In P. H. Mussen (Ed.), *Carmichael's manual of child psychology,* Vol. 1. New York: Wiley, 1970.

McCormack, J., Chalmers, A., & Gregorian, J. *Systematic instruction of the severely handicapped.* Medford, Mass.: Massachusetts Center for Program Development and Evaluation, n.d.

McGinnis, M. A. *Aphasic children.* Washington, D.C.: Alexander Graham Bell Association for the Deaf, 1963.

McReynolds, L., & Bennett, S. Distinctive feature generalizations in articulation training. *Journal of Speech and Hearing Disorders,* 1972, **37**, 462–470.

Meadow, K. P. Burnout in professionals working with deaf children. *American Annals of the Deaf,* 1981, **126**(1).

Mearham, M. L., & Wiesen, A. E. *Changing classroom behavior: A manual for precision teaching.* Scranton, Pa.: International Textbook Co., 1971.

Meichenbaum, D., Bowers, H., & Ross, R. A behavioral analysis of teacher expectancy effect. *Journal of Personality and Social Psychology,* 1969, **13**, 306–316.

Meichenbaum, D. H., & Goodman, J. Training impulsive children to talk to themselves: A means of developing self-control. *Journal of Abnormal Psychology,* 1973, **77,** 115–126.

Meier, J. *Developmental and learning disabilities.* Baltimore: University Park Press, 1976.

Mellon, J. *Transformational sentences combining a method for enhancing the development of syntactic fluency in English composition.* Harvard Research and Development Center on Educational Differences, Report No. 1, 1967.

Mercer, J. *Labelling the mentally retarded.* Berkeley: University of California Press, 1973.

Merton, R. K. *Education of handicapped children: The legal mandate.* Champaign, Ill.: Research Press Company, 1979.

Merton, R. K. The self-fulfilling prophecy. *Antioch Review,* 1948, **8,** 193–210.

Meyen, E. L. *Developing units of instruction for the mentally retarded and other children with learning problems.* Dubuque, Iowa: William C. Brown, 1972.

Meyerowitz, J. H. Self-derogation in young retardates and special class placement. *Child Development,* 1962, **33,** 443–451.

Meyerson, L. A. Somatopsychology of physical disability. In W. Cruickshank (Ed.), *Psychology of exceptional children and youth,* Englewood Cliffs, N.J.: Prentice-Hall, 1971.

Michaelis, Carol T. Chip on my shoulder. *The Exceptional Parent,* 1974, **4,** 30–35.

Milhorat, A. T. The problem of muscle disease: Muscular dystrophy. In A. T. Milhorat (Ed.), *Exploratory concepts in muscular dystrophy and related disorders.* Amsterdam: Excerpta Medica Foundation, 1967.

Miller, M. Well-planned town centers—A contemporary demand of the handicapped. Bromma, Sweden: ICTA Information Centre, 1970.

Miller, W. H. *Systematic parent training procedures: Cases and issues.* Champaign, Ill.: Research Press, 1975.

Mills v. Board of Education of District of Columbia. 348 F. Supp. 866 (D.D.C. 1972).

Mischel, W. Toward a cognitive social learning reconceptualization of personality. *Psychological Review,* 1973, **80,** 252–283.

Montessori, M. *Montessori method.* Anne E. George (Trans.). New York: Stokes, 1912.

Moore, M. G., Anderson, R. A., Frederick, H. D., Baldwin, V. L., & Moore W. G. (Eds.) *The longitudinal impact of preschool programs on mentally retarded children.* Monmouth, Oregon: Exceptional Child Department Teaching Research Division, Oregon State System of Higher Education, 1979.

Moore, M. W., & Bliss, J. C. The Optacon Reading System. *Education of the Visually Handicapped,* 1975, **7**(1), 15.

Moore, M. W., & Peabody, R. L. *A functional description of the itinerant teacher of visually handicapped children in the commonwealth of Penn-sylvania.* Pittsburgh, Pa.: University of Pittsburgh, 1976.

Moores, D.   Neo-oralism and Education of the Deaf in the Soviet Union. *Exceptional Children,* 1972, **38**, 377–384.

Moores, D.   Families and deafness. In A. Norris (Ed.), *Deafness annual.* Silver Spring, Md.: Professional Rehabilitation Workers with the Adult Deaf, 1973.

Moores, D.   *Educating the deaf: Psychology principles and practices.* Boston: Houghton Mifflin, 1978.

Moores, D.   *Educating the deaf: Psychology, principles and practices.* (2d ed.) Boston: Houghton Mifflin, 1982.

Moores, D., and Oden, C.   Educational needs of black deaf children. *American Annals of the Deaf,* 1977, **122,** 313–318.

Morkovin, B.   Experiment in teaching deaf preschool children in the Soviet Union. *Volta Review,* 1960, **62**, 260–268.

Morley, M. E.   *Cleft palate and speech.* London: E. & S. Livingstone, 1970.

Morris, P. R., & Whiting, H. T. A.   *Motor impairment and compensatory education.* Philadelphia: Lea & Febiger, 1971.

Mostofsky, D. I.   Epilepsy: Returning the ghost to psychology. *Professional Psychology,* 1978, **9**, 87–92.

Mullen, F. A., & Itkin, W.   *Achievement and adjustment of educable mentally handicapped children.* U.S. Office of Education Cooperative Research Program, Project No. OE-SAE-6529. Chicago: Board of Education, 1961.

Muma, J. R.   *Language handbook: Concepts, assessment, intervention.* Englewood Cliffs, N.J.: Prentice-Hall, 1978.

Murphy, A. T., & Fitzsimons, R. M.   *Stuttering and personality dynamics.* New York: Ronald Press, 1960.

Murphy, J. M.   Psychiatric labeling in cross-cultural perspective. *Science,* 1976, **191,** 1019–1028.

Murry, R. E., Jr.   Psychological aspects of genetic counseling. *Social Work in Health Care,* 1976, **2**, 13–23.

Mussen, P. (Ed.).   Infancy and early experience, Part II. In *Carmichael's manual of child psychology.* (3d ed.) New York: Wiley, 1970.

Myers, B. A.   The child with a chronic illness. In R. H. A. Haslam & P. J. Valletutti (Eds.), *Medical problems in the classroom.* Baltimore: University Park Press, 1975.

Myers, Patricia, & Hammill, D. D.   *Methods for learning disabilities.* (2d ed.) New York: Wiley, 1976.

Nadal, R.   A counseling program for parents of severely retarded preschool children. *Social Casework,* 1961, **42**, 78–83.

National Society for the Study of Education.   *Behavior Modification in Education.* C. Thoreson (Ed.). Chicago: University of Chicago Press, 1972.

Neelist, I.   *Planning buildings for handicapped children.* Springfield, Ill.: Charles C. Thomas, 1970.

562

Neisworth, J. T., & Smith, R. M. *Modifying retarded behavior.* Boston: Houghton Mifflin, 1973.

Neisworth, J. T., Jones, R. T., & Smith, R. M. Body-behavior problems: A conceptualization. *Education and Training of the Mentally Retarded,* 1978, **13**, 265–271.

Neisworth, J. T., Kurtz, P. D.; Jones, R. T., & Madle, R. A. Biasing of hyperkinetic behavior ratings by diagnostic reports. *Journal of Abnormal Child Psychology,* 1974, **2**(4), 323–329.

Newcomer, P., and Hammill, D. D. *Psycholinguistics in the schools.* Columbus, Ohio: Charles E. Merrill, 1976.

Newland, T. E. *Manual for the blind learning aptitude test: Experimental edition.* Urbana, Ill.: T. E. Newland, 1969.

Newland, T. E. Psychological assessment of exceptional children and youth. In W. Cruickshank (Ed.), *Psychology of exceptional children and youth.* Englewood Cliffs, N.J.: Prentice-Hall, 1971.

Newland, T. E. *The gifted in socio-educational perspective.* Englewood Cliffs, N.J.: Prentice-Hall, 1976.

Nihira, K., Foster, R., Shellhaas, M., & Leland, H. *Adaptive behavior scales,* Washington, D.C.: American Association on Mental Deficiency, 1969.

Nihira, K., Foster, R., Shellhaas, M., & Leland, H. *Adaptive behavior scales: Manual.* (2d ed.) Washington, D.C.: AAMD, 1974.

Nondiscrimination on basis of handicap. *Federal Register,* May 4, 1977 (Section 504).

Nurss, J. R., & McGauvran, M. E. *Metropolitan readiness tests.* New York: Harcourt Brace Jovanovich, 1976.

O'Brien, R. *Alive . . . aware . . . a person.* Rockville, Md.: Montgomery County Public Schools, 1976.

Ohio Department of Mental Health and Mental Retardation. *State of Ohio curriculum guide for moderately mentally retarded learners.* Columbus, Ohio: Division of Mental Retardation and Developmental Disabilities, Office of Habilitation Services, 1977.

O'Leary, K. D., & O'Leary, S. G. *Classroom management: The successful use of behavior modification.* New York: Pergamon, 1972.

O'Leary, S. G., & O'Leary, K. D. Behavior modification in the school. In H. Leitenberg (Ed.), *Handbook of behavior modification and behavior therapy.* Englewood Cliffs, N.J.: Prentice-Hall, 1976.

Orem, R. C. (Ed.) *Montessori and the special child.* New York: Putnam, 1969.

Ornitz, E. M. Neurophysiologic studies. In M. Rutter & E. Schopler (Eds.), *Autism: A reappraisal of concepts and treatment.* New York: Plenum Press, 1978.

Orton, S. T. Studies of stuttering. *Archives of Neurology and Psychiatry,* 1927, **18,** 671–672.

Osgood, C. E. A behavioristic analysis of perception and language as cognitive phenomena. In J. S. Bruner (Ed.), *Contemporary approaches to cognition.* Cambridge, Mass.: Harvard University Press, 1957.

Osgood, C. E. *Method and theory in experimental psychology.* New York: Oxford University Press, 1953.

Otto, W., McMeremy, R., & Smith, R. *Corrective and remedial teaching.* Boston: Houghton Mifflin, 1973.

Palardy, J. What teachers believe—what children achieve. *Elementary School Journal,* 1969, **69**, 370–374.

Patterson, G. R. *Families: Applications of social learning to family life.* Champaign, Ill.: Research Press, 1971a.

Patterson, G. R. Behavioral intervention procedures in the classroom and in the home. In A. Bergin & S. Garfield (Eds.), *Handbook of psychotherapy and behavior change.* New York: Wiley, 1971b.

Patterson, G. R., & Reid, J. B. Reciprocity and coercion: Two facets of social systems. In C. Neuringer & J. L. Michael (Eds.), *Behavior modification in clinical psychology.* New York: Appleton-Century-Crofts, 1970.

Pennsylvania Association for Retarded Children (PARC) v. Commonwealth of Pennsylvania. 344 F. Supp. 1257 (E.D.Pa, 1971).

Perkins, W. H. *Speech pathology: An applied behavioral science.* St. Louis: C. V. Mosby, 1971.

Peters, D. L., McConnell, H. E., & Burgess, J. *COMP-Parent: A training program for parents.* University Park, Pa.: The HICOMP Preschool Project, 1977.

Peters, L. J. *Prescriptive teaching.* New York: McGraw-Hill, 1965.

Phelps, L. A. An overview of expanding federal commitments to vocational education and employment of handicapped individuals. *Education and Training of the Mentally Retarded,* April 1977, **12** (2), 186–192.

Phillips, E. L. Achievement place: Token reinforcement procedures in a home-style rehabilitation setting for "pre-delinquent" boys. *Journal of Applied Behavior Analysis,* 1968, **1**, 213–223.

Piaget, J. *The origins of intelligence in children.* New York: International Universities Press, 1952.

Piers, E., & Harris, D. *The Piers-Harris children's self concept scale.* Nashville, Tenn.: Counselor Recordings and Tests, 1969.

Poznanski, E. O. Emotional issues in raising handicapped children. *Rehabilitation Literature,* 1973, **34**, 322–326.

President's Committee on Employment of the Handicapped. *One in eleven.* Washington, D.C.: U.S. Government Printing Office, 1975.

President's Committee on Mental Retardation. *The six-hour retarded child,* Washington, D.C.: U.S. Department of Health, Education and Welfare, 1969.

President's Committee on Mental Retardation. *Mental retardation, the known and the unknown.* Washington, D.C.: U.S. Government Printing Office, 1976.

Pressey, S. L. *Educational accelerations: Appraisal and basic problems.* Columbus, Ohio: Ohio State University, Bureau of Educational Research and Monographs, No. 31, 1949.

Provence, S., & Lipton, R. C. *Infants in institutions: A comparison of their development with family-reared infants during the first year of life.* New York: International Universities Press, 1962.

Quay, H. C., Glavin, J. P., Annesley, F. R., & Werry, J. S. The modification of problem behavior and academic achievement in a resource room. *Journal of School Psychology,* 1972, **10,** 187–198.

Quay, H. C., Morse, W. C., & Cutler, R. L. Personality patterns of pupils in special classes for the emotionally disturbed. *Exceptional Children,* 1966, **32**, 297–301.

Quigley, S. P., Jenne, W. C., & Phillips, S. B. *Deaf students in colleges and universities.* Washington, D.C.: Alexander Graham Bell Association for the Deaf, 1968.

Ramey, C. T., & Campbell, F. A. Prevention of developmental retardation in high risk children. In P. Mittler (Ed.), *Research to practice in mental retardation: Core and intervention.* Vol. 1. Baltimore, Md.: University Park Press, 1977.

Ramey, C. T., & Smith, B. J. Assessing the intellectual consequences of early intervention with high-risk infants. *American Journal of Mental Deficiency,* 1976, **81**, 318–324.

Rapier, J., Adelson, R., Carey, R., & Croke, K. Changes in children's attitudes toward the physically handicapped. *Exceptional Children,* 1972, **39**, 219–223.

Rarick, G. L., Dobbins, D. A., & Broadhead, G. D. *The motor domain and its correlates in educationally handicapped children.* Englewood Cliffs, N.J.: Prentice-Hall, 1976.

Rawlings, B. W., & Trybus, R. J. Personnel facilities and services available in schools and classes for hearing impaired children in the United States. *American Annals of the Deaf,* **123**(2), 99–114.

Rawlings, B. W., & Trybus, R. J. Update on post-secondary programs for hearing impaired students. *American Annals of the Deaf,* 1976, **121**(6), 541–546.

Ray, J. S. The family training center: An experiment in normalization. *Mental Retardation,* 1974, **2,** 12–13.

Redl, F., & Wineman, D. *Controls from within: Techniques for the treatment of the aggressive child.* Glencoe, Ill.: Free Press, 1952.

Reese, H. W. & Lipsitt, L. P. Sensory processes. *Experimental Child Psychology,* 1970a, **1,** 33–62.

Reese, H. W., and Lipsitt, L. P. Behavior modification: Clinical and educational applications. *Experimental Child Psychology,* 1970b, 643–672.

Reger, R., Schroeder, W., & Uschold, K. *Special education: Children with learning problems.* New York: Oxford University Press, 1968.

Regional Intervention Program. A parent-implemented early intervention program for preschool children. *Hospital and Community Psychiatry,* 1976, **27,** 728–731.

Report on Preschool Education, May 20, 1980, **12**(11), 3. Capitol Publications, Inc., Suite G-12, 2430 Pennsylvania Avenue, N. W., Washington, D.C. 200 37.

Reynolds, M. C. Categories and variables in special education. In M. C. Reynolds & M. D. Davis (Eds.), *Exceptional children in regular classrooms.* Minneapolis: University of Minnesota Press, 1971.

Rezulli, J. S., Hartman, R. K., & Callahan, C. M. Scale for rating the behavioral characteristics of superior students. In W. B. Barbe & J. S. Rezulli (Eds.), *Psychology and education for the gifted.* (2d ed.) New York: Irvington, 1975.

Rheingold, H. L. Controlling the infant's exploratory behavior. In B. M. Foss (Ed.), *Determinants of infant behavior.* Vol. 2. New York: Wiley, 1963.

Rhodes, S. L. The developmental approach to the life cycle of the family. *Social Casework,* 1977, **4,** 301–311.

Rhodes, W. C. The disturbing child: A problem of ecological management. *Exceptional Children,* 1967, **33,** 449–455.

Richardson, S. A. Age and sex differences in values toward physical handicaps. *Journal of Health and Social Behavior,* 1970, **11,** 207–214.

Richardson, S. A., Goodman, N., Hastorf, A. H., & Cornbusch, S. M. Cultural uniformity in reaction to physical disabilities. *American Sociological Review,* 1961, **26,** 241–247.

Richardson, S. A. The effect of physical disability on the socialization of a child. In D. Goshin (Ed.), *Handbook of socialization theory and research.* Chicago: Rand McNally, 1969.

Richens, A. *Drug treatment of epilepsy.* London: Henry Kimpton, 1976.

Riegel, K. F. Toward a dialectical theory of development. *Human Development,* 1975, **18,** 50–64.

Robb, P., Bernardoni, L. C., & Johnson, R. W. *Assessment of individual mental ability.* Scranton, Pa.: Intext Educational Publishers, 1972.

Robinson, F. B. *Introduction to stuttering.* Englewood Cliffs, N.J.: Prentice-Hall, 1964.

Robinson, N. M., & Robinson, H. B. *The mentally retarded child: A psychological approach.* (2d ed.) New York: McGraw-Hill, 1976.

Robinson, W. P. The elaborated code in working class language. *Language and Speech,* 1965, **8,** 243–252.

Robinson, W. P. Restricted codes in sociolinguistics and the sociology of education. Paper presented at Ninth International Seminar, University College, Dar-es-Salaam, December, 1968.

Rollins, B. C., & Feldman, H. Marital satisfaction over the family cycle: A reevaluation. *Journal of Marriage and the Family,* 1970, **32,** 20–38.

Rose, L. R. The functional relationship between artificial food colors and hyperactivity. *Journal of Applied Behavior Analysis,* 1978, **11,** 439–446.

Rosenthal, R., & Jacobson, L. *Pygmalion in the classroom.* New York: Holt, Rinehart and Winston, 1968.

Ross, A. O. *The exceptional child in the family.* New York: Grune & Stratton, 1964.

Ross, A. O. Behavior therapy. In H. C. Quay & J. S. Werry (Eds.), *Psychopathological disorders of childhood.* New York: Wiley, 1972.

Ross, A. O. *Child behavior therapy.* New York: Wiley, 1981.

Ross, M. Definitions and descriptions. In J. Davis (Ed.), *Our forgotten children: Hard of hearing children in the public schools.* Minneapolis: University of Minnesota, 1977. Pp. 5–18.

Rousseau, J. J. *Emile.* See William Boyd (Trans. and Ed.), *The Emile of Jean Jacques Rousseau.* New York: Teachers College Press, 1962.

Rubin, R. A., & Balow, B. Learning and behavior disorders: A longitudinal study. *Exceptional Children,* 1971, **38,** 293–299.

Rubin, R. A., & Balow, B. Prevalence of teacher identified behavior problems: A longitudinal study. *Exceptional Children,* 1978, **45,** 102–111.

Rubovits, P., & Maehr, M. Pygmalion black and white. *Journal of Personality and Social Psychology,* 1973, **25,** 210–218.

Rutter, M. Diagnosis and definition. In M. Rutter & E. Schopler (Eds.), *Autism: A reappraisal of concepts and treatment.* New York: Plenum Press, 1978a.

Rutter, M. Language disorder and infantile autism. In M. Rutter & E. Schopler (Eds.), *Autism: A reappraisal of concepts and treatment.* New York: Plenum Press, 1978 b.

Rutter, M. *Helping troubled children.* New York: Plenum, 1975.

Ryan, B. P. An illustration of operant conditioning therapy for stuttering. In C. W. Starkweather (Ed.), *Conditioning in Stuttering Therapy.* Memphis, Tenn.: Speech Foundation of America, 1972.

Sadlick, M., & Penta, F. B. Changing nurse attitudes toward quadriplegics through use of television. *Rehabilitation Literature,* 1975, **36,** 274–278.

Salvia, J. Perspectives on the nature of mental retardation. In J. T. Neisworth, & R. M. Smith, *Retardation: Issues, assessment and intervention.* New York: McGraw-Hill, 1978.

Salvia, J., & Ysseldyke, J. *Assessment in special and remedial education.* Boston: Houghton Mifflin, 1978.

Salvia, J., & Ysseldyke, J. E. *Assessment in special and remedial education.* (2d ed.) Boston: Houghton Mifflin, 1981.

Salvia, J., Clark, G., & Ysseldyke, J. Teacher retention of stereotypes of exceptionality. *Exceptional Children,* 1973, **39,** 651–652.

Salvia, J., Sheare, J. B., & Algozzine, B. Facial attractiveness and personal-social development. *Journal of Abnormal Child Psychology,* 1973, **3,** 171–178.

San Martino, M., & Newman, M. B. Siblings of retarded children: A population at risk. *Child Psychiatry and Human Development,* 1974, **4,** 168–177.

Sanford, A. R. (Ed.) *Learning accomplishment profile (LAP).* Chapel Hill, N.C.: Training Outreach Program, 1973.

Sarason, S. B. *Psychological problems in mental deficiency.* (2d ed.) New York: Harper & Row, 1953.

Sarason, S. B., & Doris, J. *Psychological problems in mental deficiency.* (4th ed.) New York: Harper & Row, 1969.

Satir, V. *Conjoint family therapy,* Palo Alto, Calif.: Science and Behavior Books, 1967.

Satterfield, J. H. Neurophysiologic studies with hyperactive children. In D. P. Cantwell (Ed.), *The hyperactive child. Diagnosis, management, current research.* New York: Spectrum Publications, 1975.

Sattler, J. M., & Tozier, L. L. A review of intelligence test modifications with cerebral palsied and other handicapped groups, *Journal of Special Education,* 1970, **4**, 391–398.

Schafler, M. Individualized educational programs in a school for the handicapped. *Social Work in Education,* **3**(1), p. 32–43, 1980.

Schein, J., & Delk, M. *The deaf population of the United States.* Silver Spring, Md.: National Association of the Deaf, 1974.

Schloss, I. P. *Implications of altering and definition of blindness.* Research Bulletin, No. 3. New York: American Foundation for the Blind, August 1963.

Schmidt, B. G. Changes in personal, social, and intellectual behavior of children originally classified as feebleminded. *Psychological Monograph,* **60,** 5, 1–144.

Schneirla, T. C. The concept of development in comparative psychology. In D. B. Harris (Ed.), *The concept of development.* Minneapolis: University of Minnesota Press, 1957.

Scholl, G. T., & Weihl, C. A. A survey of special curricular areas to be included in day programs for visually handicapped pupils. *Education of the Visually Handicapped,* 1979, **11**(1), 18–23.

Schultz, E. W., Hirshoren, A., Manton, A., & Henderson, R. Special education for the emotionally disturbed. *Exceptional Children,* 1971, **38**, 313–320.

Schwartz, M. F. *Stuttering solved.* New York: McGraw-Hill, 1976.

Schweinhart, L. J., & Weikert, D. P. Effects of the Perry preschool program on youths through age 15. Paper presented at the Conference of the Handicapped Children's Early Education Program, Washington, D.C., December 1–3, 1980.

Searl, S. J., Jr. Stages of parent reaction. *The Exceptional Parent,* 1978, **8**, F27–F29.

Seguin, E. *Idiocy and its treatment by the physiological method.* Albany, N.Y.: Brandow, 1866.

Seymour, F. W., & Stoke, T. F. Self-recording in training girls to increase work and evoke staff praise in an institution for offenders. *Journal of Applied Behavior Analysis,* 1976, **9**, 41–54.

Shames, G. H., & Sherrick, C. E. Discussion of nonfluency and stuttering as operant behavior. *Journal of Speech and Hearing Disorders,* 1963, **28,** 3–18.

Shearer, D. E., & Shearer, M. S. The portage project: A model for early childhood intervention. In T. Tjossem (Ed.), *Intervention strategies for high risk infants and young children.* Baltimore: University Park Press, 1976.

Shearer, M. S., & Shearer, D. E. The portage project: A model for early childhood education. *Exceptional Children,* 1972, **36**, 217–220.

Sheldon, W. H., Stevens, S. S., & Tucker, W. B. *The varieties of human physique: An introduction to constitutional psychology.* New York: Harper & Row, 1940.

Shere, Eugenia S. Patterns of child rearing in cerebral palsy: Effects upon the child's cognitive development. *Pediatrics Digest,* May 1971, **1**, p. 28.

Sherrill, C. *Adapted physical education and recreation.* Dubuque, Iowa: William C. Brown, 1976.

Shirer, W. *Berlin diary: The journal of a foreign correspondent, 1934–1941.* New York: Popular Library, 1961.

Shoemaker, F., & Kaplan, H. K. Observations on physical fitness and developmental skills of emotionally disturbed boys. *Therapeutic Recreation Journal,* 1972, **6**, 28–30, 35.

Shushan, R. D. Assessment and reduction of deficits in the physical appearance of mentally retarded people. Doctoral dissertation, University of California, 1974. *Dissertation Abstracts International,* 1974, **35**, 5974–5975A. (University Microfilms, No. 75–5692.)

Silbert, J., Carnine, D., & Stein, M. *Direct instruction mathematics.* Columbus, Ohio: Charles E. Merrill, 1981.

Simeonsson, R. J., & Wiegerink, R. Accountability: A dilemma in infant intervention. *Exceptional Children,* 1975, **41,** 474–481.

Sindelar, P. T., & Deno, S. L. The effectiveness of resource programming, *Journal of Special Education,* 1978, **12**(1), 17–28.

Siperstein, G. N., & Gottlieb, J. Physical stigma and academic performance as factors affecting children's first impressions of handicapped peers. *American Journal of Mental Deficiency,* 1977, **81**, 455–462.

Skeels, H. M. *Adult status of children from contrasting early life experiences.* Monographs of the Society for Research in Child Development, 1966, **31**: serial no. 105.

Skeels, H. M., & Dye, H. B. A study of the effects of differential stimulation on mentally retarded children. Proceedings and Addresses of the 63rd Annual Session of the American Association of Mental Deficiency, 1939, **44**, 114–136.

Skeels, H. M. and Harms, I. Children with inferior social histories: Their mental development in adoptive homes. *Journal of Genetic Psychology,* 1948, **72**, 283–294.

Skodak, M. and Skeels, H. M. A final follow-up study of one hundred adopted children. *Journal of Genetic Psychology,* 1949, **75**, 85–125.

Sloan, W., & Birch, J. W.   A rationale for degrees of retardation. *American Journal of Mental Deficiency,* 1955, **60**, 258–264.

Smith, B. J.   *Policy options related to the provision of appropriate early intervention services for very young exceptional children and their families.* Reston, Va.: Council for Exceptional Children, 1980.

Smith, D., & Snell, M.   Classroom management and instructional planning. In M. Snell (Ed.), *Systematic instruction of the moderately and severely handicapped.* Columbus, Ohio: Charles E. Merrill, 1978.

Smith, J., & Arkens, J.   Now more than ever: A case for the special class. *Exceptional Children,* 1974, **40**(7), 497–502.

Smith, J., Mangan, L., Fiske, L., & MacAulay, S.   Minimum objectives for incoming seventh grade students. Unpublished. North Clarendon, Vt., 1976.

Smith, M. L., & Glass, G. V.   Meta-analysis of psychotherapy outcome studies. *American Psychologist,* 1977, **32**, 752–760.

Smith, R. M.   *Teacher diagnosis of educational difficulties.* Columbus, Ohio: Charles E. Merrill, 1969.

Smith, R. M., & Neisworth, J. T.   *The exceptional child: A functional approach.* New York: McGraw-Hill, 1975.

Smith, R. M., Neisworth, J. T., & Greer, T. G.   *Evaluating educational environments.* Columbus, Ohio: Charles E. Merrill Publishing Co., 1978.

Smoll, F. L.   Motor impairment and social development. *American Corrective Therapy Journal,* 1974, **28,** 4–6.

Snell, M.   *Systematic instruction of the moderately and severely handicapped.* Columbus, Ohio: Charles E. Merill, 1978.

Snellen's Test Chart.   The National Society for the Prevention of Blindness Inc., New York.

Soderberg, G. A.   Delayed auditory feedback and the speech of stutterers. *Journal of Speech and Hearing Disorders,* 1969, **33**, 20–29.

Sontag, E., Burke, P., & York, R.   Considerations for serving the severely handicapped in the public schools. *Education and Training of the Mentally Retarded,* 1973, **8**(2).

Sontag, E., Smith, & Certo, N.   *Educational programming for the severely and profoundly handicapped.* Boothwyn, Pa.: Division of Mental Retardation, CEC, 1977.

Sparks, H. L., & Younie, W. J.   Adult adjustment of the mentally retarded: Implications for teacher education. *Exceptional Children,* 1969, **38**, 13–18.

Spivack, G., Swift, M., & Prewitt, J.   Syndromes of disturbed classroom behavior: A behavioral diagnostic system for elementary schools. *Journal of Special Education,* 1971, **5**, 269–292.

Sprague, R. L., & Werry, J. S.   Psychotropic drugs and handicapped children. In L. Mann & D. A. Sabatino (Eds.), *The second review of special education.* Philadelphia, Pa.: Journal of Special Education Press, 1974.

Sprinthall, R. C., & Sprinthall, N. A.   *Educational psychology: A developmental approach.* Reading, Mass.: Addison-Wesley, 1979.

Spurzheim, J. G. *Phrenology: Or the doctrine of the mental phenomena.* Philadelphia, Pa.: Lippincott, 1908. (Revised ed. from the 2d American ed. in two volumes published in Boston in 1833).

Stanfield, J. S. Graduation: What happens to the retarded child when he grows up. *Rehabilitation Literature,* 1974, **35**, 48–49.

Stedman, D. J. Early childhood intervention programs. In B. N. Caldwell & D. J. Stedman (Eds.), *Infant education: A guide for helping handicapped children in the first three years of life.* New York: Walker, 1977.

Stedman, D. J., and Eichorn, D. H. A comparison of the growth and development of institutionalized and home reared mongoloids during infancy and early childhood. *American Journal of Mental Deficiency,* 1964, **4**, 381–401.

Stephens, T. *Directive teaching of children with learning and behavior handicaps.* Columbus, Ohio: Charles Merrill, 1970.

Stevens, G. D., & Birch, J. W. A proposal of clarification of the terminology and a description of brain-injured children. *Exceptional Children,* 1957, **23,** 346–349.

Stokes, T. F., Fowler, S. A., & Baer, D. M. Training preschool children to recruit natural communities of reinforcement. *Journal of Applied Behavior Analysis,* 1978, **11**, 285–303.

Stokoe, W. *Sign language structure.* University of Buffalo, Studies in Linguistics, Occasional Paper No. 8, 1958.

Stotsky, B. A. Nursing home or mental retardation—Which is better for the geriatric mental patient? *Journal of Genetic Psychology,* 1969, **3**, 113–117.

Strain, P. S., Cooke, T. P., & Apolloni, T. *Teaching exceptional children: Assessing and modifying social behavior.* New York: Academic Press, 1976.

Strauss, A. A., & Lehtinen, L. E. *Psychopathology and education of the brain injured child: Fundamentals and treatment.* New York: Grune & Stratton, 1947.

Stromsta, C. Experimental blockage of phonation by distorted sidetone. *Journal of Speech and Hearing Research,* 1959, **2**, 286–301.

Stuckless, E., & Birch, J. The influence of early manual communication on the linguistic development of deaf children. *American Annals of the Deaf,* 1966, **111,** 499–504.

Sutherland, J. H., Jr. The learning disabilities label as a biasing factor in the complex visual-motor integration performance of normal fourth grade children. Unpublished doctoral dissertation, Pennsylvania State University, 1976.

Swan, W. M. The handicapped children's early education program. *Exceptional Children,* 1980, **47**, 12(b).

Talbot, M. E. *Edouard Seguin: A study of an educational approach to the treatment of mentally defective children.* New York: Teachers' College Press, 1964.

Tarver, S., & Hallahan, D. P. *Children with learning disabilities: Personal perspectives.* Columbus, Ohio: Charles E. Merrill, 1976.

Tavormina, G., Boll, T. J., Dunn, N. J., Luscomb, R. L., & Taylor, J. R. Psychosocial effects on parents of raising a physically handicapped child. *Journal of Abnormal Child Psychology,* 1981, **9**(1), 121–131.

Tawney, J. *Programmed environments for developmentally retarded children: A project for a coordinated program of research, program model development and curriculum development and dissemination.* U.S. Office of Education, Project No. 23118 (Original Proposal), 1972.

Tawney, J. *Programmed environments for developmentally retarded children* (final report). U.S. Office of Education, Bureau of Education for the Handicapped, Grant OEG-0-75-0069, 1979 (in press).

Tawney, J. Programmed language instruction for the severely developmentally retarded. *Yearbook in Special Education,* 1980, **6**, 276–278.

Tawney, J., and Hipsher, L. *Systematic language instruction: Experimental edition.* U.S. Office of Education Final Report 71205. Danville, Ill.: Interstate Press, 1970.

Tawney, J., Knapp, D., O'Reilly, C. & Pratt, S. *The programmed environments curriculum.* Columbus, Ohio: Charles E. Merrill, 1979.

Terman, L., & Merrill, M. *Stanford-Binet intelligence scale* (1972 norms ed.). Boston: Houghton Mifflin, 1973.

Terman, L. M. *Genetic studies of genius.* Vol. 1: *Mental and physical traits of a thousand gifted children.* (2d ed.) Palo Alto, Calif.: Stanford University Press, 1926.

Terman, L. M., & Oden, M. H. *The gifted child grows up.* Palo Alto, Calif.: Stanford University Press, 1947.

The school year has been a total disaster. *The Exceptional Parent,* 1977c, **7**, 25–29.

Thompson, W. R. Early environment: Its importance for later behavior. In P. H. Hock & J. Zubin (Eds.), *Psychopathology of childhood.* New York: Grune & Stratton, 1955.

Thorton, M. L. Competitive preadolescent sports. In T. T. Craig (Ed.), *The humanistic and mental aspects of sports, exercise and recreation.* Chicago: American Medical Association, 1976.

Thurman, S. K., & Lewis, M. Children's response to differences: Some possible implications for mainstreaming. Exceptional Children, 1979, **45**, 468–470.

Thurstone, T. G. *An evaluation of educating mentally handicapped children in special classes and in regular grades.* U.S. Office of Education Cooperative Research Program, Project No. OE-SAE-6452. Chapel Hill, N.C.: University of North Carolina Press, 1960.

Tizard, J., & Grad, J. C. *The mentally handicapped and their families.* London: Oxford University Press, 1961.

Torres, S. (Ed.). *A primer on individualized education programs for handicapped children.* Reston, Va.: Foundation for Exceptional Children, 1977.

572

Travis, L. E. The unspeakable feelings of people with special reference to stuttering. In L. E. Travis (Ed.), *Handbook of speech pathology.* New York: Appleton-Century-Crofts, 1957.

Tredgold, A. F. *A textbook of mental deficiency.* (6th ed.) Baltimore: Wood, 1937.

Tredgold, A. F., & Soddy, K. *A textbook of mental deficiency.* (9th ed.) London: Bailiere, 1956.

Ullman, L. P., & Krasner, L. A. *A psychological approach to abnormal behavior.* Englewood Cliffs, N.J.: Prentice-Hall, 1969.

U.S., Congress. Federal Public Law 94-142, *Congressional Record,* 94th Congress, November 29, 1975, **12,** 173-196.

U.S., Congress. *Career Education Incentive Act,* P.L. 95-207, 95th Congress, December 13, 1977.

U.S., Congress. Federal Public Law 91-517, 97th Congress. Developmental Disabilities Act (1978 revision).

U.S., Congress. *Comprehensive Employment and Training Act Amendments of 1978,* P.L. 95-524, 95th Congress, October 27, 1978.

U.S. Department of Health, Education, and Welfare. *Memorandum—Development of formal cooperative agreements between special education, vocational rehabilitation, and vocational education programs to maximize services to handicapped individuals.* Washington, D.C.: U.S. Department of Health, Education and Welfare, October 1978.

U.S. Department of Transportation. *Travel barriers.* Washington, D. C.: Office of the Secretary, Washington, D.C., May 1970.

U.S. Office of Education. *Estimated number of handicapped children in the United States, 1974-75.* Washington, D.C.: Bureau of Education for the Handicapped, 1975.

U.S. Office of Education. *Education Daily.* Washington, D.C.: Education News Service Division, Capital Publications, Inc., August 3, 1979.

Valett, R. E. The learning resource center for exceptional children. *Exceptional Children,* 1970, **36**(7), 527-530.

VanRiper, C. *The nature of stuttering.* Englewood Cliffs, N.J.: Prentice-Hall, 1971.

VanRiper, C. *The treatment of stuttering.* Englewood Cliffs, N.J.: Prentice-Hall, 1973.

Vernon, M., and Koh, S. Effects of manual communication on deaf children's educational achievement, linguistic competence, oral skills, and psychological development. *American Annals of the Deaf,* 1970, **115,** 527-536.

Vitale, F. *Individualized fitness programs.* Englewood Cliffs, N.J.: Prentice-Hall, 1973.

Vocational education. *Federal Register,* October 3, 1977 (P.L. 94-482), **42** (191).

Wald, M. S.   Legal policies affecting children: A lawyer's request for aid. *Child Development,* 1976, **1**, 1-5.

Wallace, G., & Larsen, S. C.   *Educational assessment of learning problems: Testing for teaching.* Boston: Allyn and Bacon, 1978.

Wallace, G., and McLoughlin, J.   *Learning disabilities.* Columbus, Ohio: Charles E. Merrill, 1979.

Walls, R. T., Werner, T. J., Bacon, A., & Zane, T.   Behavior checklists. In J. D. Cone & R. P. Hawkins (Eds.), *Behavioral assessment: New directions in clinical psychology.* New York: Brunner-Mazel, 1977.

Walton, J. M.   Clinical aspects of human muscular dystrophy. In G. H. Bourne & M. N. Golarz (Eds.), *Muscular dystrophy in man and animals.* New York: Hafner, 1963.

Ward, M. E., & Peabody, R. L.   *Computer-assisted remedial education No. 4: Education of the visually handicapped.* University Park, Pa.: Pennsylvania State University, 1972.

Warner, F., Golden, T., & Henteleff, M.   Health insurance: A dilemma for parents of the mentally retarded. *Exceptional Children,* 1972, **39**, 57-58.

Warren, D. H.   Cognitive development, assessment, and the I.E.P. *DVH Newsletter* (Division for the Visually Handicapped, Council for Exceptional Children), 1978, **23**, 1, 7-9, 14-15, 20.

Watson, J. B.   *Behaviorism.* New York: Norton, 1925.

Weber, C. U., Foster, P. W., & Weikert, D. P.   *An economic analysis of the Ypsilanti Perry preschool project.* Monographs of the High/Scope Educational Research Foundation, No. 4, 1978.

Wechsler, D.   *Manual for the Wechsler intelligence scale for children—revised.* New York: Psychological Corporation, 1974.

Weikert, D. P., Bond, J. T., & McNeil, J. T.   *The Ypsilanti Perry preschool project: Preschool years and longitudinal results through fourth grade.* Monographs of the High/Scope Educational Research Foundation, No. 3, 1978.

Weiner, F. F.   *Phonological process analysis.* Baltimore: University Park Press, 1979.

Weinstein, L.   Project re-ed schools for emotionally disturbed children: Effectiveness as viewed by referring agencies, parents, and teachers. *Exceptional Children,* 1969, **35**, 703-711.

Wepman, J. M.   Auditory discrimination, speech reading. *Elementary School Journal,* 1960, **3**, 245-247.

Werry, J. S.   Childhood psychosis. In H. C. Quay & J. S. Werry (Eds.), *Psychopathological disorders of childhood.* New York: Wiley, 1971.

Werry, J. S., & Quay, H. C.   The prevalence of behavior symptoms in younger elementary school children. *American Journal of Orthopsychiatry,* 1971, **41**, 136-143.

574

White, B. Informal education during the first months of life. In R. D. Hess & R. M. Baer (Eds.), *Early education: A comprehensive evaluation of current theory, research and practice.* Chicago: Aldine, 1968.

White, B. L. *Human infants: Experience and psychological development.* Englewood Cliffs, N.J.: Prentice-Hall, 1971.

White, O., & Liberty, K. Behavioral assessment and precise educational measurement. In N. Haring & R. Schiefelbusch (Eds.), *Teaching special children.* New York: McGraw-Hill, 1976.

Wiederholt, J. L. Historical perspectives on the education of the learning disabled. In L. Mann & D. Sabatino (Eds.), *The second review of special education.* Philadelphia: JSE Press, 1974.

Wiig, E. H., & Semel, E. M. *Language disabilities in children and adolescents.* Columbus, Ohio: Charles Merrill, 1976.

Wiley, J. A. A psychology of auditory impairment. In W. M. Cruickshank (Ed.), *Psychology of exceptional children and youth.* (3d ed.) Englewood Cliffs, N.J.: Prentice-Hall: 1971.

Willoughby-Herb, S., & Neisworth, J. *Hicomp curriculum.* Columbus, Ohio: Charles Merrill, 1982.

Wilson, P. T., & Spitzer, J. A comparison of three current classification systems for mental retardation. *American Journal of Mental Deficiency,* 1969, **74**, 428–435.

Winitz, H. *From syllable to conversation.* Baltimore: University Park Press, 1975.

Wolf, J. M. *Physical facilities for exceptional children in the schools.* Balboa Canal Zone: Division of Schools, 1968.

Wolf, J. M., & Anderson, R. M. *The multiple handicapped child.* Springfield, Ill.: Charles Thomas, 1969.

Wolfensberger, W. Counseling parents of retarded children. In A. Baumeister (Ed.), *Mental Retardation.* London: University of London Press, 1967.

Wolfensberger, W., & Kurtz, Richard A. (Eds.). *Management of the Family of the Mentally Retarded.* Chicago, Ill.: Follett Educational Corp., 1969.

Wolfensberger, W. A new approach to decision-making in human management services. In R. B. Kugel and W. Wolfensberger, *Changing patterns in residential services for the mentally retarded.* Washington, D.C.: President's Committee on Mental Retardation, 1969a.

Wolfensberger, W. *The principles of normalization in human services.* Toronto: National Institute on Mental Retardation, 1972.

Wood, F. H., & Zabel, R. H. Making sense of reports of incidence of behavior disorders in the elementary-age population. *Psychology in the Schools,* 1978, **15,** 45–51.

Woodcock, R. M. *Woodcock reading mastery tests.* Circle Pines, Minn.: American Guidance Service, 1973.

Worthington, M. E. Personal space as a function of the stigma effect. *Environment and Behavior,* 1974, **6**, 289–294.

Wright, B. A. *Physical disability—A Psychological Approach.* New York: Harper & Row, 1960.

REFERENCES

Ysseldyke, J. E.   Assessment of retardation. In J. T. Neisworth & R. M. Smith (Eds.), *Retardation: Issues, assessment, & intervention.* New York: McGraw-Hill, 1978.

Ysseldyke, J. E.   Validity of the Woodcock-Johnson psycho-educational battery for learning disabled youngsters. *Learning Disability Quarterly,* **4**(3), 244–249.

Ysseldyke, J. E., & Bagnato, S. J.   Assessment of exceptional students at the secondary level: A pragmatic perspective. *High School Journal,* 1976, **7**, 282–288.

Ysseldyke, J. E., & Foster, G.   Bias in teachers' observations of emotionally disturbed and learning disabled children. *Exceptional Children,* 1978, **44**, 613–615.

Zehrbach, R. R.   Determining a preschool handicapped population. *Exceptional Children,* 1975, **42**, 76–83.

Zentall, S. S.   Optimal stimulation as theoretical basis for hyperactivity. *American Journal of Orthopsychiatry,* 1975, **45**, 549–563.

Zentall, S. S.   Environmental stimulation model. *Exceptional Children,* 1977, **43**, 502–510.

Zettel, J.   State provisions for educating the gifted and talented. In *Gifted and Talented,* 78th yearbook of the National Society for the Study of Education. Chicago: University of Chicago Press, 1979.

Zigler, E.   Developmental versus difference theories of mental retardation and the problem of motivation. *American Journal of Mental Deficiency,* 1969, **73**, 536–556.

Zimmerman, I. L., Steiner, U., & Fvatt, R.   *Preschool language scale.* Columbus, Ohio: Charles Merrill, 1969.

NAME INDEX

SUBJECT INDEX

Page numbers in *italic* indicate illustrations and tables.